The Magical Play of Illusion

Kyabjé Trijang Rinpoché at Hyderabad House, New Delhi, 1956
Courtesy of Palden Tsering

The Magical Play of Illusion

The Autobiography of Trijang Rinpoché

Translated by Sharpa Tulku Tenzin Trinley

FOREWORD BY

His Holiness the Dalai Lama

Wisdom

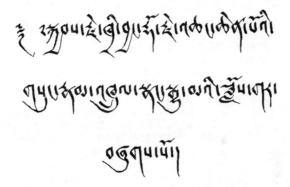

Wisdom Publications
199 Elm Street
Somerville, MA 02144 USA
wisdompubs.org

Library of Congress Cataloging-in-Publication Data

Names: Blo-bzaṅ-ye-śes-bstan-'dzin-rgya-mtsho, Khri-byaṅ, 1901–1981, author. | Sharpa Tulku, translator. | Bstan-'dzin-rgya-mtsho, Dalai Lama XIV, 1935– writer of foreword.
Title: Magical play of illusion: the autobiography of Trijang Rinpoche / Trijang Rinpoche; translated by Sharpa Tulku Tenzin Trinley; foreword by His Holiness the Dalai Lama.
Other titles: Dga'-ldan khri chen byaṅ-chub-chos-'phel gyi gral skye du rlom pa'i gyi na pa źig gis raṅ gi ṅaṅ tshul ma bcos lhug par bkod pa 'khrul snaṅ sgyu ma'i zlos gar. English
Description: Somerville, MA: Wisdom Publications, 2018. |
Includes bibliographical references and index. |
Identifiers: LCCN 2017055298 (print) | LCCN 2017061539 (ebook) | ISBN 9781614295273 (ebook) | ISBN 9780861710775 (hardback)
Subjects: LCSH: Blo-bzaṅ-ye-śes-bstan-'dzin-rgya-mtsho, Khri-byaṅ, 1901–1981. | Bstan-'dzin-rgya-mtsho, Dalai Lama XIV, 1935– —Friends and associates. | Dge-lugs-pa lamas—Tibet Region—Biography. | Dge-lugs-pa (Sect)—Biography. | BISAC: BIOGRAPHY & AUTOBIOGRAPHY / Personal Memoirs. | BIOGRAPHY & AUTOBIOGRAPHY / Cultural Heritage. | BIOGRAPHY & AUTOBIOGRAPHY / Historical.
Classification: LCC BQ968.H74 (ebook) | LCC BQ968.H74 A3 2018 (print) | DDC 294.3/923092 [B]—dc23
LC record available at https://lccn.loc.gov/2017055298

ISBN 978-0-86171-077-5   ebook ISBN 978-1-61429-527-3

22 21 20 19 18   5 4 3 2 1

The Tibetan title of *The Magical Play of Illusion* in *drutsa* style was penned by Ayetuk Jolak Chimé Gönpo in Dharamsala in 1983. He was the last surviving member of the exclusively trained calligraphers in the court of the Thirteenth Dalai Lama. Translator photo by Morgan Groves.
Cover and interior design by Gopa & Ted2, Inc. Set in Diacritical Garamond Premier Pro 11/14.16.

Wisdom Publications' books are printed on acid-free paper and meet the guidelines for permanence and durability of the Production Guidelines for Book Longevity of the Council on Library Resources.

♻ This book was produced with environmental mindfulness.
For more information, please visit wisdompubs.org/wisdom-environment.

Printed in the United States of America.

FSC www.fsc.org MIX Paper from responsible sources FSC® C013483

Please visit fscus.org.

Publisher's Acknowledgment

The publisher gratefully acknowledges the generous help of the Hershey Family Foundation in sponsoring the production of this book.

Contents

Foreword *by His Holiness the Dalai Lama* xv
Preface xvii
Translator's Introduction 1

The Magical Play of Illusion

Homage and Preliminary Remarks 13

1. The Beginning of My Life 17
   My Family Background 17
   The Death of My Predecessor 20
   My Recognition as a Reincarnation 22
   Contention Concerning a Rival Candidate 24

2. Ordination and Early Education 27
   Taking Up Official Residence and Beginning My Education 27
   The Arrival of Kyabjé Phabongkha Rinpoché 29
   Memorization of Texts 31
   My Ordination at Radreng Monastery 32
   My Mother's Difficulties 34
   My Enrollment at Ganden 35
   Meeting with Minister Shedrawa 38
   Returning to Chusang 39
   Choosing a Tutor 41
   Receiving the Kālacakra Initiation 42
   Being Awarded the First Academic Degree 43

3. Earning the Geshé Degree 45
First Meeting with His Holiness the Thirteenth Dalai Lama and Arrival of the Nationalist Chinese 45
A Smallpox Epidemic 48
Trouble with the Chinese 49
Studies and Empowerments 52
Studying Grammar and Composition 56
The Passing of Ngakrampa 57
Financial Difficulties 62
Preparations for the Geshé Lharam Degree 65
My Geshé Lharam Examination 68
Ordination, Practice, Study, and Memorization 70
Phabongkha Rinpoché's Extensive Discourse on the Stages of the Path 75
Beda Tulku's Arrival from Chatreng 76
Further Teachings and Empowerments 77
Frustrated Attempt to Solve the Estate's Problems 79
Meditation Retreats 80

4. Travels and Travails in Kham 81
Preparations for the Journey to Chatreng 81
The Journey to Chatreng 84
Teachings at Chatreng 89
Fighting 91
Travel to Gangkar Ling 92
Assassination Plot 93
Return to Chatreng 93
Construction of the Maitreya Statue 94
Overcoming Ritual Obstacles 96
Shady Dealings 97
Visit to Trehor 98

Visit to a Nomadic Community 101
Lithang Monastery 103
Pilgrimage to Kampo 104
Averting Retaliation 105
A Plot Against Me 107
At Chakra Temple 109
Visiting My Predecessor's Birthplace 111
Obstacles to My Return to Lhasa 111
The Journey Begins 115
Meeting with Gangkar Lama Rinpoché 116
Last Phase of Travel Home 119
Arrival Home 120

5. A Period of Gain and Loss 123
Cared for While Ill by Tridak Rinpoché 123
The Arrival of Palden Tsering 124
The Passing of the Ganden Throneholder and Geshé Ngawang Losang 125
The Passing of His Holiness the Thirteenth Dalai Lama 127
The Death of Losang Tsultrim 134
Tantric Teachings from Kyabjé Phabongkha Rinpoché 137
Pilgrimage to Southern District 140
Stages of the Path Teachings from Kyabjé Phabongkha Rinpoché 141
Journey to Dungkar Monastery, India, and Nepal 145
To Sakya, Tashi Lhunpo, and Back to Lhasa 149
Receiving and Giving Further Teachings 153
Appointment as Assistant Tutor and the Passing of Phabongkha Rinpoché 157
Miscellaneous Duties and Teachings 159
Pilgrimage to Phenpo 162

6. Black Clouds on the Horizon 167
Travels to Kundeling and Tölung 167
A Dispute Breaks Out 168
The Ritual to Transfer Lhamo's Shrine at Drepung 169
A New Appointment 172
Illness and Schism 175
The Formal Enrollment of His Holiness the Fourteenth Dalai Lama 179
Cataloging Religious Texts 181
Obstacles to Health 184
Renewing the Protector Support Substances in the Potala 186
Arrival of Communist Chinese and His Holiness's Enthronement 189
Flight to Dromo and the Seventeen-Point Agreement 191
Religious Activities after Returning to Lhasa 194

7. To China and Back 199
My Appointment as Junior Tutor 199
The Dalai Lama Takes Full Ordination 201
Traveling to China 203
Within China 206
Arranging a Visit to Kham 207
A Return Visit to Chatreng 211
The Journey from Chatreng to Chamdo 214
Reuniting with His Holiness and Returning to Lhasa 218

8. Storm Clouds Gathering 221
Chinese Appointments and My Mother's Passing 221
Visit to Radreng 223
Celebrating the Buddha Jayanti in Bodhgaya 225
Fears and Conflict upon Returning to Tibet 227
Visits to Tsurphu and Yerpa 230

His Holiness's Geshé Examinations 233
Portents of Trouble 237
Reflections on Impermanence 237
His Holiness's Final Examinations 239

9. The Storm Breaks 243
Tibetan Uprising 243
Divinations and a Decision to Flee 244
Long Trek through the Mountains 247
Crossing into India 249
Subjects of Chinese Propaganda 251

10. Early Years of Exile 253
Travels to Nepal and North India 253
Residences in Dharamsala and Sonada 255
Bodhgaya and Further Travels 257
Teaching in Spiti 261
Pilgrimage 264
Oral Transmission of the Works of Jé Tsongkhapa 266
The Passing of Kyabjé Simok Vajradhara 267
A Trip to Dalhousie 268
Meeting of All the Heads of the Tibetan Religious Traditions 270
Sarnath, Bodhgaya, and Return to Dharamsala 271
Bodhgaya, Sarnath, and Delhi 274
Enthronement of Kyabjé Ling Rinpoché and the Passing of Lhabu 275
Outbreak of the Indo-Pakistani War 278
Further Teachings 288

11. Distant Travels and Tragic News 291
First Visit to Switzerland 291
Germany and England 295

France, Switzerland, and Italy 299
Return to India: Dharamsala and Sarnath 302
Return to Dharamsala 306
The Passing of the Incarnation of Kyabjé Phabongkha Rinpoché 308
New Residence 311
His Holiness Requests Bodhisattva Vows 315

12. Planting Roots of Virtue 319
Invitation to Switzerland 319
England and France 327
Return to India 329
Mussoorie and Delhi 333
Averting Hindrances to His Holiness's Long Life 335
Searching for the Reincarnation of Kyabjé Phabongkha Rinpoché 338
More Teachings to His Holiness 341
Exchanging Teachings with Kyabjé Ling Rinpoché in Bodhgaya 342
His Holiness's Retreat 343

13. Twilight Years 349
Visit to the Tibetan Settlements in Southern India 349
Indo-Pakistani Conflict 351
Confirming the Recognition of the Third Phabongkha Rinpoché 354
Bodhgaya and Sarnath 356
Teachings and Retreat in Dharamsala 360
Sarnath 363
Return to South India 364
Return to Dharamsala 372
Author's Colophon 373

Translator's Colophon 377

Epilogue 379

The Final Six Years of Rinpoché's Life 379

The Special Qualities of Kyabjé Trijang Rinpoché 381

Kyabjé Trijang Rinpoché's Passing 385

The Search for His Reincarnation 390

Appendix: The Incarnation Lineage of Kyabjé Trijang Rinpoché 397

Notes 399

Glossary 423

Index 429

About the Translator 477

Foreword

BY HIS HOLINESS THE DALAI LAMA

I AM PLEASED that the autobiography of my late tutor, Kyabjé Trijang Rinpoché, is being made available in English. Rinpoché was celebrated for his erudition and eloquence, and his autobiography stands as a testimony to his remarkable skills as a writer and keen observer of human experience.

Born in 1901, in Gungthang near Lhasa, Trijang Rinpoché was recognized as the reincarnation of his predecessor when he was barely three years old. He studied at the Shartsé College of Ganden Monastic University, the seat of the great scholar and accomplished practitioner Tsongkhapa, and obtained his geshé lharam degree before reaching the age of twenty. He then joined Gyüto Tantric College, where he completed his formal education. Rinpoché's interests were varied and his field of mastery wide, ranging from classical philosophy to literature and poetry, and from traditional Tibetan healing sciences to the visual arts. The collection of his writings reflects his broad command of Tibetan cultural traditions.

In 1940 Trijang Rinpoché was appointed one of my debating assistants (*tsenshab*), and in 1952 he became my junior tutor; my senior tutor was Ling Rinpoché. I have fond memories of Rinpoché's kindness throughout my childhood.

Since his predecessors had close ties to the practice, as did his root lama Phabongkha Rinpoché, it is understandable that my late tutor followed them in propitiating Dölgyal (Dorjé Shukden). Nevertheless, the Great Fifth Dalai Lama was unequivocal in describing Dölgyal as "an oath-breaking spirit born from perverse prayers... harming the teachings and all living beings." Therefore I was deeply grateful to Rinpoché for his steadfast support when I began to express my strong objections to Dölgyal practice. He once remarked to me that the investigative procedures I had followed with regard to this issue, including my consultations with the Nechung oracle, had been consistently reliable at critical junctures for Tibet and had stood the test of time.

Trijang Rinpoché died in November 1981. The moment I received news of his imminent demise, I rushed to his residence in Gangchen Kyishong. When I arrived, sadly Rinpoché had already passed away, but I was able to pay my respects. Soon after, at the request of Rinpoché's personal staff, Ganden Shartsé Monastery, and Rinpoché's many devotees, I composed a prayer for the swift return of his reincarnation.

I feel fortunate to have been among the students of this great Tibetan master. I am profoundly grateful to Rinpoché for his kindness, for his teaching and transmissions, and for his personal friendship. It is a joy for me to add these few words of appreciation to the English translation of Trijang Rinpoché's autobiography.

10 April 2018

Preface

KYABJÉ TRIJANG RINPOCHÉ had been our family guru since long before I was born. My family sought his guidance and his divination for every major event in our lives, and the advice he gave us never failed to be beneficial. Even after 1959 Rinpoché always made me feel welcome and valued throughout the different phases of my life in exile. It was an incomprehensible loss when in 1981 Rinpoché passed away, like the sudden closure of a monumental library. I am honored to have this opportunity to share the life story of this incomparable lama with readers of the English language. Although I can scarcely hope to reproduce the beauty and free-flowing style of his writing, which in the original Tibetan is marked by elegance and candor, I hope this volume will provide even a little understanding of the immeasurable depth of his knowledge and compassion. My earnest wish is that this autobiography will reopen a small part of that huge library.

Kyabjé Trijang Rinpoché wrote *The Magical Play of Illusion* in 1975. The full Tibetan title is *Dga' ldan khri chen byang chub chos 'phel gyi skye gral du rlom pa'i gyi na pa zhig gis rang gi ngang tshul ma bcos pa lhug par bkod pa 'khrul snang sgyu ma'i zlos gar*, and it appears in volume 4 of Rinpoché's collected works as published in New Delhi by Mongolian Lama Gurudeva. Shortly after its publication, I sought Kyabjé Rinpoché's blessing and consent to translate it into English, but because of major changes in my life, I had to delay work on the translation. After I moved to New York City in 1976, my good friends Benjamin and Deborah Alterman provided much-needed encouragement to continue the work on the translation. In 1981, through the kind support and recommendations of my good friend the late Kenneth Morgan, professor emeritus and former director of the Fund for the Study of the Great Religions of the World at Colgate University, and of John Carter, professor of philosophy and religion at Colgate and then director of the fund, I received a grant enabling me to travel to Tibet and to

Dharamsala, India, where I completed the initial draft of the translation. I deeply appreciate their kindness.

The late Gyatso Tsering, former director of the Library of Tibetan Works and Archives and a devoted disciple of Kyabjé Trijang Rinpoché, provided me with accommodation and office space while in Dharamsala and helped me obtain Indian visa extensions that enabled me to complete the initial draft of this translation. I received constant support from the late Kungo Palden Tsering, lifelong attendant of Kyabjé Rinpoché, and from other staff members of Trijang Labrang. Joyce Murdoch, Elizabeth Grant, and Philippa Russell gave me invaluable suggestions. Ani Ursula Sollmann typed the original draft of the manuscript several times. My thanks to Zachary Larson for spending many hours with me in Madison preparing annotations. I deeply appreciate the valuable contributions of each of these people.

I offer my heartfelt thanks to my friend Jonathan Landaw, who rendered invaluable editorial assistance. I am very grateful to the late David Gonsalez (Losang Tsering) for his encouragement and support for this work. At my request David compiled the epilogue based on materials that I provided to him, including notes and letters from Kungo Palden Tsering and others. Sadly, David passed away in 2014 after prolonged illness. Thanks also to Andy Francis for his countless improvements to the style and clarity of the text and for his helpful annotations. Gavin Kilty lent instrumental support in interpreting difficult passages and in the rendering of verse and provided some of the glossary entries. Martin Brauen lent assistance in clarifying the identities and spellings of several European individuals mentioned in the text, and Joona Repo provided helpful information and editorial suggestions. Finally, I want to express my sincere appreciation to Daniel Aitken and Tim McNeill, publishers, and to my editor at Wisdom, David Kittelstrom, for his brilliant editorial work and sensitivity to the readers, which contributed immensely to the literary grace of this translation. I also want to thank everyone else at Wisdom Publications for their tireless work. Although I can never claim this to be a perfect translation, I am hopeful that with utmost devotion and genuine feeling for the work, I have at least not caused any damage to it.

Though begun long beforehand, *The Magical Play of Illusion* is appearing in print a year after *The Life of My Teacher*, the translation of His Holiness the Dalai Lama's biography of his other tutor, Kyabjé Ling Rinpoché. That volume parallels the present work in many respects, and the introduction by Geshé Thupten Jinpa there can in many ways be read as an introduction to this book as well. Many of the photos there also illustrate people and events that Trijang Rinpoché describes in his narrative here.

It is my sincere hope that those who read Kyabjé Trijang Rinpoché's autobiography will obtain at least a glimpse of the vast and intensive training that he and great lamas like him have undertaken. By seeing their tireless effort and dedication, we can develop a deep appreciation and gratitude for those who continue to give the authentic teachings of the unbroken lineages. We are indeed extremely fortunate to receive these teachings again and again from His Holiness the Dalai Lama, who embodies the wisdom of all the great lamas of the past. May all be greatly inspired by reading this autobiography, and may Kyabjé Trijang Rinpoché's prayers and wishes continue to guide us in our quest for enlightenment.

Sharpa Tulku Tenzin Trinley
Madison, Wisconsin

Kyabjé Trijang Rinpoché at his residence in Dharamsala, August 3, 1980
COURTESY OF PALDEN TSERING

Translator's Introduction

Historical Background

Kyabjé Trijang Rinpoché (1901–81), the author of *The Magical Play of Illusion*, was widely regarded as one of the foremost Tibetan Buddhist spiritual masters of his day. He served as the junior tutor to His Holiness the Dalai Lama alongside the senior tutor, Kyabjé Ling Rinpoché. For the benefit of those readers who are not familiar with Tibet and its Buddhist traditions, the following brief remarks may provide a context in which the life story of this great lama can be more fully appreciated.

Located north of the towering peaks of the Himalayas, the Tibetan plateau, which at an average altitude of 16,000 feet is the highest in the world, is often called the roof of the world, and the Tibetans themselves refer to their country as the "land of snows." Tibet is roughly the size of Western Europe and, contrary to popular belief, is not entirely mountainous and barren. It has vast areas rich in forest, seemingly endless pasturelands, and extensive fertile valleys. Surrounded by perennially snow-covered ranges and dotted with numerous lakes, Tibet and the area immediately adjacent to it are the source of many of Asia's greatest rivers: the Ganges, Brahmaputra, Indus, Yangtze, and Mekong, to name but a few. It borders India to the west and south, Nepal, Bhutan, and Burma to the south, East Turkestan to the north, and China to the east. Tibetan people are a distinct race with their own language belonging to the Tibeto-Burmese linguistic group. Their unique history and cultural heritage span thousands of years.

The Tibetan calendar dates from the time of King Nyatri Tsenpo in 127 BCE, and a succession of kings ruled Tibet for over a thousand years. During the reign of King Songtsen Gampo (b. 620 CE), Tibet became a great military power in Central Asia, and it was with the support of his two queens, one from Nepal and the other from China, that this leader promoted Buddhism across the region. Later, during the reign of King Trisong Detsen, the great Indian masters Śāntarakṣita and Padmasambhava were invited to Tibet, and with the founding in 790 of Samyé, the first Buddhist monastery in Tibet, Buddhism became firmly established in the land of snows. Subsequently, many other Indian masters, most notably Atiśa, whose chief Tibetan disciple, Dromtönpa (1005–64), is regarded as the predecessor of the line of Dalai Lamas, made significant contributions to the development and refinement of the Tibetan Buddhist teachings, as did hundreds of Tibetan scholars who went to India to receive their spiritual training.

Beginning in the eleventh century, during the reigns of various lamas and other rulers of the Sakya and Kaygü schools, special priest-patron relationships were established between certain highly regarded Tibetan lamas and the powerful Mongol and Chinese emperors. In 1642, the Fifth Dalai Lama assumed both spiritual and temporal authority over Tibet, and the Ming emperor of China received him not only as Tibet's head of state but as a "divinity on Earth." It is recorded that the emperor went out from Beijing to greet the Dalai Lama personally and, out of veneration, even had an inclined pathway built over the city wall so that his honored guest could enter the capital city without the indignity of having to pass through gates. Subsequent Dalai Lamas, some of whom were short lived, maintained this special priest-patron relationship with the rulers of China.

The transition to the more modern period in Tibetan history occurred during the time of the Great Thirteenth Dalai Lama, Thupten Gyatso. He was born in 1879 and took over the duties of temporal and spiritual leader of Tibet in 1895. It was during his time that various foreign powers made incursions into Tibet, and the Dalai Lama was forced into exile twice, first between 1904 and 1909 as the result of a British invasion, and again between 1910 and 1913 because of an invasion from China. The Thirteenth Dalai Lama was an intelligent reformer who proved himself a skillful politician when Tibet became a pawn in the so-called Great Game played between the Russian and British empires. After warning that Tibet would soon lose its independence, he passed away in 1933.

Gyalwa Thupten Gyatso's immediate successor, His Holiness the Fourteenth Dalai Lama Tenzin Gyatso, was born in 1935. Due to the grave situation caused by the incursion of the Communist Chinese army into Tibetan territory in 1950, he assumed full spiritual and temporal duties before he was sixteen years old. Despite these heavy responsibilities, His Holiness continued to pursue his rigorous studies and in 1959 was awarded his *geshé lharam* degree (roughly equivalent to a joint doctorate in philosophy and divinity) by the three major monasteries in Lhasa, the so-called three seats of learning. I had the great fortune of participating in many of the grand celebrations of His Holiness's geshé examinations at the monasteries concluding at the Jokhang Temple during the annual Great Prayer Festival only weeks before the tragic events of 1959. Despite the deteriorating and fearful political situation at the time, everyone enjoyed these solemn and joyous occasions. The courtyard of the Jokhang Temple was decorated with the most beautiful appliqués and ornaments, and fragrant smells of incense permeated the courtyard. His Holiness's throne was at the center of the entrance to the inner chapel of the sacred statue of the Buddha. He was flanked by his tutors: Kyabjé Ling Rinpoché on his right and Kyabjé Trijang Rinpoché on his left.

While top scholars were engaged in debate with His Holiness, high-ranking monk official Ta Lama Losang Jikmé, the medium of Nechung state oracle, was spontaneously possessed. During his possession, he was quickly whisked away by the well-trained Nechung monks, who were posted nearby in anticipation of such an occurrence. Outside the Tārā Chapel, the Nechung monks had been waiting with the full regalia, including the heavy ornate headdress. Within minutes, the Nechung oracle was escorted into the presence of His Holiness. This was the first time I had ever seen a protector in trance debate with His Holiness. After a brief exchange with His Holiness, a ceremonial white scarf was put around the neck of the oracle, who then made prostrations to His Holiness. At that moment, the oracle left the medium, who was carried away in total exhaustion. It all seems now like a beautiful dream, one that will remain forever vivid in my heart.

It was on the fateful day a week after the Tibetan national uprising against the Chinese in Lhasa on March 10, 1959, that the Dalai Lama, the senior tutor, the junior tutor, members of His Holiness's family, and key figures of the Tibetan government began their treacherous flight from occupied Tibet to seek asylum in India. Tens of thousands of Tibetans followed him and made their way to India, Nepal, Bhutan, and other lands. With the generous assistance of the Indian government under the leadership of Prime Minister Nehru, His Holiness then worked quickly to set up settlement camps for the general refugee population, establish schools for the Tibetan refugee children, and reestablish Tibet's ancient seats of learning.

With the establishment of the Central Tibetan Administration (CTA), the Dalai Lama has worked to establish democratic institutions among the refugee population. He has also attempted to forge a "middle path" solution to the Sino-Tibetan conflict by advocating Tibetan autonomy instead of full independence from China, and on March 10, 2011, he voluntarily relinquished his role as political leader.

His Holiness the Dalai Lama continues to travel extensively around the world, sharing his views on universal responsibility and supporting the desire of all beings for peace and well-being. His far-reaching efforts have touched many lives internationally. The promotion of interreligious harmony has been his unceasing mission, as are his efforts to foster mutually beneficial contact with practitioners of the physical and contemplative sciences. As a sign of the genuine appreciation felt around the world for his tireless, nonviolent, and compassionate efforts on behalf of all beings and the natural environment, His Holiness has been awarded many honors, including the Nobel Peace Prize in 1989, the U.S. Congressional Gold Medal in 2007, and the Templeton Prize in 2012.

The present work, the autobiography of the Dalai Lama's junior tutor, was written at the urging of His Holiness. His Holiness was not the only beneficiary of Kyabjé Trijang Rinpoché's wisdom, compassion, and wide-ranging expertise. First in Tibet and then afterward in exile in India, Rinpoché was much sought after for both his spiritual guidance and his advice on mundane affairs. Everyone from the highest-ranking government officials, abbots, tulkus (incarnate lamas), and geshés to the most ordinary monks, nuns, and laypeople, Tibetan and non-Tibetan alike, came to see him, and he served them all with great kindness and patience. It is from his unique vantage point at the epicenter of Tibet's spiritual and temporal life for so many decades that Rinpoché is able to provide the readers of this autobiography with such a vivid account of the momentous events that so dramatically impacted Tibet and its people in the twentieth century. Without fabrication or omission, he candidly describes the external events that unfolded before his own eyes and also gives his impressions of them. He alludes to secret visions, such as the one he had when standing before the sacred statue of Guru Padmasambhava at Sheldrak Cave.

Special Relationship of the Two Tutors

Kyabjé Ling Rinpoché and Kyabjé Trijang Rinpoché were extraordinary beings, beyond their vast learning and accomplishments. They both

Ling Rinpoché and Trijang Rinpoché sharing a laugh on the lawn of Rikon Monastery, Switzerland, 1968. COURTESY OF YONGZIN LINGTSANG LABRANG

received extensive teachings on sutra and tantra from Phabongkha Dechen Nyingpo (1878–1941), who was root guru to both of them. And they both served as tutors to His Holiness the Dalai Lama. Trijang Rinpoché was a few years older than the senior tutor, Ling Rinpoché. The term "junior tutor" merely indicates that he was appointed a few years later. Instead of experiencing rivalry and competition, the two tutors became very close. They exchanged teachings and initiations with each other in a mutual guru-disciple relationship, creating a special harmony, so vital for their roles as tutors. Whenever they attended ceremonies and functions, it was clear they were the best of friends. Kyabjé Trijang Rinpoché often made remarks that caused Ling Rinpoché to burst out laughing, which can be seen in many photographs. I witnessed a few of these occasions myself and used to wonder what it was that they could be talking about. After Trijang Rinpoché's passing, Ling Rinpoché told me several times how much he missed Trijang Rinpoché because of their unique bond.

Personal Reminiscences and Reflections

In my earliest memories of Rinpoché, he would walk to our house in Lhasa to confer White Tārā long-life initiations or to preside over special ritual offerings. All the members of my family would wear their best attire and stand in line outside the gate of our house with incense in hand to greet Rinpoché, who came a short distance from his *labrang* (official residence) together with his retinue. It was always a joyous occasion when Rinpoché came. In my memory, he is tall and slender, with sharp features, a gaze of caring tenderness, and a warm smile. He had an amazing voice: soft, deep, and melodious, and one always felt cared for and valued while in his benevolent presence. These greatly anticipated visits to our home became less frequent after Rinpoché was appointed tutor to His Holiness.

In addition to those magical occasions when he blessed our house with his visits, I have many happy memories of visiting with Rinpoché in the Potala or the Norbulingka, depending in which of these two palaces His Holiness was currently residing. And as a young boy I loved attending his teachings. Even though I was only seven years old at the time, I remember one discourse in particular that he gave in 1957. Rinpoché had returned to Tibet from two major trips accompanying His Holiness the Dalai Lama: first to China in 1954 and then India in 1956. Rinpoché was fifty-seven years old, and sadly this happened to be his last major discourse in Tibet. It was a discourse on the stages of the path (*lam rim*) and on mind training (*blo byong*). Rinpoché's teaching centered on *Liberation in the Palm of Your Hand*, a work he composed based on notes he had taken during a famous teaching given in 1921 by his main guru, the great Phabongkha Rinpoché, to a gathering of over seven hundred monks, nuns, and laypeople. Kyabjé Trijang Rinpoché edited these notes into perhaps the most widely studied stages of the path text of the past century.

This discourse in 1957 was given by Rinpoché at Shidé Monastery in Lhasa, and it lasted over a month. The sessions were long: three hours in the morning and four to five hours in the afternoon. Over four thousand people from all walks of life attended them, including abbots, tulkus, geshés, monks, government officials, and members of the general population from the Lhasa area. In the morning sessions, melodious chanting of preliminaries accompanied review meditations on the points of the teachings Rinpoché had taught the previous day. At that time there were no loudspeakers, but Rinpoché's melodious voice could be heard clearly at any location on the premises. Interspersed with readings from the text, given in order to transmit the blessings of its unbroken lineage to those in attendance, Rinpoché spoke extemporaneously. He was engaging, and as he scanned the hall from one side to the other, he made direct eye contact with all his gathered disciples. When he narrated the miseries in the lower states of cyclic existence or expounded on the heroic deeds of the bodhisattvas, audience members were visibly moved, and many had tears running down their cheeks. He had a way of drawing a wide range of reactions from his audience, often leaving them in stitches after one of his humorous anecdotes. I remember seeing a few in the audience, suddenly awakened from their momentary naps by these gleeful sounds, join in the general laughter without having any idea what the joke was about.

A few times during this discourse, Rinpoché continued to teach well into the evening and beyond. As darkness fell, the glimmering light from the hundreds of butter lamps before the holy images on the altar would illuminate the spacious assembly hall. To the right of Rinpoché's teaching throne, on a table, sat a lone kerosene lantern. I remember vividly the light this lantern cast on Rinpoché, while he sat in his typical posture, his head leaning slightly to the right. While many in attendance were apparently able to stay focused on the teachings far into the night, there were a few like me who longed for a break to relieve the pressure in our bladders. There was no shortage of people who sponsored offerings of Tibetan tea in the mornings and afternoons for the duration of the discourse. Participants brought their own wooden tea bowls. For the morning tea sessions, many brought a small pouch of roasted barley *tsampa* flour mixed with grated dried cheese. The mixture of tea and tsampa made a delicious instant meal. During the afternoon tea break, Rinpoché read announcements of the sponsors of the tea offerings and requested the audience to say prayers for them.

Despite everything else that was occurring in Tibet at that time, during the month of Rinpoché's teachings an immense feeling of joy and peace prevailed. It felt as though the grosser afflictions were dormant. Those in attendance showed kindness and love toward one another, creating an atmosphere of inspiration and hope. I remember looking forward to each day's teachings and was deeply saddened when they came to an end.

This atmosphere of love and kindness was eventually destroyed by the presence of China's People's Liberation Army. Teachings such as the ones I have described became more and more scarce in Tibet as tensions rose. The atmosphere became hostile to Tibetan culture and its unique way of life. By 1959, Tibet was an occupied country, and the values and beliefs of the Communist occupiers were in direct conflict with those of the native population, and many fled into exile in the hopes of being able to keep their culture alive.

While in exile, Rinpoché continued giving teachings and composing texts that make up the seven volumes of his collected works. I also had the good fortune to attend many of Rinpoché's teachings in India. Even though the discourses were as brilliant as before, the atmosphere in which they were given could not compare to what I experienced as a young student in Tibet. Nevertheless, the immense gratitude and appreciation I feel for the presence in exile of such great masters as His Holiness the Dalai Lama and his two tutors cannot be adequately expressed. I consider myself incredibly fortunate to share such close cultural and ethnic ties with these incomparable beings.

The Shukden Controversy

I feel it is important to clarify here the exact nature of Kyabjé Trijang Rinpoché's association with the protector Shukden, which is mentioned in the autobiography. The practice of Shukden was not a central element of Rinpoché's commitments. Shukden was one of many indigenous oath-bound protector deities that Rinpoché propitiated to bind them to their commitments to assist in Dharma activities. The practice of Shukden became widespread in certain Geluk circles in the 1970s in India, almost to the extent of taking precedence over other essential Buddhist practices, such as taking refuge in the Three Jewels. If one reads the instructional notes to the propitiation of this deity, Kyabjé Phabongkha clearly emphasizes that one should do the rituals in private and never in public. Contrary to this, Shukden was being propitiated in the general assembly halls in some monasteries. This practice was also eroding relations among the different Tibetan religious traditions. In order to promote harmony among the Tibetan lineages, His Holiness the Dalai Lama was compelled to discourage the practice of Shukden. His Holiness has clearly explained the reasons for his stand on numerous occasions and makes it clear that those who continue to pursue this divisive practice should not attend his tantric teachings, especially initiations, as this would violate sacred commitments between guru and disciple.

Contrary to some claims, there were no disagreements or breaches of guru devotion over this issue between His Holiness and Trijang Rinpoché. Many times His Holiness has expressed his deep gratitude and devotion to

Kyabjé Trijang Rinpoché as the true emanation of Cakrasaṃvara and the sole propagator of the complete transmission of the stages of the path and mind training lineages. Whenever His Holiness gives public teachings on a text that he has received from Kyabjé Trijang Rinpoché, he never fails to acknowledge and pay tribute to him as the source of the lineage. His Holiness fully discussed the conclusions of his research on the controversy with Trijang Rinpoché before declaring his stance publicly. It is not a breach of guru devotion to merely disagree with one's guru. This is clearly stipulated in verse 24 of *Fifty Verses on Guru Devotion* by Aśvaghoṣa.

Furthermore, Kyabjé Trijang Rinpoché, who was with His Holiness from the time His Holiness was only six years old, had tremendous affection for His Holiness and always marveled at the depth of his wisdom and incredible accomplishments in all aspects of learning and spiritual attainments. At the discourses in both Tibet and India, Rinpoché frequently appealed to disciples to pray for the health and long life of His Holiness. He reminded them that the Fourteenth Dalai Lama is an extraordinarily great lama who surpasses the wisdom and accomplishments of all the previous Dalai Lamas combined.

Kyabjé Trijang Rinpoché's greatest legacy is his impeccable service to His Holiness as tutor, offering instructions on all aspects of traditional Tibetan education as well as offering instructions for the training and practice of all sutra and tantra lineages. In addition to his own Dharma practice, he dedicated his entire life to preserving and propagating the sutra and tantra studies and practices for others. He is also known for his unique contributions to a wide range of other fields of knowledge such as art, drama, literature, and poetry.

After orchestrating the events at the end of his life and giving guidance for the discovery of his reincarnation, Rinpoché passed his thoughts into the state of peace at the age of eighty-one. I had the great fortune of visiting India one month before his passing. On the last day of my visit in Dharamsala before my return to New York, Rinpoché invited me to have lunch with him. He gave me much spiritual advice and lovingly held my head to his chest and blessed me. His parting words were that there will be no one like His Holiness, who can give such genuine and trustworthy advice, and that we should all follow his wishes.

The Magical Play of Illusion

A Candid Account of My Life as an Ordinary Being Claiming to Be the Reincarnation of the Great Ganden Throneholder Jangchup Chöphel

༄། །དགའ་ལྡན་ཁྲི་ཆེན་བྱང་ཆུབ་ཆོས་འཕེལ་གྱི་
སྐྱེ་གྲལ་དུ་རློམ་པའི་གྱི་ན་པ་ཞིག་གིས་
རང་གི་དང་ཚུལ་མ་བཅོས་ལྷུག་པར་བཀོད་པ་
འཁྲུལ་སྣང་སྒྱུ་མའི་ཟློས་གར།

Kyabjé Trijang Rinpoché
Losang Yeshé Tenzin Gyatso
(1901–81)

Homage and Preliminary Remarks

The immutable essence of all the victorious ones' ineffable body, speech, and mind is manifest in the form of my protectors, my twenty-two kind and venerable teachers. At their feet, I remain humbly devoted until my awakening.

Long have I lain in the bed of samsara. I despair
on seeing, in life after life, the pattern of happiness and suffering
that is like the front and back of a single brocade
woven from countless threads of karma and affliction.

But as with a flash of lightning in the dark of night,
by the kindness of the holy lamas I have caught a glimpse
of the stainless path of Dharma, and so I have hope
that my life in this world will have meaning.

Yet my heart is gripped by the demon
of clinging to things as real and lasting,
and so I tell this story of high aspiration tossed on the wind
by the ceaseless distractions of the monkey-dance appearances
of this life.[1]

I AM AN ORDINARY man called Losang Yeshé Tenzin Gyatso. It is said that I am the reincarnation of the Eighty-Fifth Ganden Throneholder[2] Losang Tsultrim Palden, who was himself the reincarnation of the Sixty-Ninth Ganden Throneholder Jangchup Chöphel. I am said to be this reincarnation, but my mind is no mystery to me, and the qualities that make those supreme beings worthy to be called incarnations of the Awakened One are no more present in me than are flowers in the sky. It is only through the immutable force of actions in previous lives that I now enjoy the fortune to have been given the title of a high incarnation.

Jé Gungthangpa[3] once said that if one has purposely reincarnated for the sake of propagating the Dharma, then one must leave a legacy of teachings and accomplishments. It is daunting to read the biographies of the holy men who were my predecessors. Their qualities arouse faith and have the power to plant the seeds of complete liberation in the minds of disciples who hear them.

Like hair on a turtle, how could any such qualities exist in one such as me, a mass of stupidity and the three poisons [of attachment, ignorance, and hatred], renowned for three things [only—sleeping, eating, and defecating]? Indeed, I have no such qualities; I possess merely the name of a master. Still, so as not to squander the name of that which I am supposed to be, I must leave at least a meager legacy of protecting and spreading the Dharma that I have heard, studied, taught, and practiced.

If one does not look closely, it may appear that I have the qualities of my predecessors or something similar to them, but these apparent qualities do not stand up to scrutiny. The qualities of greatness appearing to be mine are an illusion with the ephemeral nature of a colorful rainbow. In fact, I am an ordinary person overwhelmed by confusion about this phenomenal world. For me to write about my life may upset discriminating people because it might seem as if I, like a bat mistaking itself for a bird in the sky, have the temerity to imitate those great masters, my predecessors, who wrote their autobiographies.

Be that as it may, in the wood-dragon year (1964), the Omnipresent Protector, the Supreme Lord of the Victorious Ones, Tenzin Gyatso, His Holiness the Fourteenth Dalai Lama, said to me, "You must write the story of your life," and I received his holy command on the crown of my head. Subsequently, Geshé Tamdrin Rapten of Sera Jé and other faithful disciples insisted that I do so; the former cabinet minister Neshar Thupten Tharpa presented me with a bronze statue of the Buddha together with a ceremonial silk scarf and made this request; and more recently Dagyab Hothokthu Rinpoché asked me to do so in a letter from Germany. Moreover, Palden, who has been with me in close attendance for many years and saw everything firsthand, made a special point of taking careful notes on the conversations he overheard, and he has insisted time and again that I put them in order and edit them.

I have decided, therefore, to write candidly the story of my life, and I feel that there is nothing very wrong with this if it is considered in the context of autobiographies such as those of Depa Kyishöpa, also known as Taktsé

Shabdrung Dorjé Namgyal, the cabinet ministers Gashiwa Doring Tenzin Paljor[4] and Dokhar Shabdrung Tsering Wangyal,[5] and other well-known statesmen.

Mine is the story of how I wasted the freedom and opportunity that this life affords in the pretense of Dharma, while the happiness and suffering brought forth by my own ignorance and good and bad deeds came in turns throughout the seasons of my life. It is the story of how I received religious instructions on the vast and profound sutras and tantras from many qualified spiritual masters, who were like the Buddha himself, and yet I remained unable to show even one point that I mastered or to demonstrate with any confidence that, apart from recollection of those instructions, any of them took root in my heart through practice. As the Seventh Dalai Lama Kalsang Gyatso (1708–57) said:

> Those who teach the path to freedom to others,
> if they lack the quality of mind merged with holy Dharma
> and possess just the appearance of working for the welfare
> of others,
> cause nothing but weariness for themselves and others.
> How sad to see them fool themselves in such a way.

In brief, the feeble way in which I have propagated Dharma by teaching earnest seekers is akin to a tape recorder or a parrot reciting mantras. The Tibetan scholar Mipham Gelek once said:

> The grove of peace that has grown in my heart
> serves only to deceive myself and others,
> for I have been given a wobbly staff of morality.
> Who gave me this staff? My own unconscionable acts.

Likewise, I have deceived others and distracted myself by turning the wheel of virtuous and nonvirtuous actions, the three poisons, and the eight worldly concerns.[6] My story is one of an empty-handed vagabond in want of Dharma. It is crudely written, but it is without fabrications. I will not present what did not happen as if it had. I will not present as having been done what was not. Whatever I recall, I will openly and truthfully relate.

1 | The Beginning of My Life

My Family Background

I WAS BORN IN the land of the supreme ārya with a lotus in his hand.[7] Of Tibet's three provinces, mine was Ü-Tsang, the "province of Dharma." Among the four districts of Ü-Tsang, mine was Kyishö Tsal Gungthang. This was the birthplace of Yudrakpa, protector of the inhabitants of Shang. He founded the Tsalpa Kagyü tradition and a monastery in Gungthang district that vastly improved scholarship in the area.[8] In fact, prior to the founding of Riwo Ganden Monastery by Mañjunātha, the great Tsongkhapa, Gungthang Monastery was renowned as one of Tibet's six major centers of learning, the others being Sangphu, Ratö Dewachen, Gadong, Kyormolung, and Sulpu.

During the height of rule of the Tsalpa potentate, the monastery contained two colleges known as Tsal and Gungthang. In Tsal College there were two schools: U Ling and Yangön. In Gungthang College there were three schools: Chötri, Sim Khangshar, and Chökhor Ling. The monastery was well endowed, both spiritually and materially. Later the rule of the Tsalpa potentate declined, and in the fire-rabbit year of the ninth cycle (1507), a great fire broke out in the monastery and destroyed the main chapel, statues of Mahādeva Munīndra, Shang Rinpoché, Four-Armed Mahākāla, the Tashi Öbar mausoleum, and some extremely sacred relics of the Buddha. With only two small schools, Sim Khangshar and Chötri, remaining, the monastery deteriorated both spiritually and materially.

At the time of the Great Fifth Dalai Lama Ngawang Losang Gyatso (1617–82), Surchen Chöying Rangdröl was the presiding lama of Gungthang. After him came the ascetic from Amdo, Gendun Phuntsok, the Fiftieth Ganden Throneholder. It was he who covered Ganden's silver mausoleum of Mañjunātha Jé Tsongkhapa with gold. In appreciation of this, King Lhasang[9] bestowed upon him dominion over the Gungthang temple and its sacred treasures, the two monastic schools with a treasury for their maintenance, the land, buildings, people, and wealth of the district.

Thus Gendun Phuntsok came to be widely known as the great throneholder from Gungthang, and his subsequent reincarnations, including the revered Tenpai Drönmé, were also commonly known as men from Gungthang, even though they continued to maintain their households at Tashi Khyil Monastery in Amdo. The distance from Amdo to Gungthang was so great that the reincarnation of the great throneholder Gendun Phuntsok found it too difficult to administer his holdings in Gungthang and so eventually returned them to the central government.

In later times, when the Seventh Dalai Lama Kalsang Gyatso was in his minority, the Dalai Lama's uncle Samten Gyatso served as his devoted guardian and reading instructor. In appreciation of his services, dominion over Gungthang district, including its temple and treasury, was given in perpetuity to the entire family of Samten Gyatso, beginning with his son, a monk named Kalsang Yönten.

My own father, Tsering Döndrup, was an undisputed paternal relative of the Seventh Dalai Lama and as such became a member of the Gungthang hierarchy. An erudite man in secular matters, he was firm, subtle, and wise. Thus he came to be highly esteemed by all the inhabitants of the region and was constantly sought after for his good advice.

My father's first wife bore him two daughters and five sons and passed away at an early age. Among their children was the incarnation of the Ganden Throneholder named Khamlung Tulku, of Drati House, Sera Jé. During this time my father also had an amorous relationship with one of the household maids, and she gave birth to Phukhang Khyenrap Tulku of Ganden.

The youngest of his first wife's sons was married at the age of twenty to Tsering Drölma, a lady from the Nang Gong family of Gungthang. One day, while fording the Kyichu River on his way to Lhasa, he was swept away by the current and drowned. Later my father married the widowed Tsering Drölma, and she bore him three children. The eldest was myself, the middle child was a daughter named Jampal Chötso, and the youngest was a son, the reincarnation of Lelung Tulku. These are the origins of my immediate family.

My father was born in the water-rabbit year (1842), my mother in the wood-pig year (1874). He was fifty-nine years old and she twenty-seven

Religious dances at Gungthang Monastery, 1920 or 1921

© Rabden Lepcha, Pitt Rivers Museum, University of Oxford; 1998.285.363

when, by the force of virtuous actions I had done in previous lives, I was born as their son. I left my mother's womb at sunrise as the star Denebola appeared in the sky on Tuesday, the twelfth day of the third month of the iron-ox year of the fifteenth cycle (April 30, 1901).

My father was responsible for the overall administration of Gungthang Monastery, which included the temple and the two colleges. Among his responsibilities was the obligation to provide a monk official from the monastery's hierarchy to work in the central government. Previously some very well-known men had served in this capacity. Among them were Jampa Tengyé, who rose to become lord chamberlain, and just after him, as I recall, Tenzin Wangpo of Gungthang, who became a ministerial secretary.

My older sister, Kalsang Drölma, married a nobleman of the Khemé family named Rinchen Wangyal, who was himself a minor lay official. Thereafter the Khemé and Gungthang households were joined and became known as Khegung. As both the lay and monk officials from the household had to be at their offices in Lhasa every day, some land was bought in Lhasa when I was about three or four years old and a house constructed there called Kunsangtsé.

When I was about three years old, my father and Secretary Tenzin

Wangpo took upon themselves the responsibility of having extensive renovations made to the entire Gungthang Monastery, a small room for the Dalai Lama constructed on top, and additional monks' quarters built outside. When all was complete, they invited Dzamling Chegu Wangdü, patriarch of Sakya Phuntsok Phodrang,[10] to perform a long-life empowerment and a ceremony for the elimination of inauspiciousness. I still remember being given a sacramental tablet on a silver spoon during the long-life empowerment, people passing back and forth over a vessel filled with glowing coals, and *tsa-tsa*[11] being held over their heads while they received ablution from a ceremonial vase during the ritual for the elimination of inauspiciousness. I also remember the aged consort of the Sakya patriarch holding me in her lap with great affection and many other things that took place that day. Later, when I was about thirty-seven years old, I went on a pilgrimage in the province of Tsang and visited the Sakya Phuntsok Phodrang mausoleum where, to my amazement, I beheld something in the shape of a lotus approximately one foot high growing on the embalmed remains of that patriarch who had given us the long-life empowerment.

The Death of My Predecessor

My predecessor, Losang Tsultrim Palden, was born into the Öntön Kyergang family of Tölung Rakor in the earth-pig year (1839). In the fire-monkey year (1896) he was installed upon the golden throne of Ganden. In the iron-rat year (1900), while my predecessor still carried the responsibilities of the throneholder, the lord of the victorious ones, the Thirteenth Dalai Lama Thupten Gyatso (1876–1933), decided to make a journey to Chökhor Gyal and, as was the custom, planned to stop at Ganden en route. In order to greet the Dalai Lama according to tradition, the throneholder proceeded from Lhasa to Ganden with a golden parasol and full entourage in the third month of that year. When the procession reached a grove of willows on the Gungthang estate, the throneholder announced that he needed to rest and would stop there for a little while. His attendants asked if this would be proper, considering that they were in a formal procession and very near a village. He replied, "What is wrong with that? I shall sit for a while right here," and so the entire procession came to a brief halt. Then he commented that it would be nice if he knew someone in that area so that he could have a good place to stop when he traveled back and forth between Ganden and Lhasa.

At a later date, the Dalai Lama arrived in Ganden and the ceremonies were performed. After the Dalai Lama had departed, the throneholder's health began to deteriorate. During his daily circumambulations of Ganden, he would become tired and thirsty, and so his attendants would bring along a chair and something to drink. On the twenty-fifth day[12] of the fourth month of the iron-rat year (1900), while circumambulating Ganden, the throneholder sat down at a side entrance to the debating ground that was in front of Jé Tsongkhapa's throne room. Facing his attendants and looking at his treasurer, Ngakrampa Gyütö Losang Tendar,[13] he began to speak, saying, "This man will search out . . ." He continued speaking for a while and then faced the western sky. Laughing all the while, he said, "Ganden, Ganden,"[14] and suddenly passed into the realm of peace.

Geshé Nyitso Trinlé of Samling Monastery immediately carried the throneholder's body to the house of Jé Tsongkhapa and placed it in a small room called the Chamber of Clear Light. For one week the body remained there while offerings were made. Then it was cremated behind Ganden's Mount Gok. The smoke rising from the cremation pyre lifted the silk canopy high into the sky as if it had been blown by the wind. Both the smoke and the canopy disappeared to the west.

After one week, the cremation structure was opened, and the throneholder's heart, tongue, and eyes were discovered to have not been consumed by the fire. A reliquary stupa was built at the small monastery of Chatreng, and these parts of his body were enshrined there. Years later, when the people of Chatreng were fighting the Chinese, they found that drinking an ablution poured over these relics gave them protection against bullets, and so in order to make themselves bulletproof, they divided the relics up and ate them. In later years, Ngakrampa would refer to the natives of Chatreng as "the people who ate my lama's heart."

After the cremation, Ngakrampa assisted by Chisur Lekshé Gyatso, a nephew of the late throneholder, took primary responsibility for making ceremonial offerings and finding the throneholder's incarnation. They requested our great refuge and protector, the Thirteenth Dalai Lama, who was then staying at his paternal family's estate, to compose a prayer for the quick arrival of the reincarnation, and the Dalai Lama did so immediately.

My Recognition as a Reincarnation

The winter before I was born, a peach tree in the grove of a summer house on the Gungthang estate miraculously burst into flower, and about thirty pieces of fruit formed at the top of the tree. Before I could even walk, I displayed a fascination with deities, statues, and religious objects and took great pleasure in vajras, bells, drums, cymbals, and other ritual objects. Monks were a source of delight to me. I loved to sit among them when they were in assembly and imitate their chanting of prayers.

Since my actions showed some indication of right instincts, a geshé from Ganden who came regularly to our household to perform rituals took notice of me. He reported that there was an exceptional boy in the Gungthang household who should be considered when candidates for the throneholder's reincarnation were examined. Thus Ngakrampa and Geshé Sadul Gendun Drakpa, the monk from Chatreng who had carried the ceremonial parasol for the late throneholder, came to Gungthang to examine me.

When they arrived, I happened to be on my nanny's back just outside the fence. As we met I called out loudly, "Gendun Drakpa!" Ngakrampa inquired whether any of the family, friends, or servants had such a name and was informed that no one in the household had a name anything like that. Amazed, they went inside, and I, having followed, climbed into Gendun Drakpa's lap, extended my legs, and said, "Wash my feet!" When the late throneholder had been stricken with rheumatism, this monk had bathed the throneholder's feet with radish juice, and so it seemed to him as if I were manifesting actual remembrance of that previous life. With tears streaming down his face, he washed the bottoms of my feet by licking them with his tongue. I still remember this. Actually it must all have been nothing more than some sort of coincidence, for I myself had no actual memories of a previous life.

The household's dairyman, Tashi Döndrup—the father of both my senior attendant Lhabu and personal attendant Palden—had deep faith in the late throneholder, so when he heard while on a sojourn in Lhasa that the throneholder's reincarnation was supposed to be in Gungthang, he decided to go and see for himself. At the monastery's reception hall, he was seated at the end of a row. Seeing him, I sprang out of my seat and ran over to him. Pulling out a silver coin, I handed it to him. Not knowing what to do with it, the dairyman handed it back. I remember my father saying, "This is a gift my son made to you; it is all right for you to keep it."

The Thirteenth Dalai Lama was requested to make a divination concerning the throneholder's reincarnation. He did so and then gave the following instructions: "During the second month of the water-tiger year (1902), make a detailed investigation in the south of Lhasa." At that very time my mother went to Lhasa in order to do prostrations, circumambulations, and so on. She happened to rent a room in the house of a man called Akhu Trinlé, who was caretaker of the southern part of Lhasa's Jokhang Temple.

A tutor to the Dalai Lama, Phurchok Jampa Gyatso, said in response to a request for divination, "In a place not far to the west of Ganden, the face of that supreme emanation appears to me." The oracle of Gadong,[15] in response to the first request for a prophecy concerning the throneholder's reincarnation, said, "On the outskirts of the eastern side of the temple, examine a boy born in the iron-ox year whose mother's name ends with Drölma."

The predecessor of the present Ling Rinpoché[16] said in response to a request for divination, "Of the Buddha's five emanations,[17] this incarnation is an emanation of the Buddha's mind. He appears in a place not far to the south of Lhasa."

Responding to a second request for divination, for which he was presented with names of boys who had shown some promising signs in their examinations, the Thirteenth Dalai Lama said, "This divination indicates that the boy born in the iron-ox year to Tsering Drölma should be recognized as the late throneholder's reincarnation."

The oracle of Gadong said in his second prophecy, "The boy born in the iron-ox year to Tsering Drölma should definitely be recognized as the late throneholder's reincarnation." The Nechung oracle, when presented with the list of names, made his prophecy while in trance by stamping his seal upon the line that read, "Boy born in the iron-ox year to Tsering Drölma."

When Ngakrampa and his party made their initial examination, they showed me a statue of the Buddha that the late throneholder had received at his ordination, his prayer beads, and his wooden monk's bowl, along with other similar decoy objects. I picked up the late throneholder's statue and acted as if I wanted to put its head in my mouth. They took this as a sign that I was asserting myself as a master of the doctrine. I next picked up the late throneholder's bowl and then a string of prayer beads that had been placed among the other objects as a decoy. A little while later I put those prayer beads back, picked up the ones that had belonged to the late throneholder, and, refusing to give them back, kept them thereafter. Apparently all this gave the examiners great faith in me.

Contention Concerning a Rival Candidate

There was also another boy who had shown some good signs. He was a son of the Chagong Beda Trotitsang family from Upper Chatreng. The people of Chatreng, motivated by provincial bias, intended to have this boy recognized as the late throneholder's reincarnation, come what may. They spread rumors to the effect that a son of Lekshé Gyatso, the former governor of Gungthang, was going to be recognized as the late throneholder's reincarnation and finally wrote a letter to Ngakrampa and to the former governor Lekshé Gyatso himself that read as follows:

> The reincarnation of our lama is right here in Chatreng. You cannot give his title to some little boy from Gungthang. Since it would be wrong to give recognition to this Gungthang beggar boy, we will not allow you to take possession of the late throneholder's household or his personal possessions. They will be placed in the custody of Chatreng Monastery.

A number of heated missives like this were sent. Letters were also sent to the monks from Chatreng at Ganden and Sera monasteries apprising them of the situation. Some of the monks held the view that it would suffice to find the real reincarnation, no matter where he might come from, but the majority insisted that the boy from Chatreng be recognized regardless. These two factions remained divided and continued to argue until the Great Prayer Festival at New Year.[18] At that time representatives from Samling Mitsen and Dokhang House and the abbot and staff of Ganden Shartsé College met at the late throneholder's residence in Lhasa.[19] They argued the matter day and night until they finally came to a decision based upon the prophecies and divinations given by the oracles and masters, most especially the Dalai Lama. Thus they chose to recognize me.

The series of letters sent from Chatreng Monastery to the Trijang household with copies of the various responses, documents containing the divinations and prophecies made by the lamas (chief among them those of the Dalai Lama) and oracles, together with the formal requests, a record of the extensive rituals that were performed in order to assure discovery of the true reincarnation, and a written history of everything that transpired following the passing away of the late throneholder up to the time I was recognized and installed at the monastery—all of this was gathered together as part of the Trijang household records and kept at Chusang Hermitage near Sera. Although I was finally recognized as the late throneholder's reincarnation and installed as his successor based on the decision that had been reached at the meeting in Lhasa, the majority of the people living in Chatreng, except for a very few who remained neutral, held fast to their previous position and planned to mount a challenge.

However, in the wood-snake year (1905) a large number of Chinese soldiers led by the Chinese general Zhao Erfeng, also known as Zhao Tarin, invaded eastern Tibet and remained in occupation. Numerous monasteries in the occupied areas of Lithang, Ba Chödé, and so forth—especially Chatreng Monastery—put up an armed resistance for quite some time, but on the fifteenth day of the fourth month of the fire-horse year (1906), the monastery was lost, together with the lives of many laymen and monks.

All the laymen of those areas and the remaining monks fled to the forests and remained there in hiding. They continued to carry on their armed struggle, until finally, on the fifteenth day of the fourth month of the earth-horse year (1918), they were able to hold a service once again, in the ruins of the monastery's assembly hall. As the monastery and all the surrounding area had been in a constant state of unrest for those thirteen years, there was no opportunity to indulge in complaints to Lhasa about my installation, and so contention naturally came to a standstill during that period.

In the earth-horse year (1918) I received my geshé lharam degree, and by then many of those who had initially opposed my installation had changed their minds about me. There was still, however, a group from Beda Monastery who continued to stir up trouble until the earth-snake year (1929), when I had reached the age of twenty-eight. I shall tell about this later in its chronological place. In any case, the situation was such that the outcome could not have been altered, even by the intervention of a thousand-armed god.

2 | Ordination and Early Education

Taking Up Official Residence and Beginning My Education

In my fourth year, on the twenty-third day of the first month of the wood-dragon year (1904), I was taken for the first time from my birthplace to Trijang Labrang in Lhasa. That day was the conclusion of the Great Prayer Festival in Lhasa, and following the tradition, the current throneholder accompanied by lay and monk officials had gone in formal procession to perform the customary blessing of Lhasa's Kyichu River dam. Our party proceeded just after the throneholder's party had returned from this ceremony, and thus, without having been planned, there was a spontaneous reception as if the throneholder had come out to greet me. This was said at the time to have been an auspicious sign.

Just before we arrived at the entrance to our house, a miller's daughter carrying a large sack of wheat on her back stopped to look at our procession. The spectacle must have distracted her attention, for the rope that secured the sack slipped from her hands, and all the wheat poured onto the ground, blocking the labrang entryway. Taking this to be another auspicious sign, all who were there to greet me grabbed handfuls of the wheat and threw it at us in welcome. The bursar of our labrang had to later reimburse the miller with another sack of wheat.

Just after we arrived, a formal reception ceremony was held in the main assembly hall. Whether for a special purpose or for some other reason, my throne faced north, and the masters and staff of Ganden, who had come to welcome me, sat in a row at the north side of the hall facing south. Among them was Khedrup, the incumbent treasurer of Shartsé College, who shared the same household with Khamtruk, a man from Chatreng who had been a bodyguard of the Thirteenth Dalai Lama and had experienced some difficulties with my predecessor. Although Khedrup sat in the row with the others who were welcoming me, his were not thoughts of welcome. Staring at him I touched my finger to my cheek, indicating that he should be ashamed. Everyone was quite surprised, and naturally he became flushed with guilt.

A few days later, Ngakrampa together with Dzongsur Lekshé Gyatso and some others took me for the first time to Chusang Hermitage. When we arrived there, we were greeted by the master of the hermitage, Dromtö Geshé Rinpoché, a dignified white-haired monk who had both received from and given teachings to Kyabjé Vajradhara Phabongkha Rinpoché. In a formal receiving line there were also several other senior monks attired in their ceremonial robes and hats. A throne had been set up for me facing east in the main prayer hall, and after I was seated on it, tea and rice were served, and the monks performed the long-life ceremony of the sixteen arhats for me. I still remember that among the ritual objects that were handed to me and then taken back as part of the ceremony was a beautiful silk appliqué of a mongoose, which I refused to give back for quite some time.

About ten days later, Ngakrampa had a small wooden board for writing specially made for me. Since the translators of old had propagated the doctrine in Tibet by first studying the Indian texts written on palm leaves, he considered this to be an auspicious way of beginning my education. He printed on my wooden board the thirty letters of the Tibetan alphabet as well as all the subscripts and superscripts. He also wrote a few verses of alliterative children's poetry. In this way he taught me the alphabet, the building blocks of all literature.

I delighted my teacher by learning all thirty letters that very day. Thereafter, he would boast that his charge had learned the *ka kha ga* alphabet in a single day. Ngakrampa spent a long time teaching me to read and spell from printed editions of the Buddha's *Eight Thousand Verse Perfection of Wisdom* and the Son Teachings from the *Book of Kadam*.[20] He also had me practice on a text that had been written out in longhand with numerous abbreviations: the *Stages of the Path* by Kachen Namkha Dorjé, who was a direct disciple of Paṇchen Losang Chögyen.[21] Because of my teacher's thoughtful instructions, I was able from then on to read with ease an entire book every day, be it printed or handwritten.

Whenever Dzongsur Lekshé Gyatso would come from Lhasa to Chusang Hermitage, where I was staying, I would say before he arrived, "Mr. Dzong is coming," and then he would arrive. One day, late in the morning,

I suddenly said, "Lhundrup died." We found out later that an old servant in the Maldro Jarado Labrang, a former monk named Lhundrup, had died just at that time. Ngakrampa thought these occurrences extraordinary, and so he noted them down. Actually, they were just the babbling of a child who says whatever comes to his mind. This situation was not unlike that of the pig-headed fortune teller.[22] After all, how could I, someone who is not even sure where he will defecate at night the food he ate in the morning, know of things hidden in the future?

When I had reached the age of five, my father took the vows of a novice and a fully ordained monk from Venerable Khyenrap Yonten Gyatso, who was then the incumbent Jangtsé Chöjé and later became the Ganden Throneholder. My father was given the name of Khyenrap Chöphel. My mother Tsering Drölma, my sister Jampal Chötso, and my younger brother took up residence in the estate that my father had left to them. It was in a place called Gungthang Chökhor Ling, near the residence of an uncle named Gyatso-la, who was a monk at Chötri College of Gungthang Monastery.

When I was six years old, Demo Rinpoché[23] of Tengyé Ling Monastery, who was the same age as I, came to visit Mr. Lokhé, his monastery's bursar then staying at Chusang Hermitage. One day they came to my residence, and I met Demo for the first time. We were so small that we were both put in the same chair. Then for no apparent reason, the two of us began to cry. It seems that, ever since the time of Ganden Throneholder Jangchup Chöphel, our two labrangs had very strong religious and secular connections. Demo's predecessor had been a regent of Tibet and was imprisoned by the Thirteenth Dalai Lama. While in prison he died, and so it seemed to both Ngakrampa and Mr. Lokhé that the two of us were crying in remembrance of the difficulties that Demo's predecessor had endured. Actually this was just another coincidence, for I had no idea why I was crying.

The Arrival of Kyabjé Phabongkha Rinpoché

Later that year, Kyabjé Vajradhara Phabongkha Rinpoché came to Chusang Hermitage. This was as if the force of my prayers combined with a considerable store of accumulated merit had rolled a giant boulder of gold right up to my door. For seven years, until the end of the water-rat year (1912), he lived in the guesthouse on the debating ground of my residence.

At the beginning of this period he was twenty-nine years old and had just left Gyütö Monastery, the upper tantric college.[24] For attendants he had only his elder brother Sölpön-la, who later became the senior treasurer known as Ngawang Gyatso, and another aid named Losang, who had been provided by the Shöl Trekhang family.

Once in a while Tsangyang, a geshé from Gyalrong House of Sera Monastery who was a very talented cook, would visit Phabongkha Rinpoché for a few days and at those times would serve as chef. From time to time various masters would gather at Phabongkha Rinpoché's retreat house and exchange teachings that they had heard. Among them were Gungtrul Rinpoché, whose personal name was Khyenrap Palden Tenpai Nyima, Gangkya Rinpoché of Phenpo, Minyak Rikhü Rinpoché, who was a master from Kham, and Dromtö Geshé Rinpoché, the master of Chusang. Sometimes twenty to thirty monks from Sera and other monastic universities would come for teachings.

Between these periods Phabongkha Rinpoché would usually go into secluded retreat, after which he would perform a fire offering. He himself would make all the preparations for this ritual. He would draw the necessary hearth diagrams, arrange the ritual objects, mix the four libations, and so forth. Because I was so young, I treated these occasions as a playful distraction and would compete with Sölpön-la to assist during the ceremony by trying to hand over or receive back the offering substances before he could get to them.

Apart from an enormous number of books, the precious lama had few possessions, and his living conditions differed little from those of an average monk. After learning my lessons in the morning, I would have a break until lunch and so would go to the debating ground to play. Time and again when I came into the presence of my refuge and protector, I treated him as an equal without any reverence or courtesy, with the attitude of a child. In his presence I would perform imitations of religious dances that I had named Dance of the Lotus and Dance of White Light of Gungthang. Sometimes I would leap into his lap and play. He was a very good artist, and while sitting there he would draw all sorts of things on paper. Occasionally we would have lunch at the same time, and I would share his seat and his plate.

Although I was quite a bother, this precious lama was so very kind and gentle that he cared for me joyfully and lovingly, without ever once becoming upset or irritated. Thinking back, I received many vast and profound teachings in the presence of this incomparably kind master, who was like a father to me, but from the standpoint of practice and accomplishment, I was unable to realize the full intent of his teachings. Thus I hold the pretentious position of a fire placed in the rank of the sun, for I have been like a son who disregarded his father's last words and threw his will to the wind. Although I have propagated the discourses and esoteric practices of Dharma, principally through teaching the stages of the path, this is a mere reflection, a mimicking of my master's teachings.

When I think back on my carefree behavior as a thoughtless child, I feel that this led me not astray but rather in a good direction. It is said that devotion to one's master is the root of every good in this life and the next, and later in my life I had the opportunity of serving to the best of my ability in every way, materially and spiritually, the next incarnation of this supreme master, from the time when he was first recognized until he earned the degree of geshé lharam. I was able to serve in every way except to prevent his untimely death, which was a serious setback to the propagation of the Buddhist doctrine.[25]

Memorization of Texts

The first text that my teacher Ngakrampa had me commit to memory was *Chanting the Names of Mañjuśrī*. After I had memorized it, he required that I recite it every day without fail. He then had me memorize the short texts of worship for the red and yellow aspects of Mañjuśrī and required that I regularly repeat the mantras for increasing wisdom. In the hope of increasing my wisdom still further, I voluntarily recited one of these mantras not only every morning but every evening as well, eventually completing a hundred thousand repetitions.

Once, my elder half-brother Khamlung Rinpoché came from Sera Monastery to visit me at Chusang. He brought as a gift his monastery's reading primer, as he assumed that I had yet to learn the Tibetan alphabet. It both embarrassed and pleased him to discover that I had already memorized most of Maitreya's *Ornament of Realization* together with several different types of ritual texts.

At the age of six it is difficult to do extensive memorization, but Ngakrampa was extremely skillful in the way he raised me, applying discipline and patience in their appropriate places. Although I had no real understanding of what I was memorizing, I would make up my own interpretations, and this made it easy to hold the words in my mind. I would later ask Ngakrampa to explain the meaning of these texts, and since I had already memorized the words, the conditions were then present to support a clear comprehension.

My Ordination at Radreng Monastery

In the fourth month of the fire-sheep year (1907), at the beginning of my seventh year, I left Chusang Hermitage accompanied by Ngakrampa Losang Tendar, our treasurer Chisur Lekshé Gyatso, and Chatreng Nyitso Trinlé Tenzin of Gashar Dokhang House. Several others, including Nenang Dreshing Geshé and Sölpön Phuntsok, also joined our party. We traversed Phenpo Go Pass and stayed the night at the temple in Langthang. We then went over Chak Pass and traveled via Phödo to Radreng Monastery.[26] There, on the eighth day of the fourth month, the fourth reincarnation in the succession of the Radreng masters, the glorious and revered Ngawang Yeshé Tenpai Gyaltsen conferred upon me the precepts and vows of a layman and of a novice monk. He gave me the name Losang Yeshé Tenzin Gyatso and composed an eloquent prayer for my long life, which began with this line: "The Buddha's exquisite attributes charm the eyes of a wild mountain deer." I then received the further kindness of his oral transmission of Candrakīrti's *Entering the Middle Way* and the *Ornament of Realization*.

The fifteenth day of that month happened to be a prayer festival at Radreng Monastery. I witnessed the unfurling of their enormous silk pictorial appliqué thangka, ritual dances, and so forth. Then I went to see the monastery's most sacred image, which was a statue of the Buddha known as Lord Mañjuvajra, visited the smaller chapels, and made one thousand offerings. I also visited religious centers near Radreng, such as Tsenya Hermitage, Yangön Hermitage, and Samten Ling Nunnery, where I paid homage and made offerings.

Previously, while learning to read at Chusang Hermitage, I had read the Son Teachings of the *Book of Kadam* twice from beginning to end and so had a good recollection of the story of Atiśa's disciple in his incarnation as King Könchok Bang. Thus when our guide at Radreng explained

Radreng Monastery, 1950

points of significance, I immediately recognized them, and a certain familiarity from the associations would arise in my mind. When I practiced my reading on the Son Teachings, Ngakrampa would at the beginning explain some of the incidents in the stories. Then, as I continued reading, I was able to understand roughly most of the other episodes and the meaning of the easier verses on my own. Likewise, when memorizing the monastery's traditional prayers, I found myself for the most part able to understand roughly the meaning expressed in the aspiration prayer that concludes Śāntideva's *Guide to the Bodhisattva's Way of Life*. Considering my age, this seems to indicate that I was intelligent, at least to some degree.

While we were at Radreng, the monastery's administration had us stay in their reception room on the mezzanine and extended to our entire entourage the most cordial hospitality, seeking to provide for our every need and comfort with the utmost consideration. On the way back to Chusang, we spent a night at Taklung, a Kagyü monastery, and I visited the chapels on each floor of its temple. There I saw a most amazing thing: a statue of Dromtönpa with hair growing on its head. After that, we went to Dromtö, passing on the way Thangsak Ganden Chökhor and other monasteries. Radreng Monastery had given us so much yogurt that it lasted until Dromtö. We carried it in leather pouches and made it into a paste with roasted barley flour. Finally, we returned to Chusang Hermitage.

My Mother's Difficulties

Just before I left for the sojourn at Radreng, my father had died. Secretary Tenzin Wangpo and the other lay and monk officials residing at Kunsangtsé in Lhasa chose trustees from Gungthang for my father's estate. The trustees were a relative of my father named Ani Yangzom and her husband, a man from Kham named Bapa Apho. Those two wrote letters to Secretary Tenzin Wangpo, who was also manager of Kunsangtsé, to Rinchen Wangyal, who was an important member of the Khemé family, and to other influential people in an attempt to prejudice them against my mother. These letters made the accusation that my mother had secretly accumulated a great deal of wealth. My elder sister, Kalsang Drölma, not only failed to douse the fire of this accusation, she fueled the flames. Thus Apho-la suddenly appeared one day at my mother's house in Gungthang Chökhor Ling, locked the doors, and legally prevented anyone from entering. Now evicted, my mother and her two other children went to stay for a few days with Uncle Gyatso, who provided them with food and shelter. This was quite similar to the situation of Jetsun Milarepa's mother, Nyangtsa Kargyen, and her sister, Treta Gönkyi, who also suffered the hardship of their relations turning against them.

As soon as the news of this situation in Gungthang reached my labrang in Lhasa, my treasurer, Chisur Lekshé Gyatso, personally went to see the officials at Kunsangtsé and explained in detail what he believed to be the true factors underlying this unfortunate situation. Finally the seal on the door of my mother's house was broken and her possessions carefully examined. There was no secret accumulation of wealth as the trustees had claimed, and so the truth was revealed. On returning to Chusang, I heard about my mother's difficulties and became quite upset and worried.

My Enrollment at Ganden

During the summer retreat that year I was going to enroll at Ganden Monastery. Ngakrampa, who was well versed in astrology and accomplished in ritual procedures, did everything that was necessary to counteract negative astrological forces that might interfere with my enrollment and to remove any obstructions that might block favorable astrological influences.

On the third day of the seventh month, I left my residence in Lhasa accompanied by Ngakrampa, the treasurer Chisur, Mr. Lokhé, a monastic official named Jangchup Norsang, who represented the Dalai Lama, and several others. We set out in procession for Ganden Monastery, decked in the finest of clothing on caparisoned horses.

My late father's Gungthang estate was on our route and by all rights should have been obliged to extend hospitality to us and serve as a way station for the night, but because of the machinations of Ani Yangzom, we were not received at all and so spent the night atop the Chötri College of Gungthang. On that particular day my horse had been outfitted with a golden saddle, silk brocade caparison, and ornaments, while I myself wore an "eye of the crow" riding robe[27] and a wide-brimmed gilt lacquer hat. Being a child, I was more than happy to display such regalia.

The next day we left Gungthang and traveled to Dechen Sang-ngak Khar, where we spent the night atop the branch of Gyümé Tantric College located there. The college gave us an elaborate welcoming reception, and some friends and well-wishers who lived in that region came to present me with traditional greeting scarves and gifts. We spent the next day in the foothills of Ganden and camped that night in the willow grove of Songkhar, where monks from Samling residing at Dokhang House in Ganden Monastery had pitched a tent for us to stay in and had prepared food and drink.

The following day we left at sunrise. When we reached the Serkhang estate, we were greeted with an elaborate reception that had been set up in the courtyard there by Dokhang House. It was attended by the housemaster, administrators, and many others. They gave me the traditional rice and tea and presented me with greeting scarves and symbolic offerings of the body, speech, and mind of the Buddha.[28]

On the previous day I had been told many threatening stories to the effect that the housemaster of Dokhang was an extremely hot-tempered man and would beat little boys at the slightest provocation. When I saw him in the flesh, however, I realized that this bearded, dark-complexioned monk with padded shoulders was not really as he had been described to me, and so I was not afraid.

After this reception we continued on until reaching a grove in Tsangthok where Shartsé College of Ganden had erected a reception tent and had made elaborate preparations to receive us. The entire administrations of Shartsé and Jangtsé colleges, including the incumbent and emeritus abbots, the reincarnate masters of both colleges and the various houses, and the complete working staff of the monastery, had come to greet us and were standing in line, scarves in hand, outside the entrance of the reception tent. Amid all these people was Gajang Tridak Rinpoché. As soon as I met him, without the need for any introduction, I thought to myself, "This is Tridak Rinpoché," as if I were meeting someone I had known previously. From the reception lines, representatives of Shartsé College presented me with tea, ceremonial rice, scarves, and traditional offerings. Representatives of the overall monastic administration and colleges also presented me with these traditional offerings. Then the tulkus and the monastic staff who had come to greet me, all dressed in their finest robes, formed a line with their horses and accompanied us in a formal procession.

When we reached the top of Mount Drok, we came to the reception tent that had been set up by the administrators of the monastery as a whole. Preparations had been made to greet us, and so we took our respective positions as before. Tea and ceremonial rice were offered, and the abbots of Jangtsé and Shartsé colleges, in their capacity as representatives of the overall monastic administration, presented me with traditional offerings. Then we descended the mountain in a procession ordered according to rank. As we approached a spring near Ganden Monastery, a vast number of monks from Ganden's two colleges, all holding ceremonial banners, were arrayed on either side of the path stretching from there to the great assembly hall located in front of the monastery. Upon reaching the spring, I dismounted onto a fringed red carpet and made three fully extended prostrations toward the monastery. Then I threw some grain in that direction while reciting customary auspicious verses that Ngakrampa had taught me.

Accompanied by those who had come to greet me, all holding incense, I proceeded to the assembly hall of Dokhang House. Again they formed lines, and representatives of Ganden's administration, the two colleges, and the various houses presented me with traditional offerings. Dokhang House then gave a reception with an elaborate feast at which tea, rice, ceremonial cookies, and lunch were served to all. During the reception two students of dialectics debated on logic before the entire assembly.

After the reception I went to my suite atop Dokhang House, and there many individuals as well as representatives of various groups presented me with tea, rice, symbolic offerings of the Buddha's body, speech, and mind, greeting scarves, and so on. When all this had come to an end, I went up to the roof. As I gazed out I saw the great assembly hall, the debating courtyards, and the long streaming prayer flags. It was all in reality exactly as I had pictured it when, at Chusang Hermitage, I had heard talk of Ganden.

Following the established traditions, a few days later I was taken by the headmaster of the house to pay my respects at the feet of the incumbent Ganden Throneholder, Losang Tenpai Gyaltsen, the third reincarnation of Tsemönling Rinpoché. Then in the presence of the abbot of Shartsé College, Losang Khyenrap of Phukhang, I made offerings of tea and money and paid homage to the assembled monks of Ganden as well as to those of my college.

Then I formally enrolled in the monastery. Tsemönling Rinpoché, the precious throneholder, was invited to preside over this ceremony with the monastery's entire assembly of monks, and I presented him with offerings of the three representations.[29] A personal emissary of the Dalai Lama served me tea from a silver pot and presented me with a stack of five "donkey ear" cookies and a protection cord that had been knotted by the Dalai Lama. After that, representatives of the monastic administration, the college, and the various houses as well as other well-wishers and relatives formally congratulated me. Also, Kyabjé Phabongkha Rinpoché extended the kindness of sending his personal representative to present me with a congratulatory ceremonial scarf and rolls of silk and brocade.

Later, according to the wishes of Ngakrampa, I entered the regimen of Lekshé Kundrok Ling Dialectics School in Ganden Shartsé College. On this occasion enormous platters heaped with dried fruit were distributed to the assembled monks. From then on I attended the daily prayer assemblies of the monastery and the college, particularly the morning and evening debates, without ever missing a session. As I had previously memorized most of the prayers and rituals, I was able to participate in all the recitations except for the supplications to the lineage of abbots and the evening ritual for Tārā, the deity of enlightened activity.

Meeting with Minister Shedrawa

One day soon after my enrollment, there was a flurry of activity in the labrang. I was told that the retired cabinet minister Shedrawa[30] was coming to visit me and that preparations were being made to receive him. Soon he appeared, a portly nobleman whose balding head was crowned by a braided wreath of the little hair he still possessed. He wore an elegant gown of light blue silk brocade and looked very dignified. He presented me with a greeting scarf and gifts to congratulate me on my enrollment. Because I was so young, I could not think of anything to say, and so I just sat there stiffly. Shedrawa and Ngakrampa, however, were well acquainted and so spent quite a while recounting old times. Finally Shedrawa turned to me and said, "You are the best of everything, the yolk of the egg, the crown jewel of the Ganden lineage. You must therefore apply yourself well to your studies." He proffered much advice along these lines.

The Shedra family was a special patron of Ganden from ancient times and the patron of Dokhang House in particular. After Shedrawa had become the prime minister, he therefore visited me whenever he came to Ganden on official visits accompanying His Holiness the Thirteenth Dalai Lama. While Shedrawa was serving as a member of the council of ministers, he was placed under house arrest along with Shölkhangpa, Changkhyimpa, and Horkhangpa and confined to his residence in the Norbulingka Palace in the water-hare year (1903). This command came from His Holiness through the National Assembly. His Holiness the Dalai Lama may have made this decision for other reasons, but the apparent circumstances for Shedrawa's arrest were caused by a few jealous palace attendants of His Holiness. Later, Horkhangpa escaped to Kyichu, and the others, including Shedrawa, Shölkhangpa, and Changkhyimpa, were demoted from their cabinet posts and sent into exile but permitted to stay on their respective country estates. However, Shedrawa was ordered to stay in Orong in Kongpo. When the British army arrived in Chushur, a place near Lhasa, through Tsang province in the wood-dragon year (1904), His Holiness had to make a sudden visit to Mongolia and China. At that time a high Chinese official, General Zhang Yintang, arrived in Lhasa and insisted that

Shedrawa return to Lhasa to serve in the government. Shedrawa responded and returned from Kongpo. He resided at Lower Shedra, a family estate at the foot of Ganden Monastery. While Shedrawa was residing at that house, he insisted that, as the Dalai Lama had sent him into exile, it would not be proper for him to return to active government duty against the wishes of His Holiness.

It is clear from ancient records, such as the biography of Jé Tsongkhapa, that Shedra used to be called Sharhor. Later at the time of the Minister Shedra Desi, the name was changed to Lower Shedra as an improvement. The Shedra family had been personal patrons of Jé Tsongkhapa, and their mansion contained many relics of Jé Tsongkhapa, including his personal copy of the Kangyur, the canonical scriptures. As such it was the exclusive privilege of the Shedra family to provide the daily inner offering in the chapel of the protector Dharmarāja at Ganden. Not long after, His Holiness sent a letter of pardon from China, and subsequently Shedrawa, Shölkhangpa, and Changkhyimpa were reappointed to posts at the ministerial level. Thus Shedrawa continued to serve in the government.

Returning to Chusang

I left Ganden when the rainy-season retreat was over. On the way home we spent a little time at a reception that the Gongkotsang family of Dechen had arranged for me in a meadow in front of the Kharap Shankha estate. Afterward we spent the night at the monastic labrang of Sang-ngak Khar in Dechen. While there, the residents of our Lamotsé household in Dechen and others associated with it came to greet me with gifts. Then, further along the way, the entire monastery of Chötri at Gungthang were having their annual outdoor picnic in Jarak Park. They had pitched their assembly tent, and a performance of a dramatic opera depicting the story of Drimé Kunden[31] was underway. I briefly broke my journey there and watched the performance. As this was the first performance of that type that I had ever seen, I wanted to stay longer to enjoy it, but instead we proceeded to Lhasa that same afternoon.

It was required that I have an inaugural audience and interview with His Holiness after formally enrolling at Ganden. But as His Holiness had not yet returned to Lhasa from his journey to China and Mongolia, I petitioned the great throne in the sunlight room atop the Potala, in accordance with tradition. On the same occasion, I also had my inaugural audience with the regent, the former Ganden Throneholder Losang Gyaltsen Rinpoché, who was living in a residence on top of Meru Monastery in Lhasa.[32]

After arriving at my hermitage in Chusang, we held an outdoor picnic for two days in celebration of the completion of my enrollment activities at Ganden. A large assembly tent was pitched in our courtyard for religious activities, to which we invited the Most Venerable Kyabjé Phabongkha and Dromtö Geshé Rinpoché, the spiritual head of the hermitage, together with other resident monks. A small tent had been put up separately for myself and Demo Rinpoché, and we enjoyed playing games together. At the request of Ngakrampa, Kyabjé Phabongkha gave me the complete set of permissions for the cycle of Mañjuśrī teachings.[33] Although this series of permissions requires prior initiation into the highest yoga class of tantra, Kyabjé Phabongkha nevertheless gave the entire series exclusively to me for reasons of auspiciousness. He did this even though I had not yet received the initiation of Vajrabhairava or any other deity of this highest class.

I was too young to comprehend the entire exposition given by Kyabjé Phabongkha but remember quite distinctly a story Rinpoché told me during the permission of Dharmarāja. The story was of a lama in the past, Thoyön Lama Döndrup Gyaltsen, who when conducting the same permission, found that one of the implements—Dharmarāja's club in the shape of the upper part of a human body adorned with a skull—was not available, and so he improvised by using a chopstick with a Tibetan dumpling stuck on top. I also remember repeating after Rinpoché "I will act accordingly" a few times during the ritual.

Another time, at the request of Ngakrampa, Kyabjé Phabongkha was invited to our house and explained the measurements for diagrams of various designs used in the tantric ritual for consecrating the ground, in which different kinds of food offering substances are burned in an open flame. The instructions on these designs included four methods of accomplishment: Peace, Increase, Power, and Wrath. Except for some complicated measurements of the fire hearth related to power, I was able to comprehend these instructions quickly.

Undoubtedly, it was out of special consideration and regard for me that Kyabjé Phabongkha bestowed the above-mentioned permissions for the cycle of Mañjuśrī teachings without requiring me to have received prior initiation into the highest class of tantra. However, I did not let it suffice. As my own qualifications were known to me, I received the entire set of permissions once again from Rinpoché, complying with all the requirements, when I reached the age of twenty-one.

Choosing a Tutor

As I was in need of a regular tutor, Ngakrampa and my manager discussed a possible candidate from among a number of qualified scholars at my monastic college, Shartsé, in Ganden. They presented a list of names to Kyabjé Phabongkha and to the protector Shukden for consultation and divination for the final choice of my tutor. Both Rinpoché and the protector oracle reached a decision on the same candidate, my venerable teacher Losang Tsultrim of Phukhang House in Ganden, who was from Nangsang, a town in eastern Tibet.

In the tenth month of that year, my teacher and another monk, Dosam Nyitso Trinlé, were invited to our retreat house at Chusang. On an auspicious date determined by astrological calculations, he began to teach me. First we had a ceremony for my teacher and offered him tea and the traditional rice and scarf together with a token gift. After the ceremony my teacher started to teach me the homage verses from Ratö Monastery's[34] elementary logic textbook. I also recited for him from memory the entire text of the *Ornament of Realization* and about half of *Entering the Middle Way*. My teacher was greatly pleased with my memorization of these texts.

Previously, at an annual festival at Radreng Monastery called Khoryuk Chöpa, "environmental puja," I had witnessed a most fascinating yak dance. The dancer had done nine full turns clockwise and counterclockwise on one foot. Emulating that particular scene, I did the yak dance for my teacher. In my hand I held a brass utensil used to stir the ash in a clay container that kept the teapot warm. As I waved it around, I accidentally hit the clay container, chipping it. I was a little frightened at what my teacher might say, but I did not receive any scolding as this was our first formal meeting. From that time onward my teacher and I always remained inseparable.

That year during the months of the winter session, we returned to Ganden, and having been trained in elementary logic, I formally began to engage in the debates for solving the riddles of logic regarding color formulae.[35]

Thereafter followed four years of progressive training in elementary, intermediate, and advanced logic. From the start of my formal studies until my candidacy for the geshé examination, I never missed attending the annual winter sessions, the extracurricular summer sessions at Sangphu, and the annual Great Prayer Festival in the Jokhang Temple in Lhasa.

Receiving the Kālacakra Initiation

In my eighth year, the year of the earth-monkey (1908), at the request of the Kālacakra ritual group of Ganden, a most accomplished and highly realized master, Serkong Dorjé Chang Ngawang Tsultrim Dönden of Ganden, gave the complete three-day initiation into the deity Kālacakra in the Karmo general assembly hall at Ganden. I had the good fortune of being allowed to receive the initiation at his feet. Attendance at the initiation was so great that all the disciples could not fit into the large assembly hall, and people had to be seated in the corridors and vestibule. I was seated in front of the mandala altar behind the most venerable Kyabjé Khangsar Rinpoché[36] of Gomang College of Drepung Monastery. Serkong Rinpoché selected me to sit in the center of the purification diagrams, drawn on cloth, during the vase-initiation stage. This purification ritual is performed for novices. Whether or not Serkong Rinpoché did so for auspicious reasons, he also gave me the eye lotion used in the ritual for clarity of wisdom. The lotion contained honey, among other ingredients, and was so delicious that I ate it all. During the initiation it was most spectacular to watch some of the monks from Namgyal Monastery of the Potala Palace, His Holiness the Dalai Lama's ritual institute, performing in full tantric regalia. They each held decorated vases and chanted melodiously the verses for prosperity and auspiciousness.

Because of my immaturity I did not understand most of Rinpoché's explanations during the initiation, but I did notice his moving, expressive moods. At times tears would well up in his eyes as he explained the teachings in great detail. The next moment he would be scolding the disciples, or unexpectedly telling jokes, causing laughter. The next day, following the initiation, Rinpoché announced to the gathering that they could feel confident, without any doubt, that they each had received the initiation in its full meaning. In ancient times disciples used to receive initiation and proper blessing for their spiritual realizations with a mere slap on the cheek from a realized tantric master. Although it is difficult for this to happen nowadays, considering the type of disciples there are, without any doubt the special instructions left an impression on our mindstreams due to the power of being directed through the visualizations by such a great, realized lama.

Being Awarded the First Academic Degree

In my ninth year, the year of the earth-bird (1909), during the annual session of the disciplinarian[37] at my college, I was conferred the degree of *kachu* (covering ten subjects), and I was required to recite passages from any treatise that I had studied. At this ceremony my monastic household made offerings to the monks, and I recited by heart two pages from Jé Tsongkhapa's *Essence of Eloquence Distinguishing the Definitive and Interpretive.*[38] Everyone present at the ceremony congratulated me and commented on how well I had recited without any hesitation or nervousness despite my age. In celebration of my kachu examination, we also made extensive offerings to my main monastic house and to the other regional monastic groups with which I was affiliated.

About this time, Lhabu, who was a son of dairyman Tashi Döndrup from the pastoral region Balamshar in Dechen, arrived to become a permanent member of our labrang. He was ten years old and so became my playmate. From then on, until his death at the age of sixty-six, he served as my closest attendant. He looked after me in accordance with the finest examples of a disciple's dedicated service to his teacher as illustrated in the *Marvelous Array Sutra* with the analogies of a boat and a solid foundation, and conduct as firm as a vajra and a mountain. I am very grateful for his kind service.[39]

3 | Earning the Geshé Degree

First Meeting with His Holiness the Thirteenth Dalai Lama and Arrival of the Nationalist Chinese

In the tenth month of that year (1909), His Holiness the Thirteenth Dalai Lama returned to Tibet from China and Mongolia. There was an elaborate welcoming ceremony with the traditional arrangements of *kartro* cookies.[40] The reception was held at Ganden Chökhor Monastery in Phenpo district, northeast of Lhasa. Many dignitaries from Ganden were present, including the Ganden Throneholder, the two supreme abbots the Sharpa Chöjé and Jangtsé Chöjé,[41] the abbots of Shartsé and Jangtsé colleges, incarnate lamas, and administrators of Ganden. I was also there to welcome His Holiness the Dalai Lama. This was the first time that I saw the noble, golden face of His Holiness, complete with the mandala of physical attributes of an enlightened being. The Ganden Throneholder and other lamas and administrators went on to Lhasa for further welcoming ceremonies there. I had a strong desire to go to Lhasa, but at the wish of my labrang manager, I was excused because of my young age and left instead for Ganden.

In my tenth year, the year of the iron-dog (1910), during the annual Great Prayer Festival, the tenth incarnation of Kundeling Tatsak, Thupten Kalsang Tenpai Drönmé Rinpoché, was to pass his geshé lharam examination. Following tradition, Rinpoché extended an invitation to His Holiness to preside over the assembly of over eighteen thousand monks from Ganden, Drepung, Sera, and other monasteries. At the same festival, the fourth incarnation of the omniscient Jamyang Shepa,[42] Kalsang Thupten Wangchuk from Tashi Khyil Monastery in Amdo Province, also invited His Holiness to preside over an assembly session of the prayer festival.

The Thirteenth Dalai Lama, Darjeeling, 1910
© Thomas Paar, Newark Museum, C. Suydam Cutting Collection

It was a busy time for everyone, humans and celestial beings alike, preparing for that major ceremonial visit of His Holiness. On the third day of the first month during the evening session, after the seating arrangements had been made for the prayer festival, a large contingent of Chinese army soldiers arrived unexpectedly. Several Tibetans were killed by Chinese artillery fire at Thalphung Gang east of Lhasa. Nearby, at Lubuk Gate, the monastic government official Jamyang Gyaltsen, who was in charge of the festival, was also killed. Another high-ranking government official and member of the Eleventh Dalai Lama's family, Tashi Dorjé of Phunkhang, was injured by bullets. It was a time of turmoil and great anxiety for everyone. That night His Holiness the Dalai Lama, together with a small number of staff, left the Potala Palace and traveled via the Norbulingka for a secret journey to India. The Chinese representative by the name of Lianyu[43] sent a large number of soldiers to pursue the Dalai Lama, but they had to withdraw from the ferry dock at the Chushur bridge after a confrontation with a few Tibetans led by Dasang Dradul, a favorite special attendant to His Holiness. Dradul later married into the Tsarong family.

During that Great Prayer Festival, my venerable teacher Losang Tsultrim passed his geshé lharam examination, placing second among the learned lharam geshés. In celebration of His Holiness's safe return from Mongolia and China, the government during the festival distributed to each monk a silver coin and another commemorative coin called a *thupten*, fresh from the mint, together with a ceremonial scarf. Kundeling Tatsak Rinpoché gave a *tamkar* or *tam* and five *sho*, and Jamyang Shepa Rinpoché gave thirty-three *tam* to each of the assembled monks.[44]

During assembly sessions of the Great Prayer Festival, the Chinese showed many signs of disrespect, humiliating monks by throwing cigarette butts onto them and disrespectfully stretching their legs out on the ledge of the viewing balcony. During the early-morning discourse sessions, while the Ganden Throneholder was teaching, Chinese soldiers paraded past, sounds blasting from their marching band.

That year I went to the summer sessions at Sangphu, and in between debate sessions, besides my regular curriculum study of the texts, Ngakrampa, in his desire to aid our study of astrology, started to teach my tutor and myself how to draw the different mathematical formulae as well as other basic mathematics such as multiplication tables. Eventually we studied most of the formula drawings for astrology. I took an enthusiastic interest in the subject, to the point of making a hole in my finger from erasure, and trained myself by writing the mathematical formulae on the dust board.[45] Since I studied this subject at a very young age while simultaneously attending other core classes in addition to memorizing and studying metaphysical subjects, and since I also lacked further interest in pursuing the subject, I have forgotten most of it with almost no trace, like the trail of flying birds.

While I was attending the summer session at Sangphu, Jamyang Shepa Rinpoché of Amdo visited on pilgrimage. At the time Jamyang Shepa Rinpoché was held in high regard by the Chinese, the Chinese representative in Lhasa, and so on. Because of this Chinese support, the advance party of Rinpoché's entourage mistreated the local population, resorting to verbal and physical abuse to enforce their demands. My landlord and others at Sangphu, who were obliged to provide and perform services as part of their levies, went into hiding for three days in the Gyama Nakri hills facing Sangphu. Jamyang Shepa Rinpoché himself spent one night at Sangphu and the next day made an offering of half a *tam* to each member of the assembly, which was comprised of ten monastic institutes. After he blessed the monks, he returned to Lhasa. He was an elderly man with a long white goatee and wore a monk's robe with a yellow brocade gown—a Mongolian court robe—over it. As people from Lhasa and many others were critical of the Rinpoché, I did not have much respect for him either. On later analysis it occurred to me that, apart from the circumstances of his Chinese escorts at the time, he was a well-qualified lama.

A Smallpox Epidemic

That autumn there raged an epidemic of smallpox throughout the central province of Tibet, so I remained at Ganden for some length of time. The most venerable Kyabjé Phabongkha sent me a text on the ritual meditation practice of Viśvamātṛ[46] along with a miniature image of the deity. In accordance with his instructions and advice, my teacher and I went into retreat to perform the meditation ritual of the deity, repeating her mantra well over one hundred thousand times. We also did a retreat of White Tārā and repeated her mantra one hundred thousand times as well as one hundred thousand recitations of the *miktsema*.[47]

Since none of the methods of treatment or any of the inoculations that we have nowadays existed, the death rate among the monks at Ganden was severe. Previously interred bodies would be uncovered as new graves were being dug, a result of the shortage of space within the confines of the burial ground. In the tenth month of that year I, too, was stricken with the disease, and my face and body were covered with its pimples for many days. I made a quick recovery, mainly because of my practice of meditational rituals as advised by Kyabjé Phabongkha, and especially because of the loving care and kindness of my teacher, who looked after me for days on end without any sleep. I recovered fully and was able to attend the study and debate sessions that winter.

Once during the most serious stage of my sickness, in a quasi-dream state or fit of hallucination, I thought that I was halfway up Nyakrong Pass at Ganden, where several monks in yellow robes said to me, "Son, son, come hither. We shall go to Ganden." Uttering these words, they beckoned me. Had I died at that time, it might have been good for me, for I would not have become steeped in the ill effects of consuming offerings. In another hallucination I was holding in my lap an animal like a puppy or kitten, which was snatched away from me by a woman. On the same day my brother, who had been recognized as the reincarnation of the previous Lelung Tulku, died at Gungthang. It seems as if he passed away in my place.

Then the abbot, Losang Khyenrap of Phukhang, passed on to my teacher many experiential methods for treating the disease. He instructed my teacher that patients should take a brew of tamarisk during the initial stages and that the body should not be exposed to the wind or breezes. When the pimples filled with pus, the resin of the plant *Shorea robusta* or the shala tree should be burned. One day the pimples curved in and became cup-shaped. My teacher experienced a great deal of concern and anxiety when my condition became increasingly serious. He sought the advice of the abbot, who sent a strip of pork and gave instructions to cook it and give me a few pieces of the fat to eat. The very next day, two other pimples appeared on top of each cup-shaped pimple, like the layers of a stupa, and from that point I began to gradually recover.

After the death of my younger brother, my mother and sister were left alone. As they could not bear the ill treatment of Ani Yangzom and her husband, who were now residents of the Gungthang estate, the manager Lekshé Gyatso helped to arrange the marriage of my mother Tsering Drölma and sister Jampal Chötso to Tenzin Sangpo and his son Döndrup of the Kotsang family. This family was part of our monastic household at Dechen.

In my eleventh year, the year of the iron-pig (1911), I received an oral transmission of the exclusive or classified collected teachings of Thuken Chökyi Nyima as well as the fourteen volumes of his collected works in their entirety from the Amdo edition. I received these teachings at Meru Monastery in Lhasa from Nyal Dra-or Rinpoché, Tenzin Trinlé Öser from Deyang College of Drepung, who was the assistant tutor to His Holiness the Thirteenth Dalai Lama.

Trouble with the Chinese

Because of close connections between the monastic household of Tengyé Ling and mine, every year I was invited to the annual religious dance festival of Demo and attended it. That year, on the twenty-ninth of the eighth month, I went to attend the festival. Demo Rinpoché sat in the center of the viewing gallery, and on his right were seated other lamas: Losempa, Drakgyab Chungtsang, Tsangpa Khenchen, the tutor to Demo Rinpoché, and myself. On the left were Chinese amban Lianyu and other Chinese officials. The ministers of the Tibetan cabinet and other high-ranking officials were in front of the enclosed balconies on either side of the viewing room. The rest of the government officials were seated atop other quarters, under a tent canopy. The viewing room was filled with cigarette smoke from the Chinese, and a Tibetan official, Dzasak Chöjang Dradul, was acting in a very friendly and hospitable way to the Chinese. I was very unhappy on account of all this.

That evening, at the conclusion of the dance of Palden Lhamo Maksorma[48] and her retinue, not only did Kongtsun Demo,[49] one of the twelve *tenma* goddesses[50] that protect Tibet, faint in the vestibule entrance of the monastery, but at the end of the festival, the amban placed ceremonial scarves around the necks of each dancer. The spectators from Lhasa considered these to be bad omens. As it happened, Tengyé Ling Monastery suffered complete destruction the following year during the upheaval caused by the Chinese "War of the Water-Rat Year."[51]

That autumn following the summer session at Ganden, I was staying at my residence in Lhasa when the nationalist movement happened in China.[52] On the Day of Divine Descent,[53] political and ideological differences among the Chinese population even in Lhasa led to an outbreak of heavy conflict that resulted in casualties among themselves. This caused a great deal of turmoil, as some Chinese made forced entry into private homes, pillaging and robbing people of their horses and mules. Owing to these chaotic conditions in Lhasa, my teacher and I stayed in a corner room on the rooftop of a private house just to be safe. At that time the amban had to flee from Lhasa to Drepung.

Just before the celebration on the twenty-fifth day of the tenth month,[54] we returned to Ganden, and Ngakrampa gave us lessons on the drawing and color composition for the celestial abodes of deities such as Guhyasamāja, Cakrasaṃvara, Vajrabhairava, and Sarvavid. On our own my teacher and I drew the deities' abodes in color on a wall of our house at Ganden. The drawings came out quite well but were later destroyed in the process of completely renovating the house. During the winter session I joined the introductory Perfection of Wisdom class and engaged in the study of its texts. We avoided going to the Great Prayer Festival that year because of the dangerous situation caused by the Chinese turmoil in Lhasa and remained at Ganden instead.

That year the central government required a thousand monks to remain at each of the monasteries to defend and protect them while the rest of the monks attended the Prayer Festival, and a share of offerings received during the Prayer Festival was set aside for the monks who stayed behind. On the fifth night of the second month, the Chinese suddenly attacked Sera Monastery. The government ordered Ganden to hastily send about two hundred monks to defend Sera. Bearing daggers, spears, and muskets adorned with colored banners—weapons taken from special rooms where decorative offerings of arms had been presented to oath-bound protector deities—the monks set out. These "soldier" monks, who did not have on hand complete sets of lay clothes, were outfitted in mismatched clothing. Some wore the heavy lay robes over their monastic vests, while others wore monastic boots and wrapped their heads in the colorful cloth covers used to wrap religious texts. When our contingent of monks reached Sera, some of the elders openly wept and touched their foreheads in joy, crying out, "The monks from the senior monastery have come!"

We also heard later that some of the monks had tied small knives on the ends of sticks with bootlaces and were running about asking where the Chinese were, claiming that they would kill them. Eventually, the combined force of the Tibetan army and monk contingents from Sera and Ganden drove the Chinese out of Sera and chased them to the southern outskirts of Lhasa. My personal attendant Lhabu and other members of the labrang, which was in the region south of Lhasa, along with eight monks from Ganden who were there to read out the entire Kangyur,[55] were forced to live under Chinese control for a few months. During that time they ran short of food and other provisions and were made to dig up and transport stones to construct military barricades for the Chinese. Lhabu and others ended up with sores on their backs due to the hard labor and suffered intense hardship and anxiety. The Subsequent Prayer Session,[56] as well as the summer session at Sangphu, were canceled because of this unrest.

A classmate of mine, Ngawang Losang from the Yara region of Phukhang, became my assistant and study companion until the completion of my geshé examination. He was very intelligent and sharp in his studies, and we shared the same teacher. During the rainy-season session at Ganden, I recited a treatise on the theme of Buddha's turning the wheel of Dharma[57] and debated on the same subject in the presence of the entire assembly of monks, along with another student who excelled in his studies, Dokhang

House's Losang Chödrak from Yangteng. During this recitation, the homage procedures and debate performance were carried off without any mishap and were successful. In accordance with the tradition for this recitation, my manager, Lekshé Gyatso, took on the responsibility of making extensive offerings. All the while we could hear the sounds of cannon fire at Ganden's Nyakrong Pass.

That year, at the request of the government, Kyabjé Serkong Dorjé Chang came to Ganden to perform the exorcism ritual of most secret Dharmarāja Black Poison Mountain. On the day when the consecrated tormas were thrown into a burning haystack during the final outdoor ritual in the marketplace, I could hear Rinpoché from my room on top of Dokhang House as he made the liquid offering invoking the deity in a firm, loud tone of voice. Rinpoché also performed similar exorcism rituals as well as subjugation of demons[58] and other wrathful activities dedicated to Palden Lhamo and Hayagrīva. These rituals lasted for some months.

One day during this period, people discovered the heads and limbs of someone called Chözé, who had resided at the entrance of Ramoché, and a high-ranking Chinese officer, who had been killed by someone in the Ganden contingent earlier in the iron-dog year (1910). They had been among the volunteers who pursued the Thirteenth Dalai Lama when he fled to India. The heads and limbs of these two individuals were later used in a burial ritual near Dragoché Gate at Ganden. Serkong Dorjé Chang would perform an animated ritual dance during each exorcism. Rinpoché had very thin hair and was rather bald. Anticipating the amusement that would follow if his ritual hat were to fall off, I hoped for such an occurrence.

Studies and Empowerments

The war had not ended in Lhasa even at the conclusion of the rainy-season retreat, so I spent two months in a reading retreat at the Lamotsé estate in Dechen, not far from Ganden. My teacher instructed me to memorize Tsongkhapa's *Essence of Eloquence*. For the first few days I memorized and recited the text incoherently without full concentration, and when my teacher tested me on the memorization, I recited fifteen pages of the text looking at them upside down, as my teacher held them in his hand while checking the accuracy of my memorization. I was then scolded and punished with a lashing. I had to memorize the text from the start, including all of its seventy or so folios. I also memorized Paṇchen Sönam Drakpa's Perfection of Wisdom commentary from the topic of the twenty types of sangha up to the fourth chapter in its entirety.

At that time my mental capacity was quite good, and my abilities at memorization and debate were improving. My teacher therefore had great hopes for and confidence in me, but because I lacked diligence, he was very strict with me. Owing to this severe discipline and consequent lack of time for personal care, my body became infested with lice. One day my friend Yönten was picking lice from my woolen bedding, and he collected a large cupful of them mixed with bedding fluff.

In the ninth month I left for Gungthang with my teacher and Ngakrampa to make offerings to my birth deity.[59] My uncle, Jamyang Gyatso, who was a caretaker of the place, accommodated us in the large room with a viewing gallery on the top floor and brought me meals from his own private house for the few days I was there. Although I was born into the Gungthang estate and I am a true lineal descendant of it, Ani Yangzom and her husband did not even once, out of courtesy, extend us a dinner invitation while the estate was under their management. Another time, Rinchen Wangyal of Kunsangtsé and his wife, my half-sister, came to Gungthang from Lhasa and stayed for one week. When Ngakrampa and I went to visit them, we were served tea and a special soup dish for supper. Apart from this, I was not cared for or looked after and was rather avoided, like a tree without shade. From then on until my geshé examinations, I always stayed with my uncle at Chökhor Ling on my trips between Ganden and Lhasa during recess periods and would not go to visit the Gungthang residence.

As the war was still not over, I returned to Ganden from Dechen before the celebrations of the twenty-fifth and advanced to the senior Perfection of Wisdom class, where we picked up our study, gradually mastering and moving through "production of the enlightened attitude," "instructions," and so on.[60] In the winter recess I left for Lhasa, and on the sixteenth day of the twelfth month of that year (1912), together with other lamas, I went to pay my respects to His Holiness the Thirteenth Dalai Lama at a reception ceremony at Kyitsal Luding organized by the government on the occasion of his return to the nation's capital from India.

In my thirteenth year, the year of the water-ox (1913), I studied calligraphy following the Great Prayer Festival at the behest of Ngakrampa. Samphel-la, a retired monk official, was invited to our house to teach calligraphy to myself, Lhabu, and Tsultrim Tenzin, a nephew of Dzong Lekshé. I practiced this for about three months during intervals between my other classes and memorization and recitation periods.

After the Subsequent Prayer Session, I went to Drepung Monastery with my teacher and Ngawang Losang. There in the tantric chapel of Hardong House of Gomang College, I received oral transmission of the complete Kangyur, the teachings of the Buddha that had been translated into Tibetan, the Tengyur commentaries on them, the *Maṇi Kabum*,[61] and the Father and Son Teachings of the *Book of Kadam*. I received these from the most venerable, the great Kangyurwa,[62] Losang Dönden over a period of more than three months. The Rinpoché had a majestic presence and control over the disciples. When some of them dozed, talked to one another, or wrote, he would stare with his eyes in a triangular shape and pause for a moment, which would bring the students under control in a gentle manner. Upon completion of this discourse at Drepung, I returned to Ganden. In accordance with the wishes of my teacher, I applied myself with great zeal to the study of the Perfection of Wisdom from the twenty types of sangha up to the third topic all during the summer and autumn.[63] I practiced debate with my companion Ngawang Losang and during the winter session skipped to the advanced Perfection of Wisdom class, taking up study of the eighth topic. During the first and second periods of the winter session I studied the fourth topic.

In my fourteenth year, after the Great Prayer Festival in the year of the wood-tiger (1914), Buldü Vajradhara Jetsun Losang Yeshé Tenpai Gyaltsen of Drepung's Gomang College gave many initiations and teachings in the assembly hall of Kundeling Monastery in Lhasa at the request of Tatsak Hothokthu Rinpoché. Buldü Rinpoché was truly Vajradhara—an all-embracing lord of a hundred buddha families who establishes in the minds of the ocean of living beings whatever paths and fruits of the four bodies of enlightenment in union suit them. He gave full initiations into single-deity Vajrabhairava, thirteen-deity Vajrabhairava, the Ārya tradition of Akṣobhyavajra Guhyasamāja, the Luipa tradition of sixty-two-deity Cakrasaṃvara, the Ghaṇṭapāda tradition of five-deity Cakrasaṃvara, and the Great Compassionate One according to the Bhikṣuṇī Lakṣmī tradition, together with preparation, in a painted mandala for each. Other teachings included a discourse on three key points for the yoga of Avalokiteśvara in the Mitrayogin tradition and a discourse on the Nyen Tsembu tradition of Avalokiteśvara yoga.[64]

During these teachings the most venerable Rinpoché gave very profound and vast expositions, including the subtlest details of how to put the teachings into practice. Although, as I was of a tender age, all of the profoundly difficult points of his teachings could not penetrate the veil of my comprehension, I was able to follow his instructions on the various stages of the visualizations during the initiations and applied them in the proper context at their relevant places. Thanks to this, to this day I can vividly recall his explanations and even his countenance at those particular moments. Compared to some elders who, after receiving hundreds of initiations, could not do even rough visualizations, the way in which I understood the teachings was good, considering my age.

During the spring session, I studied the fifth topic of Perfection of Wisdom, and in the following rainy season I recited a general dissertation and performed a dialectical debate on the eighth topic of Perfection of Wisdom at Ganden's main assembly. My partner in the debate was a student from Gowo House of Ganden Jangtsé well known for his scholarship. In these performances I did well enough that I neither disappointed those erudite masters who were present nor embarrassed and disgraced myself. The most venerable Khyenrap Yönten Gyatso, then Ganden Throneholder, was invited as chief guest for the monetary and food offerings made to the assembly. These offerings were made in all stages and varied in extent according to traditions prescribed in the past. During the winter session I was passed into the introductory Middle Way (Madhyamaka philosophy) class.

In my fifteenth year, the year of the wood-rabbit (1915), the Eighty-Eighth Ganden Throneholder, Venerable Khyenrap Yönten Gyatso, gave a series of initiations commencing from the seventeenth day of the sixth month in Yangpachen Temple at Ganden at the request of Venerable Yeshé, a former disciplinarian from Tsawa House of Jangtsé College. The teachings included initiations into the forty-two mandalas of the *Vajrāvalī*,[65] as established by the great Indian master Abhayākaragupta, and initiations into the three mandalas that grant bliss and happiness in accord with the *Kriyāsamuccaya* set down by Paṇḍita Darpaṇa Ācārya. I had the great honor of receiving these forty-five initiations in their entirety along with Most Venerable Buldü Vajradhara, Venerable Geshé Sherap Gyatso (a master proponent of the five sciences[66] from Lubum House of Drepung Monastery), and other incarnate lamas and learned geshés exceeding six hundred in number. At the conduct empowerment during the initiation of

Cakrasaṃvara, I was given the elaborate costume of the deity with six bone ornaments, escorted around the mandala, and presented to the deity in a procession with ceremonial banner and parasol. Thus I was endowed with immense privilege and good fortune.

During these initiations I was seated next to Most Venerable Buldü Vajradhara. From the beginning to the conclusion of an initiation session, Vajradhara sat in deep concentration without any distraction. Because of the good example and clear exposition that Vajradhara gave during his initiations the previous year at the Kundeling Monastery, I was able to follow the visualization in a token manner. At that time I began studying grammar and composition with Kyabjé Buldü Vajradhara. Rinpoché had advised me to receive teachings on this science mainly from Venerable Geshé Sherap Gyatso. During the winter session I entered the advanced Middle Way philosophy class.

Studying Grammar and Composition

In my sixteenth year, the year of the fire-dragon (1916), after the Great Prayer Festival, my teacher and I invited Geshé Sherap Gyatso of Lubum House, Gomang College of Drepung Monastery, to our retreat house at Chusang. There we studied with him in detail the root texts the *Thirty Verses* and *Introduction to Morphology*,[67] with their commentaries by Situ and Drati Geshé, for over one month. Geshé Rinpoché always made us write exercises in verse so as to acquire skill in versified composition. As a start, for the exercise dealing with the ways to conclude sentences, I wrote my exercise in verse, beginning each line with a letter of the alphabet in sequential order. Although this was my first composition, by chance the verses were rather well written. This pleased Geshé Rinpoché very much, and he wrote:

> Not merely from my lips
> but from within, I take joy
> in your good knowledge of compiling
> according to the order of the alphabet.

He rewarded me with these words of approval likewise composed in verse following the order of the alphabet. That year at Ganden I compiled and edited a booklet of grammatical exercises.

After the completion of these grammar and composition studies, I left for the special summer session at Sangphu. As I was not so bad at making drawings of images, during the rainy season I drew the six symbols of longevity and the four harmonious friends[68] on the wall of my classmate and debate companion Ngawang Losang's room. Under each of the drawings, I composed captions in verse. As a caption to the verses of the four harmonious friends, I wrote:

> Written by the melodic swan playing in the ocean
> of lofty voice that speaks widely of the five sciences.

Since I wrote such a boastful echo, Geshé Sherap Rinpoché wrote me a letter containing the following composition to poke fun at me:

> His "lofty voice" may "speak widely of the five sciences"
> to a fool mired in the five degenerations such as I,
> but when refuted by another master wise in the five sciences
> and his claim to know the five sciences is lost, he will grieve.
>
> Ha ha! A childish jest between close acquaintances!
> I rejoice in you who's grown up like a child surpassing its mother.
> Still more do I marvel at your excellent ways
> that spread without rival your own glorious qualities.

It seems he was a bit put off by my presumption and was quite right to send me such a letter challenging my childish pride.

During the winter session, I joined the Abhidharma class. Before, when studying Perfection of Wisdom and Middle Way philosophy, I relied on the works of Jé Tsongkhapa, his chief disciples, and Paṇchen Sönam Drakpa as my primary references. On the advice of my teacher, I also studied the works of the First Dalai Lama Gendun Drup, the omniscient Jamyang Shepa, and Jetsun Chökyi Gyaltsen.

The Passing of Ngakrampa

In my seventeenth year, the year of the fire-snake (1917), I went to Drepung after the Great Prayer Festival. There with my teacher I attended the initiation into the five-deity Cakrasaṃvara and the permission for the Rinjung Hundred[69] from Most Venerable Buldü Vajradhara. While there we stayed at Geshé Sherap Rinpoché's residence at Lubum House. During the Great Prayer Festival that year, Ngakrampa was not feeling well. Before my departure for Drepung, he came to see me in my room and gave me treasured advice from his heart, concealing nothing and with tears in his eyes. I left for Drepung feeling quite sad, not knowing whether I would be able to see him again. As I set out, tears streamed uncontrollably from my eyes. Ngakrampa passed away on the seventeenth day of the second month, during the discourse at Drepung. I was tormented by intolerable grief upon hearing the news of his death.

The late Ngakrampa was born in the fourteenth cycle, in the wood-dragon year (1844), in the family of Ayik Thango of the town called Ala Ngodroké, which belonged to the three districts of Sho, Tar, and Lho in the province of Kham. He entered the monastery of Arik and studied its traditional texts. Later when he came to Central Tibet, he lived in Gungru House at Drepung and was enrolled at Gyütö Tantric College. He studied in detail the rituals of the monastery's ancient tradition. Joining the ranks of ritual masters, he became prominent among them through his expertise in the construction of the colored sand mandalas and the art of ritual sculpture. He received a vast number of discourses, oral transmissions, and initiations with devotion from numerous lamas who encompassed all good qualities. These great learned and accomplished lamas included the great tutor Tatsak Gendun Gyatso, the Kangyurwa Lhotrul Ngawang Khyenrap Tenpai Wangchuk, the great Gomang abbot Khyenrap Tenpa Chöphel, Gungtrul Rinpoché Khyenrap Palden Tenpai Nyima, and Losang Lungtok Tenzin Trinlé, the previous incarnation of Tutor Kyabjé Ling Rinpoché.

He had also studied astrology of various types to a level of mastery. At one time, on the advice of the great tutor Ling Rinpoché, he went to his native province, completed a major retreat of Vajrabhairava in its entirety, then returned to Central Tibet and remained at the tantric college as before. He held the position of house master of Amdo House and served the tantric college with loyalty and dedication in different capacities. He shared with me many accounts of his efforts at various times, but I will not relate them all here. He served for five years as the manager of my predecessor, the Eighty-Fifth Ganden Throneholder Losang Tsultrim Palden, from the time when my predecessor was the abbot of Gyütö Tantric College until he ascended the Ganden throne.

Unlike the custom that developed later, until 1920 the abbots of the tantric colleges and the Ganden Throneholder had to administer and supervise the maintenance and function of various farmlands and had to provide scheduled and special offerings to the monks of their respective monasteries. The late Ngakrampa did everything required of him according to the responsibilities of the position, without negligence. Provisions were offered to the monks with the best means, without seeking easy solutions. They were of the highest quality and not "the mildewed bits of cheese and yellowed vegetable leaves," as a Tibetan maxim says. The late Ngakrampa assumed the principal burden of responsibility after the death of my predecessor to complete various ritual offerings and to construct his reliquary stupa at Yangpachen, the memorial hall of Ganden Throneholders.

After taking care of the procedures for my discovery as the reincarnation, the late Ngakrampa handed over his responsibilities and duties to Lekshé Gyatso, a former official of the monastic management who was a nephew of my predecessor. Ngakrampa remained with me and became a constant close companion, beginning with the primary reading lessons he gave me at Chusang Retreat House and continuing until he passed away. He brought me up with a loving care and immense kindness that suffered in no way when compared to that of my own parents. As I mentioned above, he taught me recital chanting, the formulae of astrology according to the Jedrup school, line measurements and color composition of the mandalas for all tantric categories, construction of three-dimensional mandalas, the propitiation rituals for the protector deities of the traditions exclusive to the tantric colleges, and the styles of their rituals, including mudrā gestures.

He also instructed me in the various ritual offerings to Dharmarāja. Every now and then he would tell me about the traditions and procedures related to the annual curriculum and ritual sessions at the tantric college, including the rules and customs of assembly and dispersal of the daily sessions and the duties and functions of monastic officials. As he informed me of all these customs from his own experience and knowledge, fully and authoritatively, without any pretense of the eight worldly concerns, I was quite well prepared and knowledgeable about the procedures at the tantric college, even though newly enrolled, when I studied there following the completion of the course of study for the geshé degree.

During the annual study session at Drak Yerpa, I was fully prepared to demonstrate and relate to the abbot with full confidence in my knowledge of the major dimensional lines of the mandalas. I was also able to serve as a source of information on custom and tradition for junior students. This was solely due to the late Ngakrampa, the heavy burden of whose kindness would be difficult to repay even with eons spent trying.

Here is an account of his activities for a single day. He would rise early in the morning, at the first cockcrow, wash, and review the daily activities required of a monk. After this he would bless his speech, repeat mantras of transformation to intensify the effects of his deeds, and engage in the following practices in sets of one hundred: recitation of the *miktsema* with the *Hundred Deities of Tuṣita* prayer, taking refuge in the four circles of refuge, and recitation of one rosary of the hundred-syllable mantra of Vajrasattva in the context of the meditational liturgy of Vajrabhairava. After a certain number of recitations of the mantra of Vajrabhairava at leisure at about dawn, he would conclude his presentation of the torma offerings to Vajrabhairava at the section of the ritual manual for Dharmarāja. While chanting the verses of description, the long and short forms of the propitiation and declaration, as well as the praise of Dharmarāja in full, he would fill a set of one hundred offering bowls with fresh water. He undertook a longevity retreat based on White Tārā and made various other offerings in sets of one hundred specifically for my own well-being.

After these routine offerings he would have his morning tea and tsampa. Then he would tend to my studies, such as reading practice and testing me on memorization of the new material in the lessons for ritual chanting. From that point he would continue with more ritual practices, such as performing an elaborate form of purification ritual in connection with the preliminary practice entitled Practice of the Six Preliminaries Called "Dharma Ornament of Mount Meru."[70] Other practices included offering mandalas in accumulative numbers, and one hundred prostrations while reciting the confession of misdeeds. Then, while repeating five thousand times the main mantra syllables of Secret Hayagrīva in the context of its meditational liturgy for self-generation according to the Kyergang tradition,[71] he would walk through and look around the surroundings of the teaching yard and garden of Chusang.

At noon, after recitation of the *Sutra of Remembering Refuge* (*Triśaraṇagamanasūtra*), he took lunch, leaving aside a dedicated portion of food, followed by an offering of burnt sesame seeds dedicated to Vajraḍāka.[72] From the first clean portion of the food, he pressed about one hundred small statues of the Buddha, using a metal impression block, while reciting the text of request to the guru seen as inseparably one with Mahākāla as many times as he could. Then he engaged in the following routine of prayers: the mantra syllables of Samayavajra for one round of his rosary, the *Prayer of Shambhala* and, for my benefit, the *Prayer of the Sixteen Arhats*, the longevity prayer composed for me, a Hayagrīva averting ritual called Victorious Powerful Weapon, two short sutras entitled *Armlet*[73] and *Eliminating the Darkness of the Ten Directions* (*Daśadigandhakāravidhvaṃsana*), the twelve complete chapters of the root tantra of Guhyasamāja, the first chapter of the root tantra of Cakrasaṃvara, and the *Verse Summary of the Perfection of Wisdom* (*Ratnaguṇasaṃcayagathā*). At this point, he would circumambulate the outer periphery of the Chusang retreat complex.

After his afternoon tea, again for the success of my activities, he performed the mantras and self-generating liturgies of the five-deity secret Kurukulle, the meditation and recitation of Black Garuḍa, following which he would repeat the mantra of Avalokiteśvara about three-thousand times. He did the six-session guruyoga every morning and evening. On the three ninths[74] he made elaborate offerings to Dharmarāja, and on the eighth, full moon, and new moon of the month, he performed the cleansing practice for me based on the Hayagrīva and Vajravidāraṇa rituals alternately. Because he used to say his daily prayers, perform the rituals, and read the scriptures at leisure and with complete clarity without any rush, I came to remember most of them because of clearly hearing them. During my enrollment in the tantric college, I could recite the *Root Tantra of Guhyasamāja* in the company of others, the only shortcoming being my inability to recite it all by myself alone. During his stay at Lhasa and Ganden, he circumambulated their outer periphery at the start of mantra recitations of Hayagrīva, saying the mantra while walking in the mornings.

Although the late Ngakrampa did not acquire the scholastic titles of either *geshé* or *karam*, his knowledge of the teachings of both sutra and tantra was vast and diverse, as he had received discourses, oral transmissions, and initiations in the presence of many supremely qualified lamas. As mentioned earlier, the depth of his practice of what he had learned cannot be captured by the common moniker "retreat-house hermit."

He was also stable and perceptive in secular matters. The depth of his vision could be compared to that of Brahma's wisdom. Earlier, when he held the responsible position of housemaster at Amdo House of Gyütö Tantric College, all the monks had higher esteem for him than for others. As for the state of my labrang: when my predecessor died, the monasteries under its jurisdiction and many other factions within the monastery took advantage of the situation, looking for a chance to cast blame and make various accusations in order to weaken the standing of the labrang. At that time he maintained self-control and looked after the administration of the labrang without any lack of efficiency, like a majestic mountain that no one could move.

During the stages of ill health prior to his decease, he took the Mahayana precepts daily and sustained himself on just milk without any solid food. He had a set of deity costumes made to dress his body at death and had given instructions on the procedures for his cremation to Nyitso Trinlé of Chatreng and Dzongsur Lekshé, who were attending him during his sickness. For one year prior to his death he practiced the meditation of the transference of consciousness each night before going to bed. The type he practiced was called "shooting the arrow through the skylight."[75] These actions, and all other points of view, confirmed that he was truly a great spiritual master, replete with every type of quality. Upon reaching the age of seventy-four, on the seventeenth day of the second month in the fire-snake year (April 9, 1917), his thoughts ascended to a realm of peace.

Financial Difficulties

After the Subsequent Prayer Session, once again in the tantric chapel at Hardong House, Drepung, I received an initiation into Secret Hayagrīva from Most Venerable Buldü Vajradhara. Other teachings that we received included the hundred sets of permission for the Surka Cycle of sādhanas, discourses on Aśvaghoṣa's *Fifty Verses on Guru Devotion*, Candragomin's *Twenty Verses on the Bodhisattva Vow*, and a versified text explaining infractions of the root vows of tantra.

In my eighteenth year, the earth-horse year (1918), from about the beginning of the first month, the state of health of treasurer Dzongsur Lekshé Gyatso grew increasingly poor. It wasn't possible to turn his condition around with medical treatment or ritual cures, and he passed away on the first day of the third month. Up until that time Dzongsur had borne all responsibility for our labrang. My teacher and I had been fully absorbed in religious study without performing any of the duties associated with the labrang, so we had no practical experience running a labrang. In the absence of anyone else capable of carrying out those duties, the burden of maintaining the labrang fell to us. After taking stock of the records and other possessions in the treasurer's room, we found that the labrang had barely any cash—not even a hundred *sang*. As the late Dzongsur had been stricken with a prolonged illness prior to his death, there were only one and a half *tang*[76] of butter and several packages of brick tea in our stores, and all other provisions were nearly exhausted. We had to borrow money to cover the late Dzongsur's funeral, offering rituals, and other necessities.

Dzongsur appeared to have been a capable person and people held him in high regard. In his attempt to further establish the labrang, he had made extensive loans. Hoping to collect on these loans, we searched for any legal record of them. Not only did we fail to find receipts for loans made, we discovered a small black book containing a list of loans that had been made to the labrang and the monthly interest owed to various government agencies and private individuals. The grand total of the loans amounted to 294 *tamdo*. We had to take an additional loan of six *tamdo* for the late Dzongsur's memorial offering rituals, which brought the total owed to three hundred *tamdo*. As money was relatively scarce in Tibet at the time, owing three hundred *tamdo* then was an exceedingly heavy burden, like owing thirty thousand *tamdo* later when the Communist Chinese came to Tibet [in the 1950s]. Many of the merchants from whom tea, fabric for clothing, and other items had been purchased were constantly demanding payment. We were trapped in the net of serious hardship.

The attempted Chinese occupation in the water-rat year (1912) happened just after the late Ngakrampa had handed over the responsibility of managing the labrang to Dzongsur Lekshé, which greatly disrupted things. We had also spent a great sum for the feasts and offerings associated with my initial enrollment at Ganden and examinations before the assembly[77] at various stages.

Other than three dairy farms, the labrang held not even a palm-sized parcel of farmland. Although we leased these three dairy farms annually in order to cover monastic needs, most of the resident managers of the farms were related to one another, and so the income we were able to derive from them was negligible. As the great yogi Milarepa said:

> Although thunder, lightning, and southern clouds appear,
> they appear from the sky itself;
> although they disappear, they disappear into the very
> same sky—
> what naturally appears disappears naturally too.
>
> Although rainbows, fog, and morning mist appear,
> they appear from the air itself;
> although they disappear, they disappear into the very same air—
> what naturally appears disappears naturally too.

That is exactly how it was. The labrang was outwardly big but hollow within, like a Bönpo's drum. Except while attending the Great Prayer Festivals in Lhasa, my upper garment always bore five or six patches, and my other robes were also heavily patched all throughout my time at the monastery. I was forced to rely mostly on *tsampa* and vegetables for my daily sustenance. Whenever someone passing their geshé exams invited me to their celebratory feast or a monastic official made an offering required by his status, or someone invited me to perform rituals at their home, I would experience ecstatic joy in anticipation of it the night before. I used to secretly save one or two *tamkar* from the honoraria received for the performance of rituals and send Lhabu, my close attendant, to the restaurants to buy some momos during my stays in Lhasa. Sometimes I would smuggle in simple dishes from friends in the tantric college and eat them in secrecy without my steward noticing.

Money was scarce but food was cheap in that period. The cost of one quarter of a dried sheep from Yardrok was three *sho* initially and later it increased to five. I used to buy and eat it privately. Because of the paucity of my livelihood, I used to envy the affluence of the tulkus of Sera and Drepung when attending the Great Prayer Festival and subsequent sessions. Yet it is fitting that I experienced a bit of hardship at that time. As Ben Gungyal said, "Before my mouth found no food; now food doesn't find my mouth." The fact that my welfare in this life is not other than it is has been due solely to the grace of my spiritual masters.

Preparations for the Geshé Lharam Degree

That year during the summer session at Sangphu, I read and gave the transmission of *Eight Thousand Verse Perfection of Wisdom* to a group of eighty monks at the request of a monk from Dokhang House of Shartsé College. As I had memorized the root text of Vasubandhu's *Treasury of Abhidharma* in previous years, I could recite it with total mastery. By diligently studying it later along with the First Dalai Lama Gendun Drup's commentary, *Illumination of the Path to Freedom*, and investigating it closely using the step-by-step account given in the commentaries of Sera Mé Gyalwang Chöjé and Chim Jampalyang, I was able to extract the meaning of all eight chapters of the root text and commentary of the *Treasury* without error.

At that time Venerable Lodrö Chöphel of Nyakré House, the incumbent abbot of Shartsé College who Serkong Dorjé Chang of Ganden held in high esteem as one of his most learned disciples, was very fond of both my teacher and myself. Because of this, after careful consideration he promoted me as a candidate for the geshé lharam examination during the Great Prayer Festival of the earth-sheep year (1919). It is generally the tradition of Shartsé College that one cannot transfer directly from Abhidharma class to Vinaya class until one has attained the rank of geshé *doram* or *lingsé*.[78] Making an exception in my case, he permitted me to transfer to the Vinaya class during the rainy-season session in order to facilitate my study of the subject.

In addition to my complete memorization of the *Versified Vinaya* by Sharchen Ngawang Tsultrim of Mé College of Sera, I studied pertinent sections of importance from the omniscient Tsonawa's commentary on the Vinaya and received teachings on them during the rainy-season period. In accordance with the ancient traditions of the monastery, I recited a dissertation on an important chapter of the *Vinayavastu* at the common assembly and a dissertation on the *Treasury of Abhidharma* in the assembly of Shartsé College.

I took great interest and joy in the melodious chanting of the ritual invocation of the protector deities and in other uniquely stylized monastic chants and pursued their study and practice. Also I had been attending the scheduled annual sessions of the above-mentioned rituals regularly. At the insistence of the chorus and chanting experts, I compiled and wrote for the chant texts unique to the college a melody that differed from previously existing melodies. My melody was clearer and more precise and introduced new musical notation. I handwrote the book with a composition for the notes within the colophon at the end of the text.

Before the commemorative festival of the twenty-fifth of the tenth month, I recited thirty pages from Tsongkhapa's *Essence of Eloquence* and sat for exams in the main assembly hall as a requirement for the geshé doram degree. During the two-day debate session, scholars from both Shartsé and Jangtsé colleges put forth questions on various topics to me, and I answered well enough not to disgrace my status as lama. My partner at this event was Geshé Chödenpa of Tsawa House of Jangtsé College, a learned scholar and a man of good character. He was later appointed abbot of Jangtsé College by the Thirteenth Dalai Lama. On the very day of the conclusion of my doram exam, a government messenger dispatched from the court of His Holiness the Dalai Lama at the Norbulingka Palace in Lhasa arrived with an order that all those taking the geshé exams of the lharam and *tsokram* categories should come to the Kalsang Palace of the Norbulingka at sunrise in two days to appear before the exam board to debate. The next day my teacher, myself, and Ngawang Losang left Ganden on horseback and arrived in Lhasa the same day. We went to the Gak assembly court in the Norbulingka Palace at sunrise the next day.

Until the previous year, candidates for the geshé lharam degree were appointed by the abbots of the monasteries, and it wasn't customary for the government to examine lharam candidates further. Quite unexpectedly, the geshé candidates of the prior year had been examined at the Norbulingka. Following that debate examination, the abbots of the monasteries were summoned and reprimanded for choosing candidates who were not properly prepared. However, since that was the first debate examination that the government held, the abbots were told that their candidates would be approved but that if future candidates did not meet the high standards of geshé scholarship, not only would they be disqualified, but necessary action would be taken against the abbots themselves. Because of this, I was tense and apprehensive for the first two days of the exam.

The debate sessions were held in the sunlight room of the Norbulingka Palace in the presence of the lord chamberlain, Tenpa Dargyé, and Tsenshap Rinpoché from Deyang College of Drepung, assistant tutor to His Holiness the Thirteenth Dalai Lama. Sometimes His Holiness himself observed the debates inconspicuously from behind a door curtain in a room on the second floor. The geshé candidates were not allowed to discuss topics of their own choosing when their turn to debate came up. Deyang Tsenshap Rinpoché monitored the debates by selecting lines from the texts and bringing up points that were difficult to interpret. Some geshés, unable to recall the assigned topics, simply paced back and forth and were forced to switch topics. Luckily, I encountered no such obstacles. Although at times I could not defend a scriptural point when questioned, I was never left utterly in the dark due to unfamiliarity with the topics raised and was not forced to remain silent and perplexed.

After the exam I returned to Ganden feeling anxious and dreading the government's announcement. The others in my group were Uchu Muchin Sokpo Hothokthu of Gomang from Mongolia, Denma Tulku of Sera Jé, Pomra Ratak of Sera Mé, and Samling Bathar of Dokhang House. The above four colleagues were detained or told to remain in Lhasa for the time being and heard neither good nor bad news about their exam results for a month. Later, Hothokthu was fined ten gold *sang*, Denma Tulku was fined five, and Pomra Ratak and Bathar of Ganden Shartsé were fined one gold *sang* each, and they were barely allowed to retain their geshé titles.

Later, Geshé Bathar celebrated the completion of his geshé examinations and made his offerings to the monks during the second part of the winter session. I made my geshé lharam candidacy offerings at the beginning of the eleventh month during the first part of the winter session. At the main assembly I offered tea twice, a rice meal of pudding rich in butter and assorted dried fruit and monetary gifts of two *tam* for each monk. At Shartsé College, in addition to the offerings of tea and rice, each monk was offered two *tam* issued by the Ganden Phodrang government and one antique *tam* coin together with a plain ceremonial scarf. As a gift to the Shartsé College, I offered a set of three brocade appliqué thangkas of the three deities of longevity and a pair of antique cymbals for use by the chant master during the annual propitiation ritual. I made offerings to the monks of Dokhang House that were similar to the offerings made in Shartsé. A large silver butter lamp and four *drimo*[79] brought from our dairy farm at Dechen Balamshar were offered as gifts to the house. Similar offerings were made at Samling, affiliated with Dokhang House, with a donation of capital for their New Year offering fund. At Jangtsé College and at Serkong House and its branch Samling Mitsen, offerings of tea and two silver *tam* were presented to each monk.

I sat for debate questioning for two days in the debate courtyard of Shartsé and attended all-night debate sessions at Dokhang and Sokpa houses of Shartsé and at Lubum, Gyalrong, and Trehor houses of Jangtsé. After the offerings at Ganden, on the way to Lhasa we made token offerings at Chötri and Simkhang Shar at Tsal Gungthang. On the eighth of the twelfth month, the geshés drew lots to determine the dates of their exams. This was done at Drepung in the presence of a personal representative of His Holiness and two abbots who would moderate the exams. My teacher went on my behalf, and the date for my examination was set for the sixth of the first month.

My Geshé Lharam Examination

I was to take my geshé lharam examination during the Great Prayer Festival in my nineteenth year, the year of the earth-sheep (1919). On the third of the first month, the day when seating arrangements were made for the occasion, I had an audience with His Holiness at the Norbulingka. On the actual day of my examination, the sixth, I had to orally present dissertations on the five treatises on the Buddha's word[80] during the three "wet" sessions[81] and had to orally present on Logic and Epistemology in the teaching courtyard during the morning session, on the topics of Middle Way philosophy and the Perfection of Wisdom during the afternoon session, and on Vinaya and Abhidharma during the evening session. Although it would be difficult to say that my intentions were based on pure renunciation, the enlightened attitude, and so forth, my motivation was not stained by hope, fear, or arrogance. Thus I was able to respond with what I honestly knew to whatever was asked and did not pretend that I saw what I did not or knew what I did not. Although many great scholars from Sera and Drepung hurled probing questions at me, at least I did not have to answer with mere guesses, like taking measurements in the dark.

On the seventh I presented a sum of money to the offering committee for a tea offering at the noon session and offered one *tam* to each monk. The representatives of Ganden Shartsé and other houses, as well as friends and close associates, came in large numbers and presented gifts and ceremonial scarves to congratulate me on the occasion of becoming a lharam geshé. My teacher Geshé Sherap Rinpoché, other geshés, and many close friends expressed their pleasure at my performance the previous day. As mentioned earlier, since my labrang was heavily in debt and we had no resources with which to make offerings, we sold a butter lamp from the time of my predecessor, some silver objects including a tea-offering set, a large gold amulet shrine box, and some robes, the proceeds from the sale of which was just enough to cover the expenses for the money, rice, and other offerings. The quantity of butter provided from our dairy farm at Dechen Balamshar was almost sufficient, with some extra quantities borrowed from other sources, so we didn't have to take out loans specifically for the geshé offerings.

I attended all the sessions without exception during the Great Prayer Festival and fulfilled what was required according to tradition. It was customary to confer the geshé degrees in grades and present awards to outstanding geshés during a convocation ceremony at the residential palace of His Holiness the Dalai Lama in Lhasa following the torma-casting ritual.[82]

The geshés had an audience with His Holiness the Dalai Lama and received their grades and awards. That year, as His Holiness the Thirteenth Dalai Lama was engaged in a complete meditational retreat on Vajrabhairava at the Norbulingka, the abbots and we geshés were received by His Holiness in his room. At the palace court entrance, the chief secretary of the upper branch of government [consisting of monastic officials] read out the names of the geshés according to their grades. In the top category were Thupten Nyingpo of Buryatia from Hardong House of Drepung Gomang and Minyak Tashi Tongdü of Drepung Loseling, who later became Ninety-Fifth Ganden Throneholder. In the second category were Gönpo Tsering of Mongolia from Hardong House of Jé College at Sera and Tau Tsewang Gönpo from Trehor House of Jangtsé College at Ganden. In the third category were Demo Tulku Rinpoché from Loseling College and myself.

During the ceremony we sat in the order of our categories, and the others who weren't placed in any particular category sat behind us in order of monastic seniority. As the Hothokthu[83] did not attain a geshé degree with honors, he was seated behind us near the door on a throne with a backrest, to which he was entitled by his rank. Since this was unprecedented, it seemed strange. Everyone was served tea and ceremonial sweet rice, and the ranked geshés were awarded gifts. Demo Rinpoché and I received a yellow robe, an upper garment, a yellow hat, a ceremonial scarf, and two blocks of tea for our geshé category. Thus everything went well with my geshé examination, and I did not need to be depressed or feel embarrassed by disappointing my learned masters.

At this point I realized that after such a lengthy pursuit of religious study and of critical reflection on the meaning of scriptures with dedicated effort, if I did not nail down their application through practice, then my diligent study of scripture would have been merely an intellectual exercise to meet the needs of the moment, resulting only in temporary benefit, and that forgetting them as the years passed, my education would evaporate like a rainbow body of light, only to remain a half-remembered dream. After the completion of the examination activities at the Great Prayer Festival, I rested for a few days in a relaxed state of mind, like the pratyekabuddhas of the Hinayana tradition who say, "I have completed my work and know of no other state of existence than this."

Once again between the sessions of the Great Prayer Festival and the Subsequent Prayer Session, every day I went to the Norbulingka to request instruction from Geshé Sherap Gyatso, who was living there while editing a printing of the Kangyur. We studied the root text *Mirror of Poetics*[84] and the middle chapter of its commentary, *Melody to Delight Sarasvatī*.[85] Previously when I had studied grammar and composition, I had always done the exercises in verse, so I was able to present my poetry exercises at the appropriate sections due to familiarity with verse composition. I planned to study the first and last chapters in order, but this had to be postponed because I needed to attend tantric college sessions and discourses.

Ordination, Practice, Study, and Memorization

The prenatal months were added to my age,[86] and in the second month of the earth-sheep year (1919), in an assembly of ten monks at the Norbulingka Palace during the Subsequent Prayer Session, I received full ordination as a bhikṣu from the great preceptor, holder of the Vinaya, perfect lord of the Buddha's teachings, mention of whose name is meaningful, His Holiness the Great Thirteenth Dalai Lama Jetsun Ngawang Losang Thupten Gyatso Jikdral Wangchuk Choklé Nampar Gyalwai Dé Palsangpo, who acted as joint preceptor and master.[87] Deyang Tsenshap Rinpoché Tenzin Trinlé Özer[88] acted as the interviewing master,[89] and Venerable Jampa Sönam, the Kālacakra master of Namgyal Monastery, acted as timekeeper. Jangtsé Chöjé Jampa Chödrak from Trehor House of Drepung Loseling and Sharpa Chöjé Losang Gyaltsen from Lawa House of Sera Jé College—both of whom later became Ganden Throneholder—were also present.

At this point I would like to mention the following. From the time that my venerable teacher arrived at the house until I left to study at tantric college, the teacher was my constant residential companion. Daily I rose at about dawn, and after reciting the devotional practices of the *Hundred Deities of Tuṣita* and *Chanting the Names of Mañjuśrī* and the self-generation sādhana of Vajrabhairava, I would memorize about one and a half folios of whichever section of a subject I was on until morning tea. Every day after morning tea, I would attend morning and evening debates and other prayer sessions, without missing any, throughout the four seasons of Dharma instruction at the monastery. I would debate for long periods late into the evening until after ten o'clock. I would always attend either the noon prayer session or the noon debate session. In between these various sessions my teacher would instruct me or I would practice debate with my classmate Ngawang Losang. My ears and palms would become chapped and inflamed due to the extreme cold during the winter sessions. Even so, I never considered it a hardship and was not despondent or reluctant to attend debate sessions every day.

While in Lhasa, my teacher would go out on a long circumambulation of the city during recess after the morning lessons. During this time I had the opportunity to play various games or make drawings, behaviors more typical of my childish age. Just before my teacher completed his circumambulation, a nearby piece of furniture would always emit a creaking sound. If I immediately put away my toys and playthings and sat properly in the pretense of study, my teacher wouldn't scold me when he arrived. By relying on that sound, I could play totally at ease. Such instances of being cared for by the protector with name Gyalchen Dorjé during my childhood play, as if by a loving mother, are too many to count.

During recess at the monastery and while in Lhasa, I recited texts on the roof from evening until eleven at night. Whenever I omitted lines, unable to remember them, or recited the words of the texts unclearly due to sleepiness, my teacher would scold or beat me when I returned to my room. Until students reach the advanced Middle Way class, they are required to recite textbooks by heart in front of the abbot during the winter session. Two or three years in a row I was awarded first place for reciting one thousand folios from memory and received special ceremonial silk scarves for the achievement.

In addition to a set of the Narthang edition of the entire Kangyur, for several years a complete handwritten copy of a Kangyur from the library of Tengyé Ling Monastery was also kept in my residence. This Kangyur had been given to Ganden Monastery by the government after the fall of Tengyé Ling Monastery during the conflict with the Chinese in Lhasa during the water-rat year (1912). Soon after receiving the oral transmission on the Kangyur at the age of thirteen, I read all thirteen volumes on Vinaya in the Kangyur. As I found them very fascinating, I went on to gradually read the entire Kangyur with increasing enthusiasm. Afterward, I read the collection of praises and over half the sections on sutra, tantra, and many aspects of the field of Abhidharma in the Tengyur.

Expecting that my teacher would scold me for reading them, I would keep half a volume hidden in a cabinet next to my bed and read them when my teacher went out sometimes during the day. Most of the time I read them silently by the light of an oil lamp, forty to fifty folios at a time, sitting up in my bed at night after my daily recitation of texts, when my teacher had left for his room to sleep.

Also at Lhasa and at Chusang Retreat House, we kept a vast collection of books such as the collected works and biographies of Jé Tsongkhapa and his chief disciples,[90] the Dalai Lamas, the Paṇchen Lamas, and many other lamas. There were also books on sutra, tantra, general knowledge, and compendia of miscellaneous works. I can say that there is scarcely any book among those that I have not read. I would read them whenever an opportunity arose, up until my departure to Chatreng in the wood-bird year (1924). During my years in the Kham region, as well as after I returned to Central Tibet, I continued to read and study the works and teachings of many lamas from every tradition of Tibetan Buddhism. But as explained in the *Hundred Verses on Wisdom*:

> Knowledge remaining in the scriptures,
> mantra without accomplishment,
> and studies that are soon forgotten
> will all let you down at your time of need.[91]

Like a child gazing at the sights in a temple, any lasting legacy of what I had experienced was no more than the horns of a rabbit.

After the Subsequent Prayer Session, I enrolled at Gyütö Tantric College and then proceeded to Ütö Chuda to attend the spring session of tantric college. There I received the explanation and transmission of the Guhyasamāja with its four interwoven commentaries[92] from the abbot, Losang Tsöndrü of Gyalrong House of Sera Mé College. From there I went to Ganden for the summer session and successively attended the torma-casting ritual in Lhasa. Following the session at Sera, the college went to Drak Yerpa to observe the latter part of the rainy season. While in session there, the new geshés sat for examination in debate concerning tantric subjects and were trained in drawing mandala diagrams for seven days. I attended all of them, including the three-day drawing of the grid for inspection by the abbot and the dean. During this, the abbot and the dean would test the geshés on the three-dimensional mandalas of Guhyasamāja, Vajrabhairava, and Cakrasaṃvara and their symbolism. The ritual assistants were tested on the color formations and the novices on the root texts dealing with the proportions of the mandalas. I sat in the front row, and due to the kindness of the late Ngakrampa I was able to respond correctly to the questions when the geshés were examined on the three-dimensional mandalas.

At Drak Yerpa we completed the courses of study on the four interwoven commentaries on Guhyasamāja and on the *Cakrasaṃvara Root Tantra* along with its commentary, Tsongkhapa's *Elucidation of All Hidden Points*. At that time, Rikzin, a geshé and my predecessor's nephew and representative, and two monks from Gyütö Tantric College who had served as his ritual assistants returned from the Thorgö region of Mongolia after several years. They had been sent to Mongolia by the late Dzongsur Lekshé to perform religious services and to raise funds. The labrang had taken a large loan to cover the initial provisions for their journey. After the labrang had paid back the loan and the interest on the loan and divided the remaining income from the trip among the four members, the profit was negligible. It was merely enough to stir up gossip about their trip. From that point my teacher and I turned over all aspects of worldly responsibility for the labrang to Rikzin. After the session at Yerpa, I attended the two autumn sessions in Lhasa, the subsequent sessions at the Potala, the winter session at Ganden, and a session at Drepung.

When I reached my twentieth year, the year of the iron-monkey (1920), I went to Kyormolung to attend a tantric-college session after the conclusion of the Great Prayer Festival. In the past, the tradition of the tantric college was that lamas who held the rank of tulkus in the great assembly had to remain in their seats in order of seniority for three days after their enrollment and had to attend all the prayer and study sessions just as any newly joined student would. After the third day they were required to make an elaborate tea offering, called *né-ja*, similar to the administrators of the monastery, and present gifts of money to the assembly of monks. Once this was done, their seats would be moved to the section of retired monastic administrators, where they received the same privileges as the retired officials and were excused from attending sessions. Even though I had earned this privilege, I attended all the sessions just like everybody else until I completed the full year required, without looking for any special treatment. This pleased the monks greatly, and later when other tulkus entered the college, they used my behavior as an example, relating how in the past Trijang Tulku had faithfully attended the sessions.

While attending the winter session for the tantric college at Ganden, I gave an oral transmission of the three-volume *Miktsema Compendium*[93] and two volumes of the tantric rituals of Tashi Lhunpo Monastery to a group of three hundred monks of Dokhang House at the request of Geshé Gendun of Mili.

Since I had to attend the mandatory sessions following my enrollment at tantric college and I was receiving teachings at Chusang when not attending the sessions, I was unable to stay with my teacher all year round. So in the last years of his life until he passed away, he would stay at Ganden every year during the rainy-season retreat and the winter session at the invitation of many of his disciples from both Shartsé and Jangtsé colleges, and he would stay at my Lhasa residence during the spring and autumn.

In the spring of my twenty-first year, the year of the iron-bird (1921), at Chusang Hermitage, I gradually received from the supreme refuge Kyabjé Vajradhara Phabongkha the blessing of the four sindūra initiations[94] of Vajrayoginī and its profound teaching on the generation and completion stages, teachings on the Thirteen Golden Dharmas of Sakya, the Thirteen Divine Visions of Takphu, the cycle of Mañjuśrī teachings, the ear-whispered teachings of Lhodrak, and the permission of the fifteen Vaiśravaṇas.

From the third of the seventh month to the sixth of the eighth month, we received initiations into sixty-five of the mandalas unique to the mahāsiddha Mitrayogin, who fully revealed one hundred and eight of them. We received the initiations at Takdrak Hermitage, at the holy feet of the kind and glorious Takdrak Tritrul Rinpoché, Ngawang Sungrap Thuthop

Tenpai Gyaltsen, who was no different than Vajradhara, the teacher of the tantras himself. I received those teachings together with a circle of accomplished disciples, including the supreme refuge, the glorious Phabongkha Vajradhara, the all-embracing lord, as well as the great Kangyurwa Losang Dönden, Khangsar Vajradhara of Gomang, Dromo Geshé Rinpoché, Ngawang Kalsang, Ön Gyalsé Rinpoché, Tsawa Öser Tulku, Tri Ngawang Norbu Rinpoché, Tridak Rinpoché of Ganden Jangtsé, twenty-one reincarnated lamas, and Obom Tokden Jamyang Lodrö of Drakgyab along with ninety-seven geshés. Each day we received one initiation of the lower class of tantra in the morning and one initiation of the higher class in the afternoon, making two initiations per day. The preparations for each of the initiations of all the four classes of tantra were performed prior to each initiation. Thus we correctly observed the traditions of past successive lineages without negligently cutting corners.

That year, due to controversy over the selection of administrative managers at Drepung Loseling, out of ignorance a few insolent monks that the administration could not control incited a large number of monks to go to the Norbulingka Palace, where they appealed directly to His Holiness, prostrating and crying on the court platform below his residence. As this was a violation of acceptable conduct, His Holiness was very displeased with the situation and issued a summons for the principal instigators. There was talk that one of them known as Bearded Nyakré was in hiding in the Tölung area, so some government soldiers went to Taklung Drak Hermitage to search for him. Since they even ended up searching the place where we were gathered for teachings, there was fear and suspicion that anyone with a beard attending the discourse could be arrested as a suspect.

At that time, during the recess, I received the permission for the mantra extraction (*mantroddāra*) of Vajrayoginī along with teachings on the peaceful and wrathful torma offerings to Dharmarāja in sixty-four parts[95] directly from Kyabjé Phabongkha Vajradhara.

Phabongkha Rinpoché's Extensive Discourse on the Stages of the Path

After returning to Chusang from Takdrak Hermitage, as requested by Lady Yangzom Tsering, wife of Minister Lhalu, the synthesis of all refuge Kyabjé Phabongkha, who was in reality the lord of sages Losang Vajradhara,[96] gave an elaborate teaching based on his experience of the stages of the path that combined the *Words of Mañjuśrī* of the central lineage and the *Quick Path* of the southern lineage[97] to an audience of thousands of disciples, mostly tulkus and geshés, in the discourse yard of Chusang. The discourse was given from the third day of the eighth month and lasted twenty-four days. At the conclusion of the discourse, Rinpoché conducted the ceremony to generate bodhicitta, combining both the aspiring and engaging bodhisattva vows.[98]

I was most fortunate to have had the opportunity to be among the audience. Guru Vajradhara taught in accordance with the saying "Vast and profound for the intelligent; easy to grasp and put into practice for the simple minded." Thus due to his remarkable ability as a teacher, people of all different levels could easily understand him according to their own mental capacity. As his explanations were based on personal experience, rather than being mere words, they were able to have an effect on the minds of the disciples present. I am deeply grateful for the kindness he showed me by guiding my mind, which at the time ran uncontrolled like a wild horse in the hills, onto the true path of Dharma. Although there is no way that I could fully repay his kindness, I will hold it in the deepest reverence atop my head like a crown until I reach the heart of enlightenment.

At that discourse, Dongong Tulku of Drakgyab had taken rough notes, which Kyabjé Vajradhara himself checked, edited, and corrected up to the passage on invoking the field of merit within the manual of the preliminary practices (*sbyor chos*). At the request of many sincere individuals, I compiled the rest of the good points from notes taken at teachings given on the stages of the path at various other occasions, adding to them a few things I remembered from his explanations that had not appeared in the works of others. In this way I prepared the notes on the stages of the path known as *Liberation in the Palm of Your Hand*, which is now in print.

Beda Tulku's Arrival from Chatreng

Chagong Beda Tulku[99] and Lakak Tulku left from Chatreng, but Beda and his group sent a messenger ahead to seek permission from His Holiness the Thirteenth Dalai Lama for them to proceed to Trijang Labrang at Lhasa directly, as "a bird returning to its nest and sword into its sheath." They had to wait in Chamdo for over one month for the reply. Lakak Tulku, who left early, came to see me at Chusang and asked for my assistance for his enrollment at Ganden with a teacher, which I arranged according to his request.

My arrival at Mindröl Bridge at the northeast of Lhasa's outer circuit road upon my return after the completion of the stages of the path discourse coincided, like the analogy of the turtle and the yoke,[100] with the surprising and unexpected arrival in Lhasa of Beda Tulku and his group. They were met by Geshé Dapön of Pomra House of Sera Mé. In response to Beda Tulku's request, His Holiness had replied that "Trijang Tulku has been recognized in accordance with my divination and has been enrolled at Ganden. Upon completion of the activities of a geshé lharam following the conclusion of his studies, he is presently enrolled in Gyütö Tantric College. You are therefore not authorized to enter Trijang Labrang directly, but you may enter a seat of learning according to your monastic affiliation." So the tulku was enrolled at Mé college of Sera.

After the tulku had passed away, a relative of his, a humble geshé named Yeshé, gave me some documents, including the above, which were responses to letters of petition submitted to His Holiness on various occasions. He presented me with these documents before returning to his birthplace, apologizing and asking my forgiveness for many of their ignorant actions in the past.

Further Teachings and Empowerments

After a few days' recess, following the completion of the stages of the path discourse, once again in the assembly hall of Chusang, Kyabjé Vajradhara gave initiation into the five-deity outer mandala of Cakrasaṃvara in the Ghaṇṭāpāda tradition, which are the innermost secret teachings of the ultimate tantra. These are also the methods especially sought after by the yoginīs and the path traveled by millions of yogis who have attained the supreme state. After initiating us into the Cakrasaṃvara body mandala of the Ghaṇṭāpāda tradition, he gave us a complete explanation of the generation and completion stages for the body mandala, along with a commentary on the six Dharmas of Nāropa. I had the good fortune to receive the teaching with sixty others in attendance. After the regular sessions, a few of us received detailed instructions on the physical practices of the six Dharmas in reconvened sessions at night. One time, we were all sitting in complete silence as Lama Rinpoché did the yoga practices in the vase-breathing position. Just then a monk sitting in the back row broke wind loudly, which left all of us disciples and the lama in a state of laughter, breaking the continuity of the session.

After the Great Prayer Festival in my twenty-second year, the water-dog year (1922), at the behest of His Holiness the Dalai Lama, Kyabjé Vajradhara Phabongkha gave a discourse and oral reading of the *Middle-Length Stages of the Path*[101] to an assembly of four thousand disciples, myself included, in the assembly hall of Meru Monastery in Lhasa. After the Subsequent Prayer Session, the All-Embracing Lord, Takphu Vajradhara Losang Jampal Tenpai Ngödrup, or Padmavajra,[102] visited Lhasa from Kham. He stayed at the South Cabinet Ministry, and I had the great fortune of paying respects at his lotus feet. At the request of the Fourth Sharpa Tulku, son of Prime Minister Shölkhangpa, Takphu Vajradhara gave over thirty initiations on the profound teachings based on divine visions of his lineage to Kyabjé Takdrak Vajradhara, Tridak Rinpoché of Ganden, Mokchok Rinpoché of Drepung, and so on. Together with seven supreme beings, the vessel of my hopes was filled with the ambrosia of peerless blessings.

One day I invited Takphu Vajradhara to my house and received the Cittamaṇi Tārā heart-absorption permission and the longevity initiation of Chimé Palter from the Thangthong ear-whispered tradition. Takphu Vajradhara, like Takphu Tenpai Gyaltsen and Garwang Rinpoché, had visionary contact with deities and lamas in general and in particular with goddess Tārā, who appeared to him constantly, revealing prophecies. There exists a "mother" volume and three "son" volumes that contain his inconceivable secret teachings. As he was such a great being and remained in touch with an ocean of myriad mandalas, I requested his prophecy regarding my special karmic deity and the future course of my life. He conveyed this to Tārā and gave me the prophecy in a verse of eight lines. Provided what he said was not a riddle, it made for peaceful sleep.

The great Kangyur Lama Rinpoché Losang Dönden, who was always fond of me, one day came to my house and said, "If you have not received the oral transmission reading of the collected works of Jé Tsongkhapa and his spiritual sons, I will give it to you." He told me this out of compassionate care and with great pleasure, without needing me to ask or present offerings to him to do so. I received the entire transmission of the works of Jé Tsongkhapa and his disciples at the residence of the Shedra family. Because I was poor at the time, I could offer him only the sum of five *dotsé*.[103] At a later date I received the oral transmission of the five-volume collected works of Takphu Garwang directly from Kangyur Rinpoché in Shidé Monastery's *nyungné* chapel. Around this time, in consultation with the supreme refuge Vajradhara, I studied in detail the construction of the three-dimensional mandalas of Guhyasamāja, Cakrasaṃvara, and Vajrabhairava along with Ganden Jangtsé Tridak Rinpoché, Gomang Mokchok Rinpoché, Tsona Göntsé Rinpoché, and a few other tulkus and geshés at the Shesur family residence in Lhasa.

In my twenty-third year, the year of the water-pig (1923), at Chusang I received directly from Kyabjé Phabongkha Vajradhara the Bari Hundred,[104] the Ocean of Sādhanas,[105] the Narthang Hundred,[106] permission for the eighty mahāsiddhas, an experiential commentary on the generation and completion stages according to the *Sādhana Casket of Thirteen-Deity Vajrabhairava*, instruction in the *Guru Puja*'s profound path, mahāmudrā and guruyoga based on the root text of mahāmudrā, teachings on the full meditational retreat of single-deity Vajrabhairava, and many other teachings and oral transmissions.

Frustrated Attempt to Solve the Estate's Problems

Although, as stated above, we had handed responsibility for the labrang over to Rikzin, with great hope that he would straighten things out, unfortunately not only was he incompetent, he was fond of gambling. The labrang suffered great losses due to this. There wasn't even a proper supply of food for my teacher and myself, as in the saying: "pieces of meat in exchange for the carcass."

Minister Khemé Rinchen Wangyal was the most influential minister in the cabinet at the time. Hoping that, if he wanted to assist us, even a word from him would help, I went with a gift to visit him at Kunsangtsé and inform him of our situation. I had hoped that he would advise Rikzin to change his attitude and behavior and to look after the interest and affairs of the labrang in a proper manner. But apart from offering a few words of advice to the effect that I should talk to Rikzin about the matter myself, he did not take up my request. As they say, "I am my own protector. Who else could be my protector?" If you can't manage by yourself, depending on others is truly a last resort. Jé Barawa Gyaltsen Palsang said:

> Relatives ought to regard one another equally,
> and yet the wealthy are attended with special concern
> while the destitute are disparaged and suffer greatly.
> The low are neglected and the high are sought out.
> In the face of misfortune, it is hard for relatives to be sincere.

Finding this to be quite true, I gave up hoping for relief from relatives.

Meditation Retreats

After completion of the year's session at the tantric college, I stayed permanently at Chusang, where I spent most of my time attending all the teachings of Kyabjé Phabongkha Vajradhara. During recesses between discourses, I performed the meditation retreats of the special deities Vajrayoginī, single-deity and thirteen-deity Vajrabhairava, five-deity Cakrasaṃvara of the Ghaṇṭāpāda tradition, Secret Hayagrīva, and the Great Compassionate One of the Lakṣmī tradition. In the course of working to develop my mind to the best of my ability by engaging in the stages of the path meditation in conjunction with the preliminary practices of accumulating merit and purifying negative karma, I was pulled away by activities and distractions beyond my control, such as needing to visit Chatreng. I think it was my many nonvirtuous actions in previous lives that prevented me from bringing my wishes to fulfillment, causing the legacies of my experience of contemplation and meditation to evaporate like mist in the winter.

4 | Travels and Travails in Kham

Preparations for the Journey to Chatreng

In my twenty-fourth year, the year of the wood-rat (1924), I decided to travel to Chatreng at the joint invitation of the monasteries and towns there. After the Great Prayer Festival I sought resignation from the tantric college and withdrew my monastic seat cover. That day the supreme incarnation Kyabjé Ling Rinpoché enrolled at the tantric college and placed his seat cover there. By this coincidence we were together for one session at the morning assembly.

After the Subsequent Prayer Session at Tashi Rapten, my Lhasa residence, I gave the reading transmission of the collected works of Jé Tsongkhapa and his spiritual sons at the request of Samling Geshé Yönten of Dokhang House of Shartsé. At that time I was reading a volume a day. Unlike some others, it was beyond the capacity of my tongue to read two or three volumes a day.

At this point once again Geshé Palchuk Dapön of Chatreng, who was from Pomra House of Sera Mé, and Troti Tsultrim appealed to His Holiness through Minister Tsarong Dasang Dradul, whom His Holiness held in regard, causing further trouble regarding my visit to Kham. Being uncertain about entrusting the affairs of the labrang to the monastic house during the visit to Kham, I sought the prophecy of the protector in trance.

At Chusang there was a very good monk living dedicatedly in accordance with the advice of Lama Vajradhara. He was known as Shidé Tā Lama and had resigned from government service. As Shukden would rarely enter him in trance and only in strict secrecy, one day I invited him to our house. The prophecy that he delivered while in trance was as follows:

> The precious umbrella (His Holiness the Dalai Lama) is the
> best protection from heat.

The golden fish rely on the support of the vast ocean (the monastic houses).
The wish-fulfilling vase has many enemies (wrong practices).
The sun, friend of the lotus, need not doubt the moon. (The Dalai Lama will not consider the other.)

If you hold the sound of the Dharma conch, the Ganden oral tradition,
with the endless knot that is your secret heart,
I, the spirit, will turn the wheel of assistance
for the conquering victory banner of Dharma (Trijang Rinpoché).

And everything happened in exactly this way.

After that, at the request of Trungsar Rinpoché of Karzé, Trehor, I gave a reading transmission of the collected works of Thuken Chökyi Nyima, including his most exclusive sacred works, to the all-pervading master, the great Kangyurwa Losang Dönden, and to eighty other lamas and monks. At the request of nun Trinlé Dechen of Pangda, I gave the blessing of the four sindūra initiations of Vajrayoginī and teachings on its generation and completion stages to a group of sixty monks and laypeople. This was followed by initiations into five-deity Cakrasaṃvara and Secret Hayagrīva for a group of two hundred sincere people.

Nearing the time of my departure for Kham, I had an audience with His Holiness at the Norbulingka to pay my deepest respects at his lotus feet, and I received much advice for my activities in Kham. On the way up I had my farewell audience with Lord Kangyurwa Losang Dönden, who was residing at the Potala Palace to recite the extensive *Pratimokṣa Sūtra* at Namgyal Monastery during the rainy-season session at the holy command of His Holiness. The synthesis of all refuges, Phabongkha Vajradhara, was giving a discourse on Jé Tsongkhapa's *Great Treatise on the Stages of the Path* at the Loseling College of Drepung. He was staying in the Kungarawa Palace of the Dalai Lamas, and I had an audience at his feet. With great fondness he gave me gifts and much advice, essence of nectar, on the need to propagate the Geluk tradition in Kham in a pure form.

Because of the rather poor conduct of Rikzin mentioned above, and in order to prevent further negligence in the maintenance of our labrang, we requested Dokhang House to look after our residence at Ganden and to

Kyabjé Trijang Rinpoché in Lhasa bestowing empowerments of Vajrayoginī, 1924
COURTESY OF PALDEN TSERING

administer the affairs of our farm at Maldro Jarado, which we had taken on lease from Ganden Lachi.[107] We left the affairs of our labrang in Lhasa, our land on lease from Shartsé, Dechen Lamotsé, and our farms on lease in Deyangpa in the care of manager Rikzin. Of the three hundred *tam* for payment of past debts, we gave two hundred *tam* to Dokhang House and one hundred *tam* to Rikzin and gave them the responsibility to clear all the debts.

Later, on my return from Kham, Dokhang House in addition to paying all the debts had managed to amass a large amount of barley and money. Rikzin had taken an additional loan on top of existing loans. Due to the death of various managers of our labrang and continuous expenses for my geshé offerings and so on, and the lack of competent staff able to bear the responsibility, we were so poor in cash and other material possessions that we ran into great difficulty while preparing for our trip to Kham. Nevertheless, we were just able to manage to make all of our arrangements by taking loans from my patron disciples. At the beginning of the seventh month we set out from Lhasa.

The Journey to Chatreng

Our party consisted of myself, attendant Lhabu, Ngakram Budor of Gyütö Tantric College from Markham Seudru Monastery, ritual assistant Phukhang Losang Tashi of Gyütö Tantric College, cook Namgyal Dorjé, tailor Tenzin Lhawang, Sönam Wangdü and one other to look after the horses and mules, and Tendrong Palbar Thokmé and three other escorts from Chatreng. On the way we spent two nights at Gungthang. There we invoked my birth deity Drakshul Wangpo, his attendant Nyima Shönu, and so on through an oracle in trance. Although Rikzin only came along to escort us for a short distance and would not be accompanying us to Kham, Tsengö Nyima Shönu, the chief attendant of Drakshul, advised him at length regarding his attention to my food and health and to journeys through paths, narrow passages, and rivers along the way. This made no sense to me, and I thought it ludicrous.

Leaving there I spent one night in Dechen Kharap Ogong Kotsang with my mother and sister Jampal Chötso. The next day we arrived at Ganden and spent a few days at leisure visiting my teacher Losang Tsultrim. While staying there I gave an initiation into thirteen-deity Vajrabhairava, together with its preparation, for two days in the hall of Dokhang House. I also made offerings before the golden stupa of Jé Tsongkhapa and an incense offering on top of Wangkur Hill.[108] At the invitation of Shartsé College, I attended their farewell reception for me, at which time the incumbent abbot, Losang Khyenrap of Phukhang, presented me with the symbolic mandala offering along with accompanying verses. He recited the following with the presentation of the stupa:

> For inconceivable millions of eons,
> you remain, acting as a stupa.

It was patently obvious, when he recited this verse, that although he was well known for his command of philosophy, he lacked skill in literary arts.

What with the reputation of the people from Chatreng for their undaunted spirit and vigor in fighting and looting, and the existence of the faction that showed me no favor, everyone doubted my safe return to Central Tibet from Chatreng. Whatever the reason, soon after my departure from Ganden, the abbot [Losang Khyenrab] took advantage of the situation and created many problems, making accusations against Rikzin and the appointed representatives of Dokhang House. It was just as the supreme refuge Vajradhara had said:

> From the raincloud that should protect
> comes hail, lightning, and thunderbolts.
> The myriad rays of the sun on which we should rely
> are like a noose of burning hellfire.

After completing my activities of paying respect to the sacred objects and visiting friends and classmates, I made offerings to the golden stupa with the monetary gifts I had received there. Keeping about fifteen *sang* in silver for expenses, I offered the rest to my precious teacher. The day I left Ganden, my teacher, in deep grief, tears in his eyes, gave me a great deal of spiritual and worldly advice on my course of action ahead, which I carried in the innermost drop of my heart. I was forced to proceed with deep anguish, unable to bear our parting.

After spending two nights at the estate of Jarado in Maldro, we went on to Rinchen Ling, Özer Gyang, Tsomorak, Ba Pass, and Gyada in the Kongpo region. Traveling through many hazardous and fearfully difficult passages and bridges by way of Tro Pass, Lharigo, Bendha Pass, Nupgong Pass, and Alarong, we arrived in the town of Ngödroké. There I spent one night at Arik, hometown monastery of the late Ngakrampa, and made offerings there in a token form. The next day I went to visit Ayik Thango, Ngakrampa's home, and presented gifts to his relatives. At the invitation of Gyatso Ling Labrang, I stayed one night at the monastery. As I had received many teaching from the predecessor of Gungtrul Rinpoché and his lineage, I made offering to his memorial stupa. The present incarnation, Gyatso Ling Tulku, was residing there and, being young, was at play.

Crossing Shargong Pass, we arrived at Chakra Palbar. There at the request of Palbar Geshé Ngawang Chöjor, a tantric master of Gyümé Tantric College, and others I gave full ordination to a group of ten monks of Palbar Monastery. Then in Dzitho after passing through Lhatsé and Shopado with its two monasteries Nyinpa and Sipa, I spent three nights at Nyinpa at their request. I presided over the consecration of the newly made statue of the future Buddha, Maitreya, along with the ritual assembly of the monastery. The ritual performed was based on the elaborate consecration ritual Causing the Rain of Goodness to Fall.[109] I also gave longevity initiations to the people of that area.

In between religious activities, I went to Sipa Monastery and Draknak Labrang at their invitation, where I performed consecration rituals. Then I stayed at the house of Pönying Tsang, a patron of my successor in Lhozong. There, at the invitation of Shitram Monastery, I went for a brief visit and gave a short teaching to the monks. Passing through Yidak Pass, I crossed the big Right Foot Bridge over the Gyalmo Ngulchu River. Also crossing Chutsul Pass, I arrived at Wako Mari. There we met with a messenger specially dispatched from Khyungpo Tengchen by the ministerial secretary Yuthokpa Wangdü Norbu, who was the government's representative of the northern provinces, saying that he was coming to Wako Mari personally to meet me and that I should wait for him there.

After a day in Mari, the representative arrived with his entourage. I spent a whole day with him, giving him the longevity initiation in the tradition of Drupgyal. He gave me a generous sum of money as a farewell gift. I gave him a sum of money, including his gift and other offerings received on the journey, requesting him to commission two pairs of gilded bronze *tsipar* heads[110] to ornament pillar banners that I would present to Dokhang House. This ministerial secretary, in accordance with the wishes of His Holiness, had previously been in charge of the government project to restore the temple complex at Sangphu in the earth-horse year (1918). I attended the summer session that year and went daily to the courtyard to engage in the debates for the study of logical reasoning and scriptural doctrines. Seeing this, he was pleased with me, and at his request to write a complete catalog and history of the restoration to be inscribed on a wall of the temple, I wrote an opening verse of homage to His Holiness with the syllables of his full name interlaced in a poetical context.

> Friend who brings forth words of great faith and an enticing
>   fragrance to the lotuses of the senses;
> prophesied by the Sage, a beacon of samsara and nirvana, arising
>   from the mighty ocean of Dharma;
> fearless, without rival, lord of illumination, your armies
>   victorious over all demons and opposition;
> a sun for humankind, I raise you to the crown of my head.[111]

From there we proceeded through Pomda Dzogang of Tsawa region and so on, and we spent one night at the base of a pass called Jola in the Markham area. That night I dreamed of someone like my sister, Dekyi Yangchen of the Kunsangtsé family, dressed in fine clothes, wearing ornaments, and displaying many expressions of joy and happiness. In this dream she led me into a stupendous building like that of the Potala Palace. Inside a large temple with many chapels were objects of worship, statues, scriptures, and stupas and many monks making offerings. Even the staircases inside were all made of gilded bronze. This lady led me through the rooms and gave me food. The next day some people in that area told me that there was a local deity known as Tachangma who was the sister of Pawo Trobar. Later [in 1964] in Dharamsala, when I met Tachangma in a trance through the medium of Namgyal Dölma, a lady from Kham, she said, "When you came to our town previously, I indicated myself to you, meeting you in a dream. You must remember it!" It was quite convincing.

The next day we had to cross the great river Dzachu by a yak-skin ropeway called Sampa Dreng, where people and animals were tied to a rope and slid across the river to the other side. As none of us had any previous experience of using such means of travel, everyone was apprehensive, but without any mishap and after a safe journey, we arrived at Garthok in Markham, where I stayed in the residence of Özer Monastery. As I had known the previous Özer Rinpoché intimately during his residence in Lhasa, they extended warm hospitality to me during my stay in Markham.

After departing Garthok, I visited the temple at Lhadun that contained a statue of Vairocana. This stone statue is known to have been carved by the Chinese princess Wencheng on her way to Lhasa [to wed King Songtsen Gampo].

On my arrival at Seudru Monastery, also in Markham, Gangkar Lama Rinpoché Könchok Chödrak, a highly accomplished being, came to greet me at the foot of the monastery. There in the monastery I spent a few days in the newly constructed rooms of the labrang. Gangkar Rinpoché previously lived at Loseling, Drepung, but as he had not studied for any length of time, his scriptural knowledge was not advanced. Yet since he had reached a high level of insight, he possessed unobstructed clairvoyance and was a great practitioner who revealed many hidden religious objects such as statues in lakes, mountains, rocks, and so on. Still, he remained a simple monk, faithfully observing the rules of conduct of the fully ordained monks while developing the view and pursuing his practice in the pure lineage of the Geluk tradition. Although I had not met him in person, I used to receive many letters from him in Lhasa expressing his feeling that we had strong karmic connections through many of our past lives.

At the monastery I gave an initiation into thirteen-deity Vajrabhairava to the monks and the initiation of the Great Compassionate One to the general public. The Rinpoché gave me a bronze statue of one-face, two-arm Cakrasaṃvara with consort that he had removed from a rock hill on an island in a lake called Bumtso. I have carried the statue with me to this day. Then we crossed Drichu River through Gönsar Tengon Monastery in Gowo, and traveling through the very hazardous cliff passage of Tramkolam, arrived at Dzedzé Monastery. There I went to meet Dranak Lama, also known as Lama Chöphak, who had been among us when I received the oral transmission reading of the Kangyur earlier in Lhasa. This lama, for reasons of spirit possession or some other circumstances, performed *chö* rites[112] after his audience of followers had gathered around in the darkness of night, during which time much noise of conversations in Chinese and Tibetan would be heard from invisible bodies, and weapons would fire off by themselves. Many noises, such as cries of pain and agony and sounds of coins being counted, filled the room. Because of such demonstrations of supernatural powers, he gained the respect and admiration of many people, who widely talked of him as an emanation of Padmasambhava.

As people had tremendous faith in him, the lama's activities increased, and later he recruited people to fight in battles between Chinese and Tibetans and became a commander of his fighting unit. There were a large number of soldiers equipped with weapons both inside and outside the monastery. In consideration of our previous Dharma relationship, I gave him my opinion that such behavior was not proper. To this he replied that he was acting in accordance with the wishes of His Holiness. He was going to ignore my advice like wind behind the ears and place the blame upon the lama.

At the monastery I gave some teachings to the monks. Then in the town of Shokdruk Drodok, I spent one night at the home of His Holiness Tsultrim Gyatso, the Ninth Dalai Lama (1806–15). About fifty people on horseback arrived there from Chatreng to escort me. I spent one night in the Nenang household of Chatreng, passing through Raktak Monastery and others. There the abbot of Samling Monastery in Chatreng, Geshé Losang Tharchin of Nyanang Drodru, and other officials of the monastery arrived to greet me. While I was in Ganden Shartsé and this Drodru Geshé was the chant master, he used to seek forgiveness on my behalf whenever I received a scolding and punishment from my teacher. As we were very fond of one another, we were both very happy when we met. The next day, on the third of the eleventh month, we arrived at Samphel Ling Monastery in Chatreng. I rested for some time to relax and met a variety of people, who although similar in external appearance were of diverse mental attitudes and dispositions.

Teachings at Chatreng

When I was twenty-five, in the first month of the wood-ox year (1925), I went daily to the discourse yard during the monastery's prayer ceremony. I thought that it would not be suitable if, in accordance with ancient custom, I gave a discourse on Āryaśūra's *Garland of Birth Stories*, due to the poetical nature of the text and because most of the population had not heard such a religious discourse for a very long time. So I explained in colloquial Chatreng dialect the *Sutra of the Wise and the Foolish* for the sake of its easy comprehension, and because most people there had become so accustomed to a lifestyle of looting over the intervening years that they had grown ignorant of the law of cause and effect. At the request of the monastery and the region, I gave an initiation into the Great Compassionate One of the Lakṣmī tradition in the monastery courtyard after the prayer festival. On the day of the initiation, during the vase initiation, there was a sprinkle of rain and a rainbow appeared. I took these as signs that the deities and nāgas were pleased. The monastery was virtually destroyed due to the recent incursions by the Chinese army, and its inhabitants were scattered in the mountains. Due to these circumstances, the vital essence of the place and the gods, nāgas, and local deities had waned. I consecrated about twelve hundred earth vases with the *miktsema* recitation and also performed the burial rites for the vases, distributing them in all corners of the region in order to revive its vital energy.

In the third month I gave a discourse on the *Quick Path* for fifteen days to a group of two thousand people, including monks and others from various parts of the Chatreng region, in the assembly hall of the monastery. At the conclusion of the discourse, I gave the bodhisattva vows in the common dedication of everyone's virtues and good deeds toward the development of the mind of great compassion. After that I gave a teaching on the six-session guruyoga and then an initiation into thirteen-deity Vajrabhairava for two days to a group of five hundred monks who made a commitment to recite one hundred *miktsemas* daily. Then I gave an initiation into single-deity Vajrabhairava to a group of forty-eight monks who committed to performing the sādhana of self-generation daily, and to a group of sixty-three who committed themselves to completing a full meditational retreat of Vajrabhairava, I gave teachings on the generation and completion stages of Vajrabhairava on a retreat text for twelve days, all in accordance with the tradition practiced by Lama Vajradhara.

With plans to make a new gilt image of Maitreya Buddha as the main statue in the monastery, in the fourth month of the following year I sent my attendant Lhabu with some assistants to Lhasa to buy necessary materials and ornamental jewels for the image. Through Lhabu I sent offerings to His Holiness the Dalai Lama, Kyabjé Phabongkha Rinpoché, Kangyur Lama Rinpoché, my teacher Losang Tsultrim, Geshé Sherap Rinpoché, and others from whom I had received teachings directly. To Kyabjé Phabongkha I sent a letter in poetic composition requesting his prayers. I also sent a letter to Dromo Geshé Rinpoché Ngawang Kalsang and a letter to the oracle of Shukden at Dungkar Monastery in Dromo with details of the situation and circumstances at Chatreng, requesting his prediction and guidance in trance.

Fighting

In the previous year, prior to my arrival in Chatreng, it was suspected that Chaksha Tenpa and others of his clan had assassinated a well-known figure in the region, Butsa Bugen, out of jealousy and resentment. On top of that, Tenpa was also accused of being an accomplice to the theft of a large sum of money from the treasury of the monastery. A number of influential leaders who favored Bugen, including principal monks of the monastery and laypeople from the towns, caused much disturbance by way of "shaking the mountains and stirring up the lakes" in the name of a common cause with a grudge at heart. They recruited a large contingent of fighters from among their associates and supporters in various parts of the region including Gangkar Ling, Dapa, Mewo, and Mongra. Furthermore, aided by troops under the Chinese commanding officer Ma of the Division 8 border force, they made plans to capture Chaksha Tenpa on charges of being an accomplice to the theft.

While Chaksha Tenpa was staying in Dzedzé Monastery with a large party seeking the protection of the aforementioned Dranak Lama Chöphak, the militants of Chatreng were preparing to deploy for a confrontation. Although I tried to advise them against this by explaining the pros and cons to the best of my ability, just as it isn't sure that a horse's gait will match the wish of the rider, a large number of fighters set off without listening to my advice given out of kind concern. They were set against accepting any advice whatsoever and followed their own wishes. Without giving any warning, they even set fire at night to the residence in the monastery of two monks who were supporters of Chaksha Tenpa, killing them and keeping all this secret from me. They committed many perverted acts, even killing people in their own homes. As Shangshung Chöwang Drakpa said:

> Even Indra cannot lead
> those with noses of stone
> over steps of stainless crystal
> to the noble hall of victory.[113]

There was nothing I could do but think to myself that a lama of the degenerate age, such as I am, ends up with disciples like this.

Dranak Lama had a strong force of soldiers at Dzedzé, so the Chatreng fighters could not enter the monastery. They kept the monastery under siege for months without any actual confrontation. During the rainy-season retreat at the monastery, I did a meditation retreat on the Guhyasamāja of Akṣobhyavajra. When it concluded, there was still no peace due to the unrest caused by partisan fighting.

Travel to Gangkar Ling

In compliance with an invitation from the monastery and the people of Gangkar Ling, I went with a small entourage to Gangling Tsothok Pöntsang via Mongra. I spent fifteen days there and gave the initiation of five-deity Cakrasaṃvara, the blessing of the four sindūra initiations of Vajrayoginī, and brief teachings on the generation and completion stages at the request of a few earnest seekers. Gangling Sherap Tulku, a former classmate of mine at the monastery, also came to greet me.

At Gangling Monastery I was received with an elaborate reception by the monks. There I gave an initiation into Guhyasamāja Akṣobhyavajra with a painted mandala, complete with preparation, to the monks and others, about four hundred in all. I also gave Great Compassionate One and longevity initiations to more than a thousand people. At the strong request and in the company of Sherap Tulku, I then traveled for two days to visit Bumzé Belsé Pön. His family had been one of the oldest patrons of my predecessor, the Ganden Throneholder. I spent about ten days giving initiations into the Great Compassionate One and longevity to members of his estate and his people. While there I also consecrated the family's Kangyur temple and their protector chapel with the concise "horseback" consecration.[114] In their treasure chamber, I performed the enhancement of prosperity ritual of Vaiśravaṇa.

On the way back I visited a pilgrimage place known as Protectors of the Three Lineages[115] at Gangkar. I did an additional retreat on five-deity Cakrasaṃvara there at Tsogo Hermitage, reciting the mantras of the deity as many times as I could for three weeks. My stay there was very pleasant and peaceful, as I heard no contentious conversation.

The reason Gangkar Lama Rinpoché of Seudru Monastery is called Gangkar Lama is that his predecessor had lived at this place for a long time to pursue his meditational practices. While at the hermitage I gave a long-life initiation and permission for the Protectors of the Three Lineages to the resident monks and some pilgrims.

Assassination Plot

While I stayed at this place, the personal attendant of Lama Chöphak of Dzedzé Monastery conspired with a party from Chatreng who opposed the lama to kill him. They paid off a person who fought in the lama's contingent to go see the lama at night under the pretext of seeking divination advice for the lama's sister, pretending that the lama's sister was seriously ill. As soon as he called at the door, the attendant opened the gate. The person stabbed the lama with a pocket knife and killed him in his bed. Although the lama had a reputation for clairvoyance and miraculous powers, those powers failed him in his time of need. Just as when Maudgalyāyana could not remember any tricks, let alone perform miracles, when assaulted by *parivrājakas*,[116] so too this lama could not demonstrate any special qualities.

The supporters of the lama were thus left leaderless, like a corpse without its head. Their enemies could not cope with the situation either, as they had been in the battle zone for so long. Most of them drifted back to their own regions one after the other. As the fighting came to a standstill and no alternative course appeared from either side, they ultimately decided to settle the matter by a tribunal decision, and the situation was finally resolved.

Return to Chatreng

I left Nenang and visited the Siwapön household on the way, giving long-life initiations and an oral transmission of the *maṇi* mantra to people who had assembled there. After spending a few days at Gangkar Ling Monastery, I returned to the monastery of Chatreng via the Mewo region in the twelfth month.

In my twenty-sixth year, the year of the fire-tiger (1926), I continued the teaching of the previous year on the *Sutra of the Wise and the Foolish* during the discourse sessions of the prayer festival at the monastery. Lowa Goba and some others at the discourse commented that I was telling worldly stories as I had run out of religious topics to discuss.

That spring I did meditational retreats on Cakrasaṃvara of the Luipa tradition and on Sarvavid Vairocana. During the rainy-season retreat session I initiated the monks into Cakrasaṃvara of the Luipa tradition and into Sarvavid with permissions for the Rinjung Hundred.

Construction of the Maitreya Statue

My attendant Lhabu and the rest returned from Lhasa in the fourth month of that year. Through Lhabu, I received letters from His Holiness the Dalai Lama, Kyabjé Phabongkha, Geshé Sherap Rinpoché—both of the latter written in verse—and from my teacher and friends. Lhabu also brought with him various ornamental jewels and printed prayers for the statue of Maitreya Buddha. Along with Lhabu, two master craftsmen from Dzachukha region of Chamdo district arrived. On my instructions, Lhabu on his way to Central Tibet had requested cabinet minister Trimön Norbu Wangyal, then governor general of Chamdo's Domé province, to dispatch some craftsmen to construct the Maitreya statue. Thus work on the statue was begun.

In concert with some master craftsmen from Chatreng, the artisans erected a large, three-story statue of Maitreya made of gilded copper over a period of three months. In it were placed printed prayers of the four aspects of relics, the five categories of great consecration, and so on, as well as dharmakāya relics, multiplying relics of the Tathāgata, and a statue of Jé Tsongkhapa consecrated by himself, which was a treasured relic of Lower Shedra. Other relics included were self-produced sacred pills from the entombed bodies of many Indian and Tibetan masters, printed diagrams of male and female yakṣas, treasure vases, and many other items that were accumulated with great care. These were produced according to ritual, and I personally installed the relics in the statue and placed it in the inner temple of the main assembly hall. A catalog or description of the benefits of constructing statues, paying respects, and making offerings was inscribed on one wall of the Maitreya temple. Also included in the inscription was a comprehensive list of the special prayers and relics contained in the statue as well as the material and the cost of making the statue in all stages. I had also provided a complete set of water bowls and butter lamps for the thousandfold offerings, large butter lamps for daily offerings, as well as other sets of water bowls and implements in all sizes needed at the monastery for making offerings.

After the completion of all these requirements, we performed the elaborate consecration ritual Causing the Rain of Goodness to Fall according to the deity Vajrabhairava, complete in its stages of preparation, actual rite, and conclusion. I participated as the presiding master along with twenty other monks who had completed the approaching retreat of Vajrabhairava. At the section of the ritual for honoring the patrons, the staff of the committee in charge of making the statue and the senior members of the monastery's governing body were given the eight auspicious symbols and substances. The ceremony was conducted in a rather grand way.

At the end of autumn I went to Yangteng Monastery at their request and gave a discourse on the *Quick Path* for ten days. I also gave an initiation into thirteen-deity Vajrabhairava and many other initiations and permissions to those with earnest interest. Before returning to Chatreng Monastery, I visited towns and villages including Salha Dechentsang in the vicinity of the above monastery. In each place I gave various teachings in accord with the wishes of the people. Following the ancient custom of the monastery, self-initiation of Guhyasamāja, Cakrasaṃvara, and Vajrabhairava with the offering of the mandalas were performed in the style of Gyütö Tantric College. The music and chanting melody of the rituals for propitiating protectors Mahākāla and Dharmarāja were also done in the style of Gyütö. The music, chanting, and prayers for Palden Lhamo, Vaiśravaṇa, and Setrap[117] were done in the style of Ganden Shartsé.

As the monastery had been in decline for many years, only a few elder monks remained, and even they could not remember the exact melodies of the chants, which resulted in a serious deterioration of monastic activities. As this was the case, I invited Ngakrampa Bu Sönam of Gyütö Tantric College from Lura Monastery in Markham district. He and the incumbent abbot of Chatreng Monastery, Drodru Geshé Losang Tharchin, who was the former chant master of Shartsé College, were asked to train some fifty monks in the melodies of the various ritual prayers. Ngakrampa Bu Sönam and the two master craftsmen from Chamdo who had been invited to construct the image of Maitreya returned to their respective places content with their payments and gifts.

Since the costumes for the ritual dance on the occasion of the winter ritual were incomplete and mismatched, I refurbished all the costumes in matching material, having made efforts to obtain brocade the previous year. In addition to the existing dances for the winter ritual in the eleventh month, I specially invited one monk from Özer Monastery in Markham to reinstitute the ritual dances of "ācāryas and skeletons" according to the tradition of Tengyé Ling Monastery.

In the twelfth month, on an invitation from the region of Nangsang, I went to Phelgyeling Monastery of Nangsang via Palshar and Gowo Palbar monasteries. There I gave an initiation into Guhyasamāja Akṣobhyavajra to an audience of seven hundred monks, and a Great Compassionate One and a long-life empowerment to a general audience. I presented gifts of clothing and money to the family members of my esteemed teacher Losang Tsultrim.

In my twenty-seventh year, the year of the fire-rabbit (1927), I returned to Chatreng Monastery for the New Year celebrations. During the prayer festival, I gave a discourse on the Son Teachings of the *Book of Kadam* from the start. After the prayer festival, at the request of the abbot Geshé Drodru, I gave a discourse on the *Guru Puja* to about eighty monks who made the commitment to recite it daily. The discourse lasted about fifteen days.

Overcoming Ritual Obstacles

According to a message from Gangkar Lama Chödrak Rinpoché, it was said that someone with harmful intent in the time of my predecessor had buried a ritual object of black magic on a mountain peak in Chatreng. According to the physical description of the site, the mountain was shaped like a downward-facing fish with a stream running from it that merged at the mountain's base into a large river, on the bank of which lived a few lepers. He said that the harmful items had been entrusted to nāgas who live in the mountain. He stated in his message that he would be able to expose the items if the lama could come personally to the site, but doing so was inconvenient due to circumstances. Thus it was of utmost importance that a ritual counteragent be properly produced and buried at the base of the mountain. He also indicated in his letter, with a sense of great urgency, that "this mountain can be seen from the seat in your room at the monastery." Accordingly, ten monks, including the abbot Geshé Drodru, all of whom had completed a full meditational retreat on Vajrabhairava, properly produced the counteracting ritual object. Later when Geshé Drodru and my attendant Ngakram Budor went to the site to bury the substances of the counteracting ritual object, they found that the site accorded exactly with the description of Gangkar Lama in every respect.

In the eleventh month of that year, a loud sound like that of cannon fire was heard twice from the south side of the monastery just before midnight. Although I wondered what the sound might have been, I later heard a roar barely recognizable as thunder. The sound of thunder had never been heard in the winter at Chatreng before, and I therefore had some apprehension about it. After investigation, we learned from the reports of people living in the vicinity who had witnessed it that the lightning had struck the peak of the mountain where the talisman was buried at the base.

Later, soon after my return to Lhasa, I met a Nyingma lama named Tsewang Gyaltsen, the resident lama of the Kashöpa family. This lama told me that during my predecessor's time, black-magic ritual objects had been buried by others both in Kham and Central Tibet. "The one in Kham was destroyed," he said, "as you caused lightning to strike the area twice. The other is in front of Ganden, where there is a natural spring. There you must perform a rite for counteracting black magic." As no one in Lhasa knew about the events in Chatreng except myself and Lhabu, my suspicion that Lama Tsewang Gyaltsen had clairvoyance was confirmed. It seems the counteragent ritual was done properly.

Shady Dealings

While at Chatreng, Palbar Lagen Chödrak and Palchuk Dampa Chödrak came to tell me that in connection with my return from Kham there would be great expenses for making offerings at the three seats,[118] at Gyütö and Gyümé tantric colleges, at the regional houses, and so forth, as well as at the Great Prayer Festival in Lhasa. They said that the offerings that I received while in Chatreng would not begin to suffice. The two of them decided to jointly dispatch a merchant to Chamdo with horses and mules. They told me that if I sent whatever amount of money I had and joined in the trading venture, the two of them would assist me and return the capital together with profits to my table without any involvement or work on my part. Sakya Paṇḍita's *Jewel Treasury of Wise Sayings* says:

> The pleasant speech of cunning people
> is for their own ends, not to be polite.
> The laughter-like hooting of an owl
> delivers a bad omen; it's not done out of joy.

I accepted this offer without realizing that it was a deceptive scheme "to lead a calf with temptation of green grass." Assuming that their offer of assistance was genuine and that they truly intended to help me, and because they were among the senior and influential members of the monastery's governing body, I believed their words.

I made arrangements to supply them with twenty mules complete with packs and thirty thousand *tamchen*, a Chinese currency, which was all the cash that I was able to gather. The two of them made a pretense of having large sums of money as their investment, not making clear the precise amount of capital. Later, when we gathered the funds on the eve of the merchants' departure, there were the following sums from the other parties in the threeway venture in addition to my own contribution: ten thousand *tamchen* from the Palbar Tsang household and only three thousand *tamchen*—and a person called Dampa Tharchin to go on the trip with his horse—from Palchuk Dampa Chödrak. Palbar Tsang also sent twenty mules with packs as a separate business undertaking along with a person called Tenzin as his representative in our joint trading venture and in his own unrelated business.

Not only did they take for granted that any profit from their private transactions would be solely their income, but also they demanded that the net profit from our joint venture should be equally divided among the three of us, regardless of our respective contributions to the initial investment. Further, they did not offer any interest on our capital. It is quite evident that this was a deceptive act with selfish motives, to make use of my investment to do business in the name of Trijang Labrang for their private gain. Although this was the case, I went along with it, unable to withdraw from the venture because of our close connection through religious and secular relationships.

Visit to Trehor

The Shitsé Gyapöntsang family of Trehor and Yatruk Tsongpön, the manager of Beri Monastery, were known to me through their previous religious patronage in Lhasa. They had written to me many times requesting that I visit the Trehor area. That summer I left Chatreng Monastery with a small entourage and traveled through Tongjung and the nomadic colony of Gemo Ngachu. In a part of the Lithang district we traveled through a meadow area called Deshung Nakhathang, which was swathed in a riot of wildflowers in full bloom. The people, horses, and pack animals were transformed by the brilliant colors of the blossoms. The meadow, which was lined with herds of migrating antelope, extended for two days' journey.

Then through Tromthar and so forth, parts of Nyakrong district, we arrived at Trehor Beri. There, on the banks of the Beri River, the monks of Beri Monastery came to greet me headed by Getak Tulku. I arrived at Yatruk's house in a ceremonial procession. At the request of the monastery and the two patrons, I gave a discourse on the *Easy Path* to about seven hundred resident monks and others gathered there from various places. Over the next month I also gave initiations into Guhyasamāja, Cakrasaṃvara, Vajrabhairava, Sarvavid, and the Great Compassionate One as well as permissions for Mahākāla, Dharmarāja, Palden Lhamo, and Vaiśravaṇa, a long-life empowerment for Amitāyus in the tradition of Machik Drupai Gyalmo, and other teachings that they desired.

After that, at the invitation of Trungsar Rinpoché of Trehor Karzé, I went to Trungsar Hermitage and there gave Trungsar Rinpoché oral transmission of the collected works of Gyalwa Ensapa and Khedrup Sangyé Yeshé and of the *Miktsema Compendium*. In the assembly hall of the hermitage, I gave an initiation into Sarvavid to a large number of monks and laypeople. At the request of the monastery, I paid a visit to the assembly hall and the three temples, and I scattered flowers for their consecration. At the invitation of Khangsar Kyabgön Tulku, I went to his labrang and returned to Trungsar Hermitage that afternoon. At that time I wished to go meet Drakar Rinpoché of Trehor, who was widely known for his knowledge, and the previous incarnation of Lamdrak, who lived like a realized yogi. However, Drakar Tsang and the previous Khangsar, Losang Tsultrim, were exchanging criticisms with one another due to differences of religious view, and Lamdrak was ill-favored by the patroness of Khangsar, whose power and influence intimidated Trungsar Rinpoché, Gyapön Bu, and others, so it was not convenient for me to meet them.

A temple known as Dé Gönkhang, which sat in a field in front of Karzé Monastery, was known to have been built by Drogön Chögyal Phakpa[119] on his return from China. Inside were sacred images of the eight deities of Pañjaranātha Mahākāla, each one story tall, and I went to pay a visit. Once again I returned to Beri Monastery.

At that particular time Dargyé Monastery in Trehor had a large number of monks and was prosperous. The monastery was administered by members of a governing board, who were mostly of the merchant class and lacked religious education. Because of this most of the monks there took greater interest in horses, swords, guns, and so on, and monks pursuing a correct course of religious practice were few and had no influence over the religious and temporal affairs of the monastery. The father of the Gyapöntsang clan, Chögyal Gyalu, was a patron of the monastery, and he asked me to give a discourse at the monastery on the stages of the path, to which I agreed. He did this with a good intention and motive, hoping to guide the monks onto a peaceful and proper course. When he consulted the governing members about the discourse, they told him that a discourse on the stages of the path takes a long time, they had no time, and instead they requested initiation into Sarvavid Vairocana, as a large number of monks died of stroke and they often had to perform the ritual of Sarvavid for the deceased and their survivors. Gyalu, astonished and disappointed, requested me to give an initiation into Sarvavid as they wished.

When the supreme Kyabjé Phabongkha Vajradhara traveled to Dakpo for the first time to hear a discourse on the stages of the path from Kyabjé Jampal Lhundrup, Gyalu had provided all the horses and mules and had accompanied him himself. He showed me a tooth that Dakpo Lama Rinpoché [Jampal Lhundrup] had given him that had a distinct, self-produced image of the Four-Armed Avalokiteśvara on it. Gyalu himself engaged in virtuous practices and recited the manual of the preliminary practices[120] every day. At Gyalu's request, I left for Dargyé Monastery from Beri and gave the initiation of Sarvavid to the monks and people of the area, complete with preparation, for two days in a tent on the field in front of the monastery. Although I could not give a discourse on the stages of the path, I gave an elaborate introduction to the initiation, and I visited the temples in the monastery, scattering flowers for their consecration.

After that I left to visit the Shitsetsang estate, where I stayed for two weeks. There were many sacred objects in the temple, including a statue of Avalokiteśvara as the principal image and a set of the Kangyur. With the assistance of the monks of Dargyé Monastery, I did an elaborate consecration ritual for three days. I also performed the prosperity-securing ritual of Vaiśravaṇa in the family treasury. After giving a discourse on the *Seven-Point Mind Training* and a long-life initiation to a large gathering, I began my return to Chatreng.

On the way I spent one night on a slope with green grass and a stream. It was a restful place situated on a low hill in upper Tromkhok, which is part of Nyakrong. Gyapön Döndrup Namgyal, his son, and others including Tsongpön Yatruk were there to see me off. At their request I gave a brief explanation on the longevity practice of Amitāyus before they returned. In the late afternoon of that day, a black cloud suddenly formed and caused a violent hailstorm. The hail were the size of dried apricots, and it was as if earth and sky were being rent asunder by the thunder and lightning. We could see the flashes of lightning even inside the tent, and there was a smell like gunpowder, as if a thunderbolt were about to fall.

I performed the burning ritual of Sur, made offerings to local spirits, and offered tea to the protector deities and sought their active assistance. I also recited mantras of protection from lightning and hail, doing visualizations as best as I could. As these were not effective, I hastily burned some fresh human excrement in the fire, and immediately the sky directly above became clear, like the opening of a skylight. The lightning and hail vanished and sunlight shone through. Around about the middle of that night, the horses and mules suddenly became alarmed for no apparent reason, broke away from their ropes, and straying to the four directions, could not be gathered until sunrise next morning.

Later, when I arrived in Lithang, some older people informed me that owing to a certain local Bönpo spirit, lightning struck in 1567 when His Holiness the Third Dalai Lama, Sönam Gyatso, came to the area. They also told me that the weather had become very turbulent when my predecessor had visited the place as well.

Visit to a Nomadic Community

When I arrived at a place in Lithang called Bum Nyakthang, a vast green prairie, all the nomadic communities under the jurisdiction of Yönru Pön, a leader from the Washul Yönru district of Lithang, had gathered there. Geluk, Sakya, Nyingma, and other monks of Yönru district were also celebrating an annual religious festival called the Yönru Session there, in individual group assembly tents, each doing rituals of their own tradition. As I happened to arrive on this occasion, Tromthok Tulku, the incumbent abbot of the Geluk monastery of Rabgyé Ling, came to see me along with officials from the monastery. They told me that my predecessor also came there on this occasion and stayed at leisure, giving them religious discourses. They also said there were many monks and older laypeople who had seen my predecessor, and, occasioned by the unarranged spontaneity of my own visit, they insisted that I stay there until the conclusion of the session. Although I could not stay long there, I participated in the Geluk sessions, known as the Garchen Session, for about two weeks.

There were five hundred monks to whom I gave a discourse on Jé Tsongkhapa's *Song of Spiritual Experience*, an initiation into Cakrasaṃvara according to the system of Luipa together with its preparation, as well as permission for Jé Rinpoché as the triple deity.[121] The monks made ritual offerings to the mandalas of Guhyasamāja, Cakrasaṃvara, Vajrabhairava, and Sarvavid for five days each, and I attended the ritual offering to the mandala of Cakrasaṃvara for one day. The style of their ritual was almost the same as that of Gyümé Tantric College. There were a pair of brocade ornamental hanging decorations that my predecessor had presented to the monastery, in addition to which I also made an offering for the entire day with monetary gifts.

The Geluk monastery had four very large tents that could comfortably seat five hundred monks. Each tent was about two stories high and supported by four tall poles, and each tent was decorated inside with excellent religious banners. The abbot and the incarnate lamas sat on thrones made of grass bundles stacked on top of each other and covered with woolen drapes and woven carpets. It seemed quite impressive and dignified. Although I was at a nomadic monastery, meat was not allowed in accord with a good custom established by previous masters. Only tsampa, rice, melted butter, and other dairy products were given as offerings, which I found admirable.

At the invitation of the Sakya and Nyingma groups nearby, I went to visit, make offerings, and give teachings to them. During my stay I was invited by the nomadic communities living in the vicinity. Each day I visited fifteen to twenty tent dwellings, performed consecrations, and gave teachings as they wished. The nomads gave me many horses, and I ended up with about a hundred of them. Because we were staying in open fields, it was difficult to keep the horses together as they kept returning to their previous owners. I sold the horses to the nomads and offered the money from their sale as an endowment for annual offerings of food and money at Rabgyé Ling.

Lithang Monastery

Then at the insistent invitation of Lithang Monastery, whose abbot and a few of the monastic officials had come specially to see me, I arrived at Lithang Thupchen Chökhor Monastery in a procession on horseback accompanied by the leaders of the monastery and a large number of its monks. There in the courtyard of the main assembly hall, at the request of the monastery, I gave an extensive initiation into the Lakṣmī system of the Great Compassionate One together with its preparation and an Amitāyus long-life initiation according to the system of Machik Drupai Gyalmo to about three thousand monks and a large number of local people. Then in the old assembly hall, I gave a discourse on the *Quick Path* and an initiation into single-deity Vajrabhairava to about five hundred incarnate lamas and monks, including Tsatak Rinpoché and Gosap Rinpoché. In the temple of Thupchen I gave full ordination to about thirty monks, including Yongya Tulku. At this ordination I acted as the preceptor, Tsatak Rinpoché was the ritual master, and Gosap Rinpoché acted as the interviewing master. At Tsosum House I gave permission for Six-Armed Mahākāla as well as the longevity practice according to the system of Machik Drupai Gyalmo, and I gave permission for Jé Rinpoché as the triple deity to Gosap Tulku and members of his labrang. In addition I tried to fulfill the wishes of many others with a variety of teachings at their individual request. I offered food and money to the main assembly and presented gifts and funds to the monastery.

At the invitation of members of the family of His Holiness the Seventh Dalai Lama Kalsang Gyatso, who was from the town of Lithang, I went there for a day and performed rituals of purification and consecration for the image of His Holiness the Dalai Lama and other representations of the holy body, speech, and mind. I also gave a short teaching to the members of the family. At the invitation of the Otok leader of the Lithang nomadic tribes, I went there to do the rituals for securing prosperity, consecration, and to give a variety of teachings. These included a permission for Avalokiteśvara and initiation into long-life practice to the leader, Achö, members of his family, his people, monks of Otok Monastery, and many others.

The nomadic people of Washul Yönru and Otok Sumpa had great faith in religion, and there were many people who had recited the six-syllable *maṇi* mantra and the *miktsema* prayer a hundred million times each. At that time there were also many people who pledged to recite the *maṇi*, *miktsema*, and the *Prayer of Samantabhadra* a hundred million times each and do the *nyungné* fasting rite a hundred times. Like the steady flow of a stream, many families came for these, which was really something meaningful. I heard that it was the custom of the nomads to offer a feast of meat from specially slaughtered animals to lamas whom they had invited. So I made it known to anyone who came to invite me that I would accept only vegetarian food and that no meat dishes should be served. I visited many nomadic communities in Otok, where I did rituals for purification and consecration and gave various types of teachings.

Pilgrimage to Kampo

After completion of my activities in Lithang, I made a pilgrimage to Kampo, a holy place of Cakrasaṃvara, on the way back. Kampo was the place where the First Karmapa, Düsum Khyenpa, spent a long time and achieved insights. In later times his religious tradition came to be known as Kamtsang Kagyü after that place. I stayed on the upper floor of Nego Monastery, and there I did the approaching-retreat recitation of the Cakrasaṃvara deity for one week and the elaborate consecration of Cakrasaṃvara for three days. I gave an initiation into five-deity Cakrasaṃvara according to the Ghaṇṭāpāda tradition to the fifty resident monks of that place. I returned all the offerings of money and objects received at the initiation, keeping only a small thangka of Cakrasaṃvara for the sake of auspiciousness. I had it with me later even in Lhasa as an object of veneration.

I made offerings to the monks and one day visited the actual pilgrimage spot situated in the upper part of Kampo. There was a large rock with a self-emerged image of the letter *ka*. The name of the place, Kampo, was designated based on this holy rock. I made *tsok* offerings there. On the way there was a temple that had a display of the arms and armor of the heroes of the legendary King Gesar of Ling, such as the sword called Yasi Kardren that had belonged to Gyatsa Shalkar. At the Kampo pilgrimage site there was a large snow mountain where the principal Cakrasaṃvara deity abides and a row of smaller snow mountains for the retinue deities. As soon as you arrive at this place, the mind becomes clear and peaceful.

I had intended to stay there in leisure, but a messenger dispatched by the families of Palbar and Dampa arrived unexpectedly from Chatreng. The message said that our merchants, along with the pack animals and merchandise, had been robbed by a bandit militia that had lain in wait for them at Upper and Lower Bumpa. Four people—Palbar's nephew Tenzin, Dampa Chödrak's nephew Tharchin, one of Palbar's mule herders, and my mule herder—were all killed on their return from Chamdo as the merchants traveled through a narrow trail near a town called Tarkha, prior to crossing Khangtsek Pass in the region of Upper Bumpa. The bandits made off with all the merchandise, including the animals. This being the situation, the message stated that I should return immediately as retaliation was inevitable.

Averting Retaliation

When I arrived at Chatreng, Palbar Chödrak and Dampa Chödrak stated many reasons for reprisal. In response to this I told them that as my name was involved in this three-way venture, I strongly objected to plans to enact vengeance and made it clear to them that I had taken a vow to drop this matter totally. I told them that the first thing I had done upon my arrival at the monastery was to give many teachings on sutra and tantra in compliance with my position as a lama, and that to in the end engage in retaliation before my return to Central Tibet was of no use to either my reputation or activities. I said that I had given up any grasping at the people, things, and animals taken by the bandits and that I was determined not to fight and strongly objected to fighting.

Furthermore, upon later investigation, I discovered that previously Palbar Thokmé was a leader of the fighters from Chatreng when they fought the battle with Dranak Lama at Dzedzé Monastery. On that occasion many arms, ammunition, and large quantities of food provisions were taken from the people of Bumpa. Palbar Thokmé became sick and died in the war zone without having made any arrangement to repay them, so there was no one left with the responsibility for their repayment. So the reason for the robbery by the people of Bumpa was the relentless grudge that they held against the Palbar clan. They had taken it for granted that the caravan was a Palbar family business venture because a member of Palbar's group was among the traders, and so their act was not an intentional affront to me or done with knowledge of my partnership in the business.

Thus it was decided that the war on the people of Bumpa would be postponed and that we would meet in person for talks. Tendrong Samphel Tenzin represented the Palbar clan, Chödrak himself stood for Dampatsang, and our secretary Gönpo and Ngakram Budor were dispatched for discussions. Sangden, a well-known figure and manager for Jema Lama of Upper Gönsar Monastery in Gowo, near the Bumpa region, came to act as intermediary at the talks, which were held at Goworong.

The people of Bumpa, without considering our concerns or our efforts to avoid the hardship and devastation of conflict, stirred up further confusion out of spite, as a result of which the talks lasted about three months and never clearly settled the dispute. In the end the Bumpas compensated us with a small sum of cash, a few aged mules, and some clothing and objects of varying value, claiming they were of much higher value than they were, for each of the people killed. Most of the cash was counted as credit for Palbar and Dampatsang's two casualties, their bulletproof amulet boxes, meteorite vajras, weapons, and various other things that they had made claim of losing. Although the remainder of the small sum of cash, clothing, and miscellaneous things was supposed to have been divided according to the share of the original investment of capital when the caravan was dispatched, it was instead divided into three equal portions, and I received only a small amount. "Liberation and cyclic existence are of one taste," as the saying goes. We suffered losses one on top of the other, from both within and without. As Dharmarakṣita, Atiśa's guru, said:

> When I am duped by others' treachery,
> this is the wheel weapon of the wrongs I have done
> turned back on me for my vanity and selfish greed.[122]

As stated, I, a man of small mind, instead of quietly abstaining, followed the influence of others without restraint, blazing with greed. The consequences of such acts fall upon oneself. But I have no regrets and am fully satisfied that I refrained from participating in the ill deed of a conflict involving murder. Although it was their heartfelt desire to accomplish their own benefit, the others lost two of their key people and suffered other losses against their wishes, like a rain of unpleasantness. As the maxim says, "One hundred unwanted things for a single wish fulfilled."

A Plot Against Me

At that time Beda Tsultrim, uncle of the aforementioned Beda Troti Tulku who had enrolled in Pomra House at Sera Mé, arrived from Lhasa. He held a meeting consisting of prominent persons, both monks and laypeople, from Upper Chatreng under the pretext of collecting donations in the Chatreng area to cover the expense of offerings and feasts on the occasion of the tulku's geshé graduation ceremony, using it as a cover to transform "the sound of an arrow into the sound of a flute." They met for many days in the old manager's office, outwardly holding discussions about the affairs of the offering while internally conspiring with some of the tulku's relatives and prominent people closely connected with him to mount a secret surprise attack in order to assault, capture, assassinate, rob, or do whatever they could to us.

In their discussions they consulted Tendrong Samphel Tenzin, who was a relative of the tulku. He told them that they should try to capture the key person, me, first. Whether or not the people of Chatreng would rise in support of Trijang was unknown, but if they did rise up, Samphel Tenzin would stop them in the assumed guise of being nonpartisan. It would not be proper if he involved himself directly, he said, as he had a patronage relationship with Trijang Labrang. In actuality—as in the expression "Dogs collaborate with foxes"—it became apparent that they were about to launch a grave undertaking, at which point some of the people at the meeting, who were unbiased and men of discrimination, walked out. This was confided to me by Tsakha Lagen, Bali Khedrup, and others of Upper Chatreng who were loyal and faithful to me.

As we were few in number, we sought the help of some monks whom we trusted, under the pretext of their assisting us with our preparations to return to Central Tibet. We locked the doors of our residence on top of the assembly hall with additional door blocks. In my room we made a hiding place to fit one person behind my bed, between the wall and the hangings. The monks of Dargyé Ling and others in the vicinity, as well as monks from within Chatreng Monastery devoted to me, assured my attendants that if they could defend us for a short while, the monks would be prepared to come to our defense. My attendants made preparations for my temporary protection. As for myself, I prayed to the Triple Gem, requested the assistance of the protectors, and entrusted myself to the truth of karma, the results of which are inevitable once committed and cannot arise from actions not committed.

With no alternative but to wait for the results of whatever karma was in store, we had to endure under these circumstances for one month. Without our knowledge, iron bars at the gate were broken and door blocks disappeared. In this state of foreboding doom of a disaster that could happen at any time over the next ten days, one day just after nine in the evening, someone abruptly knocked on the door of our horse stable, calling us from outside. When our attendants apprehensively replied to the person, they discovered it was Wangyal, the brother of Samphel Tenzin. Wangyal had married into the family of Palbar Chödrak. He came to announce that Samphel Tenzin had just suffered a serious stroke and was afflicted with an unbearable headache, as if his head were about to split open. He came to ask that blessed substances be burned and also to ask that I come to their house to do rituals of admonition and expulsion of interference. I was unable to turn down his request, because of the close patronage relationship between myself and Samphel Tenzin, so I sent relics and so on and had to promise to go there the following day.

Ngakram Budor and other attendants suspected that it was a duplicitous scheme, but judging by Wangyal's physical and verbal demeanor, I thought the situation was probably true and was extremely pleased, unable to disguise the smile in my heart. Despite the teachings on mind training I had received at the feet of my lamas many times, I was unable to use the experience to benefit my mind, and instead I simply felt relief at the hope of escaping mortal danger. As Gungthang Jampalyang has said:

> Religious when warmed by the sun, with a full stomach;
> worldly when confronted with difficult circumstances.

Although it was most difficult for me to bestow the blessing of initiation and such on someone with a degenerate word of honor, the next day I went to Tendrong Samphel's house with a few of my attendants, outwardly for the sake of religious patronage connections. We went there fearing it might be a ruse and with other such feelings of hope and trepidation. When I arrived Tenzin was bedridden, and he told me that because I had prevented them from retaliating against the people of Bumpa and the bandits had not paid enough to recompense the damage and loss, he had in his annoyance some criticisms to level against me, but in the depths of his heart, he said, there could never be any significant change in his respect for and faith in me. He also said that if his criticism had in any way offended the Dharma protectors, who are uncompromising, he declared his faults with remorse and vowed not to repeat such actions. He requested permission for Jé Rinpoché as the triple deity, which he said that a lama in the Gorong area foretold he must receive from me. Unable to bear the weight of guilt, he insisted that I give the permission right then. I understood that he was hoping to recover from his sickness, like the retraction of a magic spell to its source, by receiving the initiation from me under the pretext of repenting his concealed wrongdoings. Judging the sincerity of his repentance, I accepted his plea for remission and gave the initiation to accord with his need. As the great Ra Lotsāwa said:

> You offer gold like a mandala,
> and I explain Yamāri like Vajrabhairava.

Signs of improvement in his condition appeared the following day, and he was able to walk within the next twenty days. Despite his recovery, he and Palbar Chödrak again continued to discuss their previous schemes to rob us. They did this while having a meal of meat and broth on the roof of their house. Thereafter Tenzin suffered another serious stroke and lost his speech. He died that night and early next morning someone was sent to fetch me to the house. I performed the ritual for transferring the consciousness and said prayers of dedication to the best of my ability.

Like the collapse of the supporting pole, the evil plans of [the uncle] Troti and his group vanished following the death of Samphel Tenzin. Just before he suffered the stroke, I dreamed that a person killed a large yak, which was indicative of the accomplishment of wrathful assistance by the protector allied with me from long ago. It was not only in this particular instance, but whenever I dreamed of the killing of yaks, sheep, and other living animals, the death of a person with perverted intentions soon occurred, either directly or indirectly. This has happened on numerous occasions.

At Chakra Temple

At the conclusion of the prayer festival in my twenty-eighth year, the year of the earth-dragon (1928), I visited various households at the invitation of the towns of Rigang and Chakragang, which are parts of Trengshok district of Chatreng. While there I gave teachings according to the wishes of the people. I spent a few days at Chakra Temple, a pilgrimage place where the Sixth Karmapa Thongwa Dönden resided for a winter. Here one could see a bodhi tree grown from a rosary bead planted by the Karmapa and a sacred image of Thongwa Dönden. I gave a long-life initiation and oral transmission of the six-syllable mantra to the general population.

In this part of Chatreng the Karma Kagyü lineage had been prevalent, and there were remains of many Kagyü temples all over the area. Each town had a descendant in the line of *ngakpas*, tantric ritualists, called Anyé who performed ritual services such as the thread-cross rites[123] and so forth. The people there made offerings on the tenth of each month to Guru Rinpoché and made propitiatory offerings in allegiance to protectors such as Bernak Mahākāla (an oath-bound protector of Tsurphu), Shingkyong Trakshé, Tashi Tseringma, and others.

All the ngakpas from the upper and lower regions gathered and requested initiations and oral transmissions. In the temple at Chakra, at their request, I gave permission for the wrathful and peaceful aspects of Guru Rinpoché according to the Second Dalai Lama Gendun Gyatso's writings concerning the practice of mind-seal deities. Permissions for Lekden, Bernak Mahākāla, Trakshé, and Tsering Chenga were given according to the Rinjung Hundred. When I gave the blessing of Guru Rinpoché, I received a bouquet of white, eight-petalled lotus blossoms from a family called Padma in Chakra. I took this as a spontaneous and impromptu sign of the auspiciousness of the occasion.

That night in my dream a person dressed in black came and spoke to me about the need to renovate the temple. Understanding this as the protector's urging or direction, the next day I made a personal request to the people of Chakra to reconstruct the temple with special chambers to be built above. They rebuilt the temple in the following year, but many years passed without the chambers being constructed. Later, in the wood-horse year (1954), the special rooms were built, and I stayed in them the following year when I visited Chakra Temple for one night on my return to Chatreng from my visit to China. Although this was no more than mere coincidence, the people believed that I had told them to build the rooms with knowledge of future events. I feel that most prophecies seemingly foretold with clairvoyance by lamas like myself are like the saying "A credulous disciple makes a fallacious lama."

Visiting My Predecessor's Birthplace

Then I went to Upper and Lower Rakpo and for health reasons spent three days at a hot spring in Upper Rakpo. At the request of the people, I composed a history of Tashi Temple of Upper Rakpo with an explanation of the benefits of circumambulating it. I visited the three towns of Dongsum at their invitation and in particular stayed for one week in the Rikngа Temple in the Dongsum region, the birthplace of my predecessor, Throneholder Jangchub Chöphel. I presented a set of ten thangkas of the thousand buddhas, mounted on brocade, to the regional institute. I gave public initiations into the Great Compassionate One and long-life practice. Then I visited the home of my predecessor at Chusang Gön, where I did a consecration ritual and presented gifts of clothing and many other things to the members of the family.

I visited all the places in the upper and lower regions of Chatreng, without consideration of difficulty or hardship, in order to give teachings and do rituals at the request of people on various occasions to satisfy their wishes—with the exception of all the families in Chagongshok, who were supporters of Troti Tulku, and a few families in the town of Söpa and Palgé, who didn't invite me because of their strong bias. As *Staff of Wisdom*[124] says:

> What can a washerman do
> in a city of naked people?

There would have been no benefit or purpose to my staying there. As the *Garland of Birth Stories* says:

> Wherever people become envious,
> they always resent the fortune of others.
> With hostile minds they become disingenuous.
> It is then I leave for a place more to my liking.

Obstacles to My Return to Lhasa

As I have said, I decided to return to Central Tibet the same year. In a letter received from Gongkar Lama Rinpoché of Seudru Monastery, I was told that there would be serious obstacles if I were unable to leave Chatreng by the fifteenth of the fourth month. But because I had to visit the families in Chakragang, Rakpo, and Dongsum, and because of insufficient preparations for the journey, my departure was postponed. That summer the Chatreng monks who had gone to study in Lhasa and merchants who had been to Lhasa the previous year reached Garthok in Markham district at the beginning of the fourth month on their return. At Markham, some local citizens, because they bore a grudge against Chatreng due to a prior conflict, used it as an excuse to charge the travelers from Chatreng with tax evasion. These people from Markham challenged them with a court case before Shelkar Lingpa, the commander in chief of the Markham border security force. The monks and fellow travelers, including the son of Drodok Chödrak, were stopped, placed under arrest, and their animals and goods were seized.

While the case was pending, Palbar Chödrak, out of firm loyalty to the late Samphel, planned to obstruct our journey to Lhasa. With malicious intent, he advised Shewa Phaktruk and other monks, the families of the traders, and Drodok Chödrak, who was very influential in Drodok area, that if they could cause a delay in our journey to Lhasa, it would be of great help in getting the governor and commanding officer of Markham to release the monks and the goods. Like wind in the folds of paper,[125] Drodok Chödrak and others, acting on the advice they received, insisted that I postpone my departure to Lhasa until their legal case was settled. I did not agree to postpone our journey and told them that it was my firm decision to leave for Central Tibet and that I had also sent a letter to His Holiness in the capital.

Palbar Lagen and Drodok Chödrak allied to recruit some armed men and prepared to rob us in ambush somewhere in the Drodok area. A monk with a goiter named Palgé Gyakser Yapa, an uncle of Troti Tulku, claimed that people should see for themselves if he would let the party of Trijang Labrang safely pursue their journey to Lhasa. This monk had previously received teachings on the stages of the path and initiations into Vajrabhairava together with its commentaries from me. He had even taken the commitment to do the full retreat of the deity. Yapa later suffered an infection of the goiter and long lingered in a limbo between life and death. Although he later sent a letter to Lhasa seeking my forgiveness, he died without any benefit.

As I mentioned above, peril confronted us from every side. Lutak Tashi Tsongpön, Nenang Phuntsok Dargyé, Shap Gyatso Nyima, and other influential people offered to escort us up to Markham with a thousand armed horsemen, saying it was better to travel straight through Drodok. Although we could have traveled without any fear if they had escorted us, they would have doubtlessly suffered tremendous casualties in conflicts on their return. Therefore we made plans to leave via Nangsang. We sent a messenger in secret to Nangsang Monastery, and in reply they said that they would take full responsibility for our safety and that we must come in that direction, so we confirmed our decision.

Drodok Chödrak, having learned of our plan, sent a warning message to Nangsang Monastery saying that he had requested me to stay for some time in order to secure the release of the detained monks and merchants and that if the monastery arranged to take us through Nangsang, even if the lama succeeded in decamping via their region, the act would become a cause for contention. In reply, the people of Nangsang said that whatever response the opposition may plan, they would take full responsibility for my journey. Thus, although we were leaving from Nangsang, the situation remained intractably difficult, and the threat of future disputes loomed.

Although we had already plans in place to depart Chatreng on the third of the sixth month, the exact route of our journey was not finalized until the day before. On that day, in desperation, I performed the dough-ball divination,[126] and in connection with the ritual of propitiation and the prayer to invoke the actions of the protectors, I asked after the best route: Drodok, Nangsang, and Lithang, as some had suggested, or via Gyalthang. It came out that Gyalthang was the better route, and we made final arrangements among ourselves in secrecy, outwardly indicating that we would depart Chatreng heading north through Drodok.

On the morning of the third, an advance party consisting of mule drivers left by the main gate of the monastery, heading south out of Chatreng in the direction of Gyalthang. Until this point, no one knew of our secret plan, and so some of our travel companions—monks and people coming to accompany us for a short distance to see us off—had already left for Shokdruk Drodok and had to return to Gyalthang. That day, after our departure from Samphel Ling Monastery of Chatreng, when I and other members of our group reached the other side of the bridge in front of the monastery, as I reflected on the hardship I had undergone on account of the various harmful acts that had flouted my good intentions, I felt like a prisoner being liberated from a dark prison cell.

Although I thought to myself that I would not return to that place ever again, in retrospect I remembered that I had left my monastic seat cover and pandit's hat on my throne in the assembly hall of the monastery. It therefore occurred to me that I might have to return to the scene, like the expression says, "to see the bad omen and smell the bad odor again." Later, when I was fifty-five years old, in the wood-sheep year (1955), I came to Chatreng again on my return from China and visited the Geluk monasteries in Lithang, Chatreng, Ba, and so forth as His Holiness's representative to southern Kham. At that time I recognized that my leaving of things behind had been a karmic sign, for it is difficult to sever the ties secured by the thread of good and bad karma, no matter how hard one tries. Further, as I joined the line of incarnations of Throneholder Jangchup Chöphel by coincidence, from my side I tried my best to act in ways that would further develop what had not degenerated and that would restore what had, by any means, for the benefit of the monastery and people of Chatreng, regardless of the physical and mental hardship involved.

The majority of monks and laypeople were very faithful, loyal, and genuinely respected and maintained good relations with me. Nonetheless, as Thuken Chökyi Nyima said:

> Harassment in return for religious teachings,
> harm in return for kindness,
> deception in return for trust:
> it is difficult to remain with the people of degenerate times.

Chöjé Surkharwa Lekshé Tsöl said:

> Though I have benefitted beings with great fairness, without discriminating whether their status is high or low, many have caused me great anguish, ungratefully returning dust for flour.

As recounted here, some people and their followers, to say nothing of repaying the kindness of the teacher, attempted on various occasions to harm me with both thought and deed, as if crushing sesame seeds on the head. However, by the compassion of the lamas and the Triple Gem, the power of the truth of cause and effect, and the ever-attentive actions of the protector with the name Dorjé, who from long ago has always been with me like a shadow with the body, I escaped the narrow ravines of all the obstructing circumstances, like the moon emerging from clouds.

The Journey Begins

We spent the night following our departure from Chatreng Monastery at a temple called Tashi in Upper Rakpo. Then, traveling through Wangshö, Gumnak, and so on, I arrived at Sumtsen Ling Monastery of Gyalthang to a grand reception held by the present and former abbots, tulkus, monastic administrators, and monks. At the monastery I stayed in a room above the assembly hall that overlooked the courtyard. I gave a commentarial discourse on the *Quick Path* and initiation into thirteen-deity Vajrabhairava to about two thousand monks in the assembly hall. I also visited the eight regional houses, including Chatreng House, at their invitation, and gave teachings and performed consecration rituals according to their wishes. I stayed there for about three weeks.

A few times during the visit I met the previous Lhakhar Rinpoché of Gyalthang Tongwa, who was in his sixties. When I first met him, he tested me by asking many questions regarding sutra and tantra. He was pleased when I was able to respond to his questions without being short of reply and came to hear my discourse on the stages of the path. Also, every year until he passed away, he sent me letters with gifts of gold through travelers from Kham. Later in Lhasa, Phabongkha Vajradhara told me that while Lhakhar Rinpoché studied in the monastery, they were in senior and junior classes and that he was very learned. I also visited Panglung Labrang, Kangyur Tsang, and other labrangs at their invitation.

Gyalthang Sumtsen Ling was established at the time of the Fifth Dalai Lama (1617–82). Due to the patron-priest relationship between successive Dalai Lamas and emperors of China, many decrees issued by Gushri Tenzin, Desi Sangyé Gyatso, and the Dalai Lamas, printed on yellow brocade, hung from the large pillars like decorative banners.[127] As for the ritual traditions and chant melodies, each of the eight houses had its own style, and the assembly hall was known to have its own as well. At their insistent request to enroll myself in the monastery, I registered my name in their book. I made token offerings with gifts of money to the assembly hall and to the houses with which I was affiliated.

After leaving Gyalthang through the upper and lower Rongpa valleys, we descended a steep mountainous track for a day, approaching the bank of the Drichu River. After the descent we arrived at Dapthang, a portage on the Drichu. There, on a raft made of logs lashed together and without any railing, we crossed the broad river with great trepidation. Then proceeding for two days on a very rough trail along the river, we arrived at the town of Kongtsé Rak or Pomtsé Rak, where Shalngo lived.[128] Then on the road up, we were well received by the previous Trathang Tulku at Shipal Hermitage.

The next day, we arrived at Jöl Döndrup Ling Monastery to a reception by the tulkus and administrators and spent a few days at Ludrup Labrang. The predecessor of the current Ludrup Tulku was then a youth of seven or eight years. I gave an initiation into the five-deity Cakrasaṃvara to Trathang Rinpoché and the entire assembly of lamas and monks. At Dechen Ling Monastery in Jöl, I stayed at Samdong Labrang for three days and gave the permission for Jé Rinpoché as the triple deity, a long-life initiation, and so forth to the monks as needed. The previous Samdong had been a good Dharma friend with whom I had received many teachings together in Lhasa. After returning to his native town, he was killed by bullets fired from a forest by a few people in the area while he was giving a long-life initiation to the townspeople.

After passing through a town called Jöldong and crossing a small pass, we spent a few days at a lake called Kamkha. There the monks of Seudru and Gangkar Lamatsang monasteries came to greet me. The escorts from Chatreng returned through Nangsang. We arrived via Tsa Pass at Dranak Monastery, where I gave teachings and oral transmissions of Jé Tsongkhapa's *Foundation of All Good Qualities* to Nyira Tulku and the monks. Again, via the towns of Chusumdo and Khawo Butsa, we arrived at Seudru Monastery and stayed more than ten days.

Meeting with Gangkar Lama Rinpoché

While there, Lamatsang extended warm hospitality to all of us with lavish feasts. Because of our very close association with Lama Rinpoché and his labrang, I felt quite at home, like being in my own house. In a relaxed state, I gave an initiation into the Great Compassionate One to the monks and laypeople there and an initiation into thirteen-deity Vajrabhairava to the monks. One day Lamatsang presented me with a long-life prayer and elaborate offerings.

On this occasion, Lama saw me as Guru Padmasambhava in a vision. Then Lama also remembered his birth at one time as the great translator Vairocana and our connection through several successive lives. He related this to Ngakram Budor and others. Although various reflections can appear to the vision of a yogin, due to our close bond and connections, and his strong liking for me, the things that appeared to him may have been reflected in a pure manner. For myself, I do not have even a whiff of such instincts and am nothing more than my present state. I did not feel the least pride, even as if in a dream, on account of Lama's vision. I, too, presented a long-life ceremony with offerings to Lama.

While I had been in Chatreng, commander Shelkar Lingpa had dispatched five hundred soldiers of the Drashi armed forces unit and regional recruits from the nine sectors of Markham district with the intention of seizing the salt flats at Tsakha Lho, which were under Lama's jurisdiction. Lamatsang was surrounded by soldiers in a surprise attack, and shots were fired from cannons and guns. Following a prophetic dream, Lama had taken relic pills called "bulletproof immortal iron pills from Jakhyung Drakar Dzong" just before the forces arrived. He opened the hidden treasure box and gave one pill each to seven specially selected monks. Arming the monks with only swords, he instructed them to drive the enemy away, up to the stupa at the foot of the monastery, which was halfway up the hill, a point from where the monks were told to return without going beyond. When the monks charged at them as instructed, the large contingent of enemy forces were driven away like a herd of sheep chased by a wolf. The soldiers were forced to flee, leaving behind weapons, rations, and so on. An artillery shell that the soldiers fired at Lama in his room did not explode. The eighteen-inch shell was there to be seen.

A medicinal odor permeated the room where the treasure box containing the iron pills was kept. One day Lama let us view the treasure box and opened it to give each of us an "iron pill." The container looked as if it were made of clay, was six inches in height and one and a half wide, with a variety of self-emerged images of deities on its sides. Inside it was filled to the brim with pills. Lama gave a large amount of pills to about twenty members of our group, including the escorts from Chatreng. The pills within the box immediately multiplied, leaving the box so full again that the Lama had to put the overflowing pills away in small packages. It was utterly convincing and extraordinary.

Before I departed, I asked Lama to perform a divination for the activities of my body, speech, and mind. Lama told me of a dream he had the previous evening in which a few people were hurriedly making a new throne in front of a large old throne in a spacious hall. Then a majestic monk official who resembled the lord chamberlain came into the room, and the people making the throne grew quiet. Someone in red garments, seemingly the official's attendant, destroyed the new throne completely, swept away its remains, and expelled all the people from the hall. Lama said, "It is certain that no external interfering forces will affect your life or activities. I will guarantee that Shukden will take care of everything." He told me this with great confidence and assurance.

Later during the Great Prayer Festival in Lhasa, in the water-monkey year (1932), Palchuk Dapön Geshé of Chatreng, who was one of the principal supporters of Troti Tulku, suffered sickness and died. Seven days later Troti Tulku himself became ill and passed away. Before that, many people in Kham who had caused me harm also died under a variety of unpleasant circumstances.

Incidentally, when Gangkar Lama Rinpoché was consulted for the discovery of new incarnations of lamas or lost objects, he would sometimes examine his dreams, and at others he would go into contemplation with his eyes half-closed and immediately point out clearly the direction of the place, town, village, or gate of a house and the family and its name. Everything happened exactly according to his prophecy. I have personally experienced it several times. Also, on my first journey to Chatreng, Lama's hair was grey, yet when I met him later on my return, his hair was black.

Lama had great devotion for His Holiness the Thirteenth Dalai Lama and had said that as long as His Holiness lived, he too would live. Later, as soon as he heard the news of His Holiness's passing, he said that it was also time for the old monk to depart. He took upon himself a mild water disease, and just before he died he called his attendants into his presence, where they recited the *Heart Sutra* together. He passed into the state of peace at the end of the recitation of the mantra in the text, following his utterance of the syllable *phat* in a loud voice. He convinced others by clearly demonstrating his achievement of insight. Lama's daily practice consisted of the *Guru Puja*, Vajrabhairava, Secret Hayagrīva, *chö* "accomplished in one sitting,"[129] and the protector Setrap. He practiced no deities or protectors apart from these.

Last Phase of Travel Home

After leaving from Seudru Monastery, I arrived at Garthok via Lhadun, Goshö Pomdatsang, and so on in Markham. There I visited the governor, Taiji Drungkhor Pelshiwa, in the district headquarters at his invitation. I gave the blessing of the four sindūra initiations of Vajrayoginī to some of the monks of Öser Monastery, the governor, and his wife and gave an initiation into the Great Compassionate One to the general public. Then at the request of the commander Shelkar Lingpa, I went to army headquarters and gave a long-life initiation to him and members of his family.

Öser Monastery had been moved from its original location and newly constructed in the upper region of Garthok. I was invited and performed a brief consecration ritual there. Then at the invitation of Khyungbum Lu Monastery, I gave the monks an initiation into thirteen-deity Vajrabhairava. Along the way I spent a night at Ribur Monastery, where I gave miscellaneous teachings and answered some questions and enquiries regarding the construction of a three-dimensional mandala of Guhyasamāja that was under preparation.

I stayed at Chakna Mutik Monastery for some days, where there lived a monk who had been master of ritual dance at Tengyé Ling Monastery in Lhasa. I was told about the good ritual performance of the deities Mahākāla, Dharmarāja, and Palden Lhamo and of the Black Hat dance in which the monks trained. They performed the dances for me, which were just the same as the dances of Demo I had previously seen at Tengyé Ling.

After crossing the Dzachu River at Sampa Dreng, I passed through Rong Dukda, Dzogang Sang-ngak Ling, Uyak, Lur Monastery, Kochen Thang, Pangda Monastery, Wako Mari, Shapyé Bridge, Lhozong Shitram Monastery, Dzitho Monastery, Shodo Monastery, Poti Monastery, and Lhatsé Monastery. After giving initiation and a variety of teachings in the monasteries and towns along the long route, I arrived in Chakra Palbar district. There at the request of the tantric adept Ngawang Chöjor of Gyümé Tantric College, I gave an explanatory reading of Tsongkhapa's *Song of Spiritual Experience* to the monks.

At that monastery there was an oracle deity called Gönpo Tsedu Nakpo. The oracle spoke through an entranced medium, whom Ngawang Chöjor brought to see me. We conducted rites to invoke the oracle and to induce trance. At the beginning of the trance, the medium held a large drum in his left hand and a drumstick in his right, participating in the invocation ritual by beating the drum. When the deity entered the medium, the drum stood alone next to the seat, and the deity made prophecies regarding the development of circumstances while beating the drum. I thought what he said was quite reliable and convincing. His prophecies regarding some of my future activities proved accurate.

Crossing Shargong Pass, I arrived at Arik Monastery. There I met the relatives of the late Ngakrampa and gave them presents. Our cook Namgyal Dorjé had preceded us on the journey and had died after falling from a cliff early one morning between Alachak Gong and Dothuk. I spent one night there to cremate his body and performed the transference of consciousness and offered prayers. Having crossed Nupgong Pass via Lharigo, Kongpo Gyada, and so on, I arrived at Özer Gyang, where some monks representing Dokhang House and Samling House had come from Ganden to greet me.

I spent one night at Tsunmo Tsal Monastery, where Dokhang House had made arrangements for my stay. There I made offerings before the stupa containing the holy body of Dulzin Drakpa Gyaltsen.[130] Not only had it been long known that the body of Dulzin Rinpoché was at Tsunmo Tsal Monastery, but it was reputed that at some point in time, when the temple housing the stupa required renovation and the monastery invited the predecessor of the current Gyalsé Tulku of Lhopa House at Ganden and Geshé Chödrak of Dokhang House to perform the construction ritual,[131] after the stupa was dismantled, the entire body was found in excellent condition in a box inside the vase structure of the stupa. Quite a lot of hair had grown on its head; the body had remained in an upright position, wrapped in two sets of monastic robes—an old and a new set—and an old wooden monk's teacup filled with dried fruit still sat in his lap. The fragrant scent of pure moral discipline permeated the entire place.[132] I had heard of this previously while at Ganden from Geshé Chödrak himself.

Arrival Home

I postponed my visit to Ganden for some time in order to prepare the offerings that I would make on my return to the monastery. At the beginning of the tenth month, I arrived safely in Lhasa at my residence, where my eyes took in the ambrosial sight of the mandala of the bodies of my teacher whose kindness is beyond measure, Geshé Sherap Rinpoché, and others.

We reunited with many a *tashi delek*,[133] and while enjoying this great happiness, we exchanged news of our lives continuously for days and nights. I met with many close associates and friends who came to call upon my return.

In accordance with ancient custom, I went to pay my respects to His Holiness the Thirteenth Dalai Lama in the sunlight room of the Norbulingka Palace. In a private audience in the Jangchup Gakhyil chamber on the top floor, I paid my respects with the crown of my head at His Holiness's lotus feet, at which all the celestial and other supreme heads of worldly existence paid tribute with their glowing crown jewel. I made symbolic mandala offerings of body, speech, and mind as well as offering one gold *sang*, five thousand Chinese silver dollars, and some goods indigenous to the province of Kham. His Holiness asked many questions about the situation in Kham, and I answered directly and frankly, without any pretense.

Afterward I went to Chusang Hermitage to be present at the feet of Kyabjé Phabongkha Vajradhara. Upon seeing the mandala of his face, meaningful to behold and like the jewel of supreme equanimity polished a hundred times, I prostrated before him, bowing the highest part of my body. I also made clouds of offerings of gold, silver, and other objects to my satisfaction and then had the pleasure of speaking fondly with him for a great length of time. The glorious Choné Lama Rinpoché Losang Gyatso Trinpal Sangpo was also staying at Chusang, so I paid my respects to him and asked permission to attend all his future discourses.

In the eleventh month I went to Ganden, where I met the incumbent abbot of Shartsé College, Losang Dargyé, and other administrators who came to greet me at a welcome reception in Bönpo Gönsar[134] at the foot of Ganden. After traveling through Nyakrong Pass, I dismounted at the market ground, where monks of Shartsé had formed a ceremonial reception line. The abbots of Shartsé and Jangtsé colleges and incarnate lamas, holding burning incense sticks in their hands, led the procession to the assembly hall of Dokhang House, where they had arranged a reception with stacked ceremonial cookies. There I accepted scarves and gifts presented to me by the main administrators of the monastery, the colleges, the houses, the regional affiliates, and many other groups and individuals. In celebration and thanksgiving for our safe return from our visit to Kham, free of tragedy, and as a token of my gratitude and appreciation, I made offerings of tea and *shethuk* pudding.[135] I also offered one *sang*, five *sho*, and one *khal*[136] of barley grain to each of the monks and established a capital fund to give one *tam* to each monk annually as an offering to the general assembly of Ganden Monastery. At Shartsé I made offerings of tea, *shethuk*, three *sang*, and one *khal* of barley to each monk. To the monastery, I presented long woven yellow carpets with lotus designs for each of the eighteen long rows of seats in the assembly hall, several handwoven square cushion covers with red woolen borders for the seats of the ranking monastic administrators, and a capital fund to give one *tam* to each monk annually. At Jangtsé I offered tea, *shethuk*, and three *sang* to the monks and established a capital fund to offer one *tam* annually. At Dokhang House I offered tea, *shethuk*, three *sang*, and one *khal* of barley. As a general offering to the house, I offered banners made of fine Russian brocade with gilded bronze *tsipar* ornamental heads for each of the four pillars, two large triangular multicolored banners, a victory banner made of *chanden* (brocade with lotus designs manufactured in Benares, India), and a capital fund to offer one *tam* annually to each monk. To the regional affiliates of Dokhang, Samling, and Serkong houses, I offered tea, money, and an annual pledge.

I made offerings of tea and money at Sang-ngak Khar Monastery at Dechen on my way from Ganden to Gongkotsang, where I met and offered gifts to my mother and other family members. At Chötri and Simshar monasteries at Gungthang, I made "daylong" offerings and monetary offerings. I also made a thanksgiving offering and presented a token sum as is customary to each of my birth deities, Drakshul Wangpo and Nyima Shönu, and their retinues through their mediums in trance and thereafter returned to my residence in Lhasa.

5 | A Period of Gain and Loss

Cared for While Ill by Tridak Rinpoché

In my twenty-ninth year, the year of the earth-snake (1929), I offered tea and three *sho* to the monks at the Great Prayer Festival. After the festival I made offerings to the assemblies of Drepung and Sera monasteries, to Gyütö and Gyümé tantric colleges, and to the monks and nuns at Chusang Hermitage. At Gyütö Tantric College I presented 150 sets of five-buddha-family headdresses, which were made specially to order to match and coated with Chinese lacquer.

That year at Chusang, at the feet of Kyabjé Phabongkha Vajradhara, I had the good fortune to receive oral teachings on the *Guru Puja* and mahāmudrā based on the great commentary on the *Guru Puja* and the root text of mahāmudrā, as well as a teaching on the generation and completion stages of thirteen-deity Vajrabhairava once again, along with many other discourses.

In my thirtieth year, the year of the iron-horse (1930), a senior staff member of the Gungthang estate, Makdrung Kalsang, established the ritual offering and practice of Vajrabhairava and restored the practice of the five-deity Cakrasaṃvara at Chötri Monastery. In order to undertake these activities, he asked that I give initiations into the deities. Although I was suffering discomfort from a kidney ailment at that time, at Makdrung Kalsang's wish, I went to Gungthang and gave the initiations, after which my condition became worse. After crossing the Brahmāputra both ways during the journey, my condition became quite serious, and later I suffered a kidney infection and swelling in the leg. I was bedridden, unable to leave my room, until the beginning of the eleventh month and suffered a great deal of difficulty.

At this time Tridak Rinpoché of Ganden Jangtsé visited me often and performed many rituals to avert the circumstances of my sickness, such as purification and nāga rituals. He also gave me permission for the practice of Striped Garuḍa and advised me to do a mantra recitation retreat for that deity. After completing the retreat according to his advice, I dreamed one night that I transformed into a striped garuḍa the size of a sheep and landed on the roof of my house. I also dreamed of a platter with many frogs on it. The platter was covered with a cloth, the ends of which I held tightly beneath the platter with my left hand. The movement of the frogs on the platter lifted the cloth cover, and when I peered into the platter by lifting one end of the cloth, two frogs leaped out, and the rest of them became soft and mushy. The skins of their backs stuck to the cloth cover, and I could see fresh red sores on their backs. I interpreted this dream as pacification of the affliction caused by spirits. I received treatment both from Dr. Jikmé of Shelkar and Kalsang-la, a teacher of medicine at the Chakpori Medical College, and recovered gradually, ignoring the beckoning of the lord of death.

Tridak Rinpoché, the incarnation of Tridakpo Ngawang Tashi, was well educated in both sutra and tantra. Not only was he well versed in poetry, literature, and Sanskrit, he was also proficient in the ritual activities of the four classes of tantra and in the diagrams and colors of the mandalas, and he was able to paint thangkas on his own. Rinpoché had received many teachings and initiations from Serkong Dorjé Chang and Kyabjé Phabongkha Vajradhara. He was not arrogant and never boasted about his knowledge; nor did he act as ordinary lamas do, advertising the little knowledge they have to others as if waving a flag. His demeanor was like a flame kindled in a container.

Since Rinpoché and I were the disciples of the same lama, we were intimately connected. Though I knew that Rinpoché had received important secret oral teachings from Serkong Dorjé Chang, as the proverb says, "The old lady of Lhasa doesn't go to see the Buddha in Lhasa."[137] So although I had intended to receive such teachings from Rinpoché, he passed away before I could do so. I greatly regretted it, but it was too late.

The Arrival of Palden Tsering

My attendant Lhabu's father, Tashi Döndrup, who looked after our dairy farm at Dechen with great loyalty and dedication, passed away after a sickness in the earth-snake year (1929). It was his wish that his youngest son, Palden Tsering, join the service of our labrang, so that autumn Palden arrived in Lhasa with an escort. I taught Palden how to read and soon after sent him to the school in Lhasa run by Dr. Rikzin Lhundrup of Nyakrong Shar and looked after him from his childhood. As it is said:

> Unspoiled although in the midst of comfort,
> not wanting to run away when times are hard,
> carrying out every task given, easy or difficult:
> this is the epitome of a loving servant.

So it is with Palden, who has served, and continues to serve, as my personal attendant with loyalty and dedication, while ignoring any difficulties of his body, speech, and mind. He is the sole supporting cane on which this old man rests his hand.

In my thirty-first year, the year of the iron-sheep (1931), I attended most of the teachings given by Lama Vajradhara at either Chusang or Tashi Chöling Hermitage. In Lhasa, from assistant tutor Kyabjé Takdrak Vajradhara, I received initiations into Vajrabhairava according to the system of Jñānapāda and Lokeśvara according to the system of Atiśa. I also received teachings on Vajrabhairava based on the texts of Ra and Pal, and many oral transmissions, such as the practice manual of great Four-Faced Mahākāla based on the root and explanatory teaching texts. At the end of that autumn, two representatives of the monastery and the people of Chatreng, Phagé Losang Yeshé of Upper Chagong and Pawo Butsa Gelong Tenpa Namgyal of Trengshok, arrived to invite me to come to Chatreng for a return visit.

The Passing of the Ganden Throneholder and Geshé Ngawang Losang

In my thirty-second year, the year of the water-monkey (1932), Chinese soldiers infiltrated through the Ba area of Kham, and the Tibetan border security forces, not able to hold them back, lost territory all the way up to Bum Lakha in Markham. Because the imminent threat of war spread throughout the country, our own government was forced to acquire weapons from the British. I spent most of the summer at Chusang, receiving teachings on the various ritual ceremonies of Vajrabhairava, and many others, from Kyabjé Lama Vajradhara. In between the teachings I did several meditational retreats on various deities.

That year, in the twelfth month, the Ninety-First Ganden Throneholder, Losang Gyaltsen of Lawa House of Sera Jé, passed away. Although I hadn't yet been called for by the throneholder's manager and staff, of his own accord His Holiness the Dalai Lama dispatched a horse groomer from Norbulingka as a messenger to fetch me. When I arrived there, I was instructed by his attendant, Thupten Kunphel, that the throneholder had passed away the previous day and that I should assist in the ritual bathing of his body as well as in the cremation and so forth. I immediately proceeded to Phurchok Labrang, where the throneholder had been staying, and found that the ritual master from Namgyal Monastery, Sönam-la, was already there. His Holiness had instructed him that he and Trijang Tulku should do what was needed and that Phurchok Tulku Rinpoché should pay careful attention to the procedures in order to acquire personal experience for his future use. In retrospect, I realized that this was done for a very special reason: His Holiness had foreseen with his clairvoyance that Phurchok Rinpoché and others, including myself, would also have to attend to the service of His Holiness's body when His Holiness's thoughts passed into the state of peace the following year.

In accord with His Holiness's wishes, we performed ritual bathing and self-initiation until the body of the Ganden Throneholder was ready to be cremated. Then I presided over the cremation ritual according to the writings of Thuken Chökyi Nyima at Phabongkha Hermitage. Phurchok Rinpoché came to observe the ritual bathing and such throughout the procedure.

In my thirty-third year, the year of the water-bird (1933), His Holiness paid a visit to Ganden Monastery during the special session at Taktsé after the annual Great Prayer Festival in Lhasa. Not daring to stay in Lhasa during his visit, I immediately left for Ganden and proceeded to participate in the Vajrabhairava ritual offerings organized by Shartsé College. I had a private audience with His Holiness in the Clear Light Chamber[138] at the Ganden Throneholder's living quarters. There His Holiness conveyed his esteemed regards to me, and I answered his questions concerning the ritual sessions that Ganden celebrated in accordance with ancient custom. After His Holiness left Ganden, I returned to Lhasa.

When I had departed for Ganden, my former classmate, Geshé Ngawang Losang of Phukhang House, whose scholarship was recognized in the three seats of learning, was sick with a fever at my house in Lhasa. When I had studied at the monastery, he had been my debate partner, and he had been a very close friend for many years. He passed away before my return to Lhasa, and I had tremendous regret at not having been able to see him at the time of his death. I made extensive offerings on his behalf.

At the end of summer, I invited Kyabjé Phabongkha to my residence at Chusang, and we were in the process of receiving permission for the seventeen emanations of Four-Faced Mahākāla[139] when a messenger specially dispatched from the stable of the Norbulingka Palace arrived with a message that I should report to the sunlight room at the Norbulingka early the next morning. I went to the Norbulingka and received through Kunphel-la the holy command, as per a letter submitted to His Holiness by the monastery and people of Chatreng requesting his consent and permission to grant me a leave of absence, that I should leave immediately for Chatreng. There I should give advice and counsel to the people to serve and support the Dharma and secular affairs. I was also told to send reports to His Holiness in the event of possible schemes for Chinese invasion. I received extensive instructions on other aspects of my activities there.

Because pack and transportation animals had not been prepared for our immediate departure, I sought and received permission to leave promptly the following year. The three permissions for the cycle of Four-Faced Mahākāla and the secret teaching of Mahākāla that I had not received were later given to me by Kyabjé Simok Rinpoché of Nalendra Monastery in Phenpo district. In preparation for my trip to Kham, I sent Losang Yeshé, one of the delegates from Chatreng, to India and instructed him to buy supplies there.

The Passing of His Holiness the Thirteenth Dalai Lama

In 1933, on the thirtieth of the tenth Tibetan month, His Holiness the Thirteenth Dalai Lama passed his thoughts into the state of peace. Phurchok Jamgön Rinpoché, assistant tutor Takdrak Vajradhara, assistant tutor Gyalwang Tulku of Kongpo House of Sera Mé, Kyabjé Ling Rinpoché, and myself, along with the master of chant and the ritual master of Namgyal Monastery, tended to the ritual procedures for the bathing and preservation of his body. I had to postpone my journey to Kham. The body of His Holiness was taken to the Sishi Palbar Chamber in the top-floor sunlight room in the Norbulingka Palace, and we started the ritual for the consecration of his body, which included bathing his body and every week changing the salt crystals in which it was kept.

Over the following days an investigation into the causes and circumstances of His Holiness's sickness and its outcome was held by the National Assembly in the Norbulingka Palace. His Holiness's attendants, including Thupten Kunphel and his physician Jampa-la, were questioned by the National Assembly about the circumstances of his death and the treatment of his illness. After this interrogation they were put under arrest and imprisoned. Thupten Kunphel was sent to Kongpo and the others to various places of exile.

In the twelfth month, the holy body of His Holiness was brought to the Ganden Nangsal Chamber in the east wing of the Potala Palace. From then on, every day for a year and a half until prayers and relics could be placed in a newly constructed golden stupa, I tended the ritual procedures of making offerings before his body. The newly appointed regent, Radreng Rinpoché,[140] and Prime Minister Yapshi Langdun Gung Kunga Wangchuk also charged us with the responsibility of drawing up plans and measurements for the memorial stupa as well as gathering the prayers and materials to be inserted in it.

When we made the diagrams for the proportions of the stupa on cloth, we laid the cloth in the vast courtyard of Deyang Shar on the east side of the Potala. We made the size of the stupa two arm lengths' larger than His Holiness the Fifth Dalai Lama's memorial stupa, the Sole Ornament of the World. The evergreen tree trunk that arrived from Radreng Monastery for the central wooden support was exactly the same size as the measurement in our plan, reaching from the top of the stupa to the lotus seat of the vase,[141] without so much as an inch difference. It was an amazing occurrence of unplanned auspiciousness. In general, the length of the wooden support for a stupa should extend from the top to the lotus petals at the base, but when the wooden support is conjoined with a mandala according to the Two Stainless Cycles,[142] the mandala diagram is to be placed at the base of the vase and the wooden support securely planted there. It was this system that we used on that occasion.

While engaged in service of His Holiness's body during my thirty-fourth year, the year of the wood-dog (1934), our manager Rikzin suddenly suffered a stroke and passed away. My attendant Lhabu and I were forced

Regent Radreng Rinpoché at Shidé Monastery, 1937

© FREDERICK SPENCER-CHAPMAN, PITT RIVERS MUSEUM, UNIVERSITY OF OXFORD; 1998.131.516

to assume responsibility for making offerings and other activities following his death. As mentioned earlier, due to lack of sufficient knowledge, ability, and success, there was a shortage of grain and other necessities at our labrang. Sometimes we were even forced to borrow from neighbors when our own supplies from our village farm estates did not come in time. With our supply of butter depleted prior to the end of the year, we had to take advance supplies from dairy farms. As our cellar storerooms only contained dried yak dung,[143] empty leather cases used for packing butter, and empty wooden boxes, we suffered great hardship for a few months due to the shortage of necessities. As Lhabu and I lacked the competence "to sacrifice a hundred in anticipation of gaining a thousand," we weren't fit to manage anything. Yet by the blessings and grace of the Triple Refuge, the status of our financial resources improved year by year, and prosperity began to return. We were able to make offerings to the objects of refuge and the monks to our hearts' content, as if drawing water from a well whose volume only seems to increase.

That year the finance minister, Lungshar Dorjé Tsegyal, and the cabinet minister Trimön Norbu Wangyal came into conflict over a disagreement with respect to governmental power and authority, which led to unrest due to factional disputes among the monastic and lay government officials as the two solicited supporters. Lungshar was arrested, and on the eighth of the fourth month, both his eyes were gouged out at the Shöl Court hearing at the base of the Potala. He was sentenced to life in prison, and some of his friends were exiled to distant estates in various districts.

Both Lungshar and Kunphel-la were well known and powerful due to the special regard that His Holiness had had for them. Kunphel-la was someone whose moods all government officials, whether high, medium, or low, had to pay attention to. Although he was someone whose words even the various political offices had to take special notice of, as it says in the Vinaya, "All compounded things are subject to decline, ruin, dispersion, and change." Both men, along with their associates and relatives, suffered sudden tremendous change. Having seen the happiness and suffering of cyclic existence and that prosperity and adversity flicker like lightning, I felt sorrow, and my renunciation increased.

While coming to the Potala every day to perform the ritual of consecrating the body and changing the salt once a week, in the autumn we began to arrange the prayers and relics to be inserted into statues and stupas. Master craftsmen constructed the wooden structures that would form the base of the golden reliquary.

Concerning the placement of mantras inside the mausoleum: among existing blockprints of protective spells, the ones that contained the widest variety of mantras were from the blocks made during the time of Desi Sangyé Gyatso. First we placed in their appropriate places, without error, the five types of great dhāraṇī, printed at the dhāraṇī printer behind the rear exit of the Potala known as Kagyama, into the places indicated for the upper, middle, and lower dhāraṇī, and diagrams of male and female yakṣas, in accord with the thought of the Great Fifth Dalai Lama's *Sun Dispelling Errors in the Placement of Dhāraṇī*[144] and Changkya's *Crystal Mirror.*[145]

We placed on boards within the base of the stupa treasure vases related to Yellow Jambhala, White Jambhala, Vaiśravaṇa, Vasudhārā, Pṛthivīdevatī, and the five buddha families as written in the catalog of Sole Ornament of the World—the Great Fifth Dalai Lama's Golden Stupa.

At the four corners and in the center of the lion-throne portion of the stupa, we placed box representations of Six-Arm Mahākāla, Dharmarāja, Palden Lhamo, Yakṣa Chamdral, and the five emanations of Nechung Dharmarāja. Inside of each we placed life-stone and life-force diagram supports for each protector; representations of body, speech, mind, qualities, activity, and so on; outer, inner, and secret representations; thread-cross supports and the various substances; and mantras and petitions to establish and consecrate it as stated in the various manuals.

Within the sun and moon ornaments at the pinnacle of the reliquary, we drew the *miktsema* diagram for pacification, increase, and subjugation; the diagram for gathering disciples; the diagram of Sitātapatrā for protecting the country; the sādhana of Jetsun Kurukulle, first among the great red goddesses among the Thirteen Golden Dharmas of glorious Sakya; *Flow of the River Ganges: Instructions on the Key Points to Conquer the Three Realms* by Tsarchen;[146] the diagram that grants one power as taught in Dakpo Tashi Namgyal's *Source of Siddhi*;[147] the diagram for controlling the three realms; and the diagram for accomplishing all aims. We drew a large Gaṇeśa as written in the *Wish-Fulfilling Tree*[148] in the manner of Mahārakta Gaṇapati, the second deity of initiation, to accomplish the four activities of the secret essence diagram. For each of the diagrams of initiation, we stacked three diagrams one on top of the other. For the third deity of initiation, the wrathful Kakchöl, we drew mother and father diagrams as written in Kāmarāja's *Blazing Jewel Sādhana.*[149] Nine diagrams of the sun, moon, and so on, which fall on the vital places, were stacked above and below.

The drawing surfaces, the substances to be applied, the time to draw the diagrams, the accomplishment, and so on were carried out according to the unerring arrangement found in the Great Fifth Dalai Lama's *Bouquet of Red Utpalas: Instructions to Undo the Knots of the Difficult Points of the Three Cycles of Red Ones*[150] and *Hook to Summon the Three Realms:*

Illumination of Diagrams.[151] The "requesting to stay" rituals are recorded in the catalog of the Thirteenth Dalai Lama's Great Golden Stupa, Granting All Goodness and Happiness.

In order to collect the materials to be inserted into the reliquary, approximately fifty sacred cases that were the property of the government and that contained self-produced relics of great realized beings from ancient India and Tibet, including their clothes, hair, bones, ashes, and many other wondrous and inconceivably precious relics, were opened in the Ganden Yangtsé Chamber of the Potala Palace in the presence of Regent Radreng Rinpoché, Prime Minister Yapshi Langdun Gung Kunga Wangchuk,[152] Cabinet Minister Trimön, the overseer of the reliquary project, four monastic governmental secretaries from the Upper Department, and those of us who were engaged in the ritual services of His Holiness's body.

A portion of each relic was made ready, presented, and inserted into the appropriate places in the various sections of the structure of the stupa. Each of us who were engaged in service to His Holiness's body were fortunate to obtain as a gift some small bits of relics. Later, as I will mention below, I came to acquire indisputably authentic relics from various monasteries during my extensive pilgrimage to holy places of Central Tibet such as the district Lhokha. I retained these with great care, as they were the most extraordinary jewels, ones that one cannot obtain on any plane of existence. I brought them with me during my flight from Tibet to India to seek asylum in the Tibetan Royal Year of 2086, the earth-pig year, 1959. Except for a small portion of the relics for my labrang, I presented the bulk of them to His Holiness the Fourteenth Dalai Lama, with a complete catalog and in labeled packages, for their perpetual use as objects in relation to which beings may accumulate merit.

We frequently changed the salt around the body of His Holiness. When the moisture of the body had nearly dried up and the body became more and more skeletal as the flesh reduced, a self-emerged image of Avalokiteśvara three inches in height, with head, hands, and feet, as well as a lotus seat, appeared very clearly on the surface of his back at the thirteenth vertebra. The sight of this filled me with great admiration and profound faith.

In the third month of my thirty-fifth year, the year of the wood-pig (1935), we completed the interment of materials in all parts of the stupa except for the vase structure. We placed ritual prayers of Sitātapatrā and *miktsema* into the gilded victory banners on the roof of the temple that would house the stupa, placed rituals of Palden Lhamo, Chamsing, and others into various adornments of the stupa, and placed protective spells into the jewel top of the gilt roof.

On an auspicious day in the month of Buddha Śākyamuni's enlightenment, the body of His Holiness was adorned with the three sets of monastic robes, crowned with the diadem of the five buddha families in the aspect of an enjoyment body, and placed inside the stupa's vase compartment. The government celebrated this occasion with elaborate ceremonies. Following this the extensive consecration ritual of Śrī Vajrabhairava was performed over three days, presided over by Radreng Rinpoché and attended by the entire assembly of Namgyal Monastery. I also attended the entire session.

To celebrate the successful completion of construction of the Dalai Lama's Great Golden Stupa, Granting All Goodness and Happiness, the government arranged an elaborate feast of ceremonial cookies in the Sishi Phuntsok Hall of the Potala Palace. There, Minister Trimön, the overseer of the stupa project, the overseer of construction, the craftsmen, and those of us who attended to His Holiness's body were honored with gifts bestowed accordingly. I was given a complete set of robes, consisting of upper and lower monastic garments, a vest, ordination robes, a monastic hat, monastic boots, as well as a case of tea, brocade and silk cloth, an honorarium, and a ceremonial scarf. I considered it a great honor and the highest good fortune to participate in the noble task of serving for one and a half years with dedication and devotion: from the very start of the ritual service to the ritual preparation of the body all the way up to the completion of the Great Golden Stupa and its foundation, with sacred material placed inside and sealed with a ritual of consecration.

During the rainy-season retreat, I went to Ganden, and at the request of Phara House of Ganden Jangtsé, I gave an initiation into Akṣobhyavajra Guhyasamāja with its preparatory rite to a large number of monks from Shartsé and Jangtsé colleges in the Jangtsé assembly hall. I attended the newly established ritual offering to Guhyasamāja at Phara House for seven days.

Since I myself was unable to go to Chatreng, Pawo Butsa Gelong Tenpa Namgyal, who had been sent as a representative of the monastery to invite me, was preparing to return to Chatreng. I wanted to send with him a large appliqué thangka as an offering to the monastery. Along with the funds for our travel expenses that the monastery had sent, donations for the thangka were also offered by members of the Chatreng community living in Lhasa. Our labrang also provided food, drink, and so on for the group of master craftsmen invited to create the thangka. The appliqué thangka, three stories high, was made of good brocade and illustrated the celestial host of Tuṣita, with Jé Tsongkhapa and his two disciples emerging from the heart of Maitreya. The two previous great throneholders were depicted on the top, and on the bottom were the protectors Dharmarāja and Trinlé Gyalpo.[153]

The Death of Losang Tsultrim

In my thirty-sixth year, the year of the fire-rat (1936), my esteemed teacher and precious mentor Losang Tsultrim, who was then sixty-seven years old, became slightly ill at the beginning of the second month. Despite relying on every possible method of treatment from the physician Jikmé of Shelkar, employing ritual offerings, and performing service and care to the best of my ability, his thoughts passed into the sphere of peace in the late afternoon on the fifteenth of the second month. My mind was tormented with unbearable grief, but as there was nothing I could do about it, I fortified myself and attended personally to his body, including the ritual bathing.

From the time I was a tender sprout at the age of seven not only did he extend to me great kindness, with untiring care in providing to me the religious instruction that has enabled this donkey to enter the ranks of humans, he took principal responsibility and gave valuable advice on secular matters following the deaths of the managers of our labrang and during that critical, most difficult phase wherein the responsibilities of the administration of the labrang had fallen to me. Even given eons the extent of the kindness he bestowed could not be measured. Although it was difficult to properly rely on my precious teacher as a spiritual friend, having been in constant companionship with him at all times, I was not the cause of any disappointment and disgust by my teacher. As the importance of properly relying on the spiritual friend is such that even the slightest mistake or act done properly can determine ruin or success, I declared openly with repentance in the presence of his body any mistakes and downfalls that may have occurred.

My teacher's body was taken to Chusang Hermitage, where together with a few ritual assistants from the Gyütö Tantric College, I cremated his body with the ritual fire offering. Each week thereafter I made offerings at the Great Prayer Festival and the subsequent session, at Gyütö and Gyümé tantric colleges, at the three monastic seats, at the three centers of Dharma,[154] and at other sacred places for the perpetual accomplishment of his wishes.

My late teacher was born into a family called Jarshing in the Nangsang region of Domé province in the iron-horse year of the fifteenth *rabjung* cycle. He enrolled in Shartsé College at Ganden, and having become a top scholar upon completion of extensive study of the five treatises, he sat for his geshé lharam examinations, receiving second position with honors. At that time, when the abbot of Shartsé, Losang Khyenrap of Phukhang House, had resigned his abbotship and was living alone, and the following abbot, Lodro Chöphel of Nyakré House, had passed away in the fifth year of his abbotship, His Holiness called "Losang Tsultrim, tutor to Trijang Tulku," by name to appear for a debate examination and was on the verge of appointing him the abbot. At this juncture, through Deyang Tsenshap Rinpoché, assistant tutor to His Holiness, and others, my teacher requested His Holiness that he be excused from this appointment due to his poor eyesight and lack of administrative knowledge and skill. Were it anyone else, an appointment with special regard by His Holiness would be considered the ultimate attainment and would have been happily accepted without hesitation. My teacher, however, was someone who did not like occupying a high post and could not sleep for days out of worry and concern, due to which he suffered from nervous tension in his chest and back and often shed tears. Nyitso Geshé Trinlé of Chatreng had to comfort him.

Generally with regard to his daily deeds and activities, he rose early in the morning and practiced the *Guru Puja*, the six-session guruyoga, the sādhanas of Vajrabhairava and Medicine Buddha, as well as various other prayers. He continuously recited the *miktsema*, the mantra of Maitreya, and the mantra of Avalokiteśvara except while teaching or studying. He never sat idle or passed time with gossip. During his stay in Ganden, many students from both Shartsé and Jangtsé came to study with him every day and he taught them without any reluctance. Many among his students became good scholars who in turn taught others. To this day there are many geshés who descend in his line of learning. As such he performed an immense service to the Dharma and left a great legacy.

His style of teaching was such that he did not give unnecessarily extensive commentaries and instead provided concise explanations on the difficult points in a manner easy to comprehend. For example, with reference to my lessons, when I studied the Perfection of Wisdom at age twelve and thirteen, my enthusiasm and comprehension were small in scope due to my age. But with the exception of the greater topic, Tsongkhapa's *Essence of Eloquence*, I was able to develop a good general understanding of the other subjects, such as going for refuge, generating bodhicitta, and the Buddha's turning of the wheel of Dharma. This was after my teacher went over the text with me once and taught me the points of debate for a penetrating understanding of the meaning. Like chasing a hundred birds with one slingshot, I had a good basic knowledge of the topics in all stages and could reconstruct them in their proper order.

Two years after my teacher passed away, in the hope of discovering his incarnation, whom I intended to personally take care of without the publicity of an official title of incarnation and enroll him for study as an ordinary monk to repay his kindness, I consulted Sengé Gangi Lama in Phenpo district. He had done the hundred thousand mantra recitations retreat of the sādhana of Yudrönma and was someone Kyabjé Phabongkha held in high regard. Based on his mirror divination, he sent this reply in verse to my questions regarding the incarnation of my teacher:

> On the full moon day, drawn up on the light-ray path
> emanated from the heart of the celestial Maitreya,
> he now dwells in the heaven of Tuṣita
> within the entourage of Ajita Deva.

Although I did not make any mention of the time of my teacher's passing away in my letter asking for his prediction, his reply stated that my teacher passed away at the full moon and was reborn in the celestial realm of Tuṣita. Though I had no further hope of discovering his incarnation, my faith and conviction in my teacher increased.

In the third month I went to Ganden to make offerings for my teacher, and there, at the request of Geshé Ngawang Tashi of Lhopa House in Shartsé, I gave to a large audience including the abbots of Shartsé and Jangtsé, as well as tulkus and monks, an initiation into sixty-two-deity Cakrasaṃvara according to the system of Mahāsiddha Luipa. That summer I began work on a project to make a decorative bejeweled appliqué drapery of multicolored brocade illustrating the thirty-five buddhas of confession and a depiction of the protector Setrap to be hung above the main entrance to the assembly hall. This large decorative drapery was to be hung on special occasions on all four of the inner sides of the clerestory of the hall, including the balcony. Twelve pillar banners made of Varanasi brocade with appliqué *tsipar* heads and twelve small hangings of triangular shape were also fabricated for Dokhang House. I went to Ganden and presented the hangings to Shartsé and Dokhang, along with tea and money offerings, during the festival of lights. I also made offerings at Jangtsé and established a capital fund for annual offerings of one *tam* to each monk.

In my thirty-seventh year, the year of the fire-ox (1937), I made offerings at the Great Prayer Festival to amass merit for the accomplishment of the wishes of my late teacher and to eliminate the obstacles of my twelve-year cycle. I made offerings at Gyütö Tantric College on the anniversary of the passing away of my late teacher and donated a capital fund to offer one *tam* every year on the fifteenth of the second month.

At the request of Lady Yangzom Tsering of the aristocratic family of Lhalu Gatsal, I constructed a shrine at the Lhalu family temple for the inner, outer, and secret objects related to the activities of the holy body, speech, and mind of the female protector goddess Palden Lhamo Maksorma, who is the aspect of Buddha's activities for sentient beings. They were constructed in the protector chamber of the family according to authoritative sources, such as the ritual manual of the goddess and the writings of the Fifth Dalai Lama and Thuken Rinpoché. I performed the ritual for seven days.

Tantric Teachings from Kyabjé Phabongkha Rinpoché

In the assembly hall of Chusang Retreat House, I received from Kyabjé Phabongkha Vajradhara a detailed explanation of Candrakīrti's *Bright Lamp* (*Pradīpoddyotana*) on the completion stage of Guhyasamāja, the secret instruction that is the best, the sublime, the ultimate pinnacle of the essence of all classes of tantra, which liberates disciples of sharp faculties from cyclic existence and delivers them onto the ground of immutable enlightenment in this very life. When we reached the explanation of the illusory body, we arranged extensive offerings of torma and tsok on the altar and offered outer, inner, and secret suchness to Lama Vajradhara conceived as the principal deity of the mandala. Then we made the request to impart the teaching on the illusory body. All this was done according to the traditions of the tantric monastery, and the offerings were well arranged. At this point I recited the following spontaneous song of joy:

Dechen Nyingpo, embodiment of all guru-buddhas,
lucidly proclaims an unending Dharma melody,
the teachings of the Glorious Guhyasamāja, the peak of all
the tantras.
What delight, this fortune that even Brahmā and Indra do
not attain!

Kyabjé Phabongkha Rinpoché
Alexandra David-Néel © Ville de Digne-les-Bains

Although lacking the ease of a melodious voice,
help me, vajra brothers of pure pledges and bonds,
to offer as a cloud of praise that pleases the incomparable guru,
this spontaneous song of joy overflowing from our rapturous delight.

Though poor in the movements gained by skill and practice,
yet by the power of Lama Akṣobhyavajra's blessing,
let us perform the joyful dance of the fortunate ones
on the swift path of the peerless great secret.

With the world of existence and appearance as myriad pure mandalas,
and the innate tones of the in and out breaths arising as secret mantra,
the army of the horses of the manifested wheels of the three realms
are harnessed on the path of dual abandonment. I take joy in
such skill![155]

The clear light of one taste with the realm of elaborations pacified
and the primordial and innate smiling youth,
a great cloud of illusion with five light rays released unhindered,
a dancer filling the vast mandalas of space.

Though appearing as a bouquet of enlightened attributes,
it is of the nature of exalted wisdom;
though existing as unobstructed exalted wisdom,
it possesses the appearance of the form body;
the joy of the stage of union, one taste appearing as many:
I yearn to dwell in the pure realm of Akaniṣṭha.

It is said that by the kindness of the siddha Indrabodhi,
many beings find freedom without relentless hardship.
E ma! Having met such an excellent and profound path,
Oḍḍiyāna must be like this, I think.

With the armor and power of patience
to free all mother living beings,
may we engage the meaning of the tantras,
garland of consonants imbued with the letter *a*,[156]

and may we thoroughly remove all stains
of erroneously clinging to duality
and sing the joyous song of *a li la mo*.[157]

Having been offered such a song, the incomparable precious guru expressed his great pleasure. Yet the fact that I lack the good fortune to materialize any of my aspirations due to being wholly entangled in distraction is certainly a result arising in accordance with unwholesome actions I performed in prior lives.

Pilgrimage to Southern District

That autumn, along with Lhabu and a few others, I left Lhasa, passing through Ganden, Maldro Katsal, Gyeteng, Cheka Monastery, Pangsa, Rinchen Ling Monastery, and Ruthok Monastery. Crossing Takar Pass, we visited Ölkha Dzingchi and Samling, and crossing Gyalong Pass we visited Chökhor Gyal, Lhamo Lhatso, Gyal Lhathok, the great temple of Daklha Gampo, and Sanglung Retreat. On the way back we went by Ölkha Chusang, Chölung, Gyasok, Lhading, and Nyima Ling. We passed a few days at the Shöl hot springs in Ölkha.

Although there were inconceivable objects of worship at Daklha Gampo,[158] the statues appeared to be neglected, which was utterly depressing. I had an audience with Daklha Gampo Rinpoché, and thinking to take advantage of the opportunity, questioned him regarding mahāmudrā and the six Dharmas of Nāropa. Perhaps he was shy. At any rate, I didn't receive satisfying replies.

We passed over Khartak Pass and visited Sangri Khangmar, Densathel, and Ön Ngari Monastery. We arrived at Tsethang having taken the Nyangpo ferry across the Tsangpo River. We visited Ngachö Monastery, Ganden Chökhor, Namgyal Temple, the congregation at Nedong Tsé, Bentsang Monastery, the chapel at Tradruk, Riwo Chöling, Yumbu Lagang, Lharu Menpai Gyalpo, one of the three sacred shrines of Yarlung, Takchen Bumpa, Tashi Chödé, Rechung Cave, Thangpoché, Songtsen's tomb, the sacred shrine of Menla Rinchen Dawa at Chenyé Monastery, the famed sacred statue of Tönpa Tsenlek at Rigang, Chongyé Riwo Dechen, Gönthang Bumoché, Tsenthang-yu Temple, Sheldrak Cave, and Jasa Temple.

At Sheldrak, when I made offerings before the statue of Padmasambhava, it appeared to me as if the statue became increasingly magnificent, as if it were Guru Rinpoché in person. It seemed as if his eyes were moving and he was about to speak. He did not do so, despite my earnest hopes, but extraordinarily on that day, an inexpressibly joyful awareness of emptiness without reference point or reason arose within me. I understood this to be a sign of having been blessed by Orgyen, the second Buddha.

At most of the above-mentioned monasteries, I gave various teachings according to particular requests and stayed for a few days at the Khemé estate. At Riwo Chöling, I offered initiation into Akṣobhyavajra Guhyasamāja as requested by the monks. Then, on the return journey, we crossed the Tsangpo River by ferry and took in the sacred sights of Samyé. Thereafter, visiting the pilgrimage sites in upper and lower Chimphu and Yamalung, we made thousandfold offerings, a hundred lamps, tsok, and food for the monks as the occasions called for and as we were able. I have not mentioned here the history of the origin of the above places and wondrous accounts of some of the special objects, as they are found in the biographies and histories and in Khyentsé's *Pilgrimage Guide.*[159]

After crossing Gökar Pass we arrived back at our residence in Lhasa. That year I went to Ganden during the winter session and made offerings to Shartsé College, on which occasion I presented to Shartsé four pillar banners to be hung on the four front pillars of the assembly hall. The banners were made of brocade with dragon designs newly manufactured in China and were attached to gilded *tsipar* heads.

Stages of the Path Teachings from Kyabjé Phabongkha Rinpoché

In my thirty-eighth year, the year of the earth-tiger (1938), I requested the sole refuge of all beings, including celestial beings, the great Phabongkha Vajradhara, to graciously consent to giving a discourse on the *Great Treatise on the Stages of the Path* with the four annotations[160] at Ganden Monastery that summer. Arriving at Ganden ahead of time, I made proper arrangements for his stay and set up a tent on Tsangthok, the green field at the foot of Ganden, for a reception ceremony in honor of my refuge and protector Vajradhara and his entourage.

Upon the arrival of the party to Tsangthok, I presented scarves and symbolic offerings of the holy body, speech, and mind to Lama Vajradhara and provided necessary services for the overnight stay. The next morning, when Kyabjé Vajradhara and his retinue arrived at Ganden, the incumbent abbot of Shartsé, Song Rinpoché Losang Tsöndrü, myself, and other incarnate lamas and monastic administrators, holding incense in our hands, led the procession from the spring, escorting Guru Vajradhara to his throne in the assembly hall of Dokhang House for an elaborate reception ceremony with stacked ceremonial cookies. After the attendants, the abbot of Shartsé, and others, including the monastic officials, had settled into the rows of seats, tea, ceremonial rice, cookies, and assorted dried fruit were offered. Following this, the officials of Shartsé and Dokhang House and I presented scarves and holy objects to Guru Vajradhara.

After the ceremony, Guru Vajradhara graciously came to stay at my residence above the assembly hall of Dokhang House, as had been arranged. The members of my labrang and I shifted quarters to the residence of the Dokhang House disciplinarian. We attended to any need of food and drink for Kyabjé Vajradhara and his attendants for a few days. Then until the conclusion of the discourse, for reasons of his health and diet, we supplied his personal attendants with staple foods, such as butter, barley flour, wheat flour, tea, and so forth, so that they did not need to purchase it from the market and offered the sums of cash needed to purchase fresh vegetables daily.

On the third day of the fifth month, an auspicious day of harmonious conjunction between the stars and the planets, the embodiment of all the victorious ones, precious guru of the beings of the three realms, entered the great assembly hall of Shartsé, Thösam Norbuling, to the tune of ceremonial music, preceded by incense holders, and placed his lotus feet on the teaching throne, the mandala of his magnificent face smiling—the sight of which was meaningful to behold.

The discourse was given to an assembly of two thousand disciples, including the incumbent and former abbots of Shartsé and Jangtsé colleges, tulkus, monastic administrators, and monks. In addition, in attendance were Drakri Rinpoché of Sera Jé, Sharpa Rinpoché of Sera Mé Kongpo House, Geshé Jampa Thayé of Sera Jé Tsawa House, who was the first great founder of the Dialectic Institute in Chamdo when it was newly established, and many other well-known holders of the Dharma, tulkus, and geshés from Sera, Drepung, Lhasa, and other places and hermits from various hermitages.

He began to deliver his discourse on the path pioneered by the vanguard Indian masters Nāgārjuna and Asaṅga, a synthesis of the essence of all the teachings of the victorious ones, the only path of fortunate beings, which possesses four preeminent qualities and three features that distinguish it above others, Jé Tsongkhapa's *Great Treatise on the Stages of the Path, Lamp of Three Worlds*, with the four annotations and with experiential teachings that detailed the ways of putting his explanation into practice, drawn from Paṇchen Losang Yeshé's *Quick Path* teaching on the stages of the path to enlightenment.

On the first day of the discourse, for reasons of auspiciousness, our precious guru recited three times the first few pages of the *Great Treatise*, following which I recited them once. I made offerings to the assembly that day. From that day on, in the beginning period of the teaching, two sessions were held daily from afternoon until dusk. In the later period of the teaching, nearing the summer session, it was necessary to hold an extra teaching session each morning. The precious guru taught without any sign of fatigue and with great pleasure and joy, upholding the deeds of compassion without the slightest reluctance. I made an offering of tea at the discourse once each day, except on occasions when others sponsored tea.

Before the discourse was completed, we suspended teachings on the fourteenth day of the sixth month in order to celebrate the sixty-first birthday of the synthesis of all refuges, our supreme guide and king of Dharma, Guru Vajradhara, with a long-life offering and the Halting the Ḍākinī's Escort ritual[161] made in conjunction with a tsok offering of the *Guru Puja*. We made these auspicious offerings so that the lama would endure for eons like an indestructible vajra. We extensively arranged thousands of the fivefold clouds of offerings.[162]

On the thirteenth we prepared for the ceremony for generating bodhicitta, and on the morning of the fourteenth, our guru graciously conferred upon us the bodhisattva vows in the manner of holding the aspiration and the engaging bodhicitta simultaneously, as is done in Śāntideva's system. Thereafter, on the occasion of offering a long-life ceremony accompanied with a *Guru Puja* of the profound path, I made, without any miserliness, elaborate offerings of food and money to the assembly. In congruence with my ability and sense of devotion, I made physical offerings to the great Guru Vajradhara, poetically praised his supreme qualities, and offered up the entire universe symbolically with an elaborate description to request that his life remain steadfast to the ends of time. He eased my mind, saying that he was greatly pleased with the meaning of the verses describing the mandala and later requested a copy of my composition, which I provided.

The Dharma discourse continued the following day, lasting until the nineteenth, on which day, for the purpose of auspiciously closing the event, I presented a mandala with the representations of body, speech, and mind and a small honorarium, and offered tea and money to the assembly. As a fitting conclusion to the Dharma teaching, with quotes from scripture, such as "I have shown you the path to liberation, but you should know that liberation is in the palm of your hands," the precious guru told those who had received the teachings that it was not enough to merely listen to them but that listening, contemplation, and meditation should be harmoniously employed in support of one another. Otherwise, if what one learns is not put into practice, then religious people run the risk of being possessed by demons, like celestial beings falling into devilish states. As in this verse from *Essence of the Middle Way*:

> By the river of the speech
> more powerful than sandalwood,
> the fire of mental afflictions
> tormenting beings is pacified.[163]

So did he exhort his disciples at length and in great detail, satisfying their hearts.

As the precious guru held Khangsar Rinpoché of Gomang and myself in highest regard among his disciples, he told the assembly by the way, "There is no doubt that their beneficial activities will expand and increase if they have long lives." Dakpo Lama Rinpoché said, "The son will be greater than the father, the nephew greater than the son, and the cousin greater than the nephew. They will be as prophesied by Lama Rinpoché; therefore everyone should earnestly pray for them." As mentioned above, many qualified lamas, tulkus, and geshés such as Drakri Rinpoché, who were quite capable of upholding and propagating the teachings, were sitting nearby. I felt quite shy about receiving such honor and praise amid such an assembly.

Afterward the precious guru spent a few days in leisure in between going to Wangkur Hill to make incense offerings and relax. Once, as we circumambulated the circuit path around Ganden, he confided in me his great pleasure at having had the opportunity to teach the stages of the path, the essence of Jé Tsongkhapa's teachings, at his own seat of learning, which I took as a treasure of nectar to my ears.

On the morning of the day he left Ganden he placed upon my head the pandit hat that he had worn and presented me a copy of the *Great Treatise on the Stages of the Path*, the first three pages of which were written in gold ink. Placing a bell and vajra in my hands, he gave me a set of silver victory and action vases filled with consecrated substances, a golden image of Tārā, a wooden teacup that Guru Vajradhara himself had used filled with precious stones of turquoise, coral, and so forth, and yellow brocade with the eight auspicious symbols. With regard to Dharma, he advised me to uphold, preserve, and propagate the sutra and tantra teachings of Mañjunātha Tsongkhapa, and I was very fortunate to have received much sincere advice from my guru.

At that time I thought that for someone such as myself, of little natural and acquired knowledge, deeply mired in unending distractions, and deprived of inner experience, it would be very difficult to find the means to serve the Dharma. Nevertheless, due to the wish of the guru and auspicious connections, I had to give many discourses, principally on the stages of the path, in the guise of the father-lama's speech after the lama had passed into the state of peace. Having to give dry explanations without the confidence of any practice was like the maxim "the donkey measuring the hour of dawn in the absence of a rooster." I interpreted the lama's regard for me as an indication of my present role.

Thereafter, the great Guru Vajradhara was invited to Sang-ngak Monastery of Dechen to give a stages of the path discourse, and I accompanied him. An annual festival of the monastery and the town of Dechen coincided, and ritual dances were presented. I enjoyed the spectacle. There were no inauspicious omens or mishaps throughout the discourse; it was supremely successful, which I took to be a consequence of virtuous karma.

Journey to Dungkar Monastery, India, and Nepal

From the time of the death of our manager Rikzin to this time of writing, Lhabu and I have assumed full responsibility for our labrang in a manner like a self-contained jewel. At that time, we retained Muli Losang Döndrup of Dokhang as an assistant manager. Later, since the labrang of Dungkar Monastery in Upper Dromo had repeatedly invited me and others to consecrate and present dhāraṇī prayers and relics to the stupa containing the embalmed body of Dromo Geshé Rinpoché Ngawang Kalsang, who had passed away the previous year, Lhabu, Phuntsok, Venerable Kalsang Wangyal of Namgyal Monastery, and I departed Lhasa in the tenth month. We crossed Gampa Pass, passing through Paldi, Nakartsé, Ralung, Gyantsé, and Phakri, finally arriving at Dungkar Monastery. There I interred the dhāraṇī in the stupa but postponed the consecration until after the New Year holiday.

Having come as far as Dromo, and seeing that it would be greatly meritorious if we made a pilgrimage to India and Nepal, we set out for Kalimpong on mules and horseback by way of Dzalep Pass, Rongling, and so on. We passed a few days in Dromo Labrang of Tharpa Chöling Monastery in Kalimpong. Then, with the assistance of an interpreter, we visited Bodhgaya, Vulture Peak, Nālandā, Kuśinagar, Śrāvastī, Varanasi, and Lumbini, and in Nepal the three stupas of Svayambunāth, Boudhanath, and Namo Buddha[164] and other holy places. When we visited the stupa at Namo Buddha, we hired a taxi and rode up to the base of the hill. But on the return trip the taxi broke down, and we had to return on foot and so did not arrive at our quarters near the Bodhanāth stupa until eleven o'clock at night. It was quite a difficult trip. At each place of pilgrimage we made offerings to the best of our abilities in order to accumulate merit.

While I was staying at the Mahabodhi Guest House in Bodhgaya, a Ladakhi monk by the name of Ngawang Samten had made secret arrangements to buy a piece of property on which to construct a Tibetan temple and asked me to do the ground consecration. As the main stupa and the surrounding sites were under the administration of Jvaki Rāja, a Hindu, I discreetly performed the ground consecration on the site of the present Tibetan temple, Ganden Phelgyé Ling. On the fifteenth of the eleventh Tibetan month, during the late afternoon moonrise, I performed the ritual seeking permission from the field protectors and deities of the area to use the site and to request them to accept, protect, and bless the site in connection with the practice of Vajrabhairava. I also performed a ritual placing a small earth vase in the ground.

In order to offer gold paint to the Vajra Seat at the Mahābodhi Temple,[165] Jvaki Rāja's permission had to be sought, so I went to meet and present some gifts to him. He was sitting on a leopard skin that had a head and four paws. When I presented him with a ceremonial scarf, he gave me a hand blessing, placing his hand on my head. He was so pleased with me that he even provided me with an elephant and provided horses for my attendants when we went to the charnel ground at Sitavana. I had never traveled on an elephant before, and though it was pleasurable at first, it soon turned to misery, as the rough and jarring motion of the animal made me feel quite dizzy and nauseous.

I gave a brief discourse and an oral transmission of Tsongkhapa's *Praise to the Buddha*, his *Praise to Dependent Arising*, the "three sets of prayers,"[166]

Kyabjé Trijang Rinpoché giving teachings in front of the Bodhi Tree at Bodhgaya in 1938 during his pilgrimage to India
COURTESY OF PALDEN TSERING

and others to a large number of Tibetan pilgrims in front of the Bodhi Tree. At the time India was still under British rule, and the country was not as developed as it is now. As there were no motor roads from railway junctions to the places of pilgrimage, it was necessary to travel either via horse and carriage or on foot.

After the pilgrimage we returned to Kalimpong, where in the open area in front of Tharpa Chöling Monastery, I granted initiation into the Great Compassionate One to a mixed crowd of over one thousand monks and laypeople as requested by a Tibetan social group. I also made short visits to Calcutta and Darjeeling to see and enjoy the benefits of those places. On the way to Darjeeling I took up an invitation to Ganden Chöling, the old monastery in Ghoom, and gave a short discourse there. In Darjeeling I gave a long-life initiation to a large number of people at the home of Lekden Babu, who had previously served His Holiness the Thirteenth Dalai Lama.

In my thirty-ninth year, I celebrated the New Year of the earth-rabbit (1939) at Tashi Chöling Monastery in Kurseong, Darjeeling. On the first day of the new year I composed a propitiation ritual for the local protector of Kurseong at the request of the patrons. We returned to Dungkar Monastery in Dromo via Kalimpong, Rongling, Dzalep Pass, and so on. I stayed there for three and a half months. After passing three days in performance of the elaborate consecration ritual for the memorial stupa, I spent fifteen days teaching a commentary on the *Quick Path*, along with a ceremony for generating bodhicitta, to a group of over two hundred monks and laypeople in the assembly hall of the monastery as requested by the monastic community and long-time patrons of the monastery, such as Phajo Dönyö of the Galingang Bönpotsang family. I gave initiations into Guhyasamāja, Vajrabhairava, five-deity Cakrasaṃvara in the tradition of Ghaṇṭāpāda, the Great Compassionate One, and permission to practice protector deities such as Mahākāla and Dharmarāja. I offered the blessing of the four sindūra initiations of Vajrayoginī and an experiential explanation of its generation and completion stages and gave a discourse on the *Guru Puja*.

We left Dromo and stayed at the house of Tsechö, a merchant chief from the Pangda family at Phakri. While there I visited the monasteries of Drakthok Gang, which the Gyütö Tantric College ran, Richung Potho Monastery, which was run by Ganden Shartsé, and the upper and lower monasteries of Tashi Lhunpo, spending one day at each monastery giving short discourses. In the courtyard of the Pangda home, I bestowed upon a large gathering an initiation into the Great Compassionate One according to the system of Bhikṣuṇī Lakṣmī. Then, for the benefit of my health, the merchant Tsechö arranged for me to spend two weeks at the Khambu hot springs in Phakri, where I met Ngaksur Ta Lama Rinpoché of Tashi Lhunpo, who had also gone there.

On the way back, I spent a day at a monastery called Khambu that had been established by Ngakchen Damchö Yarphel. Perusing some of the many texts there, I came across in one of the volumes a page containing a handwritten prophecy. Although I do not recall the exact words, it said in essence:

> Avalokiteśvara will appear with the name of Thupa.
> All his deeds and conduct will be equal to Rāhula's.
> Lightning will strike the minister Garwa.

And so on, concluding with:

> In the year of the bird, every act will be complete.

When analyzed, it is clear that the text refers to the great dignity and bearing of the late Thirteenth Dalai Lama and to the punishment that befell Demo Rinpoché. The turmoil caused by the Chinese army during the water-rat year and His Holiness's passing away for the benefit of others in the bird year were clearly predicted therein.

To Sakya, Tashi Lhunpo, and Back to Lhasa

Then we set out from Phakri to visit the sacred places in Tsang. Visiting a nunnery founded by Ra Dharma Sengé in a place called Tratsangdo, Dotra Monastery, Chilung, and so on along the way, we arrived at the glorious Sakya on the fifteenth day of the fifth month after crossing Drongdu Pass. That day, in the city quarters adjacent to the great temple at Sakya, mediums were performing trances in which local deities entered into them, just as they do in Lhasa during the universal incense-offering festival. Some of the mediums were through with trances and had joined the celebrants indulging in the drinking of beer. The Sakya township graciously made arrangements for me to stay in the house of a lay official and extended their hospitality to us, appointing an official, Mr. Maja, to be our liaison, giving us tsampa and providing food for our animals.

There were a variety of old handwritten texts in the room. Reading through them, I discovered some explanations of Logic and Epistemology, the Perfection of Wisdom, and Madhyamaka philosophy meant for recitation in the assembly hall by degree candidates, and collections of concluding auspicious verses recited by examination proctors. Except for minor differences in composition, style, and length, they were very similar to corresponding literature in the three great Geluk seats of learning and reminiscent of the style used by geshés at the Great Prayer Festival. It occurred to me that Jé Tsongkhapa and his disciples studied at Sakya, and that the tradition of the study of logic that existed at Sakya also became prevalent within our Geluk tradition.

As there were too many bedbugs in the room, I had to stay in a tent pitched on a green lawn by a stream. At that time, in order to meet with the incumbent of the Sakya throne, Dakchen Rinpoché of Phuntsok Phodrang, I had to follow his schedule and meet him during the daily morning tea ceremony. I went to his private chambers and paid my respects with prostrations. When I asked a few questions regarding the practices of the Thirteen Golden Dharmas of Sakya and the three cycles of red ones,[167] he simply told me to consult the tutor to his two sons and did not impart any in-depth advice. I was given a large amount of relic pills, including a nectar pill. When I visited the temples in the surrounding complex, the tutor to his two sons was sent to act as my guide. At leisure, we visited the statue of Mañjuśrī with eyes that follow you, the far-resounding white conch of Dharma, and the Black Skin Mask Guardian in the Gorum protector chamber.[168] I made extensive offerings and presented tea and money to the monks. The tutor and I had discussions over a variety of topics. He seemed well versed in studies concerning sutra but did not seem to have been too familiar with the Golden Dharmas or with the Path and Fruit (*lam 'bras*) oral instructions of Sakya.

From Sakya we visited the protector chapel of Palden Lhamo at Samling and Khau Drakzong, a pilgrimage site of Four-Faced Mahākāla. We crossed Atro Pass and visited the region of Charong, followed by visits along the way to Lhunpo Tsé Monastery, the great Maitreya statue at Trophu, and Gangchen Chöphel Monastery, arriving in the end at the illustrious Narthang Monastery. I visited most of the sacred images there. In one temple

I saw one of the two replicas of the Bodhgaya temple finely crafted out of sandalwood during the era of Chomden Rikral (1227–1305). I found that the actual details of the stupa and the Bodhi Tree and such were exactly as they are now, which deepened my conviction in Bodhgaya as a sacred place. Though I really wanted to visit the hermitage of Jangchen and the temple at Shalu, they had to be put off due to lack of time.

When we arrived at the seat of Tashi Lhunpo in upper Tsang, a monastic official who would act as a guide was placed at our disposal by the administration of the monastery. They also provided us with large quantities of provisions and arranged accommodations for our party at Phendé Khangsar at the labrang of the tutor Lochen Rinpoché.[169] At that time the supreme refuge Kyabjé Phabongkha Vajradhara, endowed with great compassion that leads all beings to peace, was performing a reading and giving an explanation of the *Great Treatise on the Stages of the Path* to more than a thousand disciples at Dechen Phodrang palace at the special invitation of Tashi Lhunpo Monastery. I had the good fortune of being able to touch my head to the dust of the feet of that kind, incomparable father lama and was buoyed by his expression of pleasure, like that of a father reunited with his son. Though the all-seeing Paṇchen Lama had not returned from China and Mongolia, in his absence I presented the symbolic universe and representations of the holy body, speech, and mind along with a ceremonial scarf and gifts as arrival and departure tributes during the tea ceremony sessions in accordance with ancient custom.

In the Kadam chamber of the palace of Gyaltsen Thönpo, Dzasak Lama Losang Rinchen of Kyapying sat before the seat of Paṇchen Rinpoché. I was seated in his presence, and tea, ceremonial rice, cookies, and a high stack of gifts of sacred relics, handmade clay votive statues, incense, and woolen material for an upper garment were presented to me. An inner room of the chambers had an exclusive protector chapel and a text of the *Miraculous Book of Ganden*.[170] The room was blessed with the presence of a succession of Paṇchen Lamas, beginning with Paṇchen Losang Chögyen (1570–1662), As the room had become blessed by their great works for the benefit of the Buddhist teaching, with great joy and devotion, I made strong requests and offered dedicated prayers in connection with the seven-limb practice.

Then I visited the memorial stupas of the Paṇchen lineage, the statue of Maitreya, and most of the other temples. I made offerings to the various houses and amassed heaps of merit by offering tea and money to the monks in the assembly hall of Tashi Lhunpo. I also had the great fortune, in the presence of the official Kyapying Dzasak and the chief secretary, of viewing the sacred relics of Tashi Lhunpo in their relic box. One day I respectfully offered tea and money to the assembly of disciples at the discourse in Dechen Phodrang, and I presented the representations of the three holy objects and gifts to Guru Vajradhara. I attended one session of the discourse for reasons of auspiciousness, and I am deeply indebted to him for his kindness in sharing the nectar of his speech, which is ever meaningful.

While staying at Tashi Lhunpo, many of the disciples who were attending the discourse, including a large number of monks, came to see me, and I had to give readings and explanations of the *Hundred Deities of Tuṣita* and other works, one after the other, according to their requests. Lochen Rinpoché, the predecessor to the current incarnation, was then a young lama, and on his request I conferred the permission of Jé Rinpoché as the triple deity.

We departed Tashi Lhunpo and visited Panam Gadong Monastery and Pögang Institute at Gyantsé. At both these places we saw many of their sacred objects, such as a thangka of the Hevajra mandala that had belonged to Nāropa, garments of the great Kashmiri paṇḍita,[171] and Sanskrit texts. I gave a long-life initiation to the local people at the invitation of Kashö estate of Kharkha. While staying at Serchok in Gyantsé, I made a leisurely visit to the sacred sites of Palkhor Chödé and gave a teaching on the *Hundred Deities of Tuṣita* at Shiné Monastery. Along the way I amassed merit by offering tea, money, and so on at Ralung Nunnery, Pökya Hermitage, and most of the other monasteries and sacred places.

Having traversed Kharöl Pass, Nakartsé, and so on, we crossed the Tsangpo River at Nyasok and spent one night at Nyethang.[172] There we visited and paid respects to the Tārā temple, wherein the principal statue was the "Tārā who spoke," and saw the stupa that Lord Atiśa had carried with him at all times.

We arrived back in Lhasa at the end of the sixth month. That fall, the supreme Phabongkha Vajradhara, having come to the tantric college of Sera Monastery, taught Aśvaghoṣa's *Fifty Verses on Guru Devotion* and bestowed an initiation into Akṣobhyavajra Guhyasamāja. When he conferred initiation into Vajrapāṇi Mahācakra at Hardong House of Sera Jé, I too received a flood of initiation blessings into the core of my heart.

The great fourteenth incarnation, our supreme refuge and protector of

The Nyethang statues of Tārā and Śākyamuni (left) and Atiśa (right), 1950
© HUGH RICHARDSON, PITT RIVERS MUSEUM,
UNIVERSITY OF OXFORD; 2001.59.2.70.1 AND 2001.59.13.64.1

the land of snows, the Noble Holder of the White Lotus who has manifested in the play of benefitting all beings, was in procession from Amdo, and on the occasion of his lotus feet gracing the ground of the capital city, Lhasa, at the end of the eighth month (early October 1939), I joined the tulkus of Sera, Drepung, and Ganden in a grand government reception on the plain of Gangtö Dögu. Seeing the mandala of his face endowed with the major and minor marks of enlightenment while paying respects to him, I attained the nectar that leads to liberation.

Receiving and Giving Further Teachings

In the spring of my fortieth year, the year of the iron-dragon (1940), I received the following initiations at the feet of the all-embracing lord of a hundred buddha families, the tutor Takdrak Vajradhara, at the Norbulingka: five-deity Vimaloṣṇīṣa, five-deity Viśuddhaprabhā, Amitāyus in the system of Machik Drupgyal, many peaceful and wrathful deities, the nine white deities, and Gongkhukma of Rechung. And at the feet of the supreme refuge, Ling Rinpoché Vajradhara, I also received instruction on *Ocean of Attainments of the Generation Stage of Guhyasamāja*.[173] In the rainy-season session I went to Ganden, where at the request of Phara Tulku of Ganden

Jangtsé, I gave an experiential discourse on the *Guru Puja* and mahāmudrā to an audience of former and current abbots of Jangtsé and Shartsé colleges, tulkus, and monks, more than five hundred in number, in the Phara House assembly hall.

One day during the following winter, my root guru, Phabongkha Vajradhara, sent a message to Lhasa via his attendant Namdak-la that he was going to give a detailed discourse on the generation and completion stages of Cittamaṇi Tārā, that it would be best if I came as such teachings would be difficult to receive later, and that I could stay at the retreat residence of his labrang. I left for Tashi Chöling Hermitage immediately, where I received instructions on the root text of the sādhanas of Cittamaṇi Tārā, which is a divine vision of Takphu Vajradhara, with detailed instruction on both the generation and completion stages, associated activities, and the rite for bringing rain based on commentarial texts on generation and completion composed by that lama.

At the conclusion of the teachings, I received oral instructions on the complete ritual practices related to Shukden, and saying "For the sake of auspiciousness," he gave me transmission of oral advice with detailed teachings on the methods for gaining longevity through reliance on vajra recitation of wind in connection with the longevity deity White Heruka. As I mentioned above, had Guru Vajradhara not called me for these profound teachings, I would have been deprived of them because I was involved in prayer services in Lhasa. The kindness shown to me by the father lama in holding me with his rope of compassion is as weighty as the mass of Mount Meru.

The previous year, Kyabjé Vajradhara had started having ominous dreams, and his tense looks indicated that he wished to depart to another place. So as soon as his teaching concluded, we senior incarnate lamas, including Ling Rinpoché, Demo Rinpoché, Drakri Rinpoché, Sharpa Rinpoché, and others, discussed among ourselves the idea of asking him to accept a long-life offering. Once it was settled, an elaborate long-life offering of White Heruka with ritual invocation and banishment of ḍākinī escorts was made together with all the lamas, geshés, and resident monks of the Tashi Chöling Hermitage in its assembly hall. Conjoined with the offering were our requests that his body, speech, and mind remain steadfast like an indestructible vajra throughout existence, glowing with the light of the blessings of benefit and joy, like the great life-sustaining vitality that preserves the precious Dharma in general and in its particulars. He replied to our prayer, saying, "Whatever obstacles there may have been must certainly vanish due to the ḍākinī long-life offering made by this assembly of many of my great disciples," and that Vajradhara himself will consider this to be the case. His good reply seems to have been interpretable, with the motive to soothe our minds.

On the morning of the first day of the first month of my forty-first year, the year of the iron-snake (1941), I recited upon invitation the mandala description and offered the eight auspicious symbols and substances as well as reciting inaugural words of truth at the private ceremony for the inauguration as regent of Tutor Takdrak Vajradhara. This took place at his Lhasa residence, Kunsang Phodrang, prior to the actual ceremony of investiture to the seat of regency in the Potala Palace in place of Regent Radreng Rinpoché, who had resigned as regent in the twelfth month of the previous year. I performed my duties at the ceremony satisfactorily.

That year Kyabjé Phabongkha Vajradhara made offerings to the assembly at the Great Prayer Festival. I, too, made offerings, and coincidentally we both had an audience with His Holiness the Dalai Lama on the same day to present him his share of offerings. I was supposed to sit to the front of Guru Vajradhara according to the hierarchy of my rank as Tsokchen Tulku, but I attempted to move to a seat behind him. However, Vajradhara told me to sit where I was because there are always exceptions to the rule, and so I sat there feeling very uncomfortable and nervous throughout the ceremony.

When the Great Prayer Festival concluded, I thought, "It is not right that on the tenth of each month an imagined image of guru Cakrasaṃvara is my object of worship when the real guru is physically here near me, working for the benefit of sentient beings. It will be more meaningful to make offerings to the root guru who is the embodiment of all refuges, whose presence represents the mandala of the vajra body, with all the bodily elements complete in the nature of ḍākas and ḍākinīs, who is someone to whom the offerings can actually be made and by whom they can actually be consumed." So on the twenty-fifth of the first month, I invited my only source of hope and refuge, Guru Vajradhara, and his retinue to my house for a feast in order to accumulate merit. With great pleasure, he stayed in leisure, satisfying the party, which relished myriad sublime flavors of nectar speech that radiated forth as the holy Dharma, each part of every word being noble in

Regent Takdrak Vajradhara, Lhasa, November 9, 1950
GETTY IMAGES

meaning. At one point he commented that "If His Holiness the present Dalai Lama encounters no obstacle to his life, he will rival Kalsang Gyatso, the Great Seventh Dalai Lama. Should you be called upon to serve him, you must serve him to the best of your ability." This seems to have been spoken as a prophecy, given that I later was called upon to serve him as an assistant tutor and then tutor, a service that I have continued to perform these many long years.

As Lady Yangzom Tsering of Lhalu Gatsal household had a long-standing request for Kyabjé Vajradhara to install outer, inner, and secret statues and the thread-cross abode of Shukden in their protector chapel, Vajradhara instructed me to make ready arrangements for installation of the thread cross. So I gathered the necessary items in advance and completed the preparations. That year, just after the Great Prayer Festival,

Kyabjé Vajradhara, along with eight monks from Tashi Chöling and myself as assistant, performed elaborate rituals at Lhalu Gatsal for three days. On that occasion, I received the life entrustment for Shukden together with Finance Minister Lhalu Gyurmé Tsewang Dorjé and his wife.

On the eve of Guru Vajradhara's departure from Lhalu to bestow teachings on the stages of the path at Dakpo Shedrup Ling by way of Chaksam Tsechu, I offered him my brocade monk's robe embroidered with a flower design motif, strung with a net of small pearls, and a ceremonial scarf together with mandala offering. These offerings were made primarily for him to live a long life as a protector of the teachings and all beings, such as myself, and also to offer thanks to him in advance for the composition of Shukden thread-cross rituals of providing a base, satisfying, and repelling, as well as rituals of the same protector on the torma of expelling, fire offering, and increasing wealth. He said that this would be difficult for him to do and that based on my understanding and notes, I should compile the texts. He gave me instructions on how to compose the texts, telling me to compile the ritual with the necessary supplements from other relevant ritual sources. In essence, he said that it was up to me to complete his work regarding this protector of Dharma, and therefore he was charging me with that responsibility. My thought at the time was that he was telling me this because he had little time for the work himself due to his busy schedule. Little did I realize that he was conveying to me his implicit wish that I finish his life's work. It was just as when, though the Buddha said that, if requested three times, "Tathāgatas, if they so wish, can remain for eons and eons," Ānanda, obscured by evil influences, failed to request him to stay. How I regret not asking him to live longer.

Appointment as Assistant Tutor and the Passing of Phabongkha Rinpoché

The very next day I received a summons from the office of the Norbulingka Palace saying that Trijang Tulku and Sera Mé Gyalrong Geshé Khyenrap Gyatso should come to the palace. When we arrived we were told through the lord chamberlain that the precious regent had appointed me an assistant tutor in place of Ling Rinpoché, who had been promoted to the position of tutor to His Holiness the Dalai Lama, and that Sera Mé Gyalrong Geshé Khyenrap Gyatso would assume the role of adjunct tutor. And that given these changes in title, from that time on it would be appropriate for Trijang Tulku to sit at the head of the row of senior monastic officials of the government, as had Ling Rinpoché before him, and for Geshé Khyenrap Gyatso to sit among the ranks of adjunct tutors, in order of seniority.

On an auspicious day, I appeared for an audience before His Holiness the Dalai Lama and the regent. Subsequently, on the fifteenth day of the fourth month, during the daily morning tea session in the sunlight room of the Norbulingka Palace, Geshé Khyenrap Gyatso and I presented to His Holiness and the regent silk scarves and offerings of the holy body, speech, and mind and other gifts, along with token offerings of funds for rice and tea. Following the audience, we sat in our designated seats for the tea session. That day I received well-wishers who came to offer their congratulations. Every day thereafter I fulfilled my obligation to attend the daily tea sessions and special government functions, just as all government officials must.

After several days had passed, at the behest of the precious regent, I was asked to instruct His Holiness in reading cursive and printed letters and to train him in memorization of daily prayers and religious recitations, on account of the increasing official duties of the precious regent, and to also do so whenever Kyabjé Ling Rinpoché was unavailable. On an auspicious day, with a ceremonial scarf and ritual offerings of the holy body, speech, and mind in hand, I bowed at the feet of His Holiness and began his lesson with an auspicious verse. From then on I came to serve him whenever there was time in the morning and sometimes in the evening between visits from the two tutors. I shifted my permanent residence to a room in the assistant tutors' quarters.

His Holiness seemed a bit shy on my first visit, as his personal attendants had apparently mentioned that Trijang Tulku had a short temper. On the advice of the precious regent, for my part I maintained a serious expression and did not smile. Because His Holiness was so young, when he did not properly attend to his daily memorization of texts, I would scold his elder brother Losang Samten with a grave countenance, chiding him for distracting his younger brother. This much always sufficed, so I never had to utter unpleasant words to His Holiness.

The all-embracing lord of all mandalas and buddha families, Kyabjé Phabongkha Vajradhara, set out from the Lhalu household, stopped off to give a Dharma discourse at Chaksam Tsechu Monastery in Chushul, and then pressed on to Dakpo Shedrup Ling, where at the conclusion of his discourse on the *Great Treatise on the Stages of the Path*, he passed into the sphere of peace during the evening of the first day of the sixth month. The news of his passing came like a thorn in my ear; it was like the sudden, unbidden lightning strike of past deeds to have to suffer the misfortune and sorrow of being parted from my peerless, kind lama. Tormented by unbearable grief, I prayed for the accomplishment of his wishes and made as many offerings as I could at the Tsuklakhang and elsewhere in Lhasa.

At the request of Trinlé Dargyé, my guru's nephew, I went to Tashi Chöling Hermitage to do a divination to determine whether the precious body would be preserved intact or cremated. Seeing the hermitage and his residence overcast by a grey pall and bare and his room vacant of his presence, tears streamed from my eyes. In this state of mourning, I performed the divination before the sacred statue of Dakpo Lama Rinpoché,[174] and the result was to cremate. Therefore I sent Losang Chöphel, the senior resident of Tashi Chöling, to Dakpo with careful instructions on how to serve his body.

Miscellaneous Duties and Teachings

At the wish of our refuge and protector the regent, I served a few years in a managerial capacity, along with the adjunct tutor from Sera Mé, overseeing the carving of new editions and reprinting at the Shöl printing press in Lhasa of rare texts from various places in Tibet, such as the collected works of Thuken Chökyi Nyima, Gungthang Tenpai Dronmé, and Jé Sherap Gyatso.[175] I also oversaw the completion of two great brocade appliqués sponsored by the government that would be displayed on the annual day of procession during the Subsequent Prayer Session and that were being made to replace two older ones, which were worn out after many years of use. I drew the grids for the bodies of the deities, performed the ritual of generating the artists as deities, and visited the workshop daily as the actual production was being carried out to carefully check proportions of the likenesses, correcting any mistakes.

Over the course of that year, the number of my relatives and associations increased. Even Ani Yangzom, who had been so mean to my mother, now made a show of respect toward me and expressed affection for my mother. As someone once said in homage to money, "Here's the uncle I never had!

I bow to you, O bundle of money!" Such were those apparent friends and kinsmen. The tendency to gravitate toward those who are up and to neglect those who are down is the natural disposition of ordinary folk, as Jamgön Sakya Paṇḍita wrote:

> When you are wealthy, everyone is your friend,
> but if you are poor, all become your enemies.
> A jeweled isle brings people from afar,
> but everyone leaves a dried-up lake.[176]

On the tenth day of the first month of my forty-second year, the year of the water-horse (1942), Regent Takdrak Rinpoché, acting as preceptor and master, conferred prenovitiate and novice vows on His Holiness at the Lhasa Tsuklakhang Temple. At the ceremony, I made the request to the assembly of monks for permission to confer the ordination.

Immediately following the Subsequent Prayer Session, I gave initiations of Guhyasamāja, Cakrasaṃvara, and Vajrabhairava, complete with their preparation rituals, to a gathering of more than two thousand in the Changlochen assembly hall of the Gyümé Tantric College in Lhasa. Present were all the monks from Gyümé and an assembly who had joined them from Gyütö Tantric College and the three seats of learning. This was at the request of a group of new monks from the Gyümé Tantric College who had received their full ordination, for it was the custom for groups of new bhikṣus at Gyumé to pool funds to make offerings, present objects to the monastery, and sponsor religious teachings and initiations.

During the rainy-season retreat, at the command of the precious regent, I worked on detailed catalogs of Indian and Tibetan pandits whose works came from all over Tibet, China, and Mongolia and were kept at the Druzin palace of the Norbulingka. I reviewed the previous catalogs of the handwritten and printed texts and prepared new catalogs of the new acquisitions of large collections of works of lamas and miscellaneous texts. Aside from composing catalogs for the collected works of the various lamas, I spent more than two months doing the same for miscellaneous other works, such as lists of teachings received, philosophical works (on Logic and Epistemology, Madhyamaka, Perfection of Wisdom, Vinaya, Abhidharma, and so on), sutra-level texts on the stages of the path, mind training, and so on, works on tantra such as rituals and guidebooks on the various collections of the old and new translations of tantras, as well as works of biography, religious history, history of Tibet, grammar, poetry, medicine, and astrology.

In the eighth month, I presided over the elaborate consecration of the memorial stupa containing the bone relics of Kyabjé Vajradhara at Tashi Chöling. The manager Trinlé Dargyé bore the burden of constructing the stupa, and over the course of performing the three-day consecration of Vajrabhairava together with the resident hermit monks of Tashi Chöling, I took every care, in the capacity of vajra master, to complete the ritual successfully without any negligence. During the passage for honoring the sponsors at the end of the consecration, I recalled the guru's kindness and took up the song called "Elegy for a Child Wandering on the Plain" as an appeal for the quick return of the supreme emanation. A section of the root text of Kālacakra tantra that embraces the qualities of the guru says:

> Virtues accumulated for the dead
> by the relatives who survive
> will ripen like a calf that follows
> its mother wherever she goes.
>
> Likewise, if faithful disciples observe and make offerings
> on the deceased guru's monthly and yearly anniversaries,
> his wishes will be perfectly met,
> and his disciples will follow in his footsteps.

Geshé Potowa said, "I commemorated the late Dromtönpa's death nineteen times. I expect to meet him in the next life." So I offered a fund to the assembled monks of Tashi Chöling to perform as a regular memorial ritual a *Guru Puja* and tsok in association with self-initiation into Cakrasaṃvara on the first of every month every year thereafter.

At the end of autumn that year, as requested by Khenchen Dönpalwa (a.k.a. Tashi Lingpa Khyenrap Wangchuk), I gave an explanation of the *Quick Path* and the *Words of Mañjuśrī* accompanied by a puja for generating bodhicitta to a crowd of three thousand monks and lamas in the assembly hall of Meru Monastery in Lhasa.

In the third month of my forty-third year, the year of the water-sheep (1943), at the request of Trinlé Dargyé, manager of Phabongkha Labrang, I gave an experiential explanation of the *Quick Path* and the *Words of*

Mañjuśrī over the course of a month to a gathering of three thousand monks and laypeople in the assembly hall of Meru Monastery, concluding with a puja for generating bodhicitta in the Meru courtyard. Following that, as requested by Trimön Chözé Thupten Deshek, the incumbent chant master of Namgyal Monastery, and Kalsang Wangyal, the ritual master, I taught the *Easy Path* for fifteen days to a gathering of more than seven hundred monks in the Sang-ngak Gatsal assembly hall of Namgyal Monastery, at the conclusion of which I offered initiations into Cakrasaṃvara, Vajrabhairava, Guhyasamāja, and the Great Compassionate One, with permission to practice Mahākāla, Dharmarāja, Palden Lhamo, Kubera, Four-Faced Mahākāla, Chamsing, and so on.

During the rainy-season retreat, I completed my duties as the resident abbot, and after its conclusion I went to Yaphu Ratsak Monastery in Kyishö, where I spent three days making extensive offerings in connection with the self-initiation rituals in the presence of the Vajrayoginī statue that glows with the light of blessings. This statue was the principal object of meditation of the great pandit Nāropa. I made a donation to the community of monks there and also left them funds, asking that they perform the offerings of the tenth and twenty-fifth of the month. At the request of nun Khyenrap Lhamo, I gave the blessing of the four sindūra initiations of Vajrayoginī to a gathering of a hundred monks and nuns.

At that time I had a few vivid, good dreams, but I cannot remember them now. In general, when I was young, and sometimes when I was older, too, various and sundry indistinct prophetic verses of various length were spoken to me, or shown written on scrolls, by all sorts of deities, lamas, and ordinary folk in my dreams. If the following day I let slip talk of the prophecies, I would immediately forget them. But if I didn't speak of them, I wouldn't forget them, and they would later come true, just as they did for the pig-headed fortune teller.[177] That after some time these dreams would come only rarely is, I feel, because I am saturated like drenched earth with offerings, which acts as an obstacle to such dreams.

Pilgrimage to Phenpo

In the autumn, with the permission of His Holiness and the precious regent, I went on a pilgrimage to the Phenpo area, which has been blessed by many realized Kadampa masters. I left with a small entourage, including my attendants Lhabu and Palden, and Ngakram Tsultrim Dargyé from Trehor House of Gyümé Tantric College. We crossed Gola Pass into Phenpo and visited such places as Langthang, the monastery of Geshé Langri Thangpa; Nalendra, the monastery of omniscient Rongtönpa; the reliquary stupa of Patsap Lotsāwa; Gyal Temple, which was built by Nanam Dorjé Wangchuk, an incarnation of Maitreya; Thangsak Ganden Chökhor; and the reliquary stupa of Geshé Sharawa.

Since it was well known that, given Patsap's connection with translating the *Long Life Sutra* (*Aparimitāyurjñānasūtra*), if one circumambulates Patsap's stupa, hindrances to one's life would be eliminated, many people were on the circumambulation circuit. I accumulated a moderate number of circumambulations in appreciation of his propagation of the profound view with his translation of Candrakīrti's *Entrance to the Middle Way* and his contribution to the dissemination of the Prāsaṅgika view.[178]

Previously I had heard from Kyabjé Phabongkha Vajradhara that when Simok Rinpoché Jampa Kunga Tenzin—holder of the treasury of ear-whispered lineage of the highly secret instructions of the Sakyas—first paid a visit to Chusang Retreat House, though he knew that Simok Rinpoché carried the personal instructions on the permissions and transmission of the seventeen emanations of Four-Faced Mahākāla, Kyabjé Phabongkha did not pay much attention to him, being doubtful due to underestimating the qualities of that great person. On the eve of Simok Rinpoché's departure, Phabongkha Vajradhara dreamed of a formidable old man with white hair, moustache, and beard sitting on a large throne. This old man looked greatly displeased with him for neglecting to receive the oral teachings of Four-Faced Mahākāla. So the very next day Vajradhara requested full initiation, transmission, and oral teachings, eventually receiving them. Because I heard of this incident from Guru Vajradhara himself, I had great respect and faith in Simok Rinpoché.

As Rinpoché permanently resided in Phenpo, I had not previously met him, but at that time I had the good fortune of actually looking upon his golden face when I visited him at his house at Nalendra, where I made him a token offering and requested him to give me the profound teachings. He promised to do so with great pleasure and showered me with gifts of food.

At the same time, I visited Chogyé Labrang at their invitation and met the present Chogyé Trichen Rinpoché. At Thangsak Ganden Chökhor Monastery I offered the sangha a reading transmission of the *Foundation of*

Kyabjé Simok Rinpoché of Phenpo Nalendra
COURTESY OF WWW.NALANDRA.ORG

All Good Qualities. There I was able to view an Indian text of Candrakīrti's *Bright Lamp* commentary on the five stages of the Guhyasamāja completion stage. This was the text used by the pandit Candrakīrti himself.

Although the Khamlung Tulku prior to the current one, who was a reincarnation of Throneholder Jampal Tsultrim and was my elder brother by the same father, had already passed away, since his labrang had invited me, I went to Khamlung Hermitage, the monastery of the great Geshé Khamlungpa.[179] I stayed for three days and visited the memorial stupa of Khamlungpa. It was impossible to visit some of the monastic seats of other Kadam masters, such as Neusurpa, because they were in remote mountains and caves.

As I had been invited by the family of Lhading in Upper Uru county, passing through Jeri Taktsé in Lower Phenpo, I reached the town of Lhading. As it happened to be the tenth of the month, I made an offering of tsok along with the self-initiation into Vajrayoginī together with the members of the Lhading family. At the request of the host, Rimshi Sönam Tsering, I sang "Song of the Playful Bumblebee":

Up in the heavenly realm of Khecara Akaniṣṭha,
amid a display of ten million inconceivable illusory nets,
the queen of the Conqueror's consorts, with her extraordinary
youthful charm,
guides the fortunate to Khecara paradise.

In the city of ḍākinīs, the *e* realm of the sixty-four,[180]
the most beautiful queen, Caṇḍālī, with delightful smile,
graceful and lithe, dances playfully like a lightning flash,
presenting a show of the joyfully innate *evaṃ*.

Amid the eight petals of the heart (*citta*) at the central channel
(*avadhūti*),
clear-light Ratī of the great emptiness, devoid of all fabrication,
teases seductively with her youth of illusory form, a light ray of
five colors,
presenting a show of the inconceivable stage of union.

A ho! Delightful is this profound quick path to the ultimate
secrets.
Joyful is this assembly of master and disciples with pure bonds.
In this glorious offering feast unifying joy and delight,
we establish a coming together that will never be parted.

I spent a few days and gave the blessing of the four sindūra initiations of Vajrayoginī to the members of the family and monks from the nearby monasteries. I also gave the permission for Avalokiteśvara, a long-life empowerment, and so on, to the locals. To the sangha of Thangkya Monastery, I offered at their request the great initiation into thirteen-deity Vajrabhairava.

On the way home from Lhading, I consecrated the temple at Phakmo Chödé as requested by the sangha. Passing through Dromtö thereafter, I arrived back in Lhasa. As I mentioned above, I spread clouds of offerings to various sacred places of pilgrimage and to monasteries to the best of my ability.

6 | Black Clouds on the Horizon

Travels to Kundeling and Tölung

In the fourth month of my forty-fourth year, the year of the wood-monkey (1944), I gave teachings on the *Great Treatise on the Stages of the Path* to over one thousand disciples in the assembly hall of Kundeling Monastery for one month at the request of Kundeling Tatsak Hothokthu Rinpoché.

In the summer Minister Taiji Shenkha Gyurmé Sönam Topgyé requested me to give initiations into Guhyasamaja, Cakrasaṃvara, and Vajrabhairava for the benefit of his late son, Dechen Gawai Wangchuk. I gave the initiations to about three thousand disciples for five days in the assembly hall of Meru Monastery in Lhasa.

In the eighth month, I went to the hot springs in Tölung for the sake of my health. At that time, the monks of the Gyümé Tantric College happened to be observing the late summer retreat in the nearby Chumik Valley, so at the invitation of the abbots and administrators of the monastery, I stopped by the monastery along the way. I offered the monks a reading transmission of two of the three textbooks on the five stages of Guhyasamāja that are unique to Gyümé. These three are renowned as the Three Stones Passed from Hand to Hand.[181] I presented the assembly with many donations.

I spent two weeks at the hot springs, where I met some people from Tölung Rakor, the birthplace of my predecessor, and I gave them some small gifts.

Soon after my return from Tölung, at the request of Mrs. Tsering Drölkar of the Bayer family, who were staying in the Mentö household, over the course of just a month I gave personal instructions on the *Quick Path* in connection with the *Words of Mañjuśrī*, along with offerings and the ceremony for generating bodhicitta to a gathering of around twenty-seven hundred in the assembly hall of Lhasa's Shidé Monastery. The assembly was comprised of tulkus and geshés from the three monastic seats, their students, and monks from the Gyütö and Gyümé tantric colleges as well as retreat centers.

I sent four large pillar banners of multicolored brocade appliqué in the *takshun* design, with large dragons, accompanied with appliqué forms of *tsipar* heads to be hung on the four tall pillars in the assembly hall of my monastery in Chatreng and sent a complete set of the Kangyur along with covers to Dongsum Riknga House.

A Dispute Breaks Out

If one does not avert pride in one's reputation, attire, pedigree, and status, it is difficult for a river to flow upward on a hill of arrogance unless one seeks out advice and teachings from the wise.

That winter, having invited a teacher from Lhasa's Astro-Medical Institute—a monk named Palden Gyaltsen who hailed from Yangpachen in Tölung—to my residential quarters above the Potala's school of administration, I, together with Dzemé Tulku of Ganden Shartsé, requested instruction on both Anubhūti's *Sarasvatī Grammar Treatise* (*Sarasvatīvyākaraṇa*) and its commentary *Hundred Rays of Light* by Getsé Paṇḍita Gyurmé Tsewang Chokdrup, up to the section on the five types of *sandhi*. We also studied the root text *Ratnākara's Prosody* (*Chandoratnākara*), written by the pandit Ratnākaraśānti, and its commentaries by Minling Lochen and Lama Lhaksam, up to picture prosody (*citrakavya*).[182] We were unable to fully complete the picture prosody portion due to the proliferation of distractions beyond our control.

In the tenth month of that year, fighting broke out in connection with barley debt due to a disagreement between the steward of senior secretary Chöphel Thupten's Lhundrup Dzong estate in Phenpo and Sera Jé's debt collectors, and the steward died. The senior secretary filed a report of the incident with the regent, a commission of six monastic and lay officials was appointed, and having summoned the chief culprit, details began to emerge. The investigation of this incident took place around the time of the Great Prayer Festival in Lhasa of the wood-bird year (1945), during which Tsemönling Hothokthu had invited His Holiness to preside over the assembly, as this was also the time of Tsemönling's offering for his geshé examination. There was an incident when the abbots and monks of Sera's Jé and tantric colleges boycotted the sessions for three days during the festival. An official order setting out the grave consequences of their actions of contempt was issued by the ecclesiastical offices at the Potala. Only then was the festival barely held as usual.

At the completion of the Prayer Festival and Subsequent Prayer Session, when the investigation concluded, the abbots of Jé and Ngakpa colleges were expelled along with a few of the administrators and debt collectors, who were exiled to confinement in faraway districts. On account of this, many of the monks of Jé and Ngakpa colleges badmouthed the precious regent and accrued heavy karma due to the actions of a few bad individuals. In addition, because of the expulsion of some officials who were close to Radreng Rinpoché, it was a time when bonds between guru and disciple were broken. I disliked all these events very much and gave very frank and honest advice in order to prevent further hardship for Regent Takdrak's treasurer, Tenpa Tharchin, but I could not stop it. As Sakya Paṇḍita says in his *Jewel Treasury of Wise Sayings*:

> However you may try to reverse a waterfall,
> you must accept that it only flows downward.[183]

The Ritual to Transfer Lhamo's Shrine at Drepung

In my forty-fifth year, the year of the wood-bird (1945), the government performed extensive restoration of the Ganden Phodrang Palace at Drepung Monastery. When the preparations for the demolition of the rooms on the upper floor of the western complex of the palace were ready, the protector house of the sealed statue of Gotra Lhamo (Raktamukha Devī), which is kept in a chamber of the palace, had to be moved temporarily. The precious regent told me that this protector is known to be very strict in her commands. Anyone who took even a mere scarf offered to the statue experienced immediate negative consequences. Therefore I was entrusted to oversee the proper ritual performance for the removal of the statue during the renovation phase.

After the Subsequent Prayer Session in Lhasa, I left for Drepung with the presiding master and chant master of Namgyal Monastery as ritual assistants and made propitiatory offerings to Palden Lhamo for a few days. The night before moving the chamber I dreamed I was in a huge assembly hall filled with thread-cross effigies and many large old and new torma cakes. It was so full of heaps of various things that I could find no place to step. As I looked for a path, a young lady came and, moving with a pleasing gait, showed me the way. I took this dream as a sign that the goddess was pleased and that it was time to move the protector chapel.

The next morning during the actual transfer, we opened the protector chamber in the presence of the monk-official secretary who was representing His Holiness. At first the others hesitated to touch the sacred objects and would not move them. Although I lack confidence in the view of emptiness and any meditative insight, since I had done the approaching retreat of Palden Lhamo, maintaining confidence in my being a meditational deity and in the dream I had had the previous night, I took a few objects and some scarves and moved them to the sunlight room of the palace, all the while reciting the mantra of Palden Lhamo.

Afterward, everyone—the presiding and chant masters of Namgyal Monastery (my ritual assistants), the overseer of construction and his staff, as well as the representative of His Holiness—moved the various objects, such as taxidermied animals, that had accumulated in large quantities over the years. This took three days. We then moved the main image of Palden Lhamo, which was the size of a man and was made of silver, with a representation of the sea of blood and included her mule mount and the background fire, measuring one story in height. The two attendants, one with the face of a lion and the other with the face of a *makara* sea monster, were each the size of an eight-year-old child. As the statues had originally been made individually, it did not end up being difficult to move them.

Once we had separated the main body of the statue from the sea of blood and the mule, the statue was invited to one of the rooms in the eastern wing of the palace. During the transfer I had the Namgyal monks do the elaborate invocation of Palden Lhamo, with melodious chanting together with ritual music. I along with the overseer of the restoration, the senior secretary Ngawang Söpa, and the representative of His Holiness led the procession with incense in our hands. The senior tulkus and some of the older geshés from the four colleges of Drepung carried the statue. After assembling the statue, we made a ritual of mending and restoration before the statue with extensive propitiatory and tsok offerings.

We pried open a large box containing various thangka scroll paintings that had been in the protector chapel. Inside we discovered an extremely old painting of Vajrabhairava with stacked heads that had been the personal devotional meditation object of Ra Lotsāwa and was in keeping with the *Ra Lotsāwa Collection on Vajrabhairava: Oral Transmission of the Ḍākinīs.*[184] There was also a copy of a similar thangka that the Fifth Dalai Lama had commissioned from Sur Ngakchang Trinlé Namgyal (these being both the original and its copy) and a painting of the Guardian of the Tent in standing position that was the personal meditational object of Drogön Chögyal Phakpa.[185] There were many wonderful historical paintings, including a thangka of Rishi Viṣnu hand painted by Surchen Chöying Rangdrol.[186] Moreover, there were several thangka images of Four-Faced Mahākāla and the Tent Guardian that were the personal meditation objects of some of the prior Sakya patriarchs.

In one of the cabinets for ritual cake offerings, there were some requests to the protectors written in the hand of His Holiness Tsangyang Gyatso[187] and replies to a few of the questions that he presented to the protector Lamo Tsangpa on various political matters. It also contained several rolls of flowery letters written to intimate friends in the manner of tantric conduct. His handwriting was of fair quality, but the verses he composed were excellent.

At the same time as the palace at Drepung was being restored, the palace of His Holiness at Gephel Hermitage was also to be restored. So I went to that monastery one day and did the rituals for the transfer of those deities and nāgas and the consecration ritual for construction. During these not even one among our staff, myself included, suffered any serious mishap, and I credit this success to the divine protection of the Three Jewels and the goddess protector.

Later, when the restoration of the palace at Drepung was complete, I went there with the ritual assistants of Namgyal Monastery, and we moved the statues, including that of Palden Lhamo, and the sacred objects back to the protector chapel in the renovated palace and made extensive propitiating offerings accompanied by tsok offerings over the course of seven days. Previously there had been no thread-cross abode of Palden Lhamo in the protector chamber, but as a new one had been commanded, we constructed a complete, elegant thread-cross and performed an extensive ritual for it.

That summer, in fulfillment of a request by Kusho Tserap of Namgyal

Monastery, with the aim of sowing roots of virtue for his late mother Palkyi, I taught the *Quick Path* and the *Words of Mañjuśrī* in association with its experiential commentary to an audience of more than a thousand, including the entire assembly of Namgyal Monastery, in the Jaraklingka park, where the monks of Namgyal Monastery spend their annual picnic at the conclusion of the rainy-season retreats. At the end, on the day of the ceremony for generating bodhicitta, the Dharma protector of Lhasa's Darpo Ling, Lord Chingkar, inhabiting his medium proclaimed, "Your recent discourse on the stages of the path was excellent!" He also advised the administrators of Namgyal Monastery, saying, "Beginning next year, the general assembly of Namgyal Monastery must take up the task of requesting teaching on the stages of the path and on the commentaries to the generation and completion stages of Guhyasamāja, Cakrasaṃvara, and Vajrabhairava in turn every year, without break."

That year, at the beginning of autumn, as requested by the previously mentioned Mrs. Tsering Drölkar of the Bayer family, at Lhasa's Shidé Monastery I extensively taught the profound path of *Guru Puja* and mahāmudrā combined, with its associated profound commentary, to more than two thousand monks from Sera, Drepung, and the Gyütö and Gyümé tantric colleges who had previously received initiation into the deities Guhyasamāja, Cakrasaṃvara, and Vajrabhairava.

A New Appointment

In the winter, the precious regent appointed Gyatso Ling Tulku of Gungru House of Gomang College as assistant tutor with the rank of senior ecclesiastical secretary,[188] and I was promoted to the rank of Darhan, which required me to sit before officials with ranks of Dzasak, Ta Lama, and Taiji.[189] On the occasion of my advancement to the new position of Darhan, I made offerings to His Holiness and the regent in accordance with ancient tradition.

In my forty-sixth year, the year of the fire-dog (1946), during the Great Prayer Festival, I invoked the divine presence of the Nechung protector through his medium in a trance at the temple in old Meru Monastery. The Nechung oracle gave me a scarf with the representations of the body, speech, and mind and expressed great pleasure and appreciation for the discourses I had been giving. He said that it was great that I was propagating the profound and the vast nectar-like teachings of the incomparable leader and son of Śuddhodana (i.e., Buddha Śākyamuni) at such a crucial time.

His Holiness was to commence his dialectical studies at Drepung in accordance with tradition, but a private rehearsal ceremony was held in the Ganden Yangtsé chamber of the Potala Palace. This was presided over by His Holiness in the center, with Regent Takdrak Rinpoché, Tutor Ling Rinpoché, myself, Gyatso Ling, and Geshé Khyenrap Gyatso of Sera Mé sitting in rows to the right and left. Everyone recited *Praise to the Buddha* and *Chanting the Names of Mañjuśrī.*

Because Gyatso Ling and Geshé Khyenrap Gyatso recited the texts at such disparate pitches, one high the other low, Ling Rinpoché burst into laughter. This made His Holiness laugh, and I also began to laugh uncontrollably, and the recitation was nearly interrupted. Though Regent Rinpoché wore a serious expression on his face, I could not stop laughing, even out of fear. Others present, including the chief abbot, his chief attendant, his assistant, the ritual assistant, and the lord chamberlain, all also laughed uncontrollably, like the maxim "one laughs if you look at someone else laughing." I later took this to be a sign His Holiness would attain the pinnacle of scholarly studies.

From that day forward, every day, in turn, we three serving scholars presided over His Holiness's dialectical study each afternoon, with the exception of break periods during special and scheduled government ceremonies. We were also permitted leaves of absence in exceptional cases to give teachings.

Regarding the reincarnation of my sole father in unrivaled kindness, the great Phabongkha Vajradhara: as the visions of Nakshö Takphu Rinpoché, the predictions of the Panglung Gyalchen and Gadong oracles, and my own repeated divinations were found to be in agreement, the young reincarnation, who had taken rebirth at Drigung in upper Ü, was brought to Tashi Chöling Monastery at the beginning of the second month and formally placed upon the throne of his lofty predecessor. I was present on that occasion and attended the ceremony and made offerings.

At the beginning of the third month, at the request of a group of newly ordained monks of Gyümé Tantric College, I offered initiations into Guhyasamāja, Cakrasaṃvara, and Vajrabhairava along with their preparatory rites, and explanation and transmission of Aśvaghoṣa's *Fifty Verses on Guru Devotion*, for five days to a large number of monks, primarily from

Gyütö and Gyümé tantric colleges, in the Gyümé assembly hall. At the command of Regent Takdrak Vajradhara, I compiled and edited the recitation texts of the three observances of the Vinaya monastic rules of discipline and other sutra and tantra texts recited by the monks of Takdrak Hermitage. In particular I compiled the ritual chant of the elaborate consecration, Causing the Rain of Goodness to Fall, in accordance with the tradition of the Gyümé Tantric College and the self- and front-generations, the consecration of the vase, and initiation and fire-offering rituals of Guhyasamāja Lokeśvara.

Likewise, the monks of Gyümé Tantric College had requested that the precious regent recompile their manual for subjugating demons based on the Dharmarāja rite composed by Drakar Ngakrampa,[190] since there were various readings, notes, and emendations on handwritten copies that were more reliable. Since he had no free time, he told me to do it. I therefore examined all the relevant materials, particularly chapters of Drakar Ngakram's own commentary, and compiled a reliable chanting ritual for subjugating demons called *A Yantra Wall of Vajra Mountains*.[191]

In early summer, to sow seeds of virtue on behalf of lay practitioner Tsewang Norbu at the request of Mrs. Lhamo Tsering, who lived below the meat market in Lhasa, I gave a discourse on the *Quick Path* for twenty-five days to over three thousand. This discourse was given under a large canopy in the Jarak picnic grounds of Namgyal Monastery. Following that, at the request of Namgyal Monastery, I gave discourses for fifteen days on the two stages of thirteen-deity Vajrabhairava to over one thousand disciples who had received the Vajrabhairava initiation and an explanation of the construction of the three-dimensional mandala. Scattered throughout the discourse, I gave explanations on the visualization of the fire-offering ritual, the sixty-four-part torma offering, and the great torma ritual and their different traditions and methods. I explained these as thoroughly as I myself had learned them from oral teachings without concealing anything.

Although Namgyal Monastery preserved excellent traditions of the sand and cloth mandalas for Guhyasamāja, Cakrasaṃvara, and Vajrabhairava, they did not have a tradition of instruction for the creation of three-dimensional mandalas. Therefore, in consultation with His Holiness's chief ritual assistant, Losang Samten, and the presiding master, Tenpa Dargyé, I immediately began fresh instruction on the construction of the three-dimensional mandala. I appointed Ngakrampa Tsultrim Dargyé of

Trehor House of Gyümé Tantric College as the principal instructor. Eight Namgyal monks, including the ritual master and the chant master, received thorough training, and the new mandala that they constructed as a result of their training was excellent.

Illness and Schism

I was sick for twenty days during the sixth month of that year with a serious intestinal fever, after which I was very ill with edema. Though I was on the verge of death, I recovered under the treatment of doctor Khyenrap Norbu, senior chair and director of the Tibetan government's Astro-Medical Institute, who was a master equal to the great Yuthok, the king of medicine,[192] and the treatment of His Holiness's personal physician, Khenchung Thupten Lhundrup. My recovery was helped by many religious rituals and the care that I took, but I was still barely able to go outside by the ninth month.

That winter at the request of Chözé Ngawang Dorjé of Trehor Shitsé Gyapöntsang, who was a prominent student at Sera Jé Monastery, and his brother Döndrup Namgyal, I began giving a discourse on the *Easy Path* to a group of about fifty people. Initially I held the discourse in my quarters in the Norbulingka summer palace until one day the lord chamberlain, Khenchung Thupten Lekmön, came to visit me and said: "Teaching the stages of the path to them like that here in the Norbulingka is like locking the door after letting a thief in! It would be better if you stopped for the time being."[193] I therefore moved to my residence in Lhasa and continued to teach there to about one hundred disciples. Since the protector and lord, the precious regent, could have had no such prejudice, as he is a great person, it seems that this must have been due to the lord chamberlain's own small and narrow-minded assumption, causing him to mistake his own shadow for a spirit.

The former regent Radreng Rinpoché and the incumbent regent Takdrak Rinpoché were undisputedly great beings with the highest attainments of abandonment and insight. But buddhas and bodhisattvas appear according to the dispositions of their disciples, in whatever illusory guise will best tame them—demons and devils, the pure and the impure, tamers and those to be tamed.

In my forty-seventh year, the fire-pig year (1947), Radreng Rinpoché and

Takdrak Rinpoché could have no peace with one another on account of the many false rumors of dissension and the provocations of attendants. For Takdrak Rinpoché there was Treasurer Tenpa Tharchin, Chamberlain Thupten Lekmön, and Chairman Ngawang Namgyal. Among Radreng Rinpoché's subordinates, there was his brother the Dzasak, Nyungné Tulku of Shidé, and Khardo Tulku of Sera Jé. As Sakya Paṇḍita's *Jewel Treasury of Wise Sayings* (5.34) says:

A person who constantly strives for dissension
will sever even the firmest of friends.
If water flows continually,
won't even rocks split apart?

It became apparent that the supporters of Radreng Rinpoché were plotting to harm Regent Takdrak Rinpoché, which was the first step toward their own demise. So, as soon as the meeting between the regent and his cabinet adjourned, the ministers Surkhang Wangchen Gelek and Lhalu Tsewang Dorjé were dispatched to Radreng Monastery together with a contingent of soldiers and leaders of the Drashi army base to arrest the former regent. They were dispatched suddenly in the night of the twenty-third of the second month.

I did not hear of this news until noon the next day. At that time, I was living at my residence in Lhasa and the cabinet minister Rampa Thupten Kunkhyen sent a secret message to me saying that I had better go to the Potala right away. He also said that as he needed to stay at the Potala for a few days, he would like to stay in my quarters there. I left for the Potala immediately.

Late that afternoon, at the order of the Tibetan cabinet, the Radreng labrang and the Yapshi Phunkhang mansion were sealed and locked up. The former and incumbent Dzasak of Radreng and the retired minister Gung Tashi Dorjé of Phunkhang, along with his son, were summoned to the Potala, where, stripped of rank and title, they were imprisoned in Sharchen Chok, the Great Eastern Tower prison at the Potala. The following day, the homes of Radreng Labrang's supporters—Khardo Tulku, Nyungné Tulku of Shidé, and the Sadutshang family of Trehor—were locked up, and Khardo and Gyurmé Sadutshang were also imprisoned in Sharchen Chok. Nyungné Lama escaped when arrest was imminent and shot himself.

On the twenty-seventh day of the second month, having been brought over Gola Pass of Phenpo and across the Tsesum plain at the foot of Sera, circled clockwise around the Potala, and in through the eastern gate of Shöl, Radreng Rinpoché was interned in Sharchen Chok, where he remained under heavy guard. Later Radreng Rinpoché was taken for interrogation at the meeting of the National Assembly. From my quarters at the Potala, I saw him taken back and forth through the entrance with the three staircases at Deyangshar Courtyard under tight security. It made me distraught to see such a great lama and leader who previously traveled amid a host of private and government officials in great glory and pomp now living in a dark prison cell without even one attendant, surrounded by soldiers, and having every day to go for interrogation at the National Assembly. I sensed how troubled he must have felt, but there was nothing that I could do.

I heard that Radreng Rinpoché died in prison on the night of the seventeenth of the third month. The inquiry into his case had concluded the previous day, but those attending the meeting disagreed as to his sentence. It isn't clear whether Rinpoché died of his own will in anticipation of a serious punishment or whether there were other unexpected ill circumstances. Later many rumors circulated that he was killed secretly by the leaders of the prison guards. Radreng Rinpoché's brother the Dzasak and Khardo Tulku were kept under arrest in the new prison with two rings of security in the bodyguard unit at the Norbulingka. The two of them were imprisoned for life with manacles, fetters, and wooden yokes around their necks. All the others involved were also given heavy sentences by the National Assembly. Since ex-minister Phunkhang and his son, as well as Gyurmé Sadutshang, had close connections with the Radreng labrang, they were initially suspected and kept under arrest. But later, as it became evident that they had no involvement in the intrigue, their wealth and property were returned, and they were allowed to live in peace.[194]

At that time most of the monks of Sera Jé, including Tsenya Tulku, were conspiring to rise against the government. The monastic officials had no influence in the matter, and there was much unrest. The government sent the cabinet minister Kashöpa Chögyal Nyima, General Dzasak Kalsang Tsultrim, monk-secretary Ngawang Namgyal, the finance minister Ngaphö Ngawang Jikmé, and Namling Paljor Jikmé to the Drashi military encampment, and with armed battalions they marched to Sera Jé and made a show of force. The monks of Sera surrendered, and the conflict was prevented from spreading further.

At Radreng Monastery, attendants of the Radreng labrang killed seventeen soldiers that were guarding the property. General Kalsang Tsultrim and Shakhapa Losal Döndrup, governor of the northern region, were therefore dispatched to Radreng with a large contingent of soldiers. They shelled the seat of Radreng and caused serious damage to the temples, images, and religious objects. Soldiers looted the property of Radreng Labrang, which was comparable to the treasury of Jambhala, god of wealth, and the government confiscated the rest, leaving nothing behind.

Reflecting that the joys and sorrows of samsara are unstable, changing in an instant, like a flicker of lightning, I was deeply moved to renounce forcefully all the meaningless activities of this life and withdraw into the mountains like a wounded deer, to live in the manner of āryas with the four qualities.[195] I could see the need to wholeheartedly dedicate my body, speech, and mind to practice, but because of the firm grip of my attraction to this life, I was not able to sever myself from the allure of distracting activities.

Due to the incidents related above, various prejudiced rumors regarding the precious regent and Radreng Rinpoché were spread by many from both factions. However, there is no certainty with regard to the ordinary perceptions of disciples and the power of their karma. As with what befell the ārya Maudgalyāyana, the arhat Udāyin, and the great king Ralpachen, it is best not to see faults in this situation and to withhold judgment.[196] As the "Friendship" chapter says:

> If those who have done no wrong
> associate with those who have committed evil,
> they arouse suspicion of having done wrong,
> and a bad reputation will accrue.
>
> Those who associate with those they ought not to
> themselves become tainted by the others' faults.
> An arrow, put in a quiver tainted with poison,
> though not stained with poison will become so.[197]

Mañjunātha Sakya Paṇḍita stated:

Noble beings acquire bad habits
when they befriend the wicked.
The sweet water of the Ganges becomes salty
when it reaches the ocean.[198]

As for Lord Regent Takdrak Vajradhara, he is indeed a great wielder of the vajra possessed of the three sets of vows, a lord in the sea of mandalas, and he remains as the great turner of the wheel of holy Dharma. Radreng Rinpoché, as well, while living in Dakpo in his youth, planted a wooden stake in the face of a rock and left the impression of his foot on a stone that was moved to the great chapel at Radreng, where one can examine it for oneself. He therefore is someone who bears true signs of a great being, too.

In general, due to the degenerated merit of living beings, the attendants of both Takdrak Rinpoché and Radreng Rinpoché mentioned above, and those who followed them, drunk on Manmatha's wine,[199] destroyed their present and future happiness. Many people created a tremendous amount of negativity against their gurus and the Three Jewels through their evil deeds. The deeds of these great lamas, who are protectors of beings in ordinary guise, were influenced by bad attendants. When I reflect on this, I see the truth in the Buddha's statement in many sutras, motivated by the thought that keeping good or bad company determines one's happiness, that one must keep good company.

The Formal Enrollment of His Holiness the Fourteenth Dalai Lama

That summer on the grounds of Jaraklingka, at the request of Söchö and other members of the Sadutshang family of Trehor, I gave discourses on the root text of the *Guru Puja* based on the large manual associated with the practice authored by Kachen Yeshé Gyaltsen (1713–93) and a detailed instruction on Ganden Mahāmudrā based on the root text and commentary authored by Paṇchen Chögyen. Afterward, I received directly from Kumbum Minyak Rinpoché[200] oral transmission and explanation of the *Essence of Eloquence* and *Clarifying the Intent of the Middle Way* by Jé Tsongkhapa, *Dose of Emptiness: Opening the Eyes of the Fortunate* by Khedrup Jé, the commentary *Meaningful to Behold: A Praise of Jé Tsongkhapa* by Gungthangpa, Hortön's *Rays of the Sun Mind Training*, Langri Thangpa's

Eight Verses on Mind Training, and the *Wheel of Sharp Weapons Mind Training*.

That autumn I accompanied His Holiness the Dalai Lama to Drepung Monastery in a grand procession in order to formally commence his religious studies and enrollment in the three seats of learning in accordance with ancient tradition. I stayed in a room on the middle story of the palace at Drepung. As it was tradition for the precious regent to appoint tutors from each of the seven colleges of the three seats, he added to our number by appointing as Tsenshap, in addition to we three existing assistant tutors, Geshé Losang Dönden from Gyalrong House of Loseling, Geshé Chöphel Gawa of Deyang and Geshé Ngödrup Choknyé from Hardong House of Sera Jé, and Thuksé Thupten Topjor of Serkong House of Ganden Jangtsé.

During the actual ceremony, all the monastic and lay officials of the government and the abbots and tulkus of the three monasteries were present in the courtyard of the palace. His Holiness, the regent, Kyabjé Ling Rinpoché, myself, and the rest of the seven assistant tutors recited the verses of praise of the Six Ornaments and the Two Excellent Ones entitled *Equaling Space*[201] and *Chanting the Names of Mañjuśrī* up to the passage that states "... plant well the victory banner." Then the precious regent recited a few lines from the beginning of Maitreya's *Ornament of Realization*, which His Holiness and all of us repeated. Then each of the seven assistant tutors, one by one, offered debates on the subject of the Perfection of Wisdom to His Holiness. I recited the verses of auspiciousness at the conclusion of the ceremony. As is tradition, the ceremony ended with a grand feast of ceremonial cookies.

I then accompanied His Holiness as part of his entourage to ceremonies in the great assembly hall, the four colleges, Namgyal Monastery, Tashi Khangsar, and Gephel Hermitage. After the ceremony at Drepung, His Holiness visited Nechung Monastery and invoked the great Dharmarāja Dorjé Drakden through the medium. In private, he showed His Holiness certain sacred objects, including the Sebak Mukchung mask, which I was also able to view.[202] Then we made our way through the foothills of the Pari Range to Sera Thekchen Ling Monastery. There I stayed on the upper floor of Denma House near the back door of the main prayer assembly hall. At Sera I again accompanied His Holiness to ceremonies held during visits to the great assembly hall, the three colleges, and Hardong House. His Holiness visited the Phabongkha Hermitage.[203] I sought permission to be excused and went to Tashi Chöling Hermitage to pay a visit to the incarnation of Kyabjé Vajradhara. I gave him a long-life empowerment and oral transmissions of several books. After the ceremonies at Sera, as His Holiness returned to the Potala Palace, I did as well.

The great tantric practitioner and holder of the three vows, Geshé Losang Samdrup Rinpoché of Gyalrong, had made a set of two-story-high statues of Jé Tsongkhapa and his spiritual sons that was to be placed into the chapel of Gyümé Tantric College at Changlochen in Lhasa. At his express wish, I performed, together with the monks of Gyümé Tantric College, the elaborate ritual of consecration in its entirety, Causing the Rain of Goodness to Fall in connection with Guhyasamāja. On the concluding day, Geshé Rinpoché himself, who was the patron on that occasion, and Taiji Shenkhawa, who supervised the restoration, attended the consecration ritual. I recited the descriptions of the "Celebration of the Hosts" to the best of my ability and offered the eight auspicious symbols and the eight substances.[204]

Cataloging Religious Texts

At the end of the fall, after His Holiness had settled himself at the Potala, refuge and protector the precious regent told me to complete the cataloging of all the religious texts belonging to the various Dalai Lamas that are kept in the upper and lower libraries of the Potala. Tsawa Tritrul of Sera Mé had been asked to catalog this large collection during the time of the previous Dalai Lama, but the task had been left unfinished. So I and the other assistant tutors accordingly proceeded to carefully examine the texts and complete the task as commanded. Fifteen monks from Namgyal Monastery assisted us to move nearly three thousand volumes that were housed in the library atop the northern wing of the central tower of the Red Palace and to unwrap and rewrap the books in cloth covers.

In the Sasum Chamber in the Potala, we assistant tutors carefully checked the books against the previous catalog, checked the order of their pages, and made new catalogs. Among the books were a copy of the *Ratnakūṭa Sutra* that had belonged to Jetsun Milarepa's family and a book with handwritten notations from Omniscient Butön himself. There were also handwritten copies of texts belonging to many well-known masters and realized beings such as Khedrup Norsang Gyatso and Shalu Lochen Chökyong Sangpo. These books contained many personal notes by these masters. At the end of one of the books belonging to the Fifth Dalai Lama, the Dalai Lama had written, "I, the crazy tantric practitioner of Sahor, put this into practice, and many signs of accomplishment have occurred."

There were many other writings of the Fifth Dalai Lama as well as of Desi Sangyé Gyatso and their commentaries. There were the teachings of the Buddha, the treatises on sutra and tantra that unravel the intention behind the Buddha's words authored by scholars of every sectarian and philosophical affiliation, the histories of kingdoms and religion, and many works on aspects of knowledge shared by Buddhists and non-Buddhists alike. In short, the extent and variety of the collection was inconceivable.

Among the collection were so many exceedingly rare texts that I had not even heard the names of, let alone seen. At that time I did not have an opportunity to look at them at leisure. Immediately afterward we also cataloged the many books that were housed in the sunlight room, Ganden Nangsal, in the eastern wing of the Potala. There were also many books in the library on the lower level. Although we were asked to catalog them later when we had time, they remained uncataloged.

At the beginning of the third month after the Subsequent Prayer Session in my forty-eighth year, the year of the earth-rat (1948), I gave initiations into Guhyasamāja, Vajrabhairava, and Cakrasaṃvara, along with preparations, over a period of five days at the request of the incumbent abbot of the Gyütö Tantric College, Minyak Kyorpön Losang Yönten of Drepung Loseling. These were attended by about four thousand disciples, primarily monks from Gyütö Tantric College, and took place in Ramoché, the Gyütö assembly hall in Lhasa.

At the request of a monastic government official named Losang Gyaltsen, to plant roots of merit for the late cabinet scribe Edrung Tashi Tsering, I gave the initiation of the Great Compassionate One. At that time, the precious tulku who was the supreme incarnation of my sole refuge and friend without equal, Phabongkha Vajradhara, also received initiation into the mandala of highest yoga tantra for the very first time.

The monks of Dakpo Shedrup Ling Monastery in the east came to offer an elaborate long-life ceremony on the occasion of the completion of the ceremony for His Holiness's enrollment at the seats of learning. At the request of their monastic administrators, at Shidé I gave an audience of around five hundred disciples, primarily monks from Dakpo Shedrup Ling, the initiation into the Great Compassionate One. Afterward, at the request of His Holiness's personal attendant, the monk-secretary Tsidrung Losang Kalsang, in order to plant roots of merit for his late brother Kalden Tsering, I gave the blessing of the four sindūra initiations of Vajrayoginī and an eight-day discourse on its two stages to a gathering of over three hundred at Tsemönling Monastery in Lhasa.

That year the government successfully completed the restoration of the assembly hall at Ganden. The ritual assistants from Namgyal Monastery and I accompanied Regent Takdrak Rinpoché to perform the elaborate ritual of consecration, which we did over a period of three days. As the precious regent was physically exhausted and unable to complete the repairing fire-offerings for pacification and increase, I performed them. In celebration of the full restoration of the great hall, I offered tea, sweet rice, and money to the assembly. After the precious regent had left for Lhasa, at the request of Taiji Shenkha Gyurmé Sönam Topgyé, who oversaw the restoration, I offered an initiation of Life-Sustaining Jé Tsongkhapa to the monks of Shartsé and Jangtsé and the entire team of construction workers and their leaders in the courtyard of the assembly hall.

The monks of Gyütö Tantric College are trained in the dimensions of the mandalas for Guhyasamāja, Cakrasaṃvara, and Vajrabhairava during their annual stay at Drak Yerpa to observe the rainy-season retreat. Although the abbot and chant master would administer exams on the subject, as they only gave oral exams on the three-dimensional mandala, their way of training was ineffective. Without explicitly seeing and becoming familiar with the mandalas in practice, it will be difficult for the less-sharp student to master them as written. As a result of discussing this with the abbot, lamas, and administrators, practical instruction in three-dimensional mandalas was newly instituted and undertaken every year thereafter. Around that time, together with His Holiness, I received the entire collection of initiations from the sealed, secret visionary revelations of the Great Fifth Dalai Lama from Regent Takdrak Vajradhara in the Druzin palace of the Norbulingka.

My forty-ninth year came in the year of the earth-ox (1949). That spring, in the temple of Gyümé Tantric College at the request of a group of newly ordained Gyümé monks, I gave initiations into Guhyasamāja, Cakrasaṃvara, and Vajrabhairava, permission for the collected mantras of Guhyasamāja, Cakrasaṃvara, and Vajrabhairava, and permissions for Mahākāla, Dharmarāja, Palden Lhamo, and Vaiśravaṇa to a vast audience of monks from Gyütö and Gyümé tantric colleges and tulkus and monks from

Kyabjé Trijang Rinpoché in front of his Lhasa residence, 1949
COURTESY OF PALDEN TSERING

the three seats of learning. I also offered the initiation into single-deity Vajrabhairava to over a thousand disciples who had the commitment to recite the sādhana of single-deity Vajrabhairava.

Obstacles to Health

Thinking of planting roots of virtue to counteract the bad astrological circumstances of my forty-ninth year and to support those connected to me, living and dead, in the month of Vaiśākha,[205] I sent my attendant Palden together with an assistant to build up my merit by making clouds of offerings at the various shrines and holy places in the south, such as Ölkha, Samyé, and Tradruk. At that time I gradually led His Holiness through the two main topics of Tibetan grammar.[206]

In the fifth month, to plant roots of merit for the late Losang Dolma at the request of the family of Sönam Rinchen who lived in Jeti Ling in Lhasa, I gave permissions for the deities expounded in the Rinjung Hundred to an audience of more than one thousand disciples, principally monks and incarnate lamas of the three seats of learning, in the assembly hall of Shidé Monastery.

While residing in the Norbulingka Palace during the rainy season, I suffered greatly from dysentery from the twenty-fifth of the sixth month with a relapse of the old intestinal fever. Nonetheless on the second of the seventh month, as all government officials were required to attend the opening ceremony of the Shotön, or "yogurt," summer folk-opera festival at the Norbulingka, I went to attend it for one hour. Because of this, I had excruciating stomach pain that evening and frequent diarrhea. I was so weak that I fainted and fell before reaching my bed. My attendant Palden burned tsampa mixed with the wind-disorder medicine Agar 35 and applied it to my head, face, and palms, thanks to which I just survived. Early the next morning we asked for the senior director of the Tibetan Astro-Medical Institute, Khyenrap Norbu, and the younger vice chair, Thupten Lhundrup. When they analyzed my urine and pulse, all signs indicated that there was no hope that I would survive. The two doctors would leave the Shotön festival in turns to visit and administer medicine. Thanks to their careful treatment, and by the force of many prayers said to eliminate bad circumstances, and also because my fortune to receive undeserved offerings that turn the heads of [i.e., deceive] the faithful like a whirling firebrand had not depleted, the pain lessened, and I improved slightly.

On the afternoon of the following day, the fourth, Jampa Chösang, a chamber attendant within His Holiness's personal staff, and Phalha Thupten Öden, the lord chamberlain at the Potala, requested that those who were practicing carrying His Holiness's palanquin bring over a sedan chair that they used to rehearse with. I was carried on this from the Norbulingka to my house in Lhasa. After the diarrhea had stopped, I was sick for a period of three months with edema.

I had the heads for a half-story-high statue of Amitāyus and for life-size statues of White Tārā and Uṣṇīṣavijayā made in bronze by the excellent craftsmen in Lhasa with the intention of sending them to my monastery in Chatreng, where the bodies would be made. I duly sent the gilded bronze heads, together with ornaments and dhāraṇī prayers for the interior, with Kham-bound travelers who delivered them to my monastery in Chatreng. The monastery had the bodies made and built a temple to Amitāyus to the right of the assembly hall just as I had instructed.

Renewing the Protector Support Substances in the Potala

That winter while residing at the Potala, at the request of His Holiness to renew in their entirety the outer, inner, and secret representations of the most secret Dharmarāja Black Poison Mountain, I rubbed in the substances on the shroud of the previous Dalai Lama in accordance with ancient ritual instructions. On a wrathful day of culmination of stars and planets, state artist Udrung Paljor Gyalpo generated himself as a deity. The artist had previously received Vajrabhairava initiation and had maintained daily recitation and self-generation practice of the deity. After drawing the preliminary mantra diagram on the shroud, I drew the mantra syllables at the places of the sense faculties and at the heart. With the addition of various colors, a painting of Dharmarāja was completed.

As clearly explained in the sealed teachings of the compendiums, I gathered metal name boards with life mantras and the mantra wheels of Yama and Yamāri written on them as supports of his speech and a skull-ornamented mace carved from teak with a *phurba* dagger at its handle as the support of his mind. A metal trident decorated with black banners bearing mantras was the support for the consort Cāmuṇḍā. Double-edged steel swords with scorpion hilts tempered in blood and poison were supports for the retinue of *rākṣasa* demons. A bow made from the horn of an uncastrated ox together with a bow-string made of sinews cut with a sword were the support for Viṣṇu. Figurines of a buffalo and a black long-haired yak wearing around their necks nameplates made of the wood of male trees inscribed with mantras were the outer supports. Black banners with mantras and figures drawn on them with weapon-spilled blood, sindūra, lotus blood, *ghivaṃ* bile, and musk were the inner supports. The skulls of a man and woman whose family line had been broken, on the upper part of which the faces of Yama and Yamāri had self-manifested in relief, made clear by the application of color, and that had the body of wrathful Dharmarāja drawn on a shroud placed at their union were the secret supports. I then gathered the ritual substances and the dhāraṇīs and mantras for insertion. We correctly performed sādhanas to generate the deity and to request him to remain at the end of the full completion of the supports. Having gathered these support substances, we placed them, excluding the statues and thangkas, in a series of boxes as support vessels, and we installed the boxes in the rooms and living quarters of His Holiness in the Potala.

This most secret Dharmarāja, who is a great protector of the teachings of Mañjunātha Tsongkhapa, is exceedingly mysterious and fierce, and on that occasion various signs of the oath-bound protector appeared, various eruptions of turmoil. For example, at the beginning of the process when collecting the support substances, thumping and scraping sounds were heard at night in the room where I was staying. The day when I presented a painting of Dharmarāja to His Holiness to inspect, his chief attendant[207] Khyenrap Tenzin was suddenly struck with a seizure. And once when I was leaving my house in Lhasa, the horse on which I was riding threw me off.

And just when I had completed that, His Holiness requested that I renew the ritual supports for Palden Lhamo. With respect to her images, I was not asked to renew the painting of Lhamo, as the existing one had been the support of the deity for successive Dalai Lamas and had spoken directly to His Holiness.

I correctly gathered the substances as taught in His Holiness the Second Dalai Lama Gendun Gyatso's *Presentation of the Three Acts of Lhamo*[208] and in the manual of His Holiness the Great Fifth Dalai Lama's sealed secret visionary revelations. The *Tantra of Ḍākinī Meché Barma*[209] written in gold served as the support of her speech. A mirror with *bhyōḥ* written on it was the support of her mind. A sandalwood vajra club ornamented with a black banner bearing mantras, and the skull of an illegitimate child filled with charmed substances—various types of blood and medicinal offerings—were the support for her activity. A raven figurine made from black cloth stuffed with medicinal grain and human skin on which a consecrated picture of Palden Lhamo's body had been drawn were the outer support. The faux corpse of a bastard child made of black cloth was the inner support—this was stuffed with a piece of burnt wood used in a cremation and a life-tree trident smeared with poisonous blood. These had been wrapped in a corpse shroud around which the long mantras of calling, expelling, and slaying Lhamo had been written out in weapon-spilled blood. The faux corpse had its heart stuffed with leaves that had not been blown to the ground by the wind and had the mantra of Palden Lhamo written on one side and the image of her body drawn on the other for use as dhāraṇī, and these were smeared with the juices of sexual union. The body was filled with various types of blood, grains, and mantras with interwoven text, and the whole was draped in a black coat. A victory banner was placed in its hand, and a peacock feather crest set upon the head.

One secret support was a representation of the heart of a bastard child whose three channels had not deteriorated. The heart was stuffed with pebbles drawn from the depths of Divine Lhamo Lake in Chökhorgyal and never exposed to the sky, and *phavaṃ* stones[210] upon which *bhyōḥ* was written with lotus blood. Another secret support was an arrow shaft made of a stalk of wild bamboo with seven segments, grown at Draknakpo and decorated with the unsinged feather of a crow. At the middle of the arrow was the stacked seven-part *bhyōḥ* mantra. From the base of the feather upward was drawn the tutelary deity, her mantras of calling, expelling, and slaying, along with interwoven text, and the arrow was tipped with a metal arrowhead that had been previously tempered in poisonous blood. We also gathered such things as tiger cloth and leopard cloth, a modest hair braid,[211] black banners bearing mantras, mirrors, decorative riding tassels, as well as flat-bladed swords and ritual daggers, a golden sun and silver moon fashioned by the craftsmen in a single sitting, a weapon ball made of thread,[212] fatal red curses,[213] and black and white dice stones.[214]

After having well produced and consecrated the substances and placed them in a hard black lacquer box with drawings of fearsome weapons on it, we distributed the boxes in front of the images of Palden Lhamo in the rooms and living quarters in the Potala.

At that time, His Holiness and I received initiation into seventeen-deity Sitātapatrā based on the manual by Kyishöpa[215] from Kyabjé Ling Rinpoché in the Jangchup Gakhyil quarters on the upper floor of the Norbulingka Palace.

In my fiftieth year, the year of the iron-tiger (1950), as I was requested to plant roots of merit on behalf of the late Tsamkhung nun Phuntsok, in the spring of the year at Lhasa's Tsamkhung Nunnery I gave the great initiation into Ghaṇṭāpāda's five-deity Cakrasaṃvara and Ghaṇṭāpāda's body mandala, an explanation of the generation and completion stages of

Ghaṇṭāpāda's body mandala based on experience, the blessing of the four sindūra initiations of Vajrayoginī, and an explanation of its generation and completion stages based on experience to an audience of a little more than one hundred disciples.

As requested by the abbot of Sera Jé, Thupten Samten of Trehor House, during the summer retreat in the Khenyen College assembly hall, I gave teachings based on my experience on the stages of the path using the *Easy Path*, the *Quick Path*, and the *Words of Mañjuśrī*. I also gave teachings on the *Seven-Point Mind Training* and the six-session guruyoga for over one month to about five thousand disciples, including the monks from the Jé, Mé, and Ngakpa colleges of Sera as well as many monks who came back and forth each day from Lhasa and Drepung in their fervent quest for teachings. In the middle of that sea of scholars who knew these lengthy texts by the hundred without needing to rely on others, I couldn't help but feel like a donkey disguised in leopard skin.

Among those listening to the teachings at that time was one of the most well-known among the great masters of the three seats, Geshé Yeshé Loden of Drepung Loseling. One day, after the teaching on the stages of the path, he came to visit me to express his pleasure in the discourse. He told me, "Your recent discourse was not only excellent because of your explanation of the words but was greatly beneficial in terms of their application." I appreciated his comments, but I thought to myself, "Little does he realize that I lack any personal experience and that my explanations of the teachings were like an actor's speech, narrations of the teachings without any conviction." Through the incomparable kindness of the father lama, I was merely repeating his teachings as if I were conveying messages.

Arrival of Communist Chinese and His Holiness's Enthronement

That summer brought several ominous occurrences. A comet appeared and could be seen at dawn in the skies over Bumpa Mountain to the south of Lhasa. One day at about nine in the evening while I was teaching the stages of the path at Sera, we heard a noise from the sky like gunfire that seemed to come from the area south of us where the Drashi military encampment was situated. Just afterward a strong and long earthquake struck, and the bells on the gilded roof ornaments on the top floor of Sera Jé assembly hall could be heard ringing by themselves. As I was living on the top floor, I was at first quite alarmed. But then I recalled that if I had not committed the causes, I would not meet the consequences, and that the results of actions already committed are unavoidable. Thus I maintained my composure. The sound of gunfire from the sky and the earthquake occurred in regions all over Tibet at the same time. I took this as an ominous sign portending the imminent arrival of the poisonous wave of the barbaric Red Chinese.

With the pure intention to be of help and service to Buddhism, Beri Getak Tulku Rinpoché of Trehor went to Chamdo with stainless faith and devotion to mediate between Tibet and China and to take measures to prevent the deceitful settlement of Chinese troops in Tibet. That great Rinpoché had previously received many teachings of sutra and tantra directly from the supreme presence of Regent Takdrak Rinpoché. As he and I shared a deep bond of friendship as teacher and disciple in the past, each of us showed authentic faith and affection to other. He hoped to do whatever he could to be of benefit. Although I had no concern whatsoever that he would harmfully betray us, like a karmic obstacle shared by a group, Getak Tulku came under the suspicion of his own government due to the actions of certain individuals who were seeing ghosts in their own shadows, and he was held for a long time in Chamdo and ended up dying there in custody, some say from poisoning. I was greatly distraught with sorrow when he could not return, but there was nothing I could do.

On the eighth of the ninth month, the Communist Chinese Army unexpectedly marched into Chamdo. The Tibetan soldiers stationed there were unable to defend it and lost ground. The Chinese arrested a large number of civilian and military leaders, including Minister Ngaphö, the governor general of Domé region, and his staff at Dugu Monastery. Because of this grim situation, His Holiness the Dalai Lama, Regent Rinpoché, and the cabinet and the secretariat[216] invoked the great Nechung Dharmarāja and the Dharma protector of Gadong in a trance of their mediums in the sunlight room at the Norbulingka.

The Gadong oracle made full prostrations before His Holiness and said, "The time has come for Your Holiness to assume the burden of governing the land of snows." His Holiness received again a similar prophetic statement from Nechung. Immediately afterward, the cabinet, the secretariat, and the Tibetan National Assembly formally requested His Holiness to assume religious and temporal powers, and His Holiness granted his supreme consent. On the seventh day of the tenth month, Regent Takdrak Rinpoché abdicated the highest office, and on the eighth day (November 17, 1950), the golden wheel of religious and temporal rule in the land of Tibet was placed in His Holiness's hands. His enthronement was celebrated at an elaborate ceremony held in the Sishi Phuntsok hall of the great Potala Palace. That day, every prisoner serving time in prisons throughout the entire country of Tibet—including Radreng Dzasak, Khardo Tulku, Tsenya Tulku, and Minister Kashöpa—were simultaneously pardoned and freed.

Flight to Dromo and the Seventeen-Point Agreement

Following this, on about the tenth of the eleventh month, His Holiness responded to the increased Chinese presence by appointing the ecclesiastical secretary Losang Tashi and the finance secretary Tsewang Rabten of Dekhar (Lukhangwa) as deputy prime ministers. His Holiness, the former regent Takdrak Vajradhara, Tutor Ling Rinpoché, the cabinet ministers, and a small retinue of monastic and secular members of the upper and lower departments of the government left the Potala, secretly stopping at the Norbulingka before riding to the region of Dromo. I traveled in His Holiness's party, along with Lhabu, Palden, Gyümé Ngakram Tsultrim Dargyé of Trehor, and a small number of servants. We departed Lhasa early in the morning and stopped for the night at Nyethang Tashigang. Among the statues in the Tārā temple at Nyethang, I saw the statue of Tārā that was the tutelary deity statue of Lord Atiśa that spoke, and I also got to see the memorial stupa of Serlingpa that Atiśa always carried with him.[217]

The next morning we arrived at Lower Jang, where the monks of the three seats who had been attending the Jang winter session[218] were waiting on the roadside, as they had heard that His Holiness and his entourage were coming. Because His Holiness was disguised in ordinary clothes, he passed the monks unnoticed. It was heartbreaking when Kyabjé Ling Rinpoché and I arrived there, the monks surrounded us on all sides, throwing scarves and money left and right. Openly weeping, they held on to the reins of our horses and would not let us go. We talked with them, reassuring them that they would see us again before long. We left the money that the monks had thrown to us where it fell on the roadside, so the people in the villages nearby should have found some rich pickings.

That night we stayed in a village in Chushul. Many monks of the great monasteries had followed us there. Setting out from Chaksam ferry landing, we saw the shrines of the siddha Thangtong Gyalpo at the hermitage of Chuwori. Then passing through the Gampa Pass, Yardrok, Kharo Pass, Ralung, Gyantsé, Phakri, and so on, we arrived in Chubi in Lower Dromo, where His Holiness stayed at the residence of the governor of Dromo. My retinue and I along with members of His Holiness's family—his mother, his brother Taktser Rinpoché, and so on—were distributed to sleep on the upper and lower floors of a household called Chubi Labrang. It was decided that His Holiness and his entourage would stay in Dromo, given the circumstances both domestically and abroad. From Dromo, both the negotiations for peace talks with the Chinese and the appeal to other countries for support could be carried out. Lhabu, Tsultrim Dargyé, and I remained there, but as Palden had never been on a pilgrimage to the sacred places in India and Nepal, I sent him to India with the merchant Losang Yeshé as his assistant. Since I gave him a fair amount of money with which to make clouds of offerings at the holy places, extensive offerings were made there.

On New Year's Day of the iron-rabbit year (1951), when I turned fifty-one, His Holiness, Tutor Ling Rinpoché, and I, along with the ritual assistants of Namgyal Monastery, made offerings to Palden Lhamo. The cabinet ministers and other government officials held a brief New Year ceremony at the office of the governor and presented scarves to the former regent, Takdrak Vajradhara, who was staying at Jema in Lower Dromo. On the third day of the New Year, after making offerings to the protectors, I accompanied His Holiness on a visit to the Kagyü monastery in Lower Dromo. After spending two days there, His Holiness and the entourage shifted residence to Dungkar Monastery in Upper Dromo, where I stayed in the quarters of Böntsang Ngawang Tsöndrü at Dungkar Monastery.

His Holiness upgraded my position, elevating my Darhan rank of assistant tutor so that I would sit in front of the cabinet at ceremonies, as it would be inappropriate for me to be seated behind the lay ministers. His Holiness received me in audience and held a brief ceremony with a ceremonial scarf to mark the occasion.

As Khyenrap Wangchuk of Tashi Ling, who was an acting monastic cabinet minister, had asked that I plant roots of virtue for his brother, the treasurer Gyaltsen Namgyal, I gave a discourse on the stages of the path according to the *Quick Path* and concluded with a bodhicitta-generating

Kyabjé Trijang Rinpoché on a mule en route to Dromo, 1950
COURTESY OF PALDEN TSERING

ceremony to about three hundred disciples in the assembly hall of Tashi Chöling Hermitage at Dungkar Monastery in Upper Dromo. As I had close guru-disciple connections with the Galing Gang Bönpotsang family since the time of their grandfather Pha Dönyö, at their request I went to their household and performed a prosperity ritual and gave long-life initiations, staying there for a few days. Because of my past guru-disciple connections with the previous and the most well-known Dromo Geshé Rinpoché Ngawang Kalsang and with the monks of Dungkar Monastery, I made offerings to the monks of food and money and gave four *tsipar* ornaments made of brocade appliqué with banners for the tall pillars of the assembly hall.

On the eighth day of the third month, during the traditional government torma offering of the eighth, my attendant Palden joined the monastic service of the government. While residing in Dromo, His Holiness observed an approaching retreat on the root mantra of single-deity Vajrabhairava, an approaching retreat of the Great Compassionate One according to the Lakṣmī tradition, and a retreat on the inner sādhana of Dharmarāja, for which I served as his assistant.

On that occasion, Ngaphö Ngawang Jikmé, who was a cabinet minister at the time, Dzasak Khemé Sönam Wangdü, monastic secretary

Thupten Tendar (Khendrung Lhautara), junior monastic secretary Thupten Lekmön, and others were sent to China as representatives of the Tibetan government. Coerced by the Chinese, the team signed the so-called Seventeen-Point Agreement.[219] Ngaphö and a few of his staff members returned to Tibet from China via Kham, while Dzasak Khemé and Thupten Tendar returned to Dromo via Hong Kong and India. At the very same time Zhang Jingwu, a representative of the Red Chinese that had been sent to Tibet from China, arrived in Dromo along with Alo Butang. They met with His Holiness and discussed "the peaceful liberation of Tibet" and their plans to improve the land and the lives of the people of Tibet. Making many sweet promises, they insisted that His Holiness and government officials immediately return to the capital in Lhasa. Having considered the situation, His Holiness left Dromo at the beginning of the fifth month.

Religious Activities after Returning to Lhasa

His Holiness traveled through Phakri, Gyantsé, Nakartsé, Yardrok, Samding, Taklung Monastery, Paldi, Nyasok, Sé Chökhor Yangtsé, and Nyethang Ratö, and was received by a reception party at Tsakgur Park. Then, having visited Takdrak Hermitage and other places along the way, he was received with an official government reception at Kyitsal Luding. From there His Holiness and entourage traveled in an elaborate, traditional procession to touch his foot once again to the grounds of the Kalsang Phodrang Palace, Norbulingka. To fulfill the request of monks of Nenying Monastery, Shiné Monastery in Gyantsé, and Chökhor Yangtsé, I offered summary discourses on assorted topics. I paid my respects to former regent Takdrak Vajradhara, who had left Dromo ahead of us and was staying at his hermitage.

After we arrived in Lhasa, at the invitation of the jeweler Kalsang and his daughter, the nun Ngawang Chözin of Gomang Khangsar in Lhasa, I went to Nechungri Nunnery for a few days to give the nuns the great initiation into Ghaṇṭāpāda's five-deity Cakrasaṃvara and the blessing of the four sindūra initiations of Vajrayoginī to help establish the practice of Vajrayoginī self-initiation at the nunnery. As I had been invited to visit the quarters of the monks of Samling dormitory in Pombor House at Sera, I went there and made offerings and gave them some money to put toward their

Kyabjé Trijang Rinpoché and labrang staff at his Lhasa residence, 1951. From left to right are his senior attendant Lhabu, manager Losang Döndrup, personal attendant Kungo Palden Tsering, and merchant/attendant Losang Yeshé.
COURTESY OF PALDEN TSERING

annual picnic to mark the end of the rainy season. Then as Phara Choktrul Rinpoché had invited me, I went to Ganden and gave the great initiation into Guhyasamāja Akṣobhyavajra along with its preparatory rite in Phara House over a period of three days to a large gathering of masters and lamas of both Jangtsé and Shartsé colleges.

With merchants returning to Kham, I sent gilded bronze heads for three statues that I was having erected at Samling Monastery in Chatreng—a statue of Mañjunātha Tsongkhapa one and a half stories high and statues of Gyaltsap and Khedrup that would be a little larger than life-sized—along with various printed dhāraṇīs to fill them. I had the heads of the statues produced in Lhasa because of superior craftsmanship there. The monastery itself had the bodies built and constructed the temple just as I had requested.

In the third month of my fifty-second year, the water-dragon year (1952), His Holiness received the Kālacakra initiation from his tutor Kyabjé Ling Rinpoché in the ceremonial hall of the Potala, and I received it again as well. From the tenth of the fourth month, over a period of nine days, I gave a large audience of earnest recipients the blessing of the four sindūra initiations of Vajrayoginī and its mantra extraction along with a teaching on its two stages. This teaching, given at the request of Dawa Dargyé, a staff member at Kundeling Labrang, was given according to practice of the Great Secret Explication for Disciples.[220] Sometime later, at the behest of Kyabjé Ling Rinpoché, I offered the great initiation into sixty-two-deity Cakrasaṃvara in the tradition of Luipa along with its preparatory rite.

To fulfill the request of Bayer Tsering Drolkar, the wife of Mr. Mentöpa, I gave the great initiation into five-deity Cakrasaṃvara according to the external mandala in the tradition of Ghaṇṭāpāda, the great initiation into the body mandala, instruction in the two stages of Ghaṇṭāpāda's body mandala, along with experiential teachings on the six Dharmas of Nāropa. These teachings took place over a period of about twenty days, beginning on the tenth day of the fifth month, in the assembly hall of Shidé Monastery, and were attended by an audience of nearly a thousand disciples that were mostly tulkus and geshés.

After the rainy-season retreat at the Norbulingka Palace, I went to the hot springs in Tölung. On the way, since Gyümé Tantric College was in the middle of their Dharma session while observing a later rainy-season retreat at Chumik Valley, I spent three days there and made offerings to the assembly. The monks were practicing the melodies and rhythms of the tantric college chants, and I went briefly to the individual regional houses, as they invited me. I also visited the nearby small huts where figures such as Kunkhyen Jamyang Shepa and Longdöl Lama Rinpoché had lived.

Thereafter I spent a fortnight at the hot springs for my health. It just so happened that the director of the Astro-Medical Institute, Dr. Khyenrap Norbu, and Chögön Rinpoché of Dechen Chökhor Monastery in the Gongkar Truldruk tradition were there at the same time. We all knew each other quite well. Chögön Rinpoché had a vast and profound knowledge of both religious and secular matters and was quite articulate. The director of the Astro-Medical Institute, too, was quite well versed in the ten arts and sciences,[221] with a knowledge like the great statesman Desi Sangyé Gyatso,[222] and was also learned in history. Because of their stimulating conversations, I enjoyed my visit to the hot springs so much that I didn't know where the time went.

After that encounter at the hot springs, at the request of Dingkha Rinpoché of Tölung, I went to Dingkha Monastery and gave the blessing of the four sindūra initiations of Vajrayoginī. Then, at the invitation of Chusang Monastery, the monastic seat established by the venerable Dromtsun Sherjung Lodrö, who was a direct disciple of Jé Rinpoché, I offered initiations into thirteen-deity Vajrabhairava, Sarvavid, and so on. I then went back to Lhasa.

During this same period, to support the wishes of His Holiness, I oversaw the production of new thangka paintings of single-deity Vajrabhairava, the five emanations of Nechung Dharmarāja, and Shukden in his five aspects. Since the painter, Udrung Paljor Gyalpo, had previously received the initiation of Vajrabhairava, I gave him the permissions of the five emanations of Nechung. I generated him as a deity, and the painting materials and equipment were blessed. The blessed solutions were applied to the canvases, and the mantras were written according to the manuals and texts of the individual deities. On the backs of the thangkas of the five emanations of Nechung and Shukden, I drew the life-force wheel and wrote the life-force mantras with wishes and prayers on a day when the eight classes of spirits were active.[223] When these were fully completed, the thangkas were consecrated.

7 To China and Back

My Appointment as Junior Tutor

In my fifty-third year, the year of the water-snake (1953), at the request of Chözé Gyatruk of Meru Monastery I offered initiations into Ghaṇṭāpāda's five-deity Cakrasaṃvara and thirteen-deity Vajrabhairava along with its preparatory rites to an audience of a little more than one thousand in Meru's assembly hall. Over the summer, at the wish of His Holiness, the government expanded the northern section of the Shöl Kangyur printing press at the base of the Potala Hill and constructed a new temple to enshrine the newly made statues of Vajrabhairava, Kālacakra, Palden Lhamo, and Ekajaṭī, each of which were three stories high. I took responsibility for overseeing the process at every step along the way, from blessing the materials, guiding the craftsmen to visualize themselves as the deities, and laying out measurements for the statues, to inspecting the designs and inserting the dhāraṇīs and relics inside the statues. Afterward His Holiness attended the consecration of the statues for three days and gave his blessings with the ritual tossing of grains.

I had a one-and-a-half-story appliqué thangka of Dharmarāja and his consort in union as its principal figure, surrounded by Jé Rinpoché, Vajrabhairava, Karmarāja, and Shukden, sewn from pieces of fine brocade. I had this sent to Samphel Ling Monastery in Chatreng to be displayed during the celebration at the conclusion of the *gutor* ritual.[224]

In the fall, at the request of Geshé Yeshé Gyatso of Gungru House of Gomang College of Drepung, over a period of twenty-three days in the assembly hall of Gomang College, I offered teachings on the stages of the path based on the *Easy Path*, the *Quick Path*, and the *Words of Mañjuśrī* to an audience of nearly four thousand, comprised principally of monks from the three seats, exemplified by present and former abbots and tulkus. I felt like a parrot reciting the *maṇi* as I gave dry explanations amid a sea of erudite masters. The incarnation of Kyabjé Phabongkha Vajradhara himself also attended to receive the teaching on the stages of the path for the first time. At the request of Ön Gyalsé Choktrul Rinpoché, I also offered the same gathering permission for White Mañjuśrī according to the system of Mati.[225]

At the beginning of the tenth month cabinet minister Surkhang Wangchen Gelek and monk secretary Chöphel Thupten came to visit me in my quarters in the Norbulingka. Representing the cabinet and the secretariat of the government, they told me that my duties of offering religious instructions to His Holiness alongside Kyabjé Ling Rinpoché had been well performed and that I was to be commended for it. Further, as His Holiness was to receive full ordination the following year, Ling Rinpoché would be promoted to the position of senior tutor and I should accept the position of junior tutor. They told me that at the recommendation of the cabinet and other departments, His Holiness had given his approval and that I should soon follow the necessary ceremonial procedures to assume this role in order to offer His Holiness the entire vast and profound teachings of sutra and tantra in the manner of "pouring from one vessel to another." They then presented me with a ceremonial scarf and the representations of enlightened body, speech, and mind.

The *Ornament of Realization* says of tutors:

> A mind undaunted and so forth,
> teaching the lack of a nature and so on,
> casting off all that opposes it,
> this makes for a consummate tutor.[226]

Although I did not possess even a hundredth of a hairbreadth of the inner and external qualities of a tutor as expressed in this verse, I gathered up courage to join the ranks of the fearless lions like an aged dog and accepted the offer.

Without delay I accepted the scarf symbolic of the ordered change in post and had a propitious inaugural meeting with His Holiness. On the actual day of assuming the post I made a thousand offerings[227] at Lhasa's Tsuklakhang, Ramoché, and the Avalokiteśvara temple in the Potala Palace. After visiting the sacred images, I went to the Norbulingka Palace, where I prostrated before His Holiness in the Jangchup Gakhyil chamber on the top floor and presented him with a scarf and the representations of the body, speech, and mind. His Holiness in turn gave me a scarf with the three representations and a sacred statue of Mañjuśrī made of bronze. In connection with this exchange, I gave a reading transmission of *Fifty Verses on Guru Devotion* along with a brief introductory discourse that began with the benefits of developing bodhicitta. Afterward a banquet of ceremonial cookies to mark a propitious beginning was arranged by the government in the ceremonial hall of the sunlight room. I made prostrations with the deepest reverence to the supreme leader of all beings in saṃsāra and nirvāṇa, who was seated magnificently glowing like a million suns on a throne of fearless lions. I then presented him with a scarf with the three representations and gifts. The government, as well, presented invaluable gifts to me, and in accordance with tradition, I accepted scarves from the cabinet ministers, the lord chamberlain, and other monk and lay officials, from the highest down to the sixth rank (*letsenpa*).

After the ceremonies in the Norbulingka Palace, I returned to my residence in Lhasa, where government officials of various ranks, representatives from the three seats, their colleges and labrangs, and many others with whom I had religious and secular connections came in a long line bearing gifts.

Dagyab[228] Chetsang Hothokthu first came to Lhasa that year. After he went to have an audience with His Holiness at the Potala, he came to my quarters, where I greeted him and paid my respects. That winter, I served as assistant to His Holiness as he observed the approximation retreat of the mind mandala of Buddha Kālacakra along with the repairing ritual fire offering.

The Dalai Lama Takes Full Ordination

In my fifty-fourth year, the wood-horse year (1954), His Holiness was to take full ordination as a bhikṣu at Lhasa's Tsuklakhang during the festival that commemorates the Buddha's performance of miracles in India. Dagyab Chetsang Hothokthu Rinpoché had also requested that His Holiness preside over the prayer sessions at the same time. To attend these two events, His Holiness traveled in a large ceremonial procession, as was the custom, from the great palace to the Ganden Yangtsé chambers on the top floor of Lhasa's Tsuklakhang. I also took up residence in the quarters atop the temple in the Nangsi guest room.

On the fifteenth of the first month, before the sacred Jowo Śākyamuni statue, His Holiness received his full ordination directly from the Sharpa Chöjé, Kyabjé Ling Rinpoché, who acted as both preceptor and master, attended by the incumbent Ganden Throneholder Thupten Kunga of Sera Jé, who acted as recorder of time, and myself, who acted as the interviewing master. Former Ganden Throneholder Minyak Tashi Tongdü from Drepung Loseling, the Jangtsé Chöjé, and the various adjunct tutors filled out the required assembly of ten fully ordained monks. By purely receiving the precepts and vows of a fully ordained bhikṣu, which are the basis of training, amid an assembly of ten fully ordained monks by means of the "current excellent and faultless rite," he preserved the tradition of the great ceremony that invests one as the crown jewel of all bearers of the Vinaya.

As the interviewing master, it fell to me to ask His Holiness a series of questions, such as "Are you not a non-Buddhist?" "Are you not a thief?" "Have you not killed your father?" and so forth. I felt extremely uncomfortable asking such questions to His Holiness, who is the supreme leader of the religious and temporal affairs of Tibet, the land of snows. But since this was conducted according to the ancient traditions of monastic discipline, I mustered the courage and put these questions to him.

That day during the auspicious offering of a feast of ceremonial cookies that had been arranged by the government within the vast courtyard of the Tsuklakhang, I was asked to recite the treatise for the symbolic mandala offering of the universe to His Holiness. In this treatise I recited descriptions of the supreme qualities of the enlightened body, speech, mind, and activities of His Holiness as well as the history of monastic vows in Tibet down through the ages, the fundamental importance of the Vinaya to the teachings of the Buddha, and how the monastic discipline serves as both teacher and teaching. From the following day, when the general population of Lhasa, high and low government officials, the labrang of Tashi Lhunpo, and so on made elaborate traditional offerings one after the other, I also recited explanation of the ritual mandala as requested.

After the Subsequent Prayer Session, at the request of Lady Losang Paldrön to sow roots of virtue on behalf of her late husband Rimshi Chabpel, I offered in Lhasa's Meru assembly hall the blessing of the four sindūra initiations of Vajrayoginī and an experiential discourse based on the manual *Staircase of Pure Vaiḍūrya*[229] and Shalu Khenchen's *Quick Path to Attain Khecara*[230] to an audience of nearly four hundred, including the incarnation of the supreme refuge Phabongkha Rinpoché, Dagyab Hothokthu, and Dromo Geshé Rinpoché. Following that, at the request of the monks of Dakpo Shedrub Ling Monastery who had come to make congratulatory offerings to His Holiness, I gave a discourse on the *Hundred Deities of Tuṣita* to the entire assembly of monks in Evaṃ Hall on the top floor of Lhasa's Tsuklakhang.

On the fifteenth of the fourth month, I conferred novice ordination on the incarnation of the supreme refuge Kyabjé Phabongkha Vajradhara and bestowed on him the name Ngawang Losang Trinlé Tenzin.

Traveling to China

It happened that a meeting called the National People's Congress was to be convened in Beijing.[231] The Chinese representative in Tibet Zhang Jingwu and a member of his staff, Bapa Phuntsok Wangyal, came to visit me several times to invite me to attend the conference to represent the monastic population in Tibet along with representatives from the three provinces of Tibet: Central Tibet, Kham, and Amdo. However, I declined the invitation. After they brought the situation to His Holiness's attention and pressured him, he told me, "This time you should accept it." Because I wanted to avoid causing him trouble, I could not refuse. Thereafter it was decided that His Holiness, our supreme refuge and lord, the all-seeing Paṇchen Rinpoché, we tutors, the cabinet minister Ngaphö Ngawang Jikmé, His Holiness's sister Tsering Drölma, and Dzasak Trethong of Tashi Lhunpo Labrang would go from Central Tibet.

His Holiness, Kyabjé Ling Rinpoché, Gyalwang Karmapa Rinpoché, Mindröling Chung Rinpoché, and the cabinet along with a retinue of government officials set out from the capital on the tenth day of the fifth Tibetan month. I set out with my assistants Lhabu, Palden, Losang Sherap, Losang Yeshé, and Namdröl at the same time. On the way, His Holiness kindly made a pilgrimage to Ganden Nampar Gyalwai Ling at Mount Drok. On that occasion my labrang offered clouds of offerings at the sacred objects, and I offered the gathering assembled in the great hall tea, sweet rice, and a sum of money for each monk, and I established a fund for annual monetary offerings. I invited His Holiness to preside over the prayer session on the golden throne of Lama Tsongkhapa, and with the recitation of treatises as well as an explanation of the ritual mandala, I offered as clouds of offerings whatever actual goods I had.

The high-ranking and senior members of the entourage traveled by car from Ganden up to the base of Kongpo's Ba Pass, and the rest traveled on horseback. Since the highway up to Powo Tramo had not yet been finished, the entire retinue rode on horseback through Kongpo Gyada, Ngaphö, Drul, Shokha, Nyangtri, Demo, and Lunang and eventually arrived in Powo Tongyuk. On the way we traveled through extremely thick jungle, where the branches of the trees were so densely interwoven that one could not see the sky and the terrain was very rough. Not only did we need to traverse many passes, ravines, and rivers each day, we were caught off guard by unusually strong summer rainstorms, the likes of which had not been seen before. Most of us had to walk on foot up and down the hills. We were terrified of the possibility of boulders hurtling down on us in landslides or of falling thousands of feet into deep gorges. We had to make our way falteringly across makeshift wooden bridges built over torrents swollen by the heavy rains, their spray filling the air. As Jé Lhodrak Marpa said:[232]

> Never was there an end to precipices and rivers,
> never an exit from dense jungle.
> When I recall these fearful roads,
> my breath and heart still tremble to this day.

Marpa was speaking of the notorious trails and courses of Tsari,[233] but our paths were even more dangerous and difficult. For a month it was exhausting, both physically and mentally, a great tribulation.

At Powo Tramo some Chinese motor vehicles were there to meet us, and I traveled with the entourage in these. For the overnight stopovers, the Chinese provided poor accommodation in shabby tents, and we were given clear tea to drink and had our meals in the kitchen alongside Chinese road workers. There are lines from tantric training that say, "Brahmans, outcasts, and dogs—all are seen as inseparable, manifested as one." So in this observance of sacred practice of highest yoga tantra, we all ate our meals from the same containers.

From Tramo I sent home the horses, mules, and some of the attendants that we had brought with us from Lhasa, and their return journey was even more fraught with difficulty. We went on through Tsawagang and Drakgyab Kyilthang and reached Jampaling Monastery in Chamdo district. As arrangements had been made for my stay, I spent one night at the residence of Shiwalha, where because of my past guru-disciple connection with Shisang Rinpoché in Lhasa, I was given a warm reception.

From there we crossed the great river via Kamthok portage in Dergé and crossing over a high-altitude pass in Dergé called Tro Pass, traveling via Yilhung, Dargyé Monastery in Trehor, Karzé Monastery, and Tau Monastery, we arrived at Dartsedo. At Dargyé Monastery I met the great master Geshé Jampa Khedrup Rinpoché, who had established a dialectics institute at Dargyé Monastery and had made the monks very conscientious and peaceful in their conduct by propagating teachings on the stages of the path. At Beri Monastery, I met the incarnation of Getak Tulku and Shitsé Gyapöntsang together with the members of his labrang and many other past patrons and disciples. They gave me a lot of provisions for the journey, but I was only able to carry two bags of tsampa.

Although Karzé Monastery had arranged accommodations for His Holiness's stay, the Chinese representative Zhang Jingwu ordered, "You must stay in the quarters prepared for you by the Chinese." As His Holiness had to stay in the Chinese headquarters, I also had no choice but to stay there too. Döndrup Namgyal of the Gyapöntsang family along with his son and the learned Gyapön Chözé Ngawang Dorjé came to visit me there. Lakak Tulku and some representatives of the monastery and region of Chatreng had come to Karzé to meet me and had been waiting for us for one month. As the Chinese guards would not allow them in to visit me, I went out to the tent where they were staying to meet and converse with them for an hour.

From Dartsedo, I dispatched my traveling companions Losang Yeshé and Namdröl to Chatreng via Lithang for the time being. My personal attendant Lhabu along with Palden and Losang Sherap accompanied me to China. After Dartsedo we crossed the high pass of Erlang and arrived in the first Chinese town called Ya'an. As I had been traveling all day in motor vehicles since Powo Tramo, I suffered headaches and nausea, eating less and less each day. As Muli Kyabgön Tulku and the Muli tribal king with his retinue were there, they came to visit me. At last we arrived in Chengdu, from where His Holiness and a few members of the entourage, including tutor Kyabjé Ling Rinpoché and myself with Lhabu, went to Xian by airplane. All-seeing Paṇchen Rinpoché had gone to Xian from Tsang via the northern road, and so the spiritual father and son[234] met each other there. I went along with His Holiness to visit the pilgrimage site of the temple

Kyabjé Trijang Rinpoché receiving Indian Prime Minister Nehru at Beijing airport in 1954, flanked by ministers Surkhang, Ngaphö, and Neshar, with Paṇchen Rinpoché's father and attendant Palden Tsering behind them
COURTESY OF PALDEN TSERING

wherein Lhasa's Jowo Rinpoché had previously been kept, where one can see the empty throne on which the Jowo sat. Next we went to Beijing by train. In Beijing, His Holiness, Tutor Ling Rinpoché, and myself stayed in the visitors' residences called Yikezhao.

Within China

As the congress was to commence shortly, after just two days with no time to rest we were required to attend the small preliminary committee meeting and then the actual National People's Congress, which held two sessions a day over a period of a month. It was quite a strain due to our inability to understand Chinese, the nature of the politics, and so on. Each day when the meeting adjourned, His Holiness and Paṇchen Rinpoché were invited to tour different industrial plants and to watch films and stage shows, on which occasions we were required to go along with them. In short, the fact that we were always required to be on the move from six in the morning until ten or eleven at night, with no time to rest, except during meal times, made it an exceedingly stressful ordeal.

One fortunate thing that happened during that time was that the great

Lharam Geshé Sherap Gyatso of Lubum, who was second only to youthful Mañjuśrī in his discernment of the ten arts and sciences and was overflowing with kindness, had come to the congress, and we were able to share some time with one another on several occasions. As I had not seen Geshé Rinpoché for many years, we both felt a combination of sadness and joy, like a reunion of the dead. We exchanged news of the intervening years, and I had the great opportunity to ask him questions and seek his advice. I offered him two thousand *dayang* coins.[235]

Once the Chinese asked me to broadcast a message to Lhasa over the radio about my impressions of the progress in the region of China and how the masses were free and happy, and how the Chinese had only uncontrived goodwill toward the people of Tibet. I prepared a draft of the message as I saw fit in the circumstances and gave it to the Chinese, as they had demanded to review it. I had to accept their edits and changes and was told to read it as they had written it. In Lhasa, many laymen and monks from all walks of life, not knowing that I was under the dominion of Chinese devils, thinking, "He protects and supports the Chinese with flattery," spoke disparagingly of me, like the illusion of seeing a snow mountain as blue. But how could I blame them? They weren't psychic, after all.

Since the memoir authored by His Holiness, *My Land and My People*, clearly covers the proceedings of the congress, the rights of the people, and the meetings between His Holiness and Mao Zedong on various occasions, I needn't elaborate on them here. As for the hospitality of the Chinese in terms of accommodations and food, they made a great effort to impress us during the early stages of their deception.

I then accompanied His Holiness on his visits to the great cities of China: Tianjin, Nanjing, Hangzhou, Shanghai, and so on. We were required to tour many industrial plants in those cities and found no chance to relax and rest.

Arranging a Visit to Kham

When we arrived in Shanghai, His Holiness received invitations from the monasteries of Ba, Lithang, Gyalthang,[236] and other monasteries in southern Kham. But the Chinese objected to accepting the invitations, saying that there were no motorable roads to southern Kham from China. Therefore, Tsurphu Karmapa Rinpoché, the Mindröling regent Chung Rinpoché,

The two tutors in front of the Foxiang Ge (Pavilion of the Buddha's Fragrance) at the Yiheyuan (Summer Palace) in Beijing, 1954
COURTESY OF YONGZIN LINGTSANG LABRANG

and I were dispatched to visit the monasteries of our respective religious traditions in southern Kham—Dergé, Nyakrong, and so on—as personal emissaries of His Holiness. Monastic official Ngöshiwa Thupten Samchok, physician monk Loden Chödrak, and Dzemé Rinpoché, representative of the three seats, were sent as my guides and assistants. As we were the first to be leaving China for Tibet—bearing portraits of His Holiness, his letters, and funds to make offerings at the monasteries—I requested permission to leave early and left with my attendants Lhabu, Palden, and Losang Sherap. On the day I left, I had an audience with His Holiness to take my leave. As I was to travel a great distance for a long time, I saw that His Holiness was sad. I also felt quite sad to take leave of His Holiness, as I had been with him for a long time. At the same time, I felt a great relief to be free from China. His Holiness would visit Tsongön province, Tashi Khyil, and Kumbum and arrive in Chamdo through Chengdu and Dartsedo. I was to join his entourage in Chamdo after visiting Lithang, Chatreng, Ba, and so on.

I then went to Beijing, where I spent a few days at the Bureau of the Dalai Lama. Karmapa Rinpoché, Mindröling Chung Rinpoché, and I went to visit the all-seeing Paṇchen Rinpoché, who was staying in Beijing, and receive his blessing. At that time there was a Chinese man in Beijing named Yang Daguan who had received initiation into Kālacakra from the previous Paṇchen Rinpoché and the initiations of the Mitra Hundred,[237] the *Vajrāvalī*, and so on from Ngakchen Rinpoché. As he was an observant Buddhist and requested, I secretly gave the blessing of the four sindūra initiations of Vajrayoginī to a group of about ten Chinese men and women who practiced Vajrayoginī. The important points of the visualization were translated into Chinese and explained. When we made offerings at the conclusion of the blessing, the Chinese melodiously chanted the offering and dedication prayers composed by Lama Vajradhara using Chinese phonetics. The main tsok offering was presented by two Chinese women, and they recited the verses by heart.[238] Yang Daguan placed some offerings of incense and flowers before me and said, "In the past, when I possessed great wealth, I was a patron of Ngakchen Rinpoché of Tashi Lhunpo. I requested the Mitra Hundred and made a great offering. Nowadays, since my wealth is diminished, I am unable to make such great offerings."

From Beijing, I traveled with Karmapa Rinpoché and others in a group. Traveling four or five days by boat up the Yangtze River from a city called Hankou to Chongqing, and by train in stages from Chongqing to Chengdu and Yangan, we arrived back in Tibet at Dartsedo. Representatives of Chatreng's lay and ordained populations were there in Yangan and Dartsedo, along with my attendants Losang Yeshé and Namdröl, to receive us. I gave a long-life initiation and brief teachings on the *Foundation of All Good Qualities* at Ngachö Monastery in Dartsedo.

At Dartsedo I celebrated Tibetan New Year of the wood-sheep (1955), my fifty-fifth year. At the request of Gyapön Döndrup Namgyal and Chözé Ngawang Dorjé, I offered permission for Avalokiteśvara Who Liberates from All Lower Realms[239] to about a hundred monks and laypeople in Dartsedo. When we arrived in Minyak, Karmapa Rinpoché and his retinue went to Dergé, and Mindröling Chung Rinpoché went to the Nyakrong. My retinue and I went to Ba and Lithang. As there were no motorable roads from that point on, we traveled solely on horseback from there to Chamdo.

There was a monastery called Kyilek in Minyak. According to oral accounts, my predecessor visited the monastery and gave teachings there for a few months. At the request of the administrators of the monastery, I paid a brief visit to make a token offering and give a teaching. From Minyak Rangakha, my attendants and I, Dzemé Rinpoché, the monk official representing the government, and the physician monk traveled on horses provided by the people of Chatreng. In addition to the Tibetan members of the entourage, twenty or so Chinese officers and soldiers joined us, ostensibly for our "security" but actually to spy on my activities. We did not want to bring them, but they insisted.

We crossed the Nyakchu River, and as we gradually made our way toward Lithang, we visited the family of Otok Sumpa and monasteries on the way and spent a night camping in the plains on the border of Lithang. Since the embodiment of sutra and tantra Song Rinpoché of Ganden Shartsé had been staying in Chatreng for a few years in my stead, he and Lakak Tulku came to greet me with a large number of horsemen on behalf of the monastics and laypeople of Chatreng. The following day, traveling together with the escort from Chatreng, I arrived at the great Lithang Monastery. I was received at a reception in a tent set up at the base of a nearby mountain. All the incarnate lamas and administrators in their best robes met us, and when we arrived together at Thupchen Chökhor Ling, the great monastery of Lithang, the line of escorts stretched out like a golden thread.

Arrangements had been made for me to stay on the top floor of Shiwa House, where I spent a few days and presented the offerings from His Holiness to about three thousand monks along with a portrait of His Holiness for their veneration. I also made my own offerings to the monks and at the Thupchen temple. At the request of the monastery I gave the initiation of the Great Compassionate One in the Lakṣmī tradition and an oral transmission and explanation of the *Foundation of All Good Qualities* to the monks and others in the courtyard of the assembly hall of the monastery.

At their request, I visited various houses, including Chatreng House, and the family of the Seventh Dalai Lama in the main town of Lithang and performed consecrations and gave teachings according to their wishes. On the fifteenth of the first month, they had made excellent offerings [of butter sculptures] for the Prayer Festival at the monastery; I made dedication prayers along with the offerings, which were like a mass of clouds.

From Lithang we crossed Drakar Pass and, passing through Tsosum, offered whatever Dharma teachings and consecrations were requested at various monasteries, such as Jaja Nunnery. An escort arrived from Yangteng Monastery in Dap, so we proceeded to the monastery. There I presented offerings from the government and from myself. At the request of the monastery, I gave a permission of Avalokiteśvara Who Liberates from All Lower Realms and the oral transmission and explanation of the *Foundation of All Good Qualities* to the monks and local people. As Dzemé Rinpoché had not seen the monks and his parents and family for many years, they were all overjoyed when finally reunited there. I also met some prominent citizens of Dap, including Salha Dechen Chözin, with whom I shared a patron-priest relationship during my previous visit to Kham, as well as some other seniors with whom I had relations.

Along the way Pangphuk and Drukshö Monasteries, which had been places of practice for the First Karmapa Düsum Khyenpa, offered us a reception, so I visited each place. When I asked an aged abbot from Pangphuk Monastery about their religious traditions in the monastery and whether or not they kept up the "five sets of five" that had been the principal practice of the Jé Düsum Khyenpa, the omniscient one of the past, present, and future, it seemed that he had no knowledge of the five sets. I advised him that they should uphold their own traditions and that they should live up to the name of Jé Düsum Khyenpa. I was not sure whether he liked this, but I was very sincere in my advice.

A Return Visit to Chatreng

Then after crossing Paldé Pass, we came to Upper Chatreng, where we spent two days in Chagong at the wishes of merchant Losang Yeshé at his home, called Thangteng Phakgetsang. I fulfilled the wishes of a large gathering with a Dharma teaching.

There, Gongtsen Karma Tsering, the wrathful spirit that was a local god in Chagong, suddenly possessed an oracle whose name in the local dialect was Moma. He said, "Well done!" and expressed how thankful he was, how happy he was for my recent visit to the region. When I was first recognized as an incarnate lama and later when I came to stay in Chatreng, the gods and men of Chagong didn't accept my recognition at all. Now, although I cannot be certain whether I will achieve my aims in the next life, and I play like a child at life with the title of "tutor to the Dalai Lama," a donkey draped in a leopard skin, all the people and the local deities exalt and pay respects to me. As they say, "Birds flock to the prosperous, but when you are destitute, your own son runs away." Gods, spirits, and men all act the same, it seems to me, so I find this quite humorous.

While I was at Thangteng Phakgetsang, I met my very close friend Drodru Geshé Tenzin Trinlé, who was very learned and was in the class below mine at the monastery. We then traveled through Palgé, Sölwa, and many other towns, and I stopped briefly at the full reception of Samphel Ling Monastery at Ngechi Teng. Upon my arrival, the monks provided a grand feast of ceremonial cookies at which Song Rinpoché, Lakak Tulku, and the abbot and administrators of the monastery presented scarves to me. During the ceremony, Chaklek Geshé of Yarlamgang and Butsa Nakga Geshé performed what is called "the dialogue of the ceremonial feast" perfectly in the manner as it is done in Central Tibet.

Over the fifteen days that I stayed in my own room on the top floor of the assembly hall of the monastery, I made offerings of funds on behalf of the government to over a thousand monks and presented a portrait of His Holiness to the monastery. We also offered tea and funds from our own stores to the monks. At the request of the monastery and surrounding regions, I offered the initiation into the Great Compassionate One and an explanation of the *Foundation of All Good Qualities* to a massive audience of laypeople and monks.

In order to check the quality of the rituals of propitiations and the melodies of the prayers that I had restored and introduced during my previous visit many years ago, I summoned a group of about fifty chanters and dancers to the reception hall. One day I had them perform the ritual dance, and one day I had them perform the torma-casting ritual. On that day I had put on display the brocade appliqué thangka of the *Hundred Deities of Tuṣita* that I had previously sent from Lhasa and the appliqué thangka of

Dharmarāja that is set out during the common sādhana, the torma-casting ritual, and enthronement ceremonies, and I tossed flowers to bless them.

On separate days I visited the newly constructed temples of Amitāyus and Jé Tsongkhapa and did the rituals of purification and consecration at each. They had established studies in dialectics at the temple of Jé Tsongkhapa, and thirty monks who were studying elementary dialectics debated for me. They were doing quite well, considering they were only beginners. One day a group of monks that Lakak Rinpoché had organized to perform the monthly appropriate offerings to Shukden performed the averting ritual together with its accompanying dance for me.

On another day, some of the principal monks and lay leaders from the four districts of Chatreng gathered in the reception hall to repent, from the bottom of their hearts, for breaching the guru-disciple relationship while obscured by partisanship and ignorance before when I was first recognized and when I lived in Chatreng. They asked forgiveness and promised that henceforth they would heed my advice concerning what to do and what to avoid. Asking that I love them like a mother loves a troubled child, they fervently begged me to accept their apology and care for them in all of their future lives.

In response I told them, "While it is true that each of you, layman and monk alike, have directly or indirectly entertained treacherous thoughts and actions in the past, not only have most of the principal offenders already passed, and the few that are still alive had a change of heart, since I personally bear the title 'lama,' it would go against my religious principles to hold a grudge and refuse to accept the apology of my adversaries when they hope to make amends. Since 'rejecting the apologies of those who have wronged one' contradicts the bodhisattva training, and all of you have restored your vows to perfect purity, like the sun emerging from behind the clouds, none of you need have any further misgivings." I advised everyone to live in harmony: the monks to observe the monastic discipline and work to increase their spiritual activities and the laypeople in the community to uphold the noble ideals of human conduct.

A number of villages had urged me to visit, but because I needed to be able to meet His Holiness in Chamdo, I didn't have much time, and so I gave up the idea of visiting each place individually. I arranged to meet the people from Trengshok at Chakragang, those from Rakshok at Rakmé, and those from Dongsum at Riknga Temple. After leaving the monastery,

I spent one night at Chakragang Temple and gave a long-life initiation and teachings to the people from Trengshok. There I made offerings to and consecrated a statue of Karmapa Tongwa Dönden.[240] Having met the people of northern Dongsum in the house of the Gongsum Shangmé family, I taught them Dharma. After that, I spent one night in Riknga Temple in Dongsum, where I also gave permission to practice Avalokiteśvara and taught Dharma. Then I spent one night at Rakmé Temple and gave teachings to the people of Upper and Lower Rakpo.

As I was returning from Rakmé I spent one night in the house of the Palri Yangdar family, where I met Gyalthang Abo Tulku Rinpoché, who had received many teachings from Kyabjé Vajradhara and myself. Having returned to his hometown, he had been giving extensive teachings including those on Jé Tsongkhapa's *Three Principal Aspects of the Path*. This Rinpoché had come there especially to meet me, and we performed the tenth-day tsok together.

Over the period when I stayed in Chatreng, many of my closest friends traveled over long distances to visit me: for example, Venerable Sherap Rinpoché came from Gangkar Ling; Geshé Tenzin Chöphel, with whom I had studied under the same teacher before at the monastery, came from Mili; Gyal Khangtsé Tulku and Changowa Geshé Gyaltsen, who was the student who served our precious teacher, came from Nangsang; and Lawa Geshé Khunawa, tutor to Chamdo Shiwalha, came from Kongrak.

The Journey from Chatreng to Chamdo

Mili Kyabgön Choktrul Rinpoché sent attendants bearing gifts and mules complete with saddles. Soon after that I left Chatreng with an escort of monks and laymen on horseback. After crossing the Makphak pass, we spent one night at Shokdruk Raktak Monastery where I gave a permission of Avalokiteśvara and teachings, and I consecrated the new temple dedicated to Jé Tsongkhapa. Then I visited Tongjung and Takshö and stayed in Datak Pakthang at the foothill of the snowbound Kabur region, the pilgrimage site of Heruka Cakrasaṃvara. The next morning, at their invitation, I visited Nego Monastery, where I made offerings to the monks and gave a permission of Four-Armed Avalokiteśvara to an audience of many monks and laypeople in their assembly hall.

Although I was unable to travel to the pilgrimage places due to heavy snowfall, I sent monastic official Samchok and Palden to do so and to visit Phawang Karlep, Kambur Drak, and so on to make offerings there. Nego Monastery offered me an antique thangka as an object of veneration, which I accepted. I gave them back the money and goods they offered me and supplied them with funds for making offerings to Cakrasaṃvara on the tenth of the month.

At Takpak Thang, at the request of Gyalthang Abo Rinpoché, I gave an initiation of Cakrasaṃvara body mandala combined with the preparation ritual in one day to Rinpoché himself along with Dzemé Rinpoché and Yangteng Khyenrap Tulku. The people of Ru region were lined up to receive us as we passed through Gemo Ruthok and so on, and most of the leaders of the monastery and its surrounding area, the abbots, monks, reincarnate lamas of Chödé Monastery, and so on came to escort us as we approached Lakha Hermitage in Ba. Then the monks of Chödé Lhundrup Rabten in Ba escorted us to the monastery, filing in a long line, and we stayed there in Lakha Labrang. At Chödé Monastery I offered His Holiness's letter, photographs of him as objects of veneration, and monetary offerings on behalf of the government, and I made my personal offerings. At the request of the monastery and the local population, in the great field in front of the newly erected large Buddha temple, I gave an audience of monks, lamas, and local people the initiation into the Great Compassionate One.

After stopping off to teach and perform a consecration at Bawa Gyashok House at their request, we arrived at the great Drichu River via Chisung Gang. Having crossed the river on a log raft I met an escort of horsemen waiting on the bank, including Adruk, the treasurer of Gangkar Lama's household, and others. We then passed through the village of Tarkha, the spot where our trader with horses and mules bearing merchandise were robbed together with those of the Palbar Tsang and Dampa Tsang households. After crossing Khangtsek Pass and traveling through Upper Bumpa, we arrived at Nyago Monastery in Bum. There, upon request, I gave a long-life initiation and teachings, including the oral transmission of the *maṇi* mantra.

After crossing the pass into Lower Bumpa and passing in stages through a valley called Gönang, we arrived at Gangkar Labrang at Seudru Monastery, where we were very well received and looked after for the three days we spent there. I taught Dharma to a large gathering of monks and laypeople from the monastery and its surrounding area, including giving permission to practice Avalokiteśvara Who Liberates from All Lower Realms and performed the consecration rite of Causing the Rain of Goodness to Fall for the memorial stupa of the late Gangkar Lama Rinpoché, which contains his fully preserved body that produces relics spontaneously. There is also a treasure box there containing what are called "immortal iron pills" that always miraculously replenished. There were always pills in the box until the lama passed his thoughts into peace, and thereafter they gradually diminished until the treasure box was empty. Just before the great lama passed away, for the sake of others he revealed a new treasure vessel of iron pills, shaped like an egg, but had not opened it. When I held the vessel in my hand and shook it, it sounded like there were many pills inside. The attendants of the lama asked me to open it, but I could not tell the top from the bottom. Baffled, I couldn't figure out how to open it.

At Lhadun in Markham I visited the magnificent stone image of Vairocana reputed to have been carved by the Chinese queen.[241] Passing through Gushö Pangda and so on, we stopped by Garthok Öser Monastery, Ribur Monastery, Kyungbum Lura Monastery, and others at their invitation. At each monastery I made offerings and gave teachings, oral transmissions, and initiations to satisfy their request. At the insistence of Drakpa Tulku and the denizens of Lura Monastery, I stayed there for three days. One day they put on a performance of the propitiatory ritual dance of the Seven Blazing Brothers that was said to be identical to the Demo Gucham ritual dance at Tengyé Ling in Lhasa. The moves with which the seven brothers of savage spirit Pawo Trobar of Laok blazed with a hundred expressions of wrath were magnificent and full of energy, and indeed they seemed remarkably like those used in the ritual dance at Tengyé Ling.

After a long journey, we reached the border of Drakgyab region. Drakgyab Labrang had sent a senior staff member to receive me there and assist us on the way. Excellent arrangements had been made at every place where we stopped. I was invited by the hermits of Sakar Hermitage to visit them, and although the monastery was out of our way and would take a long time to visit, because of my spiritual friendship with Lama Arap Rinpoché through our correspondence when he was still alive, I went there disregarding the inconvenience. I gave a teaching on the *Foundation of All Good Qualities* to the monks. They had recently established dialectical studies, and the students engaged in debate were quite good.

The day that I arrived at Bugön Monastery in Drakgyab, having been received by a great array of members from the labrang, a reception committee, and a long line of monks clad in yellow, I was housed in Dagyab Hothokthu Rinpoché's quarters atop the assembly hall, where I stayed for four or five days. I gave the full assembly of monks the great initiation into thirteen-deity Vajrabhairava and gave the local public permission to practice Avalokiteśvara Who Liberates from All Lower Realms.

One day I visited the historically renowned Jamdun Temple to make elaborate offerings and do a brief consecration ritual. The principal image at Jamdun Temple was a wonderful stone image of Maitreya and his retinue that had emerged from the ground up. While I was staying at Bugön Monastery, a former classmate of mine named Geshé Bu Chögyal came from his hermitage to visit me. At the beginning of our meeting he assumed a very humble attitude and showed me much respect, but as we had long been spiritual friends, once I spoke casually with him about our experiences in the old days, the geshé also began to speak freely with me about the times we had shared and any news he had to offer, just as he had when we were in school together. I gave him and a few other earnest practitioners an outline of the main points, without detailed explanation, of the *Hundred Deities of Tuṣita*. Given the season over which I stayed, hardly any vegetables were available. So each day Drakgyab Labrang served me a tray with a variety of unique dishes prepared from the same type of meat, and I ate like the king of Lanka.[242]

From Drakgyab I reached the border of Chamdo, where Shiwalha Rinpoché, who was the general manager of Chamdo, monastic official Sönam Gyaltsen, who was the elder brother of Phakchen Rinpoché, and others had come to receive us there. We spent a night there, as had been arranged, and the next morning we went on to Chamdo Chökhor Jampaling Monastery, where we stopped briefly for an elaborate reception under a tent. Afterward we proceeded to the monastery on horseback in procession with many prominent members of the monastery and the region. Just on the other side of the bridge over the Dzachu River, there stood arranged in a line a vast welcoming party comprised of military and civilian masses, students, quite a few Tibetan officers and soldiers who had been captured by the Chinese when Chamdo fell, as well as government officials, abbots and representatives of the three seats, and public representatives who had all come there to receive His Holiness as he traveled back to Lhasa. After arriving at the monastery, I was made to feel quite at home in the residence of Shiwalha.

His Holiness's arrival was briefly delayed because the motor route in the area of Dartsedo had been damaged by an earthquake, and so the large crowd was left waiting. In the meantime, at the heartfelt request of Shiwalha Rinpoché, I gave a discourse over the course of fourteen days on the stages of the path based on the *Easy Path* in the great assembly hall of Chamdo Monastery. The gathering numbered more than one thousand, including monks already living in Chamdo and those gathered there to receive and welcome His Holiness.

One day, at the invitation of Tsenyi Monastery, I gave a discourse in one session on the first few folios of the *Great Treatise on the Stages of the Path* to the monks in the debate courtyard. Then the students assembled in groups according to class level and began to debate. Thanks to the kindness of the great virtuous friend, Geshé Jampa Thayé Rinpoché, complete with the mandala of the ocean of learning, the dialectical studies were excellent, equal to the essence of dialectical studies in Sera Jé Monastery.

Reuniting with His Holiness and Returning to Lhasa

When His Holiness arrived in Chamdo, I went to the other side of the bridge across the Dzachu River to greet him. When I saw his golden countenance, exceedingly meaningful to behold and radiating with ten thousand virtues and goodnesses, he regarded me with unrestrained warmth and gladness. Shortly afterward, when he had settled in his quarters, I went to meet him in person as he had requested. He shared with me in great detail general and specific news of his trip to different regions of China, his stay in the jurisdiction of Domé, how Mao Zedong's way of speaking when he met with him made it clear his true intentions regarding Tibet, and many other things that I must keep secret within the innermost core of my heart. I too gave him a report of my travels to the different regions of Kham. This opportunity to pass the time at leisure with him refreshed the lotus of my heart with the rain of great pleasure and devotion, thus the petals of fortune unfolded. Shiwalha Rinpoché's labrang took very good care of us throughout our stay in Chamdo.

I gave Rinpoché alone all the permissions of the seventeen emanations of Four-Faced Mahākāla except for Secret Accomplishment and Black Brahman,[243] thereby fulfilling his wishes. Before I took my leave, he gave me a set of two ritual vases and inner offering cups complete with support and many other ritual objects made of gilded silver.

I left Chamdo with His Holiness and met Khargo Tulku, the general manager of Drakgyab Monastery, and others at Kyilthang in the territory of Drakgyab. Traveling in stages via Pangda in Tsawa, over the great bridge on the Gyamo River and so on, we came to Powo Tramo. A heavy rain had fallen the morning of the day we left Tramo, and boulders had spilled down the mountainside and blocked the road, holding us up for quite some time. The boulders were eventually cleared away so that the motor vehicles could just squeeze through.

Late in the afternoon just as the sun was setting, we came to a place where a waterfall from an overhanging ridge of the mountain came down in a violent torrent and had washed out one of the corner supports of the bridge we needed to cross. It was much too dangerous to cross the bridge in our vehicles, so His Holiness, Tutor Ling Rinpoché, myself, and a few other members of the entourage first crossed the bridge on foot, and then the cars were driven across one by one. Just as one of the vehicles was crossing the bridge, it gave out a loud cracking sound as the timber splintered. Although the bridge collapsed in half and plummeted down the ravine, no one was hurt, but the rest of our entourage and luggage were left on the other side of the river. The rest of us who had made it across piled into the few vehicles we had and traveled down the winding road through the night, terrified of gushing cataracts, precipices, and deep ravines, until we arrived at a place called Lunang in Kongpo around midnight.

There, without any bedding whatsoever, Losang Sherap and myself spent a cold night in a cloth tent. Mr. Mentöpa and a few government officials of the fourth rank had come there from Lhasa to receive us. I barely slept that night due to anxious worry about those left behind. That night Chinese road workers put a bridge across the river suspended on two logs bound together with ropes. His Holiness's chamber attendant and a few members of his kitchen staff then crossed the bridge. Palden also joined them, at great risk to himself, out of concern for my safety and came in a jeep to join me at the break of dawn. Lhabu and Losang Yeshé were left behind and were unable to catch up with us until we arrived at Dakpa Monastery in Maldro.

Making our way in stages along the road through places in Kongpo, such as Demo, Nyangtri, and Gyada, we crossed Ba Pass to arrive at Dakpa

Monastery in the district of Maldro, where members of Namgyal Monastery's Phendé Lekshé Ling who had prepared lodgings for His Holiness awaited us. There we were received by the estate manager of Maldro Jarado and Lhakchung from our house in Lhasa.

At the foot of Ganden I lunched together with His Holiness's entourage in a meadow as lush and green as a parrot's wings outstretched, where the governing body of Drok Riwoché Ganden Nampar Gyalwai Ling had prepared an elaborate reception in a tent. After meeting with the abbots, incarnate lamas, and monastic administrators, I went on to the temple at Tsal Gungthang, my birthplace. Every government official, of high, middling, and lower ranks, lay and ordained, and a great number of abbots and incarnate lamas from the seats of Sera and Drepung monasteries had arrived there to greet His Holiness. The government offered an elaborate welcoming feast of cookies in the temple, and Gungthang Labrang offered a separate feast in the sunlight room atop the temple. I, too, remained at Gungthang for three days, awaiting the astrologically auspicious day for the party to travel to Lhasa.

Around the thirteenth day of the fifth month, His Holiness traveled by sedan chair from Gungthang to the Norbulingka Kalsang Palace with an elaborate, traditional procession of riders on horseback. Since it rained heavily that day from the moment the procession departed Gungthang until it reached the Norbulingka, the sedan chair had to be draped with a rainproof cover, and all the members of the entourage had to wear red woolen rain capes over their best ceremonial attire. It occurred to many of us that this was not a good omen. After the reception ceremony upon our arrival at the Norbulingka, I returned to my house in Lhasa, where over the course of many days patrons and students of all levels with whom I bore religious and secular connections visited, and I accepted their offerings, which were as abundant as the cloud formations.

His Holiness the Dalai Lama with Ling Rinpoché on his right and Trijang Rinpoché on his left at Hyderabad House, New Delhi, 1956

Courtesy of Palden Tsering

His Holiness the Dalai Lama's geshé lharam examination at Drepung Monastery, 1958

Source unknown

Guests at the Office of the Tibetan Representative in Beijing, New Year's Day, February 23, 1955.
Front row from the left: Lord Chamberlain Phalha, Secretary General Ngawang Döndrup, Assistant Tutor Gyatso Ling, Deputy Minister Neshar, Minling Chung Rinpoché, Ngaphö Ngawang Jikmé, Ling Rinpoché, the Dalai Lama, Trijang Rinpoché, Karmapa Rinpoché, Minister Surkhang, the Dalai Lama's mother Dekyi Tsering, Ngari Rinpoché, the Dalai Lama's sister Tsering Drölma, Sakya Dakchen Rinpoché

Courtesy of Yongzin Lingtsang Labrang

Ganden Monastery, 1937

© Hugh Richardson, Pitt Rivers Museum, University of Oxford; 1998.131.356

Ganden Monastery in ruins, 1982

Sharpa Tulku

Kyabjé Ling Rinpoché, His Holiness the Dalai Lama, and Kyabjé Trijang Rinpoché at the Mahabodhi Stupa, Bodhgaya, 1961

Courtesy of Yongzin Lingtsang Labrang

Above: Memorial stupa of the Thirteenth Dalai Lama, Granting All Goodness and Happiness, in the Potala Palace, Lhasa
COURTESY OF YONGZIN LINGTSANG LABRANG

Left: The sacred statue of Ārya Wati Sangpo of Kyirong
© SONAM TSERING

Trijang Rinpoché and Palden Tsering in Geneva, Switzerland, 1966

Courtesy of Palden Tsering

Last known picture of Trijang Rinpoché, outside Tashi Rapten residence, 1981

Joyce Murdoch

His Holiness the Dalai Lama cutting the first snip of hair from the incarnation of Trijang Rinpoché at Thekchen Chöling, Dharamsala, 1985

Courtesy of Palden Tsering

The incarnation of Trijang Rinpoché in front of Sharpa Tulku at Tashi Rapten residence in Dharamsala, 1985. To their right is Rinpoché's father, Sönam Topgyal. Rinpoché's mother, Losang Drölma, is holding the youngest of five children.

Courtesy of Palden Tsering

Kyabjé Trijang Rinpoché in his room at Tashi Rapten House, Dharamsala, 1973
B. ALAN WALLACE

The incarnation of Trijang Rinpoché at Tashi Rapten House
DIANE BARKER. COURTESY OF TIBET IMAGES COLLECTION

8 | Storm Clouds Gathering

Chinese Appointments and My Mother's Passing

THAT YEAR, the Chinese asked me to be the principal of the Lhasa middle school. I declined, citing my lack of experience of the modern educational system so that my services would be of no benefit. The Chinese appealed to His Holiness, and I was forced to accept the position. I would go to visit the school once a week to offer my thoughts and advice to the teachers and students.

In the fall, as requested by Phakchen Hothokthu of Chamdo, I gave the complete permission of the Rinjung Hundred practice in the assembly hall of Shidé Monastery to a gathering of over three thousand including Phakchen Rinpoché, Dagyab Hothokthu, the incarnation of Kyabjé Phabongkha Vajradhara, as well as to many lamas, geshés, and monks of the three monasteries and others. As gifts for my safe return from China, I made many offerings and monetary donations for annual offerings to the three seats and the two tantric colleges. I presented Shartsé College of Ganden eight large decorative banners made of Varanasi brocade for the eight tall pillars in their assembly hall and presented Dokhang House four large pillar banners of Japanese brocade and a victory banner along with three triangular banners.

In my fifty-sixth year, the year of the fire-monkey (1956), my mother Tsering Drölma passed away at the venerable age of eighty-two after being treated for a sudden illness that lasted a few days. I had visited her often before and at the time of her death on the twelfth day of the first month, giving her advice on virtuous thoughts. Afterward I whispered the names of the tathāgatas and various types of profound dhāraṇī and mantras in her ear and then performed with care the ritual for transference of consciousness. Although my mother did not know many different practices, she was kind at heart, regularly recited the six-syllable mantra, and made great efforts to perform virtuous practices with her body and speech by doing prostrations and making offerings at the inner and outer courts of the Tsuklakhang and by circumambulating Lhasa's circular path. So she suffered not even the slightest pain from her sickness nor experienced any hopes or fears based on clinging when she died but passed from life peacefully in her sleep just as a lamp dies out when its fuel is exhausted. Since Lhasa's Great Prayer Festival was in session at the time, I made offerings on the fifteenth of the month and made offerings at various monasteries each week thereafter.

An official called Marshal Chen Yi came from China to inaugurate the Preparatory Committee for the Autonomous Region of Tibet that would be comprised of fifty-one representatives drawn from three areas: the government, Tashi Lhunpo, and the three regions including Chamdo. Again, I was required to join that committee against my will. And, again, although I had no desire to do so, I was forced to accept the title of director in an office called the Bureau of Religious Affairs. However, when the bureau actually began its work, no matter what suggestions I made, sitting at the head at the table, they did not influence matters. All the major decisions were inevitably made according to the wishes of Hui Khochang, the Chinese member. My appointment to the position of principal at the middle school was also in reality devoid of any power. My being powerless while forced against my will to bear empty civilian titles that I had no appetite for was punishment visited upon me due to past acts, such as giving Dharma talks that were mere words delivered without having practiced them myself—a grand dance to allure the faithful into the drama of the eight worldly concerns. As Mañjunātha Sakya Paṇḍita said in his *Jewel Treasury of Wise Sayings* (8.29):

> If a monkey did not dance,
> would it still be leashed at the neck?

And also (6.36):

> Because the parrot speaks, he is put in a cage,
> while the mute bird flies free.

When these meetings actually began in the fourth Tibetan month, both His Holiness the Dalai Lama and the all-seeing Paṇchen Rinpoché were required to attend them in full, and a great many representatives from the provinces of China, Amdo, Inner Mongolia, and from Kham and its regions attended. The assembly was convened with a great celebration, and afterward many days were passed with the distracting tumult.

In the sixth month at the request of the monk Gendun Chöyang, a family member of Rong Dekyi, I gave over the course of a few days initiation into Cittamaṇi Tārā according to the close transmission lineage stemming from the divine visions of Takphu Vajradhara and gave an explanation of the two stages to nearly one thousand disciples, lamas, reincarnate masters, geshés, and so on in Shidé assembly hall. After that, at the request of Dagyab Hothokthu Rinpoché, at Shidé monastic college I offered an audience of more than one thousand the great initiation of Secret Hayagrīva in the Kyergang tradition along with its preparatory practices. Right after that I offered in a series: permissions to practice the Surka Cycle of sādhanas, the eighty mahāsiddhas, and the deities of the sādhana cycles taught by Gyalwa Gendun Gyatso; four transmissions and their blessings including the distant lineage of the long-life initiation of Amitāyus, two close lineages of Drigung Chödrak's vision, and the exclusive long-life empowerment for Amitāyus as a single deity with a single vase in the tradition of Machik Drupai Gyalmo; and permission for Bhagavan Samayavajra along with permissions for the collected mantras of Guhyasamāja, Cakrasaṃvara, and Vajrabhairava.

Visit to Radreng

In the eighth month, at the invitation of Radreng Labrang, His Holiness, Tutor Ling Rinpoché, and myself traveled to Radreng Gephel Ling with a small entourage, proceeding from the Norbulingka along the northern motor roads through Tölung and Damshung. His Holiness presided over the full ritual of consecration in the main temple, which we performed over a three-day period. There we saw sacred relics such as the statue of Jowo Jampal Dorjé, the reliquary stupa of Atiśa, his monastic robes and *saṅghāṭi*,[244] his personal volumes of Indian texts, Dromtönpa's personal copy of the *Eight Thousand Verse Perfection of Wisdom*, the statue of "left-leaning" Atiśa, and the thangka of Vajrabhairava that was Guru Dharmarakṣita's principal object of meditation.

The room I stayed in was the room in which I had previously received novice ordination. Among the many texts housed in the room I found a hand-copied commentary on Asaṅga's *Compendium of Abhidharma* that the venerable Rendawa had composed at the request of Jé Tsongkhapa himself[245] and a volume of various collected teachings of Rendawa. As the commentary on the *Compendium* was exceedingly detailed, I fell asleep over it with my head swimming. The next day among the texts I found a few handwritten letters exchanged between Jé Tsongkhapa and Rendawa on matters of sutra and tantra in general and on the view of emptiness in particular. These letters were separate from the ones found in the collected works of Jé Tsongkhapa. I wanted to transcribe them but found no time, and so I wanted to borrow them and take them to Lhasa, but we were constantly distracted and the time passed. It was unfortunate, but it could not be helped. At Yangön Retreat Monastery, the site where the noble lord had composed the *Great Treatise on the Stages of the Path*, His Holiness and we his entourage read aloud the *Great Treatise*, dividing its sections among us.

Earlier when the prior regent Radreng Rinpoché and his followers fell from power in the year of the fire-pig (1947), soldiers had peeled the silver covering the reliquary stupa and had pried the jewel ornaments from the stupa and statues. They had been pockmarked with bullet holes. A three-dimensional mandala of Guhyasamāja had been smashed to pieces with cudgels like an earthen clod. When I saw the mounds of ruins and so on—evidence of the many wicked, nearly inexpiable acts, more degenerate than those of the degenerate era, that had been carried out—and thought about this special, sacred place that is the headwaters of the Kadam teachings having fallen into this state of deterioration, I was stricken with grief. With Kyabjé Ling Rinpoché acting as the preceptor and I as the master, the supreme incarnation of Radreng Rinpoché received novice ordination.

On the return journey, at the request of the renowned Gyümé Monastery, treasury of the profound tantras, which was observing the late rainy-season retreat in the valley of Chumik in Tölung, His Holiness stopped there to create a Dharma connection with the monks. By traveling there together with him, I was able to see the sacred thangkas of Jé Sherap Sengé[246] that Jé Tsongkhapa had given him. Following my return from Tölung, I went and participated in the annual consecration rituals at the invitation of Ganden Shartsé. One day I offered an explanation of the *Hundred Deities of Tuṣita* to most of the monks of Shartsé and Jangtsé in the debate courtyard of Shartsé.

Celebrating the Buddha Jayanti in Bodhgaya

That year (1956), His Holiness and the all-seeing Paṇchen Rinpoché were one after the other both extended invitations to the festival that the Mahabodhi Society in India had organized to commemorate the two thousand five hundredth anniversary of the *mahāparinirvāṇa*, or passing, of Lord Buddha (according to the Theravāda tradition). Although they both really wanted to attend, the Chinese, using various excuses, indicated that it wouldn't be good for His Holiness to go and asked that he send a representative instead.

His Holiness appointed me to the task, with Dzasak Khemé Sönam Wangdü and monk official Ngöshiwa Thupten Samchok as assistant liaisons and Rinchen Sadutshang as our interpreter.[247] On the day that we visited him to take our leave for the trip to India, Zhang Jingwu, the Chinese representative in Lhasa, came to inform His Holiness that he had received a telegram from China saying that it was all right for him to attend the religious festival in India. It had suddenly been resolved. I was told that it was necessary that I still accompany him in his entourage, and soon after His Holiness, Kyabjé Ling Rinpoché, myself, cabinet minister Ngaphö, and so on left Lhasa with a small entourage.

We traveled along the Ü-Tsang motor road through Tölung and Uyuk to Tashi Lhunpo Monastery, where after having met with the all-seeing Paṇchen Rinpoché, we passed one night.

Lord Chamberlain Phalha Thupten Öden had earnestly requested that Kyabjé Ling Rinpoché and myself spend a night at Paljor Lhundrup, his family estate in Gyantsé. So as soon as we finished paying our respects to Paṇchen Rinpoché at Tashi Lhunpo, we set out for Paljor Lhunpo, arriving at eleven o'clock that night. Although I had gone that way to Gyantsé before, due to the blackness of that moonless night, I couldn't make out the road. Not only did Kyabjé Ling Rinpoché and his entourage not know the way, neither did the Chinese driver! Because we were going along based on guesswork, we were all terrified of plummeting over the edge of a cliff—we all got a little taste of the first noble truth, the truth of suffering!

We went from Gyantsé to Jema in Lower Dromo in one day. The next morning we joined the entourage of His Holiness at Nathu Pass. The two supreme victors, spiritual father and son, traveled in a single group. Several Chinese officers and soldiers came to accompany them up to the top of the pass. Beyond it at the frontier, they were greeted by an Indian guard of honor and the representative of the Indian government. Passing Tsogo Lake we reached Gangtok, the capital of Sikkim, where we were received in the palace of the maharaja.

The next morning before dawn we left for the airport in Siliguri by car and boarded a special plane. That evening we touched down in the capital, New Delhi, where we were received by a large welcoming committee—including the vice president,[248] Prime Minister Nehru, members of the diplomatic corps, and leaders of the delegations who had come to attend the celebrations. His Holiness and his entourage stayed at Hyderabad House, a guesthouse for important foreign dignitaries. Tutor Ling Rinpoché and I stayed in the rooms adjacent to His Holiness's suite.

The following morning I went together with His Holiness and Paṇchen Rinpoché to visit Raj Ghat, the memorial place where Mahatma Gandhi was cremated. Over the next several days I was a part of the entourage that participated in the ceremonies of the Buddha Jayanti. My kind spiritual friend, that fearless lion-like exponent of the teachings, Geshé Sherap Gyatso of Lubum, who had also come from China as one of the delegates to the Jayanti, was staying at the Ashoka Hotel in Delhi. I went to pay my respects to him and he contented my heart with a stream of his ever-nourishing words of wisdom.

After the great Jayanti ceremonies were completed, I accompanied His Holiness as we toured the major sites of Buddhist pilgrimage as the guests of the government of India. We visited sites such as Bodhgaya, Varanasi, Nālandā, Kushinagar, Lumbini, Vulture Peak, Sanchi, and the Ajanta caves and Nagarjunakonda in South India, cities such as Bombay, Mysore, Bangalore, and Calcutta, and we toured some major industrial plants. When I visited holy sites like Nālandā, I thought about how the compassionate Buddha and the Six Ornaments and Two Excellent Ones[249] had done this and that at this specific place, and remembering the stories of their lives, was filled with faith. I was also happy to have been able to go to those places, but since little more than ruins remain of them now, I felt sad. Reflecting on impermanence, I was torn between equal feelings of faith, joy, and mourning.

Earlier in China and now in India we toured many industrial factories. As I watched molten iron and copper, cascading like rivers, being poured into molds and pressed out and beaten by massive machines, I was reminded of

His Holiness the Dalai Lama, the two tutors, and the rest of the official entourage at Hyderabad House in New Delhi, India, 1956
COURTESY OF OFFICE OF HIS HOLINESS THE DALAI LAMA

the torments of the hell realms, and a healthy sense of urgency would well up in me. Nevertheless, after a few days the scattered thoughts of one who has grown callous to Dharma would return anew. The fact that I was unable to wholly rid myself of the habitual undercurrent of thoughts governed by the three poisons indicates just how ingrained are the predispositions to bad behavior I have acquired through prior lifetimes.

Fears and Conflict upon Returning to Tibet

After staying in Kalimpong for several days giving Dharma discourses and so on, His Holiness went to Gangtok. Prime Minister Dekhar Tsewang Rabten (Lukhangwa), deputy cabinet minister Yuthok Tashi Döndrup, and monk official Ngawang Döndrup had arrived there from Lhasa under the pretense of escorting His Holiness back to Tibet, but in fact they had come first and foremost to report to him about the deteriorating conditions and the forceful occupation by the Chinese. As they implored him that it would be best to remain within India, about half a month passed without resolving the issue of whether to return or to stay. I stayed in Kalimpong at the house of the Sadutshang family.

All-seeing Paṇchen Rinpoché and his entourage had already left Kalimpong for Tsang ahead of us. As soon as it had been decided that His Holiness would return to Tibet, I reported to Gangtok and we all departed as a group. When we reached the top of Nathu Pass and I saw the flag of the Chinese officers and soldiers who had come to receive us, I felt great sorrow and trepidation, like someone being returned to prison.

Traveling in stages on the road through Dromo and Phakri we arrived in Gyantsé. It so happened that the new year of the fire-bird (1957) came when we were in Gyantsé, so His Holiness and the entourage spent a few days there. It was arranged that I would stay at Shiné Monastery. I fulfilled the wishes of Shiné and Rikha[250] monasteries with teachings on the *Hundred Deities of Tuṣita* and the *Foundation of All Good Qualities*, among others. On the twenty-ninth day of the twelfth month, Shiné Monastery performed a torma-casting ritual dance for His Holiness. I thought it was a good presentation and not performed merely to satisfy the shopkeepers. There was a New Year celebration with ceremonial cookies arranged by the government. At the celebration, Dzemé Rinpoché of Shartsé and Ratö Khyongla Rinpoché performed the religious dialogues.

Following New Year's, His Holiness traveled to the headquarters of the Samdrup Tsé district via Panam, where we also stayed. The population of the thirteen counties under the administration of the Tsang central government, both the upper and lower classes, offered a long-life ceremony for His Holiness, and His Holiness offered the public Dharma teachings in the district assembly hall.

Moving to the great Dharma seat of Tashi Lhunpo, His Holiness reunited with the all-seeing Paṇchen Rinpoché. He visited temples, made offerings, and consecrated images. After delivering Dharma teachings in the great assembly halls at Tashi Lhunpo and the Dechen Phodrang Palace, I was fortunate to travel together with His Holiness as he toured Ngor Evaṃ Chödé, Pal Narthang, Shalu, and Rithil and the temple of Shalu Gyangong, the place where Mañjunātha Sakya Paṇḍita took his vows of full ordination before the Kashmiri paṇḍita.[251] I was quite fortunate to have had that opportunity.

All throughout the time that His Holiness stayed at Tashi Lhunpo, the administration of Tashi Lhunpo had arranged for me to stay at Pontsang Drangkhang, which was the home of the tutor Lhopa Tulku Rinpoché. Kyabjé Ling Rinpoché and I had an audience with the all-seeing Paṇchen Rinpoché. We offered him gifts and money during a visit filled with cordial conversation. Afterward, I also visited tutor Ngulchu Rinpoché, who had invited me because in the past he received from me the oral transmission of the collected works of Jé Tsongkhapa and his two disciples.

The two supreme victors, spiritual father and son, inwardly shared the same view of things and were in fact quite close to one another, harboring not even the least bit of tension between them. Since this was the case, with the hope of further strengthening goodwill between the Ganden Phodrang government and Tashi Lhunpo—a profound connection based on pure, unsullied vows—I expressed my sincere, unvarnished opinion to many of the key figures on the staff of Tashi Lhunpo on various occasions, such as when Paṇchen Rinpoché first came to Lhasa from Amdo and during this visit. But it was as in the proverb "Profound Dharma brings powerful evils."[252] On the one hand, the Chinese were using various deceitful means to sow dissent in Tibet, and on the other hand, some officials both in the government and Tashi Lhunpo, their minds influenced by devils, were eager to cause schisms between the two lamas. The situation was fraught. It seemed as though Khardo Rikzin Chökyi Dorjé's prophecy had come to pass:

> The skein of wool of Ü and Tsang
> has been shredded by insects over many years and ruined.
> Still, in hopes of weaving fine, smooth cloth,
> you wear yourselves out searching for a weaver.

Departing Shigatsé by way of the Tak ferry, I accompanied His Holiness on a tour of monasteries he had been invited to, such as Ganden Chökhor Monastery in Shang, Dechen Rabgyé Ling, Thupten Serdokchen Monastery, the seat of Paṇchen Shākya Chokden, and Yangchen Monastery in Tölung, until his lotus feet once again graced the grounds of the Norbulingka Palace in Lhasa.

At the request of Drip Tsechok Ling Labrang, over the course of at least twenty-five days during the fourth month, I taught the root verses of the *Guru Puja* and Kachen Yeshé Gyaltsen's great instruction manual on it, along with instructions based on the root commentary on Ganden Mahāmudrā by Paṇchen Losang Chögyen.[253] The audience of around eight hundred included lamas, reincarnate masters, and geshés who had come from Sera, Drepung, and Lhasa, such as Dagyab Rinpoché and the incarnation of Kyabjé Phabongkha Rinpoché. The discourse sowed roots of virtue with meaningful exposition.

Visits to Tsurphu and Yerpa

At the invitation of Tsurphu Karmapa Rinpoché, supreme holder of the lineage of siddhas, His Holiness visited Tsurphu Monastery in Tölung. Tutor Ling Rinpoché and I accompanied His Holiness, and we were all well received. There I saw such things as the central statue called the Great Sage that Ornaments the World, which was miraculously erected by the Second Karmapa Karma Pakshi, and the memorial stupa of the First Karmapa Düsum Khyenpa called Tashi Öbar.

On the tenth day of the fifth month, we experienced the spectacle that was the festival famed as the Tsurphu Summer Dances. It included the ritual dance of the eight aspects of Guru Rinpoché, performed with graceful and relaxed movements, and Karmapa Rinpoché himself led the ritual dance of the ḍākas and ḍākinis. One day while we were there, when the great relic boxes of Tsurphu Labrang were opened for His Holiness to see, I was lucky enough to see the various relics of the golden lineage of Kagyü gurus and of many other Indian and Tibetan paṇḍits and siddhas, the black hat with golden ornament on the front, and so on.

When the Fifth Karmapa Deshin Shekpa (1384–1415) traveled to China to perform funeral rites on behalf of the Yongle emperor (1360–1424), from the fifth day until the nineteenth of the third month of the fire-pig year (1407), people witnessed rainbow-tinged clouds in various shapes, such as elephants and lions, in the sky and saw buddhas, bodhisattvas, and celestial offerings among the clouds. On the final day a golden light spread from the west throughout the entire Chinese empire. I was shown the large silk scroll, mentioned in Pawo Tsuklak Trengwa's religious history, on which, at the orders of the Yongle emperor, the many wonders that appeared were

The Sixteenth Karmapa Rangjung Rikpé Dorjé at Tsurphu Monastery, 1946
© Hugh Richardson, Pitt Rivers Museum, University of Oxford; 2001.59.7.36.1

captured each day in paintings accompanied by inscriptions in Tibetan, Chinese, and Uyghur scripts. It was an excellent piece of art in the ancient Chinese tradition. The miraculous signs and good omens that appeared at that time filled me with a wonderful joy that increased my faith and belief.

On the way back from Tsurphu, I accompanied His Holiness when he stopped by Nenang Monastery at the invitation of Pawo Rinpoché. We visited the memorial stupas of Tokden Drakpa Sengé (1283–1349)[254] and others and then returned to Lhasa.

In the eighth month, after the rainy-season retreat at the Norbulingka Palace, His Holiness visited the holy site of Drak Yerpa and stayed on the top floor of the assembly hall of Ganden Sang-ngak Yangtsé at Yerpa Monastery. I also roomed there and saw, among other things, Lord Atiśa's plate that bore an image of himself that he had drawn. At the time the monks of Gyütö Tantric College, the assembly of those who practice the secret tantra, were in the middle of their later rainy-season retreat. Together with the entire assembly of monks, I participated in the Guhyasamāja ritual of consecration for three days. His Holiness presided over this ritual of causing extensive blessings of vajra wisdom to descend on behalf of the world and the living beings supported within it. We also visited and made offerings to the large Maitreya statue that Matön Chökyi Jungné erected in the Maitreya temple, the statue of Avalokiteśvara that Rigzin Kumara made in Songtsen Cave, a statue of Vairocana dating back to the time of King Songtsen Gampo, the protector chapel of Palden Lhamo, the cave in which Lhalung Paldor[255] practiced, the Tendrel Phuk Cave of Atiśa, and the temple of Prince Gungri Gungtsen. Tsok offerings were made in the room, called Moon Cave, of Orgyen Padmasambhava, the second Buddha.

At the joint request of Gyütö Tantric College and Yerpa Monastery, His Holiness, himself an emanation of Dromtönpa, read Atiśa's *Lamp on the Path to Enlightenment* as an oral transmission to a great crowd of people gathered on the slopes of Yerpa Lhari Nyingpo. I was delighted and extremely fortunate to have been together with His Holiness when he graced the Dharma and living beings with great happiness and benefit on the very same holy spot where earlier Lord Atiśa and his spiritual sons had lit the lamp of the Kadam sevenfold divinity and teaching.[256]

After His Holiness completed his activities at Yerpa, we stopped off at Garpa Hermitage on the way back to Lhasa at the request of the all-embracing lord of a hundred buddha families, Kyabjé Ling Vajradhara. Passing just three or four days there receiving offerings of long-life prayers and consecrating images, His Holiness left ahead of us. Rinpoché said to me, "Stay and relax for a few days." So together we passed some time relaxing and having deep and wide-ranging discussions with one another and then returned to the Norbulingka.

After that, at the request of Lady Dorjé Yudrön of Yuthok Kyitsal, over the course of a month in the assembly hall of Lhasa's Shidé Monastery, to an audience of more than four thousand ordained sangha members, chief among whom were nearly fifty incarnate lamas of various ranks, such as the supreme incarnation of Kyabjé Phabongkha Vajradhara, Dagyab Hothokthu, and Chamdo Phakchen Hothokthu, and many well-known geshés like the former Sera Jé abbot Tsangpa Thapkhé, I gave the last teachings on the stages of the path I would give in Tibet. I explained, based on personal experience, the *Quick Path* and the *Easy Path*, the *Words of Mañjuśrī* according to both the central and southern lineages, and *Liberation in the Palm of Your Hand* based on my notes. In addition I taught the *Seven-Point Mind Training* and the sections from the stages of the path on equalizing and exchanging self with others, concluding with the ritual to develop bodhicitta.

After that, at the request of the exponent of the vast scriptures Geshé Ugyen Tseten from Sera Jé's Trehor House, I went to Sera and in the debate courtyard of Trehor House offered an extensive teaching on the *Hundred Deities of Tuṣita* to a large group of monks that included the supreme incarnation of Radreng Rinpoché, incumbent and retired abbots of the Jé, Mé, and Ngakpa colleges, and other lamas and geshés.

In my fifty-eighth year, the year of the earth-dog (1958), at the request of the supreme incarnation of Kyabjé Phabongkha Vajradhara, I gave teachings on the close lineage of the cycle of Mañjuśrī teachings that was transmitted to Jé Tsongkhapa by Mañjuśrī himself, the Thirteen Golden Dharmas lineage exclusive to the Sakya tradition, the permissions of the Thirteen Divine Visions of Takphu, and oral transmissions of the above teachings to an exclusive group of monks and lamas including the supreme incarnation of Kyabjé Phabongkha at his residence in Lhasa.

His Holiness's Geshé Examinations

During the sixth month, I went along with His Holiness, our supreme refuge and protector, when he made the trip to Drepung Monastery, as he was required by custom to visit the three seats upon the successful completion of his intensive study of the five great treatises.[257] I stayed with His Holiness on the upper floors of Kungarawa Palace, as had been arranged.

His Holiness stood for his geshé examination in the main courtyard of the great assembly hall amid an ocean-like assembly of intelligent and spiritually liberated monks, preceded by recitation of the verses of homage and his initial dissertation. After responding firmly and without hesitation to the challenges regarding the thornier points of the five great treatises that were mounted by the abbots of Drepung and high-ranking geshés who were well versed in the art of dialectics, His Holiness presented challenges to the abbots of Gomang and Loseling, shining a light of eloquent explanation that delighted the learned. On the same visit, he attended a grand feast of ceremonial cookies that the governing body of Drepung offered in the great assembly hall, forged a Dharma connection with the whole assembly by teaching them Dharma, and consecrated and purified the four cardinal points of the circumambulation circuit while circumambulating Drepung with his full entourage. Tutor Kyabjé Ling Rinpoché, who was Sharpa Chöjé, and his labrang made offerings of food and funds to the monks in Drepung's assembly hall, and His Holiness was invited to bless the occasion with his presence.

I was very fortunate to accompany His Holiness to various celebrations, as when he taught Dharma in the Sang-ngak Gatsal assembly hall of Namgyal Monastery at the request of the Namgyal monks. At the end of the official functions at Drepung, the government also made elaborate and generous offerings of food and funds in the assembly hall during the religious ceremonies connected with the examination.

Afterward, His Holiness visited Nechung Monastery, which was on the way back. The great Dharmarāja, through his medium in trance, came to the staircase under the western gate, respectfully bowed to His Holiness, and led him by the hand to the assembly hall, where he respectfully offered him a seat. There the monastery offered a feast of ceremonial cookies, and the Dharma protector showed us treasured ritual objects, like the Sebak Mukchung mask. Then the oracle summoned the cabinet ministers to join His Holiness, Tutor Ling Rinpoché, and myself and offered prophecies concerning religious and political life, saying things like, "There is the danger that a time may come when we are without a leader!" When he made these prophecies, I and everyone else feared that they foretold circumstances hostile to His Holiness's life. Later, after we had come to India, we understood that it must have referred to our country of Tibet being left protectorless.

Then I accompanied His Holiness to the great center of learning Sera Monastery, where he stood for his geshé examination, taught the Dharma, and was offered a great feast of ceremonial cookies. The government also made an offering of funds equal to what they had done at Drepung. While staying at Denma House over the course of our visit to Sera, I paid a visit to the supreme incarnation of my supreme refuge, Phabongkha Vajradhara, and we shared a leisurely visit. Later, the supreme lord of victors successfully completed his official functions at Sera and returned to the Norbulingka Palace.

In the eighth month when His Holiness once again traveled to Ganden, he traveled by car from Lhasa to Tsangthok, in the Ganden foothills.

On the way, he briefly stopped at Sang-ngak Khar Monastery at Dechen to pray for assistance before the principal image of the monastery, a Six-Arm Mahākāla statue that was consecrated by Khedrup Jé. His Holiness traveled from Tsangthok to Drok Riwoché Ganden Nampar Gyalwai Ling in an elaborate, traditional procession of riders on horseback. I once again stayed at my residence above the assembly hall of Dokhang House.

His Holiness had completed enrollment ceremonies at Drepung and Sera during the fire-pig year (1947), but the initial enrollment ceremonies at Ganden remained to be done. So enrollment ceremonies and geshé examination took place on that same occasion. His Holiness visited each of the colleges and attended a grand feast of ceremonial cookies. High-ranking scholars graciously presented challenges regarding the five treatises in the debate courtyard. As part of his examination, His Holiness presented challenges to the abbots of the colleges and then in turn responded to the questions they put forward. He forged a Dharma connection with each college by giving a Dharma discourse. The government offered elaborate offerings on this auspicious occasion at each of the colleges, and he attended a grand feast of ceremonial cookies that the governing body of Ganden offered in the monastery's great assembly hall. He forged a Dharma connection with the whole assembly by teaching Dharma, and he stood for his geshé examination in the monastery's great debate courtyard, just as he had done at Sera and Drebung. The labrang of the Ganden Throneholder offered a feast of ceremonial cookies in Yangpachen Temple, and the government offered a thousandfold offering and an elaborate tsok at Ganden's sacred shrines, beginning with the great golden stupa of Lama Mañjunātha Tsongkhapa.

Over the course of two or three days, a massive assembly presided over by His Holiness that included the incumbent Ganden Throneholder Thupten Kunga, Sharpa Chöjé Ling Rinpoché, myself, the ritual assistants of Namgyal Monastery, the abbots of Shartsé and Jangtsé colleges, incarnate lamas, and geshés performed an elaborate purification ritual together with tsok in the Dharmarāja chapel as part of a consecration ritual associated with Vajrabhairava. During that time, my own labrang offered tea and sweet rice to the ocean-like assembly of intelligent and spiritually liberated monks gathered in the main assembly hall of Ganden, the most potent place of merit for gods and men. Each monk was offered fifteen *sang* in silver and a ceremonial scarf, and a fund of silver *sang* for annual offerings to the monks was established.

On the same occasion, I invited the great being who embodies the wisdom, compassion, and power of the entire sea of spiritual guides throughout the ten directions, the supreme all-knowing and all-seeing lord of victors, to sit atop the golden throne of the Mañjunātha king of Dharma Tsongkhapa. I began by describing the great qualities of His Holiness's body, speech, and mind and then recited the mandala treatise and made extensive, substantial clouds of offerings to the extent of my merit, giving whatever actual money I had available. After the session in the assembly hall concluded, I graciously accepted gifts of appreciation for a job well done, which was offered by the government in the quarters above the assembly hall with a feast of ceremonial cookies.

One day, walking in an elaborate traditional procession with the full entourage, His Holiness consecrated and purified the four cardinal points of the circumambulation circuit and chanted prayers there. Stopping at the edge of the spring by the assembly hall, we chanted the prayers *Eastern Snow Mountain*[258] and *Sacred Ground*, a praise of Ganden by His Holiness Kalsang Gyatso.[259] Because *Eastern Snow Mountain* wasn't among the traditional recitations at Namgyal Monastery and because of the clamor and chatter of the crowd of people who had gathered to catch a glimpse of His Holiness that day, some confusion arose halfway through the prayer. Although I began to grow anxious that the chanters would altogether lose the thread of the prayer in front of the crowd, the strength of the voices of those monks who were skilled at chant dominated with a light and melodious tone that concealed the underlying discord, and we successfully made it to the end of the prayer.

One day, I accompanied His Holiness, who was mounted on a white yak, as he rode with a small entourage to the top of Wangkur Hill. There we performed an extensive incense offering[260] and praises to the local mountain deities.[261] Looking down from the top of the hill at Ganden spread out below, I thought of the kindness of our spiritual father Jé Tsongkhapa and his descendants and of my time in the monastery studying and taking part in the Dharma assembly. I was overcome with wistfulness and joy in equal measure.

Once during our visit, the monastery opened a sealed chest of sacred relics housed in the Throneholder's residence and showed us Jé Rinpoché's very own upper garment, his set of three monastic robes, and many other important relics, and small portions of them were given to us.

Portents of Trouble

While staying at Ganden, His Holiness came down with a serious intestinal fever for a few days, which caused everyone a great deal of concern and worry. However, the great being was fortified by his skill in cultivating spiritual protection, and thanks also to the medicine he was given, it did not worsen and he recovered fully.

After the functions at Ganden were concluded, on the way home His Holiness stopped at Tsal Gungthang, where he stayed on the top floor of the temple. Tutor Kyabjé Ling Rinpoché and I stayed in the rooms on the western side of the upper floor, which had in the past been my late father's living quarters. After attending a grand feast of ceremonial cookies that Gungthang Labrang had offered, His Holiness settled in the garden cottage and said to the officials of Kunsangtsé, "Please bring me some texts to read." Having not the slightest notion what books Gungthang Labrang held, they asked me. In the end we brought him the handwritten five-volume set of the teachings of Drogön Shang Yudrakpa[262] that was in a collection of ancient volumes kept in a cabinet in the viewing room on top of the temple.

When I went to get the texts, my younger brother Tsipön Tsewang Döndrup came along. Having a bit of fun with him, I said, "You're not capable of reading everything written in Tibetan."

"What Tibetan is there that I cannot read?!" he demanded.

I showed him a handwritten analysis of the Perfection of Wisdom that contained an abundance of abbreviations wherein four or five syllables were condensed into one. He was unable to read it and shook his head in consternation.

Reflections on Impermanence

As His Holiness relished examining the collected teachings of Lama Shang, Zhang Jingwu, the Chinese representative in Lhasa, informed him via the cabinet of the great number of casualties in Nyemo left by a confrontation between the Chushi Gangdruk militia and Chinese forces. He said that the Dalai Lama and the regional government must ensure that such attacks would cease, for if they did not, the Chinese would suppress them violently. His Holiness could not bear the news and was deeply troubled by it. The following day, he returned to the Norbulingka deep in thought.

That winter, as requested by Rabjampa Losang Wangden and others from Sera's Ngakpa College, I visited Ngakpa College and gave a gathering of at least two thousand—largely monks from Sera—initiations into Akṣobhyavajra in the Ārya tradition of Guhyasamāja, thirteen-deity Vajrabhairava, five-deity Cakrasaṃvara, and Sarvavid along with their preparatory practices. I also offered permissions for the collected mantras of Guhyasamāja, Cakrasaṃvara, and Vajrabhairava. My visit to Sera coincided with offerings that the incarnation of Dromo Geshé Rinpoché was making to mark his geshé examinations. At his invitation, I stayed at his labrang for two days. I also went to the residence of the reincarnation of my supreme refuge Phabongkha Vajradhara and had a pleasant visit with him. While there I offered prayers for the long life of his tutor Gyalrong Khentrul Rinpoché, who was unwell.

Many times over the years up to that point, at the three seats, at Gyütö and Gyümé tantric colleges, and at Meru and Shidé monasteries in Lhasa, I had taught and propagated sutra and tantra teachings, transmissions, and initiations—chief among them the stages on the path to enlightenment—to gatherings of one or two thousand and at times up to four or five thousand, chiefly monks from the area or visiting from all over. Among the disciples there were anywhere between twenty and thirty, sometimes even up to sixty or seventy, incarnate lamas of various ranks as well as many geshés headed by the incumbent and retired abbots of the three seats, and many acclaimed scholars in the audiences assembled. But inside I knew I was a charlatan, hardened to the Dharma, a hypocrite whose deeds did not correspond with his words. As Paṇchen Losang Chökyi Gyaltsen said:

> Teaching Dharma they are skilled in changing the minds
> of others,
> but the dry leather of their own minds remains hard.
> Teachers who expound like performers acting out a character
> may find they possess no genuine Dharma.

Even so, just as long ago a wicked man who had killed his own mother entered the Buddha's teaching, studied the scriptures, and led disciples to attain liberation by teaching Dharma disguised as a monk in a faraway land,[263] in the hope that one among my many students would take up the great responsibility of upholding and preserving the teachings of the Buddha, I also did my utmost to pass on, as best I could, what few drops of the nectar of teachings, which easily show the path to freedom and omniscience, that my spiritual fathers, kind gurus who embodied all the buddhas, had deposited in my ears and heart. But like a herd of drunken elephants rampaging through a garden of lotuses, the barbaric Red Chinese, messengers of the devil, destroyed every last sign of goodness in the religion and people of the land of Tibet, such that it was impossible even to catch sight of someone dressed as a monk throughout the three provinces. Many great and promising lamas, incarnate masters, and geshés were crushed beneath the anvil of Chinese oppression. A few among that small number who followed His Holiness, our great refuge and protector, into exile in India also passed away, while others could not live up to the expectations of the monastic vows. As Ācārya Vasubandhu wrote:

> When latent afflictions have not been eliminated,
> and one dwells close to their object
> with wrong and misdirected attention,
> the causes for those afflictions to manifest are complete.

When I reflect on these dashed hopes, I feel that my work, like a sand castle built by a child, has left no trace, and I am saddened. But what could I do?

His Holiness's Final Examinations

As was tradition, on the first day of the first month of my fifty-ninth year, the year of the earth-pig (1959), I participated in the atonement ritual and offering in the bedchamber of His Holiness's quarters at the Potala in front of the image of Palden Lhamo that had spoken. Early that morning, I also attended special New Year's Day torma offering to this deity on the roof of the Potala, and I attended various other ceremonies throughout the day. A light snowfall on the morning of New Year's Day seemed to be an inauspicious indication of the general disruption of religious and secular life during that time of upheaval.

That year, to mark his successful completion of intensive study of the five great treatises, His Holiness ceremonially traveled to the complex on the upper floors of the Lhasa Tsuklakhang in preparation for the final geshé examination by scholars of the highest standing, which would take place during the Great Prayer Festival.

The thirteenth day of the Great Prayer Festival, the day of His Holiness's actual geshé examination for the rank of lharam, included an early morning assembly with communal tea and oral examination in the teaching courtyard, a midday assembly with tea, an oral examination during a dry afternoon assembly, and an evening session with more debating. During each of the assemblies with tea, His Holiness would give explanations on the great treatises and offer verses of homage. Nearly thirty thousand monks, arrayed like garlands of amber or like a vast field of marigolds, attended the examinations between the morning and afternoon assemblies and the lengthy evening session.

Among the masses of great learned propounders of philosophy were geshés of the three seats as full of confidence as Dignāga and Dharmakīrti, and they mounted challenges regarding the thornier points of the treatises on logic and epistemology in the teaching courtyard during the morning. In the afternoon session, they debated Madhyamaka and the Perfection of Wisdom, and in the evening Vinaya and Abhidharma. The lotus of faith and respect bloomed in the discerning who witnessed him responding freely and without hesitation to the logical and scriptural challenges offered. I felt deeply fortunate to witness the wondrous spectacle, watching him wither the creeping vine of audacity in those who were so arrogantly proud of their learning and trample the hooded snake of pride underfoot. During the afternoon oral examination, the great Dharmarāja from Nechung, again through his medium in trance, examined His Holiness, taking up the topic of the four noble truths, and offered him congratulations.

On the fourteenth, in the great courtyard of the Tsuklakhang, the government offered His Holiness an elaborate grand feast of ceremonial cookies and a great quantity of offerings of such value and wealth as would diminish even Vaiśravaṇa's haughtiness to celebrate the successful completion of the ceremonies for his geshé examination. At the same time, the Sharpa Chöjé Kyabjé Ling Rinpoché, myself, and the assistant tutors were also each given fine gifts as a reward for successfully managing His Holiness's education.

During the annual invocation of the Nechung oracle at Lhasa's old Meru Monastery on the twelfth day of the first month, as well as during the additional invocation in the Ganden Yangtsé chamber on the upper level of the Tsuklakhang on the seventeenth, the Dharma protector spoke, saying, "I, the formless spirit, will attempt to build a bridge over the fordless Chinese river." At the time we took the statement to mean that he would search for some means of restoring and normalizing the deteriorating relations between China and Tibet. But looking back on it later, I was convinced that it was his solemn, unbreakable pledge that allowed His Holiness and his hundredfold entourage to simply walk out of the city without the slightest opposition, despite every strategic passage from Lhasa being surrounded by permanent units of Chinese troops.

As the Prayer Festival neared its conclusion, His Holiness presided over a midday assembly, as was tradition. Similar to the system of oral examinations that some schools use nowadays, after I had recited a number of different verses that appear among the five great treatises, His Holiness explained the meaning of the verses, using dialectical supports to establish his reasons. After the noontime assembly, he gave a brief discourse and engaged in debate before many scholars in the courtyard of the Tsuklakhang.

One day a message came from the Chinese officials that there would be a theatrical performance at the Siling Puwu PLA military encampment that evening and that Tutor Ling Rinpoché, myself, and members of the cabinet must attend. Prior to that, we had received reports from Kham and Amdo that many prominent lamas and leaders had been arrested, sentenced, and hauled away when they had accepted invitations to such meetings and events. With thoughts circling around in my mind, I attended in a state of terror, thinking that the Chinese would deceptively use that night to lure us into a trap. Such anxieties reveal the sense of self-preservation that lingers after empty talk of the profound view and training the mind is finished. In fact, the Chinese were just using it as a test run for their later intrigue to invite His Holiness. And so we were received with cordial hospitality in the form of food, drink, and so on and were allowed to leave amid a show of smiles and pleasantries.

As members of the Sangha, monks are worthy of respect and service and are the supreme objects to make offerings to and by which to accumulate merit. Motivated to gather merit from the practice of giving, I had every year for several years been making offerings of tea, rice meal, money, and capital funds at the Prayer Festival. I made offerings at this Prayer Festival as well, but this was the last time I gathered merit at such an event in Tibet.

I summoned Panglung Chöjē, a medium of Shukden, the chief protector, who has long looked over me, to my house and invoked the protector in trance to inquire about what future course of action should be taken. In his prophecy he said that the wicked designs of the Red Chinese, enemies of the Buddha's teaching, would soon become clear, and that it was thus imperative that His Holiness and all of us secretly depart for India. He said that it was absolutely unacceptable for me in particular to remain in Tibet, and that I must find some means of leaving. He also said that it was imperative that I urge His Holiness to go, that we must go, and that there would definitely be an occasion on which we could leave. I nevertheless remained indecisive. When His Holiness had not yet made up his mind whether to stay or leave, how could I think of leaving myself?

At the conclusion of the Prayer Festival and after the procession of Maitreya,[264] I accompanied His Holiness when he traveled from Lhasa to the Kalsang Palace at Norbulingka in a grand procession with an ocean-like entourage.

9 | The Storm Breaks

Tibetan Uprising

The Chinese military headquarters in Lhasa had extended an invitation to His Holiness, the supreme lord of victors, his two tutors, and some high-ranking government officials, chief among whom were the current cabinet ministers, to attend a theatrical show at the Chinese army camp on the evening of March 10, 1959, according to the Western calendar—the first day of the second month of the earth-pig year according to the Tibetan calendar. Phuntsok Tashi Taklha, commander of His Holiness's bodyguards, was summoned to the Chinese military camp and told that only one or two bodyguards could accompany His Holiness and they should be unarmed. The two tutors and the cabinet ministers were to come by themselves, without their staff and attendants. Judging from what they said and all their actions, their deceitful plan was evident. Because of the strength of the Red Chinese forces, His Holiness had little choice but assent to attending the show.

In general the Tibetans hated the conduct of the Chinese, but they particularly disliked this invitation for His Holiness to visit the Chinese camp. It had never happened in the eight years since the Chinese had arrived in Lhasa. Add to this the demand that His Holiness's bodyguard should be unarmed and that the government officials should come without their attendants, and the fact that it was clear the Chinese were transporting large units of military personnel to Lhasa from different parts of the country at night and amassing their forces at the encampment, it was no surprise the Tibetans' resentment reached a breaking point.

When the news of His Holiness's visit to the camp became known, the lamas and monks of the three monasteries and other monastic establishments, monks and lay officials of the government, and several tens of thousands of men and women, each on their own but as if with a single mind, thronged the main gate at the outer wall of the Norbulingka on March 10. They blocked the roads and chanted their request for His Holiness to postpone his visit, as they could not bear the responsibility for His Holiness attending the show.

On his way to the Norbulingka from Lhasa to join His Holiness's entourage, the cabinet minister Sampho Tsewang Rikzin was struck in the head with a rock and had to turn back when the crowd stoned the car he was riding in because the driver was Chinese. Then the brother of Chamdo Phakpalha, a monk official named Sönam Gyaltsen, who due to his young age often associated with the Chinese officials, came to Norbulingka on this particular day wearing a Chinese dust mask and Chinese clothing. The throng, incensed by his demeanor and suspicious behavior, stopped him at the main gate of the Norbulingka and pelted him with stones, tragically killing him. At that point His Holiness delayed his trip to the military camp.

The crowd marched through the streets of Lhasa chanting "We Tibetans are free and independent!" More than a thousand people from among the general population of the three provinces volunteered to form a militia and stand guard along the inner and outer walls of the Norbulingka, the Potala Palace, the Lhasa Tsuklakhang, and so on using their own supplies of arms and ammunition. An additional regiment of guards drafted from the crowd were stationed at Shapten Khang, the prayer hall in the Norbulingka. Thousands of Lhasa's women marched through the streets in protest against the Red Chinese, chanting, "Chinese leave Tibet!"

On the eighth day, the Chinese fired shots killing two monks just to the north of the Norbulingka and fired two cannon shots in the direction of the palace. As His Holiness made very clear in his memoirs, the situation grew extremely menacing. I and others like myself who do not have the wisdom to see all things as illusions were filled with fear.

Divinations and a Decision to Flee

Due to these circumstances, the cabinet and various government departments repeatedly asked His Holiness to leave for some suitable foreign country where his life would not be in danger. A divination was performed in front of the speaking image of Palden Lhamo, and statements from the Nechung and Gadong oracles were sought, and all unanimously agreed that His Holiness should leave immediately. At the wish of His Holiness, I secretly dispatched Ratö Chubar Rinpoché to Panglung Hermitage to request a prediction from Shukden.[265] The Dharma protector's reply came, "You must leave immediately. If you take a southwesterly route, you have my assurance that neither yourself nor anyone in your retinue will come to any harm. Someone bearing the name Dorjé must travel at the head of the victor's party, confidently wielding this sword." He then faced the direction of Ramagang to the southwest, loosed an arrow, and performed a ritual dance, gesturing with the sword.

Since the prophetic statements were in unanimous agreement, at nine o'clock in the evening on the eighth day of the second Tibetan month (March 17), the dignitaries of the Yabshi family, such as the great mother of the victor, set out ahead, after which His Holiness and a small entourage departed. After that, Tutor Kyabjé Ling Rinpoché, myself, cabinet ministers Surkhang Wangchen Gelek, Neshar Thupten Tharpa, and Shenkhawa Gyurmé Sönam Topgyal, and His Holiness's principal attendant, steward in chief, and ritual assistant took off our normal official attire and dressed as servants and laymen. We went from the Norbulingka all the way to the Ramagang ferry at the Kyichu River to the southwest of Lhasa. After exiting the ferry, we all left together on horses that had already been fitted with harnesses and so on. My attendants Lhabu, Jamyang Tashi, Norbu Chöphel, Namdröl, and Sönam Tenzin, whom I had secretly dispatched to Ramagang on the far side of the Kyichu the previous day, were waiting for us there. Palden, Losang Sherap, and Losang Yeshé came along with me at night.

When we left Norbulingka Palace, we hid in a large truck covered with a tarpaulin and drove out the main gate without any of the guards asking who was inside. Until we finally crossed the small sandy pass above Neu Dzong after reaching the far side of the Kyichu, we could clearly see the lights of the Chinese military encampment that was at Northölingka to the west of Norbulingka. The moon seemed to be shining brighter than usual, and we were afraid that the Chinese would notice us and come pursue us at any moment. Having had the fortune to make it across the Kyichu, we now made our way clinging to the hope that we could escape safely, like huntsman Gönpo Dorjé's black deer.[266] The echoes of discourses that I would thunderously proclaim from a throne, my head held high—empty talk about mind training, telling others how to bring hardship onto the path when I had yet to encounter any hardship myself—faded and deserted me.

When we reached the top of the pass at Neu Dzong, the moon set and it became pitch dark. We relaxed a little when we were past the dangers of the Chinese military camp, but we were traveling in total darkness, and as we did not dare shine any lights, our party became quite dispersed. Some went on ahead while others were left behind. I worried endlessly when my attendant Lhabu got lost, fell behind, and couldn't catch up to us until nine o'clock the following night, not knowing whether he had fallen into the hands of the Chinese.

As I had only dressed lightly for the walk from the Norbulingka to the river, now because of the icy winds I felt nauseous while riding and vomited, and my liver became upset. When we arrived at the Namgyal Gang Estate of Tsemönling, I put on a rather dirty woolen gown that the estate manager gave me, and after resting briefly and drinking a few cups of boiled water, I felt a little better.

Before Jé Pass, the manager of Takdrak Labrang was waiting for us. He had just bidden farewell to His Holiness and offered him a meal. After taking some food and drink there, we crossed Jé Pass and at sunset arrived at the Bentsa ferry on the sand bank at the conjunction of the Tsangpo and Kyichu rivers. Given the high winds, it was quite difficult for the ferry to cross the river and come back, so we waited for a long time on the near side of the crossing in the middle of a sandstorm that whipped sand at us that stung like arrows. We made it across just before dark and stayed the night on the upper floor of Rawamé Monastery, where we met His Holiness.

When we left the Norbulingka, other than the hope that no harm would come to His Holiness, as he was so very precious and important, and the hope that we would escape with our lives, we gave no thought to carrying any possessions with us. I left carrying nothing more than the robes I was wearing, my book of daily prayers, and a box of sacred relics. My attendants brought nothing more than amulet boxes for protection against weapons, a hand gun, a few bits of food and drink for the immediate future, and the clothes on their backs. It wasn't just us who left in this way. The cabinet ministers who traveled with us at the time and the many Tibetans who came after us—lay and ordained, high and low—all left behind, like dreams, everything they owned and everyone they held dear. As Jé Sakya Paṇḍita said:

Though the ignorant may amass wealth,
they benefit little from it.
Though a wish-granting cow may have milk,
the calf rarely drinks it.[267]

One would think that the experience of being forced against our will to leave behind all things and everyone that we hold most dear—friends and relatives, servants and associates, students, teachers, and patrons—would be a vivid demonstration of the reality of impermanence, that everything is like a dream, and induce people to practice more urgently. But the strength of bad habits cultivated over many lifetimes is such that after we arrived in India, the calloused mind that chases after illusions gradually reverted to squandering away this life on empty pursuits for this life alone.

After that we lodged for the night at Dophü Chökhor Monastery in Döl in the Kyidé Shöl area. The following day I visited the shrine there of the protector Gyalchen to seek his divine aid. That evening we arrived in Yoru Dranang at Drathang Monastery, founded by Drapa Ngönshé.[268] Tutor Ling Rinpoché and I stayed the night there with cabinet ministers Surkhangwa, Shenkhawa, and Nesharwa. For security reasons, His Holiness went on to the Gyango Gyalsang estate in upper Dranang.

Long Trek through the Mountains

The following day, traveling by way of the main road, we reached perhaps the most outstanding Nyingma monastery in Central Tibet, Mindröling Monastery in Drachi. This monastery was founded by the great treasure revealer Gyurmé Dorjé, a tantric yogi without rival. The monks of Mindröling upheld pure monastic discipline, beginning with practice of the three foundations,[269] and, between the Nyingma school's traditions of scripture and treasure, focused principally on the oral tradition of the scriptures. They also preserved the practice of pure revelations of the great treasure revealer himself. The monks who peacefully greeted us were wearing the yellow monastic robes and holding religious banners in their hands, but all of us, master and servant alike, were wearing chubas as if combining the taste of nirvana and samsara, and therefore I felt slightly uncomfortable.

The Mindröling regent, Chung Rinpoché, offered us lunch and an excellent reception. After we toured the monastery's group of sacred chapels, including a very magnificent protector chapel, Tutor Kyabjé Ling Rinpoché and I had a leisurely private meeting with Chung Rinpoché in his quarters on the upper floor. Since we had already been very close with Chung Rinpoché and thought well of him, we told him in detail about the situation in Lhasa, insisting that it was unsafe for him to remain in the monastery and urging him to leave. Chung Rinpoché, however, said that his departure would leave the monastery more vulnerable to harm, and so he had no wish to leave. There was nothing we could do.

We left Mindröling late in the afternoon and spent the night at the Möndro estate in the upper region of the southern district. From there we took an incredibly long path over Duchi Pass to reach Chenyé Monastery in Upper Chongyé. We made offerings and prayed before their beautiful central image of the Medicine Buddha Ratnacandra. The next morning we went to Riwo Dechen Monastery in Chongyé.

We had planned to stay the night there, as His Holiness and his entourage had arrived at the monastery a day ahead of us and had planned to spend an extra day there to rest and recuperate. However, the Red Chinese had opened fire with heavy artillery in Lhasa on the tenth of the Tibetan month, and the Norbulingka, the Potala Palace, and areas all over Lhasa had been heavily damaged, and many were lives lost. The Tibetan army was unable to hold their positions, so civilians both lay and ordained had no other choice but to run for their lives, fleeing to outlying regions in any way they could. Upon hearing of the grave situation in Lhasa, fearing for His Holiness's safety, the party set out again immediately.

Traveling by way of Dönkar Pass in Upper Chongyé, they went to Thösam Dargyé Ling Monastery in the Upper Chödegong of Yarlung. We also pushed on to reach there. All the horses and people in our group were absolutely exhausted when we finally arrived, having just made the two-day journey from Chenyé in a single day. Nevertheless we rested comfortably, as if in our own homes, thanks to the great hospitality of Ling Labrang, who was the proprietor of that monastery.

The next day, traveling by way of the great pass called Yartö Drakla that skirts Mount Yarlha Shampo, we stayed in a little village called Echudogyang, where both the people and the place were utterly impoverished. The local inhabitants' subsistence must have been driven by the results of heavy negative acts committed in previous lives. I could hardly bear to be there for even one day.

The following day after crossing Shopo Tak Pass, we arrived at Kharteng

Monastery in west Shopo, which was run by Dedruk Labrang, and on the seventeenth His Holiness reached the fort of Lhuntsé Dzong in Nyal. I attended a brief auspicious ceremony where the entire entourage gathered in the great hall of the fort and His Holiness declared a provisional government for Tibet. Tutor Ling Rinpoché offered an explanation of the ritual mandala, and I presented the eight auspicious symbols and substances, with verses describing their significance. As soon as the ceremony ended, I went with His Holiness to Dreulha Monastery, where he stayed for the night.

Then, traveling in stages, we went to Jora Monastery in Nyal and, after crossing Karpo Pass, Göntsé Monastery in Tsona. The day we reached Tsona, when we were in a curve of the hill at Gorpola, a plane flew over us. Although we could not tell which country it was from, it worried us greatly as we suspected that we were being pursued by the Chinese.

At Tsona we rejoined Dagyab Chetsang Hothokthu, his attendants, and Khenchung Tara, who had left the capital after us. According to Tara's report, from 2:00 a.m. on the tenth of the Tibetan month until 6:00 the following evening, the Norbulingka had been under continuous artillery fire, and given the thousands of rounds that were fired, the outer and inner precincts of the Norbulingka and His Holiness's personal residence within the innermost precinct of the palace were severely damaged. The Potala Palace had also sustained damage from cannon fire, and the medical college Drophen Rikché Ling on the Chakpori hill was totally destroyed. We were apprised of the grave events, the details of which His Holiness has written about in his memoirs.[270]

Traveling by way of Pö Pass from Tsona, we arrived in a place called Mangma. As I have previously stated, when traversing such high passes we were whipped by cold winds and tormented by snows. The path down from Pö Pass was quite difficult to traverse that day, because it was precipitous, long, and muddy, so I went down riding on a yak borrowed from a local dairy farm. At Mangma, His Holiness was not feeling well, so we stopped there for the day. There, a large group of people from Chatreng who had come to escort His Holiness and myself were ready to turn back, and I gave protective talismans.

Crossing into India

On the twenty-second we arrived at the Indian border town of Chudangmo, where we were received by representatives of the Indian government and provided with military bodyguards. We were given accommodation in tents. At this point, having escaped the threat of Chinese attack, my mind was released from the tight bondage of the noose of childish self-cherishing.

We set off on the long journey to the temple of Gongsum Chöten, which resembled the Boudhanath stupa in Nepal, spending nights along the way in the villages of Sharti, Lungla, and Thonglek. On the twenty-eighth, His Holiness arrived at the monastery in Tawang, and Tutor Ling Rinpoché and I stayed for a few days in a house in the village below the monastery, where an old Dharma friend, Tsona Göntsé Rinpoché, came to meet us with provisions of food. After leaving Tawang, we passed through the villages of Jang and Sengé Dzong and then crossed Sera Pass and went through a town called Dum in Dirang and a village called Rawang. On the fourth of the third Tibetan month, we reached Bomdila, where we stayed in municipal committee houses organized by the Indian government. The Indian government representative in charge of Bomdila town invited His Holiness and the entourage to a tea reception, to which I also went.

Traveling from Tsona to this place, we had suffered a great deal of hardship, for the journey had taken us on treacherous paths over high passes, through deep gorges, and through thick jungle, and when riding, I had to mount and dismount whatever creature bore me. But despite the physical difficulties and exhaustion, I inwardly felt a continuous sense of joy and relief that enabled me to tolerate the hardships and difficulties with relative ease. Here I was able to tolerate hardship in a way that I had never experienced before in my religious practice.

After three days in Bomdila, a group that included Tutor Ling Rinpoché and myself set out in advance in a jeep provided by the Indian government. We drove down very steep and dangerous roads through a village called Chaku and a town called Takma, which is part of Khelong, and eventually arrived in Phuthel on the tenth. There we had breakfast with His Holiness in the government guesthouse and traveled on to Tezpur in Shillong, where we stayed in a hilltop guesthouse. The deputy prime minister Dekharwa, the deputy cabinet minister Yuthokpa, the royal secretary to the maharaja of Sikkim, and the Indian political officer in Sikkim had come from Kalimpong to welcome His Holiness.

After lunch we left for the train station in Tezpur and boarded a special train sent by the Indian government to take His Holiness and his entourage to Siliguri, where we arrived at 11:00 on the morning of the eleventh.

There on a green lawn His Holiness was greeted by a large crowd, including local officials and dignitaries such as the maharaja of Sikkim, Tibetans from Kalimpong and Darjeeling, and many Indians. Thousands of people had gathered there like bumblebees in a lotus field, buzzing with words of sympathy for Tibet and to cheer His Holiness.

Then, progressing through Varanasi, Lucknow, Dehradun, and so on, we arrived in Mussoorie on April 20, which was the thirteenth of the third Tibetan month. His Holiness and the members of the entourage stayed at Birla House, as arranged by the government of India. Within a few days, the prime minister of India, Pandit Nehru, came to call on His Holiness. We tutors, the cabinet minister, and other officials greeted him and saw him off on his departure.

Subjects of Chinese Propaganda

After His Holiness's departure from Lhasa, the Chinese Communists branded the chief members of the cabinet, me in particular, as "reactionary leaders." I was publicly accused of fomenting rebellion by plotting with Chushi Gangdruk guerillas. They said that His Holiness had been abducted against his will and that we had secretly plotted with foreign imperialist powers. They also publicly denounced me, saying that the public had been deceived by the pretense of religion, and made up an endless list of fabricated stories against me, claiming that I had engaged in sexual assault of women and so on. They even put on a play about all this in Lhasa and plastered a portrait of me as a monster with many heads and hands in the public marketplace. Portrayals of me as a deadly toxin were broadcast repeatedly on the radio, as I later learned from people who arrived from Lhasa.

As the *Wheel of Sharp Weapons Mind Training* (verse 17) says:

> When others assail me with exaggeration or denigration,
> it is the weapon of my own evil deeds turned upon me
> for disparaging the holy beings.
> From now on I will not malign others with scathing words.

Without question, it was my own prior negative actions that brought these results. However, the immediate reasons were as follows. In the past

I had often taught and spread the Dharma all over Tibet and had religious connections with many influential and ordinary people from all the three provinces. So the Communist Chinese had appointed me principal of the Lhasa middle school in Tibet, to the Preparatory Committee for the Autonomous Region of Tibet, and as director of the Bureau of Religious Affairs, hoping that I would be their hook to win favor with the people. Because I would not enact their policies, the Red Chinese bore an intense hatred of me. I have not the slightest doubt that had I stayed behind in Tibet under Communist rule, I would have undergone all sorts of terrible tortures. By the grace of the Three Jewels and the protectors, and through the kindness of His Holiness, our great refuge and protector, who has held me with the rope of his compassion, I was able to come to India and enjoy the freedom to speak and act as I wish.

Although I am free from the terror of the Red Chinese for the time being, there is no means by which I can turn back the emissary of the south—the one who wields a club and whose might devours the three worlds[271]—whose appointed hour I cannot know. It is true I control whether I go to the unbearable prison of lower rebirths, but when I examine the present state of my own obstinate habits of body, speech, and mind, the future doesn't look promising.

10 | Early Years of Exile

Travels to Nepal and North India

DURING OUR STAY in Mussoorie, other than the small number who had already immigrated to India that came to our residence for audiences with His Holiness, visits from Tibetans were very rare, since those who had just arrived did not know the language or how to get around. Since we too did not know the country, distractions associated with the hustle and bustle of the many things to be done naturally ceased, and we were free to focus instead on daily recitations and religious practice. We observed the discipline of renunciates, setting ourselves apart from worldly activity.

At the beginning of the tenth Tibetan month, my attendants and I traveled to Nepal at the invitation of Mongolian Lama Guru Deva, director

The two tutors attending the Dalai Lama's first teaching in exile in Mussoorie, 1960
COURTESY OF TIBET DOCUMENTATION PROJECT

of Ganden Chöphel Ling Tibetan monastery in Nepal, to consecrate the monastery. Over the course of three days, accompanied by eight monks from the communities of Gyütö and Gyümé tantric colleges, I performed an extensive consecration ritual associated with Vajrabhairava and, during the same period, gave a long-life empowerment and permission to practice Avalokiteśvara Who Liberates from All Lower Realms to a large gathering of the lay and ordained in the assembly hall of the monastery.

At the request of a monk named Tashi of Zanskar, Ladakh, over two days I gave the Cakrasaṃvara body-mandala initiation in the tradition of Mahāsiddha Ghaṇṭāpāda, with its preparatory rite, to a few disciples, including Dagyab Chetsang Rinpoché, Drukpa Tsechu Tulku, and Dzemé Rinpoché. I conferred the vows of novice ordination on around twenty monastic candidates from the area and gave some of the monks life-entrustment permission for Shukden and other related practices.

I visited the various places of pilgrimage in the vicinity, principal among which were Nepal's three stupas, and made the thousandfold offering as many times as I was able.

On the way back from Nepal, I visited Kalimpong at the request of one of my patrons, Gyurmé Sadutshang. I was received by a welcoming party comprised of Kalimpong's Tharpa Chöling Monastery, some Tibetan social groups, government officials, and a few reincarnate lamas that had been waiting to greet me at a junction designated as Seventh Mile. I stayed at the Sadutshang household. At the request of the monks of Tharpa Chöling Monastery I gave the great initiation into solitary hero Vajrabhairava at the monastery. At the Sadutshang house, I fulfilled the hopes and wishes of my patron, giving quite a large group of earnest practitioners whatever Dharma they wished, including the blessing of the four sindūra initiations of Vajrayoginī and permission for the Three Wrathful Forms Combined.[272]

An old friend and benefactor of mine who was living in Kurseong, Jampal Samphel from Amdo, asked that I come to see him as he was seriously ill and on the verge of death, so I went there. On the way I paid a brief visit to the assembly of Samten Chöling Monastery in Ghoom, Darjeeling, as they had requested, and then spent one day in Kurseong, where I gave a long-life empowerment to my patron.

I then took a train by way of Siliguri to Bodhgaya to coincide with His Holiness's visit there. I took part in the ceremony that His Holiness led there for the first time to confer the vows of full ordination on a large group of novice monks. After I had made offerings and visited various sacred places around Bodhgaya, Varanasi, and so on, I returned to Mussoorie for the Tibetan New Year.

Residences in Dharamsala and Sonada

In the third Tibetan month of my sixtieth year, the year of the iron-rat (1960), as the Indian government had suggested that His Holiness and his entourage move to make their residence in Dharamsala, Himachal Pradesh, I also moved with my attendants to Nowrojee House in Dharamsala.[273]

At the command of His Holiness, over the course of many days I provided detailed instruction in the basic model for the Tibetan language, Thönmi Sambhota's *Thirty Verses* and *Introduction to Morphology*, to a group that included Dagyab Hothokthu Rinpoché, Paṇchen Ötrul, Panglung Tulku of Sera Mé, Lhakhar Tulku, Yerpa Tsenshap Tulku of Sera Mé, Chötse Tulku, Samdhong Tulku of Loseling, Yiga Tulku, Shakhor Khentrul, Nyakré Khentrul, Geshé Jampal Sengé of Sera Mé, and Geshé Tenpai Gyaltsen. During the course I had each of them write grammatical compositions and tested them regularly on each segment of grammar.

Over four days, beginning on the ninth day of the eighth Tibetan month, I offered His Holiness and a small entourage initiation into outer five-deity Cakrasaṃvara according to Ghaṇṭāpāda, the great initiation into the body mandala in Ghaṇṭāpāda's tradition, along with the blessing of the four sindūra initiations of Vajrayoginī in succession.

I went to Sonada at the appeal of Mrs. Sherpa Phurbu Lhamo, who had offered me via Ladakh Lama Ngawang Samten, former abbot of the Tibetan monastery in Bodhgaya, a two-story house situated next to the temple in the Sonada district of Darjeeling to sow roots of virtue on behalf of her late husband, Kodé Subhedar. During my visit there I gave a vast assembly of lay and ordained people the great initiation into the Bhikṣuṇī Lakṣmī tradition of the Great Compassionate One and the long-life empowerment according to Thangthong ear-whispered tradition.

During that time the monks of Dromo Dungkar Monastery invited me to Samten Chöling Monastery in Ghoom, so I went there. I stayed for seven days, giving the entire community of monks the great initiation into single-deity Vajrabhairava and gave a few groups of three monks the life-entrusting initiation and permission to practice the protector Shukden. I went to Tashi Chöling Monastery in Kurseong at the request of patrons there and gave the local people permission to practice Avalokiteśvara Who Liberates from All Lower Realms and other miscellaneous teachings.

Afterward I went to Kalimpong at the invitation of the Sadutshang family and gave the great initiation into five-deity Cakrasaṃvara in the tradition of Ghaṇṭāpāda and the blessing of the four sindūra initiations of Vajrayoginī at Tharpa Chöling Monastery. At the residence of Dromo Rinpoché, I gave an audience of about sixty monks, including the supreme incarnation of Kyabjé Phabongkha Vajradhara and Drakgyab Rinpoché of Sera Mé, the great initiation into the body mandala of Cakrasaṃvara in the tradition of Ghaṇṭāpāda.

At the request of the Friendship Society of Kalimpong, I gave a public long-life empowerment in the tradition of Machik Drupgyal in a field in front of the Sadutshang house and taught Dharma to various people from all walks of life. I had the chance to twice meet and spend a pleasant time with Tsurphu Karmapa Rinpoché while there. At the invitation of Khamtrul Rinpoché I performed the consecration for the construction of Sangdok Palri Monastery, which was in process at Dorpin in Kalimpong.

As soon as this concluded, on the nineteenth of the tenth Tibetan month, I traveled at the express wish of His Holiness to the Dharma encampment at Buxa, in West Bengal, where fifteen hundred monks from the three seats and from the Sakya, Nyingma, and Kagyü traditions who had escaped from Tibet were temporarily living. On the occasion of the festival of Ganden Ngamchö,[274] I read the monks an official letter from His Holiness and offered tea and money to the monks on behalf of the government. On the same occasion, I myself also made clouds of offerings, both of teachings and money, to the assembly.

As I had been asked both publicly and privately, I gave the entire assembly a discourse on the *Guru Puja*, the great initiation into thirteen-deity Vajrabhairava, a long-life empowerment, permission to practice the Three Wrathful Forms Combined, and gave those who had made the commitment to recite the mantra the blessing of the four sindūra initiations of Vajrayoginī. At the residence of Song Rinpoché, I gave a group of around seven hundred monks the common torma initiation into Cittamaṇi Tārā and the unique blessing of the four initiations into the body mandala. I conferred novice ordination on Kundor Tulku of Chamdo and the vows of full ordination on around sixty monks who wished to receive them, including Denma Tsenbar Tulku of Sera Jé, and gave them each teachings to fulfill their wishes.

Buxa Fort was once used as a prison camp where the British imprisoned many political activists, including India's founding fathers Gandhi and Nehru, during India's struggle for independence from British rule. It was therefore a very rough and isolated place. Yet despite the primitive nature of the place and its inhabitants, the monks bore the fourfold temperament of āryas,[275] being content with a place to sleep, the bare necessities, and so on. I was continually impressed with them throughout my stay there.

After my duties at Buxa came to an end, I went to Calcutta for a medical examination, where I stayed in the house of the Phunkhang family. I visited Tutor Kyabjé Ling Rinpoché, who was receiving medical attention in the hospital where I was undergoing my exam. At the request of a Mr. Jampa who had long lived in Calcutta, I gave the long-life empowerment of White Tārā to an audience of around a hundred Tibetans. Gyalwang Karmapa Rinpoché had also come to Calcutta, so we were once again able to meet and spend some pleasant time together. After my medical tests at the big hospital were finished, I returned to Dharamsala.

Bodhgaya and Further Travels

In the first Tibetan month of my sixty-first year, the Tibetan year of the iron-ox (1961), at His Holiness's wish, I went to Bodhgaya to give Dharma teachings at the prayer festival commemorating the display of miracles by the Buddha. This festival was organized and sponsored by the retired abbot of the Bodhgaya monastery, Lama Ngawang Samten of Ladakh, and attended by five hundred monks who had been brought to Bodhgaya from Buxa and a thousand monks who had come from other places. Every morning from the eighth to the fifteenth of the Tibetan month, in keeping with tradition, I would recite Āryaśūra's *Garland of Birth Stories* in front of the Bodhi Tree. Afterward I would give discourses on Jé Tsongkhapa's *Three Principal Aspects of the Path*, as requested by the monk official Ngawang Döndrup, who was overseeing the prayer festival. At the request of the supreme incarnation of Kyabjé Phabongkha Rinpoché, I offered the oral transmission of Śāntideva's *Guide to the Bodhisattva's Way of Life*.

In the afternoon during the dry assembly, I led the dedication prayers and recited the *Prayer for the Teachings to Flourish*[276] and Jé Tsongkhapa's

Prayer for Rebirth in Sukhāvatī just as we had done them in the Lhasa Great Prayer Festival. In the afternoon, on the order of His Holiness, I supervised the examination of that year's candidates for geshé lharampa. On the fifteenth, in front of the Bodhi Tree, I presided over the fortnightly confession ceremony and conferred the bodhisattva vows to a large crowd of monastics and laypeople in conjunction with the ceremony for generating bodhicitta. I made thousandfold offerings at the great stupa, offered money to the monks, and so on, and having completed well all my auspicious activities, I returned to Dharamsala.

Over the course of ten days beginning on the eighth day of the fourth Tibetan month, I gave His Holiness the complete set of permissions for the deities explained in the Surka Cycle of sādhanas. After that I offered a group that included Bakula Rinpoché from Ladakh the great initiations into five-deity Cakrasaṃvara and Ghaṇṭāpāda's body mandala.

In the sixth Tibetan month, I went from Dharamsala to Darjeeling, where I stayed for two months in my house in Sonada. Tutor Kyabjé Ling Rinpoché, Dromo Geshé Rinpoché, Mindröling Trichen Rinpoché, and the supreme incarnation of Kyabjé Vajradhara Rinpoché came to visit me there. I once again called on Kyabjé Ling Rinpoché while he was staying at Ghoom Monastery. I sponsored construction of a new statue of Avalokiteśvara for the Sonada temple, into which I placed dhāraṇī and many sacred relics, such as pieces of clothing and hair from many great masters of India and Tibet, and performed the rites of consecration and "opening the eyes."[277] For two days there I gave an audience of around seven hundred lay and ordained people permission to practice Avalokiteśvara Liberating from the Lower Realms and a long-life empowerment in the tradition of Machik Drupgyal.

On the twenty-fifth day of the eighth Tibetan month, Tsurphu Karmapa Rinpoché, the central pole of the practice lineage, sent a messenger inviting me to Rumtek Monastery in Gangtok. At Rumtek, I spent five days meeting with Rinpoché every day to talk at leisure about our past and present situations. We spoke freely with one another, without any pretense or artifice.

After making offerings to the monks at that Dharma institution, I went to the Sadutshang house in Kalimpong. At the request of Sönam Chöphel of Lhasa, I gave a large group of earnest practitioners at Tharpa Chöling Monastery in Kalimpong the blessing of the four sindūra initiations of

Vajrayoginī, and at the request of the supreme incarnation of Phabongkha Vajradhara Rinpoché, I offered ninety monks, including Rinpoché himself and Dromo Geshé Rinpoché, the great initiation into Cakrasaṃvara body mandala in Ghaṇṭāpāda's tradition. As soon as I had completed those, at the request of the supreme incarnation, I offered at the Sadutshang house an extensive and very detailed commentary on the generation and completion stages of the body mandala in Ghaṇṭāpāda's tradition to fifty-eight earnest disciples who had pledged to practice self-generation daily, fulfilling their wishes.

To sow roots of virtue on behalf of the late Khangsar Yeshé Nyima of Chatreng and to fulfill the request of the Friendship Society of Kalimpong, I twice gave a group of about two thousand people permission to practice Avalokiteśvara Who Liberates from All Lower Realms. At the request of Gyurmé Sadutshang, over the course of eight days beginning on the tenth day of the tenth month, I gave the initiation of Vajrayoginī and an experiential commentary on the practice of its two stages to a group of 132 earnest disciples who had committed to practice the self-generation daily and to do a retreat on the practice.

At the request of the British bhikṣu Sangharakshita, on the day of the Ganden Ngamchö festival, I gave a large crowd that included some Geluk, Kagyü, and Nyingma lamas and many devout lay and ordained men and women who had come to the festival a lecture in the town hall in Kalimpong on the great virtues of the three secrets of Jé Tsongkhapa and a general survey of the unique features of the study and practice of the Dharma as taught in the Geluk tradition.

In the eleventh Tibetan month, after I returned to Dharamsala at the feet of His Holiness, I gave the blessing of the four sindūra initiations of Vajrayoginī to a small group that included Lady Yuthok Dorjé Yudron and gave the great initiation into Secret Hayagrīva in the Kyergang tradition to a group that included the Nechung medium (Ta Lama Losang Jikmé). I began to privately give Dzemé Rinpoché of Ganden Shartsé an explanation of the *Great Treatise on the Stages of the Path* with the four annotations, which we continued whenever we had the chance until we had completed it.

In the first month of my sixty-second year, the Tibetan year of the water-tiger (1962), when Kyabjé Simok Rinpoché of Nalendra came to Dharamsala, I visited him to pay my respects. It was a thoroughly enjoyable talk, and I took the essence of his words into my heart.

Trijang Rinpoché flanked by Dudjom Rinpoché and Khamtrul Rinpoché, with Minling Trichen behind him, on the day of the Ganden Ngamchö festival at the Kalimpong town hall, 1961
COURTESY OF PALDEN TSERING

When the supreme incarnation of Phabongkha Rinpoché Vajradhara came to Dharamsala to receive full ordination, I arranged for him and his entourage to stay in my house and cared for all their needs as usual. I conferred lay and novice vows on thirty-seven monks from the road workers camp in Chamba district. I gave Powo Sumzong Lama and Tö Shungru Lama the life-entrusting initiation and permission to practice the protector Shukden. I gave Shungru Lama an explanation of the central channel according to the completion stage of Vajrayoginī. I gave the great initiation into single-deity Vajrabhairava and permissions to practice Secret Hayagrīva and Avalokiteśvara Who Liberates from All Lower Realms, respectively, to member of the Assembly of People's Deputies Samkharwa, Tsedrung Jampa Wangdü, and Töpa Tamdrin Tsering.

On the ninth and tenth of the second month, at the express wish of His Holiness, our great and supreme refuge and protector, I gave a group of about twenty that included His Holiness and Dagyab Rinpoché the great initiation into Cakrasaṃvara body mandala in Ghaṇṭāpāda's tradition along with its preparatory and actual practices at His Holiness's residence.

Over the course of seventeen days beginning on the eleventh, I gave His Holiness, Dagyab Rinpoché, Assistant Tutor Serkong Rinpoché, His

Holiness's ritual assistant, and Dzemé Rinpoché an explanation of the generation and completion stages of the Cakrasaṃvara body mandala and teachings on the six Dharmas of Nāropa based on personal experience. After that, at the request of Mr. Samkharwa from Chushur, I gave a group of about thirty lamas and monks, including Khensur Ngawang Drakpa of Sera Mé, the great initiation into single-deity Vajrabhairava, the blessing of the four sindūra initiations of Vajrayoginī, and teachings on the *Hundred Deities of Tuṣita*.

I then conferred novice ordination vows on fourteen monks from Dalhousie, on four men from Zanskar, Ladakh, as well as on Chaknang Lhawang Tsering.

Teaching in Spiti

At the request of Kyil Monastery (a.k.a. Key Gompa) in Spiti, I left Dharamsala on the third day of the sixth Tibetan month (1962) and traveled to Spiti via Mandi, Kullu, Manali, Rohtang Pass, and Chhatru. We stayed in the town temple in a village called Losel in the Spiti Valley. From Chhatru to Kyil Monastery, my attendants and I traveled on horses provided by Lochen Labrang. As we arrived at Losel a jeep suddenly rounded the bend, alarming the horse I was riding and forcing me to dismount in a hurry. In doing so I sprained my right ankle, which grew quite swollen and painful. I had to spend a week in Losel receiving treatment from the Spiti doctor Tashi Gönpo. In the meantime I gave large numbers of local people oral transmissions of the six-syllable mantra, refuge, and the *Praises to Tārā*.

When the pain had subsided, I departed Losel. Since I could not place my right foot in the stirrup, each day while riding from Losel to Kyil Monastery, I would place my left foot into the stirrup and fold my right leg around the front of the saddle and a person next to the horse would support my knee. Riding like this in the *pratyālīḍha* stance[278] was tiresome and uncomfortable. At the various villages we stopped at between Chicham and Kyil, I gave long-life initiations, oral transmissions of refuge, the six-syllable mantra, and so on.

On the nineteenth I arrived at Kyil Monastery Norbu Gephel in Spiti, the monastery of Lochen Rinpoché Losang Palden Rinchen Gyatso, a tutor to Paṇchen Lama Chökyi Nyima (1883–1937) and an incarnation of the great translator Rinchen Sangpo (958–1055). There I gave the monks of

Kyil, Drakar (Dhankar), and Takmo (Tabo) monasteries together with a large audience of lay and ordained people from the area an explanation of the *Foundation of All Good Qualities*. I gave the monks the great initiations into thirteen-deity Vajrabhairava and Akṣobhyavajra in the Ārya tradition of Guhyasamāja and permissions for Medicine Buddha, Mahākāla, Dharmarāja, Palden Lhamo, Vaiśravaṇa, and Chamsing. I conferred novice ordination on about ten monks. In the lush green field behind the monastery I gave an audience of more than one thousand local people initiation into the Great Compassionate One, a long-life empowerment in the tradition of Drupgyal, and oral transmissions of refuge and the six-syllable mantra. In Lochen Rinpoché's private quarters, I gave a few earnest disciples the blessing of the four sindūra initiations of Vajrayoginī. I therefore fulfilled the wishes of the people by giving the various teachings they had requested. Since Dr. Tashi Gönpo had treated my sprained ankle with a walnut treatment, after that I luckily no longer had to ride in the *pratyālīḍha* stance.

Previously the monasteries had traditionally served alcohol at prayer sessions and during private rituals in the homes of patrons. Also during the annual winter ceremonies they had consumed meat dishes using the meat of sheep especially slaughtered for these occasions. The local people also slaughtered goats and sheep as sacrifices to local deities to ensure a good harvest or to prevent epidemics. Since they were sure to experience unbearable hardship in future lives as the fruit of such misguided customs, which were like those of *tīrthikas* or Bönpos, I related stories of past lives found in the Buddha's Vinaya teachings and cited passages from the sutras to urge them to discontinue these practices. I strongly emphasized the view of the Dharma and the advantages of following it.

Each of the monasteries pledged, from then on, to observe the rule against drinking alcohol, to prohibit acceptance of meat slaughtered intentionally for ritual purposes, and to properly observe the three foundations of monastic discipline. The local villages also promised to prohibit blood sacrifice on behalf of their local deities and to take up customs that were in keeping with the Dharma. They have been following the good practices of observing the teachings to this day, and I continue to rejoice at the accomplishment of this good deed of discontinuing these negative customs.

The general assembly of Spiti's Kyil Monastery gave me seven thousand Indian rupees as part of an offering for my long life, which I offered back with an additional sum of five hundred rupees to use as a capital fund for observance of the annual rainy-season retreat at the monastery. On the way back from Kyil Monastery, we made our way to Manali along the road that passes through Khurik, Kiamo, Losel, and Chhatru. There I gave a large crowd of locals a long-life empowerment in the tradition of Drupgyal and oral transmissions of refuge and the six-syllable mantra.

I once again returned to Dharamsala via Kulu, arriving on the tenth day of the seventh Tibetan month. As soon as I returned His Holiness paid me a friendly visit, coming to my house to ask about the condition of my ankle, the situation in Spiti, and so on.

On the fifth day of the eighth month, I began to instruct Dagyab Rinpoché on the second chapter of Daṇḍin's *Mirror of Poetics*. On the fifteenth, Tutor Kyabjé Ling Rinpoché visited me at my home and gave me a copy of lineage prayers to my previous incarnations that he had composed, along with a ceremonial scarf and some money to stand in for a mandala offering, and told me that I must try to live a long life. I, in turn, offered him a scarf and some money as a mandala offering and requested an oral transmission of the prayer.

At the request of Venerable Chödrak of Namgyal Monastery, I gave over the course of four days to all the monks of Namgyal along with some geshés and tulkus, including Dagyab Rinpoché, Assistant Tutor Serkong Rinpoché, and Dzemé Rinpoché, an oral transmission of the ritual texts of Namgyal, which are the same as the tantric ritual texts at Tashi Lhunpo. I then offered the abbot and twenty-one monks from Gyümé Tantric College, who had come specially from Dalhousie,[279] permissions for the collected mantras of Guhyasamāja, Cakrasaṃvara, and Vajrabhairava, along with oral transmissions of the three-part Dharmarāja ritual of the Iron Fortress,[280] the wrathful fire offering, the Guhyasamāja self-generation and front-generation, the ground consecration, the peaceful fire offering, and the Magical Wheel of Stacked Vajra Mountains,[281] and a ritual for exorcising harmful spirits performed in conjunction with Dharmarāja. All of these were in the tradition of Gyümé.

On orders from His Holiness, two life-force wheels of the fivefold Dharmarāja,[282] one depicting Trinlé Gyalpo and the other Yönten Gyalpo, were made for the Nechung and Gadong mediums to wear on their bodies, and Tutor Ling Rinpoché and I blessed and consecrated the wheels. A thangka of the fivefold Dharmarāja, complete with the life-force wheel, had been made at the Norbulingka in Lhasa for His Holiness to keep close at all times, but due to its large size he commissioned a smaller one that would be more portable. The canvas was prepared with a gesso made from sacred substances, such as the relics from holy persons who had a special connection with the fivefold Dharmarāja, like Guru Rinpoché, Ngadak Nyangral,[283] Guru Chöwang, Longchenpa, and so on, and the paints were blessed. I guided the artist, Trinlé Wangyal, a monk from Namgyal Monastery, to generate himself as the deity and paint the canvas. After that, once the syllables on the three places and the mantra wheel were inscribed in the customary manner, I had His Holiness's ritual assistant (Thupten Jamyang) draw the life-force wheel on the back of the thangka.

Pilgrimage

On the third day of the eleventh Tibetan month, I traveled from Dharamsala to Bodhgaya. I met Song Rinpoché of Ganden Shartsé, who happened to be doing the burial ritual with a few ritual assistants at the behest of the government, and we talked freely. At the request of Trehor Kangyur Rinpoché of Drepung Loseling, I gave an audience of two hundred lamas, monks, and laypeople the blessing of the four sindūra initiations of Vajrayoginī at the Tibetan monastery. I made offerings of food for a complete day at the monastery and thousandfold offerings at the great stupa. To fulfill a request from Amdo Drokpa Jinpa, a monk at the Tibetan monastery, I spent two days giving a crowd of four hundred—monks at the monastery and pilgrims from various places—an explanation of Kyabjé Phabongkha Vajradhara's personal teachings on the *Hundred Deities of Tuṣita* and instruction in the six-session guruyoga.

I went to the sacred sites of Vulture's Peak and Nālandā, attended a reception given by the lamas and geshés at the Sanskrit University in Varanasi, and then went on to Sarnath, where I stayed at the Mahabodhi Guest House. At the request of Bhikṣu Thupten Jungné, the manager of Dögu Kyil Tibetan Monastery, I consecrated the statues of the temples. I invited Tutor Ling Rinpoché and made an extensive thousandfold offering in front of the Dhamek Stupa built by King Aśoka.

At the request of Geshé Khyenrap Söpa of Drepung Gowo and the bursar of the Jamyang Kyil family of Lhasa, at the Ladakhi student hostel I gave the blessing of the four sindūra initiations of Vajrayoginī to a gathering of around two hundred, comprised of abbots, lamas, and monks like Jampal

Kyabjé Song Rinpoché, 1978, Vajrapani Institute, California
LAMA YESHE WISDOM ARCHIVE

Samphel from Gyalrong, former abbot of Drepung Loseling, Shakhor abbot Phara Nyima Gyaltsen, as well as some lay men and women.

I made a pilgrimage to Kushinagar and made offerings there. At the request of Palchuk Göbu from Chatreng, I gave around five hundred people at the Chinese temple in Sarnath a long-life empowerment and permission to practice Avalokiteśvara Who Liberates from All Lower Realms. At the Tibetan monastery in Varanasi, there was a long-life ceremony with tsok offerings sponsored by the Tibetan government. Assistant Tutor Serkong Rinpoché had come to preside over the offering for my long life. It was quite auspicious.

Oral Transmission of the Works of Jé Tsongkhapa

On the afternoon of third day of the first month of my sixty-third year, the year of the water-rabbit (1963), I left Varanasi. As soon as I arrived in Dharamsala, I paid respects at His Holiness's lotus feet, and on the tenth I began to give His Holiness an oral transmission of the collected works of our gentle protector, the great Tsongkhapa. For auspiciousness, I began by offering an oral transmission of the *Abridged Stages of the Path*. Since I had already given him an oral transmission of the *Great Treatise on the Stages of the Path* in Lhasa, it wasn't necessary to redo it. We spent every day with one another from that day onward doing the oral transmission with the exception of a few days when His Holiness or I had official engagements.

Among the collected works, when doing the oral transmission of the *Highway to Enlightenment*[284] and *Exposition on the Root Tantric Vows*,[285] I also interwove explanations of Candragomin's *Twenty Verses on the Bodhisattva Vow* root text, verses on the root and secondary tantric downfalls, and *Annotations to the Root Text on the Bodhisattva and Tantric Vows* composed by Panglung Losang Thukjé, thereby achieving two goals at one time.

We suspended the transmission on the twenty-second and twenty-third so that I could offer the great initiation of Secret Hayagrīva along with its preparatory practices to eight monks from Gyümé who were planning to do an approximation retreat of Hayagrīva and a group of about fifty tulkus and monks, including Rizong Rinpoché of Ladakh and the former abbot of Gyümé, who had all come from Dalhousie.

When I gave His Holiness the oral transmissions of Jé Tsongkhapa's *Twenty-One Short Works on Guhyasamāja*,[286] I also instructed him in the recitation of Samayavajra and the fire offering of Vajraḍāka. As I gave the oral transmission of the *Jeweled Box Sādhana of Thirteen-Deity Vajrabhairava*, I offered tormas to the enlightened and worldly deities. I gave experiential commentaries on the two stages of Vajrabhairava with a fourfold explanation from memory in accordance with the tradition of Kyabjé Phabongkha Vajradhara. With the exception of *Golden Garland of Eloquent Explanation* and the *Great Commentary on Fundamental Wisdom*, I completed the oral transmissions of the collected works of Jé Tsongkhapa on the seventeenth day of the third Tibetan month. I then continued with the oral transmission of some works of Nāgārjuna and his spiritual sons contained in the Tengyur—the Guhyasamāja *Five Stages* (*Pañcakrama*), *Condensed Sādhana* (*Piṇḍīkṛtasādhana*), and *Mahāyogatantra*,[287] Nāgabodhi's *Stages of the Presentation* (*Samājasādhanavyavasthāli*), Nāgārjuna's *Explanation of Bodhicitta* (*Bodhicittavivaraṇa*), Nāgabodhi's *Twenty-Verse Mandala Ritual* (*Maṇḍalopāyikāviṃśatividhi*), and Rāhulaśrīmitra's *Illuminated Union Initiation Ritual* (*Yuganaddhaprakāśabhiṣekaprakriyā*).

The Passing of Kyabjé Simok Vajradhara

On the twenty-fourth day of the third Tibetan month, I went to visit Kyabjé Simok Vajradhara, whose physical health seemed to be deteriorating, and requested him to live longer.

I received a great many volumes of important works, like the complete collected works of Gungthang Tenpai Drönmé, that Dromo Geshé Rinpoché had sent from Kalimpong. I was fortunate to receive them and was delighted.

On the first day of the fourth month, I conferred the one-day Mahayana vows on twenty-one ordained and lay people who were undertaking the *nyungné* fasting practice.

Doctor Tashi Gönpo came to visit me from Spiti, and I sent a letter to Kachen Logyal, the abbot of Kyil Monastery, with him when he returned. I also sent a copy of an effigy ritual text and asked him to distribute copies of it to the people in the area. I had composed the ritual for their benefit so that when they wanted to help the sick, they could offer an effigy of an animal made of dough as a substitute for the life of a real animal. The ritual could also be used in lieu of actual animal sacrifice to ensure a good harvest.

At midday on the tenth of the month, Kyabjé Simok Vajradhara, Jetsun Jampa Ngawang Kunga Tenzin Trinlé Palsangpo, having lived a long life, manifested his final act, like a butter lamp flickering out when its fuel is exhausted. When he had passed into Akaniṣṭha, land of ḍākinīs, I made offerings to his body. Along with a Vajrayoginī mandala offering, I offered prayers to dedicate merit for the perpetual accomplishment of his wishes to pursue the enlightened activities of liberating beings. I also offered prayers that I might be cared for by him throughout all my future lives and composed a prayer for the swift return of his incarnation.

Some thangkas that I had been forced to leave behind during the turmoil in Lhasa had, after the passage of two years, come into the hands of the supreme incarnation of Dromo Geshé Rinpoché, who had brought them with him to India. Among them was a thangka of wrathful Gyalchen with his retinue that I had commissioned in Dromo during the year of the iron-tiger (1950) that had yet to have the brocade border attached to it. The other thangkas—of Vajrabhairava and protectors such as Mahākāla, Dharmarāja, Palden Lhamo, and so on—had been commissioned during the time of my predecessor. I used to hang these thangkas during the annual great-torma ritual at my house in Lhasa at the time of the solar equinox. When I once again received these thangkas into my hands, I felt convinced that this was significant indication of the omnipresence of the celestial assistance of my protector, and so on the twenty-ninth of the fifth month, I made extensive propitiatory offerings with tsok to the protector. On the very same day, a person came by to give me two fire-resistant statues of Jé Tsongkhapa and an old Ganden edition of the *Great Treatise on the Stages of the Path* in excellent condition. To me this was an exceedingly auspicious coincidence!

On the fifteenth day of the seventh month I gave His Holiness an oral transmission of the *Bhikṣu Pratimokṣa Sutra.* Following that I gave a permission of Palden Lhamo and oral transmission of Thuken's thread-mandala ritual of Palden Lhamo to the entire assembly of monks of Namgyal Monastery. Over the course of seven days, beginning on the eighteenth, I presided over a preliminary approximation retreat for the averting ritual associated with Palden Lhamo undertaken by the entire assembly of Namgyal and walked them through the steps of the averting-ritual sādhana. At the end we performed the torma-casting ritual.

A Trip to Dalhousie

After repeated requests from the combined assemblies of Gyütö and Gyümé tantric colleges, which had established themselves in Dalhousie, at His Holiness's wish, I left for Dalhousie on the sixteenth day of the eighth month. I arrived to an elaborate reception from tulkus and monks of the three seats, Gyütö and Gyümé tantric colleges, and other Tibetan traditions, lay and ordained members of the public, and Tibetan students. Over the following days I went to visit both of the tantric monasteries in turn. At the invitation of the monks of Ganden Shartsé, I went to where their quarters were and offered tea and money to about ninety monks. I also presented a thangka of Jé Tsongkhapa and his two disciples to the monastery.

After that I also made a brief visit to each of the houses where the monks from Drepung Loseling and Sera Jé were staying.

A tent was erected in an open field behind the living quarters, and one day I gave an audience of around seven hundred—including the abbots and disciplinarians of the two tantric colleges, the entire monastic assembly, Trehor Geshé Kyorpön Tsewang Norbu Rinpoché of Drepung, the abbots of the three seats, students, as well as a monastic assembly of lamas from other religious traditions—the preparatory rite for initiation into Akṣobhyavajra in the Ārya tradition of Guhyasamāja on one day and gave the actual initiation the following two days. I visited the residence where the monks from Gyütö Tantric College were staying and corrected a few minor mistakes in the three-dimensional mandala of Guhyasamāja that they had built.

At the invitation of Gyalwang Karmapa Rinpoché in a letter and at the invitation of Mrs. Freda Bedi,[288] I went to visit the nunnery that had just been built, which would be chiefly of the Kagyü tradition. In connection with an oral transmission of Śāntarakṣita's *Ornament of the Middle Way*, I gave a teaching to remind Taklung Matrul, Khamtrul Rinpoché, and the nuns of the precepts that they were to observe. I made an offering of funds to the nuns. Mrs. Bedi then took me to Kailash House to visit the newly established Young Lama's Home School. As a part of my offering to the school at large, I reminded them of the need to observe proper conduct. I also visited each of the dorms for the boys and girls at the Tibetan government schools and advised them of the need for study and good behavior. I gave every teacher and student a small token gift.

At Oaks Koti I made an extensive offering of funds to a group of about 330 monks from the three seats and other Buddhist traditions and from the two tantric colleges. I gave the lay and ordained Tibetan general public the permission of Avalokiteśvara Who Liberates from All Lower Realms and long-life empowerment in the tradition of Drupgyal. At the request of the two tantric colleges I gave the entire assembly permission for Six-Armed Mahākāla and Outer Dharmarāja. I repeatedly urged all the monks and laypeople to remember the kindness of His Holiness, and to accordingly take care in observing religious and secular duties in accordance with the wishes of His Holiness.

Then, at a very wonderful, auspicious occasion, the lay and ordained population that were living in Dalhousie offered me a long-life ceremony in conjunction with a *Guru Puja* and tsok at Oaks Koti. I offered the money they had given me back to them in return. After finishing my duties in Dalhousie, I went back to Dharamsala on the twenty-eighth day of the month following a warm send-off from the local people.

During the ninth month, I participated in making and consecrating the protection relics in His Holiness's residence, presided over by His Holiness, for the soldiers who volunteered to join in the special unit of the Indian army for protection from being harmed by weapons. I also attended the hundred thousand tsok offering to Guru Rinpoché to benefit the religious and secular affairs of Tibet.

Meeting of All the Heads of the Tibetan Religious Traditions

I took part in a five-day conference that was an ecumenical meeting of religious traditions, including Sakya, Geluk, Kagyü, Nyingma, and Bön. On that occasion, Sakya Trizin Rinpoché, Gyalwang Karmapa Rinpoché, Chögön Rinpoché of Druk Dechen Chökhor, Dudjom Rinpoché of the Nyingma tradition, Dilgo Khyentsé Rinpoché, and Kalu Rinpoché of the Kagyü tradition, among others, came to visit me. I myself went to have audiences with Sakya Trizin Rinpoché and Gyalwang Karmapa Rinpoché. On the twenty-eighth, when the whole conference offered His Holiness a tsok and prayers for his long life, Dilgo Khyentsé Rinpoché recited the mandala description along with a history of the Nyingma lineage and the fivefold auspiciousness. I always thought I was tall, but next to the towering girth of Dilgo Khyentsé Rinpoché I looked small. The delegates also gave me long-life offerings, and I returned all their offerings except for the scarf and the token mandala offering. I gave a dinner party to all the lamas and other participants of the meeting.

Over the course of five days, beginning on the ninth day of the tenth month, I gave His Holiness an oral transmission of Jé Tsongkhapa's *Great Commentary on Fundamental Wisdom* and *Golden Garland of Eloquent Explanation*. Following that, at the request of Prime Minister Dekharwa and Samten and Lodrö of Gyümé, I gave an audience of about 140 people—including incarnate lamas and geshés such as Dagyab Rinpoché and Chogyé Trichen Rinpoché of Nalendra, the monks of Namgyal Monastery, and various lay and ordained people—the blessing of the four sindūra initiations of Vajrayoginī. Then over eight days I gave those who had taken an oath to practice self-generation every day and to do a retreat on the practice an experiential explanation of the generation and completion stages along with permissions for the collected mantras.

When that had finished, I gave His Holiness, in sequence, practical instruction in the profound path of *Guru Puja*, based on the root verses by Paṇchen Chögyen combined with the great instruction manual on it written by Yongzin Yeshé Gyaltsen, and practical instruction in the Ganden Mahāmudrā, based on the root text by Paṇchen Chögyen combined with *Ever Brighter Lamp*, its autocommentary. In between sessions, I gave Losang Sönam of Dargyé Monastery in Trehor permission to practice Avalokiteśvara Who Liberates from All Lower Realms. I conferred full ordination on three people, including Chatreng Jungné. I gave Chamdo Dotsé permission for White Mañjuśrī and an experiential teaching on the uncommon yoga of the inconceivability of Vajrayoginī. I conferred full ordination on five novices who were students of Drukpa Tsechu Tulku from Nepal.

Sarnath, Bodhgaya, and Return to Dharamsala

I left Dharamsala on the third day of the eleventh month and on the morning of the fourth arrived in Sarnath, where I stayed at the Sangharama guesthouse. After making offerings and circumambulating the stupa for a few days, I left for Bodhgaya. There I met Tutor Kyabjé Ling Vajradhara. I made monetary offerings to the monks there for a whole day and accumulated merit by making extensive thousandfold offerings at the stupa. At the wish of the Ladakhi Losang Tashi, I consecrated the newly constructed Tibetan monastery on the site where the Buddha had practiced austerities for six years. On the twenty-fifth, as part of an offering I sponsored for all the monks in Bodhgaya, I offered Tutor Kyabjé Ling Rinpoché a long-life ceremony with the Halting the Ḍākinī's Escort ritual along with the *Guru Puja* and tsok offering related to Cakrasaṃvara, requesting that his feet remain steadfastly planted in a state of well-being. That afternoon I performed the self-initiation ritual of Vajrayoginī with Tutor Ling Rinpoché. After a long-life ceremony on my behalf that Lama Ngawang Samten of Ladakh had sponsored, I returned to Sarnath.

The overseer of the Tibetan monastery, Thupten Jungné, offered me a long-life ceremony as part of a *Guru Puja* with tsok offering. I made offerings to the monks of the monastery and offered a fund for the construction of statues. I then fulfilled the wishes of various people who asked for teachings: I composed a lineage prayer of my refuge and protector, Kyabjé Phabongkha Vajradhara, at the request of Gyara Rinpoché of Chamdo. At the request of the wife of Mensurwa, I gave the great initiation into five-deity Cakrasaṃvara in Ghaṇṭāpāda's tradition, along with its preparatory practices, and the blessing of the four sindūra initiations of Vajrayoginī at the Tibetan monastery in Sarnath to a crowd of lay and ordained people, including incarnate masters and monks. I gave oral transmissions of many texts, including the *Hundred Deities of Tuṣita* and Atiśa's *Lamp on the Path to Enlightenment* at the request of Jinpa Gyatso of Amdo. I gave the common torma initiation and the exclusive body-mandala blessings of the four initiations of Cittamaṇi Tārā at the request of the monk Gyaltsen of Ngamring. I gave Thupten Ngawang, the former manager of Ratö Monastery, instruction in the six-session guruyoga. And I gave the Chamdo monk Phurtsé permission to practice Avalokiteśvara Who Liberates from All Lower Realms.

On the twenty-sixth of February, the thirteenth day of the first Tibetan month, in my sixty-fourth year, the year of the wood-dragon (1964), I traveled from Sarnath to Dharamsala. Since the people of Chatreng had asked that a history of the region be written, I wrote a brief one even though I wasn't certain about many details.

Over the course of ten days beginning on the second day of the second month, at His Holiness's wish, I participated in the propitiation of the twelve *tenma* together with the entire assembly of Namgyal Monastery. Afterward I gave the entire assembly of Namgyal permissions to practice the shared and exclusive White Tārā and instruction in the long-life ritual associated with White Tārā. For two days, beginning on the twenty-second, I offered His Holiness an oral transmission of the *Eight Thousand Verse Perfection of Wisdom*. As soon as that was completed, I began to give His Holiness an explanation of the *Great Treatise on the Stages of the Path* with the four annotations. We worked through the text gradually, and when we reached the section "How to Train in the Bodhisattva Deeds in General," we took a break.

At the request of the attendant to the abbot of Tö Ruthok Monastery, I gave an audience of twenty-five people—eight monks from Ruthok, including the abbot, as well as some monks who were living in Dharamsala—the great initiation into single-deity Vajrabhairava, with its preparatory rite. I took the first snip of hair from Tsechok Ling Tulku and gave him an oral transmission reading of the *Hundred Deities of Tuṣita*. At the request of Drakpa Adrak of Chatreng, I gave the blessing of the four sindūra initiations of Vajrayoginī. At the request of His Holiness's ritual master, Thupten Sönam, I gave the permission of Jé Tsongkhapa as the triple deity to the three personal attendants of His Holiness and a few others. I gave innkeeper Ngödrup and his wife the long-life empowerment of White Tārā along with permission for the Three Wrathful Forms Combined. I performed the obstacle-eliminating ritual of Secret Hayagrīva for seven days for the long life of Tutor Kyabjé Ling Rinpoché. There were good indications that obstacles to his well-being had been eliminated.

On the seventeenth day of the fifth month I began to give His Holiness the transmission and explanation of how to train in the final two perfections that make up the latter half of the *Great Treatise on the Stages of the Path* with the four annotations. We continued every day until completion on the tenth day of the sixth month.

I taught for two days on the root texts of the *Thirty Verses* and *Introduction to Morphology* in conjunction with the *Wish-Fulfilling Tree of Eloquence*[289] for the abbots of the three seats who had come from Buxa. Although these abbots, being nothing but geshés of the highest rank, grasped the meaning quickly, they showed little interest in doing the written exercises. So I couldn't really tell if they had reached the point of being able to apply what they had learned from the texts. Before the abbot of Shartsé returned to Buxa, I gave him a thangka of the *Guru Puja* merit field, a horizontal thangka of the thirty-five buddhas of confession complete with brocade border, as well as many rolls of red, yellow, and blue Varanasi brocade for tantric deity costumes.

I passed three weeks performing the rituals of propitiation and invocation for celestial assistance of the protecting deities Palden Lhamo, the twelve *tenma*, fivefold Dharmarāja, and Shukden with the assembly of Namgyal Monastery. These rituals were done in accumulative numbers for the strength and success of religious and secular affairs. At the request of the former minister Shenkhawa, over the course of three days beginning on the nineteenth day of the tenth month I gave a large group of devoted students instruction in the *Wheel of Sharp Weapons Mind Training*.

Bodhgaya, Sarnath, and Delhi

On the twenty-ninth I traveled from Dharamsala to Bodhgaya, where I spent one month performing virtuous activities in the form of prostrations and circumambulations. At the wish of Mr. Jampa, a merchant from Calcutta, I gave an audience of around six hundred people a long-life empowerment in the tradition of Drupgyal and the permission of Avalokiteśvara Who Liberates from All Lower Realms at the foot of the Bodhi Tree. I invited Tutor Kyabjé Ling Rinpoché to preside over offerings at the Tibetan Monastery in Bodhgaya and over an extensive thousandfold offering at the great stupa.

On the second first day of the eleventh month,[290] I traveled from Bodhgaya to Sarnath, where I stayed at the Tibetan monastery. I offered 101 authentic sacred relics, such as pieces of clothing and hair taken from the Buddha after he passed away and from many great Indian and Tibetan masters, to be placed in the interior of the newly built statue of Śākyamuni that was to be the Tibetan monastery's principal statue and performed the ritual to bless the dhāraṇī to be inserted.

From the ninth for twenty-two days I gave experiential teachings on the *Easy Path* with the notes on the *Liberation in the Palm of Your Hand* to the abbots of the three seats and eight hundred incarnate lamas, geshés, students, and a few pilgrims who had come especially for the teachings at Shedrup Dögu Khyil Monastery, the Tibetan monastery in Sarnath. This had been requested by the Mongolian Lama Guru Deva and others, including Phakri Jolak, Serkhang Ama, and Thupten Chöjor, the former manager of Drakgyab Monastery. As soon as that finished, at the request of the above-named benefactors as well as Chamdo Dotsé and Dampa Lodrö of Tsawarong, I gave instructions over the course of five days on the *Guru Puja* based on Kachen Yeshé Gyaltsen's great instruction manual on the root text, concluding with the ceremony for generating bodhicitta. Although I did not have any personal experience, I raised my voice and gave these teachings like a donkey donning the skin of a leopard. Thinking how incredibly fortunate I was to have the opportunity to expound like an actor the methods of the stages of the path—the essence of all the paths of the buddhas of the past, present, and future, and the basis for the Buddha's turning of the wheel of Dharma—to an assembly of such distinguished masters, I accepted the challenge of doing so.

At the request of Achen of Tsawarong, I gave the initiation of Life-Sustaining Jé Tsongkhapa and the permission to practice the Three Wrathful Forms Combined.

On the eleventh day of the twelfth month I traveled from Varanasi to Delhi. At the request of Lama Losang from Ladakh, I gave a large audience at the Ladakh Buddha Vihar the long-life empowerment of White Tārā and permission to practice Avalokiteśvara Who Liberates from All Lower Realms. I also performed a short consecration in the temple.

On the seventeenth, at the invitation of my patron Gyurmé Sadutshang, I traveled from Delhi to Sehore, Bhopal. There, at my sponsor's request, I gave a group of about ten people the blessing of the four sindūra initiations of Vajrayoginī and gave an Amitāyus long-life initiation in the system of Drupgyal to the officers and staff of the G. S. Mandidip Paper Mills.[291]

Enthronement of Kyabjé Ling Rinpoché and the Passing of Lhabu

On the ninth of March in my sixty-fifth year, the sixth day of the first Tibetan month of the year of the wood-snake (1965), I traveled from Sehore to Dharamsala via Delhi. The supreme incarnation of Kyabjé Phabongkha Vajradhara came to Dharamsala for medical treatment and to receive further teachings. He stayed with me as my guest throughout his visit as usual.

On the tenth I visited His Holiness in person and delighted in seeing his face, which clearly exhibited the wondrous major and minor marks. I took part in an elaborate long-life ceremony with the ritual of five secret deities of Amitāyus, which was among the divine visions of Takphu, with the Halting the Ḍākinī's Escort ritual, all offered to His Holiness by the Tibetan government-in-exile.

The ceremony investing Tutor Kyabjé Ling Rinpoché as the holder of the throne of the second Buddha, Jé Tsongkhapa, was held in Bodhgaya. Although on that occasion I had offered him a mandala, the representations of the holy body, speech, and mind, and the pandit's hat with brocade flaps as an auspicious sign, an inaugural ceremony in the presence of His Holiness was held in Dharamsala on the sixteenth to make this enthronement official. After the ceremony I personally went to see Kyabjé Ling Rinpoché and offered him a sum of money as a token of the three representations along with a long silk scarf with auspicious symbols and a volume of Khedrup Jé's biography of Tsongkhapa *Entryway of Faith*. The following day the supreme tutor and throneholder came to my home and offered me a ceremonial scarf and the three representations in return.

At the request of His Holiness, over the course of three days beginning on the eighth day of the second month, I offered on the lawn in front of Mortimer Hall[292] very extensive instructions on the *Seven-Point Mind Training* and the *Eight Verses on Mind Training*, wherein my words belied my own actions. It was a large public gathering—including the lay and ordained staff of our own government, abbots, incarnate masters, and monks from the three seats, Gyütö and Gyümé tantric colleges, as well as various other religious traditions, and lay and ordained people living in Dharamsala.

My attendant Lhabu fell ill with a combination of bile disease and sharp shooting pains around the twentieth. I requested the general assembly of monks at Buxa, both Shartsé and Jangtsé colleges, and Gyütö and Gyümé in Dalhousie to hold prayer sessions on his behalf.

On the twenty-fourth, at the request of the supreme incarnation of Kyabjé Vajradhara Rinpoché, I began to give a group of twelve monks—including Rinpoché himself, Dagyab Rinpoché, Ratö Chubar Rinpoché, and Dzemé Rinpoché—permissions for the collections of deities included in the famed Narthang Hundred, which was edited and compiled by Chim Namkha Drak of Narthang, handed down from the glorious, incomparable Jowo Atiśa, and made the heart practice of the Kadam lamas. I gave twelve permissions on that day and twelve permissions on the twenty-fifth.

That evening my dear attendant Lhabu, who was upright by nature and without any pretension, who had been my friend and playmate since I was ten years old and he was nearly nine, who had patiently borne the burden of standing with me through whatever happened, both joys and sorrows, until he was nearly sixty-six, and who had accomplished whatever was entrusted to him with single-pointed dedication, began to irreversibly lose consciousness of the five senses despite medical treatment and prayers on his behalf. I guided his mind toward virtuous thoughts and whispered the names of buddhas, dhāraṇīs, and mantras in his ear. Since he had always recited his daily prayers and had very few thoughts of attachment or anger, he passed away peacefully in a virtuous state of mind, without the slightest feeling of hope or doubt, at eleven thirty at night. He embarked on that great path called death reflecting on the impermanent nature of all compounded phenomena. As the *Garland of Birth Stories* says:

> Even friends together for a long time
> are separated by death,
> thereby bringing great sorrow.
> That, in the world, is certain.

Although my mind was tormented with grief, I performed the ritual of transference of consciousness and said whatever prayers I knew. Every day after that day until the full forty-nine days had passed, I performed last rites, such as the purification ritual, without fail. So there was a short recess in giving the lamas and tulkus permissions for the Narthang Hundred. To sow roots of virtue on behalf of the deceased, I made monetary offerings to my sources of refuge, His Holiness being foremost of these, to the monks of the three seats, those in Gyütö and Gyümé tantric colleges in Dalhousie, and those living in Buxa. I also had offerings made at the sacred sites of India and Nepal. On the twenty-seventh his body was cremated at the cremation ground.

I gave Ngawang Drakpa, former abbot of Sera Mé, an oral transmission of various rituals I had composed in verse for Gyalchen Shukden—for establishing supports, the thread-cross ritual, fire offerings, and so on.

On the twenty-eighth day of the third month, at the request of Dampa Lodrö of Tsawarong, I conferred the one-day Mahayana vows on about three hundred people. At the beginning of the fourth month, Tutor Kyabjé Ling Rinpoché told me that he was planning to again do a retreat for Guhyasamāja Akṣobhyavajra and came to ask that I again offer him the initiation. So, over the course of two days, I gave Rinpoché alone the great initiation into Guhyasamāja along with its preparatory rite.

On the fifteenth of the fourth month, on the forty-ninth day after Lhabu's death, I made offerings of food and tsok all day to the Namgyal monks and the lamas and geshés who were living in Dharamsala in an assembly presided over by His Holiness and Kyabjé Ling Rinpoché. From the next day I repeatedly performed bone rituals with pieces of the bones of Lady Yangzom Tsering of Lhalu, which I had earlier received from Lhasa, and with the bone ashes of the late Lhabu. Then I had votive tablet statues of

Akṣobhya, Avalokiteśvara, and other deities made with the remaining bones mixed with clay.

I gave a group of around seventy lamas, geshés, and monks—including thirty monks who had come from Buxa—the blessing of the four sindūra initiations of Vajrayoginī.

On the twenty-fourth I resumed giving the remaining permissions for the Narthang Hundred to the above-mentioned tulkus and geshés. The day after that I began to give the permissions for the deities in the famed Bari Hundred, which was passed down from Lama Dorjé Denpa through Bari Lotsāwa, along with a complete oral transmission of the Indian source texts. Although the supreme incarnation of Kyabjé Phabongkha Rinpoché wanted me to give the permissions for the Ocean of Sādhanas continuously, I had to postpone it temporarily, as the Indian source texts were unavailable.

Outbreak of the Indo-Pakistani War

On the third day of the sixth month, Dagyab Rinpoché came to take his leave prior to his departure to visit a West German university that had invited him. I offered him a small departure gift and at his wish composed the following spiritual song to please his mind:

> Incomparable great master in whom the auspicious knot
> of karma, prayers, and virtuous deeds has linked together
> many lives;
> son of unsullied vows who has long been nourished by Dharma,
> though you journey countless leagues and we are separated
> for eons,
> the forever indelible picture of our warm friendship,
> placed undrawn in my heart, will be surely and vividly recalled.
>
> The brave young garuḍa son, his mental powers fully developed,
> spreads his wings to roam over the wide world,
> while his old father in hope lifts his eyelids to the skies
> to offer a prayer for success, which soars into the air.
>
> The sight of sun and moon circling the four continents
> is wondrous,

but there is danger in the vapor from the mouth of pernicious
Rahu[293]
When the striped tiger wanders near the edge of the forest,
she must beware the hidden traps of Śavaripa.[294]

In the human lands that resemble celestial realms,
the appearances of this life's happiness and wealth
are like ripples on water, more deceptive than a magician's spell.
See them as being empty of any essence.

The ever-turning water wheel of busyness and tasks
endlessly loads more suffering onto itself,
and yet the demented vainly count such burdens as badges
of honor.
See those fools who go to their deaths empty handed.

Having witnessed the ways of the barbarous lands devoid of
Dharma,
when I recall the qualities of the Dharma land of Tibet,
even the sight of an old Tibetan woman begging by the roadside
fills my heart with fondness and joy.

O cuckoo, having circled the medicinal forests of southern Mön,[295]
swiftly return and sing your sweet song.
This old decaying tree, full of leaves but fruitless,
will welcome you in the guise of a sapling swaying under its yield.

My dear friend, this little song to dispel your sadness
is offered as a parting gift by this old lion lacking the two.[296]
May the auspicious song of our reunion
arise from the treasure of your melodious voice, my friend.

On one occasion I wrote a few notes to refresh my memory of the root verses of the *Seven-Point Mind Training* based on the Hortön Namkha Pal's commentary *Mind Training Like Rays of the Sun*.

Over the course of seven days I taught the six Dharmas of Nāropa based on *Endowed with Three Convictions*[297] and the commentary by Naktsang

Tenpa Dargyé of Trehor to the supreme incarnation of Kyabjé Phabongkha Vajradhara, two of his attendants, and my own attendant Palden. At the request of the Amdo artist Dorjé, I gave thirty devout people the blessing of the four sindūra initiations of Vajrayoginī. During these times, whenever we were free, I met with the supreme incarnation to give him as much personal instruction as I could remember having seen or heard at the feet of his most kind predecessor on the traditions of initiation, oral transmission, and explanation.

One the morning of the sixth day of the seventh month, His Holiness came to visit me. At his request I offered him an oral transmission of the supplications to Guru Rinpoché called *Swiftly Accomplishing One's Wishes* and *Dispelling Obstacles on the Path*.[298] That afternoon when His Holiness, who had left on a trip, was nearing Pathankot, Pakistan launched the attack that began its war with India. Despite the danger posed by potential air raids, His Holiness and his entourage were able to pass safely through the city without incident.

Just before eleven o'clock on the night of the fourteenth, Pakistan launched an air raid, dropping bombs and firing on the military base near Dharamsala, killing two villagers and a few cows and injuring several people. There were further air raids over the next few days, and bombs were again dropped on villages near Dharamsala. Due to the emergency, nighttime use of electric or any other form of light was banned throughout Kangra district. The district magistrate ordered ditches to be dug near houses as air-raid shelters, and patrols were established to enforce the ordered blackouts. We had to live under considerable mental stress.

A few days later, His Holiness's elder brother Losang Samten arrived from Delhi and had a conference with the Tibetan cabinet ministers. It was decided that the two tutors and His Holiness's mother should go to Delhi for the time being. I advised the supreme incarnation of Phabongkha Rinpoché to stay in Dharamsala and said that I would stay in touch with him about his plans. As traditional ritual implements I offered Rinpoché a vajra and bell with silver handles, a silver grain container, a silver inner-offering cup complete with the base and cover, an ivory *ḍamaru* hand drum with a golden sash, a silver nectar vase, three silver butter lamps from large to small in size, and one thousand Indian rupees.

Tutor Kyabjé Ling Rinpoché and his retinue, my two attendants and I, and his Holiness's mother and her small entourage left Dharamsala by

The incarnation of Kyabjé Phabongkha Vajradhara in the 1960s
SOURCE UNKNOWN

car at six in the morning on the twenty-fifth. Given the wartime turmoil, we couldn't travel easily. We blew out a tire and had to travel in the dark without using the headlights at all, so we ended up on the road until at least ten o'clock that night. Accommodation had been arranged for us at Tibet House in Delhi, where it had been decided Kyabjé Ling Rinpoché and I would stay for the time being.

At the wish of the supreme incarnation of Dromo Geshé Rinpoché, who had plans to make new supplies of the precious pill known as "Dromo precious pills," I offered him about 170 kinds of most reliable and difficult to obtain relics of self-produced pills, pieces of hair and cloth of the Buddha, Indian masters, and Tibetan masters of all traditions.

Before long the Indo-Pakistani War came to an end and we were relieved.

Once, when Ganden Throneholder Kyabjé Ling Rinpoché, his labrang manager Losang Lungrik, and I were relaxing together at Tibet House, it suddenly struck me that Rinpoché looked much older, and this song arose spontaneously from my lips:[299]

> Lotus petals of past prayers may have bloomed by the thousands,
> but the frost of wandering aimlessly without thought or purpose
> has destroyed the nourishment of the good honey of enlightenment.
> Therefore, please listen to the pleas of this ignorant old lion.
>
> Having understood flawlessly and purely the transmission of Losang,
> which is the very essence of the mighty Buddha's teachings,
> proclaim down the eons the far-reaching song of your excellent deeds,
> which will show disciples in their many forms the great path of the victors.
>
> With a life reflecting the insights of the four types of āryas,
> built on the path of scripture and reasoning, and of teachings unassailable by opponents,
> the light of your perfected activities, which amaze all the buddhas,
> let it shine as the path dispelling the darkness of destructive forces.

At the same time I expressed this to his labrang manager:[300]

> Listen to me, my wise and broad-minded friend.
> By continuing to live the life of the youth Sudhana,[301]
> if you keep the ring of faith unshakable at your heart,
> it will forever be held by the hook of compassion of the master of the three families.
>
> With a mind focused on a single point, and with pure thought and deed,
> devote yourself untiringly to your kind lama,
> and without searching amid the hills and valleys,
> the wish-granting jewel will drop into your hands.

On the twenty-sixth of the eighth month, His Holiness traveled from Mysore in South India to Delhi, and Kyabjé Ling Rinpoché and I visited him to seek his advice. He advised us that it would be best if we remained in places like Bodhgaya over the winter. At the invitation of Lama Losang of Ladakh and others, Kyabjé Ling Rinpoché and I went to the Ladakh Buddha Vihar one day. There we performed a consecration ceremony, and in the afternoon the Ladakhi students put on a cultural performance of song and dance.

On the second day of the ninth month, His Holiness, we two tutors, Education Minister Chagla,[302] Dromo Geshé Rinpoché, and Indira Gandhi, daughter of Pandit Nehru, were the chief guests at the opening ceremonies for Tibet House in Delhi. After His Holiness, we two tutors, and the ritual assistants from Namgyal Monastery chanted prayers of auspiciousness amid the gathering of many distinguished guests of all types, Education Minister Chagla officiated the inauguration ceremony.

Tibet House opening ceremonies, with special guests M. C. Chagla and Indira Gandhi, October 26, 1965
COURTESY OF PALDEN TSERING

At my suggestion the supreme incarnation of Kyabjé Phabongkha Rinpoché came to Delhi from Dharamsala. At his request, over the course of eight days I gave Rinpoché himself, Dromo Rinpoché, Denma

Lochö Rinpoché, and Rizong Rinpoché of Ladakh an explanation of Jé Tsongkhapa's *Middle-Length Stages of the Path* published with headings that I had compiled. With the hope that the supreme incarnation would perform deeds that would be of great benefit to beings in the future, I presented him with a complete set of the same relics that I had given to Dromo Rinpoché and an assortment of precious pills and advised him that he must carry on the learned, disciplined, and compassionate life's work of his predecessor.

While in Delhi, I saw a vast collection of religious texts at Tibet House that contained the collected works of Bodong Choklé Namgyal, Shuchen Tsultrim Rinchen of Dergé, and many others.[303] The staff of Tibet House made me feel quite comfortable and relaxed during my stay, thanks to their generous hospitality. On the twenty-first I went to the paper factory in Sehore, Bhopal, at the invitation of Gyurmé Sadutshang.

Ganden Shartsé Monastery submitted a request to His Holiness for divination regarding the activities of my body, speech, and mind. As the outcome of the divination was apparently quite disturbing, His Holiness sent me a letter exhorting me to generate a strong intention to live a long life. In response to his letter I presented the following reply:

> Myriad mighty conquerors, inexpressible by speech,
> massive clouds of miraculous deeds, beyond the imagination,
> the beguiling dance of an enlightened body that is visible to all,
> an ocean of happiness and well-being extending beyond our sight.[304]
>
> From the waves swollen by the compassion of your mind,
> the stream of the nectar of your well-spoken words
> falls on the old crown of this ignorant old man,
> and I overflow with the bliss of the pacification of fabrication.
>
> Possessed by the devil of discursive thought,
> I perform the dance of every kind of evil conduct.
> Their vivid reverberations lead me to a dreadful abyss,
> where I turn once and knowingly jump in.[305]
>
> Desirous of the wealth provided by the patron,
> like paper caught in the wind at the paper mill,

I wander on and on, appearing to be happy,
wasting the opportunity and leisure afforded me.

From your perspective of exalted wisdom of the pure
dharmadhātu,
in which all phenomena arise simultaneously but not
indistinguishably,
seeing this piece of brass devoid of Dharma appearing as gold,
you must be thinking how all things are imputed by thought.

"Work hard to create the conditions for
your excellent human form of great value to live long."
Your weighty command, of essence and meaningful,
its profound import is absorbed in the center of my heart.

Our Dharma land, our happy celestial realm,
is destroyed by ferocious anti-Dharma forces,
and though I long to witness once again the great pageant of
Dharma and secular rule,
in which Dharma, wealth, enjoyment, and liberation flourishes,[306]
what can a powerless ordinary person like me do?

Protector whose mastery of the ten powers is complete,
when you raise the mighty army of hundreds of powerful
blessings,
the fangs of the mighty Lord of Death will surely be blunted.

Enduring friend, by your steadfastness
I clasp you firmly and forever in my heart.
With a mind of sustained unwavering hope,
protector, you who foil transience, I make this request.

How could someone like me, a mere shadow of a preserver of
the teachings
who only pretends to understand their meaning,
honorably serve the teachings of Mañjuśrī Tsongkhapa,[307]
the quintessence of the Buddhadharma?

Preserving exactly as you have realized them
the essential points of the vast and profound teachings of the
Buddha,
bringing them to bloom like a white lotus with a hundred petals,
please liberate all living beings from the ocean of samsara and
affliction.[308]

In dark and terrible times such as these
when adverse circumstances everywhere arise,
when malicious people use the machinations of deception,
you don the armor of indefatigable patience.

When from the hidden realms the buddhas and bodhisattvas
praise and exalt you as a lion of men,
apart from ignorant, stupid beasts,
who with intelligence would not revere you?

Kye! Kye! Great protector, treasure of compassion,
clearly held as an image in the center of my heart,
seize with your iron hook of compassion
this doddering old man who makes this sonorous plea.

Though this prayer lacks the music of melody,
sweetness of tone, and profundity of word and meaning,
with the candor of one long cared for by your compassion,
I respectfully offer what has flowed freely from my mind.

I gave a group of around sixty managers and laborers at the factory, including Gyurmé, long-life empowerment in the tradition of Drupgyal and oral transmissions of the fasting rite and *Guide to the Bodhisattva's Way of Life*.

I went from Bhopal to Bodhgaya, where I had an audience with His Holiness and Kyabjé Ling Rinpoché. I also met Dagyab Rinpoché, who had returned from Germany. To sow roots of virtue on behalf of the late Lhabu, I made extensive hundredfold offerings at the great stupa and made clouds of offerings of food and money for an entire day to the monks who were there.

Sakya Trizin Rinpoché and Nyingma Dudjom Rinpoché came to visit me on different occasions. During our relaxed and very friendly conversation, Dudjom Rinpoché told me how a few of the nine volumes of Ngadak Nyangral's treasure teachings called the *Eight Instructions: A Gathering of Sugatas*[309] were kept at Nyangral's home monastery of Mawo Chok in Lhodrak, and that the treasure teaching on yellow parchment seemed to be in the handwriting of Denma Tsemang.[310] When I asked him to describe the handwriting, I found that Dudjom Rinpoché's description matched two pieces of handwriting on yellow parchment that were kept in the great relic box at the Potala Palace.

On the third day of the eleventh month, I attended an auspicious restoration and purification ceremony to celebrate the completion of the extension and restoration of the assembly hall at the Tibetan monastery in Bodhgaya. When the Tibetan government made an extensive hundredfold offering at the great stupa for the general good of the Dharma and the government, His Holiness presided along with Sakya Trizin Rinpoché, Dudjom Rinpoché of the Nyingma tradition, Drukpa Thuksé and Lama Kalu Rinpoché of the Kagyü tradition, we two tutors, and others.

One day, at the invitation of an Amdo monk named Kelsang, who was the proprietor of the monastery at the Śītavana cemetery, I went there, made extensive offerings, and performed a propitiation ritual as well as a consecration. I left a newly printed volume about the five classes of tantra in the Shangpa tradition as a representation of speech in the protector chapel.

I traveled from Bodhgaya to Sarnath and stayed there. With the intention of sowing roots of virtue on behalf of the late Lhabu, I made clouds of offerings at the great stupa for an entire day, including a thousand butter lamps and so on along with tsok, to the monks who were already in Sarnath as well as fifty-four members of the scholars seminar who had been selected from among the learned masters of the three seats and from the Sakya, Nyingma, and Kagyü traditions. This seminar was organized and sponsored by the Tibetan government. One day I addressed those masters of the classics, impressing upon them that they must take as their first priority the need to explain skillfully the pure tradition of the teachings of the Buddha, sacred source of inexhaustible benefit and happiness, unerringly, just as the great Sage intended, and in a way befitting the acuity of intelligent students. When the geshés returned to Buxa, I sent Shartsé College of Ganden an excellent pair of large antique cymbals played vertically and a pair played horizontally, and to Jangtsé College of Ganden a set of antique upright cymbals.

At the request of Rizong Rinpoché from Ladakh at various times, and with personal hopes of strengthening the teachings and practice of Cakrasaṃvara in the tradition of Ghaṇṭāpāda, a path well traveled by innumerable siddhas of India and Tibet, I gave the initiation of the five-deity Cakrasaṃvara outer mandala to three hundred disciples, including lamas and monks, at the Tibetan monastery in Sarnath. At this particular time and place the teachings and practices of the body mandala of Cakrasaṃvara had declined. The supreme deity Heruka Cakrasaṃvara assured Kyabjé Phabongkha, the sole refuge and inconceivably compassionate Vajradhara, that up to the seventh generation, the glorious Cakrasaṃvara himself would personally care for his disciples. With the hope that this practice might increase, I also gave the initiation of Cakrasaṃvara body mandala to 250 who had the commitment to practice the yoga of the three purifications and gave teachings on the two stages of the body mandala to 194 who held the commitment to do the elaborate sādhana daily. I gave the teachings for seventeen days in the undegenerated traditional manner of the supreme masters. At the end of this teaching, I gave an explanation of the exclusive long-life practice of White Heruka at the request of Jinpa Gyatso, an attendant at Ling Labrang. We performed a *Guru Puja* and tsok offering in conjunction with Cakrasaṃvara, sponsored jointly by Bakula Rinpoché and Rizong Rinpoché.

On behalf of all those connected to me, I again made extensive thousandfold offerings at the stupa in Sarnath, and to sow roots of virtue on behalf of the late Lhabu, I offered ten thousand butter lamps, thereby planting the seed of omniscient enlightenment.

Further Teachings

On the tenth day of the first Tibetan month in my sixty-sixth year, the year of the fire-horse (March 2, 1966), I returned to Dharamsala from Varanasi. On the twenty-seventh, Tutor and Throneholder Kyabjé Ling Rinpoché stopped by to visit me at my home on his return from Bodhgaya. The next day I went to visit Rinpoché in his home and presented him with, among other things, a silver statue of White Tārā for auspiciousness.

Over the course of seven days, beginning on the first day of the second month, His Holiness presided over the wealth-generating rituals attended by the assembly of Namgyal monks. Kyabjé Ling Rinpoché and I attended the rituals, which were sponsored by the Tibetan government for the benefit of the Tibetans in exile. The assembly performed the Vaiśravaṇa prosperity rite and consecration of treasure vases in connection with White Jambhala, White Mahākāla, and Vaiśravaṇa.

On the twenty-seventh I began to give His Holiness an oral transmission of Gyaltsap Jé's commentary on the Perfection of Wisdom sutras entitled *Essence Ornament*,[311] and from then on, whenever His Holiness had a break in his schedule, my health permitted, and the time was available, I continued to offer him oral transmission of the collected works of Gyaltsap Jé, for which I bear the transmission lineage.

On the third day of the third month, I met with Jamyang, the son of Driwa Balsé. Driwa Balsé was a constituent of the territory of Gangkar Lama of Seudru Monastery in Markham, and he had escaped Chinese oppression in Kham. He delivered to me a very detailed account of the general situation in Markham and told me specifically that the incarnation of Gangkar Lama and treasurer Adruk had fled deep into the jungle during the Chinese takeover. Rather than fall into the hands of the Red Chinese, the tulku had passed away of his own will when he was about to be captured, while Adruk had died fighting them. When I had stayed in his monastery, the tulku had been very devoted to me and was well disciplined, but he had not seemed particularly accomplished. However, willing his own passing at the critical moment of capture struck me as an amazing demonstration of a holy person.

I gave the Gadong medium and two of his family members and the wife of Prime Minister Dekharwa (Lukhangwa) permission for the Three Wrathful Forms Combined. Former minister Shenkhawa came to clear up some questions he had about combining the practice of the sevenfold cause-and-effect instruction with the practice of equalizing and exchanging self and others, so I gave him detailed instructions.

Over the course of three days, beginning on the twelfth day of the fourth month, I offered explanation and instruction in the *Seven-Point Mind Training* to a group of around a hundred, including the entire assembly of Namgyal Monastery. The teaching was requested by Thupten Chöden of Namgyal Monastery to fulfill the dying wish of Namgyal's late Venerable Thupten Chöyang.

At the beginning of the fifth month, at the request of Ratö Khyongla Rinpoché Ngawang Losang, I gave a few people, including the tulku himself and former minister Shenkhawa, the great initiation into Cakrasaṃvara body mandala in Ghaṇṭāpāda's tradition. On the nineteenth and twentieth, at the request of the general assembly of Namgyal Monastery, I gave an audience of more than one hundred, including the Namgyal monks and other lamas, tulkus, and monks, the great initiation into Cakrasaṃvara in the tradition of Luipa along with its preparatory practices.

11 | Distant Travels and Tragic News

First Visit to Switzerland

I received an invitation to visit Switzerland from Chözé Yugyal, a member of the Sadutshang family from Trehor, who insisted that I travel there at once for medical treatment and that he would bear all of my travel expenses. So I decided to go to Switzerland. On the twenty-second of the fifth month, I had an audience with His Holiness to take my leave. On the twenty-fourth Palden and I traveled from Dharamsala to Delhi. When I departed Delhi on an Air India flight at around eleven o'clock in the morning on the twenty-seventh, the representative and staff from the Bureau of His Holiness the Dalai Lama in Delhi as well as the director and staff of Tibet House came to the airport to see me off.

I arrived at the airport in Geneva, Switzerland, at around five in the afternoon, which would have been around nine in the evening India time. I was personally welcomed there by His Holiness's representative in Europe Phalha Thupten Öden,[312] His Holiness's elder brother Losang Samten, and my benefactor, Chözé Yugyal, whose house we went to.

Since that night happened to be a Swiss holiday, a great crowd of people had gathered at Lake Geneva, and a huge display of fireworks were going off in the sky. Seeing flowers of every color appear and fall like sparkling rain from space really helped improve the way I visualized the emission and dissolution of light and the purifying rain of nectar during my daily practices. I gave Chözé Yugyal four thangkas as objects of veneration, including a thangka depicting Sukhāvatī heaven. After a few days, we moved to Mr. Phalha's apartment, as it was more spacious. Dakpo Bamchö Rinpoché left his attendant Thupten with us to assist Palden with the daily work of preparing food and drink. He was very helpful throughout my stay in Switzerland.

At the request of Ratö Khyongla Rinpoché, I gave him, Bamchö

Rinpoché, Rakra Tulku, Mr. Phalha, and Geshé Khedrup Thupten of Sera Mé the blessing of the four sindūra initiations of Vajrayoginī. They sponsored a long-life ceremony with tsok offering conjoined with the Cakrasaṃvara ritual. At that time Khyongla asked me to record a spiritual song into a tape recorder, so I sang the following:

> In this Swiss city, a meeting place of happiness and joy,
> as if Brahma, with a movement of his mind, has placed here
> the wonders of the celestial realms on high,
> we master and disciples, patron and teacher of unsullied bond,
> enjoy fully this secret gathering, an auspicious festival,
> bringing together these delightful faces.
>
> Looking up, the kind root and lineage lamas,
> their dense, limitless clouds of compassionate blessings
> let fall the gentle rain of supreme and ordinary siddhis
> of the mandalas of peaceful and wrathful meditation deities,
> and the ḍākas and ḍākinīs of the three worlds perform their dance.
> Oh, so happy to have the fortune to enjoy the wheel of secret offerings.
>
> I yearn that in the succession of our lives we will be together,
> enjoy equal shares of the nectar of the Mahayana,
> and in the Akaniṣṭha realm of effortless pleasure,
> together attain supreme enlightenment.

Chözé Yugyal arranged for me to see a private doctor named Dr. Weisman for a physical examination. Over two days my body, urine and feces, blood, and so on were closely examined. Other than low blood pressure and having a minor intestinal worm, there was nothing seriously wrong with me. The doctor prescribed some medicine and injections to strengthen me physically and various other treatments. I did everything I was told. Chözé Yugyal bore all of the costs for the doctor's visit and medications himself.

On the twenty-fourth day of the seventh month, I traveled by air from Geneva to Zürich, where I stayed at the home of a Dutch woman, Mrs. Kalff,[313] who was the sponsor of Geshé Losang Chödrak of Sera Mé. Mrs.

Kalff took me to the Zürich Zoological Garden, a place where there were all sorts of animals, including wild carnivores and every variety of bird.

I decided to visit each Tibetan resettlement area, not only because a number of them had invited me, but because I hoped that visiting each place in person might help in some small way to preserve our culture and religion. First I visited Tibetans living in the settlements of Oetwil and Rüti and gave teachings and advice to them. I stayed at the home of Gyaltsen Namdröl from Drepung Gomang in Rikon. One day I went to the settlement in Münchwilen, gave teachings, advice, and so on, and returned to Rikon.

Mr. Phalha had arranged a get-together for the Tibetan boys and girls that a number of wealthy families in Switzerland had adopted from the Tibetan Children's Village in Dharamsala. With the exception of a few families who were opposed to their adopted children having contact with Tibetans, most of the children came one at a time to see me with their Swiss families. I offered each child a gift and advised them that they should not forget their heritage and so on. Most of the children did not speak Tibetan, let alone observe Tibetan customs. They had to rely on physical gestures to try and communicate with me, which made me sad, but there was nothing I could do about it.

One day I gave about sixty people—the Tibetans living in the Rikon resettlement area along with some who had come from other settlements—the long-life empowerment of White Tārā and recited oral transmissions of the *Hundred Deities of Tuṣita*, *Praises to Tārā*, the refuge prayer, and the prayer for the long life of His Holiness. I gave them a Dharma talk on topics such as refuge and karma and conveyed the importance of abiding by the laws of the host country. I advised the children to be friendly and behave well, that they must try their best not to give up their cultural traditions, such as their language and religion, so that they could have both a secular and religious education. The next day, Tibetans from the settlement in Rikon gave me a long-life ceremony in connection with a *Guru Puja* and tsok. Not only did the two responsible for the settlement, Dr. Peter Lindegger and his wife, wear Tibetan clothing the whole time and participate in all the gatherings, but he also knew how to speak Tibetan quite well.

On the fourth day of the eighth month I traveled from Rikon to the settlement area of Reitnau. After giving Dharma teachings and advice, I traveled to Trogen, where there was a Tibetan school.[314] There I was greeted with offerings presented in the Tibetan style by a reception party that lined the road on the way to the Yumbu Lagang Tibetan home[315] comprised of Rakra Rinpoché,[316] who was overseeing the Tibetan children, Söpal,[317] the director of the village Arthur Bill,[318] the staff of the Red Cross, and the Tibetan children. There with everyone present we held a small reception with tea and ceremonial rice as a token of Tibetan tradition. Afterward I spent five days at Luksung Ngön-ga, another of the Tibetan houses, where arrangements had been made for my stay. While there, I went to visit Arthur Bill and presented him a small gift. He seemed to genuinely care about Tibetans and expressed his goodwill and sympathy for us in our conversation.

I left Trogen and spent one day in the Tibetan settlement in Waldstatt. When Mrs. Schwarzenbach, a member of the Red Cross who was in charge of all ten Tibetan settlements, came to meet me there, I gave her gifts, thanked her profoundly for her excellent work on behalf of the settlements, and expressed my hope that all future efforts would be as good as hers.

The next day I traveled to a Tibetan settlement in a small village called Samedan near the foot of a snow mountain where Lamdrak Tulku of Trehor, among others, was living. We were exhausted at the end of the day because the trip was quite long, winding around many mountains and through many tunnels. I stayed at Lamdrak Tulku's home. There I met Losang Nyima, the nephew of Gyümé Chabril Tsultrim Dargyé from Trehor, with whom I was as close as if we were family in Tibet, and my own niece Tashi Drölma and her husband and children. I gave around forty Tibetans, young and old, oral transmissions of quite a few Dharma texts, including *Chanting the Names of Mañjuśrī*, *Praise of the Exalted*,[319] *Praises to Tārā*, and the prayer for the long life of His Holiness, as well as advice on religious and secular matters. An extensive tsok offering in association with a *Guru Puja* was sponsored by the Tibetan community.

One day we took a small electric train that went straight up the side of a mountain near Samedan,[320] did some sightseeing at the peak of the mountain, and ate in a restaurant there. From Samedan I visited the four Tibetan settlements at Landquart, Buchen, Ebnat-Kappel, and Unterwasser one at a time, spending a day at each settlement giving teachings and advice similar to what I have mentioned above. In Unterwasser, at the request of Geshé Khenrab Thupten of Sera Mé, who oversaw a group of more than ten boys and girls, I gave an explanation and transmission of the *Foundation of All Good Qualities*, and when I did the *Guru Puja* with tsok with them, the children could recite the *Guru Puja* fluently. When I asked them to enumerate the eight freedoms and ten opportunities of a precious human life, the ten positive and negative actions, the sevenfold causes leading to the result of bodhicitta, and so on, the children answered correctly. I was delighted and thought how useful it is to have geshé from one of the great seats of learning as a headmaster.

I returned to Yumbu Lagang in Trogen, where over the course of an eight-day stay, I fulfilled each and every request for Dharma teaching. I gave Rakra Tulku the permission for Jé Tsongkhapa as the triple deity and the life-entrusting initiation for Shukden. I gave about seventy people, including students and staff of the Tibetan school, permission to practice Avalokiteśvara Who Liberates from All Lower Realms, the long-life empowerment of White Tārā, and oral transmissions of a number of Dharma texts, including the *Hundred Deities of Tuṣita* and *Chanting the Names of Mañjuśrī*, and advised them on religious and secular activities. At the request of Chözé Yugyal I gave seven people, including Mr. Phalha and Rakra Tulku, the great initiation into single-deity Vajrabhairava.

One evening the students put on a play about the tale of Lha Lama Jangchup Ö's efforts to invite Atiśa to Tibet. It was well done and very moving.

Germany and England

I then went to a German region called Wahlwies, where twelve Tibetan children, their religious teacher Gyalsur Tulku of Loseling, and house parent Losang Namdröl and his wife were staying.[321] I spent a day there, and the children appeared to be quite good at drawing and Tibetan writing.

Then, at the invitation of the headmaster and the general body of students and teachers of Trisong Ngön-ga Tibetan Home in England, on the thirtieth Palden, Mr. Phalha, and I left Zürich together by air, landing at the airport in the English capital, London. Geshé Tsultim Gyeltsen of Ganden Shartsé and retired government official Thupten Ngawang, who was overseeing the children, had come to welcome me. We traveled together by car to Trisong Ngön-ga in the Tibetan Children's Village, where I stayed for ten days.

I gave Geshé Gyeltsen, the headmaster, and the children the long-life empowerment of White Tārā and oral transmissions of some Dharma texts, including the refuge prayer and *Praises to Tārā*. The students gave a performance of Tibetan songs and dances. The music and the performances were excellent in every respect.

At the urging of the geshé and retired government official, one day at eight in the morning we boarded a small train and went sightseeing in London. One museum had a huge number of remarkable wax likenesses of famous leaders from all over the world—including current leaders like the queen of England and her ministers, previous kings and queens of England, prime ministers Nehru and Shastri of India, Mao Zedong and Zhou Enlai of China, and the American president, and a great number of artists and performers from the past and present. We then took an elevator up a thirty-seven-story tower to a viewing platform from which we could see the city of London.[322] The city appeared vast, reaching beyond the horizon. The houses and lanes were well arranged, and the many low family houses looked like husked rice spilled from a bag among the grass on a plain. I couldn't get enough of that view. When we finished looking, we went to a hotel where we stayed the night.

The following day we went to see a large, magnificent Christian church, famed as the place where prayers and benedictions were offered when the English monarchs were crowned.[323] In a church as prominent and imposing as that, all of the details carved in relief in the bishop's pulpit and so on are most majestic. It seemed like the preaching and listening were done with great reverence. We went around to see a few other famous places and then returned to the Trisong Ngön-ga Tibetan home.

Over the course of my stay there, to a woman who was assisting Rechung Tulku named Marianne Winder,[324] a faithful Buddhist who daily recited the mantra of White Tārā, I gave a recitation transmission for the mantra and advised her on what to visualize during prayers. I gave Geshé Tsultim Gyeltsen instruction in the *Seven-Point Mind Training*, and I gave some Tibetans, including the staff and students at Trisong Ngön-ga, permissions to practice Red and Yellow Mañjuśrī and oral transmissions of the *Guru Puja*, the *Hundred Deities of Tuṣita*, and so on.

One day we went to the city of Hastings and to the seaside nearby. We walked on the long pier extending into the sea and visited shops and restaurants.

After my visit to England was finished, Dagyab Chetsang Hothokthu in Bonn, Germany, invited me to come see him. When I arrived at the airport in London on the eleventh day of the ninth month, Mr. Richardson,[325] the former British representative in Lhasa, came to meet me. We spent quite some time having a lengthy discussion in Tibetan before I boarded the plane that took me to Cologne, Germany.

Dagyab Rinpoché came to welcome me with Phukhang Khentrul of Ganden Shartsé, Dza Rongphu Tulku, E Lama, and Pema Tsering of the Nyingma tradition, and I spent a few days at Dagyab Rinpoché's home near Bonn. While there, Khentrul and Dza Rongphu Tulku accompanied me to visit the Bonn Zentralasien Seminar,[326] an institute for the academic study of Central Asian, Mongolian, and Tibetan culture. At the department I met a professor of Indology named Hahn[327] and an ecumenical religious studies professor named Gustav Mensching. Because my visit coincided with the director of the department's visit to Japan, we were looked after by Dr. Sagaster,[328] the assistant director, who asked us many questions, such as what was the symbolism of the Buddhist depictions of the wheel of Dharma. I replied by explaining how the hub that holds the wheel, the spokes that cut, and the rim that keeps the wheel together symbolize the three higher trainings.[329] Then I was taken around to see a few libraries and various departments.

A car and guide specially provided by the tourism department of the German government took me to see an old Christian abbey called Maria Laach in order to show me the temple and the buildings in which the monks engaged in various arts and crafts with which they earned their living. I returned home when it was just getting dark. The assistant director of the Central Asian program, Dr. Sagaster, came to visit me again to ask some more questions. He expressed how happy he was with my answers. I also made a quick visit to Phukhang Khentrul's home.

At the invitation of the Kalmyk Mongolian monk Achunor and the Mongolian community in Munich, on the sixteenth I flew by Lufthansa to Munich, where I was welcomed by Venerable Achunor, Panglung Tulku of Sera Mé, Yerpa Tsenshap Tulku of Sera Mé, and a Hungarian scholar named Stephan Palos, the head of a Buddhist group who had faith in the teachings.[330] We all went together to the Mongolian temple. Over the course of the seven days that I stayed there, at the invitation of Professor Anton Spitaler, who was the head of the department where Panglung Rinpoché and Yerpa Tsenshap were working, I went to the university.[331] He gave me some reproductions of sections from very old Tibetan texts unearthed at

Dunhuang and asked me a few questions about Tibetan political and religious history, which I answered.

When the opening ceremonies for the monastery that Venerable Achunor had founded were held, the minister from the welfare department of the German government and his colleagues, the Buddhist community, Mongolians living in the area, and many other foreign guests attended. During the ceremony I cut the ribbon after chanting some preliminary auspicious verses along with Losang Dargyé of Gomang College and Panglung Tulku. I gave a brief speech about why the founding of the monastery was important. I placed ceremonial scarves on the principal statues, made offerings, performed the consecration, and gave the monastery the name Thekchen Chöphel Ling.

One day I went into the city of Munich to the huge German Museum, where I saw a variety of things, including models of ships and airplanes illustrating the history of shipping and aviation. There were exhibits on the historical development of coal mining, on the history of science and atomic energy, and on the practice of medicine in the past and present. I saw a model of a rocket with figures of people inside and an exhibit on how it is launched, travels in space, and so on.

The results of the dedicated efforts of individuals who had attained the fruit of patience through enduring great hardship and applied their human intelligence toward the development of science and technology is comparable to that of the miracles of the mahāsiddhas of the past. Considering this, the achievements of those of us who strive on the paths of sutra and tantra taught by the Buddha—who understood the ultimate nature of the four noble truths and who possessed the threefold qualities of the tathāgatas with complete command of all abandonments and insights—should be considerable. Yet people like myself can show no such accomplishments. This is because our intelligence and efforts are weak. Just as if one is wrong on the first of the month, one will be wrong to the last day of the month, likewise if one fails to establish the root of the spiritual path, guru devotion, all successive stages of the path will also fail. It is only due to our own faulty practice that attainments do not occur. We should not project our own faults onto the Dharma.

I went to see a church called Alte Peter, famous as one of the oldest Christian churches. On another occasion I went to a show with Mr. Phalha, Panglung, and Palden where only the rich and famous are allowed in and no ordinary people. The hall had five tiers of viewing galleries and was indescribably wonderful. However, due to my unfamiliarity with that type of entertainment, I was unable to really enjoy the show. At the invitation of the welfare department of the German government, I had a meeting with the director and general secretary, after which we went to visit a museum that had an exhibition of Japanese paintings, artifacts, and images as well as a great deal of African art and objects on display.

On the twenty-second, the anniversary of the Buddha's descent from Trāyastriṃśa Heaven, we and the Mongolians, as a group, performed a tsok offering with a Cakrasaṃvara *Guru Puja*, which greatly delighted the Mongolians. I offered detailed responses to questions that Pema Tsering of the Nyingma tradition had asked about developing ultimate bodhicitta according to the *Seven-Point Mind Training*. He was satisfied with my answers.

France, Switzerland, and Italy

At the invitation of the supreme incarnation of Dakpo Bamchö Rinpoché, Jampa Gyatso, in France, I flew to Paris on the twenty-third. Bamchö Rinpoché, former abbot of Gyümé Ngawang Lekden of Gomang College, and some members of the French Mongolian community came to welcome me, and I traveled with them back to Bamchö Rinpoché's home. As soon as I got there, many more Mongolians came to visit.

The following day the former Gyümé abbot came to visit me. He was so incredibly knowledgeable with regard to both sutra and tantra that his words were like the blossoming of a thousand-petalled lotus. Given his extensive intellect and enthusiasm, we passed an entire day sharing our opinions with one another on every variety of topic, from the global situation in general to the religious and political affairs of Tibet in particular.

Bamchö Rinpoché and his benefactor, Ama Yvonne Laurence (Thupten Drölkar), took me to have a look around a museum near Paris that had once been the palace of the royal family. The building was enormous, and the old frescoes and paintings inside it were very elegant. In one of the many apartments, the prior king's extremely valuable antique furniture was on display, as well as Arabian and Japanese paintings and various commodities. There were so many rooms that if one were to look closely at each one, one wouldn't finish looking at them in two or even three days.

I took an elevator to the top of the Eiffel Tower, a very tall iron tower with a restaurant on top. When I looked out at the city I saw that it stretched on, beautifully arrayed, without any end in sight.

One day at the invitation of the French professor named Stein[332] I visited him and we discussed Tibetan history. He was quite enthusiastic about the epics of Gesar.

At the sincere request of Bamchö Rinpoché, Palden and I went with Rinpoché himself and Mr. Phalha to the houses on a piece of land that had been acquired for a Tibetan monastery in a small town called La Chapelle on the outskirts of Paris. Former Abbot Ngawang Lekden, Amdo Yönten, Ngawang Drakpa, and Jamyang Mönlam were already living there. I stayed there for five days. Together with five monks who were living there, including the former abbot, and the elderly woman who was their benefactor, I offered a *Guru Puja* and tsok. At the former abbot's sincere request, I gave a brief explanation and oral transmission of the first few pages of the *Great Treatise on the Stages of Path* and a brief explanation and oral transmission of the *Foundation of All Good Qualities*.

Twenty young Tibetan boys and girls who were in the village of Bléneau to study and their host parents, Shödrung Norgyé and his wife, came to have an audience with me. I gave them teachings on the refuge prayer, the *Hundred Deities of Tuṣita*, *Praises to Tārā*, and so on and advised them about the importance of maintaining our national heritage, having faith in the teachings, and behaving well. Afterward the students nicely performed some Tibetan and French songs and dances and returned to their village that evening.

I once again visited Bamchö Rinpoché's house in Paris and visited the Grévin Museum. In this museum there were many statues of French royalty as well as contemporary leaders of various countries. This was similar to the wax museum in London. There were also many models depicting the French Revolution, when the people rose against the last king of France. The models showed many aspects of the revolution, including how the members of the royal family were put in prison. At another place, I was fascinated by the special effects achieved by colored lights and mirrors in which one could see infinite reflections of a single house or person. This was similar to the legend of the palace of the cannibal king with ten necks.[333]

On the twelfth day of the tenth month, I flew from Paris to Geneva, where I received medical treatment over several days. One day I went to visit the United Nations complex there. Surkhang Lhawang Topgyal and Lady Dekyi Lhazé came to see me, and we discussed recent events in our lives. They conveyed to me the regrets of the former cabinet minister Surkhang Wangchen Gelek at not being able to come to visit me due to some work he was doing in an American university. Surkhang Wangchen Gelek is a man of great intellect with a vast knowledge of both religious and worldly matters. He should have served His Holiness, but due to the slander and lies of certain people with the character of hungry spirits, it was impossible to make use of his services. As Sakya Paṇḍita wrote in his *Jewel Treasury of Wise Sayings* (5.6):

> Because the thieves called it a dog,
> the brahman lost the goat he was leading.

I had great regrets about this, but I was powerless to change the situation.

I returned to the settlement in Rikon once again, where at the request of Mr. Jacques Kuhn, the owner of a metalware factory, I performed a short ground ritual and consecration with auspicious verses at the site of the Tibetan monastery that Mr. Kuhn wished to build. At the invitation of the Red Cross, I went to their headquarters in Bern. There I met Mrs. Helene Vischer, vice-president of the Swiss Red Cross, and enjoyed a banquet with her. I thanked Mrs. Vischer and the Red Cross for all the help and aid they had given to the Tibetan refugees and the Tibetan settlements in Switzerland. I requested them to make provision for more Tibetans in the future, and she assured me that they would. After that I returned to Geneva for a few days.

On the ninth day of the eleventh month, I flew from Geneva to Rome, where I was met at the airport by Geshé Jampal Sengé of Sera Mé, his Italian students, and the Kagyü tulku Namkhai Norbu.[334] I stayed at Namkhai Norbu's house for three days.

In accordance with a wish expressed by His Holiness in a letter, I went to meet Pope [Paul VI], head of the Catholic Church. With me were Mr. Phalha, Palden, and Namkhai Norbu, who translated. On one corner of the Vatican complex was the Pope's multistory palace. Passing many guards, we reached the upper floor, where we were met by someone akin to a lord chamberlain. We were placed in a room for some time and then were escorted in to meet the Pope, who was standing there to receive us. I presented the Pope with a *nangzö* ceremonial scarf and a pair of antique cymbals. When we were all seated on chairs, I told the Pope that I had come upon the instruction of the Dalai Lama to extend his greetings to him. I expressed my thanks and appreciation for the aid given by various Christian organizations to the Tibetan refugees who had had to escape from their homeland. I also described how the Communist Chinese had violently invaded our humble country, with its peace-loving people, and said that since we are the same in adhering to religious principles, I am sure that we both would exert all efforts to bring peace and harmony to the world by way of our individual faiths. The Pope told me that he was pleased to receive the Dalai Lama's message of greetings and that he took a great interest in the affairs of the Dalai Lama and the Tibetans. He said that if there were anything he could do to please ask, and he asked whether there were anything he could do for me personally. I replied that I did not need any assistance but requested that he might consider providing suitable material assistance to the religious people of Tibet. We had a very cordial meeting that lasted almost an hour. He presented me with an illustrated book and a greeting card for His Holiness and a silver medallion for myself.

Return to India: Dharamsala and Sarnath

On the morning of the thirteenth day of the eleventh month, I left Italy by plane. After a brief stopover in Beirut, we arrived safely at New Delhi airport at five o'clock in the afternoon, Indian standard time. I was met by His Holiness's elder brother Gyalo Thondup, the representative and staff of the Tibetan Bureau in Delhi, and the director and staff of Tibet House. I stayed at Tibet House.

Constantly traveling, I journeyed through various countries in Europe. My impression of these countries was that the West is very prosperous and extremely developed; the cities and the towns are clean and well planned and full of many great marvels. On the other hand, people there lack spiritual depth; they are concerned with this life only and have a strong sense of grasping after permanence in all things. They are preoccupied with indulging in the mere illusion of joy and happiness. Therefore I did not feel fully satisfied.

As it says in the sutras: "The final result of accumulation is exhaustion; beings of high status fall low." Mighty and powerful kings and queens once

Trijang Rinpoché and attendant Palden Tsering visit with Pope Paul VI at the Vatican, 1966
COURTESY OF PALDEN TSERING

lived in great luxury and dignity in palaces and fortresses that ordinary beings could not even step inside. Now such luxurious places and royal palaces along with all the personal belongings of kings and queens have become objects for public viewing, and their glory remains only in name. When I saw the statues and heard the stories about the popular revolt against these powerful kings and how they were put into dark prisons and finally denied even the right to own their lives, I was convinced that even the highest marvels in existence must ultimately fall. Such a conviction should have become a deeply rooted realization, but these were only temporary thoughts of renunciation. As Jé Milarepa said:

> Solid trees and firm horns, if impacted, bend slightly,
> but at no time does this stubborn mind bend.

The fact that the calloused mindstream will not bend is due to the strength and stability of negative instincts ingrained from beginningless time. What else could it be?

I left Delhi on the night of the fifteenth and arrived in Dharamsala the following day. Immediately after I arrived, His Holiness came to call on me at my house, so I had the great fortune and pleasure of seeing the mandala of his body and receiving the nectar of his speech. On the eighteenth I went to pay my respects to His Holiness and presented him with some gifts. I reported to His Holiness about my visits to the Tibetan settlements and the situation of the tulkus, geshés, and the Tibetan students in the West. I also gave His Holiness a report on my visit with the Pope, and His Holiness was very pleased.

One day I gave His Holiness the exclusive permission of Palden Lhamo Maksorma from the collective permissions of the Rinjung Hundred. At the conclusion His Holiness made a tsok offering.

On the twenty-seventh I left Dharamsala for the Tibetan monastery at Sarnath. Before I went to Switzerland, I had asked Khemé Sönam Wangdü of Kunsangtsé and Losang Sherap to manage and supervise the painting of murals of the thousand buddhas, the host of confessional buddhas, and the sixteen arhats on the inner walls, and the four guardian kings on the walls of the entrance, of the Tibetan monastery Shedrup Dögu Khyil. This was jointly sponsored by our labrang and the Kunsangtsé family on behalf of Lhabu and my nephew Tsipön Tsewang Döndrup of Kunsangtsé. The paintings were half completed. They were being painted by the artist Ngakram Ngawang Norbu of Gyümé Tantric College and his assistants. I instructed Ngawang Norbu on a few corrections to the paintings of the sixteen arhats and the four guardian kings.

At the request of Sera Mé's Pomra House, I started the procedure to prepare Drakpa Samdrup, son of the late medium of the protector of Panglung Hermitage, to receive the protector in trance. As this was the first attempt at an invocation, he did not go into trance. I advised Drakpa Samdrup to do the invocation frequently and to do the retreat of a hundred thousand *miktsema* recitations as well as the approaching retreat of Vajrabhairava and Secret Hayagrīva. I also advised him to do a lot of purification.

At the request of Döndrup Tsering from the Hayak Nyachok area of Chatreng, I gave a long-life initiation of White Tārā to about four hundred lamas, monks, and religious and lay pilgrims. Baba Kalsang Lekshé was having a *maṇi* wheel made at the Tibetan monastery in Sarnath, to which I contributed a thousand rupees. As I could not go to Bodhgaya, I sent sums of money for offerings to Tutor Kyabjé Ling Rinpoché, a thousandfold offerings to the stupa, and offerings to the monks.

On the tenth day of the twelfth month, I performed the sindūra ritual of Vajrayoginī together with a tsok offering. That day I received a small bronze statue of Vajrayoginī made in ancient China sent to me by Khatsarwa Jampa Söpa from Nepal. It was very auspicious.

Sangra Tulku of Loseling's Trehor House came to see me, and I sent a thousand rupees with him to Buxa to the supreme incarnation of Kyabjé Phabongkha toward the expense of his geshé celebrations.

Khatsarwa Sönam Chöphel returned from his visit to Nepal. He told me that according to some people who had arrived in Nepal from Lhasa, the Chinese red guards and the youths in Lhasa had rampaged the temples, destroying all the statues in the Ramoché Temple except in the Tsepak Lhakhang. The main statue of the Buddha and of Songtsen Gampo with his queens in the Tsuklakhang had been spared, but all other statues had been broken and thrown into the streets of Lhasa. All the books had been burned—the Shöl Kangyur Press and even the books and statues in private chapels in people's homes were destroyed. The murals in the Tsuklakhang had been covered in white paint. Due to this unprecedented tragedy, many people committed suicide, throwing themselves into the Tsangpo River. Hearing this, I was despondent, thinking of how the legacies of the deeds of great religious kings of the past, those who were emanations of the protectors of the three lineages,[335] and the great translators had been brought to such a state of destruction. Their deeds, intended to last for eons, were demolished so quickly under these precipitous circumstances. Contemplating how the situation had been caused by the actions of beings, my sorrow was beyond measure.

On behalf of all those living or dead who have had connections with me, I made offerings before the sacred objects of refuge. I also made a daylong offering of food to seventy lamas and monks and thousandfold offerings and a tsok offering conjoined with the Cakrasaṃvara *Guru Puja* were also made. The abbot and the chant master of Ganden Shartsé came from Buxa and presented me with a long-life ceremony and gifts marking my return from Switzerland.

On February 11, 1967, the second day of the first Tibetan month of the fire-sheep year, my sixty-seventh year, Venerable Thupten Jungné, the manager of the Tibetan monastery in Sarnath, sponsored an offering to the resident and visiting monks and lamas of all the Tibetan religious traditions. The assembly of monks recited auspicious prayers for my long life in conjunction with a *Guru Puja* and tsok offering.

The chant master of Shartsé asked me to clarify various points about the newly made notation of the long and intermediate melodies for the propitiation rituals and other prayers in the tradition exclusive to Ganden Shartsé Monastery. As the original notation had been left in Tibet, they had made new notation in Buxa. Previously, when I was studying in the monastery, I knew the melodies very well, but almost forty-eight years had passed since my geshé examination, so I had forgotten most of them. As far as my recollected extended, I offered corrections. I also composed some prelude verses for the new notation of the melodies.

On the tenth, when the murals on the walls of the monastery were completed and the pillars and beams were freshly painted, I, along with Trehor Trungsar Rinpoché, Dromo Geshé Rinpoché, the senior and junior Rongtha Rinpoché of Sera Jé, and many other monks, performed a brief consecration ritual. On that day, our labrang and the Kunsangtsé family made a joint offering of a whole day's food and funds and a *Guru Puja* with a tsok offering to all the monks. We feasted and paid the seven artists, including Ngawang Norbu of the Gyümé Tantric College, Chatreng Rigang Aga Jamyang, Thupten Tharpa of Sera Mé, and their assistants. We also gave them each gifts.

Return to Dharamsala

On the thirteenth I left Sarnath for Dharamsala. One day I invited His Holiness and his ritual assistants and made offerings to the front and wrathful faces of the statue of Avalokiteśvara that the Chinese had damaged in Lhasa and that had been brought to India at great risk.[336]

Beginning on the nineteenth, I presided for five days over special offerings made to the twelve *tenma* goddesses, who are bound by oath to protect Tibet. The entire assembly of Namgyal monks participated in the prayers offered for the benefit of the religious and secular affairs of Tibet. Dilgo Khyentsé Rinpoché of the Nyingma tradition also presided over the prayer.

The former cabinet minister Shenkhawa Gyurmé Sönam Topgyal was very old and had become seriously ill. Because I had a close connection with him as a Dharma teacher, I called on him to inquire about his health and to give him instructions on mind training. He understood them very well.

Following the advice of the Nechung oracle, His Holiness performed the rituals of the Innermost Essence Blade based in the tradition of Tertön Sögyal Lerab Lingpa's Phurba Yangsap deity.[337] His Holiness presided over the ritual, and it was attended by Kyabjé Ling Rinpoché, Dilgo Khyentsé, and the assembly of Namgyal monks. I also attended it for five days.

Mrs. Tsamchö Drölma of Lhasa had requested me to give the blessing of the four sindūra initiations of Vajrayoginī, and I had promised her I would do so. She requested this in her will, as I was in Switzerland at the time of her passing. In order to sow roots of virtue on her behalf, I gave the blessing of Vajrayoginī on the tenth of the second month to over three hundred disciples from Dalhousie, Mussoorie, and Dharamsala in the hall of the Tibetan Children's Village. We made offerings at the conclusion of the blessing. From the next day, I gave eight days of experiential teachings on the generation and completion stages of Vajrayoginī in accordance with the undergenerated traditions of the lamas of the past. These teachings were given to 304 disciples who, in addition to the commitment to perform the sādhana daily, pledged to do the approaching retreat of 400,000 mantra recitations. I gave the life entrustment of Gyalchen Shukden to Trehor Geshé Tamdrin Rapten and Geshé Ngawang Dargyey of Sera Jé. I went to the Tibetan Transit School at their request and, at the retreat house in upper Dharamsala, gave the oral transmission of the prayers that the students recite daily.

At a meeting in Bodhgaya in 1965, a resolution had been passed at the wishes of His Holiness to reconstruct in exile the monastic headquarters for each of the four traditions. There had been no plans yet to build the Geluk monastery, so the monks in Buxa assembled and decided together to construct the monastery. They appointed six representatives, one each from the colleges of Gomang, Loseling, Jé, Mé, Shartsé, and Jangtsé. These representatives then came to Dharamsala to convey the decision to His Holiness through the Religious Affairs Office of His Holiness. They visited Throneholder Kyabjé Ling Rinpoché and myself and informed us in detail of the situation. We each donated a thousand rupees toward their immediate expenses.

On the twentieth day of the third month, the sacred statue of Avalokiteśvara called Ārya Wati Sangpo of Kyirong was brought to Dharamsala. This statue is one of four statues of Avalokiteśvara known as the "four siblings" that were all self-generated from the trunk of one sandalwood tree. Another of the four is the Ārya Lokeśvara in a temple in the Potala. The statue was brought to Nepal by the monks of Dzongkar Chödé and was kept in Nepal for a few years. When the statue arrived in Dharamsala, it was received with a procession of incense bearers. His Holiness, the two tutors, and the monks of Namgyal Monastery then made offerings and performed a purification ritual before the statue.[338]

In addition to the pieces of the head of the statue of Avalokiteśvara in Lhasa that had arrived earlier, another wrathful head of the same statue, the silver right foot of one of the four Maitreya statues in the Jokhang, and a piece of the wooden central pole of the Maitreya statue were also brought here. In addition, His Holiness received the golden statue of Guhyasamāja that Jé Tsongkhapa gave to Jetsun Sherap Sengé when he charged him with the responsibility for establishing the study and practice of tantra.

One day Ngari Rinpoché of Kyorlung came to see me to ask me some questions regarding the Madhyamaka view. I was pleased with his keen interest in Madhyamaka philosophy despite his youth, and I responded to his questions directly and spontaneously. However, Rinpoché had been examining the Madhyamaka view for a few years, and he had come to the conclusion that that which is found by the reasoning analyzing the ultimate is a coarse material form subsumed under the first of the four noble truths!

One day Ta Lama Thupten Norsang, who wished to do another Vajrayoginī retreat, asked me some questions on the practice of the three bodies of a buddha. At his request I also gave instructions on the meditation of the nine mixings of the completion stage.[339]

The Passing of the Incarnation of Kyabjé Phabongkha Rinpoché

On the seventh of the fourth month I received a telegram from Buxa saying that the supreme incarnation of my refuge and protector, Kyabjé Phabongkha Vajradhara, was critically ill. I was distressed and worried and immediately asked His Holiness and Kyabjé Ling Rinpoché for divinations and for their prayers. I sent sums of money to the monks of Sera Mé in Dalhousie to recite the *Fortunate Eon Sutra* (*Bhadrakalpika Sutra*) and to perform the prayers to the sixteen arhats as many times as Rinpoché's years.

On the thirteenth, Shenkhawa Gyurmé Sönam Topgyal, who was a former cabinet minister and a senior official of the Tibetan government, passed away at the age of seventy-two, and I offered prayers for him. The late minister had received many teachings on sutra and tantra at the feet of Phabongkha Vajradhara, Khangsar Rinpoché of Gomang, Kangyur Lama Rinpoché Losang Dönden, and many other great masters. He had managed the restoration undertaken by the government at Samyé Temple and the assembly hall of Ganden. He was a Gelukpa in the pure sense of following the views and practices of the virtuous tradition (*dge lugs*). He was a devoted practitioner, well read in the vast scriptures, and deeply familiar with the teachings of the stages of the path, such that one would hesitate to speak in his presence.

At the instruction of His Holiness, the Religious Affairs Office of the Central Tibetan Administration asked me to confer the Mahayana vows. So on the fifteenth I gave the vows in Mortimer Hall to the staff of the Central Tibetan Administration, the Namgyal monks, and a large crowd.

On the afternoon of the seventeenth I received a telegram from Kurseong, Darjeeling, with the news that the supreme incarnation had passed away at nine-thirty at night on the sixteenth at a hospital in Kurseong, where he had been transported from Buxa. When I heard that the manifestation of his three secrets had been absorbed into the *dharmadhātu* at the young age of twenty-six, it was as if the sun had suddenly vanished from the sky. My sorrow was unfathomable. I felt as if I had lost my one and only beloved child. He had all the qualities of learning, ethical discipline, and compassion and the ability to carry the responsibilities of upholding the teachings of the Geluk tradition. He was one of the best and most promising of all the lamas who had come to India and was praised by all unbiased and learned people. Both Kyabjé Ling Rinpoché and I had enthusiastically given him initiations, oral transmissions, explanations, and teachings on sutra and tantra in the hopes that he would become a preeminent bearer of the Geluk lineage.

As soon as I received the telegram, I sent a message to Kyabjé Ling Rinpoché. I made offerings before the statue of Ārya Wati Sangpo and fervently prayed for the accomplishment of the precious incarnation's wishes. I sent one thousand rupees to labrang manager Trinlé Dargyé for offerings for the late Rinpoché and as a token of condolence for Trinlé Dargyé along with a copy of a prayer I composed for the quick return of Rinpoché's incarnation.

Later I gave the initiation of single-deity Vajrabhairava to Geshé Palden Sengé of Loseling and to eight students of his who came from the Khunu area.

Mongolian Lama Guru Deva was publishing the biography of Jé Tsongkhapa,[340] and I contributed a thousand rupees for the printing of on behalf of all those connected with me, both living and dead. I contributed another thousand rupees on behalf of the late Lhabu, and I passed on twenty-eight hundred rupees donated by the late Venerable Kangyur Rinpoché. I also composed the foreword and verses of dedication for the biography.

To Geshé Ugyen Testen, Dzongtsé Tulku, and Lodrö Tulku of Sera Jé, who were going to the new Tibetan monastery in Rikon, Switzerland, I gave gifts and advice on proper conduct in both religious and secular contexts. I gave instruction to Geshé Ugyen Testen on the diagrams of the earth deity Sadak Toché for the site-consecration ritual of the monastery. I discussed with Mongolian Lama Guru Deva about giving a thousand copies of the biography of Jé Tsongkhapa to the committee for the reconstruction of a common Geluk monastery, and Lama Guru Deva agreed to this proposition. I presented a garment made of yellow brocade with a silk scarf to Lama Guru Deva for the successful publication of the biography.

I had been requested to write a commentary on the elaborate biographical praises for the protector Shukden that was composed by Kyabjé Phabongkha Vajradhara. I had previously been asked to write this commentary by a number of individuals in Lhasa, including Trungsar Rinpoché of Trehor, the resident master of Tashi Chöling Monastery Losang Chöphel, the scribe Losang Dorjé, the lord and lady of Lhalu Gatsal, and many others, and to prepare for writing the commentary, I had compiled notes from relevant biographies and documents. But then came my escape following the Chinese invasion, and in those unforeseen circumstances, I left behind all my notes and, with them, the hope of composing the text. In the meantime, however, some people who had come from Lhasa brought me my notes as well as a thangka of Shukden that was one of the very old religious artifacts of our labrang. I was fully convinced that this was due to the celestial assistance of the protector himself. When I received further requests from many individuals such as Dagyab Hothokthu and Dromo Geshé Rinpoché, I composed the commentary *Music to Please the Host of Oath-Bound Protectors*.[341]

On the ninth day of the seventh month, I finished giving His Holiness the oral transmission of the collected works of Jé Tsongkhapa and his two disciples. I also gave His Holiness the oral transmission of the *Later Tantra* of the *Root Tantra of Guhyasamāja*.[342]

Gyümé Tantric College was asked by the Tibetan government to construct a three-dimensional mandala of Avalokiteśvara for an exhibition in Bombay. In order to do this, ritual master Denma Tsültrim Dönden of Gyümé Monastery asked me to clarify some points on the mandala, and I gave him detailed instruction.

On the seventeenth day of the second seventh month, the incarnation of Lochen Rinpoché of Tashi Lhunpo came to see me from Kyil Monastery in Spiti. He was six years old and came with his teacher, Kachen Losang Gyaltsen, and twenty others. The tulku was very lively and recited the *Tibetan Trailblazer* tea-offering verse without any hesitation when tea was offered to him.[343] On a subsequent day, I gave Lochen Tulku and his entourage and many people from Spiti the initiation of Life-Sustaining Jé Tsongkhapa. I conferred lay vows on the tulku and cut the first snip of his hair. Afterward I gave him a bronze statue of the Buddha and a vajra and bell.

To mark the occasion of the recognition ceremony for the incarnation of Phara Rinpoché of Ganden Jangtsé, I sent a ceremonial scarf and a token offering of funds for the symbolic offerings of body, speech, and mind to Buxa. During the ceremony when the scarf I had sent was presented to him, he rose from his throne, placed the scarf around his neck, and then made three prostrations and joined his hands together in reverence. He then sat for some time with a serious expression on his face. I learned of this from a letter from Yeshé Tsewang of Phara Labrang in Buxa. The tulku's predecessor was a devoted disciple of mine, so it could be that such instincts were awakened.

In the eighth month, at the request of Tsechok Ling Tulku and his main attendant, I gave the permission of outer, inner, and secret Mañjuśrī, as taught in the cycle of Mañjuśrī teachings, to Rinpoché and others including Thepo Tulku, Lati Rinpoché, and many geshés.

New Residence

I was given a house on the property purchased by the Tibetan government in the mid-level of Dharamsala. Because there was a shortage of space for offices and staff, I told them that I did not need to shift my residence for the time being. However, the cabinet minister for Home Affairs, Wangdü Dorjé, and the chairman of the Tibetan People's Deputies, Kalsang Dradul, came to see me and insisted that I move to Gangchen Kyishong.[344] I therefore agreed to move. As the twenty-first day of the eighth month was an auspicious day, I sent my attendant Palden with a thangka of the *Guru Puja* merit field and a text of the *Eight Thousand Verse Perfection of Wisdom Sutra* to the new house. On the way he first encountered a person carrying milk and shepherding a herd of white goats. He then met a person who was on his way to deliver complimentary copies of a White Tārā long-life ritual text sent to me from Buxa. So these were auspicious encounters.

In the meantime I visited Kyabjé Ling Rinpoché at his request and gave him explanations on, and the oral transmission of, the *Guru Yoga of Vajrabhairava That Is a Treasury of Attainments* and the related texts the *Ways to Accomplish the Activities of Pacification and Increase*, the *Methods for Restoring the Degenerated Commitments by Relying on the Five Buddha Families of Yamāntaka*, and the *Peaceful and Wrathful Protection of Mañjuśrī*. All of the above were from the sealed works of Thuken.[345]

On the auspicious day of the third of the ninth month, I moved from Nowrojee House. Upon departing the house, my neighbors, the monks of Namgyal Monastery, presented me with scarves and bid me farewell. When I arrived at Tashi Rabten, my new residence at Gangchen Kyishong, I was ushered in by the staff of the Tibetan secretariat and the abbot of Namgyal Monastery, Ratö Rinpoché, all holding burning incense. After settling in my room, the members of the council of ministers and the Religious Affairs council offered me scarves and representations of the holy body, speech, and mind. They were followed by many individuals who came with housewarming presents to wish me well. Ratö Rinpoché privately gave me a long-life ceremony with a *Guru Puja* and tsok offering.

The following day at the request of Mr. Manithang, the bursar of the Shedra family, and his wife, I gave the blessing of the four sindūra initiations of Vajrayoginī and made tsok offerings. In the afternoon His Holiness came to my house for a leisurely visit. He declared that my house was comfortable and stressed that I should make strong intentions to live a long life. I told His Holiness that due to my deep-seated habit from time immemorial of grasping at permanence, I hope and will myself to live a long time even in my dreams.

Following the wishes of Rikya Tulku of Sera Jé, I gave the most secret Heart Absorption permission of Cittamaṇi Tārā, which is only given to single recipients. I also gave the oral transmission of the *Diamond-Cutter Sutra* and the *Heart Sutra*.

On the twenty-third His Holiness came to my house to tell me about his visit to Thailand, where he had attended a Buddhist conference. He told me of how the king and the people there have great respect for Buddhist monks. His Holiness also told me of how he was deeply impressed with the calm, peaceful, and sincere demeanor of many monks of the Theravada tradition and with their rigorous observance of the Vinaya monastic rules. He related his discussion with them on various Buddhist topics, including concentration meditation, penetrative insight, the thirty-seven aspects of enlightenment, and so on.

Tutor Kyabjé Ling Rinpoché visited me on his way to Bodhgaya. I gave him the oral transmission of the methods for averting frost by the four letters relying on Vajrabhairava and performed the purification ritual of the Ḍākinīs that Dispel Obscurations. I sent Losang Yeshé to Bodhgaya on a pilgrimage to make twenty thousand butter-lamp offerings on behalf of the late Lhabu and another twenty thousand on behalf of all others connected with me. I told him to divide the offerings between Bodhgaya and Varanasi.

On the fourth day of the eleventh month, based on the root text and His Holiness Kalsang Gyatso's commentary the *Source of All Attainments*,[346] I taught the *Hundred Deities of Tuṣita* to Lati Rinpoché of Ganden Shartsé, Thepo Tulku, and Geshé Rapten of Sera Jé.

On the tenth day of the twelfth month, on the anniversary of the parinirvāṇa of Serkong Dorjé Chang, Assistant Tutor Serkong Rinpoché requested me to give the blessing of the four sindūra initiations of Vajrayoginī. At his wish I gave the blessings to Rinpoché himself and other lamas and geshés, including Ratö Rinpoché, to monks from Namgyal and Dzongkar Chödé monasteries, and to some lay practitioners, a hundred people in all. At the conclusion we offered an extensive tsok.

On February 29, 1968, the first day of the Tibetan earth-monkey year and my sixty-eighth year, I paid my New Year's respects at the feet of His Holiness, and I attended the offerings to Palden Lhamo. After the New Year celebration, I visited with His Holiness at his residence, and we discussed various topics. His Holiness asked in particular about whether nirvana is emptiness and about the distinction between the delusions that arise from grasping the I as self-sufficient substantially existent, asserted by the lower schools of tenets, and the delusions arising from grasping the I as truly existent, asserted by the Prāsaṅgikas. According to the Prāsaṅgikas, all delusions are similar to that of the grasping of true existence, but if that is the case, then it is not possible to abandon even the coarse delusions by the method of meditation on selflessness that accords with the teachings of the lower tenets.

To these and many other questions His Holiness asked, I answered that there are differences of opinion as to whether nirvana is emptiness, and that there are coarse and subtle differences between the above-mentioned delusions. According to the Prāsaṅgikas, coarse delusions can be suppressed by meditating on selflessness as taught by the lower tenets, but they cannot be entirely abandoned. That is the reason for the explanation of the arhat found in the Abhidharma. I offered these replies according to what struck me at the time, but I do not know whether they served any purpose.

On the eleventh His Holiness came to my house and told me about the discourse he was going to give on the *Great Treatise on the Stages of the Path* beginning on the fifteenth at the request of His Holiness's ritual assistant. I expressed my profound gratitude for this kindness on behalf of the Buddhadharma and for all beings. In this connection I presented His Holiness with the old Ganden edition of the *Great Treatise on the Stages of the Path* that I had received in the water-rabbit year, as mentioned above,[347] together with a ceremonial scarf and a token sum for the three representations. On the first page of the text I wrote the following:

> This text of the supreme path of millions of buddhas and
> bodhisattvas,
> with its complete stages, to be completely traveled,
> well illumined by the conquering Losang, treasure of wisdom,
> containing the four supreme and excellent features,
> is offered by an ignorant one with no excellent qualities of mind,
> but with firm faith from time immemorial,
> to the great guide of samsara and nirvana so that he may turn
> the wheel of the Mahayana for as long as samsara lasts.

On the fifteenth, at the request of the Religious Affairs Office, I gave Mahayana vows to seventy staff members of the Central Tibetan Administration and other monks and laypeople. On the twenty-sixth I finished compiling the outlines of the stages of the path to incorporate further subdivisions into the text of the *Middle-Length Stages of the Path* by Jé Tsongkhapa. I had started to do this many years ago and had put a great deal of effort into it. Denma Jampa Chögyal started to write the master copy for publication.

On the fifth day of the second month, the abbot and disciplinarian as well as the monks of the Gyütö Tantric College recited prayers for my long life in connection with a *Guru Puja* and tsok offering. At the request of Trehor Samten of the Gyümé Tantric College, I gave explanations on the exclusive practice of the *Hundred Deities of Tuṣita* based on the recitation text compiled by Kyabjé Vajradhara. I gave these teachings on the lawn of my house to about four hundred disciples, including monks from Namgyal and Dzongkar Chödé monasteries as well as the monks of the three seats and the two tantric colleges in Dalhousie. On the first of the third month, at the request of Chogyé Trichen Rinpoché of Phenpo Nalendra, I bestowed a White Tārā long-life initiation on Rinpoché and his entourage.

Geshé Rapgyé of Sera Jé's Tsangpa House came to see me. He confided that he had been unable to accomplish śamatha despite applying himself to single-pointed concentration for over six months. He asked me for special methods to rein in the mind from habitual wandering. I instructed him to imagine the mind mixing with or dissolving into the object of concentration. I also told him that it is possible to stabilize the mind by thinking that the mind abides within the object. If that did not help, then he should take a break from meditation and instead engage in the practices of accumulating merit, purifying mental obstacles, and making requests to the gurus. He later told me that my suggestions had been helpful.

Ganden Shartsé Monastery had written to Thepo Tulku and other lamas and geshés in Dharamsala to arrange for a long-life offering to remove obstacles to my longevity. On the third, they organized a long-life ceremony with a *Guru Puja* and tsok offering. This was attended by all the Shartsé monks in Dharamsala.

His Holiness Requests Bodhisattva Vows

On the twentieth, His Holiness, Tutor Kyabjé Ling Rinpoché, and I attended the ceremony commemorating the founding of the Tibetan

Children's Village in Dharamsala. There, in the course of our private conversations, His Holiness raised the topic of the twelve links of dependent origination as they appear in the teachings on the stages of the path. His Holiness said that it is not possible to complete one full cycle of the twelve links in fewer than four or five lives.[348] He gave the example of a being in the bardo destined for hell who is transferred by force of its virtue to the bardo of a god. Such a being does not take birth in hell even though it had the establishing links of desire and craving that propelled it into the hell bardo. When the being does land in hell at some point in the future, does the earlier activation of desire and craving suffice, or must that series of links repeat itself? If it does suffice, then the full cycle can be completed within four or five lives. I told His Holiness that it seems that desire and craving would have to be activated again before the being is again born in hell, so the cycle may not necessarily be completed in four or five lives. His Holiness also raised many issues regarding the Cittamātra view on external phenomena.

In the evening the children presented a play reenacting the story of Atiśa being invited to Tibet by Lha Lama Yeshé Ö and his nephew Jangchup Ö. The play was well performed. It had been drawn from reliable sources and had engaging narration.

On the twelfth day of the fourth month, a long-life ceremony conjoined with the ritual of sixteen arhats was offered to me by the monks of the three seats settled in Dalhousie along with the monks who had come to receive His Holiness's discourse on the stages of the path. The long-life ceremony was sponsored by the monks from Dalhousie, and I gave back to them the offerings they made to me.

His Holiness asked me to arrange for an elaborate offering for the occasion for him to take the bodhisattva vows from me, and for these offerings, he contributed a thousand rupees. Since my house had insufficient space and inadequate facilities in which to arrange extensive offerings, I had three hundred large torma offerings prepared with the best ingredients, including the three sweets and clarified butter.[349] I also filled several baskets with a variety of the highest-quality fruit.

On the thirteenth, the prescribed day, His Holiness came to my house at eight in the morning to take the bodhisattva vows. I had risen at dawn that day and had taken the aspiring and engaging bodhisattva vows myself in conjunction with the practice of the six preliminaries.[350] After that, His Holiness and I made offerings with the six preliminaries first, and then I offered His Holiness the aspiring and engaging bodhisattva vows simultaneously according to the tradition of Śāntideva. His Holiness then gave me a monk's begging bowl filled with fruit as a token of bodhicitta, and we recited the "On that day in Bodhgaya" verse three times[351] and the *Guide to the Bodhisattva's Way of Life*. After following the uncorrupted traditions established by the lamas of the past in this manner, His Holiness returned to his compound and gave bodhisattva vows to those attending his discourse on the stages of the path. Thus he planted the seeds of enlightenment in the minds of many.

On the eighth day of the fifth month, the people of Chatreng offered me a long-life ceremony. At their invitation, the ceremony was conducted by Song Rinpoché and Dzemé Rinpoché, among other lamas and monks. Later, following a unanimous decision by the people of Chatreng to form an association, I contributed two thousand rupees to the association's general fund.

On the eighth day of the seventh month (August 31, 1968), I attended the celebration to mark the shifting of His Holiness's residence from Swarg Ashram to Thekchen Chöling. I presented a scarf and the three representations during the ceremony. The remaining faces of the Lhasa Lokeśvara statue and the Kyirong statue of Ārya Wati Sangpo were invited to the ceremonial hall in procession. Afterward, His Holiness, the two tutors, and the monks of Namgyal Monastery made offerings to the statue and performed the rituals of purification and consecration. The auspicious confession ceremony was then held, after which the pages of the sutra *Perfection of Wisdom in Twenty-Five Thousand Lines* were distributed, so that the entire text could be recited.

On the twelfth, ten monks from the Gyümé Tantric College, including the abbot and the disciplinarian along with a few monks of Namgyal Monastery, performed the elaborate ritual of consecration related to Guhyasamāja in the new palace. Then ten monks from the Gyütö Tantric College, including the abbot and the chant master along with eight Namgyal monks, performed the consecration according to the Cakrasaṃvara ritual. On the day of the consecration, Kyabjé Ling Rinpoché presided over the Guhyasamāja ritual, and I presided over the Cakrasaṃvara ritual. At this time Denma Jampa Chögyal of Sera Jé had finished copying the text of the *Middle-Length Stages of the Path* with my supplementary outline. One thousand copies of the text were printed at the press in Dharamsala. Jampa Chögyal was well rewarded for the work.

The incarnation of Muli Khentrul Thupten Lamsang of Shartsé was brought to see me by a disciple of his predecessor named Gendun. The predecessor had been the abbot of Richung Pothö Monastery in Phakri, and his eight-year-old incarnation had been born in Bhutan. I took the first snip of his hair and gave him the name Losang Dönyö Palden.

The monks of Seudru Monastery and the people of Tsakha Lhopa asked me to discover the reincarnation of Gangkar Lama Rinpoché Könchok Chödrak of Seudru Monastery. As described above, his prior incarnation had died from illness during the war with the Chinese. I sought out his incarnation not simply because they asked me to but also because I had very close karmic connections with the two previous incarnations. I therefore asked the Gadong oracle for predictions about the whereabouts of the incarnation on three separate occasions, and all three predictions were unanimous. Each time the oracle said the incarnation would be found to the east of Dharamsala, born among his own townspeople.

My own divination indicated that the boy was called Karma Lhundrup and was born to a mother named Kalsang from Tsakha Lhopa. She was working at a road workers' camp in Gangtok. I instructed Apho Wangden, an old-time attendant of Gangkar Lama, to test the boy secretly. On the morning of the day Wangden was to arrive at the house, the boy said a visitor would come that day. After Wangden arrived at the house, the boy put a silver butter lamp and a set of seven water-offering bowls that belonged to the family into Wangden's bag. This, and many other circumstances, gave convincing proof that this was the correct incarnation. I therefore made a final determination that the boy was the true incarnation of Gangkar Lama.

12 | Planting Roots of Virtue

Invitation to Switzerland

Kyabjé Ling Rinpoché and I had received repeated invitations from Mr. Kuhn, the owner of the metalware factory at Rikon in Switzerland, to inaugurate and consecrate the newly constructed Tibetan monastery there. Having received His Holiness's consent to the trip, I visited His Holiness on the twenty-third to take my leave. At the same time I presented His Holiness with a complimentary copy of the *Middle-Length Stages of the Path* published with the enhanced outline.

On the twenty-fifth, I left Dharamsala with my attendants Palden and Norbu Chöphel. When we reached Pathankot, Kyabjé Ling Rinpoché and his entourage had also arrived there. We left by train together and arrived the next morning at the old Delhi railway station. There we were met by His Holiness's elder brother Gyalo Thondup, the representative and the staff of the Bureau of the Dalai Lama in Delhi, the director and the staff of Tibet House, and many other Tibetans. We stayed at Tibet House and left from the Delhi airport via Air France at ten in the evening on the twenty-seventh (September 20, 1968).

After brief stops at Cairo and Tel Aviv, the capitals of Egypt and Israel, respectively, we arrived in Paris at seven in the morning on the twenty-eighth. There we changed to another plane and flew to Zürich, Switzerland, where we were welcomed by the Tibetan representative Mr. Phalha, Mr. Kuhn, Geshé Ugyen Tseten of Sera Jé, who was the abbot of the new monastery, and many other Tibetans. After a brief rest in the VIP lounge, we left for the monastery in Rikon, where we received a traditional ceremony of welcome before settling into our quarters.

On the first day of the eighth month, Mr. Kuhn invited all of us on a sightseeing trip up the slopes of Mount Rigi. We traveled to the top of the mountain in a large electric cable car that could transport twenty people.

We rested and had a meal in a grand restaurant. After touring clockwise around the mountain, viewing the vast and picturesque Swiss towns spread out below and the diverse landscape, we returned by cable car. Then, while touring the surrounding area, we visited a large Christian church where we saw many people attending a religious service.[352] That day we were out from about eight in the morning to ten at night. Except for the stops at the mountaintop and in the church, we traveled in vehicles along winding roads for long distances, which made me tired and nauseous. The kind and generous hospitality of our patron became my suffering!

The opening ceremony of the monastery took place on the seventh day of the eighth month and was attended by most of the Tibetans in the area and many Swiss people carrying colorful banners. With people playing musical instruments on either side of the road, Kyabjé Ling Rinpoché, myself, and the resident monks processed. All of us monks wore our three sets of yellow monastic robes and walked slowly and peacefully in the manner of Ārya Aśvajit.[353] When we reached the entrance of the monastery, Kyabjé Ling Rinpoché inaugurated the opening ceremony by cutting the ribbon. After taking our seats in the prayer hall, we performed the blessing of the site and the facilities as well as invocation and purification rituals, the seven-limb prayer, and so forth. We all then presented scarves to the main Buddha image. Panglung Tulku read His Holiness's message in German, and Mr. Kuhn gave an address about the monastery. I then spoke about Buddhism's unique qualities, its culture, and its extensive spread in Tibet. I emphasized how Buddhism in Tibet was genuine in its teachings and practice, no different from what was taught by the Buddha himself; it was not a spurious creation with no framework. The ceremony was then concluded.

On the morning of the eighth, Kyabjé Ling Rinpoché gave a long-life initiation of White Tārā, and I gave permission to practice Avalokiteśvara Who Liberates from All Lower Realms, with brief advice on religious and worldly matters, to the people. In the afternoon, the Office of Tibet hosted a banquet in honor of the Kuhn family, Dr. Lindegger, and ourselves, and it was attended by many guests.

At the wish of Kyabjé Ling Rinpoché, I gave him a teaching and oral transmission of the *Great Treatise on the Stages of the Path* in the lineage of Kyabjé Phabongkha Vajradhara. Kyabjé Ling Rinpoché told me that he had received the lineage of the teachings from His Holiness the Thirteenth Dalai Lama but had been very young at the time. He had not been able to receive the complete teachings from Phabongkha Vajradhara, so I fulfilled his wish by giving him this teaching. Beginning on the seventeenth day of the eighth month, I offered this teaching to Rinpoché alone. In doing so, I did not bother to repeat points or elaborate unnecessarily. It was a concise, symbolic discourse meant to transmit the lineage. I was like a firefly in the presence of the brilliant thousand rays of the sun.

Ling Rinpoché and Trijang Rinpoché exchanging teachings during their visit in Switzerland, 1968
COURTESY OF PALDEN TSERING

At the request of the Tibetan settlement in Rikon, Kyabjé Ling Rinpoché gave the permission of Green Tārā, and I gave a long-life empowerment of Amitāyus in the system of Drupgyal. On the morning of the twenty-third, a doctor gave me a complete physical exam, testing my heart in particular. He told me I had no health problems.

On the twenty-seventh, Kyabjé Ling Rinpoché and I along with Geshé Ugyen Tseten and three monks performed the ritual of blessing the relics and the printed prayers to be placed inside the main statue of the Buddha. Kyabjé Ling Rinpoché and I then carefully inserted the relics and the prayers into the statue.

On the twenty-eighth the doctor came to see me to again check my health. He said that my blood pressure was only 100, which was below the recommended pressure of 140. He advised me to increase my protein intake and to include more milk, yogurt, and vegetables in my diet.

At the invitation of the director of the Pestalozzi Children's Village and the Tibetan school in Trogen, Kyabjé Ling Rinpoché and I visited the village on the second day of the ninth month. When we arrived at the Yumbu Lagang Tibetan home, we were received by the Tibetan students, who held flowers and incense and religious banners. After a brief welcome ceremony in the chapel, we settled into our rooms. To fulfill an earlier request made by Trethong Rakra Tulku, I gave Rakra Tulku and Mr. Phalha a concise teaching on the exclusive practice of the *Hundred Deities of Tuṣita* compiled by Phabongkha Vajradhara.

Ling Rinpoché and Trijang Rinpoché visiting Tibetan students at Trogen, Switzerland, October 23, 1968
COURTESY OF YONGZIN LINGTSANG LABRANG

On the sixth, Kyabjé Ling Rinpoché gave the permissions of Yellow and Red Mañjuśrī and of Green Tārā, and I gave the permission of White Sarasvatī, to the Tibetan students of Yumbu Lagang and Luksang Ngön-ga along with their principal, Trethong Rakra Tulku, Trethong Söpal, the Tibetan teacher Shödrung Rapgang, Mr. Phalha, and others. As I did not have the text for the permission of Sarasvatī, I recited the rituals of the self- and front-generations according to the system found in kriyā tantra. For the actual permission, I followed the usual format for granting deity permissions, and during the recitation of the mantra, I supplemented it with the emanation and dissolution based on the diagram wheel of Sarasvatī. Thus I tried to follow the procedure correctly, in accordance with reliable sources, so as not to be like those who are careless and ignorant and, without any valid references, perform the rites however they please in order to deceive others.

On the seventh, at the invitation of Arthur Bill, the director of the Pestalozzi Children's Village, Kyabjé Ling Rinpoché and I visited him at his house. We presented him with token gifts. Mr. Bill had a genuine sympathy and love for the Tibetans. He was not only concerned with reducing the temporary difficulties of our people; he gave valuable suggestions and assistance to aid the Tibetans over the long term. He asked why the Tibetans use the symbol of the dragon on Tibetan rugs and so forth. In our reply we told him that this design was auspicious, symbolizing prosperity and renown, like the sound of a dragon's roar reaching far and beyond. We explained that the Tibetan use of the symbol differs from that of the Chinese.

The next day I gave Rakra Tulku the permissions of Nīlagrīva Vajrapāṇi, Five Wrathful Garuḍa, and Vajrapāṇi Mahācakra.

On the morning of the ninth, Kyabjé Ling Rinpoché and I went to the village chapel, where we performed a consecration and made offerings. In the afternoon we went to the monastery in Rikon. Professor Palos, who is a German citizen of Hungarian origin, repeatedly asked me to give him the prenovice, novice, and full ordination vows. After checking to see whether there were any negative indications, I conferred ordination on him in the presence of five monks, including Geshé Ugyen Tseten and Lodrö Tulku. I gave him the name Tenzin Chöphel.

Apart from the Tibetan children in the Swiss settlements and those at Trogen, the Tibetan children who have been adopted into Swiss families have forgotten their native language and will soon forget their national heritage, despite their excellent living conditions. Given the serious threat that many of them will be lost, Mr. Phalha had previously tried to arrange for these adopted children to gather together at the annual commemoration of the March 10 uprising, but so far his wishes had not been realized. Therefore, at Mr. Phalha's suggestion, Kyabjé Ling Rinpoché and I invited the children and their adopted families to a tea party at the Rikon monastery. About sixty children and their families attended the party, where tea, cookies, fruit juices, and other snacks were served. Both Kyabjé Ling Rinpoché and I thanked the parents for caring for their children and asked them to make efforts to ensure that the children did not forget the Tibetan language and customs. We gave the children advice on how to behave properly and on how important it is for them, as Tibetans, to know Tibet's language and customs. We asked them to gather at the monastery each year at His Holiness's birthday celebrations. We both gave a token sum of a thousand Swiss francs toward their annual gatherings. Then Dr. Aeschimann, who was the first to adopt Tibetan children, announced to those present his full agreement to do this. The children and the parents with their voices and gestures exhibited great pleasure and enthusiasm.

The next day, Kyabjé Ling Rinpoché and I hosted a dinner for the members of the Kuhn family; Dr. Lindegger, president of the monastery; Mrs. Vischer, vice-president of the Swiss Red Cross; Mrs. Chöden Bar, director of the Tibetan settlements; and Dr. Aeschimann. In addition to those dignitaries, who all played significant roles on behalf of the Tibetans, we also invited Mr. Phalha and His Holiness's elder brother Losang Samten. At the dinner we thanked everyone for their efforts and appealed to them to continue their assistance.

On the fifteenth, Kyabjé Ling Rinpoché and I, along with Geshé Ugyen Tseten and three other monks, performed the intermediate version of the consecration called *Sheaves of Auspiciousness*[354] after doing the sādhana of single-deity Vajrabhairava. This was to consecrate the temple as well as the statue of the Buddha and so forth. Supplementing the ritual of consecration, we performed the ordinary ritual of purification and the supramundane ritual of purification in an elaborate manner. During the ritual of consecration, at the section for honoring the patrons, the symbols of the eight auspicious substances were passed around to the members of the Kuhn family and Dr. Lindegger.

On the eighteenth, at the invitation of the Dzarong family and Trehor Draksé Tulku's family, I went to Ebnat-Kappel with Palden and Norbu Chöphel. I enjoyed their generous hospitality for three days. On the twenty-second, at the invitation of the Tsāriwa Phuntsok family, Kyabjé Ling Rinpoché gave the permission of the Three Wrathful Forms Combined, and I gave an Amitāyus long-life initiation in the system of Drupgyal, to about a hundred people at the Rikon temple. In the afternoon the Phuntsok family sponsored a *Guru Puja* with a tsok offering, which everyone attended.

At the invitation of twenty-one Tibetans who had recently arrived in Switzerland, I went to the settlement in Bauma. I performed purification and consecration rituals in their quarters and gave general teachings and advice. Following that I went to Wald and had lunch at the house of Trehor Losang Nyima and my niece Tashi Drölma. Then, at the invitation of Dagyab Rinpoché, Shakor Khentrul, and Yiga Tulku, I went to Landquart, where I stayed for a week enjoying their generous hospitality. I gave experiential teachings on the two stages of Kurukulle to Dagyab Rinpoché alone for three days. This teaching was based on the teachings of Dergé Shar Lama. The other tulku had brought a large tape recorder and asked me to record some spiritual songs, so I recited what occurred spontaneously to me.

Mr. Phalha and Dr. Lindegger had arranged for Palden and I to stay in a big state-run hospital in Winterthur to rest and improve our health for two weeks beginning the sixth day of the tenth month. The furnishings and the facilities, such as telephones, were excellent. We were examined by various specialists, and all parts of our bodies were tested with electronic equipment. They also repeatedly tested our blood, urine, sputum, and so on. In the meantime, I sent Norbu Chöphel to Bonn with Dagyab Rinpoché to do some sightseeing. At the end of our hospital stay, on the twenty-sixth, the doctor told me that I had tuberculosis in a small area of my lung but that I had nearly recovered from it. He advised that I should get further treatment for it at the hospital in Wald.

At his direction, Palden and I stayed in a private room at the hospital in Wald. Norbu Chöphel returned from Germany and stayed at the house of Losang Nyima and my niece near the hospital. Norbu Chöphel came to see us at the hospital frequently. The hospital, situated on a lush green hill, was several stories high. The ground floor contained recreation facilities and a television lounge for the patients. There were also large gardens for walks and outings. The meals were clean and excellent. The doctors performed medical tests with x-rays and injections.

I took two days' leave from the hospital and went to the monastery to give the blessing of the four sindūra initiations of Vajrayoginī to twenty-one people on the twenty-fifth day of the eleventh month at the request of Ratö Losang Jamyang. The next day I gave the oral transmission of the texts of Cittamaṇi Tārā to Lodrö Tulku. I gave instructions on the ritual of "reviving the lost vital life energy"[355] to Geshé Ugyen Testen. In the afternoon I returned to the hospital. Lodrö Tulku brought me a book on the life of the Buddha composed by Jampa Kalsang Gyatso and printed in China, which I read daily. On the fifth day of the twelfth month, Dr. Barun, a well-known psychiatrist who lived in Zürich, came to visit me. He asked questions about the transition from one life to the next, about the process of reincarnation, as well as about the methods for attaining enlightenment and meditating on emptiness. I responded to each of his questions. On the thirteenth, my doctor told us that the tuberculosis in my lung had responded well and Palden's sickness in his left side was completely cured.

On the sixteenth, I sent New Year greeting cards to His Holiness, Tutor Ling Rinpoché, Sakya Trichen, Karmapa Rinpoché, and other high lamas as well as to old Tibetan acquaintances. The cards had a color picture depicting the life of Atiśa. On the back of the cards I wrote the following verse of greeting:

> In the garden of the thousand-petalled lotuses of prosperity,
> the melodious song of the strutting celestial peacock
> rings out from the Turquoise Leaf realm of happiness
> to invite the guests of the goodness of the three worlds.

When I left the hospital on the twenty-fifth, I gave a square Tibetan carpet and various drawings of yaks to the doctor who was primarily responsible for my treatment, as token of my appreciation for his excellent care. He said that both Palden and I had no health problems. Rikzin Jikmé Lingpa said:

> Except for those who see the truth,
> of all those called bhikṣus, brahmans, and lamas,
> there are none who are not tied and bound
> by the eight worldly concerns, such as gain and loss.

Bound tightly in this way by the eight worldly concerns, I received the doctor's assurance with pleasure and satisfaction. We were given a supply of medicine to be taken regularly, and we left the hospital. I then stayed with Losang Nyima and Tashi Drölma and made the tsok offering of the twenty-fifth on that day. From there, we departed for Rikon and stayed at the home of Gyaltsen Namdröl.

England and France

At the insistent invitation of Özer Ngawang and his wife, who were the house parents of the Tibetan house at the Pestalozzi Children's Village in England,[356] and also Geshé Tsultim Gyeltsen, the religious instructor there, I left Zürich for London by air on the twenty-ninth at eleven in the morning. When I arrived at London airport, some staff members of the UK Tibet Society, Rechung Tulku and his wife, Özer Ngawang, and others were there to greet me. We all boarded a train and arrived at the Tibetan house at four in the afternoon.

In 1969, my sixty-ninth year, on the first day of the first Tibetan month in the earth-bird year, all of us, including the staff and students of the Tibetan house Trisong Ngön-ga, celebrated Tibetan New Year with the traditional ceremonies in the prayer hall. We all recited the verses of refuge, generating the mind of enlightenment, the *Gangloma* prayer to Mañjuśrī, and the long-life prayer for His Holiness. That day, many Tibetan boys and girls from London and other places came to see me. Extending my greeting to them, I advised them on the importance of faith in the Dharma and of maintaining our customs and our cultural heritage.

After the New Year, I gave the initiation of Cakrasaṃvara body mandala to Geshé Tsultim Gyeltsen alone and the blessing of the four sindūra initiations of Vajrayoginī to Geshé-la, Öser Ngawang, and his wife. I gave an Amitāyus long-life initiation in the system of Drupgyal and the oral transmission of the *Abridged Stages of the Path* and the *Song of Spiritual Experience* to the staff and students. I told everyone there that they should make efforts to increase their knowledge of both the religious and worldly arenas and that they should observe good conduct in order to support the prestige of the Tibetans.

One day I was taken to Hastings, where we walked on the pier and visited the shops, some restaurants, and various amusement facilities.

I threw a dinner for about fifteen dignitaries, including the chairman of the Pestalozzi village, and expressed my appreciation for their past assistance and care for the Tibetan children and requested their continued help. On the sixteenth I left Trisong Ngön-ga and went to London, where I stayed in a hotel. In London I visited the planetarium, where I watched a fascinating show about the planets and the constellations accompanied by narration. The planets and stars were projected on the ceiling of the dome and gave an illusion of the vast space at night. They showed the progression of a lunar eclipse as if it were actually happening.

In the afternoon I gave instructions on how to practice single-pointed concentration to a British friend of Rechung Tulku. I went sightseeing around a famous ancient royal palace [the Tower of London] where many precious crowns of the British rulers along with many regal vestments were on display. In the palace was a garden with a variety of birds and animals.

On the eighteenth I was invited by the UK Tibet Society to attend a March 10 commemoration organized by the society. This was attended by over two hundred British nationals and fifty Tibetans. At the meeting, I read His Holiness's personal message and gave a brief talk, which was translated into English by Mrs. Rinchen Dolma Taring.[357] The Tibetan children sang the Tibetan national anthem and performed Tibetan songs and dances, which was a token demonstration of our Tibetan heritage.

On the nineteenth I left London by air for Paris, where I was met by the incarnation of the Most Venerable Dakpo Bamchö Jampal Lhundrup Gyatso and Shödrung Norgyé as well as some Kalmyk Mongolians. I stayed at Dakpo Rinpoché's house. There I met Kyabjé Ling Rinpoché, who was there for medical treatment. Kyabjé Ling Rinpoché and I exchanged news of recent events and discussed the date of our return to India.

Kyabjé Ling Rinpoché and I were invited by the Mongolian community to their New Year celebrations. Extending our greetings to them, we expressed our view that the younger generation of the community should preserve the Dharma and maintain the good customs and traditions of their elders and past generations. The next morning I escorted Kyabjé Ling Rinpoché to the airport as he left for Switzerland. The next day I gave a brief teaching and oral transmission of the *Three Principal Aspects of the Path* and the first few pages of the *Great Exposition of Secret Mantra* to Dakpo Bamchö Rinpoché, Thupten, Ngawang Drakpa, and their two landladies.

One day I visited a museum presenting the history of humankind's evolution from monkeys.[358] I saw the gradual changes in the bone structure. There were also exhibits of various tools from the Stone Age, through human history, up to the modern scientific instruments. A great variety of costumes was also on display.

On the twenty-seventh, twenty Tibetan students and their house parents, Shödrung Norgyé and his wife, invited me to visit them in Bléneau;

I went and spent one night there. I gave teachings and oral transmission of the *Hundred Deities of Tuṣita* and the *Gangloma* prayer to Mañjuśrī as well as advice to the students. The students performed some Tibetan songs and dances. Their Tibetan writing, drawing, and conduct were excellent in every respect.

Return to India

On leaving Paris, I traveled to Geneva, where I stayed at the home of Mr. Phalha. On the eleventh day of the second Tibetan month, I visited the Tibetan settlement in Reitnau, spending a night there and giving teachings and performing consecrations. En route, I stopped over at the settlement in Oetweil am See, where I gave the permission of the Three Wrathful Forms Combined, before returning again to Rikon, where I stayed at Gyaltsen Namdröl's house. There I met Tutor Ling Rinpoché, and on the thirteenth, Kyabjé Ling Rinpoché left for Paris ahead of me, for further medical tests. I left for Paris myself on the twentieth from the Zürich airport and met up with Kyabjé Ling Rinpoché and his entourage in the airport in Paris. I saw Dakpo Bamchö Rinpoché there briefly, and at nine at night, we flew out of Paris on an Air France flight.

On the twenty-first we arrived at the Delhi airport at noon. We were met by the officers and staff of the Bureau of His Holiness in Delhi and Tibet House, Bakula Rinpoché from Ladakh, Nyakré Khentrul, Mongolian Lama Guru Deva, and others. We stayed at Tibet House. At the request of Nyakré Khentrul, I gave a brief teaching and oral transmission of the *Abridged Stages of the Path* and the *Song of Spiritual Experience* to about a hundred people at Tibet House.

On the twenty-third I left Delhi for Dharamsala, where I settled into my house. Some days later I went to visit His Holiness with some offerings to pay him my respects and had the pleasure of receiving his words. At the request of Nepo Ngödrup I gave the blessing of the four sindūra initiations of Vajrayoginī to a large gathering in connection with the tenth-day offerings in the third month.

I contributed five thousand rupees toward the silver statue of Avalokiteśvara and the gilded bronze statues of Guru Rinpoché and Buddha Śākyamuni that were being created at the wish of His Holiness. His Holiness placed the heads of the statue of Avalokiteśvara destroyed by the Chinese in Lhasa inside the new silver statue. I dedicated this contribution to the welfare of all the beings connected with me.

On the tenth day of the fourth month, His Holiness was to start his discourse on the *Great Exposition on the Stages of Tantra* to the monks from Dharamsala as well as the Gyütö and Gyümé Tantric College monks and others who came from different places. For this occasion I presented His Holiness with a true Ganden edition of the text. The woodblocks of this particular text were sponsored by Pön Shizom, who was appointed governor of Lhokha Gongkar by Nedong Desi Drakpa Gyaltsen. Woodblocks were made at the requests of Gyaltsap Jé, Tokden Jampal Gyatso, and Sempa Chenpo Kunsangpa. Work on the woodblocks began in the earth-pig year, six years after the parinirvāṇa of Jé Tsongkhapa (1425). The woodblocks were presented to Ganden during Gyaltsap Jé's seventh year as Ganden Throneholder. I presented a copy of the text to His Holiness and wrote the following verses on the first page of the text:

> This meaningful work bringing joy to the fortunate,
> which lays out the stages to be traveled
> within the quick path of extraordinary yogic practice
> leading to the place of the all-pervading, glorious Vajradhara,
> is presented to the supreme guide of samsara and nirvana
> by an old man whose mental ability is far too low
> to practice the unmistaken path to enlightenment,
> so difficult to encounter even within a billion eons.

On the twenty-fourth, seventy monks including the abbot and chant master of Gyütö Tantric College, who had come to attend His Holiness's discourse on the *Great Exposition of Secret Mantra*, came and presented me with a scarf and a token sum of money to symbolize the enlightened body, speech, and mind and recited prayers for my long life. To fulfill the requests of both tantric monasteries, I gave the initiations of sixty-two-deity Cakrasaṃvara in the tradition of the mahāsiddha Luipa to over a thousand monks, including the monks of the tantric monasteries and the three seats as well as to monks from Ladakh, Kinnaur, and Spiti. This initiation was given for two days after His Holiness's discourse on tantra in the hall of the Tibetan Children's Village.

On the twenty-ninth I gave the life entrustment of the protector Shukden to two monks of Sera Mé and one monk from Ganden Jangtsé in conjunction with my monthly propitiation offering to the protector. Just as I started to do the propitiation rituals, the monk Losang Dorjé of Dromo, who had come from Gangtok, brought me the first copy of the commentary to the biographical praise of the protector that I had composed. It was a very auspicious coincidence.

On the first day of the fifth month, a hundred monks from the Gyümé Tantric College came to my house and offered me a scarf and a sum as a token of the three representations. They recited the prayers to the sixteen arhats for my long life and asked me to make a strong intention to live a long life. I replied that I would offer prayers to live long and advised the monks that they should observe the traditions of the lineage of the great masters of tantra.

On the ninth, I met the incarnation of Gangkar Lama of Seudru Monastery, who had come to Dharamsala once he had been recognized beyond doubt. The day he came to see me, the monks of Seudru Monastery invoked the presence of the Gadong oracle in a trance. Although the tulku was only five, he showed no apprehension or shyness in the presence of the oracle. The oracle gave him sips of his tea and a scarf and then picked him up to hold him in his lap, telling those present including Tārā Tulku, Geshé Yeshé Thupten, and other monks of Seudru Monastery that they should sever all their doubts about the incarnation and should make efforts to ensure the tulku's longevity.

Dakpo Bamchö had come from France and was staying in Dharamsala. At his request I gave the initiation of Cakrasaṃvara body mandala for two days to Rinpoché, Assistant Tutor Serkong Rinpoché, and seven others.

Beginning on the first day of the sixth month, I presided as vajra master over the fulfillment and confession ritual, together with an accumulation of tsok offerings, to the fivefold Dharmarāja Dorjé Drakden with the Nechung monks at their monastery. The rituals were made for seven days for the benefit of the religious and secular affairs of Tibet at the wishes of His Holiness.

On the fourth day of the sixth month, I gave novice ordination to a German man named Roland and to six Tibetans. I gave Roland the novice name Losang Kalden. When Losang Kalden left for Varanasi to study Tibetan Buddhism, I gave him a copy of the *Fifty Verses on Vinaya* on the vows and conduct of novices.[359] From the tenth I gave experiential teachings on the two stages of Vajrayoginī secretly to Assistant Tutor Serkong Rinpoché, Dakpo Bamchö Rinpoché, and Palden for seven days at the wish of the two Rinpochés.

Drakpa Samdrup was the son of the late Panglung Gyalchen Shukden medium, and at the urging of those monks from Pomra House of Sera Mé who were caretakers of the protector, I invoked Gyalchen in my residence several times in the hope that the protector would enter Drakpa Samdrup. There were a few signs that he had entered. After that I invited the local protector of Panglung, Tsengö Khaché Marpo. The signs were more evident than before, but he did not stay long, probably because the oracle had not been trained. I left it at that for the time being. It seemed that the protector would appear with further practice.

At the request of Assistant Tutor Serkong Rinpoché, I gave a White Tārā long-life initiation to Rinpoché and his attendants. Then, in the afternoons over a period of eight days, I gave an explanation of the *Middle-Length Stages of the Path* with my expanded outlines to Tsenshap Rinpoché, Dakpo Bamchö Rinpoché, Ratö Chubar Rinpoché, Thepo Tulku of Ganden Shartsé, Lati Rinpoché, and Geshé Rapten—eight of them all together. As all of them were very learned, I did not bother to explain the text word by word, as I would for beginners. Instead I explained the main points briefly and gave detailed instructions on meditation on certain points from my personal experience.

On the fourth day of the eighth month, I visited His Holiness at his request to offer the White Heruka long-life initiation according to the teachings of Mañjuśrī. From then on in the afternoons, over a period of fifteen days, I offered the experiential teachings and oral transmission of the *Middle-Length Stages of Path*, the *Easy Path*, the *Words of Mañjuśrī* according to the southern lineage, and the explanation of the notes on *Liberation in the Palm of Your Hand* simultaneously. After that I gave the initiation of the close lineage of longevity practice, the *Vajra Life-Tree of Immortality*, to His Holiness. This practice was given to the Third Dalai Lama, Sönam Gyatso, by Drupchen Palden Dorjé.

From the twenty-third, for three days, I completed the explanation and oral transmission of the *Great Treatise on the Stages of the Path* that I had previously begun giving to Kyabjé Ling Rinpoché.[360] Tutor Kyabjé Ling Rinpoché is a master of all the teachings of sutra and tantra and remains a teacher continuously giving teachings, which he has thoroughly perceived, to his disciples, and when I gave him this explanation, I added nothing new to his knowledge. Therefore, instead of explaining the words, I offered him an explanation for the methods of meditating on the points of the teachings. With this brief explanation, I made offerings to please him.

At the wish of Assistant Tutor Serkong Rinpoché, I gave the transmission of two chapters from the Iron Fortress cycle found within the sealed writings of Paṇchen Chökyi Gyaltsen, which included the ritual of the sixty-four-part torma offering known as the *Magical Wheel of the Blazing Weapon of Death*, and so on, as well as a work composed by myself on a site ritual known as the *Iron Fortress Sixty-Four-Part Ritual with Reliance upon External Dharmarāja*,[361] together with the recitations.

Mussoorie and Delhi

At the invitation of the Central School for Tibetans and the Tibetan Homes Foundation, I left Dharamsala for Mussoorie on the seventh day of the ninth month. The next day I arrived at the Tibetan monastery in Mussoorie. The following morning, on the tenth, Sakya Dakchen Rinpoché of Drölma Phodrang came to visit me and asked me to come to visit the center in Rajpur on my return to Dharamsala. In the afternoon, at the wish of Gomo Tulku, I gave the blessing of the four sindūra initiations of Vajrayoginī to about a hundred people in the assembly hall of the monastery. The next day I paid a visit to Dakchen Rinpoché. Although Rinpoché was very young, his learning and behavior revealed the true nature of this lineage inherited from Khön Mañjuśrī. I was very pleased and was moved with respect.[362]

Thereafter I gave a White Tārā long-life initiation and the oral transmission of the *Three Principal Aspects of the Path* to the boys and girls of the school and the homes as well as to a large crowd from the Mussoorie area. At the end I advised the students on the importance of their religious and secular studies. I gave lay, prenovice, and novice ordination to sixty-two boys and one girl and presided over the monthly confession ceremony. Each day I visited the school and the homes and performed consecrations. On the seventeenth I left Mussoorie and was seen off by the principal and the director of the Central School for Tibetans and the Tibetan Homes Foundation, Mr. and Mrs. Taring, along with the teachers and the students.

On the way I went to Rajpur to visit the Sakya center as Sakya Dakchen

Rinpoché had requested. All together there were over fifty monks of all ages. I presented a sum of money with which to make offerings to them. I expressed my hope that they would uphold the pure Sakya tradition of sutra and tantra while living in perfect harmony. On the way back I spent one night in a hotel in Ambala and arrived in Dharamsala the following day.

On the twenty-eighth at the wish of Assistant Tutor Serkong Rinpoché I gave Rinpoché, his attendants, and Chokteng Ta Lama the blessing of the four sindūra initiations of Vajrayoginī and the oral transmission of the wrathful fire offering of Vajrabhairava in the tradition of the Gyümé Tantric College, which I had composed, along with the burial ritual.

On the first day of the tenth month, I participated in the blessings of the relics and printed prayers that were to be placed in the statues of Guru Rinpoché and Buddha Śākyamuni. This took place in His Holiness's residence. I gave a White Tārā long-life initiation and the oral transmission and some instructions on the practice of the Mahākāla prayer composed by Khedrup Jé, *Wish-Fulfilling Jewel*, to a few monks of Gyümé Tantric College, including the abbot and the chant master. I also gave instructions on the five points of protection and repulsion by the ten wrathful deities and offered instructions on the visualization of the rituals of protection, repulsion, and destruction to nine monks of Gyütö Tantric College, including the abbot and the chant master, who had come to do some ritual prayers for the success of religious and secular pursuits.

At one point, I offered His Holiness the initiation of Secret Hayagrīva in the system of Kyergang based on the text by Gyal Khenchen Drakpa Gyaltsen.[363]

Bakula Rinpoché from Ladakh came to see me and insisted that I should attend the annual twenty-fifth day of the tenth month commemoration that was to be held at the Ladakh Buddha Vihar in Delhi and would be sponsored by the Geluk Buddhist Cultural Society.[364] I left for Delhi on the twenty-second. At the meeting on the morning of the twenty-fifth, I delivered a lecture on the principal deeds of Jé Tsongkhapa, such as his discourses, dialectics, and compositions, and his pursuit of studies and learning. This was translated into English by Lobsang P. Lhalungpa. At the meeting Dr. Suni Sahib and Dr. Rao asked me questions concerning the deeds of Jé Tsongkhapa, and I replied accordingly. Attending the actual celebration of the event in the evening were the cabinet minister Dr. Karan Singh, ambassadors from countries such as Sri Lanka, as well as both foreigners and Tibetans. At this large gathering Dr. Singh, Bakula Rinpoché, and other dignitaries gave talks. I also gave a talk on the life of Jé Tsongkhapa and how the followers of the Geluk tradition combine study, contemplation, and meditation with scholarship, ethics, and compassion all as complementary to one another without any contradiction. This was again translated into English by Lobsang Lhalungpa. I left for Dharamsala on the evening of the twenty-seventh.

Averting Hindrances to His Holiness's Long Life

From the sixth of the eleventh month I gave experiential teachings over the course of three days on the *Seven-Point Mind Training* to Barshi Phuntsok Wangyal, the instructor of Tibetan medicine and astrology at the Astro-Medical Institute. Mr. Barshi had a profound and vast knowledge of this science of learning.

At the request of the *nyungné* fasting group, I gave a White Tārā long-life initiation and oral transmission of the essence of dependent origination mantra to a large gathering of people in the Avalokiteśvara temple in

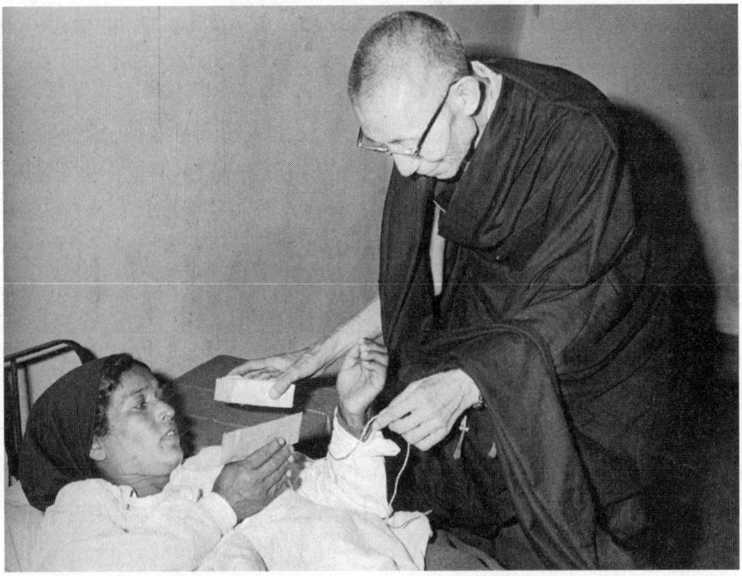

Trijang Rinpoché blessing a hospital patient in India, date unknown
COURTESY OF PALDEN TSERING

upper Dharamsala.[365] As part of my explanation of this four-line verse, which starts with the line "All things originate from causes," I presented the meaning of the four noble truths in both their forward (evolution) and reverse (involution) order. I also explained the meaning of the six-syllable *maṇi* mantra.

On the nineteenth, His Holiness came to visit me and gave me some long-life pills and other substances from his retreat practice of long-life White Heruka. He related to me his auspicious dreams during his Vajrabhairava retreat. His Holiness discussed with me some points of interpretation he was not clear about after reading Jé Tsongkhapa's *Great Commentary on Fundamental Wisdom*, *Clarifying the Intent of the Middle Way*, and *Essence of Eloquence.* I was deeply moved with faith and truly impressed with his understanding, which was a manifestation of the qualities of the supreme masters.

On the twenty-fifth day of the eleventh month, I gave the blessing of the four sindūra initiations of Vajrayoginī to Sherpa Karma Wangchuk, the Dromo monk Chödar, and others. As His Holiness's thirty-seventh year, considered year of obstacles, was approaching, I proceeded to perform the long-life retreat of White Tārā starting on the fifth day of the twelfth month. On the eighth I attended the auspicious confession ceremony at the completion of the statues of the Buddha and Guru Rinpoché installed at the Thekchen Chöling temple. I presented His Holiness with 320 different types of sacred relics of Indian and Tibetan great realized masters. As mentioned earlier, I had received some of these relics from the Tibetan government's relics box when I was engaged in the task of making His Holiness the Thirteenth Dalai Lama's golden memorial stupa. Others were relics I was able to accumulate from most reliable sources during my pilgrimages to holy places. I presented these to His Holiness in separate yellow brocade bags of the relics divided into Indian, Sakya, Geluk, Kagyü, and Nyingma sources along with a catalog of their contents.

Beginning on the tenth, I attended the elaborate three-day consecration performed in conjunction with the Cakrasaṃvara ritual with thirty-two monks, including the abbot and the chant master of Gyütö Tantric College. This was presided over by His Holiness, and all stages—the preparation, the actual consecration, and the conclusion—were performed in the most effective manner so that the wisdom beings should become indivisible with the statues—the commitment beings.[366] On the thirteenth, I invited the monks of Gyütö Tantric College to my house, where they performed purification and consecration rituals. In the afternoon I gave instructions on the purpose and the significance of the mundane and supramundane purification and elimination rituals of the elaborate consecration. I also explained the meaning of the Iron Fortress of the sixty-four-part torma offering and the significance of the number of tormas in these rituals according to the instructions and traditions of past lamas.

On the twenty-third, Tsurphu Karmapa Rinpoché along with the Shamar, Kathok Situ, Drungpa Gyaltsab, and Kongtrul Rinpochés[367] came to visit me, and I offered a dinner in their honor. Karmapa Rinpoché asked me to compose a long-life prayer for His Holiness because His Holiness was approaching his perilous thirty-seventh year. At his wish I composed a prayer in conjunction with supplications to the sixteen arhats. It was entitled the *Long-Life Prayer of the Melodious Words of Truth.*[368]

In 1970, the iron-dog year, I entered my seventieth year. On the ninth day of the first Tibetan month (February 13), I presided over a long-life ceremony of the five secret deities of Amitāyus with the Halting the Ḍākinī's Escort ritual offered to His Holiness by the staff of the Central Tibetan Administration, representatives of the four lineages, and the Assembly of Tibetan People's Deputies. This long-life ritual was based on the divine visions of Takphu Garwang.[369]

On the fifteenth, at the request of Kachen Losang Gyaltsen, I composed a biographical supplication to Lochen Tulku of Tashi Lhunpo. I based this supplication on a previous edition of the biographies of the Paṇchen Lamas. I presented the text to Lochen Tulku with a scarf.

I gave the permission of Secret Hayagrīva and a distant lineage of Amitāyus long-life ritual to Rikya Rinpoché and his attendants from Sera Jé. At the request of the monk Losang Dorjé of Dungkar Monastery in Dromo, I gave the initiations of the Cakrasaṃvara body mandala in the Ghaṇṭāpāda tradition to Losang Dorjé, Ngakram Tsering Wangdü of Tashi Lhunpo, and the three others. As Losang Dorjé was to do a retreat of the Cakrasaṃvara body mandala, I gave him detailed instructions on the retreat procedure.

For some time I had been having persistent disturbing dreams due to certain spirits. I therefore asked Song Rinpoché and two monks who had done the retreat of Hayagrīva to perform remedial rituals. On the ninth day of the second month, after three days of rituals, an effigy with various types of gifts was sent away to pacify the spirits. I also recited the *Heart Sutra* many times and meditated on the ultimate lack of inherent existence of the disturbances and on how their nature on a relative level is as illusory and deceptive as a dream. As I did this contemplation to dissolve the effects of the harm, my unpleasant dreams ceased.

Over one hundred people from the Chatreng area were gathered in Dharamsala for the Kālacakra initiation to be given by His Holiness around the fifteenth day of the second month. At their insistence, they offered me a long-life ceremony, which was performed with a *Guru Puja* and tsok offering conducted by some monks and presided over by Song Rinpoché. The group offered me a sum of 2,100 rupees as a gift. I kept 600 rupees and offered 1,500 rupees to the general fund of the Chatreng association, supplementing the 2,000 rupees I had given previously.[370]

At the request of the Kālacakra sponsors Amdowa Jinpa Gyatso from the Tibetan monastery in Bodhgaya and Pasho Thupten, Kyabjé Ling Rinpoché gave the permission to practice Avalokiteśvara Who Liberates from All Lower Realms one morning, and then I gave the permission of the twenty-one Tārās in the system of Atiśa. These were attended by over twenty thousand people who had come for the Kālacakra initiation at the Thekchen Chöling temple.

On the thirtieth, at the request of the nun Ngawang Paldrön, I gave Mahayana one-day precepts to a large gathering at the temple.

Searching for the Reincarnation of Kyabjé Phabongkha Rinpoché

On the eighth day of the third month I invoked the protector Shukden through the medium of Lhokha Riwo Chöling Monastery for prophetic advice on the discovery of the new incarnation of the late supreme incarnation of Kyabjé Phabongkha Vajradhara. The protector said the indications would be revealed but did not give specific details. Early the next day I had a dream of the late regent Takdrak Rinpoché sitting in a ceremonial hall flooded with sunlight. He seemed very pleased to see me and advised me that I would live long and work for the service of the Dharma. In my reply I told him that due to my old age I did not hold out much hope of serving the Dharma. I also told him that the late supreme incarnation passed away suddenly even though I had had great hopes in him, as he had acquired the qualities of learning, ethics, and compassion. Other young incarnations have not become mature in their learning, and therefore the state of the upholders of the Geluk tradition is grim. I told him this in great despair. In reply he said, "The verse of your poem—'The *mai-na-ka* manifested by the might of the ten forces'—was excellent." He said this emphatically so that even in the dream I repeated the line "The manifestation of *ka-da-ka* by the might of the ten forces" again and again. Later it turned out that these syllables formed part of the name of the new incarnation's mother.

On the twenty-second I invoked Shukden through the medium of the Ganden Chöphel Ling Tibetan monastery in Nepal. He said that the incarnation had been born the previous year and he was nearly twenty-two months old. Now we know that this corresponded to the date of the birth of the young incarnation, who was born on the fourth day of the seventh month of the bird year.

Starting on the twenty-third, I gave experiential teachings to His Holiness and Assistant Tutor Serkong Rinpoché on the generation and completion stages of the controlling force of the Jetsun Kurukulle based on the writings of Dergé Shar Lama Kunga Palden.[371] I gave these teaching in the manner of the fourfold explanations in accordance with the traditions of the lamas. At the same time I offered them the oral transmission of the *Flow of the River Ganges* on the permissions of the Thirteen Golden Dharmas of Sakya formulated by Takphu Garwang Rinpoché.

From the third day of the fourth month, I stopped receiving visitors so that I could perform a retreat on the sixteen drops of the Kadam lineage at the instruction of His Holiness.[372] Subsequently I did a retreat on the White Tārā longevity practice for His Holiness's long life. I concluded the retreats on the twenty-fourth of the second fourth month.[373]

At the wish of the monk Tenzin Chöphel from Hungary, I gave him and a few others the initiation of single-deity Vajrabhairava and the blessing of the four sindūra initiations of Vajrayoginī. On the fifteenth day of the sixth month, I offered the initiation of the sixteen drops of the Kadam lineage based on the writings of Kachen Yeshé Gyaltsen and Ngulchu Dharmabhadra.

Beginning on the sixteenth, I gave experiential teachings for six days to Dzemé Rinpoché on the generation and completion stages of Jetsun Kurukulle based on the writing of Dergé Shar Lama. In this teaching I followed the tradition of "letting go of mental fixation" and so forth.[374]

Subsequently I gave Dzemé Rinpoché explanations on the following teachings: the Amitāyus root text *Life Accomplishment of Kurava* by Jé Tsongkhapa,[375] the *Life Accomplishment in Verse* by Phabongkha Vajradhara,[376] the Amitāyus life accomplishment based on the two commentaries by Jé Sherap Gyatso,[377] meditation and recitation of Samayavajra from *Twenty-One Short Works on Guhyasamāja* by Jé Tsongkhapa, teachings on the Vajraḍāka fire offering, teachings on Avalokiteśvara according to the Nyen Tsembu tradition[378] by Changkya Rölpai Dorjé, teachings on the Mitrayogin system of Avalokiteśvara using the *Three Essential Moments* explanation of Jamyang Shepa Jikmé Wangpo,[379] as well as teachings on the blessing of speech by Jé Sherap Gyatso.

At the request of the Hungarian monk Tenzin Chöphel and the German monk Losang Kalden, I spoke to them before they returned to their countries on the need to regularly apply the opponents to the three poisons, on the way to examine one's body, speech, and mind, as well as on a brief introduction to the Middle Way view. These were recorded on tape.

From the first day of the seventh month I gave Ratö Chubar Rinpoché, Dzemé Rinpoché, Lati Rinpoché, and my attendant Palden long-life initiations with the blessings of the four initiations of the twenty-three deities of Secret Wrathful Amitāyus in the system of Drupgyal, the nine red deities in the *Very Secret Instructions of Rechungpa*, and nine deities of Amitāyus.

At the invitation of the commander and the troops of the defense training establishment in Dehradun, I left Dharamsala on the twelfth day of the eighth month, and traveling by various modes of public transport, I arrived at the base camp in Chakrata the next day. On the fifteenth, four thousand Tibetans, including the officers and the trainees of the 22nd Establishment and some students, gathered in the training camps. There I gave them the permission of Avalokiteśvara Liberating from All Lower Realms. The next day I gave them an Amitāyus long-life initiation in the system of Drupgyal.

On the following days I met some high-ranking Indian military advisors. I visited the chapels of the individual companies and gave teachings and oral transmissions. I also visited the army school and the hospital and gave appropriate teachings and advice. I left the establishment on the twentieth, and on my return trip I visited with disabled servicemen and with some wives of the personnel at the handicraft unit. There I gave teachings and performed a consecration and the like. Then, leaving via Saharanpur and so forth, I arrived in Dharamsala the following day, on the twenty-first.

More Teachings to His Holiness

Beginning on the first day of the ninth month, I offered His Holiness experiential teachings for three days on the root text of the "close lineage" of Takphu's divine visions of the practice of Cittamaṇi Tārā combined with Phabongkha Vajradhara's writings on the generation and completion stages of the practice. I offered him experiential teachings on the two stages of Vajrayoginī using the Vajrayoginī sādhana called *Quick Path to Great Bliss*[380] as the base text and giving oral transmissions of the commentaries on the two stages by Takphu, Ngulchu, and the Shalu Trisur Losang Khyenrap. With these four used for a single purpose, I gave the explanation from memory. I offered these teachings for seven days with the wish to "cut fabrications" and "let go of mental fixation" in accordance with the Sakya tradition. I offered His Holiness the permission for the mantra extraction of Vajrayoginī and the oral transmission Causing the Rain of Goodness to Fall and other ritual practices of Cittamaṇi Tārā. Following this, when Kyabjé Ling Rinpoché offered His Holiness the performance-tantra initiation Vairocana Abhisaṃbodhi, I also had the great fortune to attend the initiation to enforce the fruition of liberation.[381]

I offered a contribution of five thousand rupees and a set of gilded bronze statues of Jé Tsongkhapa and his main disciples complete with pandit hats and robes for the main assembly hall being constructed at Ganden Monastery. The statue of Jé Tsongkhapa measured two feet eight inches including the lotus seat, and the statues of the two disciples measured two feet and five inches including the cushions.

Mongolian Lama Guru Deva came to visit me on the twenty-fourth. He had just returned from a trip to Ulan Bator, where he had attended a religious conference. He gave me the collected works of Chahar Geshé Losang Tsultrim in ten volumes, a definitive clarification on the stages of the path by the Mongolian Losang Dorjé, a book comparing the establishment of the two truths in the four tenets schools, a definitive clarification of the *Treasury of Abhidharma* written by Palden Chöjé, biographies of Paṇchen Sönam Drakpa and Shukden written by the hermit Lhawang Gyatso and others, and a volume on the stages of the path by Thoyön Lama Döndrup Gyaltsen. He also gave me a pair of large vertically played cymbals. I was delighted to receive the invaluable books, more precious than gold.

By this time, novice monk Thupten Phelgyé [a.k.a. Drakpa Samdrup], the son of the late medium of Panglung Hermitage, was reliably receiving Shukden and his retinue in trance. On the twenty-sixth we invoked Shukden, Setrap, Chingkarwa, and Yumar Tsengö in succession. I requested of them their dutiful protection, bound them to their oaths, and formally accepted the new medium in the presence of the incarnation of Dromo Geshé Rinpoché, Ratö Rinpoché, and others.

Exchanging Teachings with Kyabjé Ling Rinpoché in Bodhgaya

On the fourth of the tenth month I left for Bodhgaya. On the sixth Tutor Kyabjé Ling Rinpoché's labrang sponsored a long-life ceremony for me. This was held in the assembly hall of the Tibetan monastery, and the monks performed the tsok offering ritual. At the ceremony, Kyabjé Ling Rinpoché presented me with the eight auspicious symbols and substances along with melodious, descriptive verses.

In fulfillment of my previous request, the incomparable and dauntless master of the profound meaning of secret tantra, Tutor Kyabjé Ling Vajradhara, on the eighth began giving me alone teachings on and the oral transmission of Jé Tsongkhapa's *Great Exposition of Secret Mantra*. He gave me the teachings every day from two in the afternoon until late in the evening without any breaks. Remembering the essential benefits of making offerings to the Three Refuges, I made daily offerings of over ten thousand butter lamps at the stupa. On the fifteenth I made offerings to the monks for the entire day and contributed a thousand rupees for the new murals on the inner walls of the monastery's assembly hall. In the afternoon I requested Kyabjé Ling Rinpoché to preside over the thousandfold offerings I made at the Mahābodhi stupa on behalf of all those connected with me, both living and dead. The teaching on the *Great Exposition of Secret Mantra* concluded on the sixteenth. Maintaining the form of even a mere human being becomes very meaningful when that form becomes the vessel in which to receive the nectar of the great secret teaching that is the life-sustaining essence of peerless liberation.

The next day at the request of the monk Tsöndrü Gyatso of the Tibetan monastery in Bodhgaya, I gave the blessing of the four sindūra initiations of Vajrayoginī to fifty monks. On the eighteenth and nineteenth, I offered the initiations of the single-deity and thirteen-deity Vajrabhairava in the cloth-drawn mandala to Kyabjé Ling Rinpoché alone. As Kyabjé Ling Rinpoché is a master of the twenty inner and outer qualities of a vajra master, I did not bother to give elaborate explanations of the initiations and offered the initiation in a brief manner.

On the twentieth, I invited Kyabjé Ling Rinpoché to preside over a long-life ceremony in conjunction with a tsok offering conducted by the monks in the assembly hall of the monastery. I made sincere requests to Kyabjé Ling Rinpoché to firmly plant his feet on the ground throughout existence and made some material offerings. On the twenty-first, at the wish of Kyabjé Ling Rinpoché and the request of the monks, I gave teachings and the oral transmission of the *Hundred Deities of Tuṣita* and the *Foundation of All Good Qualities* to over two hundred disciples.

The following day I departed for Varanasi. On the twenty-fifth, at the request of Ama Mikmar Drölma, I gave the blessing of the four sindūra initiations of Vajrayoginī at the Tibetan monastery to over two hundred disciples, including tulkus and geshés who were students at the Institute of Higher Tibetan Studies in Sarnath. In the evening I made the thousand-fold offering at the holy stupa. The next day I gave the oral transmission of my commentary to the biographical praises of Shukden to Song Rinpoché, Assistant Tutor Serkong Rinpoché, Chamdo Gyara Rinpoché, and Doboom Tulku of Trehor's Dargyé Monastery. On the eighth day of the eleventh month, I returned from Varanasi to Dharamsala via Delhi.

His Holiness's Retreat

To avert any obstacles to His Holiness's long life during his thirty-seventh year, I did a retreat of the thirty-three peaceful deities of inner Amitāyus in the system of Drupgyal beginning on the twenty-seventh of the eleventh month. During this time I did not receive any visitors.

On the tenth day of the twelfth month, His Holiness sent me a letter informing me of his wish to do daily practice of the completion stage in conjunction with the yoga of inner heat (*caṇḍālī*, Tib. *tumo*) in the six Dharmas of Nāropa, and he sent me 1,125 rupees for offerings on the tenth of every waxing and waning moon from that day forward, for three years and three half months. He told me to have a special lunch with this money on those offering days. In response to his great regard for me, which is like seeing a clod of earth as gold, I composed the following poems.

The wish-granting jewel of the three realms
has seen this lump of brass as gold,
and when this compassionate letter of generosity arrived,
joy, faith, and reverence all strove to surpass each other within me.

If this rotten old dog is granted a holiday
for a while by the messengers of death from the south,
the tenth-day meals granted to me for three years
will be devoured with tongue-smacking relish.

Inner heat's short *a* vowel is the cornerstone of the completion stage,
the mental sustenance of the siddhas of India and Tibet,
and the hook to gather emptiness and wind in the central channel.
Your embarking on such a practice is the way of supreme beings.

The inner woman Rati plays within the central channel,
and with the lightning-flash movement of her noose,
all proliferation is at once bound within the dharmadhātu.
Such a performance strikes me as truly wondrous.

This profound yoga of the completion stage
is weighted down by the essence of bliss and emptiness.
If sustained in a well-balanced way, without laxity or intensity
but consistently, it will definitely bring results.

These beautiful words, though colorful as a rainbow,
are not found upon examination; they are in nature emptiness.
This life wasted in deception and superficial activity
moves me to sorrow.

In 1971, the Tibetan iron-pig year, I turned seventy-one. On the second of March, the sixth day of the first Tibetan month, I performed the amending ritual fire offerings on the successful completion of the long-life retreat. On the thirteenth the ministers and the staff of the Central Tibetan Administration as well as the Tibetan People's Deputies offered an elaborate long-life ceremony with the ritual of White Tārā to His Holiness in order to pacify and eliminate the obstacles to his thirty-seventh year. After attending the ceremony, I visited His Holiness at his residence and paid my New Year respects to him.

Nyakré House of Ganden Shartsé Monastery had previously requested me to compose new rituals of propitiating, wealth gathering, and tsok offering to their protector Red Spear Vaiśravaṇa and his retinue.[382] This had been put off for several years, but now, due to definitive indications in my dreams of the protector's wish that I quickly write the rituals, I composed the rituals of propitiation and wealth gathering. I compiled the tsok offering from the writings of Thuken and sent the texts to Nyakré House.

Thepo Tulku, Lati Rinpoché, and others residing in Dharamsala received a letter from Ganden Shartsé Monastery asking them to make arrangements to offer me a long-life ceremony. Therefore, on the fourth day of the second month, forty tulkus and geshés, including Thepo Tulku and Lati Rinpoché, and other Shartsé monks on break from the Institute of Higher Tibetan Studies in Sarnath, offered me a *Guru Puja* with tsok offering and recited prayers for my long life.

At the wish of Assistant Tutor Serkong Rinpoché, I gave the initiation of the five-deity Cakrasaṃvara to a select group of nineteen tulkus and geshés, including Lochen Tulku, beginning on the nineteenth. At the request of Mongolian Lama Guru Deva, I gave experiential teachings on the *Easy Path* to seventeen senior tulkus and geshés. As this group was already well versed in the teachings and was learned, I did not elaborate on the general points of the teachings and gave instead a rather extensive discourse to draw meditational experience from visualizations. To conclude I performed the ceremony for generating bodhicitta. Lama Guru Deva sponsored a tsok offering and, as an offering for the bodhicitta ceremony, presented me a copy of the *Great Treatise on the Stages of the Path* written in gold.

On the tenth day of the third month, I gave the blessing of the four sindūra initiations of Vajrayoginī to Barshi Jampa Tenkyong before he emigrated to Canada. Following that, for four days I gave experiential teachings on the six Dharmas of Nāropa, based on the writings of Trehor Naktsang, to the monk Losang Dorjé of Dungkar Monastery in Dromo. On the second day of the fourth month, at the request of Assistant Tutor Serkong Rinpoché, I gave the permissions of Garuḍa and of White Tārā Endowed with Nine Lineages[383] to a few tulkus. This was followed by teachings on Samayavajra from Jé Tsongkhapa's *Twenty-One Short Works on Guhyasamāja* and the ritual fire offerings of Vajraḍāka.

Jamgön Sakya Dakchen Rinpoché came to Dharamsala to offer a long-life ceremony to His Holiness. During his stay, we called on each other. I also met Chogyé Trichen Rinpoché of Nalendra and questioned him about the custom of preliminary meditation retreats as preparation for conferring initiations of the Compendium of All Tantras.[384] Rinpoché told me that when the initiations of the *Vajrāvalī* and Mitra Hundred are conferred separately, the mandala they have in common does not suffice to have one general initiation. He said that there are elaborate and abbreviated methods of doing the retreats of the deities, and they can be performed either individually or by combining groups of deities.

In the fifth month, I gave the permission to practice Avalokiteśvara Who Liberates from All Lower Realms at Namgyal Monastery to the abbot, the chant master, and the monks. I gave the permission of [an aspect of Avalokiteśvara called the] Black Liberating Standing Lion to Thubten Yeshe of Sera Jé's Tsawa House, his American student Losang Chökyi, and others. At the request of Thepo Tulku, I gave a permission of Four-Faced Mahākāla Time of Approximation.[385]

On the eighth of the seventh month, at the wish of Assistant Tutor Serkong Rinpoché, I gave the permission of Jé Rinpoché as the triple deity and teachings on the *Hundred Deities of Tuṣita* based on the commentary by the Seventh Dalai Lama Kalsang Gyatso, *Source of All Attainments*, to thirty tulkus and geshés. In the days following, at the wish of His Holiness, I gave various long-life initiations to His Holiness, Shakor Khentrul Nyima Gyaltsen, the abbot and chant master of Namgyal Monastery, Assistant Tutor Serkong Rinpoché, and other tulkus and geshés including hermits and the senior monks of Namgyal Monastery. These initiations included the preparation and initiation of the thirty-three peaceful deities of inner Amitāyus in the Drupgyal system, which was passed from Machik Drupai Gyalmo to Rechungpa. This initiation, in conjunction with the long-life empowerment, comes from the rituals of Amitāyus explained in the *Blue Book of Synonyms* of the Cakrasaṃvara explanatory tantras.[386]

Other initiations were the long-life empowerment in conjunction with blessing of the four initiations of the twenty-three wrathful deities of Secret Amitāyus, the nine red deities of Extremely Secret Amitāyus of Rechung, the long-life empowerment of nine white deities of Amitāyus, the long-life empowerment in conjunction with the blessings of the four initiations of the exclusive one deity and one vase of Red Amitāyus, and the permission of Samayavajra and consort as explained in Guhyasamāja. Each day after giving the long-life empowerment I gave teachings on and the oral transmission of the root text of the *Wheel of Sharp Weapons Mind Training*. As Dza Paltrul said:

> These days when I give teachings,
> it is an experience of narrating my own faults,
> like a ghost hypnotized by a mantra.
> How shameful is that!

This is how I also felt.

At the wish of His Holiness I also gave the preparation and initiation of the thirty-seven deities of the root Sarvavid tantra deriving from the ritual that removes negativities called *Victorious over the Three Realms*, which is the second section of the yoga tantra *Compendium of Reality* (*Tattvasaṃgraha*). This initiation was given in accordance with *Illuminating the Meaning of the Sarvavid Tantra*[387] by Dulzin Drakpa Gyaltsen and was attended by seven hundred people, including His Holiness, various tulkus and geshés, the Namgyal monks, and other monks and laypeople from Dharamsala and elsewhere.

At the request of the nun Losang Wangmo, a member of the staff of the Tibetan Children's Village, I gave the blessing of the four sindūra initiations of Vajrayoginī to three hundred disciples, including lamas, monks, and laypeople, in the Avalokiteśvara temple in upper Dharamsala.

One day I offered the oral transmission of Guhyasamāja texts such as the *Vajra Garland Tantra* (*Vajrāmālātantra*), *Explanation of the Intention* (*Sandhivyākaraṇa*), the *Vajra Wisdom Compendium* (*Vajrajñānasamuccaya*), and the *Tantra Requested by the Four Goddesses* (*Caturdevīparipṛcchātantra*).

On the seventeenth day of the eighth month, Kyabjé Ling Rinpoché and I, as part of a tsok, made extensive offerings to five hundred monks, including the monks of Gyütö and Gyümé tantric colleges who had come to receive his Holiness's teachings on four interwoven commentaries on the *Guhyasamāja Root Tantra*.[388] On this occasion I made material offerings dedicated with prayers that the presence of His Holiness's three secrets[389] be as solid as a vajra and that no negative circumstances arise in his obstacle year.

After His Holiness's discourse, at the request of Jangchup Gyaltsen of

Markham, I gave the initiation of the sixty-two deity Cakrasaṃvara in the system of the mahāsiddha Luipa. This was attended by His Holiness and seven hundred others, mostly monks, including the monks of Gyütö and Gyümé tantric colleges. During the initiation I gave full explanations of the stages of the initiation, even though I do not have even the complete qualities of a disciple let alone the qualities of a vajra master. In this present degenerate age, I am simply looked up to as a master like a nomad who reaches the front row because he is chased by dogs. I merely followed the traditions of the lineage of kind lamas.

13 | Twilight Years

Visit to the Tibetan Settlements in Southern India

In response to repeated invitations for some years by the nun Gyaltsen Palmo from the settlement in Mysore and various invitations from the monasteries and other Tibetan settlements, I left Dharamsala on the fourth day of the ninth month. I flew from Delhi to Bangalore, where I was met at the airport by the head of the settlement in Mundgod and by the abbots and administrators of the Sakya, Geluk, Kagyü, and Nyingma monasteries, including the major monasteries of Sera, Drepung, and Ganden. I spent a night in a government circuit house in Bangalore. The next morning, when I arrived at the Mysore settlement, I was greeted by the ordained and lay members of the communities. It was arranged for me to stay in His Holiness's residence.

At the request of the Jé and Mé colleges, I gave teachings at Sera Monastery on the *Three Principal Aspects of the Path*. Then, at the request of the nun Gyaltsen Palmo, I gave the complete initiation of single-deity Vajrabhairava. On the thirteenth I offered tea, bread, and five rupees to each of the Sera monks together with a ceremonial scarf. I offered one thousand rupees to the construction of a new assembly hall.

On that day I invoked protectors Shukden, Setrap, and Yumar Tsengö in trances through the new Panglung medium, Thupten Phelgyé, at which time the protector gave prophetic advice for a brief moment. On the fourteenth, I visited and made offerings at the Nyingma monastery Namdröling, the Sakya monastery, and the Geluk monastery Thekchen Chöling. At each monastery I gave teachings and performed consecrations. I also visited the administrative offices of the settlement as well as the hospital and the school and performed consecrations. On the sixteenth, I gave the permission of the Three Wrathful Forms Combined and the Amitāyus long-life initiation in the system of Drupgyal to a large gathering of monks and laypeople at the request of the settlement. These were given in the spacious green field in front of His Holiness's residence, and afterward I advised everyone to carry out their religious and secular duties in accord with the wishes of His Holiness.

The next day I visited the settlement in Hunsur and gave the oral transmission of the refuge verse, the *Praises to Tārā*, and His Holiness's long-life prayer to about eight hundred Tibetans who had come to the settlement from Gangtok. On the way I visited the future site of the headquarters for the Association for the Preservation of the Geluk Tradition as well as settlements 5 and 6 and performed consecrations.

On the eighteenth I gave prenovice and novice ordinations to eighty-three young monks of Sera Jé and Sera Mé. The following day the Sera Lachi administrations and the settlements offered me a long-life ceremony with *Guru Puja* and tsok offerings conducted by the monks. In the afternoon at the request of Sera Jé, I gave the permission of Lion-Faced Ḍākinī to the monks.

On the twentieth I left Bylakuppe by car for Mundgod and spent one night in a guesthouse at Shomogang. The next day when I arrived at the settlement in Mundgod, I was received by the Ganden, Drepung, Sakya, and Nyingma abbots and monks and by the officers and members of the settlement community. I stayed in His Holiness's residence. On the twenty-second, on the occasion of Lord Buddha's descent from the celestial realms, I performed the consecration of the statues of Jé Tsongkhapa and disciples that I had previously offered to the great assembly of Ganden Monastery. The statues were placed in a small chapel until the completion of the assembly hall. I offered seventeen thangkas complete with brocade borders and colored silk tassels to Ganden Shartsé. The thangkas included a depiction of the Buddha surrounded by the sixteen arhats and a set of Chinese embroidered thangkas depicting the lives of the Paṇchen Lamas.

In the following day, at the request of the administrations of Drepung and Ganden, I gave teachings based on the root text of the *Hundred Deities of Tuṣita* in the assembly hall of Ganden Jangtsé Monastery. I gave the permission of Lion-Faced Ḍākinī and teachings on the six-session guruyoga to the monks in the debate yard of Drepung Loseling. To sixty-five novices of Ganden and Drepung I gave prenovice and novice ordination. At the request of Ganden Shartsé I gave the permission of Jé Rinpoché as the triple deity to the monks of Ganden and Drepung. I visited Drepung Gomang and performed consecrations and gave the oral transmissions of the *Praise of Dependent Arising*. At the request of Ganden Jangtsé, I gave the permission of Palden Lhamo Maksorma. I offered tea, bread, and five rupees each with scarves to the Drepung, Ganden, Sakya, and Nyingma monks.

On the thirtieth the monasteries and the settlements offered me a long-life ceremony with a *Guru Puja* and tsok offering. On the first of the tenth month, I visited the retirement home, the hospital, the handicraft center, and the schools of the settlements. At each place I performed consecrations and offered words of advice. On the second, at the request of the settlements, I gave the permission of the Three Wrathful Forms Combined and the Amitāyus long-life initiation in the system of Drupgyal to a large gathering of tulkus, monks, and the public in the open area of the palace compound. I advised everyone that in their daily activities they should never do anything to undermine the wishes of His Holiness.

On the third I left Mundgod and went to Hubli and Bangalore by train. From Bangalore I flew to Delhi. In Delhi I stayed at the house of Mongolian Lama Guru Deva. On the eighth, at the request of Ama Chözom, proprietor of the York Hotel, I gave a long-life initiation of White Tārā to a large gathering of monks and laypeople at the Ladakh Buddha Vihar. On the tenth I left Delhi for Dharamsala, and on the fourteenth I paid my respects to His Holiness.

Indo-Pakistani Conflict

In the afternoon of the sixteenth, a border conflict broke out between India and Pakistan, and for a few days everyone lived in a state of anxiety. On the night of the twentieth, having just drafted a letter to the manager of Phabongkha Labrang, Trinlé Dargyé, about the final determination for the recognition of the incarnation, I dreamed of my refuge and protector Kyabjé Phabongkha Vajradhara. He was sitting on a lofty throne, and the benefactor Lady Lhalu Lhacham Yangzom Tsering[390] presented him with a scarf in an elaborate ceremony. Lama Vajradhara wore a ceremonial brocade gown, which he showed to me holding it up by the collar. Proudly he told me that he was dressed up for his birthday celebration.

Dagyab Hothokthu Rinpoché came to Dharamsala from Germany and stayed at our house. At his request, beginning on the eighteenth day of the eleventh month, I gave fifteen days of teachings on the *Middle-Length Stages of the Path* to Rinpoché and others, including Sera Jé Khamlung Tulku, Gönsar Tulku, Trehor Thupten Tulku, Sera Mé Sharpa Tulku, Sera Jé Trehor Geshé Ngawang Dargyey, Loseling Jangmar Tulku, and Ganden Shartsé Geshé Asong. Then I gave the blessing of the four sindūra initiations of Vajrayoginī to Rinpoché and a few others. Again I gave initiation of the sixteen drops of the Kadam lineage to twenty-nine tulkus and geshés including Rinpoché, Loseling Denma Lochö Rinpoché, and Ratö Chubar Rinpoché. I gave the oral transmission of the commentary to the praise of Shukden to nine tulkus and geshés, including Rinpoché himself. To Rinpoché alone, I taught on the long-life practice of Amitāyus based on the following four commentaries: the root text by Jé Rinpoché, a long-life practice compiled by Phabongkha Vajradhara, and two commentarial texts of the practice from the collected works of Jé Sherap Gyatso.[391] After these teachings Rinpoché returned to Germany.

The Tibetan water-bird year, 1972, was my seventy-second year. On the morning of February 15, the first day of the Tibetan year, I offered His Holiness the substances of longevity from my White Tārā long-life retreat. During the Annual Prayer Festival at the Thekchen Chöling temple, in the morning discourse on the tenth, I fulfilled the instructions of His Holiness by explaining the reasons for and the benefits of Mahayana mind training, the methods for practicing of the six perfections, and the way they should be practiced when following in the footsteps of the past buddhas, in conjunction with the oral teachings on the stages of the path. I covered these topics in my prefatory comments to a discourse on the *Garland of Birth Stories*—the past lives of the Buddha—in accord with the traditions of past masters. This discourse was attended by a large number of monks and laypeople. During the noon tea session, I led the prayers of refuge and bodhicitta. In the afternoon dry assembly, I led the dedication prayers and recited the *Prayer for the Teachings to Flourish* and the *Prayer for Rebirth in Sukhāvatī* in accordance with the tradition. On the twelfth I made offerings of tea, a meal of rice, and money to 550 monks attending the prayer festival, thus accumulating merit.

On the fifteenth, His Holiness presided over the sessions, and I attended them all from early morning throughout the day, including the confession ceremony. While attending the sessions, I reflected on the great qualities and achievements of both the Buddha and Mañjuśrī Lama Tsongkhapa, and I offered sincere prayers to the best of my ability.

On the sixth day of the second month, at the request of Yangdhar Chözin of Chatreng, Galu Losang Gyaltsen, and Töpa Kako Tashi, I gave the permission of Avalokiteśvara Who Liberates from All Lower Realms to a large number of monks and laypeople who had come to receive His Holiness's teachings on the stages of the path at the Thekchen Chöling temple. At the request of the Lhasa nun Thupten Chödrön and Yangdhar Chözin of Chatreng, I gave the blessing of the four sindūra initiations of Vajrayoginī to six hundred monastics, including abbots and ex-abbots of the three seats and the two tantric monasteries, and to tulkus and two hundred laypeople. The following day, I gave experiential teachings on the two stages of Vajrayoginī to six hundred disciples who pledged to perform the retreat of the deity in addition to upholding a daily sādhana commitment. I gave teachings for seven days with four explanations, as is done in the Sakya tradition. At the conclusion of this discourse, for auspicious reasons, I gave an explanation and oral transmission of the long-life practice by way of vajra recitation with breath yoga.

I sent three thousand rupees through the former chant master of Ganden Jangtsé, who was returning to Mundgod, as a contribution to new statues being made, and an excellent pair of antique cymbals to be presented to Jangtsé College. Starting the thirteenth day of the third month, at the request of the two tantric monasteries, I gave teachings on the six Dharmas of Nāropa based on the commentary of Jé Tsongkhapa entitled *Endowed with the Three Convictions* and the teachings of Trehor Naktsang Tenpa Dargyé along with physical exercise yogas to 715 people, including abbots, masters, senior geshés, and resident monks from Dharamsala as well as tulkus and monks from other places. Although I lacked the confidence of having valid experience of them, I delivered the oral teachings of the compassionate lamas like a messenger. As there were many learned geshés and hermits present, I held the hope that they would preserve and make the teachings known through further explanations and practice.

Afterward, to the same group, I gave the permissions of the deities from the close lineage of the cycle of Mañjuśrī teachings that Lama Umapa transmitted to Jé Tsongkhapa and the permission of the thirteen aspects of Six-Armed Mahākāla. I also gave the oral transmission of the following:

the Luipa tradition of Cakrasaṃvara's self- and front-generation, initiation ritual, site ritual, and ritual fire offerings, Gyümé Tantric College's manual of the Iron Fortress ritual, its supplement, and the eight major explanations, the Magical Wheel of Stacked Vajras Mountain for dispelling spirits, the ritual fire offering of the force of Vajrabhairava, Gyütö Tantric College's supplement to the consecration ritual in conjunction with Cakrasaṃvara and Guhyasamāja, Thuken's self- and front-generation of Secret Hayagrīva, the propitiation of Hayagrīva, its spirit-dispelling ritual, Throneholder Tenpa Rapgyé's White Mahākāla treasure-vase ritual, and teachings on *Fifty Verses on Guru Devotion*, the *Twenty Verses on the Bodhisattva Vow*, and verses on the root and secondary tantric downfalls.

To three hundred disciples, including the above group, I gave the common torma initiation and uncommon body-mandala initiation of Cittamaṇi Tārā at the request of Drakgyab Ngawang Tsephel. After this I gave the permission of the mantra extraction of Vajrayoginī to forty-six tulkus and monks.

Confirming the Recognition of the Third Phabongkha Rinpoché

On the eighth I mailed Trinlé Dargyé, the manager of Phabongkha Labrang, the unanimous determinations along with the questions regarding the incarnation of the late supreme incarnation of Kyabjé Phabongkha Vajradhara. The results of His Holiness and Kyabjé Ling Rinpoché's divinations as well as my own divinations and dreams and the predictions of the Gadong oracle and Shukden all agreed on the same candidate, Sönam Gyatso. He was born in Darjeeling to Drölkar and Tsewang Norbu. The parents ran the Lhasa Restaurant at Shipal Dora in Darjeeling. Together with a letter and so on, I sent a sum of money as a token of the three representations and a verse of auspiciousness.

On the second day of the fifth month, Khemé Sönam Wangdü of the Kunsangtsé family fell ill for a few days. All the members of our labrang did their best to provide medical treatment for him and make religious offerings. Despite our efforts, he passed away in dignity. He had reached the age of seventy-three and had been sick with various illnesses. When his condition became acute, I visited him, instructed him to reflect on virtuous topics, and recited sacred mantras into his ear. After he had passed away, I offered prayers on his behalf. As I am the only surviving member of the Kunsangtsé family and descendent of the Gungthang estate, I did all the things that were necessary and disposed of all his belongings for virtuous purposes, wasting nothing.

Starting on the third day of the sixth month, I did a retreat on Guhyasamāja in the Mañjuvajra system of Jñānapāda at the wish of His Holiness. I saw no visitors during the retreat.

On the tenth I received a letter from Trinlé Dargyé in which he said that although the incarnation was only thirty-four months old, his bearing was dignified during the recognition ceremony at which robes were put on him and a long-life ceremony offered. Trinlé Dargyé also mentioned that the incarnation was relaxed and smiling with him, as if he had known him as his manager for a long time. These seemed like clear indications of instincts from his predecessor. Trinlé Dargyé was very pleased with how well everything went during the ceremonies, and he sent me photos of the incarnation. I was naturally filled with joy and felt relieved of a great burden of responsibility.

On the twenty-eighth day of the seventh month, I finished my retreat and did the compensating ritual fire offering. From the twelfth day of the eighth month, I did a retreat of Jinasāgara Avalokiteśvara, which is among the one hundred special mandalas of the mahāsiddha Mitrayogin. Upon the conclusion of the retreat I did the ritual fire offering.

One day, at the request of Barkham Shodo Dragom Tulku, I gave him the life entrustment of the protector Shukden and oral transmission of the ritual practices of the protector. Dragom Tulku's predecessor was not only a Dharma friend but was also responsible for requesting many of the rituals of the protector in writing. Shukden was his main protector. I also lent Dragom Tulku my notes on the special points of the visualizations for the Shukden retreat.

On the fourth of the tenth month I gave prenovice and novice ordinations to Nadia from France and gave her the ordination name Losang Chödrön. Beginning on the fifteenth, I offered His Holiness a number of permissions starting with the common torma initiation and the exclusive body-mandala initiation of Cittamaṇi Tārā together with the most secret Heart Absorption permission. I went on to offer him the permissions of the seventeen emanations of Four-Faced Mahākāla Robber of Strength[392] in order, including Split Faces, Striking the Vital Point, and Secret Accomplishment but excluding Entrusted Black Brahman.[393]

Bodhgaya and Sarnath

On the twenty-first, I left Dharamsala for Bodhgaya with Palden and Norbu Chöphel. The illuminator of the practice lineage, Gyalwang Karmapa Rinpoché, was also in Bodhgaya. Because of our close connections, we were very pleased to see each other and visited one another several times.

From the ninth of the eleventh month, at the request of Chatreng Jungné, I gave the permission of Avalokiteśvara Who Liberates from All Lower Realms, and at the requests of the Shedra family bursar Mr. Manithang and his wife, I gave the blessing of the four sindūra initiations of Vajrayoginī to 150 people in the assembly hall of the Tibetan monastery. Also at the request of the monk Tsöndrü Gyatso of the Tibetan monastery, I gave experiential teachings on the two stages of Vajrayoginī to ninety-one disciples, who took the commitment to do the retreat of the deity.

On the morning of the seventeenth, the incarnation of Phabongkha Rinpoché and Trinlé Dargyé showed up from Darjeeling to meet me. I received them in my quarters. That day it so happened that I was to give the initiation of long-life deity White Heruka from the teachings of Mañjuśrī to Sera Jé Rikya Tulku, the abbot of the monastery in Tawang in the Mön region. The incarnation and Trinlé Dargyé also attended the initiation. When I was seven years old, Kyabjé Phabongkha Vajradhara was staying in our hermitage at Chusang. At the request of the late kind Ngakrampa, he gave the complete set of permissions of the cycle of Mañjuśrī teachings, and I received these as my first teachings from him. The coincidence that I was to give the White Heruka long-life initiation when I met the young incarnation for the first time felt like an auspicious indication of the continuous golden samaya bond with my most kind lama, who compassionately cares for me throughout my successive lives. Not only that, Heruka Cakrasaṃvara was the principal practice deity of Kyabjé Phabongkha Rinpoché.

On the eighteenth I paid my respects to the feet of Kyabjé Ling Rinpoché, who arrived in Bodhgaya after showering a rain of profound, vast, and magnificent teachings on the fortunate disciples in the Mysore area in South India. On the twenty-second, Kyabjé Ling Rinpoché's labrang sponsored a long-life ceremony for me. This was done in conjunction with a *Guru Puja* and tsok offering conducted by both monks resident in Bodhgaya and those who had gathered from various places. During the ceremony Kyabjé Ling Rinpoché presented the eight auspicious symbols and substances to me, thus making firm the vajra-pillar of life. Afterward, I took the first snip of hair of the young incarnation and bestowed on him the name Losang Thupten Trinlé Kunkhyap with a scarf. At the request of Kyabjé Ling Rinpoché I offered him experiential teachings on the profound path of the *Guru Puja* based on the root text and Kachen Yeshé Gyaltsen's commentary, teaching continuously until I had completed the explanation. In this way I made offerings of practice to the lama. On the twenty-fourth our labrang sponsored a long-life ceremony in conjunction with a *Guru Puja* and tsok offering to Kyabjé Ling Rinpoché, so that his feet might be firmly planted in the nature of indestructibility. During the rituals conducted by the monks, I presented the eight auspicious symbols and substances to Rinpoché followed by material offerings.

On the twenty-fifth I gave the first teachings of the Tibetan alphabet to the incarnation. Along with a scarf and the three representations, I presented the following verse, which I wrote spontaneously:

> The young sun that was the supreme incarnation of Dechen Nyingpo,
> the most incomparable spiritual father, has set in the celestial sphere,
> but the enchanting smile on the beautiful face
> of the new moon of his reincarnation
> appearing over the eastern mountain of the fortunate
> makes this day a happy one.
>
> By hearing, contemplating, and meditating upon
> the great ocean of sutra and tantra literature,
> by holding the wonderful qualities of learning, ethics, and compassion,
> by performing wonderful deeds of preserving, developing,
> and propagating the teachings of the conqueror Losang,
> I pray and yearn that you emulate the life of the former incarnation.

The next day the monk Tsöndrü Gyatso, who was the disciplinarian of the Tibetan monastery, sponsored a long-life ceremony in conjunction with a *Guru Puja* and tsok offering to Tutor Ling Rinpoché and myself.

At the feet of Kyabjé Ling Rinpoché I received teachings on the Dharmarāja sixteen-point Iron Fortress ritual, ground ritual, and supplement in the tradition of Gyütö Tantric College and the *Iron Fortress of the Magical Wheel of the Torma Ritual* of Vajrabhairava composed in three parts by the predecessor of Kyabjé Ling Rinpoché. As I had already studied the diagrams of collected mantras, Rinpoché proceeded with the textual explanations without practical demonstration of the diagram lines. This was very convenient, as Rinpoché was very busy and his disciple indolent, caught up in distracting activities. At the wish of Kyabjé Rinpoché I offered explanations on the root text of the *Self-Accomplishment of the Peaceful and Wrathful Mañjuśrī*, the *Vajra Words* by Jé Tsongkhapa, and the commentary by Jamyang Shepa, the *Wish Fulfilling Hope of the Fortunate*. Then, for the benefit of all beings, especially those connected with me, I made a thousandfold offering at the stupa, presented an all-day food offering at the monastery, and donated a thousand rupees toward the rainy-season retreat. While staying in Bodhgaya, I offered over ten thousand butter lamps.

On the twenty-ninth I left Bodhgaya for Varanasi and stayed at Guru Deva's residence at the Chinese temple in Sarnath, where I met the incarnation of Kyabjé Phabongkha Vajradhara. For two days, many teachers and students from the Institute of Higher Tibetan Studies came to visit me, as did the incarnation of Dergé Dzokchen Pema Rikzin.[394] On the fourth of the twelfth month, at the request of a disciple from Phakri living in Bhutan, I gave a White Tārā long-life initiation to three hundred monks and laypeople at the Tibetan monastery. On the seventh, the incarnation of Kyabjé Vajradhara went back to Kalimpong. I presented Rinpoché with a thousand rupees, a ceremonial scarf, and a token sum of the three representations. I gave gifts to the manager as well as to the attendants and parents of Rinpoché and advised them regarding his education and proper care. On the eighth, I made daylong offerings to all the monks and thousandfold offerings at the stupa. I gave prenovice and novice ordinations to the students of the institute. At the request of Ashé Yangkyi, the mistress of the late King Jikmé Sengé Wangchuk of Bhutan, I gave a long-life initiation of White Tārā to five hundred people. I gave the permission of Secret

Hayagrīva according to the Kyergang tradition to Yangkyi and members of her family.

Lati Rinpoché came to see me. He had sponsored the teachings on Nāgārjuna's six treatises on reasoning and Āryadeva's *Four Hundred* (*Catuḥśataka*) given by His Holiness in Mundgod. Lati Rinpoché brought me a letter from Ganden Shartsé with the pictures of the gilded bronze statue of the Buddha that I had had made and presented to Shartsé to be their principal statue in the college's assembly hall. The statue is four feet wide at the base of the lotus seat, and it was made well, as I had hoped. The statue contains many rare and precious relics, including pieces of clothes and hair of many Indian and Tibetan masters, as well as printed prayers.

At the request of the Geluk Students Association of the Institute of Higher Tibetan Studies, starting the first day of the second twelfth month I taught for three days on Jé Tsongkhapa's *Three Principal Aspects of the Path* and gave the permission of Avalokiteśvara Who Liberates from All Lower Realms. This was attended by four hundred monks, including the geshés, students, tulkus, and other monks who had gathered there, as well as two hundred laypeople.

Shakabpa Wangchuk Deden came to visit me, and he left with me three volumes of his writings on the political history of Tibet and asked me to go over them and give my suggestions and comments. He told me that the library in Patna contained a history of Ganden Shartsé. As this text was very difficult to obtain in India, I dispatched Sokpa Achok Tulku and Thupten Gönpo of Shartsé to copy the manuscript. On the tenth, at the invitation of Samdhong Rinpoché of Drepung's Tsawa House, the principal of the institute, I went to his residence and gave him the life entrustment of Shukden in the morning and made tsok offerings in the afternoon. That day I made offerings of tea and money to all the teachers and students of the four traditions at the institute. I received the copy of the history of Shartsé in *khyuk* Tibetan script by Achok and Thupten Gönpo.

On the fifteenth I went to the banks of the Ganges River and released a large quantity of fish to save their lives from fisherman and dedicated prayers for the enlightenment of these creatures. As streams of pilgrims came to visit me without any break during my stay in Bodhgaya and Sarnath, it was very distracting and tired me out. On the twentieth, I left by night train for New Delhi and stayed at Guru Deva's house.

On March 5, 1973, the first day of the Tibetan water-ox year, my seventy-third year, the representative, director, and the staff of the Bureau of His Holiness in Delhi and Tibet House, as well as many Tibetans staying at Ladakh Buddha Vihar, came to give me New Year greetings.

With the help of Bakula Rinpoché of Ladakh, I went to the Wellington Hospital for a medical check-up. After the doctors had carefully examined me, they told me that my health was good. On the night of the ninth, I left for Dharamsala by train and arrived at my house, Tashi Rabten. The following day Kyabjé Ling Rinpoché and his entourage arrived from Bodhgaya, and he called on me on his way home. We offered each other New Year scarves and had lunch together. One day I went to pay my respects to His Holiness, and I joyfully took the essence of his words into my heart.

Teachings and Retreat in Dharamsala

When the monks of Gyütö Tantric College arrived from Dalhousie to attend the Annual Prayer Festival, I requested them to make propitiation offerings to all the protectors and made offerings to the protectors for an entire day. I attended one session of prayer with them, when the monks chanted the propitiation of Mahākāla and Dharmarāja. It seemed their chanting melody was somewhat different from when I had attended Gyütö Tantric College. I can't say whether my recollection was mistaken or whether this slight discrepancy was because there were now fewer senior monks than there had been before.

At the request of Assistant Tutor Serkong Rinpoché, I gave him teachings on the "three essential moments" in the Mitrayogin system of Avalokiteśvara. I gave prenovice and novice ordinations to the young incarnation of Gangkar Lama Rinpoché and five novices of Gyütö Tantric College, bestowing the name Losang Könchok Tenzin on the incarnation. Gyütö Tantric College sponsored a long-life ceremony in conjunction with a *Guru Puja* and tsok offering and the Halting the Ḍākinī's Escort ritual for Kyabjé Ling Rinpoché and myself at the Nyungné temple in upper Dharamsala. The blessings of the monks strengthened our tree of life.

On the first of the second month I gave the permission of the Three Wrathful Forms Combined to Chokteng Thupten Norsang and others. I gave the permission of Siṃhanāda Avalokiteśvara and an Amitāyus long-life initiation in the system of Drupgyal.

Dromo Geshé Rinpoché offered me the complete set of the Lhasa edition of the Kangyur printed on high-quality Tibetan paper. I sent Norbu Chöphel to Ghoom Monastery in Darjeeling to receive the gift. He then conveyed the set to my house in Mundgod before returning to Dharamsala.

The upholder of the Nyingma tradition Dilgo Khyentsé Rinpoché came to Dharamsala to conduct the full consecration at the Thekchen Chöling temple. During his visit he called on me, bringing with him the young incarnation of Dergé Dzongsar Khyentsé Rinpoché. As Dilgo Khyentsé Rinpoché and I knew each other well, we had a very pleasant time together.

On my seventy-second birthday, on the twelfth day of the third month,[395] Dzemé Rinpoché came to Dharamsala from Dalhousie. In order to eliminate the negative circumstances of my difficult seventy-third year, he along with a large number of tulkus and monks offered me a long-life ceremony with a Halting the Ḍākinī's Escort ritual in conjunction with a *Guru Puja* and tsok offering. Because of the bond of our stainless guru-disciple relationship, it was very beneficial.

Kyabjé Trijang Rinpoché giving teachings at the Tibetan Children's Village, Dharamsala, mid 1970s
ALEXANDER BERZIN

On the seventeenth, at the request of Assistant Tutor Serkong Rinpoché, I gave the long-life initiation of five-deity Amitāyus in the Mañjuśrī lineage from Jé Tsongkhapa, the distant lineage of the long-life initiation of Amitāyus, and teachings on the practice of Avalokiteśvara in the Nyen Tsembu tradition. These were attended by twenty-five tulkus and geshés, including Serkong Rinpoché, the former abbot of Gyümé Tantric College Samten Chöphel, Ratö Chubar Rinpoché, Denma Lochö Rinpoché, Lati Rinpoché, Dzemé Rinpoché, Lochen Tulku, Śrī Chusang Tulku, Geshé Rapten, Kangyurwa Losang Thupten, Geshé Ngawang Dargyey, and Geshé Rikzin Tenpa.

On the tenth of the fourth month, with instructions from His Holiness, I began the retreat of the protector Time of Approximation,[396] one of the seventeen emanations of Four-Faced Mahākāla Robber of Strength. During the retreat I did not receive any visitors. That night in a dream I was in an unfamiliar room. Suddenly the place became filled with many people. Then an old man claiming to be the king of Muli,[397] with a beard and moustache and dressed in a blue brocade robe, came into the room. I gave him a chair to sit on, but instead he sat on a thin cushion in front of me and appeared to be very pleased with me. Afterward, someone like the head lama of Muli came into the room and sat on the chair. Still in my dream I vaguely wondered why the king of Muli was wearing a chupa robe since he was a monk and so on. I thought these dreams might be an indication of the establishment of a close link with Mahākāla.

At the conclusion on my retreats on the emanations of Four-Faced Mahākāla called Time of Approximation, Time of Accomplishment, and Secret Accomplishment, I performed elaborate propitiation with offerings of tsok and ritual torma offerings with the monks of Namgyal Monastery. Near the conclusion of the retreats, I also had a few dreams of my closeness to the protectors. Within the same retreat boundaries, I started the long-life retreat of White Tārā for the longevity of Kyabjé Ling Rinpoché. On the conclusion of the retreat on the seventeenth, I went to visit Kyabjé Ling Rinpoché and presented him with the blessed substances of longevity with fervent requests that he firmly plant his feet to extend his life. Then I went to pay my respects to His Holiness and reported to him about the successful conclusion of the Four-Faced Mahākāla retreats.

I gave a long-life initiation to Shödrung Norgyé and his wife, the house parents to Tibetan students in the school in Bléneau, France, and to Mrs.

Pasang Lhamo from Bombay. I gave the permission of the Adhipati Lords of the Cemetery to Sera Jé Lawudo Tulku, his teacher Thubten Yeshe, and their Western students Thubten Dönyö and Thubten Ngawang.[398] I gave the life entrustment of Shukden to three of them, excluding Thubten Ngawang.

On the eighth of the seventh month I offered His Holiness permission of the very sensitive Stacked Faces, Striking the Vital Point, Secret Accomplishment, and Black Brahman from among the seventeen emanations of Four-Faced Mahākāla. At the end a tsok offering was made. On the fourteenth of the ninth month, I gave the permission of Jé Rinpoché as the triple deity to the incarnation of Geshé Jampa Khedrup of Dargyé Monastery in Trehor, Losang Tenzin, and Geshé Rapten. To Tseten Phuntsok, the bursar of the Marlam family, and four others I gave novice ordinations.

Gyütö Tantric College had made a statue of Lord Akṣobhyavajra[399] in place of the former statue in Ramoché Temple in Lhasa that was destroyed by the Red Chinese. The new statue was made in Nepal and brought to the Thekchen Chöling temple in Dharamsala. At their request, I gave them fifty different types of sacred relics of Indian and Tibetan masters of all traditions to be put into the statue. On the nineteenth, Kyabjé Ling Rinpoché and myself along with the abbot and chant master and forty monks of Gyütö Tantric College blessed the prayers and relics and placed them inside the statue. In conjunction with the occasion of the Buddha's descent from the deva realms, the monks performed the elaborate ritual of consecration of the statue by way of Vajrabhairava complete in all three stages—preliminary, actual, and concluding. On the day of the actual consecration, Kyabjé Ling Rinpoché presided over the rituals, and I attended the sessions for the entire day, engaging in the combined practice of self- and front-generation in the morning and continuing on to the conclusion of the ritual. His Holiness attended the ritual from the invitation of wisdom deities of the consecration to the conclusion of the initiations of the deities.

Sarnath

On the twenty-ninth I left Dharamsala for Sarnath with Palden, Norbu Chöphel, Jamyang Tashi, and Sönam Tenzin, arriving there on the evening of the thirtieth. Starting on the eighth day of the tenth month, I gave the preparation and the actual initiation of five-deity Cakrasaṃvara on two consecutive days at the request of Tau Losang Jampa. This was attended by seven hundred monks, including forty abbots and tulkus, at the Tibetan monastery. On the tenth, at the request of the nun Namgyal Chözom on behalf of her late husband the prime minister, and also at the additional request of Ngawang Tenzin, a former chef in the kitchen of His Holiness, I gave the blessing of the four sindūra initiations of Vajrayoginī with the commitment to practice the Vajrayoginī sādhana daily. This was concluded with elaborate tsok offerings.

On the following day, I began experiential teachings from memory on the basic sādhana of Vajrayoginī. The teaching lasted four days and was attended by 670 people, monastic and lay, including tulkus, with the commitment to do the retreat of Vajrayoginī. I gave the teachings in accordance with the Sakya method of teaching, fully explaining the oral teachings and the traditions of the lamas in hopes that it would further the continuity of the teachings.

During the initiation I did not feel well due to the cold, and as I continued teaching despite discomfort, I became seriously ill. After the teaching I had to undergo medical treatment and stopped seeing people for a few days. I had planned to leave for Mysore and Mundgod on the second day of the eleventh month, and train tickets had been bought, but because of my health and also because of a nationwide mass-transit strike in India, I remained in Sarnath and rested.

On the ninth day of the twelfth month, the young incarnation of Sera Jé Denma Tengyé Rinpoché came to meet me for the first time. I gave him prenovice and novice ordinations and the name Losang Thupten Gyaltsen. The incarnation revealed clear instincts from his predecessor. On the fifteenth I went to the bank of the Ganges to release fish, following in the footsteps of the merchant's son Jalavāhana.[400] On behalf of all those connected with me, both living and dead, I sent four thousand rupees through Tashi Gyaltsen, the manager of Samten Ling Monastery, to offer fresh coats of whitewash to the three stupas in Nepal and to make thousandfold offerings there. On the twenty-third, I left Sarnath for Dharamsala.

Return to South India

The year 1974 was my seventy-fourth year. On February 22, the first day of the wood-tiger year, I attended the New Year celebration at Thekchen

Chöling and visited His Holiness at his residence to pay my respects. On the twenty-fifth, Geshé Tamdrin Rapten sponsored a *Guru Puja* with tsok offering in conjunction with Cakrasaṃvara that was attended by the hermits living in the hills of Dharamsala. I appreciated the simple offerings made without unnecessary elaborations or false pretenses. On the twenty-ninth, Tutor Kyabjé Ling Rinpoché arrived from Mundgod and came to visit me. We offered each other scarves for the New Year. After that I did Gyalsong effigy rituals of Hayagrīva at Ratö Rinpoché's house for his well-being.[401]

On the fifteenth of the second month, I gave long-life initiations of White Tārā to Rikya Rinpoché, his attendants, and Swiss nun Anne Ansermet.[402] I gave oral transmissions and uncommon teachings of bodhicitta generation to Denma Lochö Rinpoché. On the eleventh day of the fourth month, at His Holiness's instruction, Assistant Tutor Serkong Rinpoché along with the Namgyal monks performed the long-life ritual in conjunction with the deity White Heruka for me. The private secretary, the Kungo Tara, presented me with a scarf and gifts.

On the ninth day of the sixth month, I gave the following teachings to Serkong Rinpoché and Denma Lochö Rinpoché: the *Life Accomplishment of Kurava* by Jé Tsongkhapa, the *Guru Yoga of Vajrabhairava That Is a Treasury of Attainments: The Way to Accomplish the Secondary Limbs*, the *Peaceful and Wrathful Protection of Mañjuśrī*, and *Methods for Restoring the Degenerated Commitments by Relying on the Five Buddha Families of Yamāntaka*. On the night of the tenth, I dreamed of His Holiness the Thirteenth Dalai Lama. On the way to my house, he did not take any notice of the horses and cows that were there but toyed with a large black monkey with his rosary while the monkey remained indifferent. Then a monk bodyguard lifted up the door curtain for him to enter, and I greeted him. Looking very pleased, he gave me a scarf of the highest quality[403] and a plate bearing two red tormas, which I received with respect. Then, among the gifts of His Holiness, an attendant placed before me a round metal plate bearing a carcass of fresh meat. When I had this dream, I was composing the wealth-generating rituals of one of the five emanations of Shukden. I interpreted this as an indication that the protector was pleased.

On the eighteenth day of the eighth month, I went to see His Holiness on his return from Switzerland, where he had been for medical treatment, to pay my respects and to take my leave, as I was going to Mysore and

Mundgod. His Holiness told me of his medical checks and described his successful activities during his visit to the West.

I left Dharamsala on the third day of the ninth month and stayed at Nyakré Khentrul Ngawang Gelek's house in Delhi. The next morning I flew to Bangalore, arriving at noon. I was greeted in Bylakuppe, Karnataka, by the Sera Monastery abbots, Lama Guru Deva, and the head of the settlement. I went to the new monastery of Tashi Lhunpo and officiated at its opening ceremony. For three days beginning on the eighth, I performed with the Tashi Lhunpo monks the full ritual of consecration in conjunction with Vajrabhairava according to the tradition of Tashi Lhunpo's tantric college. At the conclusion of the consecration, the eight auspicious symbols and substances were presented to Lama Guru Deva and other patrons of the monastery. I made offerings of tea and funds to the monks and presented the monastery with a thousand rupees.

On the morning of the eleventh, the monastery offered me a long-life ceremony. I gave the initiation of thirteen-deity Vajrabhairava to a large number of monks, including the monks of Tashi Lhunpo, Gyümé Tantric College, and Sera, with the preparation on one day and the actual initiation on the day following. On the thirteenth, at their invitation, I went to Gyümé Tantric College in Hunsur, where I stayed in His Holiness's residence. I accepted the invitation of the settlement of the people from Chatreng and visited them and gave them words of advice and then returned to the residence. The next morning I gave the oral transmission of the *Praises to Tārā*, the *maṇi* mantra, and His Holiness's long-life prayer to the people of the settlement in Hunsur. I visited Dzongkar Chödé Monastery and performed a brief consecration.

On the morning of the fifteenth, I gave the permission of Jé Rinpoché as the triple deity to the monks of Gyümé Tantric College and advised them that they should preserve the past traditions of study of the tantric teachings and ritual methods. I had previously offered a contribution of a thousand rupees for the reconstruction of their monastery, and this time I made offerings of tea, bread, and five rupees with a scarf to each of the monks. After I left Hunsur, I visited Thekchen Chöling Monastery in settlement number 2, which was on my way, and performed purification and consecration rituals there.

I was received by the monks at Sera Monastery with a grand ceremonial welcome, and I stayed in the library of Jé College. Beginning on the seventeenth, at the requests of Sera Jé Denma Geshé Ngawang Lekden, I gave experiential teachings on the root text of the profound path of the *Guru Puja* with the commentary by Kachen Yeshé Gyaltsen to about eight hundred monks, including the monks of Sera, Gyümé Tantric College, and others who had come from Mundgod especially for the teachings. I gave the teachings in the assembly hall of Sera. It says in *Staff of Wisdom*:

> Some volunteer to preach,
> while others accomplish through silence.
> The water lily bears no fruit,
> but the walnut bears both flower and fruit.[404]

I, who am like the water lily and played the part of a speaker, gave teachings continuously for six days from one in the afternoon until six in the evening. On the morning of the eighteenth, the Sera administration with the Geluk Association and Geshé Lekden offered me a sutra-tradition long-life ceremony, which was attended by all the monks. I had previously given a contribution of a thousand rupees for the reconstruction of the assembly hall. On this occasion I offered tea, bread, five rupees, and a scarf to each of the monks. On the morning of the twenty-second, I gave oral transmission of the *Praises to Tārā*, Samayavajra, and so on, to all the people of the new and old settlements. On the twenty-third, at the request of Sera Jé Monastery, I gave the permission of Yakṣa Yamayamī,[405] and at the request of Samlho Geshé Losang, I gave oral transmission of the *Ornament of Realization* and *Entering the Middle Way*. I told the monks that they themselves should become ornaments of the teachings through the path of study and practice. The next day at the invitation of Sera Mé, I attended a ceremony in their library. Arrangements were made by Pomra House for me to invoke the presence of Shukden and his retinue through the medium. At my insistent requests for prophetic advice, the protector gave a few predictions. On the twenty-fifth, I left Sera and performed consecrations in the new office complex of the settlement and in the temple of settlement number 1.

I left by train from Mysore and arrived in Hubli the next day, where I was received by the abbots of Ganden and Drepung monasteries and the head of the settlement, T. C. Tethong. I spent the night in a guesthouse. The next morning I left for Mundgod by car. There I was received with a ceremonial welcome by abbots, tulkus, monks, the lay populace, and schoolchildren.

First I went to the general assembly hall of Ganden, where there was a brief ceremony with tea and rice. The administrations of Ganden Monastery and its colleges, Shartsé and Jangtsé, presented me with scarves and the three representations. Then I proceeded to my new house, Phuntsok Rapten. There the administrations of Ganden, Drepung, and the other monasteries as well as many individuals came to give me housewarming scarves and gifts to please a worldly being.

As had been requested, Shartsé Monastery had taken full responsibility for the construction of our house. The monastery had appointed Geshé Jampa Rapjor of Nyakré House to oversee this, and he went to a great deal of trouble and did his utmost to make the house excellent both in appearance and in durability. I was very pleased with the house. Although I am quite old and experiencing the suffering of aging, my disciples and patrons with genuine concern for the future had conveyed their hopes through Palden and other members of the labrang that we build a house in Mundgod at a convenient location, near Ganden Monastery. Everyone spoke in favor of this suggestion. As for myself, such a house would be but a guesthouse for an overnight stay, but because I could see various reasons and purposes for it, I transgressed and turned the wheel of holding to true existence, erroneously clinging to the appearances of this life. As Jé Kharak Gomchung said:

> Building the walls of samsara's prison rather than inhabiting
> a mountain retreat is a mistake.
> Teaching the Dharma before crowds of disciples rather than
> reflecting on the truth in solitude is a mistake.[406]

Nāgārjuna said:

> Some fools forget about death
> and busy themselves with many works.
> Are they not deceived by Māra?[407]

As stated by these masters, this clearly revealed my hypocrisy, the contradiction between what I teach and what I do.

On the third day of the tenth month, the members of my labrang invited Dzemé Rinpoché and some other monks and sponsored a long-life ceremony in conjunction with a *Guru Puja* and tsok offering for my longevity. The people of Chatreng also gave donations for the long-life ceremony and offered gifts. On the same day the administrations of Ganden and Drepung, Shartsé and Jangtsé, and the abbots of Sera's Jé and Mé colleges came specially and gave me housewarming gifts.

One day I invoked the presence of the peaceful emanation of Shukden, who commended me for my efforts to further the excellent traditions of Jé Tsongkhapa through my teachings by living a long life. On the ninth, I made offerings of tea, ceremonial rice, and three rupees with a scarf to each of the monks of Ganden and to the tulkus and monks of Sera who had come for religious discourse. I invited Kyabjé Ling Rinpoché to preside over the offering, and in conjunction with a *Guru Puja* and tsok offering, I made dedicated requests for Kyabjé Ling Rinpoché to live to the end of the eon. I made offerings of gifts and presentations of the eight auspicious symbols and substances to him. Afterward Kyabjé Ling Rinpoché and his attendants came to my house and gave me housewarming gifts, and we had lunch together. About this time I made offerings of tea, bread, and three rupees to each of the Jangtsé monks and gave a large thangka of Jé Tsongkhapa with his two main disciples, complete with brocade borders and silk covers, to the monastery.

At Shartsé I made similar offerings and presented a set of nine thangkas of the Buddha, the Six Ornaments, and the Two Excellent Ones. The thangkas were framed in antique Russian brocade that had once been the outer layer of a ceremonial gown belonging to His Holiness the Thirteenth Dalai Lama. I had received it through a merchant who brought it from Lhasa. The thangka set was completed with silk covers and a pair of silver knobs for each. I also offered five volumes of the collected works of Paṇchen Losang Chökyi Gyaltsen and two pairs of antique cymbals. To Dokhang House I offered a pair of antique cymbals. At the Drepung assembly hall, I made similar offerings of tea and so forth and also gave a contribution of a thousand rupees for the reconstruction of the assembly hall. At the Sakya monastery, I made similar offerings of tea and so forth to sixty monks, and I gave two hundred rupees to the monastery, and I did the same for the Nyingma monastery and its thirty monks.

On the morning of the sixteenth, I went to Drepung Monastery and was given a ceremonial welcome by the monks of Gomang and Loseling colleges. I went to the assembly hall of Gomang, where the administration of Drepung and the two colleges presented me with scarves and the three representations during a ceremony with tea and rice. After that, in the debate courtyard of Loseling, I attended a long-life ceremony in conjunction with a *Guru Puja* and tsok offering sponsored by Ling Labrang. Kyabjé Ling Rinpoché presided over the ceremony, which was attended by the entire assembly of Drepung and by monks of Sera who had come to attend the teachings on the stages of the path. Kyabjé Ling Rinpoché presented the eight auspicious symbols and substances to me and recited the verses of auspiciousness. Thus the premise that all composite phenomena are impermanent as explained in the teachings was made insignificant. After that I went to the Ling Labrang and presented housewarming gifts to Kyabjé Ling Rinpoché and his attendants at his new residence. The labrang served us lunch.

On the eighth day of the eleventh month, Ganden and Drepung monasteries along with the Sakya and Nyingma monks and the people of Mundgod settlement made a long-life offering in conjunction with a *Guru Puja* and tsok offering to Kyabjé Ling Rinpoché and myself in the debate courtyard of Loseling. This was attended by the monks there and others. On the seventeenth, at the request of the administration of Drepung, I gave the permission of Vajravidāraṇa to the monks and a large number of settlers. At the request of Loseling College, I gave teachings on the *Seven-Point Mind Training*. The next day Loseling College made a long-life offering in conjunction with a *Guru Puja* and tsok offering to Kyabjé Ling Rinpoché and myself. At the request of Shartsé and Jangtsé colleges, I gave initiations of Guhyasamāja in the Ārya system of Akṣobhya and of thirteen-deity Vajrabhairava for three days starting on the twentieth. These were attended by over a thousand monks from Drepung, Ganden, and Sera. On the twenty-third, the administration of Ganden Monastery offered a sutra-tradition long-life offering ceremony to Kyabjé Ling Rinpoché and myself. That afternoon, Kyabjé Ling Rinpoché and I along with the abbots of Shartsé and Jangtsé, tulkus, geshés, and others performed the short ritual of consecration for the assembly hall and the sacred statues.

On the twenty-fifth, at the request of the mendicant Sönam Losang Tharchin of Chatreng to accumulate positive roots of virtue on behalf of the late Losang Bumkyi, I gave the blessing of the four sindūra initiations of Vajrayoginī to those who had attended the initiations of Guhyasamāja and Vajrabhairava earlier. The next day at the request of Apho Söpa Thokmé of

Chatreng, I gave the permission of Medicine Buddha and the initiation of Life-Sustaining Jé Tsongkhapa to a large number of monks and laypeople on behalf of the late bhikṣu Geshé Gyaltsen.

On the first day of the twelfth month the Association for the Preservation of the Geluk Tradition awarded certificates of geshé lharam and ngakram to Kyabjé Ling Rinpoché, myself, and others who had taken the examinations in Tibet and later in India. The ceremony was held in the assembly hall of Ganden and was attended by the abbots and monks of the three seats and the two tantric colleges. Samdhong Rinpoché gave the opening speech, and the abbot of Namgyal Monastery, Samten Chöphel, gave an introductory speech. Then Kyabjé Ling Rinpoché and I were each given the certificate and a gold medal with the highest quality scarves. The other geshés were given certificates and flower garlands with scarves. After that Kyabjé Ling Rinpoché and I sat on thrones and were given congratulatory scarves by various institutions and individuals. The ceremony concluded with the chanting of verses of auspiciousness. On the third, the Association for the Preservation of the Geluk Tradition gave Kyabjé Ling Rinpoché and myself a sutra-tradition long-life ceremony in the assembly hall of Ganden.

On the morning of the eighth, at the request of Gomang College, Kyabjé Ling Rinpoché and I, along with their abbots, tulkus, and geshés, performed a brief consecration of their assembly hall. In the afternoon, at the wish of the local drama troupe, we attended an opera depicting the life story of King Sudhana. This was performed in the open area in front of His Holiness's residence. We watched the performance for two hours and presented the dance troupe with gifts. Watching the performance made me recall a verse form the *Garland of Birth Stories*, and I even muttered the words of the verse:

> Alas, this world is transient.
> It will not remain. It will not bring joy.
> Even the wonders of the *kumuda* lily
> will become just a memory.[408]

This was not the first occasion that I had recalled the verse. It had often come to my mind when I attended government ceremonies and opera performances in the Norbulingka during the four-day Shotön summer festival as assistant tutor and later as tutor, and I did not enjoy the performances very much.[409]

Shartsé and Jangtsé colleges held a debate contest session for two days where most of the debates were on the Abhidharma. Since many years had passed since I took the examination, I could no longer remember enumerations in the Abhidharma. As stated in *Guide to the Bodhisattva's Way of Life* (5.25):

> Whatever has been learned, contemplated,
> and meditated upon by one who lacks awareness,
> like water in a leaky pot,
> will not be held by the memory.

As most of the topics had been stolen by the thief of forgetfulness, I was not able to judge the quality of the debaters' erudition. I gave gifts to young novices of the two colleges who had memorized either the *Ornament of Realization* or *Entering the Middle Way* or both and advised them of the importance of putting effort into their studies. On the fifteenth, I gave pre-novice and novice ordinations to fifty young monks of Shartsé and Jangtsé including Phara Tulku.

On the morning of the eighth, I left Mundgod by car for Belgaum, from where I flew to Delhi. There I stayed at Lama Guru Deva's house.

Return to Dharamsala

In 1975 I was seventy-five. On February 11, the first day of the Tibetan year, I performed a token New Year ceremony. The directors and staff of the Bureau of His Holiness and of Tibet House came to offer New Year greetings to me. On the sixth, I left Delhi, and the following day I arrived at my house in Dharamsala. The next day I visited His Holiness and paid my respects to him. On the third day of the second month, Kyabjé Ling Rinpoché returned to Dharamsala from Bodhgaya and on the way he came to my house. We exchanged New Year greetings.

On the fourth, at the request of Mrs. Pasang Lhamo to sow roots of virtue on behalf of her late husband, Karma Wangchuk, I gave the initiation of five-deity Cakrasaṃvara with the preparation on two consecutive days at the Thekchen Chöling temple. This was attended by 650 disciples, including the abbots of the three seats, the two tantric monasteries, Tashi Lhunpo Monastery, tulkus, geshés, hermits, the resident monks, laypeople of Dharamsala, and others who came from various places. The following day I gave the initiation of Cakrasaṃvara body mandala to 560 of the above-mentioned disciples who committed to perform daily the yoga of the three purifications. Beginning on the eighth I gave twelve days of experiential teachings on the generation and completion stages of the Cakrasaṃvara body mandala to 183 disciples who daily recited the full sādhana of the deity. This was given at the Library of Tibetan Works and Archives. Following this I gave teachings on the long-life practice with reliance on vajra recitation with breath yoga in conjunction with the yoga of the White Heruka longevity deity.

Author's Colophon

Paṇchen Losang Chökyi Gyaltsen said:

> Teaching others while not practicing oneself
> is shameful in the presence of those with eyes of wisdom.
> However, the teachings of the Tathāgata, just by transmission,
> are said by the peerless Teacher himself to be meaningful.

As stated by the Paṇchen Lama, I accomplished the virtuous deed of disseminating the meaningful teachings of the compassionate spiritual father so others could receive the nectar. Also Āryadeva's *Four Hundred Verses* states:

> If by having an unstable mind
> one is said to be mad,
> then how could a wise one say
> that anyone in this world is not mad?

Although I am aware that I do not possess even a fraction of the qualities of learning and practice required for others to regard me as their lama, many people, mistaking copper for gold, have shown me esteem, respect, and veneration. Due to this, like a crazy person with an unnatural state of mind, the nature of my life is the play of the mere form of a lama in this degenerate time, as stated by the omniscient Longchenpa:

> Not realizing that gatherings and crowds of people
> are just the devils of deceptive distraction,
> you may think to give advice, teach the Dharma, and work
> for others,
> but ask yourself, "Will they truly benefit by such behavior?"

Furthermore, Kadam Geshé Shawo Gangpa said:

> Be not like those who, while lacking higher qualities within
> their mindstreams, aspire to be others' masters. . . .
> Be not like those who, while their teachings are high, have
> low realization.[410]

My life has not been beyond what these masters have related. It has been a story of a life set within the scene of an illusory play that accords with the norms of neither the Dharma nor the world. I have nothing to present here in writing about my life like the biographies of masters that inspire faith and admiration. Despite this, many have asked me to write the story of my life, especially Dagyab Rinpoché, who in a letter and when we met in person told me time after time that I should quickly finish writing my autobiography, as he wished to publish it and translate it into English. I also wrote thinking that in the future, whenever anyone wished to discuss my life, this work would help eliminate speculations based on fabrications and false assumptions. I also felt that writing the story of my life candidly would not be improper, telling of the alternating waves of positive and negative karma in the ocean of this deceptive life like the biographies of others who are comparable to myself.

Being in the lineage of the Ganden Throneholder Jangchup Chöphel by mere chance, I, Losang Yeshé Tenzin Gyatso, completed this autobiography in my seventy-fifth year in 1975, covering the story of my life up to the second month of the wood-rabbit year. Herein I have written the account of my life as far as I can remember it, supplemented by Palden's diary of the events of my life up to the unforgettable happenings in 1959 in Lhasa. I was not able to write in much detail as a lot has been forgotten. I have eliminated here accounts of unnecessary distracting activities since my arrival in India and have presented an account of suitable length. Thus many years of my life have passed, but as the Tibetan master Mipham states:

> Composite phenomena are like the play of the seductive maid of lightning.
> Happiness and suffering are the wheels of a chariot.
> I have seen the strange and wondrous expressions of samsara,
> but unyielding karma is my share.

All composite phenomena possess the nature of transience and are subject to destruction, while all places, possessions, and our own bodies, brought together by contaminated samsara, are in the nature of suffering. This can be directly seen and experienced, as taught in the great scriptures. However, this spoiled and wild mind, clinging to reality and permanence, with its play of deception and guile, immerses itself only in actions that snatch away the very life of liberation and does not move at all to take the upward steps to the wisdom that thinks about the next life. This, I think, is the proliferation of my share of powerful imprints of previous habituation with bad karma.

In the delightful unexamined city of deception
are the thousand illusory dramas of the eight worldly concerns of this life.
To look at these wonders, transforming incessantly like lightning,
grandfather must manifest four faces, I think.

May goodness prevail!

Translator's Colophon

With ineffable gratitude for the threefold kindness of Lama Vajradhara, whose name I find difficult to express yet mention for a purpose, Kyabjé Vajradhara Jetsun Losang Yeshé Tenzin Gyatso, the third incarnation of Throneholder Jangchup Chöphel, the translation of his esteemed autobiography *The Magical Play of Illusion* was completed on the auspicious occasion of the tenth day of the first seventh month of the fire-horse year in the sixteenth rabjung cycle, the royal year of Tibet 2113, Friday the fifteenth of August, 1986, on the thirty-ninth anniversary of India's Independence Day.

The translation was completed in the very room of the late Kyabjé Vajradhara, where he completed the writing of the autobiography in Tibetan, at his residence Tashi Rapten, at Gangchen Kyishong, Dharamsala, Kangra district, Himachal Pradesh, India. A tsok offering of the tenth was made to dedicate the merits of this translation for the perpetual accomplishment of Kyabjé Vajradhara's wishes.

May everyone share and be benefitted by the boundless wisdom and compassion of Kyabjé Trijang Vajradhara.

Epilogue

THE ACTIVITIES of enlightened beings are beyond the scope of ordinary beings, therefore any attempt to summarize their lives is fraught with limitations. What ordinary beings perceive is a mere reflection of their karma and does not truly represent such an enlightened being's activities. Nevertheless, the life that Kyabjé Trijang Rinpoché displayed can be characterized as the closest to the actions of a fully enlightened being that any ordinary being will ever witness. With that in mind, I will present events in the way that the fully enlightened Kyabjé Trijang Vajradhara revealed them to the ordinary beings of this world.

The Final Six Years of Rinpoché's Life

As Kyabjé Rinpoché advanced in years, his activities lessened, and he spent more and more time absorbed in meditation. Nevertheless he continued to give numerous teachings to many fortunate disciples. Here I present a mere portion of his enlightened activities during the six and a half years prior to his passing.

In 1975, when Kyabjé Rinpoché was seventy-five years old, he gave the Cakrasaṃvara five-deity and body-mandala initiations to about 650 disciples in the Thekchen Chöling temple in Dharamsala. Afterward he gave an experiential commentary on the generation and completion stages of the Cakrasaṃvara body mandala to about 180 disciples at the Library of Tibetan Works and Archives. He gave the Mañjuvajra initiation of Guhyasamāja in the tradition of Jñānapada to our great refuge and protector, the Fourteenth Dalai Lama, as well as the great initiation of nine-deity Jinasāgara Avalokiteśvara. At the Ganden assembly hall, he gave a commentary on the stages of the path according to *Liberation in the Palm of Your Hand* to more than a thousand monastics and about eight hundred laypeople.

In 1976, Kyabjé Rinpoché's seventy-sixth year, he gave a commentary on the *Hundred Deities of Tuṣita* to more than one hundred who assembled in the nunnery in Dharamsala. In Delhi, he gave the blessing of the four sindūra initiations of Vajrayoginī as well as the commentary on its generation and completion stages to about two hundred disciples who assembled in the temple built by the Gyakar Khampa, Indians of Tibetan origin. At Ganden Shartsé he gave the Mañjuvajra initiation of Guhyasamāja and so forth.

In 1977, Kyabjé Rinpoché's seventy-seventh year, he gave the initiation of five-deity Cakrasaṃvara in the tradition of Mahāsiddha Ghaṇṭāpāda as well as the blessing of the four sindūra initiations of Vajrayoginī and so forth in Ganden Thekchok Ling in Manali, in Kullu Valley, to about two hundred disciples. To more than two thousand ordained and lay disciples he gave the permission of Avalokiteśvara and so forth. He gave a commentary on the *Three Principal Aspects of the Path* to a vast number of disciples in Sangyé Chöling Monastery in Shimla. At Ganden Monastery he gave a commentary on the *Wheel of Sharp Weapons Mind Training* as well as the initiations of five-deity Cakrasaṃvara and the body mandala in the tradition of Mahāsiddha Ghaṇṭāpāda and a commentary on the generation and completion stages of the body mandala.

In 1978, Kyabjé Rinpoché's seventy-eighth year, he conferred novice ordination vows on twenty-five disciples at Sera Monastery. At the Kagyü monastery of Drukpa Thugsé Rinpoché in Darjeeling, he gave a reading transmission of Atiśa's *Lamp on the Path to Enlightenment*. At Samten Chöling in Darjeeling, he conferred novice vows on about thirty newly ordained young monks. In Kalimpong he gave the blessing of the four sindūra initiations of Vajrayoginī to about three hundred disciples as well as a commentary on its generation and completion stages. In the assembly hall at Ganden Monastery he gave an experiential commentary on the stages of the path by combining the *Easy Path* and the *Quick Path* to more than two thousand disciples. At the residence of Phuntsok Rapten, to his faithful disciples Dzemé Rinpoché and Kachen Söpa of Tashi Lhunpo Monastery, Kyabjé Vajradhara gave the reading transmission of the sections of his collected works that had been published. In the assembly hall at Ganden Shartsé, he gave thirteen of the seventeen permissions of Four-Faced Mahākāla.

In 1979, Rinpoché's seventy-ninth year, he gave a commentary on Jé Tsongkhapa's *Middle-Length Stages of the Path* to a vast assembly of disciples at Sera Monastery.

In 1980, Rinpoché's eightieth year, he gave a commentary on the *Hundred Deities of Tuṣita* to a vast assembly of disciples at the Sera Jé assembly hall, and at the Sera Mé assembly hall, he gave the permissions of the sixteen arhats and White Mañjuśrī.

In 1981, Rinpoché's eighty-first year, he gave a commentary on the *Praise of Avalokiteśvara*[411] as well as a profound commentary on the essential definitive meaning concerning the composition on the *Gangloma* prayer to Mañjuśrī to about eighteen hundred students. For this teaching he merely gave a general outline of the main sections. Because his mind was completely filled with love, compassion, and bodhicitta, he was able to establish countless fortunate disciples on the path to enlightenment.

The Special Qualities of Kyabjé Trijang Rinpoché

Kyabjé Trijang Rinpoché had forsaken all inferior motivations. He had overcome any sense of self-cherishing, and his great compassion was free from the defects of lassitude and agitation. He also accomplished the realization of bliss and emptiness through the completion stage and mastered the meditations for causing the winds to enter, abide, and dissolve within the central channel. Furthermore, when Trijang Rinpoché was twenty-five, he traveled to an amazing place in Chatreng, the abode of Avalokiteśvara called Protectors of the Three Lineages at Gangkar (Gangkar Riksum Gönpo). Each year, on the fifteenth day of the fourth month (Vaiśākha), a spring of water spontaneously emerged. During his visit, again and again, the sounds of various musical instruments could be heard. Also, on the tenth day of the twelfth month during the special month of Cakrasaṃvara and Vajrayoginī called Puṣya—a time when the ḍākinīs congregate—Trijang Rinpoché performed self-initiation in the sindūra mandala of Vajrayoginī and performed an extensive tsok offering, and while in a state of meditation, he completely stopped breathing, during which time his attendants and disciples made as many prostrations and supplications as possible. When he commenced breathing again, he immediately began singing songs of spiritual realizations, one of which began:

> The powerful conqueror Jé Losang
> dwells in the pure Dharma land of Ganden,

> inseparable from the kind Śrī Cakrasaṃvara—Dechen Nyingpo—
> who remains on anthers of the eight-petalled lotus of my heart.

This was a clear indication that he had mastered the realization of the exalted wisdom of bliss and emptiness by causing the winds to enter, abide, and dissolve within the central channel. Later, when he was twenty-seven, he sang more songs of spiritual realization while presenting a tsok offering in conjunction with Cakrasaṃvara at Kampo Mountain—a sacred site of Heruka Cakrasaṃvara in Domé Kampo—at which time the sound of ḍākas and ḍākinīs singing spontaneous vajra songs arose together with the sound of instruments.

Concerning his good qualities of training in wisdom, he had the wisdom that realizes the ultimate mode of existence of all phenomena, conventional wisdom such as the knowledge of the five sciences, and wisdom understanding the various ways of benefiting living beings according to their various dispositions. He had also fully mastered the wisdoms of explaining, debating, and composing as well as the profound, clear, great, and quick wisdoms. He had both innate and acquired wisdom due to his vast experience in listening, contemplating, and meditating. In short, he was the embodiment of wisdom that is matched only by fully enlightened beings revealing the aspect of great scholars. He had absolutely perfect reliance upon his own spiritual masters through his realization of the proper way to rely upon one's guru as presented in such texts as the *Marvelous Array Sutra* and the *Great Treatise on the Stages of the Path.* Trijang Rinpoché himself had said that he had one hundred root gurus but that, among his root gurus, Kyabjé Phabongkha was his primary guru. This is similar to the way in which Atiśa held Serlingpa as his primary guru out of his 157 gurus.

With regard to his studies of sutra and tantra, he had grasped all the teachings of the Conqueror embodied in scripture and realization. Seeing the great importance of hearing many teachings, he studied the great texts, debated their meaning, and eliminated uncertainties whereby he came to grasp the true intent of the scriptures of sutra and tantra. Through combining view, meditation, and action—or in other words, the three higher trainings—he studied at Ganden Shartsé Monastery, where he received the highest degree available, that of a lharam geshé. Afterward he went to Gyütö Tantric College and studied the four classes of tantra in general and highest yoga tantra in particular. Among the highest yoga tantric practices,

A drawing of the Buddha that Trijang Rinpoché sketched on the spot at the request of a visitor from South Africa
COURTESY OF PALDEN TSERING

he mastered the root and explanatory tantras of Guhyasamāja and the commentaries composed by Tibetan and Indian masters.

Concerning the way he attained the state of an unparalleled scholar of explanation, debate, and composition, his qualities of explanation are without compare and are free from all faults; he was an outstanding debater, and his teachings perfectly reveal the true intent of the great scriptures, such as those composed by Nāgārjuna, Āryadeva, Candrakīrti, Asaṅga, and others. Above all, he was the foremost exponent of the profound teachings of Lama Tsongkhapa and his disciples. Whatever he taught was supremely effective for the mind, and were you to ask his disciples, they would all leave his discourses having received exactly what was needed to transform their minds. He always acted in the most humble manner, free of any pretense or arrogance. Although he never revealed any of his realizations or good qualities, one only needed to listen to his profound expositions to immediately understand the depth of his knowledge and realization.

Some of his more well-known disciples include His Holiness the Fourteenth Dalai Lama, Kyabjé Ling Rinpoché, Drepung Gomang Kangyurwa Chenpo Losang Dönden, Kumbum Minyak Rinpoché, Kyabjé Simok Rinpoché, Drupwang Geshé Losang Samdrup Rinpoché, Ratö Chubar Rinpoché, Gashar Song Rinpoché, Gashar Dzemé Rinpoché, the Second Phabongkha Rinpoché, Sera Mé Gyalrong Khentrul, Sera Mé Dagyab Rinpoché, Assistant Tutor Serkong Rinpoché, and countless other lamas and geshés too many to mention, "like the host of stars in the sky," as we say in Tibetan.

As for Trijang Rinpoché's writings, his collected works fill eight volumes and cover a wide variety of topics, such as the stages of the path, commentaries and sādhanas on both the action tantra practice of White Tārā Wish-Fulfilling Wheel and the highest yoga tantra practice of Cittamaṇi Tārā, various Dharma protectors, the practices of Cakrasaṃvara, and many other minor domains of knowledge. He is known for his spontaneous composition of brilliant poetic verses on any topic.

With regard to his moral discipline, he saw that maintaining pure moral discipline is extremely important and is the foundation of all paths to enlightenment. He perfectly maintained the prātimokṣa vows as set forth in the Vinaya, the bodhisattva vows and conduct as set forth in such texts as the *Guide to the Bodhisattva's Way of Life*, and the tantric vows as set forth in such texts as Jé Tsongkhapa's *Cluster of Attainments.* Thus, without any sense of self-concern, he maintained the three sets of vows, thereby setting a perfect example for his faithful disciples to emulate. Dedicating his entire life to others, Kyabjé Trijang Rinpoché lived and breathed the peerless path to enlightenment as revealed by all the previous enlightened beings, not wavering even for an instant.

To give a few examples of his magical powers,[412] in 1958, when my parents were returning to Lhasa after my father had completed his tour of duty as the representative of His Holiness the Dalai Lama at the Bureau of the Dalai Lama in Beijing, my sister made requests to Kyabjé Trijang Rinpoché for divinations and prayers. Trijang Rinpoché responded by indicating that there would be some obstacles on the day the party reached Lhasa. In order to avert hindrances, Trijang Rinpoché suggested having a number of sixty-four-part torma rituals performed in conjunction with the protector Dharmarāja. My sister invited a group of monks from Gyümé Tantric College to perform the ritual offering. Of course, on the day they approached Lhasa, as they were crossing the narrow Kuru Bridge on the outskirts of Lhasa, passing motor vehicles startled the horses, causing them to become frantic. Apart from a few minor injuries, the party made it safely to the Rampa House. My family members were extraordinarily grateful to Trijang Rinpoché for his compassionate advice and display of his foreknowledge that guided them home safely that day.

Another fascinating story is told by the father of Lama Kunga, the nobleman Tsipön Shuguba, in his book *In the Presence of My Enemies*. When Lama Kunga was first born, he was on the brink of death, so his father invited Trijang Rinpoché to come to their home and say prayers on behalf of his ailing son. It seemed certain that the tiny infant that was to become Lama Kunga would pass from this world at any moment. Before beginning the ritual, Trijang Rinpoché said, "If you give me your son, I will save his life." It seemed as though Rinpoché may have just been joking, but after a few moments of intense meditation, the child began to exhibit signs of a complete recovery. Afterward Rinpoché strongly suggested that the father send the boy to be a monk at any monastery, it didn't matter which tradition. Kyabjé Trijang Rinpoché gave this boy his name Losang Kunga Gyurmé. Lama Kunga to this day lives as the spiritual director of Ngor Ewam Chöden Sakya Center in Kensington, California.

Some of Kyabjé Trijang Rinpoché's previous lives include Buddha Śākyamuni's charioteer Candaka, Arhat Madhughoṣa, Candrakīrti, Atiśa, the Eighth Karmapa Mikyö Dorjé, and many others.[413] There were many prophecies made about Trijang Rinpoché stating that he was in fact an emanation of Padmasambhava, Jé Tsongkhapa, Atiśa, and others.

Kyabjé Trijang Rinpoché's Passing

Just as the Buddha's final teaching to his disciples was to reveal the importance of realizing death and impermanence, during the last several years of his life, Kyabjé Trijang Rinpoché revealed the aspect of approaching his parinirvāṇa. He was spending more and more time in a state of meditation while his disciples from various monasteries offered prayers and requests for his long life.

The labrang had purchased train tickets on October 10, 1981, for him and his entourage to travel from Dharamsala to Ganden Shartsé in South India. Rinpoché had been going to South India for the winter for several years, and this year was no exception. They were to depart November 15. Despite contracting an illness on October 23, Trijang Rinpoché decided to make the trip as planned. He told his attendants that if there were any special rituals that needed to be done that they should be done at Ganden Monastery after their arrival.

On November 3, 1981, Ling Rinpoché came to Kyabjé Trijang Rinpoché's residence and made prayers and requests for Kyabjé Rinpoché not to pass into the sphere of nirvana. At this time, the two tutors made plans to travel to Ganden together. On November 5, Trijang Rinpoché stated, "I must leave for Ganden on November 15." This carried a special significance because Jangchup Chöphel, the first incarnation in the line of those bearing the name Trijang Rinpoché, also went to Tuṣita (Tibetan: Ganden) at the time of his passing; therefore this statement indicated that our root guru, the Third Trijang Rinpoché, was also definitely going to the pure land of Tuṣita.

On the morning of November 5, His Holiness the Dalai Lama had just returned from Sikkim. He came immediately to Kyabjé Rinpoché's residence and requested him to remain in this world for the welfare of living beings. Soon after this, Trijang Rinpoché reported, "My leg is swelling up a bit," at which time his attendants examined his leg and the physician Yeshé Dönden gave him some medicine. Rinpoché's disciples inquired as to which ritual would be best to perform for his health, at which point Trijang Rinpoché replied, "Until now I haven't experienced any serious illness; yet at this time there are no special rituals to be done, since there isn't much hope that I will remain in the world much longer." He also advised Kungo Palden Tsering, his lifelong attendant, to not consult other lamas about performing more rituals for his long life.

However, Kungo Palden was quite concerned and had prayers and extensive offerings made at Sera, Drepung, Ganden, and so forth for Trijang Rinpoché's long life, including a recitation of the Kangyur. Kungo Palden also made extensive prayers of his own, performing all the requests perfectly, after which he made the obligatory request for Rinpoché's quick return by asking, "However, in case you have completed your work here, will you please return to us quickly in the most auspicious aspect?"

Trijang Rinpoché told his disciples, "Whether I get well or not, we must travel to Ganden during the ninth month. Rinpoché later said, "I had a vision of Tuṣita that is the result of the virtuous actions performed in my previous lives. You must stop making offerings for my long life and make offerings instead for my rebirth in Tuṣita." On November 9, the Ganden Throneholder Kyabjé Ling Rinpoché once again returned and requested Trijang Rinpoché to remain in this world. Despite his disciples' best efforts, the merit of living beings in this world was not sufficient to maintain the presence of Cakrasaṃvara's supreme emanation body. That same morning, Rinpoché asked when the study session was to begin at Ganden, and his attendant replied that he wasn't certain. After some consideration, Trijang Rinpoché said, "I think it is starting today." These were his last words.

The previous Trijang Rinpoché, Ganden Throneholder Losang Tsultrim, as Rinpoché narrates at the outset of his memoir, would circumambulate Ganden Monastery during his final days. On his final day, as he approached the throne room of Jé Tsongkhapa, he paused to sit on a chair. After conversing with his attendant, he faced the western sky and, laughing all the while, said, "Ganden, Ganden, Ganden . . . ," and passed away. Like this, all three incarnations bearing the name Trijang Rinpoché passed into the sphere of peace with their minds focused on Ganden.

Therefore, at nine-thirty in the morning on November 9, the omniscient mind of Kyabjé Trijang Vajradhara was withdrawn into the sphere of the dharmakāya. However, Kyabjé Rinpoché had yet to reveal his final teaching. To display to the world and his faithful disciples the way in which a fully enlightened being passes from this world, for the next two days his consciousness remained in single-pointed meditation on clear light of death absorbed inseparably with the omniscient mind of all the buddhas. His Holiness the Dalai Lama came immediately upon his passing and performed a *Guru Puja* and prayers to Cakrasaṃvara.

News of Kyabjé Rinpoché's parinirvāṇa spread quickly throughout the Tibetan community, sending his disciples into a state of shock. Gen Losang Chöphel told me that when he heard of Kyabjé Rinpoché's passing, he felt as though his heart had been ripped out and he could not eat or sleep for several days. He told me the passing of his mother and father could not compare to the loss he felt upon the passing of Kyabjé Trijang Vajradhara. By ten o'clock, disciples started gathering around Kyabjé Rinpoché's residence to offer their prayers and express their faith and devotion while focusing their minds single-pointedly on Rinpoché's private quarters. The Tibetan people described it has having their most precious jewel stolen by a thief or the moon turning black. To mark this great tragedy, all the government offices remained closed. During this time, His Holiness instructed his private secretary to offer his services in any way possible, such as assisting with the cremation ceremony and so forth. All the monasteries throughout India, Nepal, Bhutan, and Ladakh held special services in honor of his passing.

Kyabjé Rinpoché's mind remained absorbed in the clear light, while his body sustained without any signs of deterioration, until ten in morning on November 11. While Kyabjé Rinpoché was absorbed in the clear light of death, the weather had been calm and serene. However, as soon as he passed from the clear light of death, a heavy rain and a powerful wind arose. A magical presence seemed to fill the air, some of the children from the Tibetan Children's Village reported seeing visions, and the surrounding area had the aura of being bathed in rainbow light.

At four-thirty on the morning of thirteenth, the Ganden Throneholder Kyabjé Ling Rinpoché came to oversee the preparations for the cremation rituals. On the fourteenth, various lamas and officials as well as all the monks and laypeople transported his holy body to the cremation site. The entire path from the Tibetan's Children Village to the cremation site was lined with schoolchildren. Upon reaching the site, the Ganden Shartsé abbot Lati Rinpoché presided as the ritual master of the cremation ceremony. On this particular morning, the moon appeared larger than usual, as was witnessed by all present, who interpreted it as the moon coming closer to the earth to pay its final respects to Kyabjé Trijang Rinpoché. Numerous auspicious signs occurred, such as when the fire was lit, the smoke appeared in the aspect of the eight auspicious symbols. Also, when the ritual was begun, two large vultures circumambulated the cremation site counterclockwise, specially signifying Trijang Rinpoché's practice of Cakrasaṃvara.

During the ritual, five-colored rainbow light appeared around the residences of both Kyabjé Trijang Rinpoché and Kyabjé Ling Rinpoché. When the holy body of Kyabjé Trijang Vajradhara was cremated, the smoke went toward the northeast, and the banner covering the cremation site flew off to the east. When the hearth was opened, two small footprints heading east were revealed in the ashes.

Lati Rinpoché describes this miraculous occurrence that took place during the cremation site.[414] Kyabjé Trijang Rinpoché's cremation stupa was lit by a young boy at the Tibetan Children's Village. This boy had recently arrived from Tibet and had not received any teachings from Kyabjé Trijang Rinpoché. As the pyre was lit, white smoke arose in the northeasterly direction. Right then, the wind lifted up in the same direction the skirt of a yellow parasol that was placed above the stupa. As the ritual offerings proceeded, Lati Rinpoché witnessed some self-emerging relics being produced on a silver platter on which a small statue of the Buddha was placed in anticipation of such rare occurrences. Lati Rinpoché, as the presiding vajra master, placed this statue on the main altar in front of the stupa on the advice of Ratö Chubar Rinpoché, who had instructed him to be on the lookout for such relics. The relics slowly started to emerge as Lati Rinpoché watched in amazement. The relics consisted of one large and many tiny crystal-like balls. As this phenomenon was unfolding, Lati Rinpoché recalls telling Ratö Rinpoché's attendant Ngawang Gendun about it. Ngawang Gendun told this to a few who were there. Soon, many devotees who attended the cremation ceremony witnessed this miracle unfolding and converged at the altar to view them. Suddenly, the relics began to disappear before Lati Rinpoché's eyes, and he quickly tried to rescue them from the silver platter. Lati Rinpoché regretted telling Gendun, as this process should have been left to complete its course without so many people watching.

Every morning for several days, many of the highest lamas of the Geluk tradition made offerings in front of the cremation site and made prayers. When the cremation site was opened, his body had shrunk to one cubit in height, while his torso and heart remained undamaged by the fire. There was also one Buddha statue placed on a platter, and within it was one large self-emerging relic. His ashes were put in a special urn, wrapped in ritual attire, and a crown of the five buddha families was placed upon it.

After the cremation, as the party proceeded to Rinpoché's residence at Gangchen Kyishong, two big vultures were once again circumambulating his residence. The main entrance to his residence overflowed with a vast crowd of devotees, including the highest lamas and government officials together with a vast assembly of monks who had gathered there to welcome his holy relics. When his holy relics arrived at his residence, Kungo Palden offered the three supports of enlightened body, speech, and mind, after which all the devotees made a request to His Holiness the Dalai Lama to compose a prayer for the quick return of Kyabjé Rinpoché. The labrang prepared a vast tsok offering where all the tulkus, geshés, monks, and so forth gathered to make offerings and pay their respects to the holy relics of Kyabjé Trijang Vajradhara.

On the twenty-second day of the ninth Tibetan month, during the special occasion of Buddha's Descent from the Pure Land, a vast assembly of many thousands of disciples consisting of high lamas from numerous monasteries gathered to perform vast offerings presided over by Ganden Throneholder Kyabjé Ling Rinpoché.

The Search for His Reincarnation

In 1980, Trijang Rinpoché had advised Kungo Palden on what do to with his relics to help them to locate his reincarnation, and he also gave him some letters and a diary. Concerning his reincarnation, Rinpoché said that they should look in northeastern India to see if there were any special boys as possible candidates. He also informed him of which oracles to consult for the search.

In the Tibetan year of the water-dog on New Year's Day, at Ganden Shartsé Monastery, the Setrap oracle put a white scarf on a pillar in the eastern direction and another in the northeastern direction. Then, on July 8, 1983, Kungo Palden asked His Holiness, who said, "I believe he will be reborn in northwestern India, therefore you should search for his reincarnation there."

Then, both Losang Thupten and Sera Mé Sharpa Rinpoché sent a letter to Kungo Palden and said that they feel that Kyabjé Rinpoché may have been reborn as the son of Phenpo Sönam Topgyal and Losang Drölma, who worked in a carpet factory in Dalhousie. The letter stated, "On October 15, they gave birth to a special child. You should examine this boy." Five or six years prior to his passing, when Sönam Topgyal had an audience with Trijang Rinpoché, Rinpoché mentioned that Drakri Rinpoché is being cared for by Sera Mé Geshé Yeshé Wangchuk and is a very good tulku, and Drakri Rinpoché, Khamlung Rinpoché, and Gashar Phukang Khenrap Paljor are all related.[415] Kyabjé Trijang Rinpoché said casually to Sönam Topgyal, "In my future life, if I am born in your family lineage, we will all have the same name under Gungthang Labrang, and we will all be related." Kungo Palden was present, and he thought that the fact that Rinpoché was speaking in this way must have some significant meaning.

As His Holiness felt certain that Trijang Rinpoché's reincarnation had been reborn in northwestern India, Kungo Palden, full of hope, went with Jamyang Tashi to Dalhousie on May 8, 1983, and stayed with Losang Thupten. They mentioned nothing about looking for Kyabjé Rinpoché's reincarnation. Instead, they went to visit Sönam Topgyal and engaged him in discussion about business, pretending that they were interested in buying carpets, all the while secretly examining the child. The child was very fond of religious articles and had a very special disposition. He also was quite fond of Kungo Palden and of Jamyang Tashi, who had been one of Trijang Rinpoché's attendants from a young age. The child wasn't very articulate, however, and therefore it was difficult to understand him. Nevertheless he seemed intent on speaking and hugged both Kungo Palden and Jamyang Tashi several times. His particular fondness for Jamyang Tashi made Kungo Palden very hopeful that it might be the true reincarnation.

Beginning from January 31, 1984, Shartsé Abbot Lati Rinpoché, Jangchup Tsultrim, Phukhang Geshé Tashi Norbu, and Ngakré Phuntsok Tsultrim, together with Kungo Palden, traveled all throughout India and Nepal searching for the correct reincarnation. When there was an area they could not get to, they sent correspondence by various means. They next assembled the names of the best of the 544 candidates, selecting from them ninety-nine special children. Among them there were eight particularly special children whose names were presented to His Holiness. His Holiness said, "Now it is very important that we not only do a divination but that it should be done in the presence of Kyabjé Rinpoché's holy relics housed in the sacred stupa at Ganden Monastery." Therefore, when His Holiness went to Mundgod in South India in December, he did the divination in the presence of Trijang Rinpoché's holy relics. On the twenty-third, he made all the necessary preparations. On the twenty-fourth, he performed the actual divination, and it came out that the child from Dalhousie was the best candidate. Based on this outcome, they did another divination as to when they should make contact with the tulku, and the decision was to wait. Therefore, they suspended their inquiry temporarily. On April 4, 1985, Kungo Palden again asked His Holiness about the reincarnation, and His Holiness said he should do another divination in the presence of the Avalokiteśvara called the Ārya Wati Sangpo of Kyirong. His Holiness performed the divination on April 22, alongside Shartsé Abbot Lati Rinpoché and Kungo Palden, and the result was that it was now time to confirm the reincarnation and that the son of Sönam Topgyal and Losang Drölma is the unmistaken reincarnation of Kyabjé Trijang Vajradhara.

On April 23, 1985, Gyatso Tsering, director of the Library of Tibetan Works and Archives and a devoted disciple of Kyabjé Trijang Rinpoché, sent a letter from Dharamsala to Sharpa Tulku, who was translating for Tārā Rinpoché in Hawaii, describing the situation in Dharamsala:[416]

> Early on the morning of April 22, His Holiness the Dalai Lama retreated into meditation concentrating on the name mantra of Kyabjé Trijang Vajradhara. When he was finished, Kungo Palden and Lati Rinpoché were called to His Holiness's private residence, and in their presence the necessary rituals were performed under the benign presence of the Ārya Avalokiteśvara [statue]. There, His Holiness gave the verdict that Sönam Topgyal's child was the true reincarnation of Kyabjé Trijang Vajradhara. With a beaming expression on his face, His Holiness then charged Lati Rinpoché and Kungo Palden with responsibility of caring for the child.

Next, His Holiness gave instructions concerning which ritual should be performed to remove obstacles and create favorable conditions. After this, it was announced on the Tibetan-language channel of All-India Radio that the unmistaken reincarnation of Kyabjé Trijang Vajradhara had been discovered. Everyone was ecstatic. As Gyatso Tsering wrote:

> The news spread like wildfire, bringing joy everywhere—you should have seen the joy bursting in Kungo Palden's face. That evening he treated the residence of Trijang Labrang to an extravagant meal amid much talk of Kyabjé Rinpoché's amazing deeds and exemplary life. The chanting was most boisterous. They went up the mountain that evening, performing prayers and rituals all night, and ended with an early-morning incense ritual.
>
> Now everyone's attention is focused on Dalhousie. Sönam Topgyal's family has become famous overnight, and right now this is the most talked-about subject in Dharamsala. Topgyal's other child in Sursok school has also become the object of attention.
>
> In a week's time, on an auspicious day, Kungo Palden and Lati Rinpoché will be leaving for Dalhousie to seek formal permission from his parents and to present offerings to the supreme incarnation of Kyabjé Trijang Vajradhara. They will then return

> to Dharamsala, make the necessary preparations—which Kungo Palden says will take about a month—and then escort the supreme incarnation to Dharamsala from Dalhousie amid ceremonial procession.

On May 17, 1985, in Dalhousie, the incarnation of Kyabjé Rinpoché was dressed in the attire of a follower of the Buddha, and everything went without incident. The party accompanying the incarnation left Dalhousie, and preparations were made at Tilokpur, not far from Dharamsala, to welcome the supreme incarnation. For two days the party stayed at the Indian government guesthouse in Kangra while they prepared for two groups to proceed to Dharamsala. Rinpoché's incarnation was first brought to the branch of Ganden Shartsé Monastery in Dharamsala for a welcome reception. Then on June 10, an auspicious day, Rinpoché was received by the Tibetan government, by the monks of Sera, Ganden, and Drepung, as well as by the monks of Gyütö and Gyümé tantric colleges. They then proceeded to the Tashi Rapten residence at Gangchen Kyishong, where they performed a vast ceremony amid various offerings and perfectly enthroned him as the supreme incarnation of Kyabjé Trijang Vajradhara.

Among the many indications that this child was the correct reincarnation was his reaction on first encountering his former attendants Kungo Palden and Jamyang Tashi—his great happiness at meeting them, as though reunited after a long separation. He was also very fond of vajras, bells, and other ritual items, just as the previous Trijang Rinpoché was.

Many people said that Tsering Gyurmé (the birth name of Trijang Rinpoché's incarnation) was obviously someone very special and must be the incarnation of a high lama. Therefore, the former abbot of Ratö Monastery invited him to his residence for an examination, at which time Tsering Gyurmé identified many photos of various lamas that the abbot showed him. While Rinpoché's incarnation was looking at these photos, he pointed to the photo of the previous Trijang Rinpoché and said, "This is a photo of me!"

Rinpoché's incarnation would often drink a lot of milk, so much so that his parents said, "It will be hard to cover our expenses if you keep drinking so much milk."

Rinpoché reassured them, "Don't worry I have lots of cows."

His father Topgyal had a new pair of shoes that he didn't usually wear, saving them for special occasions. Rinpoché told him, "Now it is time to wear your special shoes."

His father replied, "I need to save them. I don't have another pair this nice."

To this, Rinpoché said, "Don't worry! Palden will buy you another pair."

Also, Rinpoché was always talking about going to Dharamsala. Kyabjé Rinpoché had a unique way of calling for Palden, and the incarnation did so in exactly the same way. Also, when they arrived in Dharamsala, he took charge of all of the previous Trijang Rinpoché's belongings just as if they were his own.

On July 1, 1986, Rinpoché's incarnation had his first audience with His Holiness the Dalai Lama. At this hair-cutting ceremony, His Holiness recited the *Hundred Deities of Tuṣita*, named Rinpoché Tenzin Losang Yeshé Gyatso, and gave him a sacred statue of Buddha.

On July 14, Rinpoché was invited to Ganden Monastery. On his way, he traveled through Delhi, Poona, and Hubli, and on July 21, a very auspicious day, he arrived in Mundgod, South India, and was welcomed at the Phuntsok Rapten residence at Ganden Shartsé, where they had a vast celebration and enthroned him as the supreme incarnation of Kyabjé Trijang Vajradhara.

Later, in 1987, His Holiness gave the empowerment of Life-Sustaining Jé Rinpoché, which Rinpoché attended.

On February 22, 1988, he was received as an official member of Ganden Shartsé amid the entire assembly of monks, and the next day there was a vast celebration in honor of his official enrollment at Ganden Shartsé. As a component of that celebration, Shartsé's Dokhang House as well as the monks of Drepung Monastery partook in the Great Prayer Festival, which Rinpoché attended. This event was sponsored by Trijang Labrang, and a token monetary offering was made to all the monks.

Rinpoché visited the monasteries of Ganden Jangtsé and Sera, Gyütö and Gyümé tantric colleges, Tashi Lhunpo, Gyümé Tantric College in Hunsur, Dzongkar Chödé, Drepung Monastery in Mundgod, the Sakya monastery, and the Nyingma monastery Taklung Chödé, where he made vast offerings to these respective monasteries and their resident monks while visiting all of their respective temples. When he arrived in Dharamsala after having completed all religious obligations, he had an audience with His Holiness.

Today Trijang Choktrul Rinpoché resides in Vermont as the spiritual director of the Trijang Buddhist Institute, where he continues his studies while providing teachings and guidance to his disciples.

Appendix: The Incarnation Lineage of Kyabjé Trijang Rinpoché[417]

Buddha's charioteer Candaka
Arhat Madhughoṣa
Kuśala Rasadhara
Master Vimalaśrī
Candrakīrti (600–ca. 650)
Bodhisattva Dharmamitra
Śāntarakṣita (eighth century)
Atiśa Dīpaṃkara Śrījñāna (980–1054)
Geshé Langri Thangpa (Kadam) (1054–1123)
Lotsāwa Jampal Dorjé (Sakya) (1485–1533)
Chöjé Mönlam Palwa (early Ganden Throneholder) (1414–91)
Chöjé Lodrö Palsang
Karmapa Mikyö Dorjé (Kagyü) (1507–54)
Surchen Chöying Rangdröl (Nyingma) (1604–69)
The First Trijang Rinpoché, Tri Jangchup Chöphel (1756–1838)
The Second Trijang Rinpoché, Tri Tsultrim Palden (1839–99)
The Third Trijang Rinpoché, Trijang Losang Yeshé Tenzin Gyatso (1901–81)

Notes

1. The reference is to a saying of Sakya Paṇḍita about how when a wise person speaks, no one listens, but when a monkey dances, everybody looks.
2. The Ganden Throneholder, or Ganden Tripa, is the highest lama in the Geluk tradition, holding the throne of its founder, Tsongkhapa (1357–1419).
3. Gungthang Könchok Tenpai Drönmé (1762–1823) was one of Tibet's great literary figures, with a vast and diverse body of work. He was especially renowned in his home region of Amdo.
4. The autobiography of Doring Tenzin Paljor (b. 1760), a Tibetan civil servant, includes a biography of his father, Doring Paṇḍita Ngödrup Rapten (1721–92).
5. Possibly *Bka' blon rtogs brjod*, an autobiographical work by scholar and political leader Dokharwa Tsering Wangyal (1697–1763).
6. The three poisons are desire, hatred, and ignorance. The eight worldly concerns are worldly motivations that undermine the practice of Dharma. They are concerns about (1–2) gain and loss, (3–4) pleasure and pain, (5–6) praise and blame, (7–8) fame and disrepute.
7. "The supreme ārya with a lotus in the hand" is an epithet for Avalokiteśvara, and the entire phrase is in reference to him as the protector of Tibet.
8. Lama Shang Yudrakpa Tsöndrü Drakpa (1122–93) founded Tsal Gungthang Monastery in 1175 just north of Lhasa and ruled over Central Tibet for a number of years. The Tsalpa Kagyü tradition no longer exists as a distinct school.
9. King Lhasang, a.k.a. Lajang Khan, was a Mongol ruler who held dominion over Tibet between the Fifth and the Seventh Dalai Lamas in the early eighteenth century.
10. Dzamling Chegu Wangdü (1855–1919) was the thirty-eighth patriarch of Phuntsok Phodrang. The Sakya Phuntsok Phodrang supplies one of the patriarchs of the Sakya school, while the other comes from Drölma Phodrang. In the past, these two patriarchs alternated as heads of the Sakya school, and until 2017, that appointment was for life. Now the throneholder position is appointed every three years from among qualified members of the two Phodrangs. The first to be enthroned under the new system is the son of the previous Sakya Trizin.
11. *Tsa-tsa* are small clay images of enlightened beings.
12. The day of the third-quarter moon. One of the two *tshes bcu*, or half-moon days, in a month; they are treated as auspicious days in the Tibetan calendar.
13. Sngags rams pa Rgyud stod Blo bzang bstan dar. The title Ngakrampa indicates that Losang Tendar was a tantric graduate, i.e., a Geluk geshé who earned a tantric degree from either of the two Geluk tantric colleges of Lhasa—Gyütö and Gyumé.
14. Ganden is not only the name of Ganden Monastery but is the name of Maitreya's pure land (Sanskrit: Tuṣita), where Lama Tsongkhapa is said to reside.

15. One of the two principal state oracles of Tibet, the other being the Nechung oracle.
16. The Fifth Ling Rinpoché Losang Lungtok Tenzin Trinlé (1856–1902), a tutor to the Thirteenth Dalai Lama.
17. Of body, speech, mind, qualities, and activities.
18. The Great Prayer Festival (*smon lam chen mo*) was initiated by Tsongkhapa in 1409 to commemorate Buddha Śākyamuni's victory over five rival teachers who challenged him in a contest of supernatural feats. Celebrated in Lhasa in the Jokhang Temple complex, the festival takes place over two weeks during the waxing moon of the first Tibetan month. The festival focuses around the chanting of praises to the Buddha and other great masters by large congregations of monks from all over Tibet. It is during the Great Prayer Festival that the geshé lharam candidates of that year sit for their final examinations.
19. Samling Mitsen is a group of Chatreng monks at Sera, Dokhang House was the late throneholder's house at Ganden, and Shartsé College is where the late throneholder had studied.
20. The *Book of Kadam* consists of two distinct volumes, the Father Teachings and the Son Teachings. The Son Teachings is a collection of twenty-two stories, narrated by Atiśa, relating the past lives of his student, the Kadam school founder Dromtönpa (1005–64). The stories are reminiscent of the well-known *Jātakas*, which chronicle the past lives of the Buddha. For more, see the introduction to Thupten Jinpa, trans., *The Book of Kadam: The Core Texts* (Boston: Wisdom, 2008).
21. The First Paṇchen Lama Losang Chökyi Gyaltsen (1567–1662) was tutor to the Fifth Dalai Lama, and Kachen was also born in the sixteenth century. The text in question is likely the *Lam rim khrid yig zhal shes man ngag*.
22. The "pig-headed fortune teller" was a charlatan psychic who wore a pig's head and would predict the future. Of course, some of what he said turned out to be true.
23. This is the incarnation of Ngawang Losang Trinlé Rapgyé, the Ninth Demo Rinpoché (1855–99), who was charged with plotting against the Thirteenth Dalai Lama. See Tsepon W. D. Shakabpa, *Tibet: A Political History* (New Haven, CT: Yale University Press, 1967), 194–96.
24. The upper tantric college of Gyütö, established in 1474 by Jetsun Kunga Döndrup (1419–86), is one of two major tantric colleges of the Geluk tradition. Gyümé, the lower tantric college, was established in 1433 by Kunga Döndrup's teacher Jetsun Sherap Sengé (1383–1445). The colleges are called "upper" and "lower" based on their relative locations.
25. Rinpoché contracted tuberculosis at a young age after getting his geshé lharampa degree in exile at the monastic encampment at Buxa, West Bengal. See chapter 11.
26. Radreng (or Reting) is the first monastery of the Kadam school founded by Dromtönpa, the chief Tibetan disciple of Atiśa. In 1738, the Seventh Dalai Lama offered this monastery to his teacher, Ganden Throneholder Ngawang Chokden. Since then, the reincarnations of Ngawang Chokden have been called Radreng Tulku.
27. A red ceremonial robe made of wool with "crow's eye" designs on the back worn by high-ranking lamas and abbots while riding horses in ceremonial processions.
28. Typically, such offerings consist of a mandala base symbolizing the offering of the universe, a statue to represent the Buddha's body, a text to represent his speech, and a stupa to represent his mind. Sometimes a small sum of money is put in a specially folded envelope, called *shokchak*, with "Token offering of mandala with body, speech, and mind" written in the front in ornate *drutsa* script.

29. The "three representations" are the representations of body, speech, and mind described in the preceding note.
30. A former *kalön* of the council of ministers, the *kashak*. The account of Shedrawa can be found in Shakabpa, *Tibet: A Political History*, 208.
31. The Drimé Kunden drama is a Tibetan retelling of the popular *Viśvantara Jātaka*, the story of how the Buddha in his past life as Prince Viśvantara perfected his practice of generosity by giving away the national treasury, then his children, and finally his own eyes.
32. Losang Gyaltsen (b. 1840) served as Ganden Throneholder for seven years in the first decade of the twentieth century and was elected by the National Assembly to rule in the absence of His Holiness.
33. *'Jam dbyangs chos skor*. This is a cycle of empowerments that Tsongkhapa received directly from the bodhisattva Mañjuśrī.
34. Ratö, founded in 1205, was a small but renowned monastery in Chushur known as the center for training in logic in Tibet.
35. The debate manuals called Collected Topics (*bsdus grwa*) are used as introductory textbooks in Geluk monasteries, and they usually begin with basic arguments about the classification of colors. Learning how to apply simple logical reasoning to these categories prepares one to study more difficult issues.
36. Khangsar Dorjé Chang Ngawang Thupten Chökyi Wangchuk (ca. 1888–1941). Phabongkha and Khangsar are together called the sun and moon of the Buddha's teachings.
37. During this session a new monastic disciplinarian (*dge bskos*) is inaugurated from among the scholarly members of the monastery to ensure strict enforcement of monastic discipline as well as the study curriculum.
38. *Drang nges legs bshad snying po*, hereafter referred to as the *Essence of Eloquence*.
39. The *Marvelous Array Sutra* (*Gaṇḍavyūhasūtra*) narrates the story of Sudhana, who receives teachings from fifty-two different masters in his quest for enlightenment. This sutra illustrates many types of guru devotion.
40. Ceremonial cookies in festive shapes made of dough and deep-fried in butter or oil.
41. The Dharma masters (*chos rje*) Sharpa Chöjé and Jangtsé Chöjé represent the penultimate stations of ecclesiastical authority in the Geluk order. Only someone holding one of these two positions may ascend the Ganden throne. Ascension alternates between the Sharpa Chöjé and Jangtsé Chöjé.
42. The First Jamyang Shepa, Ngawang Tsöndrü (1648–1721), was the founder of Tashi Khyil Monastery and composed the textbooks for Drepung Gomang and Ganden Shartsé.
43. Lianyu was the last Qing amban stationed in Lhasa, a position he held from 1906–12. Ambans operated as Qing imperial residents in protectorate regions of the Qing state.
44. Tibet had a complex system of currency in the first half of the twentieth century, with the most common coins called the *sho* (*zho*), *sang* (*srang*), and *tam* (*tam*). These were composed of various metals depending on the minting, with shifting denominations that increased over the period. Tibet also had paper currency starting from 1913, also using *tam* and *sang* denominations. In general, ten *sho* was worth one *sang*, and fifty *sang* made a *dotsé* (*rdo tshad*). Gold *sang*, issued between 1918 and 1921, were worth twenty *sang*. The value of the *tam*, *tamdo* (*tam rdo*), *tangka*, or *tamkar* (*tam dkar*), the most common and longstanding form of coinage, is hard to pinpoint relative to the *sang*, as there were several varieties. When the *sang* coin, or *ngulsang*

(*dngul srang*), first appeared in 1909, it was worth about seven silver *tam*, but the final *tamkar*, issued in 1953–54 for distribution to monks, was valued at five *sang*.

45. A wooden board covered with fine dust particles would have been used by each student as a blackboard for this practice.
46. *Sna tshogs yum*. This deity is the consort of Kālacakra and is particularly associated with the power to ward off sickness.
47. A popular verse of praise for Tsongkhapa, which begins with the words *mikmé tsewai* ("Immeasurable compassion . . .") and so is called the *miktsema* for short.
48. Skt. Devīkoṭī. A form of Palden Lhamo (Skt. Śrīdevī), the principal protector goddess of Tibet.
49. Another protector goddess of Tibet who hails from Kongpo, where she encountered Padmasambhava as he traveled to Tibet, swearing an oath to protect the country and its religious practitioners from then on. According to lore, this goddess is an incarnation of Chinnamuṇḍā Vajravārāhī.
50. *Bstan ma bcu gnyis*. These are twelve female spirits of Tibet that Padmasambhava subjugated and converted to protectors of the Buddhist teachings.
51. When the eighteenth infantry division of the Qing dynasty's army invaded Tibet.
52. The nationalist revolution against the reign of the emperor of the Manchu Qing dynasty.
53. *Lha babs dus chen*. One of the four major Buddhist holidays celebrated in Tibetan culture. It commemorates the Buddha's return from Tuṣita heaven after journeying there to teach Dharma to his deceased mother.
54. *Dga' ldan lnga mchod*. A festival of lights commemorating Jé Tsongkhapa.
55. Reading out the entire Buddhist canon is traditional means of dispelling obstacles and gathering merit.
56. *Tshogs mchod*. Here this refers to the great offering ceremony performed in the waning fortnight of the second Tibetan month.
57. A subject in Perfection of Wisdom studies.
58. *Sri mnan*. "Demons" (*sri*) here are interfering spirits that are ritually summoned and then buried during this rite.
59. A "birth deity" is a local god or spirit who follows you from one life to the next. If you make offerings to your birth deity, he or she will provide you with favorable conditions.
60. These two open the list of topics treated in Maitreya's *Ornament of Realization* (*Abhisamayālaṃkāra*).
61. A vast collection of teachings covering the history and activities of the Dharma king Songtsen Gampo as well as numerous sādhanas and discourses on the practice of Avalokiteśvara and his six-syllable mantra.
62. A title denoting one who has received transmission of the teachings of the Buddha in their entirety.
63. This indicates an intensive period of study that covered in a few months material that would typically take about a year.
64. According to the *Blue Annals*, the siddha Tsembupa (*tshem bu pa*) received the lineage of the Great Compassionate One from the goddess Nairātmyā and practiced on Mount Yeru (*g.yas ru*).
65. The Tibetan *Rdor phreng* encompasses the *Vajrāvalī* description of the forty-two mandalas by the twelfth-century Abhayākaragupta with the accompanying *Niṣpan-*

nayogāvalī, which describes how deities are added to these, and the *Jyotirmañjarī* description of the fire offerings for each practice.

66. The five sciences are language, crafts, medicine, logic, and Dharma.
67. These are classical texts on Tibetan language by Thönmi Sambhota. The *Thirty Verses* (*Sum cu pa*) is a work on grammar, and *Introduction to Morphology* (*Rtags kyi 'jug pa*) is a text on Tibetan word forms.
68. The six signs of longevity are a wise man, water, a cliff, a crane, a tree, and a deer. The four harmonious friends are from a story about an elephant, monkey, rabbit, and bird.
69. *Rin 'byung brgya rtsa*. A collection of sādhanas compiled by Tāranātha. Though called a "Hundred," it contains more than four hundred sādhanas, or ritual deity practices.
70. *Sbyor chos thub stan lhun po'i mzdes rgyan*.
71. Kyergangpa Chökyi Sengé (1143–1216) was a founding member of the Shangpa Kagyü lineage.
72. Za byed mkha' 'gro, the "devouring ḍāka," one of nine preliminary practices of the Ganden oral tradition. In this purification rite, offerings are poured into Vajraḍāka's mouth in the form of sesame seeds cast into a fire.
73. *Dpung rgyan*. The identity of this text is uncertain.
74. The ninth, nineteenth, and twenty-ninth of the lunar month.
75. *'Pho ba dkar khyung mda' 'phen*.
76. A *tang* is a yak-skin container for storing butter.
77. *Tshogs langs*. An examination wherein the candidate must stand, debate, and recite in the monastic assembly. It is customary that the candidate make an offering to the assembly on such occasions.
78. *Doram* (*rdo rams*) is a rank of geshé not universally accepted by all three monastic seats. It is so called because the debates were held in front of a large stone (*do*) on which was placed the throne of the Dalai Lamas. The term *lingsé* (*gling bsres*), "mixing of the communities," dates to a time when candidates were examined by more than one college within the same monastery.
79. *'Bri mo*, the female of a particular species of yak.
80. The five classical Indian books studied at the heart of the geshé curriculum are Dharmakīrti's *Treatise of Valid Cognition* (*Pramāṇavārttika*), Maitreya's *Ornament of Realization* (*Abhisamayālaṃkāra*), Candrakīrti's *Entering the Middle Way* (*Madhyamakāvatāra*), Guṇaprabha's *Vinaya Sutra*, and Vasubandhu's *Treasury of Abhidharma* (*Abhidharmakośa*).
81. This refers to those prayer sessions where tea is served.
82. An important ceremony on the twenty-ninth day of the new year in which a sacrificial cake (*gtor ma*) is thrown into a bonfire to dispel obstacles.
83. Uchu Muchin Sokpo Hothokthu, mentioned above. "Hothokthu" is a title for high lamas bestowed by the Manchu emperor.
84. Daṇḍin's *Kāvyādārśa*, the principal text on classical Indian poetics studied in Tibet.
85. *Snyan ngag me long gi rtsa ba dang dka' 'grel dbyangs can dgyes glu*. This commentary was written by the Fifth Dalai Lama, Ngawang Losang Gyatso.
86. Sometimes in Tibetan monastic culture the prenatal months of a person's life (*mngal shol gyi zla ba*) are added to their postnatal age in order to allow their full ordination earlier than would otherwise be possible.

87. Full monastic ordination as a bhikṣu must be overseen by both a preceptor (*upādhyāya*) and a master (*ācārya*). His Holiness the Thirteenth Dalai Lama filled both of these roles for Trijang Rinpoché.
88. Assistant tutor to His Holiness from Deyang College of Drepung Monastery.
89. The interviewing master (*raho'nuśāsakācārya*) asks a series of standard questions to validate the ordinand's candidacy for ordination.
90. Tsongkhapa's collected works comprise eighteen volumes. The works of his two principal disciples, Gyaltsap Darma Rinchen (1364–1432) and Khedrup Gelek Palsangpo (1385–1438), comprise eight and twelve volumes, respectively.
91. *Prajñāśataka* (*Shes rab brgya pa*), attributed to Nāgārjuna.
92. Of the four interwoven commentaries on Guhyasamāja, the first is Candrakīrti's *Bright Lamp* (*Pradīpoddyotana*), and the other three are commentaries by Tsongkhapa on Candrakīrti's text: general interlinear annotations, an analysis of difficult points called the *Precious Sprout* (*Rin chen myu gu*), and a summary outline.
93. *Be'u bum*. A collection compiled by Khyenrap Tenpa Chöphel of ritual texts associated with the *miktsema* verse.
94. *Sindura'i dbang bzhi byin rlabs.*
95. *Drug bcu ma*. The sixty-four-part torma-offering ritual made to the protector Dharmarāja and the fifteen direction protectors.
96. *Blo bzang thub dbang rdo rje 'chang*. An epithet of Tsongkhapa Losang Drakpa as an embodiment of both the Buddha and Vajradhara.
97. The *Words of Mañjuśrī*, composed by the Fifth Dalai Lama, is one of the so-called eight great texts on the stages of the path (*lam rim*). The *Quick Path*, another of the eight, was composed by the Second Paṇchen Lama as a commentary on the First Paṇchen Lama's *Easy Path*.
98. These teachings became the basis for the very popular text that Trijang Rinpoché compiled from notes taken on the occasion. The work is available in multiple English translations, including *Liberation in the Palm of Your Hand*, translated by Michael Richards (Boston: Wisdom, 1991).
99. The rival candidate for the Trijang Rinpoché reincarnation from Chatreng.
100. This is in reference to the famous analogy used to exemplify the difficulty in obtaining rebirth as a human being: the chance that a blind turtle that resides on the bottom of a great ocean and surfaces only once every hundred years will poke its head through a golden yoke floating randomly upon the surface.
101. This text was composed by Tsongkhapa. It is almost half the length of the *Great Exposition on the Stages of the Path* and focuses more on the practical application of the stages of the path.
102. Padmavajra was his secret, tantric name.
103. *Rdo tshad*. See note 44 above.
104. *Ba ri brgya rtsa*. A set of one hundred initiations collected by Bari Lotsāwa Rinchen Drak (1040–1111), the Second Sakya Trizin.
105. *Grub thabs rgya mtsho*. A set of initiations collected by Kunkhyen Pema Karpo (1527–92), the Fourth Gyalwang Drukpa.
106. *Nar thang brgya rtsa*. A set of one hundred initiations collected by the Kadam master Chim Namkha Drak (1210–85), the seventh abbot of Narthang Monastery.
107. The main administrative body of Ganden Monastery.
108. A hilltop at Ganden where prayer flags are hung and incense is burned.
109. *Rab gnas dge legs char 'bebs.*

110. A *tsipar* is an imaginary animal used in various decorations, especially in colorful brocade banners hung on the pillars inside temples.
111. The syllables of the full name of the Thirteenth Dalai Lama, Ngawang Losang Thupten Gyatso Jikdral Wangchuk Choklé Namgyal Dé, are woven into the poem. The verse is taking the sun as a metaphor. The sun is known as the friend of the lotus; it is a beacon, and in Vedic myth it arose from the ocean.
112. *Gcod*, literally "cutting through," a practice lineage originating with the female practitioner Machik Labdrön (1055–1143), who in turn extracted it from a teaching in the Perfection of Wisdom sutras.
113. This is in reference to the Tibetan custom of placing rings in the noses of livestock to lead them. If you are not receptive (i.e., made of stone), higher beings cannot possibly lead you.
114. *Rta thog ma*. A consecration ceremony so brief, it is said to be possible to perform it without getting off your horse. The full consecration takes three days with elaborate rituals.
115. *Rigs gsum mgon po*—that is, Avalokiteśvara, Vajrapāṇi, and Mañjuśrī.
116. *Kun tu rgyu*, wandering ascetics. Trijang Rinpoché is referring to the story of one of Buddha's chief disciples. Maudgalyāyana was widely known to possess supernatural powers, but when he was under attack by his assailants, his powers failed him, and he was beaten to death. Buddha later revealed that the disappearance of his powers at his moment of need was a karmic result of thinking about beating his parents in a previous life.
117. *Mgon po bse khrab*, the main protector of Ganden Shartsé, is also associated with Sangphu Monastery. Sangphu and Shartsé recognize Setrap as an emanation of Buddha Amitābha.
118. That is, Sera, Ganden, and Drepung monasteries.
119. Drogön Chögyal Phakpa (1235–80) was the fifth patriarch of the Sakya school of Tibetan Buddhism and the nephew of Sakya Paṇḍita. He is known for developing an alliance with Kublai Khan of the Yuan dynasty.
120. Jampal Lhundrup's *Preliminary Practices: A Necklace for the Fortunate* (*Sbyor chos skal bzang mgrin rgyan*).
121. *Rje rigs gsum spyi sgrub*.
122. *Wheel of Sharp Weapons Mind Training* (*Blo sbyong mtshon cha 'khor lo*), v. 42.
123. A *thread cross*, in its simplest form, is two crossed sticks woven together with thread. Thread crosses act as containers for ritual substances or effigies of victims in rites to dispel harm.
124. *Prajñādaṇḍa* (*Shes rab sdong po*). This is a collection of sayings attributed to Nāgārjuna.
125. An idiomatic phrase indicating a conspiracy behind events.
126. A dough-ball divination is performed by placing various answers to a question that you ask of a certain protector or other enlightened being inside dough balls, typically three. After a preparatory ritual, the dough balls are swirled around in a cup until one "leaps" from the cup, thus revealing the correct answer through the blessing of the particular enlightened being.
127. Gushri Tenzin Chögyal (1582–1655) was a Mongol khan who patronized the Dalai Lamas. Desi Sangyé Gyatso (1653–1705) was the regent of Tibet during the interregnum after the passing of the Fifth Dalai Lama. The town of Gyalthang was renamed Shangri-la by Chinese authorities in the mid 1990s to boost tourism.

128. Shalngo Sönam Chöphel (1595–1657), a chief minister of the Fifth Dalai Lama who helped establish the Ganden Phodrang.
129. *Gcod stan thog gcig ma.*
130. Dulwa Dzinpa Drakpa Gyaltsen (1374–1434) was a senior and early disciple of Jé Tsongkhapa and a specialist in the monastic discipline.
131. This refers to a ritual to request the holy essence of religious objects to depart to their respective pure lands so that the dismantling of a sacred building will not be a sacrilegious act.
132. A sweet scent reminiscent of flowers is said to exude from the bodies of highly realized beings who keep pure discipline, extending to the period in which they remain absorbed in clear-light meditation after passing away.
133. A common Tibetan greeting, which means "May it be auspicious and good!"
134. A labrang of Shartsé College.
135. Rice pudding cooked with butter and several kinds of dried fruit.
136. Twenty kilograms.
137. This is in reference to taking Dharma for granted, like a person who lives in Lhasa yet never goes to see the Buddha in the Jokhang Temple there.
138. The Ösal Buk is the room at Ganden Monastery where Lama Tsongkhapa passed away and is the residence of all subsequent Ganden Throneholders.
139. Joona Repo kindly compiled this list of the seventeen aspects from the titles of the permissions in the collected works of Phabongkha Rinpoché: (1) Mahākāla Time of Approximation: Four-Faced Lord, Robber of Strength (Stobs 'phrog dbang po gdong bzhi pa bsnyen dus mgon po), (2) Uncommon Mahākāla Time of Approximation (Bsnyen dus thun mong ma yin pa), (3) Mahākāla Time of Accomplishment: Multicolored Faces (Sgrub dus kyi mgon po zhal khra can), (4) Uncommon Mahākāla Time of Accomplishment (Sgrub dus thun mong ma yin pa), (5) Śrī Mahākāla with a Mask in the lineage of Paṇḍita Bumtrak Sumpa (Paṇḍi ta 'bum phrag gsum pa nas brgyud pa'i dpal mgon gdong brnyan can), (6) Common White Five-Deity Longevity [Mahākāla] (Dkar po tshe 'phel lha lnga thun mong ba), (7) Uncommon White Longevity [Mahākāla] (Dkar po tshe 'phel thun mong ma yin pa), (8) Yellow Five-Deity Four-Faced Śrī Mahākāla Increasing Merit (Dpal mgon zhal bzhi pa ser po bsod nams rgyas byed lha lnga), (9) Uncommon Yellow Four-Faced Śrī Mahākāla Increasing Merit (Dpal mgon zhal bzhi pa ser po rgyas byed thun mong ma yin pa), (10) Five-Deity Four-Faced Śrī Mahākāla Bringing All under His Power (Dpal mgon zhal bzhi pa dbang sdud lha lnga), (11) Four-Faced Śrī Mahākāla, principal and fourfold retinue, called Destroying Obstacles (Dpal mgon zhal bzhi pa bgegs 'joms gtso 'khor lnga), (12) Utterly Fierce and Secret Displaying Auspiciousness, or "Split Faces" and "Stacked Faces" (Shin tu gnyan cing gsang ba shis bstan pa'am gdong bkas ma dang brtsegs zhal mar grags pa), (13) Extremely Fierce Mahākāla Striking the Vital Point Practiced Like the Inner Yama (Ches shin tu gnyan pa nang gshin rje ltar sgrub pa gnad dbab kyi mgon po), (14) Utterly Secret and Fierce Commander, the Secret Accomplishment Mahākāla (Ches shin tu gsang zhing bka' gnyan pa gsang 'khrid), (15) Four-Faced Śrī Mahākāla with the Face of a Garuḍa, or "The Mahākāla General" (Dpal mgon zhal bzhi pa khyung zhal can nam, dmag dpon mgon por grags pa), (16) Four-Faced Śrī Mahākāla Black Lion (Dpal mgon zhal bzhi pa seng+ge nag po), (17) Śrī Mahākāla Black Brahman and the Six Butchers (Dpal mgon bram gzugs bshan pa drug).
140. Jetsun Thupten Jampal Yeshé Tenpai Gyaltsen (1912–42).

141. "The vase" refers to the bulbous portion of the structure, where the body of His Holiness would be housed.
142. The Two Stainless Cycles (*dri med rnam gnyis*) are two cycles of instructions given by the Buddha Śākyamuni on how to build, fill, and consecrate stupas. Regardless of the outer form of a stupa, the inner consecration is identical in every case when based on these two cycles.
143. Dried yak dung was used as fuel for cooking.
144. *Gzungs 'bul 'khrul spong nyin byed.*
145. *Shel dkar me long.* That is, Changkya Ngawang Losang Chöden (1642–1714), *Dpal rdo rje 'jigs byed kyi zhi ba'i sbyin sreg bya tshul gyi cho ga blo bzang dgongs rgyan shel dkar me long.*
146. *Khams gsum dbang du bsdu ba'i gnad yig gangga'i chu rgyun.* We could not locate this title among Tsarchen's collected works. Tsarchen Losal Gyatso (1502–66) was a Sakya master and a prolific author. The Fifth Dalai Lama wrote a biography of him, praising the quality of his writing. For more on Tsarchen, see Cyrus Stearns, *Song of the Road: The Poetic Travel Journal of Tsarchen Losal Gyatso* (Boston: Wisdom, 2012).
147. *Dngos grub 'byung gnas.*
148. *Rin chen ljon shing.*
149. *Sgrub thabs nor bu gsal 'bar ma.*
150. *Dmar po 'khor gsum gyi dka' gnad mdud grol reg gzigs utpala dmar po'i chun po.*
151. *'Khor lo'i gsal byed khams gsum g'ugs pa'i lcags kyu.*
152. 1906–81. The younger brother of His Holiness the Thirteenth Dalai Lama.
153. The thangka referred to depicts an image common in the Geluk order. The founder of the order, Jé Tsongkhapa, is depicted flanked by his two chief disciples, Gyaltsap Jé and Khedrup Jé, seated on a billowing formation of white clouds that emanate from the heart of Maitreya, who sits above delivering a Dharma discourse to the gods of Tuṣita.
154. The three ancient doctrinal centers in Tibet: Samyé Monastery, the Jokhang Temple in Lhasa, and Tradruk Temple in Yarlung.
155. Rinpoché is expressing the five stages of the Guhyasamāja completion stage. This verse is the body and speech isolation, which are counted as one stage. The next verse expresses mind isolation, clear light, and the illusory body, and that is followed by a verse on the stage of union.
156. This likely refers to the fact that all Tibetan consonants have the letter *a* as their default vowel sound.
157. Here Trijang Rinpoché begins each couplet with the vowels represented in the Tibetan alphabet (*i, u, e, o, a*), repeating the vowel *a* at the beginning of each couplet in the last verse.
158. As the monastery of the Kagyü forefather Gampopa Sönam Rinchen (1079–1153), Daklha Gampo is effectively the mother monastery of all the various Kagyü lineages.
159. *Dbus gtsang gnas yig ngo mtshar lung ston me long*, the guide to the holy places of central Tibet composed in the nineteenth century by Jamyang Khyentsé Wangpo (1820–92).
160. *Mchan bzhi sbrags ma*; four sets of annotation interwoven into Tsongkhapa's text—annotations by Baso Lhawang Chökyi Gyaltsen (1537–1605), the First Jamyang Shepa (1648–1721), Kharok Khenchen Ngawang Rapten (b. seventeenth century), and Trati Geshé Rinchen Döndrup of Sera Jé (b. seventeenth century).
161. *Mkha' 'gro bsu zlog.*

162. The five types of offerings are flowers, incense, light, water, and ritual cakes.
163. *Madhyamakahṛdaya* (*Dbu ma snying po*) by the Indian master Bhāviviveka. In Sanskrit Buddhist literature, sandalwood is said to have special cooling powers.
164. Namo Buddha is the location where, in a previous life during his career as a bodhisattva, the Buddha is said to have fed his own body to a tigress so that she could feed her starving tiger cubs.
165. The seat on which the Buddha sat and gained enlightenment under the Bodhi Tree.
166. Three sets of prayers, *smon lam rnam gsum*, are the *Prayer of Samantabhadra*, the *Prayer to Be Born in the Coming of Maitreya*, and chapter 10 of *Guide to the Bodhisattva's Way of Life*.
167. The three "red ones" (*dmar mo*) referred to are the cycles of Vajrayoginī in the system of Nāropa, Vajrayoginī in the system of Indrabhūti, and Vajrayoginī in the system of Maitripa—all derived from the Cakrasaṃvara tantras. The three "great red ones" (*dmar chen*) are the cycle of Kurukulle from the Hevajra Tantra and the cycles of Great Red Gaṇapati and the wrathful Kakchöl Kāmarāja on the basis of Cakrasaṃvara tantra. The three "minor red ones" (*dmar chung*) are Kurukulle Garbhasuvarṇasūtra Śrī, Red Vasudhārā, and the goddess Tinuma. These comprise the first nine of the Thirteen Golden Dharmas. The remaining four are Blue Siṃhamukha, Black Mañjuśrī, Vajragaruḍa, and the longevity practice of Red Jambhala.
168. The conch shell is believed to be from the time of the historical Buddha. The Black Skin Mask Guardian is a form of Mahākāla. His physical representation in the form of a dance mask was housed at Gorum, Sakya's original temple founded by Khön Könchok Gyalpo (1034–1102).
169. The Lochen Rinpochés are said to be reincarnations of Lochen, or "great translator," Rinchen Sangpo (958–1055). This particular incarnation, Losang Palden Rinchen Gyatso (dates unknown), had been tutor to the Ninth Paṇchen Lama Chökyi Nyima (1883–1937).
170. *Dga' ldan sprul pa'i glegs bam*, a.k.a. the *Ganden Emanation Scripture*, is the root text of the Geluk mahāmudrā oral lineage, which tradition says was a magical revealed book that Tsongkhapa passed to his disciple Tokden Jampal Gyatso. Paṇchen Losang Chögyen received the oral lineage from his teacher, but it is said he also had access to the mystical book before he put the oral instructions down in writing. See Joona Repo, "Phabongkha Dechen Nyingpo: His Collected Works and the Guru-Deity-Protector Triad," *Revue d'Études Tibétaines* 33 (October 2015): 5–72, esp. 36–37.
171. Śākya Śrībhadra (1127–1225), an Indian scholar who visited Tibet at the behest of Trophu Lotsāwa, oversaw the construction of the great Maitreya statue at Trophu Monastery, translated many Sanskrit works into Tibetan, and founded an ordination lineage.
172. A favorite place of Atiśa, where he spent the last few years of his life and passed away in 1054.
173. *Gsang 'dus bskyed rim dngos grub rgya mtsho*, a commentary on Guhyasamāja by Tsongkhapa's disciple Khedrup Jé Gelek Palsang (1385–1438).
174. Jampal Lhundrup (1845–1919) of Dakpo Shedrup Ling Monastery was one of Phabongkha Rinpoché's teachers. An eighty-three-folio biography of him appears in Phabongkha's collected works.
175. Thuken Losang Chökyi Nyima (1737–1802), Gungthang Könchok Tenpai Drönmé (1762–1823), and Jé Sherap Gyatso (1803–75) were all born in Amdo and spent much of their lives there.

176. Chapter 4, verse 10, of Sakya Paṇḍita's *Jewel Treasury of Wise Sayings.*
177. See note 22 above.
178. Patsap Nyima Drak (b. 1055) studied with Indian masters in Kashmir for twenty-three years before returning to Tibet and popularizing the study of Madhyamaka via Candrakīrti's *Entrance to the Middle Way* (*Madhyamakāvatāra*) and *Clear Words* (*Prasannapadā*), both of which he translated into Tibetan.
179. Khamlungpa Shākya Yönten (1025–1115) was one of the principal students of Dromtönpa. See Thupten Jinpa, *Wisdom of the Kadam Masters* (Boston: Wisdom, 2013), 72.
180. This refers to the center of the sixty-four-petal navel cakra, and *caṇḍalī* alludes to the practice of "inner heat" (Tib. *tumo*).
181. *Rdo lag brgyud ma gsum.* The imagery here is of workers passing building stones from hand to hand through a construction site. It refers to the fact that the texts were transmitted through a direct transmission.
182. *Sgra'i ri mo*, a form of Sanskrit poetry in which the words can be arranged on the page in the form of an image. Minling Lochen is the great Nyingma polymath Dharmaśrī (1654–1717/18). Lama Lhaksam may be Lhaksam Tenpai Gyaltsen, a nineteenth-century abbot of Palpung Monastery.
183. Chapter 3, verse 1.
184. *Rwa khrid mkha 'gro snyan brgyud.* Ra Lotsāwa Dorjé Drak (b. 1016), or Ralo, introduced Vajrabhairava tantra to Tibet. He is reputed to have had a penchant for magical combat.
185. On Chögyal Phakpa, see note 119 above. Guardian of the Tent (*gur gyi mgon po*) is a two-faced form of Mahākāla that is a central protector deity of the Sakya lineage.
186. Surchen (1604–69) was an important holder of both Nyingma and Geluk lineages. He and his own teacher, Khöntön Paljor Lhundup, were the main early teachers of the Fifth Dalai Lama.
187. The Sixth Dalai Lama (1683–1706).
188. *Khendé chekhak.* Assistant tutors (*mtshan zhabs*) are the very best geshés who serve as instructors and debate partners to the young Dalai Lama. Only one is selected from each of the colleges at the three seats of learning.
189. These are Mongolian titles for high government positions of the fourth level.
190. The First Drakar Ngakrampa, Losang Tenpa Rapgyé, was born in the seventeenth century and hailed from Amdo.
191. *Rdo rje'i ri rab brtsegs pa'i 'phrul 'khor.*
192. Yuthok Yönten Gönpo merged Indic and indigenous Tibetan medical practices into a new edition of the *Four Medical Tantras* in the eleventh century and was a prolific author of medical texts. He was a descendant of another physician of the same name who lived in the time of King Trisong Detsen.
193. Because of the ill feelings of Sera Jé monks toward the government due to tensions surrounding treatment of the previous regent, Radreng Rinpoché, it was feared that some of the monks might harm Takdrak Rinpoché. Trijang Rinpoché is suggesting the lord chamberlain was being overly suspicious.
194. The Sadutshang family were not part of the ruling class but had become wealthy through trans-Himalayan trade. In an effort to redress the losses sustained by the family in the Radreng affair, a government post was offered to the family. That post was filled by Gyurmé's cousin, Rinchen Sadutshang, whose memoir is found in *A Life Unforeseen* (Somerville, MA: Wisdom, 2016).

195. The four qualities are contentment with (1) clothing, (2) shelter, and (3) food and (4) enthusiasm for practice and meditation.
196. Maudgalyāyana, although a clairvoyant disciple of the Buddha, was stoned to death by a mob. Arhat Udāyin was sometimes praised by the Buddha for his intelligence, but he had a habit of saying the wrong thing at the wrong time, which Buddha explained was a habit that followed him from prior lives. Ralpachen (806–38), also known as Tri Tsukdetsen, was one of the three great Dharma kings of Tibet's imperial period. He was assassinated by ministers who placed his anti-Buddhist brother Langdarma on the throne.
197. *Collection of Aphorisms* (*Udānavarga*) 25.9–10.
198. *Jewel Treasury of Wise Sayings* 4.41.
199. Manmatha, "churner of hearts," is an epithet of Māra, the incarnation of temptation in Buddhism.
200. The Fourth Kumbum Minyak Rinpoché, Ngawang Lekshé Gyatso, 1902–58.
201. *Mkha' mnyam ma*, by Tsongkhapa's teacher Rendawa Shönu Lodrö. The Six Ornaments are Nāgārjuna, Asaṅga, Āryadeva, Vasubandhu, Dignāga, and Dharmakīrti, and the Two Excellent Ones are Guṇaprabha and Śākyaprabha.
202. *Bse 'bag smug chung.*
203. Phabongkha Hermitage sits on the side of Mount Uduk northwest of Sera. It was originally the site of a castle of King Songtsen Gampo but was early on converted to a monastery. Tsongkhapa spent time at the monastery as a hermit, after which it eventually became a Geluk institution.
204. Within the consecration ritual is a "Celebration of the Hosts," where the sponsors of the elaborate consecration are exalted with verses of praise by the presiding ritual master. The eight auspicious signs are the lotus, parasol, wheel, banner, golden fish, endless knot, vase, and conch. The eight substances are a mirror, yogurt, *durva* grass, *bilva* fruit, a right-spiraling conch, *ghivaṃ* bile medicine, vermillion powder, and white mustard seed.
205. Vaiśākha, the fourth month in the lunar calendar, is considered an extremely auspicious month, as the Buddha's birth, enlightenment, and death are held to have happened in this month.
206. Likely the two works of Thönmi Sambhota mentioned above. See note 67.
207. *Spyi khyab mkhan po*, the chief monastic official in the government.
208. *Lha mo'i las gsum rnam gzhag.*
209. *Mkha' 'gro ma me lce 'bar ma'i rgyud.*
210. Possibly meaning *pha wang*, "bat." According to Dan Martin, "*pha wang long bu* seems to have literal meaning 'bat's anklebone.' This is a stone said to serve as a soul stone of the *btsan* demons. My guess is it's galena (lead ore)."
211. *Ngo tsha bsnol ba'i skra*. Meaning obscure.
212. *Mtshon gru.*
213. *Byang dmar.* Read as *byad dmar.*
214. *Sho rde dkar nag.*
215. Likely Kyishö Shapdrung Ngawang Tenzin Trinlé (1639–82).
216. The cabinet (*kashak*) is the council of ministers (*kalöns*). The secretariat (*drungtsi*) is the secretarial and finance committee, consisting of four monastic secretaries (*drung*) and four lay officials (*tsi*).
217. On page 152 above, Trijang Rinpoché narrates seeing the same objects on an earlier visit.

218. *Ljang dgun chos*. For a full description of the Jang winter session, see Geshé Lhundub Sopa, *Like a Waking Dream* (Boston: Wisdom, 2012), 135–37.
219. The government of the People's Republic of China holds the Seventeen-Point Agreement for the Peaceful Liberation of Tibet (十七條協議) to be a legally binding document. Tibetans, however, hold that the document was signed under duress, and its contents have been repudiated many times by His Holiness the Fourteenth Dalai Lama. The document essentially states that Tibet acknowledges that it is a part of China and wishes to be under the control of the Communist government.
220. *Gsang chen slob bshad*. There are two traditions for transmitting the Sakya school's oral instructions on the Path and Fruit (*lam 'bras*): the explication for disciples (*slob bshad*), which was originally a secret oral lineage, and the explication for the masses (*tshogs bshad*).
221. The traditional list of ten arts and sciences is Buddhist philosophy, logic, language, medicine, crafts, *kāvya* poetics, prosody, lexicography, drama, and astronomy and divination.
222. Trijang Rinpoché here refers to the polymath sovereign Desi Sangyé Gyatso (1653–1705) as Buddhasāra, a Sanskrit version of his name.
223. These diagrams, mantras, and prayers commit a protector to give assistance. The eight classes of spirits (*sde brgyad*) are enumerated in various ways but typically include beings such as māras, *tsen* demons, nāgas, and yakṣas.
224. The *gutor* (*dgu gtor*) is a ritual in conjunction with Dharmarāja that lasts about one week and is generally performed at the end of the year to overcome obstacles. A central part of the ritual consists of throwing conical torma cakes made of butter and barley flour into a massive bonfire.
225. The practice of White Mañjuśrī composed by Lalitavajra and passed down from Sasang Mati Paṇchen (Sa bzang Ma ti paṇ chen, 1294–1376).
226. Maitreya, *Abhisamayālaṃkāra* 1.37.
227. An offering of torma, incense, butter lamps, bowls of grain, and so on, each numbering one thousand.
228. *Brag gyab*. In other contexts in this book, this name is rendered Drakgyab to conform with the book's phonetic style, but the spelling here reflects the personal preference of this contemporary figure, who now lives in Germany.
229. *Baiḍūrya zhun ma'i them skas*. The *vaiḍūrya* gem, sometimes translated as lapis, is likely beryl.
230. *Mkha' spyod sgrub pa'i nye lam*. The great abbot of Shalu indicated here is likely Tsarchen Losal Gyatso. See note 146 above.
231. This was to be the very first meeting of the National People's Congress.
232. Marpa Lotsāwa (1012–97), the first Tibetan master in the Kagyü lineage, made several trips to India in his career as a translator before he became Milarepa's guru.
233. Tsari is a pilgrimage place associated with the deity Heruka Cakrasaṃvara, situated near the border with Assam, India.
234. This refers to the guru-disciple relationship that the Dalai Lamas and Paṇchen Lamas are held to have shared over many lives.
235. These were a silver currency used by the previous Chinese regime.
236. That is, Ba Chödé Monastery, Lithang Thupchen Chökhor Ling, and Gyalthang Sumtsen Ling.
237. The Mitra Hundred is a cycle of 108 tantric practices compiled by Mitrayogin (twelfth–thirteenth century).

238. During this portion of the tsok ritual, the main portion of the tsok offering is presented to the presiding lama.
239. *Spyan ras gzigs ngan song kun sgrol*. A one-faced, two-armed aspect of Avalokiteśvara flanked by Tārā and Ekajaṭī originating from the Indian mahāsiddha Mitrayogin. In a vision, Mitrayogin was told by Avalokiteśvara that anyone who receives this empowerment will not be reborn in the lower realms in their next life.
240. The Sixth Karmapa (1416–53).
241. Wencheng Gongzhu, the Chinese bride of the Songtsen Gampo (d. 649), founder of the Tibetan empire. She is credited in Tibetan lore as one of the earliest people to bring Buddhism to Tibet.
242. This is a reference to Rāvaṇa, the mythical meat-eating demon king of Śrī Laṅka, who is the antagonist to King Rāma in the Indian epic the *Rāmāyaṇa*.
243. *Gsang sgrub* (Skt. Guhyasādhana) and *Bram ze nag po*, a.k.a. *Bram gzugs* (Skt. Brahmarūpa).
244. The *saṅghāṭi* is a large robe made of a patchwork of thirty-two pieces of cloth, usually yellow in color, that is worn as a mantle over ordinary robes on special occasions.
245. *Rje bdag nyid chen po*, literally, "the lord, the great being." Rendawa Shönu Lodrö (1348–1413) was Tsongkhapa's guru.
246. Founder of Gyümé Tantric College.
247. Sadutshang gives his own account of these events in *A Life Unforeseen*, 193–200.
248. Sarvepalli Radhakrishnan, who served as vice president of India from 1952–62 and as president from 1962–67.
249. *Rgyan drug mchog gnyis*. See note 201 above. In recent times, His Holiness the Dalai Lama has expanded the list to include seventeen masters of Nālandā.
250. Rikha Ganden Shedrup Dargyé Ling. The monastery was founded in the eleventh century by Geshé Rikharwa, a student of the Kadampa master Potowa.
251. Śākya Śrībhadra. See note 171 above.
252. *Chos zab bdud zab*. Literally, "profound Dharma; profound devil." The gist of this proverb is that profound evil follows profound good, causing severe hindrances.
253. Drip Tsechok Ling Monastery was founded by Kachen (a.k.a. Yongzin) Yeshé Gyaltsen (1713–93), the author of the commentary mentioned here.
254. The First Shamarpa, reputed to be the founder of Nenang Monastery.
255. Lhalung Palgyi Dorjé, the ninth-century disciple of Padmasambhava who is said to have assassinated King Langdarma.
256. The sevenfold divinity and teaching of the Kadam tradition refers to the practice of four meditational divinities (Buddha, Avalokiteśvara, Tārā, and Acala) and the teachings of the three baskets of scripture (Vinaya, Abhidharma, and Sutra).
257. See note 80.
258. A prayer about the beauty of Ganden Monastery composed by the First Dalai Lama Gendun Drup (1391–1474).
259. That is, *Gnas sa 'dzin ma*, by the Seventh Dalai Lama (1708–57).
260. *Lha bsangs*. A ritual in which juniper and other aromatic plants are burned to produce smoke offerings to remove obstacles when beginning a new endeavor as well as to remove obstacles to health and good fortune.
261. *Dgra lha dpang bstod*. This is a very old Tibetan custom of praising local gods and protectors from atop their mountain homes. One praises and makes smoke offerings to them in their primordial struggle against negative forces. The offerings are

typically accompanied by cries of *Kye kye so so! Lha gyalo!* ("So be it! The gods are victorious!).

262. See note 8.
263. The story of Mahādeva appears, for instance, in Tāranātha's history of Buddhism in India. For a book-length investigation of the many variations of the Mahādeva legend in Buddhist literature, see Jonathan Silk, *Riven by Lust* (Honolulu: University of Hawai'i Press, 2009).
264. In this procession, a statue of Maitreya, the future buddha, is carried through the streets of Lhasa along the circumambulation circuit around the Jokhang Temple to celebrate his pending arrival in the world.
265. Because of the critical gravity of the situation for the safety of His Holiness, Trijang Rinpoché sent Ratö Chubar Rinpoché to Panglung Hermitage to consult the Shukden oracle. However, according to His Holiness in *Freedom in Exile* (London: Hodder and Stoughton, 1990), 149, the actual decision for His Holiness's departure was made on the prediction of the Nechung oracle, who while in trance drew a map of the exact location for the escape party to ford the Tsangpo River at the Ramagang ferry on the night of escape.
266. This reference is to a story about the famed Tibetan yogi Milarepa. A black deer pursued by a hunter finds safety by the side of the meditating yogi, who then disarms the hunter and sings a song that causes him to have a change of heart.
267. *Jewel Treasury of Wise Sayings* 3.30.
268. Drapa Ngönshé (1012–90) was a treasure revealer and builder of temples renowned for his revelation of the four medical tantras (*rgyud bzhi*) that form the basis of Tibetan medicine.
269. These are the three practices fundamental to preserving Buddhist monastic discipline: twice-monthly confession and mending of vows, observing the rainy-season retreat, and releasing restrictions at the end of the retreat.
270. See *My Land and My People* (New York: Potala Corporation, 1977), 206–8. His Holiness the Dalai Lama remembers this news reaching him near Chenyé Monastery via a letter that Khenchung Tara dispatched from Rawamé Monastery after fleeing the bombardment in Lhasa.
271. Yama, the Indian personification of death. The three worlds are the three realms of samsara into which beings may be born.
272. *Drag po gsum bsgril*. Vajrapāni, Hayagrīva, and Garuḍa combined into a single deity. Vajrapāni is the principal deity and displays Hayagrīva's "horse head" upon his head. Above this appears Garuḍa. It is said that its practice can overcome obstacles from all types of interfering spirits.
273. This house, originally the home of the Nowrojee family, was later purchased by Lama Yeshe and Lama Zopa Rinpoché, two of Trijang Rinpoché's students, and converted into Tushita Meditation Centre.
274. A festival of lights to commemorate the passing of Jé Tsongkhapa.
275. The penetrative insight into the nature of reality that distinguishes āryas from ordinary beings induces a change in behavior and perspective. The fourfold temperament is contentment with simple food, clothing, dwelling place, and possessions.
276. *Bstan 'bar ma*, an oft-recited prayer taken from the sutras, with the last verse added by Tibetans.
277. A ritual performed upon the completion of the consecration of a statue in a Buddhist temple, in which the eyes of the statue are either painted onto the statue or a

blindfold is removed from them, symbolizing the presence of the deity inhabiting the statue itself.

278. The *pratyālīḍha* stance, with right leg bent and left extended, is found in the depiction of wrathful deities in particular in Buddhist iconography.
279. The two tantric colleges had been reestablished in exile in Dalhousie.
280. *Lcags mkhar.* A wrathful ritual that uses a torma constructed in the shape of Yama's iron fortress, with nine or sixteen sides. It was instituted at Gyümé by Losang Tenpa Rabgyé in the late seventeenth or early eighteenth century.
281. *Rdo rje'i ri rab brtsegs pa'i 'khrul 'khor.*
282. *Rgyal po sku lnga*, "the king with five bodies." The five emanations—Pehar, Gyajin, Mönbuputra, Shingjachen, and Dralha Kyechikbu—correspond to those of body, speech, mind, activity, and qualities. The five were originally tamed by Padmasambhava as protectors of Samyé Monastery.
283. Nyangral Nyima Öser (1124–92). For more on the life of this pivotal figure in Tibetan history, see Daniel Hirshberg, *Remembering the Lotus Born* (Somerville, MA: Wisdom, 2016).
284. *Byang chub sems dpa' tshul khrims kyi rnam bshad byang chub gzhung lam*, Tsongkhapa's commentary on the chapter on ethical discipline in Asaṅga's *Bodhisattvabhūmi*. The work contains a ritual for conferring the bodhisattva vows.
285. *Rtsa ltung gi rnam bshad*, a.k.a. *Cluster of Siddhis* (*Gsang sngags kyi tshul khrims rnam bshad dngos grub kyi snye ma*), a commentary on the tantric vows.
286. *Gsang 'dus yig chung nyer gcig sogs.*
287. Nāgārjuna, *Meditation on the Generation Stage of Glorious Guhyasamāja Mahāyoga Tantra Related to the Sutra* (*Śrīguhyasamājamahāyogatantrotpādakramasādhanasūtramelāpaka*).
288. Mrs. Freda Bedi (*née* Houlston, 1911–77) was a British woman who married B. P. L. Bedi, an Indian, in 1933 and moved to India in 1934. Mrs. Bedi and her husband were active in the Indian independence movement, and she served the Indian government in a number of capacities throughout her life, primarily in the area of social welfare. In 1959 she was tasked by Jawaharlal Nehru to help the Tibetan refugees that were streaming into the country. Among other things, she founded the Young Lamas Home School, which was responsible for the early education of a number of well-known Tibetan lamas, including Chögyam Trungpa Rinpoché, Akong Rinpoché, Thubten Zopa Rinpoché, and Chökyi Nyima Rinpoché. Late in her life, Mrs. Bedi took *śrāmaṇerikā* ordination under the Sixteenth Gyalwang Karmapa and then traveled to receive full *bhikṣuṇī* ordination in Hong Kong. She is very fondly remembered by those among the first generation of Tibetan refugees in India who knew her.
289. *Legs bshad ljon dbang.* A grammar treatise by Yangchen Drupai Dorjé (1809–87) on Thönmi Sambhota's *Thirty Verses.*
290. Sometimes months in the lunar calendar require an extra day added to stay synchronized with the moon phases.
291. This was a private enterprise organized by Tibetans in exile in which the government in Dharamsala invested. See Sadutshang, *A Life Unforeseen*, 241–48.
292. The former site of the Tibetan exile government opposite the new Bhagsu Hotel.
293. *Sgra can.* In traditional Indian astronomical lore, Rāhu is one of the nine planets, specifically related to the phenomenon of solar eclipses. Mythologically speaking, Rāhu is the severed head of a demigod that swims through space, occasionally swallowing the sun, which then reappears in the sky when it falls through its neck.

294. Śavaripa, one of the eighty-four Indian mahāsiddhas, was a hunter by trade.
295. The Mön valley straddles the border of Tibet and the Indian state of Arunachal Pradesh. In Tibetan literature it evokes a wild and lush place.
296. *Gnyis med sengge.* The lion of the analogy lacks the beautiful mane and ferocious claws of the Himalayan snow lion. This is a colloquial Tibetan way to refer to someone who lacks reasoning and learning.
297. Jé Tsongkhapa's *Yid ches gsum ldan.* These six practices are inner heat, illusory body, clear light, dream yoga, intermediate state, and transference of consciousness.
298. The *Bsam pa lhun grub* and *Bar chad lam sel.*
299. Literally, "from my *sambhogacakra*," which is located at the throat and connected with speech. Trijang Rinpoché uses a poetic convention that weaves the names of the people his verses refer to into the verses themselves. He identifies the first verse with himself (Trijang) and the following two with Ling Rinpoché (Thupten Lungtok Namgyal Trinlé).
300. Here again, Trijang Rinpoché weaves the name Losang Lungrik into each verse.
301. Sudhana is a youth from the *Marvelous Array Sutra* renowned for his reliance upon his gurus. See note 39.
302. M. C. Chagla (1900–81) was a prominent Indian statesman, well known for his time as chief justice of Bombay High Court, cabinet minister under Nehru, and member of the first Indian delegation to the United Nations.
303. Choklé Namgyal, a.k.a. Bodong Paṇchen (1375–1451), was a renowned scholar and siddha whose teachings survived as an independent lineage for a few generations before being absorbed into the Sakya and Geluk lineages. He was a teacher to Gendun Drup, the First Dalai Lama. His collected works are said to fill more than a hundred volumes. Shuchen (Zhu chen, 1697–1774) was a master of the Sakya tradition from Dergé. He edited the Tengyur there and is regarded as a major figure in the transmission lineage of literary and grammatical arts.
304. Here Trijang Rinpoché weaves His Holiness's proper name, Ngawang Losang Yeshé Tenzin Gyatso, into his verse of praise of the same.
305. Into this self-deprecating verse about himself, Trijang Rinpoché weaves his own proper name, Losang Yeshé.
306. These are elsewhere enumerated as the "four prosperities" (*phun tsog sde bzhi*).
307. Tsongkhapa is here addressed as *blo gter rgyal ba*, literally, "conqueror who is a treasury of wisdom," an epithet of Tsongkhapa as an emanation of Mañjuśrī.
308. Here again, into two verses about himself and His Holiness the Dalai Lama, respectively, Trijang Rinpoché weaves his own and the Dalai Lama's proper names.
309. *Bka' brgyad bde gshegs 'dus pa*, a diverse collection of practice texts centered around eight wrathful deities. It is Nyangral's most extensive collection of rediscovered treasure texts.
310. A ninth-century translator known to have produced many of the earliest canonical translations, and his style of calligraphy has been handed down to the present day. He was said to be the chief scribe to Padmasambhava and to have written down many of his treasure teachings.
311. Gyaltsap Darma Rinchen, *Essence Ornament to Haribhadra's Clarification of the Meaning of the Ornament of Realization. Shes rab kyi pha rol tu phyin pa'i man ngag gi bstan bcos mngon par rtogs pa'i rgyan gyi 'grel pa don gsal ba'i rnam bshad snying po'i rgyan.*
312. This is the same Phalha as the lord chamberlain mentioned above.

313. Dora M. Kalff (1904–90), a Swiss woman of Dutch origin, well known as the founder of Sandplay Therapy. Mrs. Kalff hosted Geshé Losang Chödrak in her home for eight years, became a practitioner of Tibetan Buddhism and Japanese Zen, and formed friendships with many Tibetan lamas throughout her life, including His Holiness the Fourteenth Dalai Lama.
314. This was the Pestalozzi Children's Village in Trogen.
315. A private Swiss organization called the Association of Tibetan Homes (Verein Tibeter Heimstätten), in cooperation with the Swiss Red Cross and the Intergovernmental Committee for European Migration, established a series of so-called Tibetan homes (*Tibeter Heim*) to house groups of Tibetan refugees arriving in Switzerland to ease them into Swiss life. Tibetan homes were established in Samedan in the canton of Graubünden; Buchen im Prättigau, Landquart, and Igis in the canton of Graubünden; Waldstatt in the canton of Appenzell Ausserrhoden; Wattwil, Lichtensteig, Ebnat-Kappel, Flawil, Rapperswil, and Wil in the canton of St. Gallen; Münchwilen in the canton of Thurgau; and Rikon, Umgebung, Turbenthal, Bauma, Rüti, Oetwil am See, and Horgen in the canton of Zürich.
316. Rakra Thubten Chödhar (1925–2012).
317. Tethong Söpal, the sister of Rakra Rinpoché, who also served as a house mother in Pestalozzi Children's Village.
318. Arthur Bill (1916–2011) was director of the Pestalozzi Children's Village in Trogen from 1949 to 1972 and worked in many humanitarian capacities throughout his life, including work for UNESCO and Swiss Humanitarian Aid.
319. *Viśeṣastāva*. This praise in verse of the qualities of the Buddha, attributed to Udbhaṭasiddhasvāmin, opens the Tengyur.
320. Likely Blais da Muottas, which has a restaurant on its slopes accessed by a funicular railway.
321. Wahlwies is the site of another Pestalozzi Children's Village, where Losang Namdröl and his wife were house parents.
322. This was presumably BT Tower, known then as Post Office Tower, which opened to the public in 1966.
323. Westminster Abbey.
324. Marianne Winder (1918–2001), a historian of medicine, helped Rechung Rinpoché Jampal Kunsang to publish *Tibetan Medicine* with the University of California Press in 1976.
325. Hugh Edward Richardson (1905–2000) represented the British in Gyantsé and Lhasa from 1936–40 and again from 1946–50. Richardson was also an early Western chronicler of Tibetan history and advocate for Tibetan independence and self-determination.
326. Seminar für Sprach und Kulturwissenschaft Zentralasiens at Rheinischen Friedrich-Wilhelms-Universität Bonn.
327. Michael Hahn (1941–2014) was a German Indologist and Tibetologist who made his career at Philipps-Universität Marburg. During this time period, Hahn would have just been beginning a period of study under Walther Heissig, who was the director of the Bonn program.
328. Klaus Sagaster is currently Professor Emeritus Rheinischen Friedrich-Wilhelms-Universität Bonn. He had a lengthy career as a Sinologist, Mongologist, and Tibetologist in Germany.
329. That is, the hub symbolizes training in ethical conduct, which supports all the other

qualities. The spokes, like those on chariot wheels with blades sticking out of them, cut, symbolizing the training in the wisdom that cuts through all the mental afflictions. And the rim, which "holds in" or "gathers together" the wheel to prevent it from falling apart, represents the training in concentration, which collects the mind and prevents it from wandering.

330. Palos was at this time involved with the community of Lama Govinda called Arya Maitreya Mandala.
331. Ludwig-Maximilian-University, Munich (LMU).
332. Rolf Stein (1911–99) was a German-born French Sinologist and Tibetologist known for his work on the Tibetan epic of Gesar.
333. This is a reference to the demon king of Laṅka, Rāvaṇa, who in the *Rāmāyaṇa* epic is defeated by Rāma. The story of Rāvaṇa appears in many Buddhist texts. He was said to have ten heads that he cut off to propitiate Śiva, and his palace was inconceivably large.
334. For the record, Namkhai Norbu does not consider himself a Kagyü lama. Educated in the Sakya tradition, he teaches a nonsectarian Dzokchen practice.
335. Avalokiteśvara, Mañjuśrī, and Vajrapāṇi.
336. This clay statue of Ārya Lokeśvara, an Avalokiteśvara with a thousand arms and eleven faces, was one of the statues in the Tsuklakhang Temple and one of the four ārya sibling statues (see note 338 below). Some histories report that King Songtsen Gampo dissolved into the heart of this statue at the end of his life. This was one of the many sacred historical images the Red Guards destroyed during the Cultural Revolution in the 1960s. The above-mentioned faces of this statue were found in the rubble and were smuggled out of Tibet and presented to His Holiness.
337. A *phurba* is a ritual dagger, and the Phurba Yangsap deity is the focus of a cycle of practices.
338. All four sibling statues are renowned as having self-arisen during Tibet's imperial period and were popular sites of pilgrimage. When deciding matters of great importance, His Holiness performs divinations before this sacred statue. The remaining two siblings, Ārya Jamali (a.k.a. Seto Macchendranath) and Ārya Ukhang (a.k.a. Rato Macchendranath), are housed in Nepal—in Kathmandu and Patan, respectively.
339. In the completion stage of tantra, basic-state experiences are "mixed" (*bsre ba*) with the three enlightened bodies to bring one closer to the resultant state. There are three categories of experience—sleep, death, and meditative experience—each divided into three, thereby making nine mixings.
340. This biography is the *Jewel Garland Beautifying the Buddha's Teachings* (*Thub bstan mdzes pa'i rgyan gcig ngo mtshar nor bu'i phreng ba*) by Gyalwang Chöjé Losang Trinlé Namgyal, a tutor to both the tenth and eleventh Dalai Lamas. The bibliographic title for this volume published in Sarnath in 1967 was *'Jam mgon chos kyi rgyal po tsong kha pa chen po'i rnam thar.*
341. (*Rdo rje shugs ldan gyi gsang gsum rmad du byung ba'i rtogs brjod*) *dam can rgya mtsho dgyes pa'i rol mo.*
342. The *Root Tantra of Guhyasamāja* has seventeen chapters, with an eighteenth chapter, the *Later Tantra*, often classified as a distinct work.
343. This offering verse is a praise to Tsongkhapa and his two disciples that begins *Gangs can shing rta'i srol 'byed tsong kha pa.*
344. Gangchen Kyishong (*gangs can skyid gshongs*) is below McLeod Ganj, where the Dalai Lama currently lives, and above the Indian town of Dharamsala. It is the

name given to the complex that includes the offices of the Central Tibetan Administration, the Library of Tibetan Works and Archives, and other buildings.

345. This is the *'Jigs byed kyi bla ma'i rnal 'byor dngos grub gter mdzod/ gshin rje rigs lnga la brten nas nyams chag gso ba/ 'jam dpal zhi drag gi bsrung ba/ dus min 'chi ba zhi ba/ bla ma'i rnal 'byor gyi sgo nas zhi rgyas kyi las sgrub tshul sogs* of Thuken Chökyi Nyima.
346. Seventh Dalai Lama Kalsang Gyatso, *Source of All Attainments: Instructions on the Hundred Deities of Tuṣita* (*Dga' ldan lha brgya ma'i khrid yig dngos grub kun 'byung*).
347. See page 268.
348. For a detailed presentation of the twelve links of dependent origination see His Holiness the Dalai Lama, *The Meaning of Life from a Buddhist Perspective* (Boston: Wisdom, 1992).
349. The three sweets are sugar, molasses, and honey.
350. In other words, performing the preliminary-practice ritual called *Necklace for the Fortunate* (see note 120). These six preliminary practices are (1) cleaning the room and arranging symbols of the buddhas' body, speech, and mind; (2) obtaining offerings honestly and arranging them beautifully; (3) sitting in the eightfold posture of Vairocana and then taking refuge and generating bodhicitta; (4) visualizing the merit field; (5) performing the seven-limb prayer and offering a mandala; and (6) making further prayers according to the oral instructions.
351. "On that day in Bodhgaya, when the sun-like Maitreya rises above the hills, may the lotus blossom of my mind open, so that I may satisfy the bee-like fortunate ones."
352. Einsiedeln Abbey, a Benedictine monastery.
353. One of Buddha's first five disciples.
354. *Bkra shis snye ma*, by Choné Lama Drakpa Shedrup (1675–1748).
355. *Bla 'gugs tshe 'gugs*.
356. In Sedlescombe, Sussex, England.
357. For Ms. Taring's memoir, written in 1969, see *Daughter of Tibet* (Boston: Wisdom, 1986). Taring was the first Tibetan woman to leave Tibet for an education in Darjeeling, in 1922. She was also the first director of the Tibetan Homes Foundation in Mussoorie.
358. Presumably the National Museum of Natural History in Paris.
359. *'Dul ba lnga bcu pa*. That is, the *Śramaṇapañcāśatkārikāpadābhismaraṇa* of Kamalaśīla.
360. See pages 320–21 above.
361. *Dam can chos rgyal phyi sgrub la brten nas gtor chen drug cu pa'i rnam bzhag rdo rje gnam lcags 'bar ba'i phreng ba*.
362. From its inception, leadership of the Sakya lineage has descended through members of the Khön family, and the Khön family in turn is said to have descended from gods. The founder of the Sakya sect was Khön Könchok Gyalpo (1034–1102), said to be a manifestation of the bodhisattva Mañjuśrī. Dakchen Rinpoché here is not the Dakchen Rinpoché of Phuntsok Phodrang who migrated to Seattle in 1960 but the Forty-First Sakya Trizin (b. 1945) of Drölma Phodrang.
363. Born in Amdo in 1762, Gyal Khenchen Drakpa Gyaltsen was a student of the Second Jamyang Shepa and studied at Drepung Gomang. He was appointed abbot of Chökhor Gyal Monastery in 1786 and later sat on the throne of Labrang Monastery. He died in 1836.

364. *Dge lugs rig gzhung gces skyong lhan tshogs.*
365. This mantra, actually a canonical verse that begins *ye dharmā hetuprabhavā*, has since ancient times figured prominently in inscriptions and elsewhere to distill the nature of the Buddha's teachings. It is frequently recited as a dhāraṇī, especially in conjunction with consecration rituals. "All things originate from causes. The Tathāgata taught these causes. Also that which puts a stop to these causes—this too was taught by the great ascetic."
366. In other words so that the blissful, empty essence of the enlightened deities—the wisdom beings (*jñānasattva*)—should come and inhabit the statues—the commitment beings (*samayasattva*).
367. The last four are the four regents below the Karmapa in the Karma Kagyü clerical hierarchy.
368. *Zhabs brtan smon tshig drang srong bden pa'i dbyangs snyan.*
369. Takphu Garwang Chökyi Wangchuk dates from the eighteenth or nineteenth century. Trijang Rinpoché later arranged the publication of a corpus of ritual texts based on Garwang's visions. *Sgrol ma'i chos skor* (New Delhi: Ngawang Topgyal, 1975). See also page 78 above.
370. See page 317 above.
371. Kunga Palden was a Sakya lama of the nineteenth century. His title of Shar Lama comes from his position at Dergé Monastery, where there was an eastern (*shar*) master and a western (*nub*) master.
372. The sixteen drops, the heart practice of the *Book of Kadam*, are a meditation that goes from the broadest scope of the entire universe down through progressively smaller objects, ending at the drop of great awakening at the meditator's heart. For a description of this practice, see Jinpa, *Book of Kadam*, especially Khenchen Nyima Gyaltsen's *Elucidation of the Heart-Drop Practice* on pages 395–452.
373. This is somewhat equivalent to a leap year in the Tibetan calendar.
374. *Sems 'dzin gtong ba.* This is a reference to the cycle of texts and practices based on the root verse "Parting from the Four Attachments" attributed to the Sakya forefather Sachen Kunga Nyingpo (1092–1158): "If you are attached to this life, you are not practicing Dharma. If you are attached to the realms of existence, there is no renunciation. If you are attached to your own interest, you do not have bodhicitta. If grasping arises, you do not have the view."
375. *Sgra mi snyan gyi tshe grub.* Kurava is the northern continent among the four continents of Buddhist cosmology.
376. *Tshe sgrub tshigs bcad ma.*
377. A khu ching Shes rab rgya mtsho, 1803–75.
378. *Gnyan tshem bu pa'i lugs.* See note 64 above and the *Tshem bu pa'i lugs kyi spyan ras gzigs kyi dmar khrid* in volume 3 of Changkya's collected works.
379. *Don gsum*, by the Second Jamyang Shepa, Könchok Jikmé Wangpo (1728–91).
380. Phabongkha Rinpoché's *Nā ro mkha' spyod kyi sgrub thabs thun min bde chen nye lam.*
381. This initiation took place November 9–10, 1970. The *Mahāvairocanābhisaṃbodhi* is perhaps the oldest tantric text and is the main practice of the performance tantra (*caryātantra*) class. Because of its rarity, His Holiness had specially requested Ling Rinpoché to do the retreat on this deity so that he could bestow this initiation.
382. *Rnam sras mdung dmar.*
383. *Sgrol dkar bka' babs dgu ldan.*

384. *Rgyud sde kun btus*. Compiled by Loter Wangpo (1847–1914), this thirty-volume compendium collects practices from all classes of tantra from all the Tibetan schools. Within the compendium, one finds such collections as the *Vajrāvalī* and the *Mitra Hundred* as well as depictions of 139 different mandalas.
385. *Dpal mgon zhal sgrub dus mgon po*.
386. *'Khor lo sdom pa'i bshad rgyud mngon brjod 'bum pa*.
387. *Kun rig rnam bshad*, a survey of practices related to the *Sarvadurgatipariśodhana Tantra*. Dulzin (1374–1434) was one of Tsongkhapa's primary disciples.
388. See note 92 above.
389. The "three secrets" refer to his body, speech, and mind.
390. See Joona Repo, "Phabongkha and the Yoginī: The Life, Patronage and Devotion of the Lhasa Aristocrat, Lady Lhalu Lhacham Yangdzom Tsering," *Journal of the Oxford Centre for Buddhist Studies* 9 (November 2015): 109–42.
391. On these practices, see above, page 340.
392. *Stobs 'phrog dbang po*.
393. *Bram ze nag po mngags gtad*.
394. Pema Rikzin (1625–97) was the First Dzokchen Rinpoché, and this incarnation would have been the seventh, born in 1964.
395. This is the same lunar date as his date of birth but not the same Western calendrical date. This would be May 12, 1973, whereas he was born April 30, 1901.
396. *Bsnyen dus mgon po*, the most commonly bestowed form of this deity.
397. *Mu le*, a region in eastern Tibet.
398. Lawudo Tulku is Lama Thubten Zopa Rinpoché. Thubten Dönyö and Thubten Ngawang are Italian students Piero Cerri and Claudio Cipullo.
399. *Jo bo mi bskyod rdo rje*, the image of the Buddha as a child that Queen Bhṛkuṭī brought to Lhasa from Nepal in the seventh century.
400. *Khye'u chu 'bebs*, the "water bringer," a former birth of the Buddha who in the *Sutra of Golden Light* saves ten thousand fish disciples from dehydration.
401. In an effigy ritual for health and long life, an effigy of the person being targeted by spirits is offered up as a substitute.
402. Anne Ansermet, daughter of the Swiss conductor Ernest Ansermet, was instrumental in the founding of Tharpa Choeling in Le Mont-Pèlerin in the 1970s, a Dharma center centered around Geshé Tamdrin Rapten. It was renamed Rabten Choeling after his passing in 1986.
403. *Nang mdzod nyin mo bde legs*. This ceremonial scarf comes from the ancient dynasties of China and would cost approximately US$1,000 today.
404. Nāgārjuna's *Prajñādaṇḍa*, v. 167.
405. *Gnod sbyin lcam dral*.
406. For the full text of Kharak Gomchung's advice, see Thupten Jinpa, *Wisdom of the Kadam Masters* (Boston: Wisdom, 2013), 99–108.
407. *Staff of Wisdom* (*Prajñādaṇḍa*).
408. This is from jātaka 32 of Āryaśūra's collection. The *kumuda* lily is a white lotus, but the Sanskrit of this verse suggests the line is referring to a magnificent festival named for the flower.
409. See page 185 above, where Trijang Rinpoché became seriously ill while attending the Shotön summer opera performances.
410. For the full text of Shawo Gangpa's advice, see Jinpa, *Wisdom of the Kadam Masters*, 92–98.

411. The Seventh Dalai Lama's *'Phags bstod.*
412. This story is from Sharpa Tulku's firsthand experience.
413. For a complete list of Trijang Rinpoché's previous lives see the appendix.
414. The following account was related to Sharpa Tulku by Lati Rinpoché during Rinpoché's visit to Tushita Mahayana Meditation Center in New Delhi on August 8, 1989.
415. Kyabjé Trijang Rinpoché, Drakri (Bari) Rinpoché, Khamlung Rinpoché, and Phukhang Rinpoché were close relatives, and their reincarnations were again all related, all born to the families of brothers in the Nachuk household in Phenpo, Tibet.
416. The following letter has been lightly edited from the original.
417. Many websites claim that the current Trijang Rinpoché is the eighteenth, but only the last three on this list held the title Trijang Rinpoché, making the current Trijang Rinpoché the fourth.

Glossary

Abhidharma. One of the five main subjects of the monastic curriculum, systematically presenting phenomena whose analysis and contemplation will bring one closer to nirvana. Also a genre of texts on this topic.

assistant tutor (Tib. *tsenshap*). Literally, an attendant to a lama who helps him in his philosophy studies.

Avalokiteśvara. Known as Chenrezik in Tibetan, this bodhisattva is the manifestation of the compassion of all buddhas. Common aspects include the white form with one face and four arms and the white form with eleven faces and a thousand arms. Jinasāgara Avalokiteśvara (Tib. Gyalwa Gyatso) is a red, four-armed form. Avalokiteśvara is the patron deity of Tibet, and the Dalai Lamas are thought to be incarnations of Avalokiteśvara. *See also* Great Compassionate One; *maṇi*.

Avalokiteśvara Who Liberates from All Lower Realms (Tib. Chenrezik Ngensong Kundröl). A practice of the one-face, two-arm aspect of Avalokiteśvara flanked by Tārā and Ekajaṭī originating from the Indian mahāsiddha Mitrayogin. In a vision of Avalokiteśvara, Mitrayogin was told that anyone who merely receives this initiation will not be reborn in the lower realms in their next life, hence its name.

bodhicitta. The intention to become enlightened for the welfare of all living beings motivated by love and compassion that sees the suffering nature of samsara and seeks to liberate all living beings from it.

bodhisattva. An individual who has generated bodhicitta and has entered the path to enlightenment.

Bodhi Tree. The tree in Bodhgaya, India, where Buddha attained enlightenment some twenty-five hundred years ago.

body mandala. Tantric practice where one's body is taken to be the mandala of the particular tantra.

Cakrasaṃvara. Sometimes referred to as Heruka, he is one of the three main deities of the Geluk tradition utilized to attain realizations of the clear light and transform attachment into the path to enlightenment.

chant master (Tib. *umzé*). Monk trained in chanting techniques and styles who leads the assembly in ritual chanting. A *lama umzé* can also refer to a deputy abbot.

Cittamaṇi Tārā. A highest yoga tantra aspect of Green Tārā originating from a divine vision of Takphu Vajradhara.

clear light (Tib. *ösal*). Also translated as "luminosity," it refers to the dawn-like luminous appearance occurring at the last stage of the death process before the consciousness enters the intermediate state. A facsimile of this state for the purposes of practice is designated to the period of dreamless sleep.

completion stage. The second of two stages of highest yoga tantra, following the generation stage. The completion stage itself has five stages: (1) speech isolation, (2) mental isolation, (3) illusory body, (4) clear light, and (5) union.

cyclic existence (Skt. *saṃsāra*). The series of uncontrolled rebirths brought about by karma and afflictive emotions. The point of all Buddhist practice is to bring an end to samsaric rebirth.

dharmakāya. At the level of the complete enlightenment of a buddha, it refers to the body of enlightened qualities that make up the enlightened mind, and to the ultimate-truth emptiness of that mind.

Dharmarāja. (Tib. Chögyal; a.k.a. Kālarūpa). Wrathful oath-bound protector associated with the deity Vajrabhairava. He is black in color with a single buffalo head, two arms, and an equally wrathful female companion, both sitting astride a buffalo.

equalizing and exchanging self with others. An important Mahayana practice for generating bodhicitta by transforming self-centeredness into a mind cherishing others and ultimately the firm determination to become enlightened for the welfare of all living beings.

emanation body (Skt. *nirmāṇakāya*). A coarse form body of an enlightened being that is emanated for the welfare of ordinary beings.

enjoyment body (Skt. *saṃbhogakāya*). The subtle body of an enlightened being that can only be perceived by bodhisattvas who have attained the path of seeing.

Entering the Middle Way (Skt. *Madhyamakāvatāra*). Candrakīrti's seminal work on Madhyamaka philosophy presented around the framework of the ten spiritual levels of a bodhisattva.

Essence of Eloquence Distinguishing the Definitive and Interpretive. Tsongkhapa's philosophical masterpiece of Indian philosophical systems. It is often referred to as the "iron bow" because it is so difficult to comprehend.

Fifty Verses on Guru Devotion (Skt. *Gurupañcāśikā*). A famous text by Aśvaghoṣa containing the proper attitude and behavior that the spiritual practitioner must keep in relation to his or her spiritual master.

five buddha families. The purified aspects of an enlightened being's five aggregates. Consciousness manifests as Akṣobhya, discrimination as Amitābha, feeling as Ratnasambhava, form as Vairocana, and compositional factors as Amoghasiddhi.

Foundation of All Good Qualities. A verse text by Tsongkhapa covering the stages of the path of both sutra and tantra.

four noble truths. The basis of all Buddhist teachings. They are: (1) true suffering, (2) true origin, (3) true path, and (4) true cessation.

Ganden. The first monastery of the Geluk tradition built by Tsongkhapa. "Ganden" is Tibetan for Tuṣita, the name of Maitreya's pure land.

Garland of Birth Stories (Skt. *Jātakamālā*). A series of stories based on the previous lives of Buddha Śākyamuni compiled by Āryaśūra.

generation stage. The first of two stages of highest yoga tantra, where the mind is prepared for the dissolution of the winds in the central channel during the completion stage by mimicking the dissolution process at the time of death, bardo, and rebirth.

geshé (Skt. *kalyāṇamitra*). Literally "spiritual friend." Originally used as a general title for Buddhist teachers and mentors, but these days in the Geluk tradition it is a degree or title awarded to monks who have passed a rigorous examination of their studies. It is of varying grades, the highest of which is lharampa, awarded to those who have successfully sat in debate in all three monastic seats. Lower grades are karampa, tsokrampa, lingsé, and dorampa.

Great Compassionate One (Mahākaruṇika). Avalokiteśvara in his thousand-arm, eleven-face form. This is the central deity in the nyungné purification practice that descends from the nun Bhikṣuṇī Lakṣmī (Tib. Gelongma Palmo).

Great Treatise on the Stages of the Path (Tib. *Lamrim Chenmo*). Tsongkhapa's magnum opus dealing with the stages of the path in sutra.

Guhyasamāja. One of the three main deities of the Geluk tradition, he is utilized to attain the illusory body and transform ignorance into the path to enlightenment.

Guide to the Bodhisattva's Way of Life (Skt. *Bodhicaryāvatāra*). Śāntideva's eloquent verse masterpiece dealing with the generation of bodhicitta and the practice of the six perfections.

Guru Vajradhara (Tib. Lama Dorjé Chang). An epithet used for one's teacher. Throughout this text Kyabjé Trijang Rinpoché often uses it to refer to Phabongkha Rinpoché. Vajradhara is the enjoyment body of Buddha Śākyamuni, his form as the teacher of Buddhist tantra.

Guru Puja (Tib. *Lama Chöpa*). Rite of offering and praise focused on the guru as the personification of all the buddhas, meditation deities, ḍākinīs, and so on. The text of this name was composed by the First Paṇchen Lama Losang Chökyi Gyaltsen.

Heart Sutra. One of the most concise of the Perfection of Wisdom sutras. It is often recited before spiritual teachings.

Iron Fortress. A torma used in a wrathful ritual constructed in the shape of Yama's iron fortress and with nine or sixteen sides.

Jé Rinpoché as the triple deity. An aspect of Tsongkhapa with Mañjuśrī at his crown, Avalokiteśvara at his throat, and Vajrapāṇi at his heart.

Jewel Treasury of Wise Sayings (Tib. *Sakya Lekshé*). A famous text by Sakya Paṇḍita (1182–1251) focusing on both worldly and enlightened advice for living.

Kangyur. The Tibetan Buddhist canon, i.e., the sutras, tantras, and Vinaya texts of Buddha Śākyamuni translated into Tibetan and published in 108 volumes.

Kyabjé. Master for refuge and protection. A term of great respect given to high lamas.

labrang. Monastic household of a lama, managing his or her personal, business, and religious affairs through a manager and support staff.

Lamp on the Path to Enlightenment (Skt. *Bodhipathapradīpa*). The first text Atiśa composed upon arriving in Tibet, laying out the entire path in forty-one verses. It became the prototype for all subsequent texts of its genre, such as the Path and Fruit in the Sakya tradition, the Kagyü *Ornament of Precious Liberation* of Gampopa, and the Geluk stages of the path texts.

life entrustment. Often taken to mean a ritual whereby the practitioner entrusts their life to a protector, but according to His Holiness the Dalai Lama should be the practice of the protector entrusting itself to the practitioner.

Madhyamaka. The Middle Way philosophy propounded by Nāgārjuna and elucidated by Candrakīrti and others.

maṇi. The *maṇi* mantra is the six-syllable mantra of Avalokiteśvara *Oṃ maṇi padme hūṃ*.

māra. Obstacles to spiritual development, whether demons or other obstacles, such as distractions and death.

miktsema. A four-line verse that is used as a praise, request, and mantra centered on Tsongkhapa.

Nāgārjuna. The first Madhyamaka philosopher, who is said to have traveled to the subterranean land of the nāgas to obtain the Perfection of Wisdom sutras.

nāgas. A type of serpent spirit. There are numerous types of nāgas; some are benign or even helpful while others are malignant.

Nechung. The main protector, and counsel by way of oracle, for the Ganden Phodrang Tibetan government and the Dalai Lama.

ngakpa. A lay tantric yogi.

Ornament of Realization (Skt. *Abhisamayālaṃkāra*). A famous Mahayana text that was revealed to Asaṅga by Buddha Maitreya revealing the meaning of the Perfection of Wisdom sutras.

Palden Lhamo (Skt. Śrīdevī). Female protector deity of Tibet with a close connection to the first and subsequent Dalai Lamas. She is wrathful in appearance, dark blue, and riding a mule.

Perfection of Wisdom (Skt. *prajñāpāramitā*). As a topic of monastic curriculum, it is the systematic study of the Perfection of Wisdom sutras from the perspective of their concealed teachings on the paths, levels, and practices leading to the goals of nirvana and enlightenment.

Prāsaṅgika. Of the four Buddhist philosophical schools of India, the highest is the Madhyamaka school, and the Prāsaṅgika subschool is the highest within the Madhyamaka. It is called Prāsaṅgika "Consequentialist," because it proceeds by exposing the flawed consequences in the positions of other schools without advancing any of its own.

Prayer of Samantabhadra. Often used to pray for the deceased, this famous aspirational prayer of the bodhisattva Samantabhadra is sometimes called the *King of Prayers*. Its formal title is *Vows of Good Conduct* (Skt. *Bhadracaryāpraṇidhāna*).

Rinpoché. A term of high respect meaning "precious one" bestowed by disciples. It most typically is applied to reincarnated lamas.

sādhana. A ritual text for generation-stage practice focused on a particular deity.

Samayavajra. A deity of the Guhyasamāja tantra with the special capacity to purify one's broken or defiled tantric vows.

samsara. *See* cyclic existence.

sevenfold cause-and-effect instruction. A method for generating bodhicitta based on the following six causes and one effect: (1) recognizing all beings as your mother, (2) remembering their kindness, (3) wishing to repay their kindness, and developing (4) affectionate love, (5) great compassion, (6) the universal wish, and (7) bodhicitta.

Seven-Point Mind Training. A teaching brought to Tibet by Atiśa and written down by Geshé Chekawa. It is a series of one-line aphorisms divided into seven topics: (1) preliminaries, (2) main practice, (3) transforming adversity, (4) applying the teachings to one's entire life, (5) the measure of having trained the mind, (6) commitments of training the mind, and (7) precepts for training the mind.

six-session guruyoga. A practice performed six times a day focusing on one's guru. It is the commitment of all highest yoga tantra practitioners in the Geluk tradition.

sixty-four-part torma ritual. Known in Tibetan as *drukchuma*, this practice in conjunction with the Dharma protector Dharmarāja is used to accomplish various actions, most notably overcoming obstacles from spirits.

six perfections. The basis for all Mahayana practices, they are: (1) generosity, (2) moral discipline, (3) patience, (4) joyous effort, (5) concentration, and (6) wisdom.

six Dharmas of Nāropa. A series of completion-stage practices of highest yoga tantra taught by the Indian mahāsiddha Nāropa: inner heat, illusory body, clear light, dream yoga, transference of consciousness, and the bardo.

Song of Spiritual Experience. A verse-poem on the stages of the path written by Tsongkhapa based on his own personal experience.

stages of the path. Known as the *lamrim* in Tibetan, the stages of the path provide all the Buddha's teachings in systematic order intended to be put into practice.

Sukhāvatī (Tib. Dewachen). The pure land of Buddha Amitābha.

Sutra of the Wise and the Foolish. A famous sutra that explains karma and its effects using stories.

Tengyur. The collected teachings of Indian scholars and siddhas translated into Tibetan in just over 250 volumes.

thangka. A scroll painting of religious significance, usually depicting various enlightened beings.

three principal aspects of the path. (1) Renunciation, (2) bodhicitta, and (3) emptiness, central pillars of all Mahayana teachings and practices. Tsongkhapa wrote a short verse text by this name.

three representations. A buddha statue, scripture, and a stupa as representations of the body, speech, and mind of the buddhas; traditional offering to a lama along with a mandala that symbolizes an offering of the universe.

torma. A ritual cake that is blessed and offered to various mundane and enlightened beings.

tsok offering (Skt. *gaṇacakra*). A tantric feast involving ritual music and sacred substances for invoking the blessing of the ḍākas and ḍākinīs and strengthening your tantric commitments.

Tsongkhapa (1357–1419). Great Tibetan scholar and yogi who founded the Geluk tradition of Tibetan Buddhism.

tulku. Literally "emanation body," refers to the incarnation of a highly realized lama. It has become a title for high lamas and originated with the First Karmapa, Dusum Khyenpa.

twelve *tenma*. Twelve female spirits of Tibet who were subjugated by Padmasambhava and transformed into protectors of the Buddhist teachings.

Vajrabhairava. Also referred to as Yamantaka, he is one of the three principal deities of the Geluk tradition. He is the wrathful manifestation of Mañjuśrī utilized by the practitioner to overcome obstacles to enlightenment and transform anger into the path to enlightenment.

Vajrasattva. A white deity who embodies the purificatory powers of all enlightened beings.

Vajrayoginī. Although she is the female counterpart to Cakrasaṃvara, she is also a very popular deity in her own right, known for bestowing attainments quickly and assisting devotees to attain rebirth in her pure land.

Vinaya. The monastic discipline or code set down by the Buddha for the ordained, as well as a genre of texts in the Buddhist canon that elucidates these rules, often with elaborate stories about the Buddha and his disciples.

Wheel of Sharp Weapons Mind Training. A mind-training (Tib. *lojong*) teaching popularized in Tibet by Atiśa, who learned it from his Sumatran guru Dharmarakṣita.

yoga of the three purifications. A practice of Cakrasaṃvara utilized to purify one's body, speech, and mind.

Index

Note: Titles of works may be listed under author name.

A

Abhayākaragupta, 55, 402n65
Abhidharma, 57, 65, 68, 72, 160, 240, 314
"ācāryas and skeletons" ritual dance, 96
accumulation, final result of, 302–4
Achen of Tsawarong, 275
Achunor, 297, 298
Adhipati Lords of the Cemetery, 363
Adruk, 215, 289
Aeschimann, Dr., 324
Ajanta caves, 226
Akaniṣṭha, 139
Akhu Trinlé, 23
Akṣobhyavajra Guhyasamāja, 91, 92, 96, 128, 139, 141, 152, 238, 262, 269, 370
Akṣobhyavajra statue, 363, 420n399
Ala Ngodroké, 58
Alachak Gong, 120
Alarong, 85
alcohol, 262
All-India Radio, 392
Alo Butang, 194
Alte Peter church (Munich), 298
Ama Chözom, 351
Ama Mikmar Drölma, 343
ambans, Qing, 401n43
Amdo, 18, 45, 153, 159, 229, 241
Amdo Drokpa Jinpa, 264
Amdo House, 58, 62
Amitābha, 405n117
Amitāyus, 153, 346–47
  distant lineage, 337, 362
  five secret deities of, 275, 337
  inner, 346
  longevity practice of, 101
  long-life empowerments, 99, 103, 223, 275, 321, 324, 327, 349–50, 351, 360, 414n291
  nine deities of, 340
  root texts and commentaries on, 340, 352
  statue, 185–86
  temple of, 213
analogies
  chasing hundred birds with one slingshot, 135
  drunken elephants, 239
  leading calf with temptation of green grass, 98
  offering gold like a mandala, 109
  parrot reciting *maṇi* mantra, 199–200
  sesame seeds, crushing on head, 114
  turtle and yoke, 77, 404n100
  washerman in city of naked people, 111
  wind in folds of paper, 112, 405n125
  wish-granting jewel, 344
Ānanda, 157
Ani Yangzom, 34, 35, 49, 53, 159
animal sacrifice, prohibition of, 262, 267
Annual Prayer Festival, 352, 360. *See also* Great Prayer Festival
Ansermet, Anne, 365, 420n402
Anubhūti, *Sarasvatī Grammar Treatise*, 168
Apho Söpa Thokmé, 370–71
Apho Wangden, 318
Arap Rinpoché, 216
Arhat Madhughoṣa, 385, 397
arhats, sixteen, 28, 304, 308, 316, 331, 337, 350, 381
Arik Monastery, 58, 85–86, 120
Armlet, 61
Ārya Lokeśvara statue, 306, 308, 317, 392, 417n336

Ārya sibling statues, 308, 416n338, 417n336
Ārya tradition of Guhyasamāja, 54, 238, 262, 269, 370
Ārya Wati Sangpo of Kyirong statue, 307–8, 309, 317, 391, 417n338
Āryadeva, 359, 373, 383, 410n201
āryas, four qualities/fourfold temperament of, 178, 257, 282, 410n195, 413n275
Āryaśūra. See *Garland of Birth Stories* (*Jātakamālā*, Āryaśūra)
Asaṅga, 143, 383, 410n201
Bodhisattvabhūmi, 414n284
Compendium of Abhidharma, 224
Ashé Yangkyi, 358–59
Aśoka, 264
Asong, Ganden Shartsé Geshé, 352
Assembly of People's Deputies, 260, 337, 344
Association for the Preservation of the Geluk Tradition, 350, 371
Association of Tibetan Homes, 416n315
astrology, 47, 58, 59, 160, 402n45
Astro-Medical Institute (Lhasa), 168, 175, 185, 196, 335
Aśvaghoṣa. See *Fifty Verses on Guru Devotion*
Aśvajit, 320, 418n353
Atiśa, 2, 106, 153, 191, 276, 382, 385, 397, 408n172
in *Book of Kadam*, 400n20
cave of, 232
Lamp on the Path to Enlightenment, 232, 272, 380
play about, 295, 316
relics of, 223, 231
statue, "left-leaning," 223
system of, 125, 338
Atro Pass, 150
Avalokiteśvara, 405n115
epithet of, 17, 399n7
image of on body of Thirteenth Dalai Lama, 132
Jinasāgara, 355, 379
in *Maṇi Kabum*, 402n61
mantra of, 61
permissions given, 103, 165, 214, 380
Potala temple of, 200
Siṃhanāda, 360
statues of, 100, 232, 258, 306, 329–30, 417n336
teachings on, 340, 362
"three essential moments," 360
three-dimensional mandala of, 311
yoga of, 54
See also Great Compassionate One
Avalokiteśvara temple (Dharmasala), 335–36, 347
Avalokiteśvara Who Liberates from All Lower Realms, 412n239
in Bodhgaya, 338, 356
at Chakrata base camp, 340
in Dartsedo, 210
in Delhi, 275
in Dharamsala, 260, 271, 274, 352
in Kalimpong, 259
at Namgyal, 346
in Nepal, 254
public permission, 217, 269
in Sarnath, 265, 272, 359
at Seudru, 216
in Sonada, 258
in Switzerland, 295, 320
at Tashi Chöling, 256
at Yangteng, 211
Ayik Thango family, 58, 86

B

Ba, 125, 210
Ba Chödé Monastery, 25, 207, 209, 215
Ba Pass, 85, 204, 219
Baba Kalsang Lekshé, 304–5
Bakula Rinpoché, 258, 329, 334, 335, 360
Bali Khedrup, 107
Bapa Apho, 34
Bapa Phuntsok Wangyal, 203
Barawa Gyaltsen Palsang, 79–80
Bari Hundred, 79, 278, 404n104
Bari Lotsāwa Rinchen Drak (second Sakya Trizin), 278, 404n104
Barkham Shodo Dragom Tulku, 355
Barshi Phuntsok Wangyal, 335, 345
Barun, Dr., 326
Baso Chökyi Gyaltsen, First Jamyang Shepa, 407n160
Bawa Gyashok House, 215

Bayer family, 167, 172
Bearded Nyakré, 75
Beda Monastery, 25
Beda Troti Tsultrim, 81, 107, 109
Beda Tulku. *See* Chagong Beda Tulku
Bedi, Freda, 269, 414n288
Ben Gungyal, 64
Bendha Pass, 85
Bentsang Monastery, 140
Bentse ferry, 246
Beri Getak Tulku Rinpoché, 190
Beri Monastery, 98–99, 205
Bernak Mahākāla, 110
Bhāvaviveka. See *Essence of the Middle Way* (Bhāvaviveka)
Bhikṣu Pratimokṣa Sutra, 268
Bhikṣuṇī Lakṣmī tradition. *See* Lakṣmī tradition
Bhṛkuṭī, Queen, 420n399
Bill, Arthur, 294, 323, 416n318
Birla House, 251
Black Garuḍa, 61
Black Hat dance, 119
Black Liberating Standing Lion, 346
black magic, ritual counteragent to, 96–97
Black Skin Mask Guardian (mask), 150, 408n168
bliss and emptiness, 344, 381, 382
Blue Book of Synonyms, 346
Bodhgaya
  Jayanti celebration in, 225–27
  offerings in, 313
  ordination in, 254–55
  pilgrimage to, 146–48, 264
  reconstruction resolution in, 307
  sacredness of, 151
  teachings in, 257–58, 271–72, 342–43, 356–58
  virtuous activities in, 274, 286
Bodhi Tree, 147, 148, 151, 257, 258, 274, 408n165
bodhicitta, 135, 201
  ceremonies generating, 76, 143, 148, 161, 162, 167–68, 172, 192–93, 233, 258, 274, 345
  of Trijang Rinpoché, 381
  ultimate, 299
Bomdila, 250
Bön tradition, 101, 270
Bonn Zentralasien Seminar, 297
Bönpo Gönsar, 121, 406n134
Böntsang Ngawang Tsöndrü, 192
Book of Kadam, 28, 32–33, 54, 96, 400n20, 419n372
Boudhanāth, 146, 250
Bramāputra River, 123
breath yoga, 352, 373
British army, 2, 38, 125
Bu Chögyal, Geshé, 217
Bu Sönam, Ngakrampa, 95
Buddha Śākyamuni, 410n205
  festivals of, 50, 133, 201, 225–27, 257, 299, 350, 390, 402n53
  five emanations of, 23, 400n17
  Great Prayer Festival and, 400n18
  on keeping good company, 179
  past lives of, 262
  praise of, 294, 416n319
  relics of, 94
  sacred sites of, 146, 271, 408nn164–65
  statues of, 274, 305, 324, 329, 334, 336, 359
  Trijang Rinpoché's drawing of, 383
  white conch of, 150, 408n168
Bugön Monastery, 216–17
Buldü Vajradhara Jetsun Losang Yeshé Tenpai Gylatsen, 54–55, 56, 58, 62
Bum Lakha, 125
Bum Nyakthang, 101–2
Bumpa, 105–6, 108, 215
Bumpa Mountain, 189
Bumtso Lake, 88
Bumzé Belsé Pön, 92
Butön, 181
Butsa Bugen, 91
Butsa Nakga Geshé, 212
Buxa encampment, 256–57, 305, 307

C

Cakrasaṃvara, 155
  body-mandala initiation, 215, 254, 256, 259, 260, 288, 290, 327, 331, 337, 373
  consecration rituals, 317, 336
  drawing, 50
  explanatory tantras, 346
  generation and completion stage of, 172, 261, 373

holy site of (Kampo), 104–5, 382
initiations given, 99, 102, 160, 162, 167, 173, 182, 183, 290
initiations received, 54, 55–56
mandala of, 73, 79, 102
mantra permissions, 223, 238, 263
prayers, at Trijang Rinpoché's passing, 387
retreats, 80, 92, 93
self- and front-generation of, 354
self-initiation of, 95, 161
signs of practice of, 388, 389
sixty-two-deity initiation, 136, 196, 330, 348
statue of, 88
three "red ones" in, 408n167
Trijang Rinpoché as emanation of, 9
tsok offering of, 271
Cakrasaṃvara, five-deity initiation, 380
in Chatreng, 82
at Chötri Monastery, 123
in Dharamsala, 255, 258, 345, 372–73, 379
in Gangkar Ling, 92
at Jöl Döndrup Ling, 116
at Meru Monastery, 199
at Nechungri Nunnery, 194
at Ngakpa College, 238
received, 58, 77
in Sarnath, 272, 288, 363–64
at Shidé, 196
at Tashi Chöling, 148
at Tharpa Chöling, 256
at Tsamkhung Nunnery, 188–89
Cakrasaṃvara Root Tantra, 61, 73
Calcutta, 148, 257
calligraphy studies, 53–54
Cāmuṇḍa, 186–87
Candaka, 385, 397
Caṇḍālī, 165, 409n180
Candrakīrti, 383, 385, 397
Bright Lamp (*Pradīpoddyotana*), 137, 164, 404n92
Clear Words (*Prasannapadā*), 409n178
Entering the Middle Way (*Madhyamakāvatāra*), 32, 41, 163, 367, 372, 403n80, 409n178
Candrogomin. See *Twenty Verses on the Bodhisattva Vow*
Causing the Rain of Goodness to Fall, 86, 95, 174, 181, 216, 341
"Celebration of the Hosts," 181, 410n204
Central School for Tibetans, 333
Central Tibetan Administration (CRA), 3–4, 309, 314–15, 337, 344, 417–18n344
Cerri, Piero, 420n398
Chagla, M. C., 283, 415n302
Chagong, acceptance in, 211–13
Chagong Beda Trotitsang family, 24
Chagong Beda Tulku, 76–77, 107, 111, 112, 118, 404n99
Chagongshok, 111
Chahar Geshé Losang Tsultrim, collected works of, 341
Chak Pass, 32
Chaklek Geshé of Yarlamgang, 212
Chakna Mutik Monastery, 119
Chaknang Lhawang Tsering, 261
Chakpori Medical College, 124
Chakra Palbar district, 119–20
Chakra Temple, 110
Chakragang, 110, 112
Chakragang Temple, 213, 214
Chakrata base camp, 340
Chaksam ferry landing, 192
Chaksam Tsechu Monastery, 157, 158
Chaksha Tenpa, 91
Chamdo, 94, 142, 190, 204–5, 209, 210, 217–18
Chamdo Chökhor Jampaling Monastery, 204–5, 217
Chamdo Dotsé, 271, 274
Chamdo Gyara Rinpoché, 343
Chamdo Monastery, 218
Chamdo Phakchen Hothokthu, 232–33
Chamdo Shiwalha. *See* Shiwalha Rinpoché
Chamsing, 133, 162, 262
Changkhyimpa, 38, 39
Changkya Nagwang Losang Chöden, *Crystal Mirror*, 131
Changkya Rölpai Dorjé, 340
Changowa Geshé Gyaltsen, 214
chanting, skill of, 6, 22, 59, 60, 65–66
Chanting the Names of Mañjuśrī, 31, 71, 173, 180, 294, 295
Charong region, 150

Chatreng, 24, 80, 81, 249
 departing from, obstacles to, 110–15
 exile community of, 317, 338, 366, 369, 370–71
 fighting in, 91–92
 history of, composition of, 272
 invitation to return to, 125, 127
 plot against Trijang Rinpoché in, 107–9
 reputation of people of, 85, 89
 second visit to, 114, 211–14
 visit to, 11, 84–89, 93, 110
Chatreng House, 115, 211
Chatreng Jungné, 271, 356
Chatreng Monastery, 21, 24, 25, 95–96, 98, 107, 115, 168
Chatreng Nyitso Trinlé Tenzin, 32
Chatreng Rigang Aga Jamyang, 306
Cheka Monastery, 140
Chen Yi, Marshal, 222
Chengdu, 205–6, 209
Chenyé Monastery, 140, 248, 413n270
Chilung, 149
Chim Jampalyang, 65
Chim Namkha Drak, 276, 404n106. *See also* Narthang Hundred
Chimé Palter longevity initiation, 78
Chimphu, 141
China
 emperors of and Dalai Lamas, historical relationship of, 115
 journey to, 203–6
 nationalist movement in, 50, 402n52
 Thirteenth Dalai Lama's visits to, 38, 39
Chinese army and officials
 in Chatreng, 90, 91, 127
 at Demo festival, 49–50
 escorts by, 210, 225–26, 228
 at Great Prayer Festival, 46–47, 50–51
 in Kham, 125
 in Lhasa, 245
Chinese Communists
 armed conflict with, 237–38, 243–44, 248
 destruction of Lhasa by, 305, 417n336
 dissent and schisms provoked by, 229
 invasion by, 2, 302
 in Markham, 289
 mediation and peace talks with, 190, 192, 194, 222–23, 411n219
 oppression by, 239
 propaganda of, 251–52
 Tibetan attitudes toward, 243
Chinese "War of the Water-Rat Year," 50, 63, 72, 149, 402n51
Chingkarwa, 172, 342
Chinnamuṇḍā Vajravārāhī, 402n49
Chisung Gang, 215
Chisur Lekshé Gyatso, 21, 32, 34, 35
chö ritual, 88, 118, 405n112
Chöden Bar, Mrs., 324
Chögon Rinpoché of Dechen Chökhor, 196, 270
Chögyal Gyalu, 100
Chogyé Labrang, 163
Chogyé Trichen Rinpoché, 163, 270, 315, 346
Chöjé Lodrö Palsang, 397
Chöjé Mönlam Palwa, 397
Chöjé Surkharwa Lekshé Tsöl, 114
Chökhor Gyal Monastery, 20, 45, 53, 140, 188, 418n363
Chökhor Yangtsé, 194
Choklé Namgyal, Bodong Paṇchen, 284, 415n303
Chokteng Ta Lama, 334
Chokteng Thupten Norsang, 360
Chökyi Gyaltsen, Jetsun, 57
Chölung, 140
Chomden Rikral, 151
Choné Lama Drakpa Shedrup, *Sheaves of Auspiciousness*, 324, 418n354
Choné Lama Rinpoché Losang Gyatso Trinpal Sangpo, 121
Chongyé Riwo Dechen, 140, 248
Chöphel Gawa, Geshé, 180
Chöphel Thupten, 169, 200
Chötri College, 29, 35, 39
Chötri Monastery, 122, 123
Chötse Tulku, 255
Chözé, remains of, 52
Chözé Gyatruk, 199
Chözé Ngawang Dorjé, 175, 210
Chözé Yugyal, 291, 292, 295
Chubi Labrang, 192
Chudangmo, 249–50
Chumik Valley, 167, 196, 224
Chusang Hermitage, 32, 34

book collection at, 72
celebrations at, 40
Losang Tsultrim's cremation at, 134
offerings to, 123
Phabongkha Rinpoché at, 29, 121, 163
records on throneholder's recognition at, 25
studies at, 56, 59
teachings received at, 41, 74, 75–76, 79, 123, 125, 127, 137–40
Trijang Rinpoché's arrival at, 28, 29
visit to, 111
Chusang Monastery, 197
Chushi Gangdruk militia, 237–38, 251
Chushul, 158–59, 192
Chushur, 38, 46
Chusumdo, 116
Chutsul Pass, 86
Chuwori Hermitage, 192
Cipullo, Claudio, 420n398
circumambulations
around Ganden, 144–45
benefits of, 111, 163
in Bodhgaya, 274
consecration of cardinal points, 234, 236
by Geshé Sherap, 71
Lhasa's circular path, 222
by Ngakrampa, 61
procession of Maitreya, 242, 413n264
Cittamaṇi Tārā
body-mandala initiation of, 354, 355
close lineage of, 341
generation and completion stages of, 154
Heart Absorption permission, 78, 313, 355
initiations given, 223, 256, 272
transmission of, 325
Trijang Rinpoché's commentary on, 384
Cittamātra view, 316
clairvoyance
of Dranak Lama, 93
of Gangkar Rinpoché, 88
of Thirteenth Dalai Lama, 126
of Trijang Rinpoché, 110
of Tsewang Gyaltsen, 97
Collected Topics, 41, 401n35
commitment beings (*samayasattva*), 336, 419n366
compassion, 4, 78, 90, 114–15, 143, 151, 154, 252, 309, 381, 385
Compendium of Reality (*Tattvasaṃgraha*), 347
completion stage, 308, 344, 381, 417n399
conduct empowerment, 55–56
confession ceremony, 258, 317, 331, 333, 336, 352
confidence, 15, 53, 60, 118, 145, 170, 240, 353
cremation rituals
for Losang Gyaltsen, 126
for Losang Tsultrim (tutor), 134
for Losang Tsultrim Palden, 21
for Ngakrampa Gyütö Losang Tendar, 62
for Trijang Rinpoché, 388–90

D

Dagyab Chetsang Hothokthu, 217, 310, 384, 411n228
arrival in Lhasa, 201, 202
in Bodhgaya, 286
escape from Tibet, 249
in Germany, 278–79, 296–97
language instruction received, 255, 263
permissions received, 221
requests Trijang Rinpoché's autobiography, 14, 374
in Switzerland, 325
teachings received, 230, 232–33, 254, 260–61, 263, 270–71, 276
teachings requested, 223, 351–52
ḍākas and ḍākinīs, 154–55, 230, 292, 382
Dakchen Rinpoché (Sakya thronholder), 150
Ḍākinīs that Dispel Obscurations, 313
Daklha Gampo Rinpoché, 140, 407n158
Dakpa Monastery, 219–20
Dakpo Bamchö Rinpoché, 291, 299, 300, 328, 329, 331, 332
Dakpo Lama Rinpoché. *See* Jampal Lhundrup (Dakpo Lama Rinpoché)
Dakpo Shedrup Ling, 157, 159, 182, 408n174
Dakpo Tashi Namgyal, *Source of Siddhi*, 131
Dalai Lamas
assistant tutor positions, 2, 409n188

and Paṇchen Lamas, connection between, 229, 411n234
patron-priest relationships of, 115, 405n127
tenth and eleventh's tutor, 417n340
See also Gendun Drup, First Dalai Lama; Gendun Gyatso, Second Dalai Lama; Kalsang Gyatso, Seventh Dalai Lama; Khedrup Gyatso, Eleventh Dalai Lama; Ngawang Losang Gyatso, Fifth Dalai Lama; Ngawang Losang Thupten Gyatso, Thirteenth Dalai Lama; Sönam Gyatso, Third Dalai Lama; Tsangyang Gyatso, Sixth Dalai Lama; Tsultrim Gyatso, Ninth Dalai Lama
Dalhousie, 390, 391, 393. *See also* Gyümé Tantric College (Dalhousie); Gyütö Tantric College (Dalhousie)
Dampa Lodrö of Tsawarong, 274, 277
Dampa Tharchin, 98
Dampa Tsang, 215
Damshung, 223
dances, ritual, 30
at Chakna Muntik, 119
costumes for, at Chatreng Monastery, 95–96
in Dechen, 145
Demo Gucham, 216
at Samphel Ling, 212–13
Seven Blazing Brothers, 216
of Shukden, 245
at Tsurphu, 230
Daṇḍin, *Mirror of Poetics* (*Kāvyādārśa*), 70, 263, 403n84
Dap, 211
Dapa, 91
Dargyé Monastery, 99–100, 107, 205
Darjeeling, 46, 148, 251, 254, 255, 258, 354, 361, 380, 418n357
Darpo Ling, 172
Dartsedo, 205, 209–10
Dasang Dradul, 46
Datak Pakthang, 214
Dawa Dargyé, 196
Dé Gönkhang temple, 99
debates
on Abhidharma, 372
at Chamdo, 218
examinations, 66–67, 240
for Fourteenth Dalai Lama's enrollment ceremony, 180
at Ganden, 51–52
on Perfection of Wisdom, 55
on tantric subjects, 73
training in, 41–42, 53, 54, 55, 71, 135
Trijang Rinpoché's mastery of, 383
Dechen, 43, 122, 235
Dechen Balamshar, 67, 69
Dechen Gawai Wangchuk, 167
Dechen Kharap Ogong Kotsang, 84
Dechen Lamotsé, 83
Dechen Nyingpo, 138
Dechen Phodrang Palace, 151, 152, 228–29
Dechen Rabgyé Ling, 229
Dechen Sang-ngak Khar, 35
Dedruk Labrang, 249
Dedrung Khenchen Ngawang Rapten, 407n160
degenerate age, 91, 114, 348
Dehradun, 340
deities
birth, 53, 84, 122, 402n59
costumes of, 56, 62, 273
drawing, training in, 50
mind-seal, 110
praising local, 236, 412n261
signs of pleasing, 90
wisdom and commitment, 336, 363, 419n366
Dekyi Lhazé, Lady, 301
Dekyi Yangchen (sister), 87
Demo, 204, 219
Demo Rinpoché, 29, 40, 49, 69, 149, 154, 400n23
demons, subjugation of, 52, 402n58
Denma Geshé Ngawang Lekden, 300, 367
Denma House, 180, 234
Denma Jampa Chögyal, 315, 317
Denma Lochö Rinpoché, 283–84, 352, 362, 365
Denma Tengyé Rinpoché incarnation, 364
Denma Tsemang, 287, 415n310
Denma Tsenbar Tulku of Sera Jé, 67, 257
Denma Tsültrim Dönden, 311
Densathel, 140

Depa Kyishöpa (a.k.a. Taktsé Shabdrung Dorjé Namgyal), 14–15
dependent origination, 316, 335, 419n365
Dergé, 205, 208, 210, 415n303
Dergé Shar Lama. *See* Kunga Palden, Dergé Shar Lama
Deshung Nakhathang, 99
Desi Sangyé Gyatso, 115, 130, 182, 196, 411n222
devotion, 8–9, 31, 143–44, 157, 159, 298, 401n39. *See also* guru-disciple connection
Deyang College, 49, 66, 180
Deyang Shar Courtyard, 128, 177
Deyang Tsenshap Rinpoché, 66, 67, 70, 135, 404n88
Deyangpa, 83
Dharamsala, 9, 372–73, 379–80, 394
  air raids in, 280–81
  move to, 255
  offerings and rituals in, 306–7
  teachings in, 259–61, 272–74, 288–90, 334
dhāraṇīs, 130–31, 146, 187, 188, 195, 274
Dharma teaching, reflections on, 238–39, 245–46, 274–75, 352, 373–74
dharmakāya relics, 94
Dharmakīrti, 240, 403n80, 410n201
Dharmamitra, 397
Dharmarāja, 61, 134
  fivefold, 263–64, 273, 414n282
  inner sādhana of, 193
  Iron Fortress ritual, 263, 414n280
  Outer, 269
  permission received, 40
  permissions given, 99, 148, 162, 183, 262
  representations of, 131
  ritual performance of, 119
  rituals of, 59, 60, 95, 174, 263, 360, 384–85
  sixty-four-part torma offering to, 75, 404n95
  thangkas of, 199, 213, 268
Dharmarāja Black Poison Mountain, 52, 186–87
Dharmarāja chapel, 39
Dharmarakṣita, 106, 223
diagrams, 131–32, 186, 197, 310, 358, 411n223
Dialectic Institute, Chamdo, 142
dialectics, 173, 216, 218, 233
Diamond-Cutter Sutra (*Vajracchedikāsūtra*), 313
Dignāga, 240, 410n201
Dilgo Khyentsé Rinpoché, 270, 306, 307, 361
Dingkha Monastery, 197
Dingkha Rinpoché of Tölung, 197
Dispelling Obstacles on the Path, 280
divinations. *See* oracles; prophesies and divinations
Divine Lhamo Lake, 188
Doboom Tulku, 343
Dokhang House, 24, 51–52, 81, 120, 235, 394, 400n19
  accusations against, 85
  gifts and offerings to, 67, 86
  management of Trijang Labrang by, 82–84
  offerings at, 122
  pillar banners for, 137, 221
  receptions at, 121, 142
  Shedra family patronage of, 38
  teachings given at, 65, 74, 84
Dokhar Shabdrung Tsering Wangyal, 15, 399n5
Döl, 247
Döndrup Namgyal, 175, 205
Döndrup Tsering, 304
Dongong Tulku of Drakgyab, 76
Dongsum, 111, 112
Dongsum Rikngа House, 168
Dönkar Pass, 248
Dophü Chökhor Monastery, 247
Doring Paṇḍita Ngödrup Rapten, 399n4
Doring Tenzin Paljor, 15, 399n4
Dorjé (Amdo artist), 280
Dorjé Denpa, 278
Dorjé Drakden, 180, 331
Dorjé Yudrön, Lady, 232, 259
Dosam Nyitso Trinlé, 41
Dothuk, 120
Dotra Monastery, 149
Drachi, 247
Dragoché Gate, 52
dragon, symbolism of, 323
Drakgyab Kyilthang, 204, 219
Drak Yerpa, 60, 73, 183, 231

Drakar (Dhankar) Monastery, 262
Drakar Pass, 211
Drakar Rinpoché of Trehor, 99
Drakgyab, 216–17
Drakgyab Chungtsang, 49
Drakgyab Labrang, 216, 217
Drakgyab Ngawang Tsephel, 354
Drakgyab Rinpoché, 256
Draknak Labrang, 86
Draknakpo, 188
Drakpa Adrak, 273
Drakpa Gyaltsen. *See* Dulwa Dzinpa Drakpa Gyaltsen
Drakpa Samdrup. *See* Thupten Phelgyé (a.k.a. Drakpa Samdrup)
Drakpa Tulku, 216
Drakri Rinpoché, 142, 144, 154
Drakri Rinpoché, incarnation of, 390, 421n415
Drakshul Wangpo, 84, 122
Drakthok Gang, 148
Dranak Lama (a.k.a. Lama Chöphak), 88–89, 91–92, 93, 105
Dranak Monastery, 116
Drapa Ngönshé, 247, 413n268
Drashi armed forces, 117, 176, 177–78, 189
Drathang Monastery, 247, 413n268
Drati Geshé, 56
Drati House (Sera Jé), 18
drawing skills, 57, 383
dreams
  disturbing, 337–38
  forgotten, 162
  of Fourteenth Dalai Lama, 336
  Gangkar Lama's, 117, 118
  of killing animals, 109
  of king of Muli, 362, 420n397
  of moving protector chapel at Drepung, 170
  of pacification of illness, 124
  of Phabongkha Rinpoché, 351
  Phabongkha Rinpoché's, 154, 163
  on renovating Chakra Temple, 110
  of Tachangma, 87
  on third incarnation of Phabongkha Rinpoché, 338–39, 354
  of Thirteenth Dalai Lama, 365
Drepung Gomang, 42, 54, 56, 58, 172, 199–200, 401n42, 418n363
Drepung Gomang (Mundgod), 371–72
Drepung Gomang (Rikon), 293
Drepung Loseling, 69, 75, 82, 88
Drepung Loseling (Mundgod), 350, 370
Drepung Monastery
  Fourteenth Dalai Lama at, 180, 233–34
  Lhamo's shrine transfer at, 169–71
  offerings to, 123
  studies at, 73
  transmissions received at, 54–55, 57–58
  See also Deyang College
Drepung Monastery (Mundgod), 369–70, 394
Dreulha Monastery, 249
Drichu River, 88, 116, 215
Drigung, 173
Drigung Chödrak's vision, lineages of, 223
Drimé Kunden drama, 39, 401n31
Drip Tsechok Ling Labrang, 230, 412n253
Driwa Balsé, 289
Drodok Chödrak, 112, 113
Drodok region, 112
Drodru Geshé Losang Tharchin, 95, 96
Drodru Geshé Tenzin Trinlé, 212
Drogön Chögyal Phakpa, 99, 171, 405n119
Drok, Mount, 203
Drok Riwoché Ganden Nampar Gyalwai Ling, 203, 220, 235. *See also* Ganden Monastery
Drölma Phodrang, 333, 334, 399n10
Dromo, 148, 191–94, 225, 228
Dromo Dungkar Monastery, 255
Dromo Geshé Rinpoché Ngawang Kalsang, 75, 146, 193, 310
  gifts from, 267–68
  incarnation of, 238, 281, 283–84, 306, 342, 360–61
  initiations received, 259
  request for guidance to, 90
  residence of, 256
  in Sonada, 258
Dromo Labrang, 146
Dromtö, 34, 165
Dromtö Geshé Rinpoché, 28, 30, 40

Dromtönpa, 2, 34, 161, 223, 232, 400n20, 400n26, 409n179
Dromtsun Sherjung Lodrö, 197
Drophen Rikché Ling medical college, 249
Drukpa Thuksé, 287, 380
Drukpa Tsechu Tulku, 254, 271
Drul, 204
Drupchen Palden Dorjé, 332
Drupgyal tradition, 86, 262, 263, 269, 274, 286, 321, 324, 327, 340, 343, 346, 350, 351, 360
Druzin palace, 160–61, 183
Duchi Pass, 248
Dudjom Rinpoché, 260, 270, 287
Dugu Monastery, 190
Dulwa Dzinpa Drakpa Gyaltsen, 120, 347, 406nn130–32, 420n387
Dungkar Monastery, 90, 146, 148, 192, 193
Dunhuang texts, 298
Dza Rongphu Tulku, 297
Dzachu River, 87, 119, 217, 218
Dzachukha region, 94
Dzalep Pass, 148
Dzamling Chegu Wangdü, 20, 399n10
Dzarong family, 324
Dzasak Chöjang Dradul, 50
Dzasak Kalsang Tsultrim, General, 177, 178
Dzasak Khemé Sönam Wangdü. *See* Khemé Sönam Wangdü
Dzasak Lama Losang Rinchen of Kyapying, 151
Dzasak of Radreng, 176
Dzasak Trethong of Tashi Lhunpo, 203
Dzedzé Monastery, 88–89, 91, 93, 105
Dzemé Rinpoché, 168, 228, 384
  China visit, 208, 210, 211, 215
  initiations received, 259
  long-life ceremonies offered by, 317, 368–69
  offerings from, 361
  teachings received, 261, 263, 276, 339, 340, 362, 380
Dzitho, 86
Dzitho Monastery, 119
Dzogang Sang-ngak Ling, 119
Dzongkar Chödé, 308, 313, 315, 366, 394
Dzongsar Khyentsé Rinpoché, 361
Dzongsur Lekshé Gyatso. *See* Lekshé Gyatso
Dzongtsé Tulku, 310

E

E Lama, 297
earth vase, 146
Easy Path (First Paṇchen Lama), 99, 162, 175, 189, 199, 218, 232, 274, 332, 345, 380, 404n97
Echudogyan village, 248
Edrung Tashi Tsering, 182
eight auspicious symbols and substances, 181, 249, 324, 342, 357, 366, 370, 410n204
Eight Thousand Verse Perfection of Wisdom, 28, 65, 223, 272, 312
Eight Verses on Mind Training, 276
eight worldly concerns, 15, 59, 222, 326, 375, 399n6
Ekajaṭī, 199, 412n239
"Elegy for a Child Wandering on the Plain," 161
Eliminating the Darkness of the Ten Directions, 61
emptiness, 313–14, 326, 338. *See also* bliss and emptiness
England, 295–96
equalizing and exchanging self with others, 233, 289
Essence of the Middle Way (*Madhyamakahṛdaya*, Bhāvaviveka), 144, 408n163
Europe, impressions of, 302–4
"eye of the crow" riding robe, 35, 400n27

F

festivals
  of Buddha Śākyamuni, 50, 133, 201, 225–27, 257, 299, 350, 390, 402n53
  of Demo, 49–50
  Ganden Ngamchö, 256, 259, 260, 413n274
  Khoryuk Chöpa (Radreng), 32, 41
  of lights commemorating Tsongkhapa, 402n54
  Shotön folk-opera, 185, 372, 420n409
  Tsurphu Summer Dances, 230

universal incense-offering, 149
Yönru Session, 101–2
Fifty Verses on Guru Devotion (*Gurupañcāśikā*, Aśvaghoṣa), 9, 62, 152, 173, 201, 354
fireworks display (Lake Geneva), 291
five buddha families, 131, 133
five great treatises on Buddha's word, 68, 233, 235, 239–40, 241, 403n80
five sciences, 55, 57, 403n66
"five sets of five" practice, 211
Five Wrathful Garuḍa, 323
Flow of the River Ganges, 339
Fortune Eon Sutra (*Bhadrakalpika Sutra*), 308
four classes of tantra, 75, 124, 382–83. *See also* kriyā tantra; performance tantra (*caryātantra*); yoga tantra
four harmonious friends, 57, 403n68
Four Hundred Verses (*Catuḥśataka*, Āryadeva), 359, 373
Four Medical Tantras (Yuthok), 409n192
four noble truths, 240, 298, 308, 336
Four-Armed Avalokiteśvara, 100, 214
Four-Armed Mahākāla, destruction of statue of, 17
Four-Faced Mahākāla, 125, 150
permission given, 162, 380
Robber of Strength, 356, 362
seventeen emanations of, 127, 163, 218, 363, 406n139
thangkas of, 171
Time of Approximation, 346, 362, 420n396
France, 299–300, 328
Friendship Society of Kalimpong, 256, 259

G

G. S. Mandidip Paper Mills, 275, 284, 286, 414n291
Gadong Monastery, 17, 152
Gadong oracle, 400n15
on exile from Tibet, 244–45
on Fourteenth Dalai Lama's enthronement, 190–91
on Gankar Lama's reincarnation, 318, 331
life-force wheels for, 263
on Phabongkha's reincarnation, 173
teachings received, 289
on throneholder's reincarnation, 23
Galingang Bönpotsang family, 148, 193
Galu Losang Gyaltsen, 352
Gampa Pass, 146, 192
Gampopa Sönam Rinchen, 407n158
Ganden (pure land), 21, 386, 387, 399n14
Ganden Chökhor, 140, 229
Ganden Chöling (Ghoom), 148
Ganden Chöpel Ling (Nepal), 254, 339
Ganden Emanation Scripture. See *Miraculous Book of Ganden*
Ganden Jangtsé College, 36, 51–52, 55, 66, 67, 69, 74, 121, 122, 128, 133, 136, 142, 154, 180
Ganden Jangtsé College (Mundgod), 288, 352, 395
Ganden Lachi, 83, 404n107
Ganden Mahāmudrā, 179, 230, 271, 408n170
Ganden Monastery, 136, 141, 220, 309
administrative body of, 83, 404n107
arrival at, 35–37
assembly hall restoration, 183
black-magic, counteracting at, 97
debate at, 55
defense from Chinese by, 51
drapery project for, 136–37
examinations before assembly at, 63, 403n77
founding of, 17
Fourteenth Dalai Lama at, 234–36, 237
Kālacakra initiation at, 42
Losang Tsultrim Palden at, 20–21
return to, after visit to Kham, 121–22
Shedra family patronage of, 38, 39
Sherap Geshé at, 74
smallpox epidemic at, 48–49
studies at, 73, 74
teachings given at, 141–44, 154
Thirteenth Dalai Lama's visit to, 126
visits to, 84–85
See also Ganden Shartsé College
Ganden Monastery (Mundgod), 350–51, 366–68, 380, 391, 394
Ganden Nangsal Chamber, 128, 182

Ganden Ngamchö festival, 256, 259, 260, 413n274
Ganden Phelgyé Ling, 146
Ganden Phodrang, 67, 229, 406n128
Ganden Phodrang Palace, restoration of, 169–71
Ganden Sang-ngak Yangtsé at Yerpa, 231–32
Ganden Shartsé College, 36, 74, 121, 142, 406n134
  abbots of, 65, 154
  annual consecration rituals at, 224
  banners for, 221
  debate training at, 41–42
  enrollment at, 37–38
  history of, text of, 359
  initiations given at, 128, 133, 136
  land leased from, 83
  Losang Tsultrim at, 135
  melodies exclusive to, 306
  monastic disciplinarian at, 43, 401n37
  offerings at, 67, 122
  pillar banners, gift of, 141
  protector of, 405n117
  reception at, 84–85
  studies at, 382
  style of, 95
  textbooks of, 401n42
  See also Dokhang House
Ganden Shartsé College (Mundgod), 284, 287–88, 315, 345, 390, 393, 394
Ganden Thekchok Ling, 380
Ganden Throneholders, 70, 202, 399n2
  duties of, 59
  Eighty-Sixth, rival candidate for, 24–25
  lineage of, 374
  prior incumbents, 17, 18, 20, 29, 37, 55, 69
  residence of, 126, 406n138
  Trijang Rinpoché as, 13
  See also Jangchup Chöphel; Losang Gyaltsen
Ganden Yangtsé Chamber, 132, 173, 201, 241
Gandhi, Indira, 283
Gandhi, Mohandas, 226, 257
Gaṇeśa, 131
Gangchen Chöpel Monastery, 150
Gangchen Kyishong, 312, 360, 377, 389, 393, 417n344
Ganges River, release of fish at, 359, 364, 420n400
Gangkar, 92, 381
Gangkar Labrang, 215
Gangkar Lama Rinpoché Könchok Chödrak, 88, 92–93, 96, 117–18, 216
Gangkar Lama Rinpoché Könchok Chödrak, incarnation of, 289, 318, 331, 360
Gangkar Lamatsang Monastery, 116–18
Gangkar Ling, 91, 92, 93
Gangkya Rinpoché of Phenpo, 30
Gangling Sherap Tulku, 92
Gangling Tsothok Pöntsang, 92
Gangloma prayer, 327, 329, 381
Gangtö Dögu, 153
Gangtok, Sikkim, 226, 227
Garchen Session at Bum Nyakthang, 102
Garland of Birth Stories (*Jātakamālā*, Āryaśūra), 89, 111, 257, 277, 352, 371–72
Garpa Hermitage, 232
Garthok, 87–88, 112, 119
Garthok Öser Monastery, 119, 216
Garuḍa, 345, 413n272
Gashar Dokhang House, 32
Geluk Buddhist Cultural Society, 334
Geluk Students Association, 359
Geluk tradition, 270, 335
  Ganden Throneholder, position of in, 399n2
  geshé curriculum in, 68, 403n80
  in Kham, 82, 101–2, 114
  lecture on, 259
  mahāmudrā oral lineage of, 408n170. *See also* Ganden Mahāmudrā
  monastic reconstruction in India, 307, 310
  pure sense of, 309
  and Sakya, commonalties between, 150
  Shukden in, 8
  state of, 339
  tantric colleges in, 400n24
  thangka images of, 134, 407n153
Gemo Ngachu, 98
Gemo Ruthok, 215

Gen Losang Chöphel, 387
Gendun Chöyang, 223
Gendun Drakpa, Geshé Sadul, 22
Gendun Drup, First Dalai Lama, 57, 415n303
  Eastern Snow Mountain, 236, 412n258
  Illumination of the Path to Freedom, 65
Gendun Gyatso, Second Dalai Lama, 110, 187, 223
  Presentation of the Three Acts of Lhamo, 187
Gendun Phuntsok, Fiftieth Ganden Throneholder, 17, 18
Gephel Hermitage, 171, 180
Germany, 295, 296–99
Gesar of Ling, 104, 300, 417n332
Geshé Chödenpa, 66
Geshé Chödrak, 120
Geshé Dapön, 77
geshé doram, 65, 66, 403n78
Geshé Gendun of Mili, 74
geshé lharam degree, 45–47, 400n18
  candidacy for, 65–68
  examination for, 68–69
  of Fourteenth Dalai Lama, 2–3, 240–42
  in India, 258, 371
  of Phabongkha's incarnation, 31, 400n25
  of Trijang Rinpoché, 25, 382
Geshé Potowa, 161
Geshé Rapgyé, 315
Geshé Sharawa, 163
Geshé Sherap. *See* Sherap Gyatso, Venerable Geshé
Getak Tulku, 99, 205
Getsé Paṇḍita Gyurmé Tsewang Chokdrup, *Hundred Rays of Light*, 168
Ghaṇṭapāda tradition, 54, 77, 80, 104, 148, 188–89, 194, 196, 199, 254, 255, 256, 258, 259, 260, 288, 290, 337, 380
Ghoom Monastery, 258, 361
Gok, Mount, 21
Gökar Pass, 141
Gola Pass, 163, 177
Gomang College. *See* Drepung Gomang
Gomang Mokchok Rinpoché, 78, 79
Gomo Tulku, 333
Gönang (valley), 215
Gongkar Lama Rinpoché of Seudru, 111
Gongkar Truldruk tradition, 196
Gongkhukma of Rechung initiation, 153
Gongkotsang, 122
Gongkotsang family, 39
Gongsum Chöten, 250
Gongsum Shangmé, 214
Gongtsen Karma Tsering, 211–12
Gönpo (secretary), 106
Gönpo Dorjé's black deer, 245, 413n266
Gönpo Tsedu Nakpo, 119–20
Gönpo Tsering of Mongolia, 69
Gönsar Tengon Monastery, 88
Gönsar Tulku, 352
Gönthang Bumoché, 140
Göntsé Monastery, 249
Gorum Temple, 150, 408n168
Gosap Rinpoché, 103
Goshö Pomdatsang, 119
Gotra Lhamo (Raktamukha Devī), 169–71. *See also* Palden Lhamo
Gowo House, 55
Gowo Palbar Monastery, 96
Gowo region, 88
Goworong, 106
grammar and composition studies, 56–57, 185, 255
Great Compassionate One, 54, 402n64
  in India, initiations given, 148, 149, 255
  initiations given, 99, 103, 116, 162, 182, 210, 212, 262
  public initiations, 88, 89–90, 92, 96, 111, 119, 215
  retreat on, 80, 193
  See also Avalokiteśvara
Great Game, 2
Great Golden Stupa, Granting All Goodness and Happiness, 128, 131–33, 407n141
Great Prayer Festival, 24, 27, 118, 126, 400n18
  attendance at, 42, 64
  Chinese trouble during, 45–47, 50
  geshé examinations during, 3, 68–69, 240–42
  literature at, 150
  in Mundgod, 394
  Nechung divination at, 172–73

Ngakrampa's illness at, 58
offerings at, 123, 135, 137, 155, 211, 222, 241
Sera Jé boycott of, 168–69
See also Annual Prayer Festival
Great Red Gaṇapati, 408n167
Great Sage that Ornaments the World statue, 230
Great Secret Explication for Disciples, 196, 411n220
Great Treatise on the Stages of the Path (Tsongkhapa), 404n101
copy written in gold, 345
four annotations on, 143, 407n160
Fourteenth Dalai Lama's discourse on, 314, 316, 317, 330
Fourteenth Dalai Lama's receipt of, 270, 273
Ganden edition of, 268, 314, 330
Phabongkha lineage of, 82, 141, 142–43, 151, 159, 320–21
Phabongkha's gift of, 145
reading aloud, 224
teachings given on, 167, 218, 259
transmissions given, 300, 332
Trijang Rinpoché's mastery of, 382
Green Tārā, 321, 322
Guardian of the Tent, 171, 409n185
Guhyasamāja, 50
of Akṣobhyavajra, 91, 92, 96, 370
completion stage, 137, 138–40, 164, 407nn155–57
consecration ritual, 232, 317
four interwoven commentaries, 73, 347, 404n92
generation and completion stage of, 172
initiations given, 99, 148, 160, 162, 167, 173, 182, 183
mandalas of, 73, 79, 102, 119, 224, 269
mantra permissions, 223, 238, 263
oral transmission of texts of, 347
root tantra, 61
self- and front-generation, 263
self-initiation of, 95
statue, 308
transmission received, 73
Trijang Rinpoché's mastery of, 383
unique Gyümé transmissions of, 167
Guhyasamāja Lokeśvara, 174
Guhyasamāja Root Tantra
four interwoven commentaries, 73, 347, 404n92
Later Tantra of, 311, 417n342
recitation of, 61
Guṇaprabha, 403n80, 410n201
Gung Tashi Dorjé of Phunkhang, 46, 176, 177
Gungri Gungtsen, temple of, 232
Gungru House, 58, 172
Gungthang, 84, 122
Gungthang Chökhor Ling, 29, 34
Gungthang College, 17
Gungthang estate, 20, 22, 35, 49, 53, 123, 355
Gungthang Jampalyang, 108
Gungthang Könchok Tenpai Drönmé, 13–14, 18, 159, 267, 399n3, 408n175
Meaningful to Behold, 179
Gungthang Labrang, 220, 237, 390
Gungthang Monastery, 17–18, 19, 20, 22–23, 53, 237, 399n8
Gungtrul Rinpoché Khyenrap Palden Tenpai Nyima, 58, 86
Guru Chöwang, 264
Guru Deva, Lama, 253–54, 274, 310, 329, 341, 345, 351, 358, 366
Guru Puja, 79, 123, 357
in Bodhgaya, 358
at Buxa, 256
daily practice of, 118, 135
in Dharamsala, 365
discourses given on, 96, 148, 154, 179, 230
at Drepung (Mundgod), 370
experiential teachings on, 367
in France, 300
in Germany, 299
instructions given on, 271, 274
in London, 296
and mahāmudrā combined, 172
at Oaks Koti, 270
for Phabongkha Rinpoché, 161
in Sarnath, 288, 306
in Switzerland, 293, 294–95, 324
thangkas of, 273, 312
for Trijang Rinpoché, 345, 350, 351, 360, 361, 368–69

at Trijang Rinpoché's passing, 387
tsok offering of, 143
Guru Rinpoché. *See* Padmasambhava
Guru Yoga of Vajrabhairava That Is a Treasury of Attainments, 365
guru-disciple connection, 169, 205, 213, 361, 382, 411n234
gurus, qualities of, 161
guruyoga, six-session, 61, 79, 90, 135, 189, 264, 272, 350
Gushö Pangda, 216
Gushri Tenzin Chögyal, 115, 405n127
gutor ritual, 199, 411n224
Gyada, 85, 219
Gyakar Khampa, 380
Gyal Khangtsé Tulku, 214
Gyal Khenchen Drakpa Gyaltsen, 334, 418n363
Gyal Lhathok, 140
Gyal Temple, 163
Gyalchen. *See* Shukden
Gyalchen Dorjé, 71. *See also* Sherap Gyatso, Venerable Geshé
Gyalmo Ngulchu River, 86
Gyalo Thondup, 302, 319
Gyalong Pass, 140
Gyalrong House, 30, 73, 180
Gyalrong Khentrul Rinpoché, 238
Gyalsur Tulku, 295
Gyalthang, 113, 115, 405n127
Gyalthang Abo Tulku Rinpoché, 214, 215
Gyalthang Sumtsen Ling, 115, 207, 209
Gyaltsap Darma Rinchen, 195, 330, 404n90, 407n153
Essence Ornament, 289
Gyaltsé Tulku of Lhopa House, 120
Gyaltsen Namdröl, 293, 326, 329
Gyaltsen Palmo, 349
Gyaltsen Thönpo, palace of, 151
Gyalwa Ensapa, collected works of, 99
Gyalwang Chöjé Losang Trinlé Namgyal, *Jewel Garland Beautifying the Buddha's Teachings*, 417n340
Gyalwang Tulku of Kongpo House, 127
Gyama Nakri hills, 47
Gyamo River bridge, 219
Gyango Gyalsang estate, 247
Gyantsé, 146, 152, 192, 194, 225, 228
Gyapön Bu, 99
Gyapön Chözé Ngawang Dorjé, 205
Gyapön Döndrup Namgyal, 101, 210
Gyapöntsang clan, 100, 205
Gyara Rinpoché of Chamdo, 272
Gyasok, 140
Gyatsa Shalkar, 104
Gyatso Ling Labrang, 86
Gyatso Ling Tulku, 86, 172, 173
Gyatso Tsering, 391–93
Gyatso-la (uncle), 29, 34, 53
Gyümé Chabril Tsultrim Dargyé, 294
Gyümé Tantric College, 334, 399n13, 400n24, 412n246
abbots' duties, 59
Dechen Sang-ngak Khar branch, 35
Fourteenth Dalai Lama visits, 224
initiations given at, 160, 183–84
offerings at, 123, 135, 196
statues of Tsongkhapa at, 181
style of, 102, 360
summer retreat of, 167
teachings requested by, 173–74
Gyümé Tantric College (Dalhousie), 395, 414n279
mandala construction at, 311
offerings by, 315, 360
permissions given, 263
prayers offered by, 331
rituals performed by, 317
teachings received by, 268–69, 330, 353–54
Gyümé Tantric College (Hunsur), 366, 394
Gyurmé Dorjé, 247
Gyurmé Sadutshang, 176, 177, 254, 259, 275, 284, 286
Gyütö Tantric College, 399n13
abbots' duties, 59
enrollment at, 72, 77
Guhyasamāja ritual at, 231–32
initiations and teachings given at, 182
Losang Tsultrim Palden at, 59
Ngakrampa at, 58, 62
offerings at, 123, 135
Phabongkha Rinpoché at, 30, 400n24
resignation from, 81
studies at, 72–75, 382–83
style of, 95

three-dimensional mandala training at, 183
Gyütö Tantric College (Dalhousie), 394, 414n279
Akṣobhyavajra statue offering, 363, 420n399
offerings by, 315
rituals performed by, 317, 336, 337
teachings received by, 268–69, 330, 334, 353–54

H

Hahn, Michael, 297, 416n327
Halting the Ḍākinī's Escort ritual, 143, 271, 275, 337, 360, 361
Hardong House, 54, 62, 69, 152, 180
Hayagrīva, 52, 61, 337, 354, 365, 413n272, 420n401
Heart Sutra, 118, 313, 338
hell realms, torments of, 226–27
Heruka Cakrasaṃvara, 214, 288, 356, 382, 411n233. *See also* Cakrasaṃvara, five-deity initiation
Hevajra Tantra, 408n167
highest yoga tantra, 382–83
Hinayana tradition, 70
Horkhangpa, 38
Hortön Namkha Pal, *Rays of the Sun Mind Training*, 179, 279
Hothokthu title, 403n83
Hui Khochang, 222
Hundred Deities of Tuṣita
in Bodhgaya, 343
commentary on, 380
in Dharamsala, 346, 379–80
in France, 300, 329
at Gangchen Kyishong, 313
in London, 296
in Mundgod, 350
outline of, 217
Phabongkha's personal teachings on, 264, 315, 322
recitations of, 60, 71, 394
in Switzerland, 293, 295
teachings on, 152, 224, 228, 233, 261, 272
thangka of, 212–13
transmission of, 273
Hunsur, 350, 366, 394
Hyderbad House, 226, 227

I

Illuminating the Meaning of Sarvavid Tantra, 347, 420n387
illusory body, 137–38
impermanence, 130, 237–39, 247, 375
India
arrival in, 249–51
asylum in, 132
Buddhist pilgrimage sites in, 226
pilgrimage to, 146
Shukden practice in, 8
Tibetan exile in, 239
Indian army, 270
Indo-Pakistani war and conflicts, 280–81, 351
Indrabhūti, 408n167
Indrabodhi, 139
initiations, methods used in, 42–43
inner heat yoga, 165, 343, 344, 409n180
Innermost Essence Blade ritual, 307, 417n337
Institute of Higher Tibetan Studies (Sarnath), 343, 345, 358, 359
Iron Fortress of the Magical Wheel of the Torma Ritual, 358
Iron Fortress ritual, 263, 333, 337, 354, 358, 414n280
Iron Fortress Sixty-Four Part Ritual with Reliance upon External Dharmarāja, 333

J

Jaja Nunnery, 211
Jakhyung Drakar Dzong, 117
Jalavāhana, 364, 420n400
Jambhala, 131, 178, 289
Jamdun Temple, 217
Jampa, Mr., 257, 274
Jampa Chödrak, Jangtsé Chöjé, 70
Jampa Chösang, 185
Jampa Kalsang Gyatso, 326
Jampa Khedrup Rinpoché, 205
Jampa Khedrup Rinpoché, incarnation of, 363
Jampa Rapjor, Geshé, 368
Jampa Sönam, Venerable, 70
Jampa Tengyé, 19
Jampa Thayé Rinpoché, Geshé, 218

Jampal Chötso (sister), 18, 29, 49, 84
Jampal Dorjé, Lotsāwa, 397
Jampal Lhundrup (Dakpo Lama Rinpoché), 100, 144, 159, 408n174
Jampal Samphel, 254, 264–65
Jampal Sengé, 255, 301
Jampa-la (doctor), 128
Jampaling Monastery of Chamdo, 204–5, 217
Jamyang Gyaltsen, 46
Jamyang Khyentsé Wangpo, *Pilgrimage Guide*, 141, 407n159
Jamyang Kyil family, 264
Jamyang Mönlam, 300
Jamyang Shepa Ngawang Tsöndrü, 45, 57, 401n42
Jamyang Tashi, 245, 363, 390–91
Jangchup Chöphel, Sixty-Ninth Ganden Throneholder, 13, 29, 111, 114, 386, 397
Jangchup Gakhyil chamber, 121, 188, 200–201
Jangchup Gyaltsen of Markham, 347–48
Jangchup Norsang, 35
Jangchup Ö, play about, 295, 316
Jangchup Tsultrim, 391
Jangtsé Chöjé, 29, 45, 401n41
Jaraklingka park, 39, 172, 174, 179
Jasa Temple, 140
Jātakas, 400n20, 401n31
Jé Pass, 246
Jé Rinpoche as triple deity, 102, 103, 109, 116, 152, 273, 295, 346, 350–51, 363, 366
Jedrup school, 59
Jema Lama, 106
Jeri Taktsé, 164
Jeti Ling, 185
Jetsun Thupten Jampal Yeshé Tenpai Gyaltsen. *See* Radreng Rinpoché
Jikmé Lingpa, Rikzin, 326
Jikmé of Shelkar, Dr., 124, 134
Jikmé Sengé Wangchuck, King of Bhutan, 358
Jinpa Gyatso, 272, 288, 338
Jñānapāda system, 125, 355, 379
Jokhang Temple, 23, 308, 406n137, 407n154, 413n264
Jöl Dechen Ling Monastery, 116
Jöl Döndrup Ling Monastery, 116
Jola Pass, 87
Jora Monastery, 249
Jowo Jampal Dorjé statue, 223
Jowo Śākyamuni, 201–2, 206
Jvaki Rāja, 146–47
Jyotirmañjarī, 402–3n65

K

Kabur region, 214
Kachen Logyal, 267
Kachen Namkha Dorjé, *Stages of the Path*, 28, 400n21
Kachen Söpa, 380
Kachen Yeshé Gyaltsen. *See* Yeshé Gyaltsen (Yongzin/Kachen)
kachu degree, 43
Kadam school
  Narthag Hundred in, 276
  pilgrimages places of, 162–64
  Radreng Monastery and, 224, 400n26
  sevenfold divinity and teaching of, 232, 412n256
  sixteen drops practice, 339, 352, 419n372
Kagyü tradition, 104, 110, 211, 230, 269, 270, 287, 407n158, 411n232. *See also* Karma Kagyü lineage
Kailash House, 269
Kakchöl, 131, 408n167
Kālacakra, 199, 201, 402n46
  initiations, 42–43, 195–96, 209, 338
  tantra, 161
Kalff, Dora M., 292–93, 416n313
Kalimpong, 146, 148, 227–28, 254, 256–57, 258–59, 260, 380
Kalsang Dradul, 312
Kalsang Drölma (sister), 19, 34
Kalsang Gyatso, Seventh Dalai Lama, 15, 18, 103, 156, 236, 313, 346, 400n26, 412n259
  Praise of Avalokiteśvara, 380
  Sacred Ground, 236, 412n259
  Source of All Attainments, 313, 346
Kalsang Palace (Norbulingka), 66, 242
Kalsang Thupten Wangchuk, Fourth Jamyang Shepa, 45, 47–48
Kalsang Wangyal, Venerable, 146, 162
Kalsang Yönten, 18
Kalsang-la, 124

Kalu Rinpoché, 270, 287
Kamalaśīla, *Fifty Verses on Vinaya*, 331, 418n359
Kāmarāja, *Blazing Jewel Sādhana*, 131
Kambur Drak, 215
Kamkha Lake, 116
Kampo pilgrimage, 104–5, 382
Kamtsang Kagyü tradition, 104
Kangyur
- editing and printing, 70
- gifts of, 168, 360–61
- oral transmission of, 54
- recitation of, 51, 401n55
- study of, 71–72

Kangyur Tsang, 115
Kangyurwa title, 402n62
karma, 80, 108, 114, 145, 169, 178, 190, 293, 375
Karma Kagyü lineage, 110, 337, 419n367
Karmapa Rinpoché (Ranjung Rigpe Dorjé, Sixteenth Karmapa), 270
- China visit, 203, 209, 210
- connection with, 258, 356
- Fourteenth Dalai Lama's visit with, 230–31
- Freda Bedi and, 269, 414n288
- in India, 257, 337, 356
- in Kalimpong, 256
- in Kham, 207–8
- photograph of, 230

Karmapas
- Deshin Shekpa, Fifth, 230–31
- Düsum Khyenpa, First, 104, 211, 230
- Karma Pakshi, Second, 230
- Mikyö Dorjé, Eighth, 385, 397
- *See also* Karmapa Rinpoché (Ranjung Rigpe Dorjé, Sixteenth Karmapa)

Karmarāja, 199
Karpo Pass, 249
Karzé Monastery, 99, 205
Kashmiri Paṇḍita Śakya Śrībhadra, 152, 229, 408n171
Kashöpa Chögyal Nyima, 177, 191
Kashöpa family, 97, 152
Kāvyādārśa. *See* Daṇḍin, *Mirror of Poetics*
Kham, 58, 72, 78, 81, 82, 97, 207–11, 241
Khambu hot springs, 149
Khambu Monastery, 149
Khamlung Hermitage, 164
Khamlung Rinpoché, 390, 421n415
Khamlung Tulku/Rinpoché (half-brother), 18, 31, 164
Khamlungpa Shākya Yönten, 164, 409n179
Khamtruk of Chatreng, 27
Khamtrul Rinpoché, 256, 260, 269
Khangsar Dorjé Chang Ngawang Thupten Chökyi Wangchuk, 42, 144, 309, 401n36
Khangsar Kyabgön Tulku, 99
Khangsar Losang Tsultrim, 99
Khangsar Vajradhara of Gomang, 75
Khangsar Yeshé Nyima, 259
Khangtsek Pass, 215
Kharak Gomchung, 368
Kharap Shankha estate, 39
Khardo Rikzin Chökyi Dorjé, 229
Khardo Tulku of Sera Jé, 176, 177, 191
Khargo Tulku, 219
Kharo Pass, 192
Kharöl Pass, 152
Khartak Pass, 140
Kharteng Monastery, 248–49
Khatsarwa Jampa Söpa, 305
Khau Drakzong, 150
Khawo Butsa, 116
Khecara Akaniṣṭha, 165
Khedrup, treasurer of Shartsé College, 27
Khedrup Gelek Palsang (Khedrup Jé), 235, 404n90, 407n153, 408n173
- *Dose of Emptiness*, 179
- *Entryway of Faith*, 276
- *Ocean of Attainments of the Generation Stage of Guhyasamāja*, 153, 408n173
- statue of, 195
- *Wish-Fulfilling Jewel*, 334

Khedrup Gyatso, Eleventh Dalai Lama, 46, 417n340
Khedrup Norsang Gyatso, 181
Khedrup Sangyé Yeshé, collected works of, 99
Khegung family, 19
Khemé family, 19, 34, 141
Khemé Rinchen Wangyal, 79
Khemé Sönam Wangdü, 193–94, 225, 304, 354–55
Khenchen Dönpalwa (a.k.a. Tashi Lingpa Khyenrap Wangchuk), 161

Khenchen Tara, 249, 413n270
Khendrup Thupten, Geshé, 292
Khenrab Thupten, Geshé, 294–95
Khensur Ngawang Drakpa, 261
Khenyen College, 189
Khön Könchok Gyalpo (Khön Mañjuśrī), 333, 408n168, 418n362
Khöntön Paljor Lhundup, 409n186
Khoryuk Chöpa, 41
Khyenrap Gyatso, Geshé, 157–58, 159. 173
Khyenrap Lhamo, 162
Khyenrap Norbu (doctor), 175, 185, 196
Khyenrap Palden Tenpai Nyima (Gungtrul Rinpoché), 30
Khyenrap Söpa, Geshé, 264
Khyenrap Tenpa Chöphel, 58, 404n93
Khyenrap Tenzin, 187
Khyenrap Wangchuk, 192
Khyenrap Yonten Gyatso, 29, 55
Khyungbum Lu Monastery, 119
Khyungpo Tengchen, 86
Könchok Bang, King, 32
Könchok Jikmé Wangpo, Second Jamyang Shepa, 340, 419n379
Kongpo, 38, 39, 50, 85, 128, 204, 219–20, 402n49
Kongpo House, 127, 142
Kongtsé/Pomtsé Rak, 116
Kongtsun Demo, 50, 402n49
Kotsang family, 49
kriyā tantra, 322
Kriyāsamuccaya, 55
Kubera, 162
Kublai Khan, 405n119
Kuhn, Jacques, 301, 319, 320
Kuhn family, 320, 324
Kumbum, 209
Kumbum Minyak Rinpoché, Ngawang Lekshé Gyatso (fourth), 179, 384, 410n200
Kundeling Labrang, 196
Kundeling Monastery, 54, 56, 167
Kundeling Tatsak Hothokthu Rinpoché, 54, 167
Kundeling Tatsak Thupten Kalsang Tenpai Drönmé, 45, 47
Kundor Tulku, 257
Kunga Döndrup, Jetsun, 400n24
Kunga Palden, Dergé Shar Lama, 325, 339, 419n371
Kungarawa Palace, 82, 233
Kungo Palden Tsering. *See* Palden Tsering (attendant)
Kungo Tara, 365
Kunkhyen Jamyang Shepa, 196
Kunphel-la. *See* Thupten Kunphel (attendant to Thirteenth Dalai Lama)
Kunsang Phodrang, 155
Kunsangtsé, 53, 79
Kunsangtsé family, 19, 34, 87, 304, 306, 355
Kurseong, 148, 254, 256, 309
Kuru Bridge, 385
Kurukulle, 61, 131, 325, 339, 408n167
Kuśala Rasadhara, 397
Kushinagar, 146, 226, 265
Kusho Tserap, 171–72
Kyapying Dzasak, 152
Kyergang tradition, 60, 223, 259, 334, 403n71
Kyergangpa Chökyi Sengé, 403n71
Kyichu River, 18, 27, 245, 246
Kyil Monastery (a.k.a. Key Gompa), 261–63, 264, 311
Kyilek Monastery, 210
Kyishö Shapdrung Ngawang Tenzin Trinlé, 188, 410n215
Kyishö Tsal Gungthang district, 17, 162
Kyitsal Luding, 53, 194
Kyormolung Monastery, 17, 73
Kyungbum Lura Monastery, 216

L

Labrang Monastery, 418n363
Ladakh Buddha Vihar, 275, 283, 334–35, 351, 360
Ladakhi Losang Tashi, 271, 275, 283
Lajang Khan (a.k.a. King Lhasang), 17, 399n9
Lakak Tulku, 76–77, 205, 210, 212, 213
Lakha Hermitage, 215
Lakṣmī tradition, 54, 80, 90, 103, 193, 210, 255
Lalitavajra, 411n225
Lama Chöphak. *See* Dranak Lama (a.k.a. Lama Chöphak)
Lama Kunga. *See* Losang Kunga Gyurmé

Lama Lhaksam, 168, 409n182
Lama Umapa, 352
Lamdrak, 99
Lamdrak Tulku of Trehor, 294
Lamo Tsangpa, 171
Lamotsé household and estate, 39, 52
lamrim. *See* stages of the path (*lam rim*)
Langdarma, 410n196, 412n255
Langri Thangpa, Geshé, 163, 397
  Eight Verses on Mind Training, 179–80
Langthang, 32, 163
Lati Rinpoché
  offerings by, 345
  permissions and initiations received, 311, 340
  teachings received, 313, 332, 362
  at Trijang Rinpoché's passing, 388, 389
  Trijang Rinpoché's reincarnation and, 391, 392
  visit from, 359
Laurence, Ama Yvonne, 299
Lawa Geshé Khunawa, 214
Lawa House, 70
Lawudo Tulku. *See* Thubten Zopa Rinpoché
Lekden, 110
Lekden Babu, 148
Lekshé Gyatso, 24, 28, 49, 52, 54, 59, 62–63, 73
Lekshé Kundrok Ling Dialectics School (Shartsé), 37–38
Lelung Tulku (brother), 18, 48–49
"letting go of mental fixation" practice, 339, 341, 419n374
Lhabu (senior attendant), 22, 43, 97, 124
  China visit, 203, 205, 209, 219
  under Chinese control, 51
  death of Rikzin and, 128–29, 130
  escape from Tibet, 245, 246
  flight to Dromo, 191, 192
  illness and passing of, 276–77
  Kham journey, 84
  Lhasa journey, 90, 94
  management of labrang and, 145–46
  photograph, 195
  pilgrimages with, 140, 163
  sowing virtue roots for, 277, 286, 287, 304, 310, 313
  studies of, 54
Lhading, 140, 164–65
Lhadun, 88, 119, 216
Lhakchung, 220
Lhakhar Rinpoché, 115, 255
Lhalu Gatsal family, 137, 156–57, 158, 310. *See also* Yangzom Tsering, Lady Lhalu
Lhalu Gyurmé Tsewang Dorjé (finance minister), 75, 157, 176
Lhalung Palgyi Dorjé, 232, 412n255
Lhalungpa, Lobsang, 334, 335
Lhamo Lhatso, 140
Lharam Geshé Sherap Gyatso of Lubum, 207
Lharigo, 85
Lharu Menpai Gyalpo, 140
Lhasa
  armed conflict in, 248
  Beda Tulku's arrival in, 77
  broadcast message ordered by Chinese, 207
  Chinese turmoil in, 50–52, 53
  destruction in, 305
  Fourteenth Dalai Lama's arrival in, 152–53
  Kunsangtsé house, 19
  Qing ambans in, 401n43
  return to, 115–20
  three seats of learning, 3, 405n118
  Tibetan uprising in, 3, 243–44, 323, 328
  Zhang Yintang in, 38–39
Lhatsé, 86
Lhatsé Monastery, 119
Lhawang Gyatso, 341
Lhodrak, ear-whispered teachings of, 74
Lhokha district, 132, 330
Lhopa House, 120, 136
Lhopa Tulku Rinpoché, 229
Lhotrul Ngawang Khyenrap Tenpai Wangchuk, Kangyurwa, 58
Lhozong Shitram Monastery, 86, 119
Lhundrup, death of, 29
Lhundrup Dzong estate, 168–69
Lhunpo Tsé Monastery, 150
Lhuntsé Dzong, 249
Lianyu, 46, 50, 401n43
Liberation in the Palm of Your Hand, 5, 76, 233, 274, 332, 379, 404n98

Library of Tibetan Works and Archives, 373, 379, 391–92, 417–18n344
life-force wheel, 197
Life-Sustaining Jé Tsongkhapa initiation, 183, 275, 311, 394
Lindegger, Peter, 293, 320, 324, 325
Ling Labrang, 248, 288, 342, 356–57, 370
Ling Rinpoché, 1, 154, 232, 263, 360, 384
  arrival in India, 250
  audience with Paṇchen Rinpoché, 229
  audiences with Fourteenth Dalai Lama, 173, 180, 283, 286
  in Bodhgaya, 225–27, 271, 274, 356–57
  China visit, 203, 205, 206, 219
  consecrations given, 263
  Delhi relocation, 280–81, 282
  in Dharamsala, 288–89, 347, 365
  Dharma conversation with Trijang Rinpoché, 315–16
  divination by, 308
  donation for monastic reconstruction project, 307
  in Dromo, 191, 192
  enrolls at tantric college, 81
  enthronement as Ganden Thronholder, 275–76
  escape from Tibet, 245, 247, 248, 249
  at geshé examinations for Fourteenth Dalai Lama, 3, 234, 235, 240
  initiations and permissions given, 153, 188, 195–96, 338, 341
  longevity of, retreats for, 362
  medical treatment, 257, 328, 329
  Ngakrampa and, 58
  obstacle-eliminating ritual for, 273
  offerings for, 305
  ordains Fourteenth Dalai Lama, 202
  Phabongkha Rinpoché's third incarnation and, 309, 354
  photographs of, 5, 209, 227, 253, 321, 322
  previous, 23, 400n16
  Radreng visit, 223–24
  requests Trijang Rinpoché to remain, 386, 387
  rituals performed, 307, 317, 363, 369, 370, 390
  in Sarnath, 264
  in Sonada, 258
  in Switzerland, 319–24
  theater invitation from Chinese, 241
  at Thirteenth Dalai Lama's passing, 127
  transmissions and teachings received, 277, 312, 313, 320–21, 332–33
  Tsurphu visit, 230
  tutor appointments, 157–58, 200
lingsé examination, 65, 403n78
Lion-Faced Ḍākinī, 350, 351
Lithang district, 25, 98–99, 101–2, 114, 210
Lithang Monastery, 103–4, 207, 209, 210–11, 411n236
Lochen Labrang, 261
Lochen Rinpoché line, 337, 408n169
Lochen Rinpoché Losang Palden Rinchen Gyatso, 150, 152, 261, 408n169
Lochen Rinpoché Losang Palden Rinchen Gyatso, incarnation of, 311, 362
Loden Chödrak, 208
Lodrö Chöpel, Venerable, 65, 135
Lodrö Tulku, 310, 323, 325, 326
Logic and Epistemology, 41–42, 68, 150, 160, 401n34
Lokeśvara, teachings received, 125
Lokhé, Mr., 29, 35
London, sightseeing in, 296, 327–28
Long Life Sutra (*Aparimitāyurjñānasūtra*), 163
Longchenpa, 264, 374
Longdöl Lama Rinpoché, 196
longevity, six symbols of, 57, 403n68
long-life ceremonies
  for Fourteenth Dalai Lama, 228, 232, 275, 344–45, 346
  for Ling Rinpoché, 271
  for Phabongkha Rinpoché, 143, 154–55
  for Trijang Rinpoché, 28, 265, 269–70, 271, 272, 293, 305, 312, 316, 317, 338, 361, 366
long-life empowerments, 193
  of Amitāyus, 99
  in Bhopal, 275, 286
  in Bodhgaya, 274
  in Dharmasala, 346–47
  in Gangkar, 92–93
  at Gungthang Monastery, 20
  in Kurseong, 254, 256
  in Nepal, 254

in Oaks Koti, 269
at Otok Monastery, 103
at Phelgyeling, 96
public, 110, 111, 152, 165, 256
at Samdong Labrang, 116
in Sarnath, 265
for Shelkar Lingap, 119
at Shitsetsang estate, 100
in Sonada, 255, 258
in Spiti, 262
at Tashi Chöling, 148
See also under Amitāyus; White Tārā
long-life pills, 336
Long-Life Prayer of the Melodious Words of Truth, 337
long-life prayers
for Fourteenth Dalai Lama, 270, 293, 294, 327, 337, 350, 366
for Trijang Rinpoché, 32, 116, 306, 315
Losang (aid to Phabongkha Rinpoché), 30
Losang Chödrak, Geshé, 292, 416n313
Losang Chödrak from Yangteng, 52
Losang Chöphel of Tashi Chöling, 156, 310
Losang Dargyé, abbot of Shartsé, 121
Losang Dargyé of Gomang College, 298
Losang Dolma, 185
Losang Dönden, Geshé, 180
Losang Dönden, Kangyurwa, 54, 75, 78–79, 82, 90, 309, 310, 384
Losang Döndrup, 195
Losang Dönyö Palden (Muli Khentrul Thupten Lamsang incarnation), 318
Losang Dorjé (Mongolian), 341
Losang Dorjé of Dromo, 331, 337, 345
Losang Drölma (mother of reincarnation), 390, 391
Losang Gyaltsen (government official), 182
Losang Gyaltsen, Kachen (teacher of Lochen Rinpoché's incarnation), 311, 337
Losang Gyaltsen, Ninety-First Ganden Throneholder, 70, 126, 401n32
Losang Kalden, 340
Losang Khyenrap of Phukhang, 37, 49, 85, 135
Losang Kunga Gyurmé, 385
Losang Lungrik, 282, 415n300
Losang Lungtok Tenzin Trinlé, Fifth Ling Rinpoché, 58, 400n16. *See also* Ling Rinpoché
Losang Namdröl, 295, 416n321
Losang Nyima, 294, 325, 326
Losang Paldrön, Lady, 202
Losang Samdrup Rinpoché, 181, 384
Losang Samten (brother of Fourteenth Dalai Lama), 158, 280, 291, 324
Losang Samten (ritual assistant), 174
Losang Sherap (assistant), 203, 205, 209, 219, 245, 304
Losang Sönam of Dargyé, 271
Losang Tashi, 191
Losang Tenpa Rapgyé, First Drakar Ngakrampa, 174, 409n190, 414n280
Losang Tenpai Gyaltsen, 37
Losang Thupten, Kangyurwa, 362, 390
Losang Thupten Trinlé Kunkhyap, Third Phabongkha Rinpoché, 354, 355, 356, 357, 358
Losang Tsöndrü, 73
Losang Tsultrim (tutor), 94
appointment of, 41
family of, 96
geshé lharam awarded to, 46–47
incarnation of, 136
life and teachings of, 135–36
offerings to, 90
passing of, 134–35
relationship with, 84, 85, 134
Losang Tsultrim Palden, Eighty-Fifth Ganden Throneholder, 13, 20–21, 22–25, 45, 58–59, 387
Losang Vajradhara, 75, 404n96
Losang Wangmo, 347
Losang Yeshé of Chatreng, 127, 195, 203, 205, 211, 245, 313
Losang Yeshé Tenzin Gyatso (ordination name), 32
Loseling College. *See* Drepung Loseling
Losempa, 49
Loter Wangpo, Compendium of All Tantras, 346, 420n384
Lowa Goba, 93
Lubuk Gate, 46
Lubum House, 55, 56, 58
Ludrup Labrang, 116

Ludrup Tulku, 116
Luipa tradition, 54, 93, 102, 136, 196, 290, 330, 348, 354
Luksang Ngön-ga, 322–23
Lumbini, 146, 226
Lunang, 204, 219–20
Lungshar Dorjé Tsegyal, 130
Lur Monastery, 119
Lura Monastery, 95
Lutak Tashi Tsongpön, 112

M

Ma (Chinese military officer), 91
Machik Drupai Gyalmo tradition, 99, 103, 153, 223, 256, 258, 346
Machik Labdrön, 405n112
Magical Play of Illusion, The, 1
  author's colophon, 373–75
  request to compose, 14
  translator's colophon, 377
Magical Wheel of Stacked Vajra Mountains, 263, 354
Magical Wheel of the Blazing Weapon of Death, 333
Mahābhodhi Temple, 146–47
Mahabodhi Guest House, 146, 264
Mahabodhi Society, 225
Mahādeva legend, 238–39, 413n263
Mahādeva Munīndra, destruction of statue of, 17
Mahākāla, 408n168
  guru as inseparable with, 61
  permissions given, 99, 148, 162, 183, 262
  prayer, 334
  propitiating ritual, 95, 360
  ritual performance of, 119
  secret teaching of, 127
  thangka of, 268
mahāmudrā, 79, 123, 140, 154, 172, 179, 230, 271, 408n170
Mahārakta Gaṇapati, 131
mahāsiddhas
  eighty, permission for, 79, 223
  miracles of, 298
Mahāvairocanābhisaṃbodhi, 419n381
Maitreya, 134, 407n153
  incarnation of, 163
  mantra of, 135
  Ornament of Realization (*Abhisamayālaṃkāra*), 31, 32, 41, 180, 200, 367, 372, 402n60, 403n80
  procession of, 242, 413n264
  pure land of, 399n14
Maitreya statues, 150, 151, 408n171
  at Jamdun, 217
  in Jokhang, 308
  at Nyinpa, 86
  at Samphel Ling, 90, 94–95
  at Yerpa, 232
Maitripa, 408n167
Maja, Mr., 150
Makdrung Kalsang, 123
Makphak Pass, 214
Maldro district, 219–20
Maldro Jarado Labrang, 29, 83, 85, 220
Maldro Katsal, 140
Manchu Qing dynasty, 402n52
mandalas
  drawing and construction of, 57, 59, 73
  knowledge of, 60
  offering, 95
  three-dimensional, 59, 73, 79, 119, 174–75, 183, 224, 269, 311
Mangma, 249
Mani Kabum, 54, 402n61
maṇi mantras, 93, 103–4, 110, 215, 305, 336, 366
Manithang, Mr., 312, 356
Mañjuśrī, 285, 405n115, 415n307
  Gangloma prayer to, 327, 329, 381
  Red and Yellow, 296, 322
  statues of, 150, 201
  See also *Chanting the Names of Mañjuśrī*
Mañjuśrī cycle, 40–41, 74, 233, 311, 352, 356, 401n33
Mañjuvajra, 32, 355, 379, 380
Manmatha's wine, 179, 410n199
mantra wheels, 186
mantras
  dependent origination, 335–36, 419n365
  life-force, 197
  of Maitreya, 135
  of protection from lightning and hail, 101
  in protector shrines, 187–88

recitation in retreats, 92, 124
six-syllable (Avalokiteśvara), 110, 135, 221, 261, 262, 263, 402n61. See also *maṇi* mantras
for Thirteenth Dalai Lama's mausoleum, 130–31
Mao Zedong, 207, 218, 296
Māra, 410n199
March 10 Uprising, 3, 243–44, 323, 328
Maria Laach abbey (Bonn), 297
Markham district, 87, 88, 95, 96, 112, 117, 125, 216, 289
Marpa Lotsāwa, 204, 411n232
Marvelous Array Sutra (*Gaṇḍavyūhasūtra*), 43, 401n39, 415n301
Mati system, 200
Matön Chökyi Jungné, 232
Maudgalyāyana, 93, 178, 405n116, 410n196
Mawo Chok Monastery, 287
maxims and expressions
birds flock to the prosperous, 212
dogs collaborate with foxes, 107
donkey disguised in leopard skin, 189, 212, 274
donkey measuring the hour, 145
on laughing, 173
lion lacking the two, 279, 415n296
mildewed bits of cheese, 59
one hundred unwanted things, 106
parrot reciting *maṇi*, 199–200
profound Dharma; powerful evil, 229, 412n252
reunion of the dead, 207
river/waterfall flowing upward, 168, 169
seeing bad omen and smelling bad odor, 114
on seeing the Buddha in Lhasa, 124, 406n137
sound of arrow into sound of flue, 107
McLeod Ganj, 417n344
meat eating, 262
medical tantras, 413n268
Medicine Buddha, 135, 248, 262, 371
Menla Rinchen Dawa shrine, 140
Mensching, Gustav, 297
Mentö household, 167
Mentöpa, Mr., 196, 219
merit, 80, 132, 137, 155–56, 179, 241
Meru Monastery, 40, 49, 78, 161–62, 167, 172–73, 199, 240–41
Methods for Restoring the Degenerated Commitments by Relying on the Five Buddha Families of Yamāntaka, 365
Mewo, 91
Middle Way (Madhyamaka philosophy)
debates on, 240
mistaken conclusion on, 308
Patsap Lotsāwa's role in, 409n178
presentation on, 68
studies of, 55, 57, 71
teachings on, 340
works on, 150, 160
miktsema
diagram of, 131, 132–33
recitation of, 48, 60, 90, 104, 135, 304, 402n47
Miktsema Compendium (Khyenrap Tenpa Chöpel), 74, 99, 404n93
Milarepa, 34, 64, 181, 303, 411n232, 413n266
Mili Kabgön Choktrul Rinpoché, 214
mind training, 5, 9, 108, 160, 307, 352
Mindröl Bridge, 77
Mindröling Chung Rinpoché, 203, 207, 209, 210, 247–48
Mindröling Monastery, 247–48
Mindröling Trichen Rinpoché, 258, 260
Minling Lochen Dharmaśrī, 168, 409n182
Minyak, 210
Minyak Kyorpön Losang Yönten, 182
Minyak Rikhü Rinpoché, 30
Minyak Tashi Tongdü, Ganden Throneholder, 69, 202
Mipham, 375
Mipham Gelek, 15
Miraculous Book of Ganden (a.k.a. *Ganden Emanation Scripture*), 151, 408n170
Mitra Hundred, 209, 346, 411n237, 420n384
Mitrayogin / Mitrayogin tradition, 54, 74, 340, 355, 360, 411n237, 412n239
Mön valley, 279, 415n295
monastic discipline, 202, 247, 262, 313, 413n269
monastic headquarters reconstruction, 307, 310

Möndro estate, 248
Mongolia, 38, 73
Mongolian communities, 297–98, 299, 328
Mongra, 91, 92
monkey-dance appearances, 13, 399n1
Mortimer Hall, 276, 414n292
Muli Kyabgön Tulku, 205
Muli Losang Döndrup, 145–46
murals, 304, 305, 306, 342
Music to Please the Host of Oath-Bound Protectors, 310, 331, 343
Mussoorie, 251, 253, 255, 307, 333–34

N

Nāgabodhi, 267
Nāgārjuna, 143, 383, 410n201
  Hundred Verses on Wisdom (*Prajñāśataka*), 72, 404n91
  six treatises on reasoning, 359
  Staff of Wisdom (*Prajñādaṇḍa*), 111, 367, 368, 405n124
  transmission of works of, 266–67
Nagarjunakonda, 226
nāgas, 90, 124
Nairātmyā, 402n64
Nakartsé, 146, 152, 194
Nakshö Takphu Rinpoché, 173
Naktsang Tenpa Dargyé, 279–80
Nālandā, 146, 226, 264, 412n249
Nalendra Monastaery, 127, 163
Namdak-la (Phabongkha's attendant), 154
Namdröl (assistant), 203, 205, 209, 245
Namdröling Monastery (Mysore), 349
Namgyal Chözam, 364
Namgyal Dölma, 87
Namgyal Dorjé (cook), 84, 120
Namgyal Gang Estate, 246
Namgyal Monastery, 70, 126, 133, 234, 263
  assistance in cataloging project from, 181
  ceremonies at, 180
  monastic performers from, 42
  recitations at, 82, 236
  teachings given at, 162, 172
  three-dimensional mandala instruction at, 174–75
Namgyal Monastery (India)
  permissions given to, 346
  prayers offered by, 306
  requests by, 290
  rituals performed with, 272, 273, 283, 289, 307, 308, 312, 317, 362, 365
  teachings given to, 268, 270–71, 289, 315
Namgyal Temple, 140
Namkhai Norbu, 301, 417n334
Namo Buddha stupa, 146, 408n167
Nanam Dorjé Wangchuk, 163
Nang Gong family, 18
Nangsang (eastern Tibet), 41, 96, 116, 135
Nangsang Monastery, 112
Nāropa, 152, 162, 408n167
Narthang Hundred, 79, 276, 277, 278, 404n106
Narthang Monastery, 150–51
Nathu Pass, 225, 228
National Assembly, 38, 128, 177, 190–91, 401n32
National People's Congress, 203, 206–7, 411n231
Nechung Monastery, 180, 234, 331
Nechung oracle, 400n15
  on exile from Tibet, 234, 240–41, 244–45, 413n265
  five emanations of, 131, 197
  on Fourteenth Dalai Lama's enthronement, 190–91
  on Fourteenth Dalai Lama's examinations, 240
  at Great Prayer Festival, 3
  initiations received, 259
  life-force wheels for, 263
  on propagating Dharma, 172–73
  ritual advice of, 307
  on throneholder's reincarnation, 23
Nechungri Nunnery, 194
Nedong Desi Drakpa Gyaltsen, 330
Nedong Tsé, 140
Nego Monastery, 104, 214, 215
Nehru, Jawaharlal, 3, 206, 226, 251, 257, 414n288
Nenang, 93
Nenang Dreshing Geshé, 32
Nenang family, 89
Nenang Monastery, 230, 412n254
Nenang Phuntsok Dargyé, 112
Nenying Monastery, 194

Nepal, 3, 146, 192, 250, 253–54, 277, 305, 308, 339, 362, 388
Nepo Ngödrup, 329
Neshar Thupten Tharpa, 14, 206, 245, 247
Neu Dzong, 245–46
New Delhi, 226, 227, 275, 280–86, 304, 334–35, 351, 380, 394
New Year celebration
  at Chatreng Monastery, 96
  in Darjeeling, 148
  at Dartsedo, 209–10
  in Delhi, 372
  in Domo, 192
  at Gangchen Kyishong, 313
  greeting cards for, 326
  in Gyantsé, 228
  in Lhasa, 239
  in Paris, 328
  at Thekchen Chöling, 364–65
  in Trisong Ngön-ga, 327
Ngachö Monastery, 140, 209
Ngadak Nyangral, *Eight Instructions*, 287, 415n309
Ngakchen Damchö Yarphel, 149
Ngakchen Rinpoché, 209
ngakpas (tantric ritualists), 110
Ngakram Budor (attendant), 84, 96, 106, 108, 117
Ngakram Tsering Wangdü, 337
Ngakrampa Gyütö Losang Tendar, 21, 41, 53, 63, 73, 120, 399n13
  astrology teachings of, 47
  drawing teachings of, 50
  hometown monastery of, 85–86
  life of, 58–62
  passing of, 58, 62
  with Shedrawa, 38
  teachings requested by, 40
  throneholder's recognition and, 22, 23, 24
  with Trijang Rinpoché at Ganden Shartsé, 35, 37
  in Trijang Rinpoché's early education, 28, 29, 31–32, 33
Ngakrampa title, 399n13
Ngakrampa Tsultrim Dargyé, 163, 174–75, 191, 192
Ngakré Phuntsok Tsultrim, 391
Ngaksur Ta Lama Rinpoché, 149
Ngaphö Ngawang Jikmé, 177, 190, 193–94, 203, 204, 206, 225
Ngari Rinpoché of Kyorlung, 308
Ngawang Chöjor, 119–20, 221
Ngawang Chokden, 400n26
Ngawang Chözin of Gomang Khangsar, 194
Ngawang Dargyey, Geshé, 307, 352, 362
Ngawang Döndrup, 227–28, 257
Ngawang Drakpa, 277, 328
Ngawang Gendun, 389
Ngawang Gyatso (Sölpön-la), 30, 32
Ngawang Losang, Geshé (classmate), 51, 54, 57, 71, 126–27
Ngawang Losang Gyatso, Fifth Dalai Lama, 17, 115, 171, 405n127, 406n128, 407n146
  authority of, 2
  Bouquet of Red Utpalas, 131
  Hook to Summon the Three Realms, 131–32
  Melody to Delight Sarasvatī, 70, 403n85
  revelations of, 183, 187
  ritual manuals of, 137
  stupa of, 128
  Sun Dispelling Errors in the Placement of Dhāraṇī, 131
  teachers of, 400n21, 409n185
  Words of Mañjuśrī, 76, 404n97
  writings of in Potala library collections, 182
Ngawang Losang Thupten Gyatso, Thirteenth Dalai Lama, 2, 81, 94, 148, 369
  administrative problems at Loseling and, 75
  assistant tutor to, 49
  audiences with, 68, 82, 121, 126
  first meeting with, 45
  full ordination given by, 70, 404n87
  Gangkar Lama Rinpoché's devotion for, 118
  at geshé exams, 66–67
  homage verse to, 87, 405n111
  India, secret journey to, 46, 52
  Ling Rinpoché and, 320–21
  Losang Gyaltsen's passing, instructions upon, 126
  with Losang Tsultrim Palden, 20, 21
  offerings to, 90

passing of, 127–33
photograph, 46
plot against, 29, 400n23
prophecy concerning, 82
reception at Kyitsal Luding, 53
and Shedrawa, arrest and pardon of, 38, 39
teachings requested by, 78, 82
on Trijang Rinpoché's reincarnation, 23, 25, 76–77
Ngawang Losang Trinlé Rapgyé, 400n23
Ngawang Losang Trinlé Tenzin (Phabongkha tulku), 203
gifts for, 280, 305
illness and passing of, 308–9
initiations and teachings received, 221, 230, 232, 256, 280
ordination of, 260
personal instruction received, 280
photograph of, 281
reincarnation of, 338, 354, 358
teachings requested by, 233, 257, 259, 276, 278, 283–84
visits with, 234, 238, 258, 275
Ngawang Namgyal, Chairman, 176
Ngawang Norbu, Ngakram (artist), 304, 306
Ngawang Paldrön, 338
Ngawang Samten, Ladakh Lama, 146, 255, 257, 271
Ngawang Söpa, 170
Ngawang Tashi, Geshé, 136
Ngawang Tenzin (chef), 364
Ngawang Yeshé Tenpai Gyaltsen, 32
Ngechi Teng, 212
Ngödroké, 85
Ngödrup Choknyé, Geshé, 180
Ngor Evaṃ Chödé, 228
Ngor Ewam Chöden Sakya Center (California), 385
Ngöshiwa Thupten Samchok, 208, 215, 225
Ngulchu Dharmabhadra, 339, 341
Ngulchu Rinpoché, 229
Nīlagrīva Vajrapāṇi, 323
nirvana, 313–14
Niṣpannayogāvalī, 402n65
Norbu Chöpel, 245, 319, 324, 325, 356, 361, 363
Norbulingka Palace, 5, 121
audiences at, 82
catalogs of teachings at, 160–61
ceremonies at, 200–201
daily tea sessions at, 158
damage to, 248, 249
Fourteenth Dalai Lama's returns to, 194, 220
full ordination at, 70
geshé examinations at, 66–67
initiations and teachings at, 153
Shedrawa's confinement at, 38
summons from, 127, 157
teaching at during Radreng affair, 175, 409n193
uprising at, 244
Nowrojee House, 255, 312, 413n273
Nupgong Pass, 85, 120
Nyago Monastery, 215
Nyakchu River, 210
Nyakré House, 65, 344
Nyakré Khentrul Ngawang Gelek, 255, 329, 366
Nyakrong district, 99, 101, 208, 210
Nyakrong Pass, 48, 52, 121
Nyal, 249
Nyal Dra-or Rinpoché, Tenzin Trinlé Öser, 49
Nyangral Nyima Öser, 264, 414n283
Nyangtri, 204, 219
Nyangtsa Kargyen, 34
Nyasok, 194
Nyatri Tsenpo, 1
Nyemo, armed conflict in, 237–38
Nyen Tsembu tradition, 54, 340, 362, 402n64
Nyethang, 152, 408n172
Nyethang Ratö, 194
Nyethang Tashigang, 191
Nyima Ling, 140
Nyima Shönu, 122
Nyingma tradition, 101, 102, 247, 270, 287, 369, 394
Nyinpa Monastery, 86
Nyira Tulku, 116
Nyitso Trinlé, Geshé, 21, 62, 135
nyungné fasting rite, 104, 267, 286, 335
Nyungné temple (Dharamsala), 360
Nyungné Tulku of Shidé, 176

O

Oaks Koti, 269, 270
Obom Tokden Jamyang Lodrö of Drakgyab, 75
obstacles
  averting, for Fourteenth Dalai Lama, 336, 343–44, 384–85
  to dreams, 162
  to health, 184–86
  mental, purifying, 315
  prayer for removing, 155
  to return from Kham, 111–15
  ritual, overcoming, 96–97
  rituals to eliminate, 199, 273, 402n55, 403n82, 411n224, 412n260, 413n272
  in twelve-year cycles, 137, 336
Ocean of Sādhanas, 79, 278, 404n105
Oḍḍiyāna, 139
offerings, 123, 130, 172, 305
  at Arik Monastery, 86
  to birth deity, 53, 402n59
  in Bodhgaya, 264, 342–43
  of Buddha's body, speech, mind, 35, 37, 141–42, 400n28
  butter lamps, 94, 287, 288, 313, 342, 358
  at Chakra Temple, 110
  daily, of Ngakrampa, 60–61
  deception involving, 97–98
  to Dharmarāja, 39
  extensive incense (*lha bsangs*), 236, 412n260
  fire, 30, 61, 157, 174, 183, 201, 263, 266, 334, 344, 355, 402–3n65, 403n72
  fivefold clouds of, 143, 165, 192, 203, 408n162
  for Fourteenth Dalai Lama's well-being, 347, 352
  at geshé lharam candidacy, 67–68
  at geshé lharam examination, 68–69
  at Great Prayer Festival, 123, 135, 137, 155, 211, 222, 241
  hundredfold, 286, 287
  implements for, 94
  mandala, 95, 102, 144, 202
  né-ja (special tea offering), 74
  to Phabongkha Rinpoché, 121, 155–56
  on pilgrimage, 141
  at Rabgyé Ling, 102
  in Spiti, 262–63
  of spontaneous song, 138–40
  Subsequent Prayer Session, 51, 401n56
  tantric, 137–38
  at Tashi Lhunpo, 151, 152
  to teachers, 85
  for teachings, 78–79
  to Thirteenth Dalai Lama, 121
  thousandfold, 200, 235, 254, 258, 264, 271, 274, 305, 411n227
  Tibetan Trailbalzer tea-offering, 311, 417n343
  to Tsongkhapa's golden stupa, 84–85
  upon return to Ganden, 121–22
  See also torma offerings; tsok offerings
Ölkha, 185
Ölkha Chusang, 140
Ölkha Dzingchi, 140
Ön Gyalsé Choktrul Rinpoché, 75, 200
Ön Ngari Monastery, 140
one taste, 106, 139
Öntön Kyergang family, 20
oracles, 84
  in Chagong, 212
  Gönpo Tsedu Nakpo, 119–20
  of Lord Chingkar, 172
  Namgyal Dölma, 87
  at Sakya, 149
  training, 304, 332
  on Trijang Rinpoché's reincarnation, 390
  See also Gadong oracle; Nechung oracle; prophesies and divinations
ordinations, 29, 404n89
  age requirement for, 70, 403n86
  in Bodhgaya, 254–55
  in Buxa, 256–57
  in Dharamsala, 260, 261, 271, 331, 355, 360
  of Fourteenth Dalai Lama, 201–3
  full, 70, 404n87
  in Mussoorie, 333
  in Nepal, 254
  novice, 32–34
  of Radreng Rinpoché's incarnation, novice, 224
  in Sarnath, 364
  in South India, 350, 380
  in Spiti, 262

in Switzerland, 323
in Tibet, 86, 103, 160
in Varanasi, 358
Ornament of the Middle Way (*Madhyamakālaṃkāra*, Śāntarakṣita), 269
Otok Monastery, 103–4
Otok Sumpa, 103–4, 210
Özer Gyang, 85, 120
Özer Monastery, 87, 96
Özer Ngawang, 327
Özer Rinpoché, 87

P

Padma family, 110
Padmasambhava, 1–2, 264, 385, 402nn49–50, 414n282, 415n310
Dranak Lama as emanation of, 88
eight aspects, ritual dance of, 230
offerings to, 110, 270
statues of, 4, 140–41, 329, 334, 336
supplications to, 280
wrathful and peaceful aspects, permission for, 110
Pakchen Rinpoché, 217
Pal Lotsāwa, 125
Pal Narthang, 228
Palbar clan, 105–6
Palbar Lagen Chödrak, 97–98, 105, 108, 109, 112
Palbar Monastery, 86
Palbar Thokmé. *See* Tendrong Palbar Thokmé
Palbar Tsang family, 98, 215
Palchuk Dampa Chödrak, 97–98, 105–6
Palchuk Dapön Geshé, 81, 118
Palchuk Göbu, 265
Paldé Pass, 211
Palden Chöjé, 341
Palden Gyaltsen of Yangpachen, 168
Palden Lhamo, 119
chapels of, 150, 232
offerings to, 192, 239, 313
permissions given, 99, 162, 183, 262
renewing ritual supports for, 187–88
representations of, 131, 133
rituals for, 52, 95, 268, 273
speaking image of, 244
statues of, 199
thread-cross abode of, 171
Palden Lhamo Maksorma, 137, 304, 351
Palden Lhamo Maksorma dance, 50, 402n48
Palden Sengé, Geshé, 310
Palden Tsering (attendant), 14, 22, 215, 368, 374
arrival of, 124–25
in Bodhgaya, 356
China visit, 203, 205, 206, 209, 219
escape from Tibet, 245
European visits, 291, 295, 298–99, 301, 319, 324
flight to Dromo, 191
at Gangchen Kyishong, 312
joins government, 193
journey to India, 192
making offerings for Trijang Rinpoché's merit, 184–85
medical treatment, 325, 326
photographs, 195, 303
pilgrimages with, 163
in Sarnath, 363–64
teachings received, 280, 340
at Trijang Rinpoché's passing, 389, 390
Trijang Rinpoché's reincarnation and, 390–91, 392–94
during Trijang Rinpoché's illnesses, 185, 386
Paldi, 146, 194
Palgé, 212
Palgé Gyakser Yapa, 112
Paljor Lhundrup, 225
Palkhor Chöde, 152
Palos, Stephan, 297, 323, 417n330
Palri Yangdar family, 214
Palshar Monastery, 96
Panam Gadong Monastery, 152
Paṇchen Lamas, 337, 350
Chökyi Gyeltsen, Tenth, 151, 203, 205, 209, 222–23, 225–27, 228, 229
Chökyi Nyima, Ninth, 261, 408n169
Losang Chökyi Gyaltsen, First, 28, 151, 230, 238, 271, 333, 369, 373, 400n21, 408n170. See also *Easy Path* (First Paṇchen Lama)
Losang Yeshe, Second. See *Quick Path* (Second Paṇchen Lama)

Paṇchen Ötrul, 255
Paṇchen Shākya Chokden, 229
Paṇchen Sönam Drakpa, 53, 57, 341
Paṇḍita Darpaṇa Ācārya, 55
Pangda family, 148–49
Pangda Monastery, 119
Panglung Chöjé, 242
Panglung Gyalchen, 173, 332
Panglung Labrang/Hermitage, 115, 304, 342
Panglung Losang Thukjé, *Annotations to the Root Text on the Bodhisattva and Tantric Vows*, 266
Panglung Tulku of Sera Mé, 255, 297, 298–99, 320
Pañjaranātha Mahākāla, 99
Pari Range, 180
Pasang Lhamo, Mrs., 363, 372
Pasho Thupten, 338
Path and Fruit (*lam 'bras*), 150, 411n220
patience, 4, 139–40, 286, 298
Patna library, 359
Patrul Rinpoché, 347
Patsap Lotsāwa Nyima Drak, 163, 409n178
Pawo Butsa Gelong Tenpa Namgyal, 125, 133–34
Pawo Trobar, 87, 216
Pawo Tsuklak Trengwa, 230
Peaceful and Wrathful Protection of Mañjuśrī, 365
Pema Karpo, Kunkhyen (Fourth Gyalwang Drukpa), 79, 404n105
Pema Rikzin, Dergé Dzokchen, 358, 420n394
Pema Tsering, 297, 299
People's Liberation Army, 7
People's Republic of China, 411n219. *See also* Chinese Communists
Perfection of Wisdom
  commentary on, 53
  debates on, 180, 240
  handwritten analysis of, 237
  presentation on, 68
  studies of, 50, 51–52, 53, 54, 55, 57, 135, 402n57, 402n60, 402n63
  sutras, 405n112
  works on, 150, 160
Perfection of Wisdom in Twenty-Five Thousand Lines, 317
performance tantra (*caryātantra*), 341, 419n381
Pestalozzi Children's Villages, 293–94, 295, 322, 323–24, 327, 416n314, 416n321, 416nn317–18
Pha Dönyö, 193
Phabongkha Hermitage/Labrang, 126, 161–62, 180, 351, 354, 410n203
Phabongkha Rinpoché, 5, 28, 37, 75, 94, 136, 382, 401n36
  audience with, 82
  biographical praise to Shukden by, 310
  birthday celebration of, 143
  on Cakrasaṃvara, 288
  Chögyal Gyalu and, 100
  on choice of tutor, 41
  collected works of, 406n139
  early studies with, 29–31
  gifts from, 145
  lamrim teachings of, 75–76, 141–44, 157
  on Lhakar Rinpoché, 115
  Life Accomplishment in Verse, 340
  lineage prayer for, 272
  offerings to, 90, 155–56, 157
  passing of, 158–59
  photograph, 138
  reincarnation of, 173, 181, 182, 200, 202. *See also* Ngawang Losang Trinlé Tenzin
  requesting to remain, missed opportunity, 157
  at Sera, 152
  Simok Rinpoché and, 163
  stupa of, 161
  at Tashi Lhunpo, 151, 152
  teachings received from, 5, 40–41, 48, 74, 75, 77–78, 79, 80, 123, 125, 127, 137–40, 154
  third incarnation of, 338–39. *See also* Losang Thupten Trinlé Kunkhyap, Third Phabongkha Rinpoché
  tradition of, 90
  Tridak Rinpoché and, 124
  on turmoil, 85
  on two stages, 341
Phagé Losang Yeshé, 125
Phajo Dönyö, 148

Phakchen Hothokthu of Chamdo, 221
Phakmo Chödé, 165
Phakri, 146, 148, 149, 192, 194, 228
Phakri Jolak, 274
Phalha Thupten Öden (lord chamberlain), 185, 225
  in France, 300
  in Germany, 298–99
  in Rome, 301
  in Switzerland, 291, 292, 293, 295, 319, 322, 323, 324, 325, 329
Phara Choktrul Rinpoché, 195
Phara House, 128, 154, 195
Phara Labrang (Buxa), 311
Phara Rinpoché incarnation, 311
Phara Tulku, 154–55
Phawang Karlep, 215
Phelgyeling Monastery of Nangsang, 96
Phendé Khangsar, 151
Phendé Lekshé Ling, 220
Phenpo district, 45, 127, 136, 162–65, 168
Phenpo Go Pass, 32
Phukhang family, 257
Phukhang Geshé Tashi Norbu, 391
Phukhang House, 41, 126
Phukhang Khenrap Paljor, 390, 421n415
Phukhang Khentrul, 297
Phukhang Khyenrap Tulku, 18
Phukhang Losang Tashi, 84
Phuntsok Phodrang, 150
Phuntsok Rapten residence (Mundgod), 368, 380, 394
Phuntsok Tashi Taklha, 243
Phurba Yangsap, 307, 417n337
Phurchok Jamgön Rinpoché, 127
Phurchok Jampa Gyatso, 23
Phurchok Labrang, 126
Phurchok Tulku Rinpoché, 126
Phurtsé (Chamdo monk), 272
Phuthel, 250
pig-headed fortune teller, 29, 162, 400n22
pilgrimages, 132
  in India, 146–49, 264
  Kampo, 104–5
  to Protectors of the Three Lineages, 92, 405n115
  to Southern District, 140–41
  in Tsang, 20
pillar banners, 86, 137, 141, 168, 193, 221
Pö Pass, 249
Pögang Institute (Gyantsé), 152
Pökya Hermitage, 152
Pombor House, 194–95
Pomda Dzogang, 87
Pomra House, 77, 81, 107, 304, 332
Pomra Ratak, 67
Pön Shizom, 330
Pontsang Drangkhang, 229
Pönying Tsang, 86
Pope Paul VI, 301–2, 303
Potala Hill, 199
Potala Palace, 5
  consecration rituals for Thirteenth Dalai Lama at, 128, 130–33
  damage to, 248, 249
  Kangyurwa Losang Dönden at, 82
  libraries of, text cataloging in, 181–82
  protector support substance renewals at, 186–88
  relic box at, 287
  uprising at, 244
Poti Monastery, 119
Powo Sumzong Lama, 260
Powo Tongyuk, 204
Powo Tramo, 204, 219
Practice of the Six Preliminaries Called "Dharma Ornament of Mount Meru," 60
Praise of the Exalted (*Viśeṣastāva*), 294, 416n319
Praises to Tārā, 261, 293, 294, 296, 300, 350, 366, 367
Prāsaṅgika view, 163, 314, 409n178
Pratimokṣa Sūtra, 82
pratyālīḍha stance, 261, 262, 414n278
pratyekabuddhas, 70
Prayer for Rebirth in Sukhāvatī, 352
Prayer for the Teachings to Flourish, 257–58, 352, 413n276
Prayer of Samantabhadra, 104, 408n166
Prayer of Shambhala, 61
Prayer of the Sixteen Arhats, 61
prayers, three sets of, 147, 408n166
preliminary practices, 80, 100, 316–71, 405n120, 418n350
Preliminary Practices: A Necklace for the Fortunate, 100, 405n120, 418n350

Preparatory Committee for the Autonomous Region of Tibet, 222–23, 252
pride, 57, 168
prophecies and divinations
  on choice of tutor, 41
  dough-ball, 113, 405n126
  on exile from Tibet, 242, 244–45
  by Gangkar Lama Rinpoché, 118
  on Gankar Lama's reincarnation, 318
  on karmic deity, 78
  mirror divination, 136
  for Phabongkha's body, 159
  on Phabongkha's reincarnations, 173, 354
  on schisms, 229
  on Thirteenth Dalai Lama, 149
  on Tibetan exile, 234
  on Trijang Labrang, 81–82
  on Trijang Rinpoché's activities, 284
  Trijang Rinpoché's comments on, 110
  on Trijang Rinpoché's reincarnation, 23, 24–25, 77, 390, 391
  on tutor appointment, 156
  See also Gadong oracle; Nechung oracle; oracles
prosperities, four, 285, 415n306
prostrations, 60, 201, 274
Protectors of the Three Lineages, 92, 93, 305, 381–82, 405n115
Pṛthivīdevatī, 131
purifications, yoga of three, 288

Q

Quick Path (Second Paṇchen Lama), 76, 143, 404n97
  discourses on, 90, 95, 103, 115, 148, 161, 172, 174, 189, 192–93, 199
  personal instructions given on, 167–68, 232–33, 380
Quick Path to Attain Khecara (Shalu Kenchen), 202, 411n230
Quick Path to Great Bliss (sādhana), 341

R

Ra Dharma Sengé, 149
Ra Lotsāwa Dorjé Drak, 109, 125, 171, 409n184
Rabgyé Ling, 101–2
Rabjampa Losang Wangden, 238
Radhakrishnan, Sarvepalli, 412n249
Radreng Labrang, 176, 178, 223
Radreng Monastery, 32–34, 33, 41, 128, 176, 178, 223–24, 400n26
Radreng Rinpoché (Jetsun Thupten Jampal Yeshé Tenpai Gyaltsen), 169, 224, 406n140
  arrest of, 176
  imprisonment and death of, 177
  incarnation of, 233
  photograph, 129
  in regency schism, 175–76, 178
  resignation as regent, 155
  signs of great being of, 179
  at Thirteenth Dalai Lama's passing, 128, 132, 133
Rāhu, 279, 414n293
Rāhulaśrīmitra, *Illuminated Union Initiation Ritual*, 267
Raj Ghat, 226
Rakmé Temple, 213, 214
Rakpo, Upper and Lower, 111, 112, 115
Rakra Thubten Chödhar, 292, 294, 295, 322, 323
Ralpachen, 178, 410n196
Ralung, 146, 192
Ralung Nunnery, 152
Ramagang ferry, 245, 413n265
Ramoché Temple, 52, 182, 200, 305, 363
Rampa House, 385
Rampa Thupten Kunkhyen, 176
Rao, Dr., 334
Rapten, Geshé Tamdrin, 14, 307, 365, 420n402
Ratnākaraśānti, *Ratnākara's Prosody*, 168
Ratnakūṭa Sūtra, Milarepa's copy of, 181
Ratö Chubar Rinpoché, 245, 276, 312, 313, 332, 340, 342, 352, 362, 384, 389, 413n265
Ratö Khyongla Rinpoché, 228, 290, 291–92
Ratö Losang Jamyang, 325
Ratö Monastery, 17, 41, 401n34
Rāvaṇa (cannibal king), 300, 417n333
Rawamé Monastery, 246
rebirth/reincarnation, 326, 404n100
Rechung Cave, 140
Rechung Tulku, 296, 327, 416n324

Rechungpa, 346
Red Cross, 294, 301, 324, 416n315
Red Spear Vaiśravaṇa, 345
refuge, 135, 261, 262, 263
  four cycles of, 60
  offerings to, 305
  prayer, 293, 296, 300, 327
relatives, advice on, 80
relic pills, 150, 284
  "Dromo precious pills," 281
  "immortal iron," 117, 216
relics
  offering, 274
  of Phabongkha Rinpoché, 161
  powers of, 21
  protection, 270
  at Radreng, 223
  in statues, 94, 334, 363
  for stupa of Thirteenth Dalai Lama, 132, 336
  of Tashi Lhunpo, 152
  in thangka preparation, 264
  tooth with Avalokiteśvara image, 100
  of Trijang Rinpoché, 389, 391
  of Tsongkhapa, 236
  at Tsurphu Labrang, 230
Rendawa Shönu Lodrö, 224, 412n245
  Equaling Space, 180, 410n201
renunciation, 130, 178, 253, 303–4
retreats, 125
  completion of, 80
  Four-Faced Mahākāla, 362
  on Guhyasamāja, 91, 355
  inner Amitāyus, 343
  long-life, 344, 352
  by Ngakrampa, 58
  preliminary meditation, 346
  reading, 52–53
  on sixteen drops of Kadam, 339, 419n372
  on Striped Garuḍa, 124
  by Thirteenth Dalai Lama, 69
  on Viśvamātṛ and White Tārā, 48
  White Tārā, 362
"reviving the lost vital life energy" ritual, 325–26
Ribur Monastery, 119, 216
Richardson, Hugh E., 297, 416n325
Richung Pothö Monastery, 148, 318
Rigang, 110, 140
Right Foot Bridge, 86
Rigi, Mount, 319–20
Rigzin Kumara, 232
Rikha Ganden Shedrup Dargyé Ling, 228, 412n250
Riknga Temple, 111, 213, 214
Rikon Monastery, 5, 319, 320, 323, 324
Rikya Tulku, 313, 337, 356, 365
Rikzin (labrang manger), 73, 79, 82, 83–84, 85, 128, 145
Rikzin Lhundrup, Dr., 125
Rikzin Tenpa, Geshé, 362
Rimshi Chabpel, 202
Rimshi Sönam Tsering, 165
Rinchen Dolma Taring, Mrs., 328, 333, 418n357
Rinchen Ling, 85, 140
Rinchen Sadutshang, 225, 409n194
Rinchen Sangpo (Lochen), 261, 408n169
Rinchen Wangyal, 19, 34, 53
Rinjung Hundred (Taranatha), 58, 93, 110, 185, 221, 304, 403n69
Rithil, 228
rituals
  atonement, 239
  bathing of deceased bodies, 126, 134
  bone, 277–78
  burial, 334
  for ceremonial brocades, 159
  in Chatreng, to revive vital energy of, 90
  at Chatreng Monastery, retraining in, 95–96
  chö, 88, 405n112
  composition of, 345
  consecrations, 86, 90, 100, 111, 119, 146, 148, 213, 223, 271, 301, 306. *See also* Causing the Rain of Goodness to Fall
  daily, Ngakrampa's, 60–61
  for dismantling sacred buildings, 120, 406n131
  for disturbing dreams, pacifying, 337–38
  effigy, text for, 267
  elimination of inauspiciousness, 20
  exorcism, 52, 263, 402n58
  gutor, 199, 411n224
  for healing, 108–9, 123–24
  "horseback" consecration, 92, 405n114

Innermost Essence Blade, 307, 417n337
Ngakrampa's teachings on, 59
for nomadic tribes, 102, 103–4
nyungné fasting rite, 104, 267, 335
"opening the eyes," 258, 413n277
for passing of Thirteenth Dalai Lama, 127–33
proper performance of, 323
of propitiation, 113
prosperity, 193
of protection, repulsion, destruction, 334
relic blessing, 321
"reviving the lost vital life energy" ritual, 325–26
for subjugating demons, 174
Sur, 101
thread-cross, 110, 405n123
torma-casting, 69, 73, 212–13, 228, 268, 403n82
for transferring protector shrines and images, 169–71
of Vaiśravaṇa, 92
See also cremation rituals; Halting the Ḍākinī's Escort ritual
Riwo Chöling, 140, 141
Riwo Ganden Monastery. *See* Ganden Monastery
Rizong Rinpoché of Ladakh, 266, 284, 288
Rome, 301–2
Rong Dekyi, 223
Rong Dukda, 119
Rongling, 148
Rongpa valleys, 115
Rongtönpa, 163
Ru region, 215
Rumtek Monastery (Gangtok), 258
Ruthok Monastery, 140

S

Sachen Kunga Nyingpo, 419n374
Sadak Toché, 310
Sādhana Casket of Thirteen-Deity Vajrabhairava, 79
Sadutshang family, 176, 177, 179, 228, 254, 256, 258, 259, 291, 409n194. *See also* Gyurmé Sadutshang; Rinchen Sadutshang
Sagaster, Klaus, 297, 416n328
Sahib, Suni, 334
Sakar Hermitage, 216
Sakya Dakchen Rinpoché, 333–34, 346, 418n362
Sakya monastery (Mysore), 349, 369, 394
Sakya Paṇḍita
Jewel Treasury of Wise Sayings, 97, 160, 169, 176, 178–79, 222, 246–47, 301
ordination of, 228–29
Sakya Phuntsok Phodrang, 20, 399n10
Śākya Śrībhadra (Kashmiri paṇḍita), 152, 229, 408n171
Sakya temple, 149–50
Sakya tradition, 101, 102, 270, 287, 334, 341, 405n119, 418n362
ear-whispered lineage of, 163
Path and Fruit in, 150, 411n220
patriarchs of, 399n10
protectors of, 171, 409n185
teaching method of, 353, 364
See also Thirteen Golden Dharmas of Sakya
Sakya Trizin Rinpoché, 270, 287
Śākyaprabha, 410n201
Salha Dechen Chözin, 211
Salha Dechentsang, 95
śamatha, advice on, 315
Samayavajra, 61, 223, 266, 340, 345, 347, 367
Samdhong Tulku, 255, 359, 371
Samding, 194
Samdong Labrang, 116
Samdrup Tsé district, 228
Samkharwa, 260, 261
Samlho Geshé Losang, 367
Samling Bathar, 67
Samling Geshé Yönten, 81
Samling House, 120, 122
Samling Mitsen, 24, 67, 400n19
Samling Monastery (Chatreng), 67, 140, 150
Sampa Dreng ropeway, 87, 119
Samphel Ling Monastery, 89, 113–14, 199, 212–13
Samphel-la (calligraphy teacher), 53–54
Sampho Tsewang Rikzin, 244
Samten Chöling Monastery, 254, 255–56, 380
Samten Chöphel, 362, 371

Samten Gyatso (uncle of Seventh Dalai Lama), 18
Samten Ling Monastery, 364
Samten Ling Nunnery, 32
Samyé Monastery, 2, 141, 185, 309, 407n154, 414n282
Sanchi, 226
Sangden, 106
Sang-dok Palri Monastery, 256
Sangharakshita, 259
Sangharama guesthouse, 271
Sanglung Retreat, 140
Sang-ngak Gatsal hall, 162, 234
Sang-ngak Khar labrang, 39
Sang-ngak Khar Monastery, 122, 145, 235
Sangphu Monastery, 17, 42, 47, 51, 57, 65, 86–87, 405n117
Sangra Tulku, 305
Sangri Khangmar, 140
Sangyé Chöling Monastery, 380
Sanskrit picture prosody, 168, 409n182
Sanskrit University (Varanasi), 264
Śāntarakṣita, 1–2, 269, 397
Śāntideva
  bodhisattva vow system of, 143, 317, 418m351
  Guide to the Bodhisattva's Way of Life (*Bodhicaryāvatāra*), 33, 257, 286, 317, 372, 384, 408n166
Sarnath, 264, 265, 271, 272, 274, 287, 304–6, 363–64
Sarvavid, 50
  initiations given, 99, 100, 197, 238, 347
  mandala of, 102
  retreat on, 93
Sasang Mati Paṇchen, 411n225
Sasum Chamber, 181–82
Śavaripa, 279, 415n294
Schwarzenbach, Mrs., 294
science and technology, mahāsiddhas and, 298
Sé Chökhor Yangtsé, 194
Sebak Mukchung mask, 180, 234
Secret Hayagrīva
  as daily practice of Gangkar Lama Rinpoché, 118
  initiation received, 62
  initiations given, 82, 223, 259, 266, 334, 354
  liturgy of, 60
  obstacle-eliminating ritual of, 273
  permissions given, 260, 337, 358–59
  retreat practice, 80, 304
Secret Wrathful Amitāyus, 340
Self-Accomplishment of the Peaceful and Wrathful Mañjuśrī, 358
selflessness, 314
Sempa Chenpo Kunsangpa, 330
Sengé Gangi Lama, 136
Sera Jé, 69, 70
  bells ringing by themselves, 189–90
  conspiracies at, 177–78, 409n193
  Drati house, 18
  financial disputes involving, 168–69
  at stages of path teachings, 142
Sera Jé (India), 350
Sera Mé, 65, 77, 81, 107, 127, 142, 304, 332
Sera Mé (Dalhousie), 308, 350
Sera Mé Gyalwang Chöje, 65
Sera Monastery, 51, 123, 152, 180–81, 189, 234
Sera Monastery (Mysore), 349, 366–67, 380–81
Sera Ngakpa College, 169, 189, 233, 238
Sera Pass, 250
Serchok, 152
Serkhang Ama, 274
Serkhang estate, 35
Serkong Dorjé Chang Ngawang Tsultrim Dönden, 42, 52, 65, 124, 313
Serkong House, 67, 122, 180
Serkong Rinpoché (assistant tutor), 265, 384
  teachings received, 260–61, 263, 331, 339, 343, 365
  teachings requested by, 313, 332, 333, 334, 345, 346, 360, 362
Serlingpa, 382
Setrap, 95, 118, 137, 342, 349, 390, 405n117
Seudru Monastery, 84, 88, 92, 111, 116, 215–16
Seudru Monastery (India), 318
Seven-Point Mind Training (Atiśa), 100,

189, 233, 276, 279, 289, 296, 299, 335, 370
Seventeen-Point Agreement, 194, 411n219
Shakabpa Wangchuk Deden, 359
Shakhor abbot Phara Nyima Gyaltsen, 265
Shakhor Khentrul, 255, 346
Shakhapa Losal Döndrup, 178
Shakor Khentrul, 325
Shalngo Sönam Chöphel, 116, 406n128
Shalu, 228
Shalu Gyangong temple, 228–29
Shalu Lochen Chökyong Sangpo, 181
Shalu Trisur Losang Khyenrap, 341
Shang, 229
Shang Yudrakpa Tsöndrü Drakpa, 17, 237, 399n8
Shangpa Kagyü, 287, 403n71
Shangri-la, Gyalthang renamed as, 405n127
Shangshung Chöwang Drakpa, 91
Shap Gyatso Nyima, 112
Shapten Khang, 244
Shapyé Bridge, 119
Sharchen Chok prison, 176, 177
Sharchen Ngawang Tsultrim, *Versified Vinaya*, 65
Shargong Pass, 120
Sharpa Chöjé, 45, 401n41
Sharpa Rinpoché, Sera Mé, 142, 154, 390, 392
Sharpa Tulku, the Fourth, 78
Shartsé College. *See* Ganden Shartsé College
Shawo Gangpa, Kadam Geshé, 374
Shedra family, 38, 39, 78, 312
Shedrawa, 38–39, 401n30
Shedrup Dögu Khyil Monastery, 274, 304
Sheldrak Cave, 4, 140–41
Shelkar Lingpa, 112, 117, 119
Shenkhawa Gyurmé Sönam Topgyal, 245, 247, 273–74, 289, 290, 306–7, 309
Sherap Gyatso, Jé, 159, 340, 408n175
Sherap Gyatso, Venerable Geshé, 55, 94
  in Bodhgaya, 226
  at geshé exam, 68
  notes to Trijang Rinpoché, 56, 57
  offerings to, 90
  seasonal schedule of, 74
  teachings received from, 70
  and Trijang Rinpoché, relationship between, 71–72, 74, 120–21, 214
Sherap Sengé, Jetsun, 224, 308, 400n24, 412n246
Sherpa Karma Wangchuk, 336
Sherpa Phurbu Lhamo, Mrs., 255
Shesur family, 79
Shewa Phaktruk, 112
Shidé Monastery, 221
  audiences at, 182
  lamrim discourse at, 5
  Radreng Rinpoché at, 129
  teachings given at, 168, 172, 185, 196, 223, 232–33
  teachings received at, 79
Shidé Tā Lama, 81
Shigatsé, 229
Shiné Monastery, 152, 194, 228
Shingkyong Trakshé, 110
Shipal Hermitage, 116
Shitsé Gyapöntsang, 98, 100, 205
Shiwa House, 210, 218–19
Shiwalha family, 205, 214
Shiwalha Rinpoché, 214, 217, 218–19
Shodo Monastery, 119
Shödrung Norgyé, 300, 328–29, 362
Shödrung Rapgang, 322
Shokdruk Drodok, 89
Shokdruk Raktak Monastery, 89, 214
Shokha, 204
Shöl Court, 130
Shöl hot springs, 140
Shöl Kangyur Press, 156–61, 199, 305
Shöl Trekhang family, 30
Shölkhangpa, 38, 39, 78
Shopado, 86
Shopo Tak Pass, 248
Shotön folk-opera festival, 185, 372, 420n409
Shuchen Tsultrim Rinchen, 284, 415n303
Shukden (a.k.a. Gyalchen)
  acceptance of Drakpa Samdrup as medium, 342
  biographical praises to, commentary on, 310, 331, 343, 352
  biography of, 341
  on choice of tutor, 41
  controversy surrounding, 8–9

on exile from Tibet, 242, 245, 413n265
Gangkar Lama on, 118
installation in Lhalu Gatsal protector chapel, 156–57
instructions received on, 154, 157
invocation of, 247, 349, 367, 369
life entrustment received, 157
life entrustments given, 254, 255, 260, 295, 307, 330–31, 355, 359, 363
offerings to, 213
oracle of, 81–82, 90
protection of, 114–15
rituals for, 273, 277, 365
thangkas of, 197, 199, 268
on third incarnation of Phabongkha Rinpoché, 338, 354
Shungru Lama, 260
signs and miracles, 93
of auspiciousness, 110
Avalokiteśvara image on body of Thirteenth Dalai Lama, 132
of Communist Chinese invasion, 189–90
of Dharmarāja, 187
at Dulzin Drakpa Gyaltsen's stupa, 120, 406n132
on first trip to Gangchen Kyishong, 312
of Fourteenth Dalai Lama's scholarly achievement, 173
at Gankar Riksum Gönpo, 381
of incarnation, 22
ka on rock at Kampo, 104
lightning strike at black magic counteragent, 97
of multiplying iron relic pills, 117
at Samphel Ling, 90
at Trijang Rinpoché's passing, 388–89
at Trijang's arrival at Trijang Labrang, 27
turbulent weather at Tromkhok, 101
at Yongle emperor's funeral, 230–31
Sikkim, 226
Siliguri, 250–51
Siling Puwu PLA encampment, performances at, 241, 243
Simok Rinpoché Jampa Kunga Tenzin, 127, 163, 164, 259, 267, 384
Simshar Monastery, 122
Singh, Karan, 334–35
Sino-Tibetan conflict, 4
Sipa Monastery, 86
Sishi Palbar Chamber, 127–28
Sishi Phuntsok Hall, 128, 191
Sitātapatrā, 131, 132, 188
Śītavana charnel ground, 147, 287
Situ, 56
Siwapön family, 93
six Dharmas of Nāropa, 77–78, 140, 196, 261, 279–80, 343, 345, 353, 415n297
Six Ornaments, 180, 226, 369, 410n201
Six-Armed Mahākāla, 103, 131, 235, 269, 352, 353
Söchö, 179
Sögyal Lerab Lingpa, 307
Sokpa Achok Tulku, 359
"soldier" monks, 51, 52, 89
Sole Ornament of the World, 128, 131
Sonada, 255, 258
Sönam Chöphel, 258, 305
Sönam Gyaltsen, 217, 244
Sönam Gyatso (third Phabongkha incarnation). *See* Losang Thupten Trinlé Kunkhyap, Third Phabongkha Rinpoché
Sönam Gyatso, Third Dalai Lama, 101, 332
Sönam Losang Tharchin, 370
Sönam Rinchen, 185
Sönam Tenzin, 245, 363
Sönam Topgyal, Phenpo (father of reincarnation), 390, 391, 392, 393–94
Sönam Wangü, 84
Sönam-la (Namgyal's ritual master), 126, 127
Song Rinpoché Losang Tsöndrü, 142, 210, 212, 256, 264, 265, 317, 337, 338, 343, 384
Songkhar willow grove, 35
songs and poems, 325, 384
of accomplishment, 381–82
for Dagyab Rinpoché's departure, 278–79
on first visit to Switzerland, 292
for Fourteenth Dalai Lama, 344
on Guhyasamāja completion stage, 138–40, 407nn155–57
for Ling Rinpoché, 282, 415n299
for Losang Lungrik, 282, 415n300

as reply to Fourteenth Dalai Lama, 284–86, 415nn304–8
"Song of the Playful Bumblebee," 165
for third Phabongkha incarnation, 357
Songtsen Cave, 232
Songtsen Gampo, 1, 88, 140, 232, 305, 402n61, 410n203, 412n241, 417n336
spirits, eight classes of, 197, 411n223
spiritual path, roots of, 298
Spitaler, Anton, 297
Spiti, 261–63, 311
Śrāvastī, 146
Śrī Chusang Tulku, 362
stages of the path (*lam rim*), 76
compliment on teaching, 189
discourse requested, 100
Jé Chingkar's advice on, 172
meditation on, 80
Phabongkha's teachings on, 75–76, 141–44, 157
teachings given, 112, 115, 145, 199–200, 232–33, 238
Trijang Rinpoché's teachings on, 6–7, 76, 352
twelve links and, 316
Staircase of Pure Vaiḍūrya, 202, 411n229
Stein, Rolf, 300, 417n332
Striped Garuḍa practice, 124
study, 70, 71–72, 333
stupas, 152
of Atiśa, 223
in Bodhgaya, 146, 258, 264, 274, 286, 287, 358
construction of, 120, 406n131, 407n142
Dhamek, 264, 358
of Dromo Geshé Rinpoché Ngawang Kalsang, 146
of Dulzin Drakpa Gyaltsen, 120, 406nn130–32
of Fifth Dalai Lama, 128, 131
of Gangkar Lama Rinpoché, 216
of Khamlungpa, 164
of Losang Tsultrim Palden, 21, 59
in Nepal, 146, 254, 364, 408n167
of Paṇchen lineage, 151
of Phabongkha Rinpoché, 161
in Phenpo, 163
of Serlingpa, Atiśa's, 152, 191
of Thirteenth Dalai Lama, 128, 131–33, 336, 407n141
of Tsongkhapa, 84–85, 235
Subsequent Prayer Session, 51, 54, 70, 159, 401n56
Sudhana, 282, 371, 415n301
Sukhāvatī, 291
Sulpu Monastery, 17
supernatural powers, 88, 384–85, 405n116
Sur Ngakchang Trinlé Namgyal, 171
Surchen Chöying Rangdröl, 17, 171, 397, 409n186
Surka Cycle, 62, 223, 258
Surkhang Lhawang Topgyal, 301
Surkhang Wangchen Gelek, 176, 200, 206, 245, 247, 301
Sutra of Remembering Refuge, 60
Sutra of the Wise and the Foolish, 89, 93
Svayambunāth, 146
Swarg Ashram, 317
Swiftly Accomplishing One's Wishes, 280
Switzerland, 291–95, 300–301, 310, 319–26

T

Ta Lama Losang Jikmé, 3
Ta Lama Thupten Norsang, 308
Tachangma (local deity), 87
Taiji Drungkhor Pelshiwa, 119
Taiji Shenkha Gyurmé Sönam Topgyé, 167, 181, 183
Tak ferry, 229
Takar Pass, 140
Takchen Bumpa, 140
Takdrak Hermitage, 74–75, 174, 194
Takdrak Labrang, 246
Takdrak Tritrul Rinpoché, Ngawang Sungrap Thuthop Tenpai Gyaltsen, 74–75, 78, 127, 194
abdication of, 191
consecration at Ganden, 183
in Domo, 192
dream of, 338–39
with Fourteenth Dalai Lama, 180
initiations received from, 125, 153, 183
photograph, 156
regency of, 155, 160, 173, 174, 179, 190, 409n193

in regency schism, 175–76, 178
Taklung Chödé, 394
Taklung Matrul, 269
Taklung Monastery, 34, 194
Takmo (Tabo) Monastery, 262
Takpak Thang, 215
Takphu Garwang Chökyi Wangchuk, 79, 337, 339, 419n369
Takphu Tenpai Gyaltsen, 78
Takphu Vajradhara Losang Jampal Tenpai Ngödrup, 78, 154, 223, 404n102
Takshö, 214
Takster Rinpoché, 192
Tantra of Ḍākinī Meché Barma, 187
Tārā, 412n239
ritual at Ganden Shartsé, 38
statue at Nyethang, 152, 153, 191
Takphu's visions of, 78
twenty-one forms, 338
See also Cittamaṇi Tārā
Tārā Chapel, 3
Tārā Tulku, 331, 392
Taring, Mr. and Mrs., 333. *See also* Rinchen Dolma Taring, Mrs.
Tarkha, 215
Tashi Chödé, 140
Tashi Chöling Hermitage, 125, 154–55, 159, 161, 181, 193
Tashi Chöling Monastery, 148, 173, 256, 310
Tashi Döndrup, 22–23, 43, 124
Tashi Dorjé of Phunkhang. *See* Gung Tashi Dorjé of Phunkhang
Tashi Drölma (niece), 294, 325, 326
Tashi Gönpo (doctor), 261, 262, 267
Tashi Gyaltsen, 364
Tashi Khangsar, 180
Tashi Khyil Monastery, 18, 45, 209, 401n42
Tashi Lhunpo Monastery, 74, 148, 149, 151–52, 225, 228–29
Tashi Lhunpo Monastery (Bangalore), 366
Tashi Öbar mausoleum, destruction of, 17
Tashi Rapten
Gangchen Kyishong, 312, 360, 377, 389, 393
Lhasa, 81
Tashi Temple of Upper Rakpo, 111, 115
Tashi Tseringma, 110
Tatsak Gendun Gyatso, 58
Tau Losang Jampa, 364
Tau Monastery, 205
Tau Tsewang Gönpo, 69
ten arts and sciences, traditional, 196, 207, 411n221
Tendrel Phuk Cave, 232
Tendrong Palbar Thokmé, 84, 105
Tendrong Samphel Tenzin, 106, 107, 108–9, 112
tenet systems, 314
Tengyé Ling Monastery, 29, 49, 50, 72, 96, 119, 216
Tengyur, 54, 72, 415n303
tenma goddesses, twelve, 50, 272, 273, 306, 402n50
Tenpa Dargyé (lord chamberlain), 66, 174
Tenpa Tharchin, 169, 176
Ṭenpai Gyaltsen, 255
Tenzin Chöpel (Hungarian monk), 339, 340
Tenzin Chöpel, Geshé, 214
Tenzin Gyatso, His Holiness the Fourteenth Dalai Lama, 1, 186, 384
arrival in Lhasa, 152–53
audience with Trijang Rinpoché's reincarnation, 394
audiences and visits with, 155, 158, 192, 200–201, 209, 218, 280, 283, 286, 291, 304, 312, 313–14, 329, 332, 336, 386
awards and honors, 4
enrollment in three seats, 180–81, 182
enthronement of, 190–91
escape from Tibet, 245–49, 413n265, 413n270
first instructions from Trijang Rinpoché, 158
flight from Tibet, 3
geshé examinations, 233–35
at Great Prayer Festival, 168–69
humorous recitation session with, 173
illness of, 237
initiations received, 188, 195–96
Jayanti in Bodhgaya, 225–27
letter requesting long life, 284
life of, 2–3
My Land and My People, 207

negotiations with Chinese, 192, 194, 222–23
obstacle year of, 336–38
offerings to, 352
oracles invoked by, 190–91
ordination of, full, 201–3
photographs of, 227, 253
pilgrimages of, 203
prenovitiate and novice vows of, 160
Radreng visit, 223–24
relics presented to, 132
relinquishment of political role, 4
requests Trilang's autobiography, 14
retreats of, 193, 201
return to Lhasa, 220
on Shukden practice, 8–9
teachings and transmissions received, 266–67, 268, 270–71, 272, 273, 280, 289, 311, 332, 334, 341–42, 348, 355–56, 363, 379
teachings requested by, 260–61, 276, 344, 347
on Trijang Rinpoché's reincarnation, 390–91
tutors of, 5, 180, 200
visit to Trijang Rinpoché, 263
Tenzin Lhawang (tailor), 84
Tenzin Sangpo, 49
Tenzin Wangpo of Gungthang, 19–20, 34
Tethong, T. C., 367
Tethong Söpal, 294, 416n317
Thailand, 313
Thalphung Gang, 46
thangkas
of Dharmarāja, fivefold, 263–64
at Ganden Shartsé (Mundgod), 350
gifts of, 291, 369
of *Guru Puja* merit field, 273, 312
at Gyüme, 224
of Hevajra, 152
from Lhamo chapel in Drepung, 171
from Lhasa, return of, 267–68
from Nego Monastery, 215
overseeing production of, 197
of Samphel Ling, 199, 212–13
of Shukden, brought from Tibet, 310
for stupa of Thirteenth Dalai Lama, 134
of thousand buddhas, gift of, 111
of three longevity deities, gift of, 67
Thangkya Monastery, 165
Thangpoché, 140
Thangsak Ganden Chökhor, 34, 163–64
Thangten Phakgetsang, 211, 212
Thangthong ear-whispered tradition, 78, 255
Thangthong Gyalpo, 192
Tharpa Chöling Monastery, 146, 148, 254, 258–59
theft, 91
Thekchen Chöling, 317, 336, 338, 349, 352, 361, 363, 364–65, 366, 373, 379
Thekchen Chöpel Ling (Munich), 298
Thepo Tulku, 313, 315, 332, 345, 346
Theravada tradition, 313
Thirteen Divine Visions of Takphu, 74, 233, 275, 341. *See also* Takphu Garwang Chökyi Wangchuk
Thirteen Golden Dharmas of Sakya, 74, 131, 150, 233, 339, 408n167
thirty-five buddhas of confession, 136–37
Thongwa Dönden, Sixth Karmapa, 110
Thönmi Sambhota, 403n67
Introduction to Morphology, 56, 255, 273, 403n67
Thirty Verses, 56, 255, 273, 403n67, 414n289
Thösam Dargyé Ling, 248
Thösam Norbuling hall, 142
Thoyön Lama Döndrup Gyaltsen, 40, 341
three centers of Dharma, 135, 407n154
three higher trainings, 297, 416n329
three poisons, 15, 227, 340, 399n6
three "red ones," 150, 408n167
Three Stones Passed from Hand to Hand, 167, 409n181
three worlds (of samsara), 252, 413n271
Three Wrathful Forms Combined, 254, 256, 273, 275, 289, 324, 329, 349, 351, 360, 413n272
Thuken Chökyi Nyima, 49, 82, 114, 126, 137, 159, 312, 408n175, 418n345
Thuksé Thupten Topjor, 180
Thupten (attendant to Dakpo Bamchö), 291
Thupten Chöden, 289
Thupten Chödrön, 352

Thupten Chöjor, 274
Thupten Chöyang, 289
Thupten Gönpo, 359
Thupten Gyatso. *See* Ngawang Losang Thupten Gyatso, Thirteenth Dalai Lama
Thupten Jamyang (ritual assistant), 264
Thupten Jungné, 264, 271–72, 305
Thupten Kalsang Tenpai Drönmé Rinpoché, 45
Thupten Kunga, Ganden Throneholder, 202, 235
Thupten Kunphel (attendant to Thirteenth Dalai Lama), 126, 127, 128, 130
Thupten Lekmön, Chamberlain, 175, 176, 194
Thupten Lhundrup, 185
Thupten Ngawang, 272, 295
Thupten Nyingpo of Buryatia, 69
Thupten Phelgyé (a.k.a. Drakpa Samdrup), 304, 332, 341–42, 349
Thupten Samten, 189
Thupten Serdokchen Monastery, 229
Thupten Sönam, 273
Thupten Tendar (Khendrung Lhautara), 194
Thupten Tharpa, 306
Tibet
  Chinese occupation of, 7–8, 25, 228. *See also* Chinese Communists
  currency of, 63, 74, 401n44
  dissent and schisms provoked by Chinese, 229
  escape from, 8, 245–49
  geography of, 1
  government in exile, 3–4
  imperial period, 1–2, 410n196
  invasions of, 2
  Nationalist Chinese in, 50–52
  priest-patron relationships in, 2
  provisional government, declaration of, 249
  uprising of March 10, 3, 243–44
Tibet House (Delhi), 281, 282, 283, 284, 302, 319, 329, 360, 372
Tibetan alphabet, 28, 31, 357
Tibetan Buddhism
  ecumenical conference on, 270
  establishment of, 2
  lineages of, relationship between, 8
  remarks on, 320
  study of all traditions of, 72
  Wenchen Gongzhu and, 412n241
Tibetan Children's Village (Dharamsala), 293, 307, 315–16, 330, 347, 361, 388
Tibetan government, 201
  cabinet and secretariat, 190, 410n216
  ranks, 172, 409n189
Tibetan heritage, importance of in exile, 324, 327, 328
Tibetan Homes Foundation, 333, 418n357
Tibetan settlements
  in Buxa, 256–57, 305, 307
  in Hunsur, 350, 366
  in Mundgod, 350–51, 367–72
  in Mysore, 349–50, 367
  in Switzerland, 293–95, 301, 323–25, 329
Tibetan Trailbalzer tea-offering, 311, 417n343
Tibetan Transit School (Dharamsala), 307
Tibeto-Burmese linguistic group, 1
Time of Approximation. *See under* Four-Faced Mahākāla
Tö Shungru Lama, 260
Tokden Drakpa Sengé, First Shamarpa, 230, 412n254
Tokden Jampal Gyatso, 330, 408n170
Tölung, 75, 168, 223, 224, 225, 229, 230
Tölung hot springs, 167, 196
Tölung Rakor, 20, 167
Tongjung, 98, 214
Tongwa Dönden, Sixth Karmapa, 214
Tönpa Tsenlek statue, 140
Töpa Kako Tashi, 352
Töpa Tamdring Tsering, 260
torma offerings
  at bodhisattva vows of Fourteenth Dalai Lama, 316
  at end of retreats, 362
  in exorcism rituals, 52
  with Fourteenth Dalai Lama, 266
  for Fourteenth Dalai Lama's bodhisattva vows, 316, 418n349
  governmental, 193
  on New Year's Day, 239

by Ngakrampa Gyütö Losang Tendar, 60
to Shukden, 157
sixty-four-part, 75, 174, 333, 337, 384–85, 404n95
at solar equinox, 268
torma-casting rituals, 69, 73, 212–13, 228, 268, 403n82
for teachings, 137
during Tsongkhapa's collected works transmission, 266
Tradruk Temple, 140, 185, 407n154
Tramkolam, 88
transference of consciousness
for Lhabu, 277
for mother, 221
for Namgyal Dorjé, 120
by Ngakrampa, 62
Trathang Tulku, 116
Trati Geshé Rinchen Döndrup, 407n160
Tratsangdo, 149
Trāyastriṃśa Heaven, 299
treachery, teachings on, 106
treasure revealers, 247, 287, 413n268, 415n309
treasure vases, 94, 131, 289, 354
Treasury of Abhidharma (*Abhidharmakośa*, Vasubandhu), 65, 341, 403n80
Treatise of Valid Cognition (*Pramāṇavarttika*, Dharmakīrti), 403n80
Trehor, 98–101
Trehor Draksé Tulku, 324
Trehor House, 69, 70, 163, 175, 233
Trehor Kangyur Rinpoché, 264
Trehor Naktsang, 345, 352
Trehor Samten, 315
Trehor Thupten Tulku, 352
Trehor Trungsar Rinpoché, 306
Treta Gönkyi, 34
Trethong Söpal, 322
Tri Ngawang Norbu Rinpoché, 75
Tridak Rinpoché, Ganden Jangtsé, 36, 75, 78, 79, 123–24
Tridakpo Ngawang Tashi, 124
Trijang Buddhist Institute (Vermont), 395
Trijang Choktrul Rinpoché, 390–95, 421n415
Trijang Labrang, 134, 394
arrival at, 27–28
Beda Tulku and, 76–77
financial difficulties at, 63–64, 73, 79–80, 84, 97–98, 129–30
Geshé Sherap at, 74
management of, 82–84, 145–46
Ngakrampa at, 62
prophecy on, 81–82
Trijang Rinpoché, 1, 397, 421n417
academic abilities of, 53, 55, 56, 81
affection for Fourteenth Dalai Lama, 9
birth date of, 361, 420n395
birth of, 17
childhood prescience of, 28–29
civilian titles imposed by Chinese, 221, 222, 252
daily routine, prior to full ordination, 71–72
Darhan rank, 172, 192
denounced by Chinese, 251–52
Dharma conversation with Ling Rinpoché, 315–16
disciples of, 384
donation for monastic reconstruction project, 307
early education, 28
forty-ninth year obstacles, 184–85
hardships of, 63–64, 250
illnesses and injuries of, 48–49, 123–24, 175, 185, 205, 246, 261, 262, 364, 386–87
incarnation lineage of, 397, 421n417
initiations received, 54, 55, 62, 74–75, 77–79, 153, 155
kachu degree awarded, 43
legacy of, 4, 9
and Ling Rinpoché, relationship between, 4–5, 232, 263, 282, 288, 312, 332–33, 360, 365
magical powers of, 384–85
medical treatments, 291, 292, 300–301, 321–22, 325–26, 360
memory, 31–32, 33, 372
and Ngakrampa, relationship between, 58, 59–60
ordination of, 32–34
parents and siblings of, 18–19
passing of, 9, 387–90
photographs in Europe, 303, 321, 322

photographs in India, 147, 227, 253, 260, 335, 361
photographs in Tibet and China, 5, 83, 184, 193, 195, 206, 209
plot against, 107–9
previous lives of, 13–14, 385
realization of, 381–82
recognition of, 22–24, 25
on regency dispute, 175, 178–79
reincarnation of, 390–95, 421n415
special treatment, declining, 74
teaching ability of, 6–7
translator's personal recollections of, 5–8
Tsokchen Tulku rank of, 155
tutor appointments, 157–58, 200
wisdom of, 382–83
on writing his autobiography, 14–15
writings of, 8, 384
See also *Liberation in the Palm of Your Hand*; *Music to Please the Host of Oath-Bound Protectors*
Trimön Chözé Thupten Deshek, 162
Trimön Norbu Wangyal (minister), 94, 128, 130, 132
Trinlé Dargyé, 159, 161, 309, 351, 354, 355, 356
Trinlé Dechen of Pangda, 82
Trinlé Gyalpo, 134, 263
Trinlé Wangyal (artist), 264
Trisong Detsen, 1, 409n192
Trisong Ngön-ga Tibetan Home, 295–96, 327
Tro Pass, 85, 205
Tromkhok, 101
Tromkhok Tulku, 101–2
Tromthar, 99
Trophu, 150
Trophu Lotsāwa, 408n171
Trophu Monastery, 408n171
Troti Tsultrim, 81
Troti Tulku. *See* Chagong Beda Tulku
Trungsar Hermitage, 99
Trungsar Rinpoché of Karzé, 82, 99
Trungsar Rinpoché of Trehor, 310
Tsa Pass, 116
Tsakgur Pass, 194
Tsakha Lagen, 107
Tsakha Lho, salt flats at, 117
Tsakha Lhopa, 318
Tsal College, 17
Tsal Gungthang Monastery, 220
Tsalpa Kagyü, 17, 399n8
Tsalpa potentate, 17
Tsamchö Drölma, Mrs., 307
Tsamkhung nun Phuntsok, 188
Tsamkhung Nunnery, 188–89
Tsang, 149–52, 228
Tsangpa Khenchen, 49
Tsangpa Thapkhé, 232–33
Tsangpo River, 140, 141, 152, 246, 305, 413n265
Tsangthok field, 141–42
Tsangyang, Geshé, 30
Tsangyang Gyatso, Sixth Dalai Lama, 171
Tsarchen Losal Gyatso, 131, 407n146, 411n230
Tsari, 204, 411n233
Tsāriwa Phuntsok family, 324
Tsarong Dasand Dradul (minister), 81
Tsarong family, 46
Tsatak Rinpoché, 103
Tsawa House, 55, 66, 142
Tsawa Öser Tulku, 75
Tsawa region, 87
Tsawa Tritrul of Sera Mé, 181–82
Tsawagang, 204
Tsechok Ling Tulku, 273, 311
Tsedrung Jampa Wangdü, 260
Tsemönling, 246
Tsemönling Monastery, 183
Tsemönling Rinpoché, 37, 168–69
Tsengö Khaché Marpo, 332
Tsengö Nyima Shönu, 84
Tsenshap Rinpoché, 332
Tsenthang-yu Temple, 140
Tsenya Hermitage, 32
Tsenya Tulku, 177, 191
Tsenyi Monastery, 218
Tsepak Lhakhang, 305
Tsering, Mrs. Lhamo, 174
Tsering Chenga, 110
Tsering Dölma, 221
Tsering Döndrup (father), 18–19, 28, 34
Tsering Drölkar, Mrs., 167, 172, 196
Tsering Drölma (Fourteenth Dalai Lama's sister), 203

Tsering Drölma (mother), 18–19, 23, 29, 34, 49, 84, 122, 221–22
Tseten Phuntsok, 363
Tsethang, 140
Tsewang Gyaltsen, 97
Tsewang Norbu, 174
Tsewang Rabten (Lukhangwa), 191, 227–28, 250, 270, 289
Tsidrung Losang Kalsang (attendant to Fourteenth Dalai Lama), 183
tsipars, 86, 122, 137, 141, 168, 193, 405n110
Tsipön Shuguba, *In the Presence of My Enemies*, 385
Tsipön Tsewang Döndrup, 237, 304
Tsogo Hermitage, 92
Tsogo Lake, 226
tsok offerings, 143
  in Bodhgaya, 342, 343
  of Cakrasaṃvara, 271
  in China, 209, 412n238
  by Fourteenth Dalai Lama, 304
  for Fourteenth Dalai Lama, 270
  in France, 300
  at Ganden, 235
  at Gangchen Kyishong, 312
  in Germany, 299
  hundred thousand, 270
  for illusory body teachings, 137–38
  at Kampo, 104
  in Lhading, 164–65
  for merit of translation, 377
  at Oaks Koti, 270
  for Phabongkha Rinpoché, 161
  in protector relocation, 170, 171
  in Sarnath, 288, 305, 306, 364
  in Switzerland, 293, 294, 324
  tenth-day, in Chatreng, 214
  at Trijang Rinpoché's passing, 389
  in Varanasi, 265
  at Yerpa, 232
Tsomorak, 85
Tsona, 249
Tsona Göntsé Rinpoché, 79, 250
Tsonawa, Vinaya commentary of, 65
Tsöndrü Gyatso, 342, 356, 358
Tsongkhapa, 17, 308, 385, 399n14, 410n203
  Abridged Stages of the Path, 266, 327, 329
  biography of, 310, 417n340
  Clarifying the Intent of the Middle Way, 179, 336
  Cluster of Attainments, 384
  collected works of, 72, 78, 81, 229, 266–67, 404n90
  commentaries on Guhyasamāja, 404n92
  disciples of, 197, 406n130, 408n170. *See also* Gyaltsap Darma Rinchen; Khedrup Gelek Palsang
  Elucidation of All Hidden Points, 73
  Endowed with Three Convictions, 279, 352
  epithets of, 75, 285, 404n96, 415n307
  Essence of Eloquence Distinguishing the Definitive and Interpretive, 43, 52–53, 66, 135, 179, 336
  Exposition on the Root Tantric Vows, 266, 414n285
  Foundation of All Good Qualities, 116, 163–64, 209, 210, 211, 212, 216, 228, 262, 294–95, 300, 343
  in Ganden curriculum, 57
  Golden Garland of Eloquent Explanation, 266, 270
  Great Commentary on Fundamental Wisdom, 266, 270, 336
  Great Exposition of Secret Mantra, 328, 342
  Great Prayer Festival, initiation of, 400n18
  Highway to Enlightenment, 266, 414n284
  house of, 21
  Jeweled Box Sādhana of Thirteen-Deity Vajrabhairava, 266
  lectures on life and deeds of, 334, 335
  letters exchanged with Rendawa, 224
  Life Accomplishment of Kurava, 340, 365
  mausoleum of, 17
  Middle-Length Stages of the Path, 78, 284, 315, 317, 319, 332, 352, 380, 404n101
  miktsema recitation for, 402n47
  parinirvāṇa of, 330
  passing of, 406n138
  Praise to Dependent Arising, 147, 351

Praise to the Buddha, 147, 173
Prayer for Rebirth in Sukhāvatī, 257–58
Precious Sprout, 404n92
protector of, 187
relics of, 94
Shedra family's patronage of, 39
Song of Spiritual Experience, 102, 119, 327, 329
statues of, 181, 195, 268, 341, 350
temples of, 213, 214
thangkas of, 134, 199, 268, 407n153
Three Principal Aspects of the Path, 214, 257, 328, 333, 349, 359, 380
three secrets of, 259
throne of, 203, 236, 399n2
Trijang Rinpoché's knowledge and realization of, 383
Twenty-One Short Works on Guhyasamāja, 266, 340, 345
Vajra Words, 358
See also *Great Treatise on the Stages of the Path*; Jé Rinpoche as triple deity
Tsongön province, 209
Tsongpön Yatruk, 101
Tsosum, 211
Tsosum House, 103
Tsuklakhang, 159, 200, 201–3, 222, 240, 241, 244, 305, 417n336
Tsultrim Gyatso, Ninth Dali Lama, 89
Tsultrim Gyeltsen, Geshé, 295, 296, 327
Tsultrim Palden, Second Trijang Rinpoché, 397
Tsultrim Tenzin, 54
Tsunmo Tsal Monastery, 120
Tsurphu Monastery, 110, 230–31
Tuṣita, 134, 136, 399n14, 402n53, 407n153
Tushita Meditation Centre, 413n273
tutors, qualities of, 200
Twang, 250
Twenty Verses on the Bodhisattva Vow (Candrogomin), 62, 266, 354
Two Excellent Ones, 180, 226, 369, 410n201
Two Stainless Cycles, 128, 407n142

U

Uchu Muchin Sokpo Hothokthu, 67, 69, 403n83
Udānavarga, 178
Udāyin, 178, 410n196
Udrung Paljor Gyalpo (artist), 186, 197
Ugyen Testen, Geshé, 233, 310, 319, 321, 323, 324, 325
UK Tibet Society, 327, 328
Upper Gonsar Monastery, 106
Uṣṇīṣavijayā statue, 185–86
Ütö Chuda, 72
Ü-Tsang, 17, 225
Uyuk, 225

V

Vairocana, 88, 117, 216, 232, 412n241
Vairocana Abhisaṃbodhi initiation, 341, 419n381
Vaiśākha, 184, 410n205
Vaiśravaṇa, 95, 131, 240
fifteen forms of, 74
initiation given, 262
permissions given, 99, 183–84
prosperity rituals of, 92, 100, 289
See also Red Spear Vaiśravaṇa
Vajra Life-Tree of Immortality, 332
vajra masters, 161, 331, 343, 348, 389
vajra recitation, 154, 352
Vajra Seat, 146–47, 408n165
Vajrabhairava
averting frost by four letters relying on, 313
blessing of, 146
at Chötri Monastery, 123
in cloth-drawn mandala, 342–43
consecration ritual of, 95, 133, 161, 235, 254
for countering black magic, 96
as daily practice of Gangkar Lama Rinpoché, 118
drawing of, 50
fire offering of, 354
generation and completion stage of, 172
initiations given, 99, 112, 148, 160, 162, 167, 173, 182, 183
initiations received, 40, 125
mandala of, 73, 79, 102

mantra permissions, 223, 238, 263
Ngakrampa's practice of, 60
retreat practices of, 69, 79, 80, 304
ritual offerings to, 126
sādhanas of, 71, 135
self-initiation of, 95
solitary hero initiation, 254
statues of, 199
thangkas of, 171, 199, 223, 268
wrathful fire offering, 334
Vajrabhairava, single-deity
approaching retreat, 193
initiation received, 54
initiations given, 90, 103, 184, 255, 260, 261, 273, 295, 310, 339, 349
sādhana of, 324
thangka paintings of, 197
Vajrabhairava, thirteen-deity, 262, 366, 370
generation and completion stages, teachings received on, 123
initiations given, 84, 88, 90, 95, 115, 116, 119, 165, 197, 199, 217, 238, 256
Vajraḍāka, 61, 266, 340, 345, 403n72
Vajradāraṇa, 61, 370
Vajradhara, seeing great teachers as, 54, 74–75
Vajrapāṇi, 405n115, 413n272
Vajrapāṇi Mahācakra, 152, 323
Vajrasattva, hundred-syllable mantra of, 60
Vajrāvalī, 55, 209, 346, 402n65, 420n384
Vajrayoginī
completion stage, 260
empowerments of, 83
initiation given, 259
mandala offering, 267
mantra extraction of, 75, 196, 341, 354
meditation retreat of, 80
practices given to Fourteenth Dalai Lama, 341
sādhana of, 364
self-initiation offerings/ritual, 162, 164–65, 271
statues of, 305
three cycles of red ones, 150, 408n167
two stages of, 307, 332, 341, 352, 356, 380
uncommon yoga of, 271
Vajrayoginī, four sindūra initiations of, 380
in Bodhgaya, 264, 342, 356
in China, 209
in Dharamsala, 255, 256, 259, 261, 270–71, 273, 278, 280, 329, 334, 336, 339, 345, 347, 352
in Dromo, 148
in England, 327
at G. S. Mandidip Paper Mills, 275, 414n291
at Gangchen Kyishong, 312, 313
at Gangling, 92
in Garthok, 119
in Kalimpong, 254
in Lhading, 165
in Lhasa, 183, 189, 194, 196, 197, 202
in Mundgod, 370
in Mussoorie, 333
performance of, 305
receipt of, 74
in Sarnath, 272, 343, 364
in Spiti, 262
in Switzerland, 292, 325
Trijang Rinpoché's self-initiation in, 381–82
for Tsamchö Drölma, 307
at Yaphu Ratsak, 162
Varanasi, 146, 226, 251, 265, 313, 343, 358–60
vase initiation, 90
vase-breathing position, 77–78
Vasubandhu, 239, 410n201. See also *Treasury of Abhidharma*
Vasudhāra, 131
Venerable Chödrak of Namgyal, 263
Venerable Yeshé, 55
Verse Summary of the Perfection of Wisdom (*Ratnaguṇasaṃcayagathā*), 61
Very Secret Instructions of Rechungpa, 340
Victorious over the Three Realms, 347
Victorious Powerful Weapon ritual, 61
Vimalaśrī, 397
Vimaloṣṇīṣa initiation, 153
Vinaya, 130, 160, 262
compilation and editing of, 174
debates on, 240
ordination ceremony in, 202
presentation on, 68
studies of, 65, 72
Theravada observance of, 313

Vinaya Sutra (Guṇaprabha), 403n80
Vinayavastu, 65
Vischer, Helen, 301, 324
Viṣṇu, 186–87
visions, 4, 78, 117
Viśuddhaprabhā initiation, 153
Viśvamātṛ, 48, 402n46
Viśvantara Jātaka, 401n31
vows and precepts
  bodhisattva, 76, 90, 143, 258, 316–17, 414n284
  lay, 311
  Mahayana, 62, 309, 314–15
  monastic, 239
  one-day Mahayana, 267, 277, 338
  tantric, 62, 354
Vulture Peak, 146, 226, 264

W

Wako Mari, 86, 119
Wangdü Dorjé, 312
Wangkur Hill, 84, 144, 236, 404n108
Wangyal (brother of Samphel Tenzin), 108
Washul Yönru, 103–4
Wati Sangpo. *See* Ārya Wati Sangpo of Kyirong statue
Weisman, Dr., 292
Wenchen Gongzhu, 412n241
Wencheng (Chinese princess), 88
wheel of Dharma, 51, 135, 297, 402n57, 416n329
Wheel of Sharp Weapons Mind Training, 180, 251, 274, 347, 380
White Heruka, 154, 288, 336, 356, 365, 373
White Mahākāla, 289, 354
White Mañjuśrī, 200, 271, 381, 411n225
White Sarasvatī, 322–23
White Tārā
  Endowed with Nine Lineages, 345
  long-life empowerments, 5, 257, 272, 273, 293, 295, 304, 315, 320, 332, 333, 334, 335, 344, 351, 358, 365
  mantra of, 296
  retreat, 48, 60, 336, 339, 352, 362
  ritual text, 312
  statues, 185–86, 288
  Trijang Rinpoché's commentary on, 384
Winder, Marianne, 296, 416n324
wisdom beings (*jñānasattva*), 336, 363, 419n366
Wish Fulfilling Hope of the Fortunate (Jamyang Shepa), 358
Wish-Fulfilling Tree, 131
Words of Mañjuśrī, 76, 161–62, 167–68, 172, 189, 199, 232–33, 332, 404n97

Y

Yabshi family, escape from Tibet, 245
yak dances, 41
Yakṣa Chamdral, 131
Yakṣa Yamayamī, 367
Yama, 186–87, 413n271
Yamalung, 141
Yamāri, 186–87
Yang Daguan, 209
Yangan, 209
Yangchen Drupai Dorjé, *Wish-Fulfilling Tree of Eloquence*, 273, 414n289
Yangchen Monastery, 229
Yangdhar Chözin, 352
Yangön Hermitage, 32, 224
Yangpachen Temple, 55, 59, 235
Yangteng Khyenrap Tulku, 215
Yangteng Monastery, 95
Yangtze River, 209
Yangzom Tsering, Lady Lhalu, 75, 137, 156, 157, 277, 351. *See also* Lhalu Gatsal family
Yantra Wall of Vajra Mountains, A, 174
Yaphu Ratsak Monastery, 162
Yapshi Langdun Gung Kunga Wangchuk, Prime Minister, 128, 132, 407n152
Yapshi Phunkhang mansion, 176
Yardrok, 192, 194
Yarlha Shampo, Mount, 248
Yarlung, 140, 248
Yartö Drakla Pass, 248
Yasi Kardren (sword), 104
Yatruk Tsongpön, 98, 99
Yerpa Lhari Nyinpo, 232
Yerpa Monastery, 231–32
Yerpa Tsenshap Tulku, 255, 297
Yeru, Mount, 402n64
Yeshé, Lama Thubten, 346, 363
Yeshé Dönden (physician), 386

Yeshé Gyaltsen (Yongzin/Kachen), 179, 230, 271, 274, 339, 357, 367, 412n253
Yeshé Gyatso, Geshé, 199
Yeshé Loden, Geshé, 189
Yeshé Ö, 316
Yeshé Thupten, Geshé, 331
Yeshé Tsewang of Phara Labrang, 311
Yidak Pass, 86
Yiga Tulku, 255, 325
yoga tantra, 347
Yongle emperor, 230–31
Yongteng Monastery, 211
Yongya Tulku, 103
Yönru Pön, 101
Yönru Session, 101–2
Yönten (friend), 53
Yönten Gyalpo, 263
Yönten Ngawang Drakpa, 300
Young Lama's Home School, 269, 414n288
Yudrakpa. *See* Shang Yudrakpa Tsöndrü Drakpa
Yudrönma, 136
Yumar Tsengö, 342, 349
Yumbu Lagang, 140, 294, 295, 322, 416n315
Yuthok Kyitsal, 232
Yuthok Tashi Döndrup, 227–28
Yuthok Yönten Gönpo, 175, 409n192
Yuthokpa Wangdü Norbu (minister), 86, 250

Z

Zhang Jingwu, 194, 203, 205, 225, 237
Zhang Yintang, 38–39
Zhao Erfeng/Tarin, 25
Zopa Rinpoché, Thubten, (Lawudo Tulku), 363, 413n273, 414n288, 420n398

About the Translator

Sharpa Tulku Tenzin Trinley was born in Lhasa, Tibet, into the Rampa family, whose members served in Tibet's Ganden Phodrang government until 1959. He left Tibet following the Chinese occupation, and in India he spent time at the monastic settlement in Buxa and at Freda Bedi's Young Lamas Home School before being sent to the United States in 1962 for Western education along with Geshé Lhundub Sopa and two other tulkus. In 1966, he returned to Dharamsala, where he served on the Tibetan Council for Religious Affairs. Subsequently he joined the newly established Library of Tibetan Works and Archives, where he translated for Dharma classes and worked on many translations of Buddhist texts, including the *Yamantaka Cycle Classics* published by Tibet House, New Delhi, in 1990. He has translated orally for His Holiness the Dalai Lama, Kaybjé Ling Rinpoché, Kyabjé Trijang Rinpoché, Assistant Tutor Serkong Rinpoché, the Ninety-Eighth Ganden Throneholder Jampal Shenphen, Lati Rinpoché, and many other lamas and geshés. He moved to the United States in 1976 and currently resides in Madison, Wisconsin, with his family.

What to Read Next from Wisdom Publications

The Life of My Teacher
A Biography of Ling Rinpoché
His Holiness the Dalai Lama
Translated by Gavin Kilty

"This rare and oftentimes tender life story is a gift to us all. Its publication should be greeted with much rejoicing."
—Jan Willis, author of *Enlightened Beings: Life Stories from the Ganden Oral Tradition*

Like a Waking Dream
The Autobiography of Geshe Lhundub Sopa
Geshe Lhundub Sopa with Paul Donnelly
Foreword by His Holiness the Dalai Lama

"Geshe Sopa is one of the greatest living Buddhist masters of his generation. This marvelous lifestory, rich in detail and told in his own words, will captivate the hearts and minds of anyone who reads it."
—José Ignacio Cabezón, Dalai Lama Professor and Chair of the Religious Studies Department, UC Santa Barbara

A Life Unforeseen
A Memoir of Service to Tibet
Rinchen Sadutshang
Foreword by His Holiness the Dalai Lama

One of the only government officials in pre-Communist Tibet to have been educated in English recounts the pivotal events that changed his homeland, and the fate of his people, forever.

The Lawudo Lama
Stories of Reincarnation from the Mount Everest Region
Jamyang Wangmo
Foreword by His Holiness the Dalai Lama

"It will stretch your mind and move your heart."
—Lorne Ladner, author of *The Lost Art of Compassion*

Liberation in the Palm of Your Hand
A Concise Discourse on the Path to Enlightenment
Pabongka Rinpoche
Edited by Trijang Rinpoche
Translated by Michael Richards

"The richest and most enjoyable volume from the lamrim tradition published to date."
—*Golden Drum*

Steps on the Path to Enlightenment
A Commentary on Tsongkhapa's Lamrim Chenmo—Volume 5: Insight
Geshe Lhundub Sopa with Dechen Rochard
Foreword by His Holiness the Dalai Lama

The final installment of the *Steps on the Path to Enlightenment* series examines the nature of reality with a master class in Buddhist Middle Way philosophy and meditation.

Approaching the Buddhist Path
His Holiness the Dalai Lama and Thubten Chodron

"A distillation of all Buddhist wisdom, *Approaching the Buddhist Path* covers its history, philosophy, and meditation. Flowing in limpid language and powered by the dynamic reasoning of eminent Dharma authorities, it is suitable for all readers, beginner and advanced."
—Tulku Thondup, author of *The Heart of Unconditional Love*

The Foundation of Buddhist Practice
His Holiness the Dalai Lama and Thubten Chodron

The second volume in the Dalai Lama's definitive and comprehensive series on the stages of the Buddhist path, *The Library of Wisdom and Compassion.*

The Voice That Remembers
One Woman's Historic Fight to Free Tibet
Ama Adhe as told to Joy Blakeslee

"A riveting account of the desecration of a culture, a religion, a family, and a landscape."
—Mickey Spiegel, Human Rights Watch

A Hundred Thousand White Stones
An Ordinary Tibetan's Extraordinary Journey
Kunsang Dolma

"Refreshingly honest and brave, this book leaves us looking at our lives with completely new eyes."
—Jaimal Yogis, author of *Saltwater Buddha*

Vast as the Heavens, Deep as the Sea
Verses in Praise of Bodhicitta
Khunu Rinpoche
Foreword by His Holiness the Dalai Lama

Revered by many—especially His Holiness the Dalai Lama—as the very embodiment of altruism, the late Khunu Rinpoche Tenzin Gyaltsen devoted his life to the development of bodhicitta—the aspiration to achieve enlightenment for the sake of all sentient beings. Presented in both English and the original Tibetan, this modern classic is a collection of Khunu Rinpoche's inspirational verse.

The Easy Path
Illuminating the First Panchen Lama's Secret Instructions
Gyumed Khensur Lobsang Jampa
Edited by Lorne Ladner

"A marvel."
—Jan Willis, author of *Dreaming Me: Black, Baptist, and Buddhist*

Mind Training
The Great Collection
Thupten Jinpa

"For the first time, the instructions of the great Kadampa masters have been translated in their entirety. Their clarity and raw power are astonishingly fresh."
—*Buddhadharma*

The Book of Kadam
The Core Texts
Thupten Jinpa

"This volume brings key classical Tibetan texts to the Western world."
—*Eastern Horizon*

The Crystal Mirror of Philosophical Systems
A Tibetan Study of Asian Religious Thought
Thuken Losang Chökyi Nyima
Translated by Geshe Lhundub Sopa
Edited by Roger Jackson

"An impressive translation of a fascinating and vitally important book. Its broad scope and keen observation makes it an invaluable resource."
—Guy Newland, Central Michigan University, author of *Introduction to Emptiness*

A Lamp to Illuminate the Five Stages
Teachings on Guhyasamāja Tantra
Tsongkhapa
Translated by Gavin Kilty

"Tsongkhapa's *Lamp to Illuminate the Five Stages* stands as one of the greatest literary contributions to the genre of highest yoga tantra ever written. In his translation of this extremely profound text, Gavin Kilty has successfully captured both its meaning and eloquence with such precision and grace that it will stand as the benchmark to which future translations of similar material must aspire."
—David Gonsalez, translator of *Source of Supreme Bliss*

About Wisdom Publications

Wisdom Publications is the leading publisher of classic and contemporary Buddhist books and practical works on mindfulness. To learn more about us or to explore our other books, please visit our website at wisdompubs.org or contact us at the address below.

Wisdom Publications
199 Elm Street
Somerville, MA 02144 USA

We are a 501(c)(3) organization, and donations in support of our mission are tax deductible.

Wisdom Publications is affiliated with the Foundation for the Preservation of the Mahayana Tradition (FPMT).